M. Lasi /86   26.50
                       T

D1613894

KEY ENVIRONMENTS

General Editor: J. E. Treherne

AMAZONIA

The International Union for Conservation of Nature and Natural Resources (IUCN), founded in 1948, is the leading independent international organization concerned with conservation. It is a network of governments, non-governmental organizations, scientists and other specialists dedicated to the conservation and sustainable use of living resources.

The unique role of IUCN is based on its 502 member organizations in 114 countries. The membership includes 57 States, 121 government agencies and virtually all major national and international non-governmental conservation organizations.

Some 2000 experts support the work of IUCN's six Commissions: ecology; education; environmental planning; environmental policy, law and administration; national parks and protected areas; and the survival of species.

The IUCN Secretariat conducts or facilitates IUCN's major functions: monitoring the status of ecosystems and species around the world; developing plans (such as the World Conservation Strategy) for dealing with conservation problems, supporting action arising from these plans by governments or other appropriate organizations, and finding ways and means to implement them. The Secretariat co-ordinates the development, selection and management of the World Wildlife Fund's international conservation projects. IUCN provides the Secretariat for the Ramsar Convention (Convention on Wetlands of International Importance especially as Waterfowl Habitat). It services the CITES convention on trade in endangered species and the World Heritage Site programme of UNESCO.

IUCN, through its network of specialists, is collaborating in the Key Environments Series by providing information, advice on the selection of critical environments, and experts to discuss the relevant issues.

KEY ENVIRONMENTS
AMAZONIA

Edited by

GHILLEAN T. PRANCE

The New York Botanical Garden, U.S.A.

and

THOMAS E. LOVEJOY

World Wildlife Fund, U.S.A.

Foreword by

HRH THE DUKE OF EDINBURGH

Published in collaboration with the

INTERNATIONAL UNION FOR CONSERVATION OF NATURE AND NATURAL RESOURCES

by

PERGAMON PRESS

OXFORD · NEW YORK · TORONTO · SYDNEY · FRANKFURT

U.K.	Pergamon Press Ltd., Headington Hill Hall, Oxford OX3 0BW, England.
U.S.A.	Pergamon Press Inc., Maxwell House, Fairview Park, Elmsford, New York 10523, U.S.A.
CANADA	Pergamon Press Canada Ltd., Suite 104, 150 Consumers Road, Willowdale, Ontario M2J 1P9, Canada
AUSTRALIA	Pergamon Press (Aust.) Pty. Ltd., PO Box 544, Potts Point, N.S.W. 2011, Australia.
FEDERAL REPUBLIC OF GERMANY	Pergamon Press GmbH, Hammerweg 6, D-6242 Kronberg-Taunus, Federal Republic of Germany

First edition 1985

Library of Congress Cataloging in Publication Data
Main entry under title:
Key environments:—Amazonia.
(Key environments)
Includes bibliographical references and index.
1. Natural history—Amazon River Region.
2. Man—Influence on nature—Amazon River Region.
3. Amazon River Region. I. Prance, Ghillean T., 1937–
II. Lovejoy, Thomas E. III. Series.
QH112.A43 1985   508.81′1   84-11050

British Library Cataloguing in Publication Data

Amazonia—(Key environments)
1. Natural history—Amazon River Valley
I. Prance, Ghillean T. II. Lovejoy, Thomas E. III. Series
508.81′1   QH112

ISBN 0-08-030776-0

Printed in Great Britain by A. Wheaton & Co. Ltd., Exeter

The general problems of conservation are understood by most people who take an intelligent interest in the state of the natural environment. But if adequate measures are to be taken, there is an urgent need for the problems to be spelled out in accurate detail.

This series of volumes on "Key Environments" concentrates attention on those areas of the world of nature that are under the most severe threat of disturbance and destruction. The authors expose the stark reality of the situation without rhetoric or prejudice.

The value of this project is that it provides specialists, as well as those who have an interest in the conservation of nature as a whole, with the essential facts without which it is quite impossible to develop any practical and effective conservation action.

1984

General Preface

The increasing rates of exploitation and pollution are producing unprecedented environmental changes in all parts of the world. In many cases it is not possible to predict the ultimate consequences of such changes, while in some, environmental destruction has already resulted in ecological disasters.

A major obstacle, which hinders the formulation of rational strategies of conservation and management, is the difficulty in obtaining reliable information. At the present time the results of scientific research in many threatened environments are scattered in various specialist journals, in the reports of expeditions and scientific commissions and in a variety of conference proceedings. It is, thus, frequently difficult even for professional biologists to locate important information. There is consequently an urgent need for scientifically accurate, concise and well-illustrated accounts of major environments which are now or soon will be, under threat. It is this need which these volumes attempt to meet.

The series is produced in collaboration with the International Union for the Conservation of Nature. It aims to identify environments of international ecological importance, to summarize the present knowledge of the flora and fauna, to relate this to recent environmental changes and to suggest where possible, effective management and conservation strategies for the future. The selected environments will be re-examined in subsequent editions to indicate the extent and characteristics of significant changes.

The volume editors and authors are all acknowledged experts who have contributed significantly to the knowledge of their particular environments.

The volumes are aimed at a wide readership, including: academic biologists, environmentalists, conservationists, professional ecologists, some geographers as well as graduate students and informed lay people.

John Treherne

Preface

Inside and outside Brazil there is a growing interest in Amazonia and its future. People want to know more and more about the destruction of tropical forests, the impact of huge hydroelectric dams, the consequences of opening roads, the effects of the discoveries of new mineral deposits, the unstable situation in Indian lands, etc. In the beginning of the seventies, the average Brazilian cared very little about the future of the Amazonian forests. The official attitude at that time was this was strictly an internal affair that should not concern anybody outside the country, except our neighbors in the same region. ''If other people want the oxygen produced by our forests, they should pay for it'', former Minister Delfim Neto announced to the press.

Nowadays, on the one hand, the oxygen issue is no longer an issue, after it was explained to the general public that climax forests are more or less in a state of equilibrium, regarding oxygen production and consumption. On the other hand, scientific research has increasingly revealed that large scale human activities in Amazonia will certainly affect the climate of the region and possibly also that of the whole world. In any case, the cost of such changes, to humankind, could be immense. We also know that future generations cannot afford to lose genetic material of enormous and irreplaceable value.

We must consider, too, as Philip Fearnside shows (Chapter 21), that if, in absurdity, the entire Brazilian 'Amazonia Legal' is divided in lots of 100 hectares (the minimum acceptable size for new settlements), it would only accommodate 25 million people in five million holdings. This dispels the myth that Amazonia, because of its size, could receive untold millions of humans. Also, by now, everyone should know the clearing of the dense tropical rain forest for the establishment of large cattle ranches was generally a failure, economically and ecologically; the notion such clearings improve the soil is simply not true. These and other data presented and discussed in this book should make people reconsider, in a new light, many of the old, simplistic and disastrous views that the destruction of the forest and its substitution by large ranches or by small farms could be a good solution to the pressing social and development needs of Amazon nations.

The heart of the problem is how to show to the economic planners, and also to the general public, what the true realities of Amazonia are, as they emerge from the scientific studies made in recent years. From my personal experience, in more than twelve years as head of Brazil's Federal Environmental Agency (SEMA), this is a very difficult task. Many decision makers only make a pretense of interest in ecological matters when approached in relation to such subjects. This book, however, presents an impressive array of arguments and facts that no one can or should ignore. These facts should go to the press, radio and TV so that decision makers, together with the general public, will hear about them not only in their offices, but also in their homes.

With the money spent in buying, let us say, two or three jet-fighter planes, which for the great world powers would be considered very small spending, the Amazonian countries could firmly establish or complete networks of protected areas extremely valuable as genetic banks for future generations. Also, with relatively small amounts of funds, such countries could intensify tropical forest research. If we don't learn quickly how to benefit from the rational use of forest products, without destroying the forest, conservation will be a lost cause in Amazonia.

We have little time left to act before it is too late. Let us hope that this book will circulate widely and quickly so as to soon deliver its messages.

PAULO NOGUEIRA-NETO
Secretaria Especial do Meio Ambiente
Special Secretary of the Environment
Brasília

Contents

Introduction

Recently there has been a spate of books about the Amazon but they have tended to dwell on specific aspects, or particular groups of organisms. Meanwhile, a book presenting a more comprehensive review of the state of knowledge has been lacking, although there have been many exciting developments in this vast and scarcely known realm. The book which comes close to such a review is the just published volume by Salati *et. al.* (1983), which covers some areas. So far it is only available in Portuguese but it deserves wider attention. Sioli's monumental recent tome (1984) appeared while this was in press and represents a major contribution on Amazonian limnology and landscape ecology.

The lack made the idea of a volume for the Key Environments Series seem exceedingly timely, and, in any event, how could any environment be more key than the Amazon? It certainly has managed to absorb a great deal of the attention of these editors (over a combined period of 38 years). The best way to approach such a book seemed to be to ask the authorities themselves to contribute chapters.

We also felt that it would be more interesting and useful to approach the subject on a topical basis, rather than on a taxonomic or geographical one. Such an approach seemed appropriate, because the recent advances in Amazonian science have emphasised relationships and interaction more than the descriptive sciences. So there is not a chapter on the taxonomy of birds, nor one on fish systematics. There is, however, one on primates, but its emphasis is on community structure and ecology, and the one about fish concentrates on the interactions between fish and the forest.

An effort was also made to include a goodly number of scientists who work in the region itself. This likewise reflects a change in Amazon science, namely the growing number of scientists permanently based in the Amazon at institutions, such as Brazil's National Institute for Research on Amazonia (Instituto Nacional de Pesquisas da Amazônia = INPA). Most of the authors have ongoing research in Amazonia and work with institutions such as INPA or the Museu Goeldi. This represents the growing capacity for science in these nations, one that we hope will not be jeopardized by serious economic problems which cloud the horizon. While short-term economic crises may occupy centre stage, it is the institutional strength in areas such as science which will make the greatest difference to the future welfare of the Amazon and Amazonian nations.

Obviously this is a time of change for more than Amazonian science and scientists. It is a time of change for the interaction of the people with the Amazonian ecology. Consequently a section on human impact was added to the ones on the physical and biological setting. In many ways the major purpose of this volume relates to this: up-to-date information about the Amazon, its biota, and its processes can provide a basis for better management.

The Amazon with its great wealth of species (probably in excess of a tenth of the world total) represents a special challenge to science and society. The secrets locked within Amazonia hold enormous potential for bettering the human condition, but they are easily destroyed by unwise development. The myth that the Amazon has the potential to be the greatest breadbasket of the planet is largely dispelled, swept away by the failures of the TransAmazon colonization scheme. Neither is the Amazon a perpetual economic wasteland best left to mosquitoes, snakes and tropical diseases. What becomes increasingly clear is the fact that what naturally occurs there has a lot to reveal about intelligent and sustainable use of the Amazon. The challenge for science, then, is to probe the Amazon's rich fragility so we can understand without destroying, for understanding is a necessary precursor to use and benefit without destruction.

The Amazon contributed and does contribute important products to our daily lives, ones which are often used in ignorance of their origin. There are undoubtedly a very large number of useful products yet to be discovered within the reaches of the basin. In addition to these utilitarian products the basin must be considered as an important fount of *knowledge* about biological systems, how they work, and how they might be of use. This is reaffirmed, really in a very minor way, every time a pharmaceutical laboratory succeeds in synthesizing an important phytochemical substance of Amazon origin. We can expect such useful discovery to happen over and over again, and to be of considerable human benefit.

Recently the Amazon has provided a setting requisite to discovering how forests can make their own rainfall (Chapter 2), a regional echo of the repeated recognition of how life modifies its environment, often to its own benefit. Deforestation would not only lower rainfall in the basin, but affect central Brazil, and by affecting the heat transfer mechanism of clouds, perhaps affect global climatic patterns. The potential of Amazon deforestation to affect global cycling of elements such as carbon, could independently have an effect on global weather patterns, although the details are ill-defined. In these senses as well as reducing the capacity of the land, massive Amazon deforestation would modify our environment to our disadvantage. In this sense the Amazon is a key environment on a global scale.

The importance of greater knowledge about the Amazon then is obvious, and we hope this book makes a small contribution in that direction. The practical consequences of ignorance and misuse cannot be ignored. Yet neither should it be overlooked that the Amazon has great worth in itself, as a source of interest, wonder and beauty.

Ghillean T. Prance
Thomas E. Lovejoy

REFERENCE

Salati, E., H. O. R. Shubart, W. Junk and A. D. de Oliveira (1983). *Amazônia: Desenvolvimento, integração e ecologia*. Editora brasiliense, Rio de Janeiro and Conselho Nacional de Desenvolvimento Científico e Tecnológico.

Sioli, Harald, ed. (1984). The Amazon: Limnology and landscape ecology of a mighty tropical river and its basin. Dr. W. Junk Publishers, Dordrecht, Boston, Lancaster.

PART I

The Physical Setting

CHAPTER 1

The Physical and Chemical Properties of Amazonian Waters and their Relationships with the Biota

WOLFGANG J. JUNK and KARIN FURCH

Max-Planck-Institut für Limnologie, Plön, Federal Republic of Germany *in cooperation with* Instituto
Nacional de Pesquisas da Amazonia (INPA), Manaus, Amazonas, Brazil

CONTENTS

1.1. INTRODUCTION

Water is one of the principal features of the Amazonian landscape. The Amazon and its affluents
represent the greatest river system on earth — its catchment areas covering about six million square
kilometres. About one sixth of all freshwater transported by rivers to the oceans passes through the
Amazon river. High precipitation rates of 2 − 3 m per year result in a dense network of streams and
rivers which gives the Amazon landscape its specific character. Most conspicuous for man are erosion
and sedimentation processes which demonstrate the results of the kinetic energy of flowing water. The
Amazon itself and its enormous floodplain is a beautiful example for these processes. Other examples for

the erosive force of water can be observed in Amazonia where man cuts the natural vegetation cover. Quickly, erosion starts, flushing away the fertile top layer of the soil, sometimes cutting deep valleys into the slopes of the hills.

A less conspicuous, but extremely important property of the water is its ability to dissolve many solid and gaseous substances. The dipole character of the water molecules makes it one of the best solvents existing. Due to the abundance of water in Amazonia, its property to act as a solvent has an enormous importance for the ecosystems.

In the soil many inorganic and organic substances occur in soluble form and can be leached by the rainwater. As a source of plant nutrients soils can become impoverished, losing their fertility. On the other hand, the dissolved compounds give to the water itself specific characteristics or a 'specific quality'.

Quantity and quality of water are of fundamental importance for life. The plant cover of the Amazon Basin in its actual appearance depends upon the amount of water in the atmosphere and the amount and distribution of precipitation during the year. Plants and animals in the water itself are affected by the water quality. The amount of dissolved substances will have direct and indirect influence on the occurrence and frequency of the species. Interaction between water, land and the biota in Amazonia will be shown in the following chapters. Considering the fact that the total quantity of water, its distribution and its pathways in the Amazon Basin are of fundamental importance for the evaluation of its impact, some basic information on climate, hydrology and water balance will be given, too.

1.2. CLIMATE, HYDROLOGY AND WATER BALANCE

The climate in the Amazon Basin is permanently hot and humid. Average temperature is 27.9°C during dry season, and 25.8°C during rainy season. Daily fluctuations in temperature are greater than seasonal variations. Average maximum temperature in September is 33.1°C and average minimum temperature is 23.9°C. Air humidity is permanently high, varying between 88% in the rainy season and 77% in the dry season (Falesi et al., 1971). The total amount of water vapour in the atmosphere in Central Amazonia corresponds to about 45 mm of precipitation. This quantity is easily reached in a heavy rainfall. The mean recycling time of water vapour is only about 5.5 days (Marques et al., 1979).

Precipitation varies between 1500 mm per year in the northern and southern parts of the basin to more than 6000 mm per year on some slopes of the Andes, however $2 - 3$ m being typical for most parts of the basin. The distribution of rainfall varies, showing a more or less developed dry and rainy season during the year. The rainy season starts first in the southern part of the basin. Porto Velho, for instance, has high rainfall from October to April. In Manaus, in the middle of the basin, it begins 1 month later and lasts from November to May, and in Barcellos, in the northern part, the period of greatest rainfall is between April and June.

About half the total precipitation is carried by wind into the Amazon Basin from the Atlantic Ocean. The other half is derived from the evapotranspiration of the basin itself and its plant cover (Marques et al., 1977; Villa Nova et al., 1976; Salati et al., 1979, this volume). In the rainforest proper, the evapotranspiration may contribute up to 75% of total precipitation. This shows the close relationship between plants and climate inside the basin: the rainforest depends on high precipitation, which to a considerable extent is the result of its own evapotranspiration.

High precipitation rates result in an extremely dense net of watercourses to collect the surplus water and to transport it to the Amazon river and back to the Atlantic Ocean. There are approximately 2 km of streams per 1 km^2 of surface area around Manaus. Differences in precipitation rates during the year affect stream and river levels. Smaller streams react strongly to local rainfalls because of their small catchment area. Their discharge also shows considerable short term oscillations (Fig. 1.1). The discharge of large rivers represents the average rainfall of a large catchment area, local rains being of little

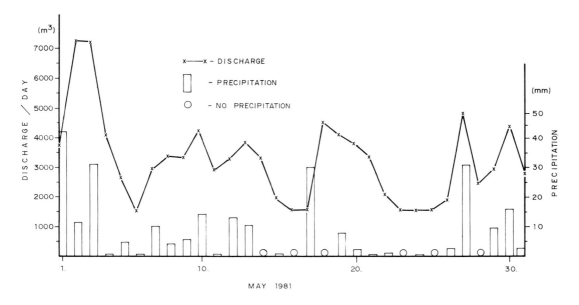

Fig. 1.1. Daily discharge of the stream 'Barro Branco' in the forest reserve 'Reserva Ducke' near Manaus, in May 1981, and precipitation data from its catchment area during the same period (Discharge data: W. Franken, INPA, unpubl. data; precipitation data: M. N. Goes Ribeiro, INPA, Manaus).

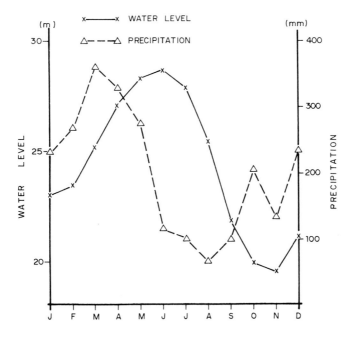

Fig. 1.2. Average monthly water level* of the Rio Negro/Amazon river at Manaus and mean precipitation in the Manaus area (1975-1979). Absolute maximum and minimum of river level since 1902: 29.70 m in 1953 and 13.64 m in 1963. Level from last day of the respective month. Data from Manaus harbour authorities; precipitation data: M. N. Goes Ribeiro, INPA, Manaus.

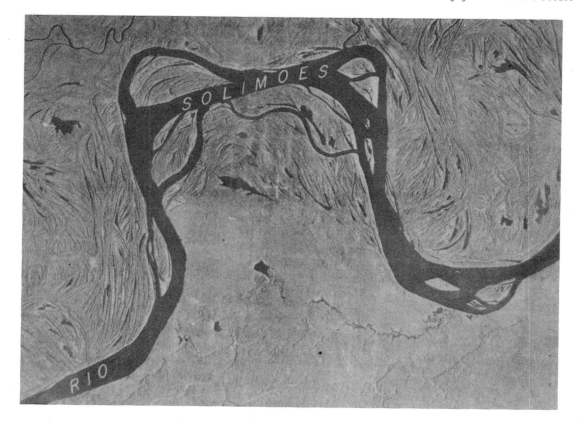

Fig. 1.3. Floodplain of the Rio Solimões* near Fonte Boa (* In Brazil, the Amazon between the Peruvian border and the confluence with the Rio Negro is called Rio Solimões).

importance. The time difference in the rainy season in the Amazon river system is such that the southern affluents reach peak flood some months earlier than northern affluents. The Amazon itself reaches its maximum at Manaus in May—June, several weeks after the beginning of the dry season, showing that local rains have little impact on its discharge (Fig. 1.2). Its waterlevel changes as well as that of most of its large tributaries which follow a sinoidal curve. Their amplitude varies between a few metres up to 15 m.

Most of the great rivers have built large fringing floodplains which are regularly inundated during high water (Fig. 1.3). Sedimentation and erosion processes in the floodplains are related to the sediment load and currents of rivers. Quantity as well as quality of sediment of the big Amazonian rivers differ considerably, depending on the respective catchment areas, as will be shown later.

1.3. PHYSICAL AND CHEMICAL ASPECTS OF AMAZONIAN WATERS

1.3.1. The rainwater

Rainwater is not like distilled water. Passing through the atmosphere, it dissolves and collects substances existing there and transports them to the ground. Among these substances are principally gases composing the atmosphere, such as oxygen, nitrogen, carbon dioxide, the inert gases and many

TABLE 1.1. Chemical composition of rainwater, throughfall and stem flow in Central Amazonia, in comparison with the water of Central Amazonian forest streams.

	forest streams*	rainwater**	throughfall†	stem flow†
pH	4.5	4.65	5.3	5.2
El. Cond. μS/cm(20°C)	10.0	7.2	26.1	32.5
Na mg/l	0.22	0.12*	0.27	2.11
K mg/l	0.15	0.10*	1.24	6.58
Ca mg/l	0.04	0.07*	0.25	1.72
Mg mg/l	0.04	0.02*	0.19	0.97
N(NH_4) mg/l	N.D.	0.169	<0.05	9.20
N(NO_3) mg/l	0.004††	0.110	0.56	0.27
N(NO_2) mg/l	0.002††	0.002	<0.01	0.02
N tot. mg/l	0.30††	0.41	N.D.	N.D.
Cl mg/l	2.2	1.9	1.03	3.73
P(PO_4) mg/l	N.D.	0.003	0.151	0.095
P tot. mg/l	0.01	0.011	N.D.	N.D.

* Furch 1984   ** Anonymous 1972
† unpublished data from W. Franken, INPA, collected 1981 near Manaus. Average values from 10 measurements throughout the year.
†† Schmidt 1972.
N.D. no data available.

others of biotic as well as abiotic origin. One result of the dissolving of carbon dioxide is that rainwater has a low pH value. A further fraction are solids in the form of small particles, e.g. volcanic ashes, dust from the soil, or ash from burnings carried by the wind sometimes at high altitudes and over long distances. Additionally, there exists a small fraction of compounds, which develop in the atmosphere itself, due to physical and chemical processes induced by high energy solar radiation in the upper layer of the atmosphere and by electrical discharges in thunderstorms. The nitrogen compounds which are derived from such processes are very important. Most of the plants are not able to transfer the stable nitrogen molecules to a form suitable for biochemical processes. Nitrogen being an essential element for plant growth, often becomes a limiting factor in the ecosystem. This happens frequently in Amazonia. Nitrogen compounds and other mineral nutrients like phosphorus, potassium and calcium are transported in small concentrations by the rain into the system (Table 1.1). Considering the data given in Table 1.1 and considering for Central Amazonia an average yearly precipitation of 2 m, rains add about 8.2 kg nitrogen, 0.22 kg phosphorus, 2.0 kg potassium, 1.4 kg calcium per ha per year to the ecosystem. These quantities are of fundamental importance for the nutrient budget of the Amazon Basin, as will be shown later.

In the last decade air pollution during the dry season in Amazonia has increased considerably through an increased rate of forest burning. We may suppose that rainwater collected in areas recently affected by fire will show considerably higher concentrations of dissolved and suspended matter than indicated by the values given above. Air pollution by heavy industry is still negligible in the Amazon Basin.

1.3.2. Throughfall and stem flow

Before reaching the ground most of the rainwater passes through the canopy of the forest. Here its chemical composition is modified due to soluble inorganic and organic substances, which are leached directly from the leaves and stems of the trees and from the excrement of the many animals living in the canopy of the forest. At first glance it may seem astonishing that many epiphytic plants are able to live attached to trees extending their roots on the surface of the bark with little or no substrate and having 'just rainwater' at their disposal. However, a chemical analysis of stem flow water reveals that it has much higher concentrations of dissolved mineral nutrients than the original rainwater (Table 1.1).

Nitrogen compounds are on an average 15 times higher, phosphorus 30 times, potassium 65 times and calcium 25 times. Nutrient levels of stem flow and throughfall water are the highest measured in Central Amazonian waters in respect to nitrogen compounds.

Of course, there are great differences in the concentrations of organic and inorganic substances in the water from stem flow and throughfall. In part this is due to differences in the vegetation and vegetation structure. Furthermore, at the beginning of the rain, concentrations may be high, whereas they reduce after a few hours, as happens in rainwater too.

1.3.3. Relationships between water and its catchment areas

Before it becomes a part of the dense network of Amazonian watercourses, rainwater enters the ground or passes over its surface. This period is very important, because it determines the final chemical composition of the river water. During this period, very complex processes occur, involving the biota as well as the abiotic environment. As water leaches the ground and the organic material in its upper layer, plants take up with their roots the nutrients which are important for their growth. Additionally, complex adsorption and exchange processes between water and substrate occur. In very general terms we may consider the chemical composition of creek and river water as the expression of the chemical conditions of their catchment areas and the result of chemical and biological processes occurring there. For instance, water from Carboniferous areas will show high concentrations of calcium and magnesium, whereas these elements will occur in small quantities only when the catchment area is formed by granite and other archaic formations poor in alkali-earth metals. Water from a swamp has higher concentrations of organic material than water originating from areas where organic material is scarce. However, it has to be considered that the chemical composition of the water represents an integral value of the whole catchment area. The larger the catchment area is, the greater the geochemical differences between its different parts can be. Additionally, human impact can modify considerably the hydrochemical conditions of a river by pollution. However, in the big Amazonian rivers human impact on the hydrochemical conditions is still negligible.

1.3.4. Typology of Amazonian waters

The concept that waters of different qualities may exist in Amazonia is supported by the existence of rivers and creeks with different water colours.

This can be shown by local names like Rio Negro (black river), Rio Branco (white river), Rio Verde (green river), etc. Already at the beginning of systematic limnological studies in Amazonia, Sioli (1950) classified Amazonian rivers into three types, according to their colour: whitewater, blackwater and clearwater rivers.

The name 'whitewater' is given to the muddy water, rich in fine suspended inorganic solids of the Amazon itself and some of its tributaries, like Rio Madeira, Rio Purus, Rio Juruá, and Rio Jutai. 'Clearwater' is the designation given to all rivers with transparent greenish water. This category is represented by the Rio Tapajós, Rio Trombetas, Rio Xingú, and Rio Curuá Una. 'Blackwater' is transparent but has a dark brownish or reddish colour. Representative of this type are the Rio Negro and Rio Urubú.

Sioli related the water colour to specific conditions of the catchment areas. Whitewater was related to areas with intensive erosion processes like for instance the Andean and Pre-Andean region.

Clearwater rivers were related to areas where erosion processes are less intensive, like in the archaic shield of Central Brazil and Guianas, as well as the Central Amazon Basin.

The origin of blackwater is a result of organogenic processes. The dark colour of the water is caused by dissolved organic substances (humic and fulvic acids). These substances are derived from the breakdown of the leaf litter under acid conditions and subsequent edaphic processes that happen in Amazonian soils. They may have high molecular weight, are resistant to further decomposition and they contribute to the low pH value of the water because of their acidity. Furthermore, they are able to capture dissolved metals which are already scarce in the water.

In kaolinitic soils, a great part of the humic substances are fixed on the clay particles. In sandy soils a great part is swept away to the streams, giving the water a dark colour. Certain sandy soils, the so-called podzols, are the main sources of blackwater in Amazonia. The other sources are the swampy areas where organic material from the flooded forest is accumulated and leached out by the water. Both conditions are frequently found in Central Amazonia, and in the northern peripheric region. Intensity of the colour of stream or river water depends on the percentage of such areas in the catchment areas and the quantity of organic material available. Normally organic substances are accumulated during the dry season and leached during the rainy season. Therefore, stream water has a darker colour at the beginning of the rainy season than in the dry season. Podzols occupy limited areas only in Central Amazonia. Therefore, the water of one stream may have a dark colour, whereas the water of the next one may be nearly colourless.

More studies on Amazonian waters have shown that there are gradients between these three water types. Rivers may change in colour, their water being 'white' because of an increased load of suspended solids during the rainy season, whereas it is 'clear' in the dry season. This happens for instance, in the Rio Branco, an affluent of the Rio Negro. Streams in Central Amazonia often have clearwater during the dry season and blackwater during the rainy season because of leached humic substances from podzol areas.

The water of the Amazon, entering the floodplain, loses its white colour because of sedimentation of inorganic suspensoids and becomes transparent, brownish or greenish. Modifications in the catchment areas by man may increase erosion processes, producing in Central Amazonia a 'man-made whitewater'. This often makes an identification of the water types according to water colour difficult, and shows the need for further parameters for a more precise classification.

In addition to their colour, the water types may be characterised by some hydrochemical parameters. Whitewater has relatively high concentrations of total electrolytes and a pH value near 7, whereas blackwater has low concentrations of electrolytes and a very low pH value of about 4. Clearwater is placed between these two types, showing however, a great hydrochemical heterogeneity (Sioli, 1965).

Fittkau (1971) related the hydrochemical conditions in Amazonian rivers and streams to geochemical conditions of the basin. He divided the basin into 3 basic geochemical provinces (Fig. 1.4).
1. The Andean and pre-Andean region (western peripheral region);
2. The archaic shields of Guiana and Central Brazil (northern and southern peripheric region);
3. Central Amazonia.

These three provinces differ considerably in respect to their geochemistry and geomorphology. The Andes are young mountains which started to rise in the Tertiary. The intensive erosion processes affect former marine sediments rich in mineral elements, especially calcium and magnesium. Consequently, rivers with their catchment areas in the Andes and pre-Andean region contain high sediment loads and high concentrations in mineral salts with a large percentage of alkali-earth metals and neutral pH.

The archaic shields of Guiana and Central Brazil belong to the oldest geological formations on earth. In comparison to the Andes the relief is low, erosion processes being relatively minor. However, the weathering of the rocks delivers small quantities of mineral nutrients. Water derived from these areas has little sediment load and is poor in mineral elements, especially in alkali-earth metals, thus having low pH value.

Central Amazonia is covered with tertiary sediments of fluviatile and lacustrine origin. These soils

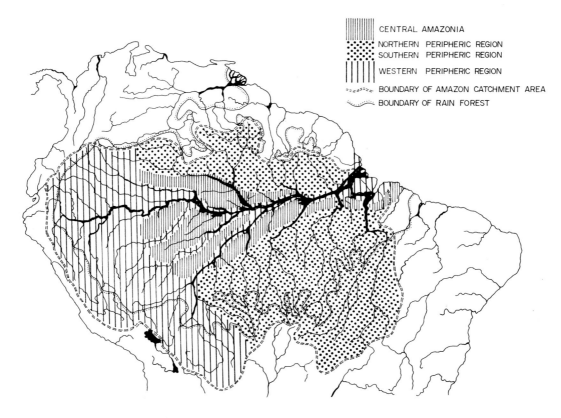

Fig. 1.4. Geochemical classification of the Amazon basin (according to Fittkau, 1971).

have high fractions of sandy and kaolinitic material. The availability of mineral nutrients and the pH value are extremely low. The relief is low and gradients in elevation are small. Dense vegetation cover inhibits intensive erosion processes. Rivers with catchment areas in Central Amazonia have transparent and very acid water with extremely low concentrations of dissolved minerals.

The differentiation of Amazonia into 3 geochemical provinces is a rather generalised one. A large scale investigation program of the Brazilian government, using remote sensing techniques in combination with ground data collection (Projeto RADAMBRASIL) has shown that the geology of the basin is much more complex. This heterogeneity is reflected by the hydrochemical conditions of the streams as well (Furch and Junk, 1980). In very general terms, the classification nevertheless is very useful as a first approach for the description and the understanding of the geochemical conditions in Amazonia.

According to Furch (1984) most of the dissolved compounds including trace elements actually measured do not seem to be useful for a detailed classification, because their variability is great and there is little evidence for a characteristic distribution pattern. More suitable criteria in addition to those already used are the relationships between the absolute and relative amounts of alkali, alkali-earth and trace metals and possibly the amounts of total phosphorus.

Most freshwaters of the world are characterized by high percentages of alkali-earth metals, mainly calcium, with a high percentage of bicarbonate and are called carbonate waters. The characterization of carbonate water agrees with Sioli's definition of whitewater rivers from the Andean region (Fittkau's western peripheral region). Blackwaters, and clearwaters with low ion content, are characterized by high percentages of alkali metals (mostly sodium and potassium) and high percentages of trace metals such as iron, manganese, copper, zinc and aluminum. Bicarbonate concentration is normally very low in these types of water. Their catchment areas are situated in the northern and southern peripheral regions and in Central Amazonia.

Total phosphorus may be used as an additional criterion for the description of water types. There seems to be a gradient in the concentration of this element, whitewater being rich in total phosphorus, blackwater, extremely poor and clearwater intermediate. Considering the fact that phosphorus can be a limiting factor for plant growth, this parameter is important in respect to the evaluation of the fertility of Amazonian waters.

1.3.5. Amazonian lakes

Whereas water in streams and rivers is permanently renewed and mixed by the current, lake water persists at least for certain periods in the same area. Therefore, streams and rivers are considered as open systems with discharging character, whereas lakes are considered as closed systems with accumulating character. This differentiation indicates that lake water is subjected strongly to internal biotic and abiotic processes, which may accumulate or reduce substances in different ways to that which happens in rivers or streams.

Amazonian lakes are mostly floodplain lakes (Junk, 1980). These lakes receive water when the river rises, store it during flood period and return it, in part, to the river when the level goes down. Consequently, they are intermediate between open and closed systems. The basic pattern of hydrochemical parameters is strongly influenced by respective connected rivers. However, inside the floodplain lakes current is reduced. A thermal stratification of $2-4°C$ difference in temperature between surface water layer (epilimnion) and the water near the bottom (hypolimnion) develops. This stratification is not very stable, however, it hinders the mixture of the whole water body during high water.

Biotic and abiotic processes modify the chemical composition of the water. In the surface layer of $2-4$ m in depth, aquatic plants such as algae and floating aquatic macrophytes take up mineral nutrients and produce organic material and oxygen. Dead plants sink to the bottom and decompose, consuming the oxygen available and release mineral nutrients. After a short period of time a chemical stratification develops, showing an increasing amount of mineral nutrients but a strong reduction in oxygen and even the production of hydrogen sulphide near the bottom. In comparison to temperate lakes the reduction of oxygen is accelerated because of high temperatures accelerating the decomposition processes, diminishing at the same time the solubility of oxygen in the water. Whereas in water of 10°C 10.92 mg/l oxygen are soluble to reach 100% of saturation, in water of 30°C there are only 7.53 mg/l. Hypoxic or even anoxic conditions in the hypolimnion are therefore characteristic for all Amazonian lakes.

Exchange processes with the sediment and leaching of the shores lead to further modification in the chemical composition of the water. During low water period, when little water covers the sediment, concentration of dissolved mineral salts may increase about 15 times in comparison with the original concentration in the respective river water.

1.3.6. Amazonian waters in comparison with the world's freshwater

A comparison of the chemical composition of Amazon waters with that of freshwaters of other parts of the world seems to be a very ambitious and difficult task because of its enormous heterogeneity. However, there exists a theoretical 'world average freshwater' whose chemical composition has been calculated from hydrochemical information existing from inland waters all over the world (Livingstone, 1963). This will be used as a standard for comparison (Furch, 1976).

The world average freshwater is carbonate water with a high percentage of alkali-earth metals in comparison to alkali metals. The total concentration of electrolytes (major cations and anions), is about $185\mu S/cm(20°C)$. Whitewater from the Amazon river reflects very well the chemical properties of average world freshwater. However, the total amount of electrolytes measured near Manaus is only one third of the world average. Blackwater and frequently clearwater, too, differ considerably from the average world freshwater (Fig. 1.5a,b). These waters have a very low carbonate content, a high percentage of alkali metals and are extremely poor in electrolytes. Often the amount of electrolytes and the distribution of major cations is comparable to the amount in rainwater (Fig. 1.5a,b). This indicates the extremely low content of mineral salts in the soils of the catchment areas of respective rivers.

A further specific property of these waters with low ionic content is the greater amount of dissolved barium than strontium. In most freshwaters on earth, as well as in Amazonian whitewaters, the relationship between these elements is the contrary. In comparison with other freshwaters on earth, Amazonian blackwaters and many clearwaters can be considered as unusual in respect to the total amount of dissolved minerals as well as their overall chemical composition (Furch et al., 1982).

1.4. INTERACTIONS BETWEEN HYDROCHEMICAL CONDITIONS AND PLANT AND ANIMAL LIFE

1.4.1. The rainforest

As has already been mentioned, plants have a strong influence on the chemical composition of the water by uptake and release of substances. The trees of the Amazonian rainforest have a very small supply of mineral nutrients from the soil itself, because it is extremely poor. Therefore, vegetation has developed strategies to reduce as much as possible losses of nutrients by leaching. This guarantees that the amount necessary for growth is maintained in the system. Considering an average precipitation of about 2 m per year and a low ion exchange capacity of the soils this requires very effective absorption mechanisms able to quickly retain nutrients in even small concentrations.

In the Central Amazon rainforest the roots of the trees form a very dense layer on the soil surface, absorbing nutrients directly from litter, reducing losses by surface run-off and water infiltrating the ground. About half the total quantity of fine roots were found to extend just beneath the surface of the soil in Amazonian rainforests (Klinge, 1976). This indicates that the deeper soil is used by the trees principally as a substrate for mechanical anchoring rather than as a medium of nutrient supply.

The enormous diversity of tree species — about 500 species in 2000 m^2 surface — is considered as a response of the plant community to the extremely low nutrient concentrations of the soil too (Klinge, 1973; Fittkau, 1973). Different species are supposed to have slightly different requirements for nutrients and different capacities of nutrient uptake. Because of these very effective retentive mechanisms, the Amazonian rainforest responds to mineral nutrients as a nearly closed system, in spite of the high precipitation. Most of the nutrients are stored in the plants and circulate between dead and living organic matter. Of course, some losses are inevitable. However, the quantity of dissolved minerals leaving the system with stream and river water from the nutrient poor Central Amazonia is very small and comparable to the amount brought in by the rain. This shows on one side the importance of rains on the nutrient budget of the Amazonian rainforest. On the other hand, it indicates that high species diversity and closed vegetation cover are necessary to maintain the basic nutrient level in a system with low nutrient levels. Removal of the vegetation cover and/or reduction of the species diversity will

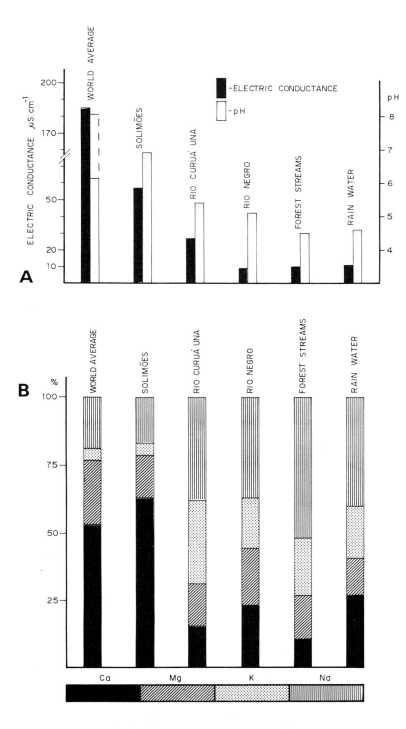

Fig. 1.5a,b. Electric conductance, pH value (Fig. 5a), and distribution of alkali and alkali-earth metals (Fig. 5b) of Amazonian rivers and streams near Manaus in comparison to rainwater and to the world average (according to Furch, 1984*, Junk *et al.*, 1981).

reduce the effectiveness of the filter system and result in substantial nutrient losses through the dense network of streams and rivers. This impoverishment quickly reaches a critical point, as can be seen by the shifting cultivation practised in Amazonia. After burning the forest, the concentration of mineral nutrients in the ash allows crop plantation. However, after only a few years crop plantation is no longer feasible, because of lack of nutrients in the soils due to lixiviation. The people have to shift to another place with untouched forest and start cutting and burning again.

Contrary to the small amount of mineral nutrients existing in most parts of the basin, organic carbon is produced in great quantity by the rainforest. Considerable amounts enter the streams and rivers and are transported in soluble and particulate form to the ocean. Richey et al. (1980) calculated that a total amount of $100 \cdot 10^6$ t of organic carbon is transported yearly from the basin to the ocean by the Amazon.

1.4.2. Aquatic plants and animals

Aquatic plants and animals can be influenced directly and indirectly by the chemical properties of the water. As direct influence we may consider any impact of dissolved substances on the physiology of the biota. Snails and bivalves for instance, do not occur in very acid blackwater, whereas they are frequently present in slightly acid clearwater with higher amounts of calcium, and in whitewater. Probably this is due to the fact that they are not able to develop their shells at such low concentrations of calcium and/or that such acidic pH of the water attacks the calcium in the shells, destroying them quickly. There is one exception: the snail, *Ampullaria papyracea*, occurs in blackwater. However, its shell is composed almost entirely of an organic substance, conchiolin, which normally constitutes only a small part of the structure of the molluscan shells. A similar difference can be found in the eggs of this snail. The representatives of the genus *Ampullaria* deposit their eggs in clumps outside the water. Whereas the eggs of the species occurring in whitewater are covered with a reddish or whitish hard calcareous shell, the eggs of *Ampullaria papyracea* are covered by a greenish gelatinous material only.

Some fish species prefer either electrolyte rich and little acid water, or electrolyte poor and acid rich one. The cardinal fish, *Cheirodon axelrodi*, a famous ornamental fish, occurs only in electrolyte poor streams. Of the two species of discus, *Symphysodon aequifasciatus* is restricted to whitewater, whereas *Symphysodon discus* occurs in clearwater. According to Geisler and Schneider (1976), the difference in calcium content in the water is reflected in the chemical composition of the skeleton of both species. In comparison to *Symphysodon aequifasciatus*, *S. discus* had a smaller percentage of calcium in its skeleton and a higher amount of magnesium and barium. The freshwater shrimp, *Macrobrachium amazonicum* occurs in great quantities in whitewater, whereas *Macrobrachium nattereri* occurs in blackwater.

Growth of aquatic plants strongly differs in the different water types. In whitewater the water hyacinth, *Eichhornia crassipes*, the aquatic fern *Salvinia auriculata*, the famous *Victoria amazonica*, and many other floating species are very common. Some aquatic grasses like *Echinochloa polystachya*, *Paspalum repens* and *Hymenachne amplexicaulis* form floating meadows of enormous extent during high water in the floodplains of whitewater rivers. With diminishing amounts of mineral nutrients in clearwater, their quantity is less and these species are completely absent in blackwater. Extremely low pH values may also have a negative effect on some of these species. Electrolyte-poor clearwater creeks are colonised by other aquatic plant species, for instance by members of the genus *Echinodorus*. They are rooted in the ground, and it is supposed that they take up part of the nutrients from the sediments (Junk and Howard-Williams, 1984).

Besides the direct impacts of the hydrochemical conditions on plants and animals, there exist many indirect ones. Blackwater creeks are for instance not colonised by submerged aquatic macrophytes, probably due to low light intensities caused by the coloured humic substances.

The most important indirect impact of waterchemical conditions on the fauna is due to the production of organic material. Production of organic material is high in nutrient-rich whitewater and low in nutrient-poor blackwater. In clearwater it is supposed to be of intermediate level. Phytoplankton produces in the floodplain lakes of the Amazon about 6 t dry matter/ha/year, whereas in blackwater there are only 60 kg (Schmidt, 1973, 1976). The great difference between blackwater and whitewater in respect to aquatic macrophyte development has already been mentioned. Animals dependent upon autochthonous primary production have little food available in blackwater and are scarce. Aquatic insects and crustaceans occur in blackwater in much smaller numbers than in whitewater. The same happens with fish and fish-feeding birds. Herons, kingfishers and cormorants occur in great numbers along the whitewater rivers, whereas they are seldom found along blackwater rivers.

In small blackwater streams we may find a relatively great number of fish but this is not due to the production capacity of the water itself. In these streams fish and most other aquatic animals depend on insects, fruit, pollen and other food items falling into the water from the surrounding forest (allochthonous material).

1.5. INTERACTION BETWEEN MAN AND HYDROCHEMICAL CONDITIONS

The innumerable watercourses of the Amazon Basin have been of great importance for man in his conquest of Amazonia and have been the natural water-highways for the penetration of immigrants. However, hydrochemical conditions influenced and are still influencing the colonisation and the development of the region.

The state capital, Manaus, was constructed on the shores of the Rio Negro near its confluence with the Amazon. Later the administration was transferred from Manaus to Barcellos, in the middle of Rio Negro, but fish were scarce and fishermen had to travel to the Amazon for fishing. Finally, the government decided to go back to the old place near the Amazon again, where fish are abundant. Whitewater rivers provide more than 90% of total catch of inland fishery of the state of Amazonas, fish being the principal source of protein for the Amazonian population (Bayley, 1981).

High fertility of whitewater is also reflected in the great amount of aquatic insects. Mosquitos are plentiful in the floodplains of the Amazon, making the use of the mosquito net essential, whereas in blackwater they are scarce.

Fertility of the water is to a certain extent correlated with the sediment carried by the river. Floodplains of whitewater rivers (várzea) are composed of sediments derived from the Andes and are rich in nutrients, being used by man for crop plantation and farming during low water periods. Soils of floodplains of blackwater rivers are poor in nutrients, and their production potential is consequently low. Sediments of clearwater rivers may have an intermediate status. Therefore, since the beginning of colonisation of Amazonia, the shores of whitewater rivers have in general shown a higher population density than the shores of blackwater rivers, which are locally termed 'hunger rivers' (rios de fome). Any further plans to use Amazonian floodplains for agriculture and husbandry should take this into account. The floodforests (igapós) of blackwater rivers and in part those of clearwater rivers have such a low production potential that their use is not to be recommended. Plantations would not compensate for the destruction of natural vegetation.

In whitewater floodplains, inundations are fundamentally important for the high productivity of the system, because the river water adds annually new sediments and dissolved mineral nutrients to the system. Large-scale flood control would interfere with the water regime and consequently with the nutrient budget of the system (Junk, 1982).

Another effect of hydrochemical conditions on man is due to water borne diseases. In streams rich in calcium and of slightly acidic pH, snails of the genus Biomphalaria occur, which are the hosts of

Schistosoma mansoni, vector of the schistosomiasis. Until 1949 the disease had not been reported in Amazonia. Probably it was introduced from highly infected regions of northeastern Brazil. Nowadays the disease occurs in the Carboniferous areas along the Transamazonian highway near Santarém (Sioli, 1953). Infested people may propagate the disease further into areas which actually are not yet infected, when hydrochemical conditions are suitable for the snails.

Today man is beginning to interfere with the hydrologic regime of Amazonian rivers on a large scale, due to the construction of enormous man-made lakes for the generation of hydroelectric energy. Hydrochemical conditions will have strong impacts on these development schemes. Water, not acid, and relatively rich in nutrients, will show high productivity, including mass development of aquatic macrophytes with all the negative consequences (Junk *et al.*, 1981). High oxygen consumption and H_2S development in the benthic zone occurs, because great quantities of organic material are produced and decomposed in the reservoirs. Suitable habitats for vectors of waterborne diseases develop, problems for navigation and fishery are created, etc. In the acidic black- and clearwater areas production of organic material will be low, and macrophyte growth will be strongly reduced. This will, however, reduce fish production, which is often considered as a very attractive byproduct of man-made lakes. Furthermore, acid water will attack the dam construction and turbines.

Other development schemes, such as large-scale deforestation and agricultural activities, mining and development of industries will in future have impact on the hydrological regime of Amazonian waters and its hydrochemical conditions, which at present are difficult to evaluate. This indicates the great importance of further studies on the hydrochemistry and its role in the Amazonian ecosystem in order to diminish negative impacts and avoid irreversible modifications by man's activity.

REFERENCES

Anonymous (1972) Regenwasseranalysen aus Zentralamazonien, ausgeführt in Manaus, Amazonas, Brasilien von Dr. Harald Ungemach. *Amazoniana* 3(2), 186 – 198.

Bayley, P. B. (1981) Fish yield from the Amazon in Brazil: comparison with African river yields and management possibilities. *Trans. Am. Fish. Soc.* 110, 351 – 359.

Falesi, I. C., Rodrigues, T. E., Morikawa, I. K. and Reis, R. S. (1971) Solos do Distrito Agropecuário de SUFRAMA (Trencho: km 30 – km 79, Rod. BR-174). Instituto da Pesquisa e Experimentação Agropecuária da Amazônia Ocidental (IPEAAOc), Serie Solos: 99 pp.

Fittkau, E. J. (1971) Ökologische Gliederung des Amazonas-Gebietes auf geochemischer Grundlage. *Münster. Forsch. Geol. Paläont.* 20/21, 35 – 50.

Fittkau, E. J. (1973) Artenmannigfaltigkeit amazonischer Lebensräume aus ökologischer Sicht. *Amazoniana* 4(3), 321 – 340.

Furch, K. (1976) Haupt- und Spurenmetallgehalte zentralamazonischer Gewässertypen (Erste Ergebnisse). *Biogeographica* 7, 27 – 43.

Furch, K. (1984) Water chemistry of the Amazon: The distribution of chemical elements among freshwaters. In *The Amazon. Limnology and Landscape Ecology of a Mighty Tropical River and its Basin*, Ed. H. Sioli. Dr. W. Junk Publ., The Hague, pp. 167 – 199.

Furch, K. and Junk W. J. (1980) Water chemistry and macrophytes of creeks and rivers in Southern Amazonia and the Central Brazilian Shield. In *Tropical Ecology and Development*, Ed. J. I. Furtado, pp.771 – 796. The International Society of Tropical Ecology, Kuala Lumpur.

Furch, K., Junk, W. J. and Klinge, H. (1982) Unusual chemistry of natural Amazonian water. *Acta Cient. Venezolana* 33, 269 – 273.

Geisler, R. and Schneider, J. (1976) The element matrix of Amazon waters and its relationship with the mineral content of fishes (Determination using neutron activation analysis). *Amazoniana* 6(1), 47 – 65.

Junk, W. J. (1980). Áreas inundáveis – um desafio para limnologia. *Acta Amazonica* 10(4), 775 – 795.

Junk, W. J. (1982) Amazonian floodplains: their ecology and potential use. *Rev. d'Hydrobiol. Trop.* 15(4), 285 – 301.

Junk, W. J. and Howard-Williams, C. (1984) Ecology of aquatic macrophytes in Amazonia. In *The Amazon. Limnology and Landscape Ecology of a Mighty Tropical River and its Basin*, Ed. H. Sioli. Dr. W. Junk Publ., The Hague, pp. 269 – 293.

Junk, W. J., Robertson, B. A., Darwich, A. J. and Vieira, I. (1981) Investigações limnológicas e ictiológicas em Curuá-Una, a primeira represa hidrelétrica na Amazônia Central. *Acta Amazonica* 11(4), 689 – 716.

Klinge, H. (1976) Nährstoffe, Wasser und Durchwurzelung von Podsolen und Latosolen unter tropischem Regenwald bei Manaus/Amazonien. *Biogeographica* 7, 45 – 58.

Klinge, H. (1973) Struktur und Artenreichtum des zentral-amazonischen Regenwaldes. *Amazoniana* 4(3), 283 − 292.

Livingstone, D. A. (1963) Chemical composition of rivers and lakes. U.S. Geological Survey, Professional Paper 440 − G, 1 − 64.

Marques, J., Santos, J. M., Villa Nova, N. A. and Salati, E. (1977) Precipitable water and water vapour flux between Belém and Manaus. *Acta Amazonica* 7(3), 355 − 362.

Marques, J., Santos, J. M. and Salati, E. (1979) O armazenamento atmosférico de vapor d'água sobre a região Amazônica. *Acta Amazônica* 9(4), 715 − 721.

Richey, J. E., Brock, J. T., Naiman, R. J., Wissmar, R. C. and Stallard, R. F. (1980) Organic carbon: oxidation and transport in the Amazon river. *Science* 207, 1348 − 1351.

Salati, E., Dall'Olio, A., Matsui, E. and Bat, J. A. (1979) Recycling of water in the Amazon basin. An isotopic study. *Wat. Resources Res.* 15(5), 1250 − 1258.

Schmidt, G. W. (1972) Chemical properties of some waters in the tropical rain-forest region of central Amazonia along the new road Manaus — Caracaraí. *Amazoniana* 3(2), 199 − 207.

Schmidt, G. W. (1973) Primary production of phytoplankton in the three types of Amazonian waters. III. Primary productivity of phytoplankton in a tropical floodplain lake of Central Amazonia, Lago do Castanho, Amazonas, Brazil. *Amazoniana* 4(4), 379 − 404.

Schmidt, G. W. (1976): Primary production of phytoplankton in the three types of Amazonian waters. IV. On the primary productivity of phytoplankton in a bay of the lower Rio Negro (Amazonas, Brazil). *Amazoniana* 5(4), 517 − 528.

Sioli, H. (1950) Das Wasser im Amazonasgebiet. *Forsch. Fortschr.* 26(21/22), 274 − 280.

Sioli, H. (1953) Schistosomiasis and limnology in the Amazon region. *Amer. J. Trop. Med. Hyg.* 2(4), 700 − 707.

Sioli, H. (1965) Bemerkungen zur Typologie amazonischer Flüsse. *Amazoniana* 1(1), 74 − 83.

Villa Nova, N. A., Salati, E. and Matsui, E. (1976) Estimativa de evapotranspiração na Bacia Amazônica. *Acta Amazonica* 6(2), 215 − 228.

CHAPTER 2

The Climatology and Hydrology of Amazonia

ENEAS SALATI

(Formerly of INPA - Manaus), Centro de Energia Nuclear na Agriculture/USP, Piracicaba, Brazil

CONTENTS

2.1. INTRODUCTION

Throughout development of civilisations, although not always well documented, there have always been modifications to the environment, especially due to the substitution of forest and other natural ecological systems for agricultural ones. Deforestation was often necessary to utilise the soil for agricultural production and in previous times to provide fuel for heating and cooking. Even today, a large part of the world's population uses wood as a source of energy, and in the last quarter of the present century, forested regions (particularly those of the humid tropics) are being cleared in an attempt

18

to enlarge the agricultural frontiers. However, the speed of the present modifications is accelerated by the use of advanced technology (bulldozers, power-saws, defoliants, etc).

In the last millenia many ecological modifications have resulted from the human need to provide sustenance. The lack of data on the areas actually covered by the different natural ecosystems, especially in Europe, Asia and Africa at the beginning of civilisation (4 – 5,000 B.C.), coupled with a lack of scientific methods for measuring and recording physical atmospheric parameters, prevent a complete analysis of man-made modifications on these continents. In addition to the anthropogenic variations there are also those resulting from natural causes.

Slight climatic oscillations, can, through positive feedbacks, produce large ecological modifications. It is known that climatic changes occurred in relatively recent times and still continue today. There is much evidence of climatic oscillations in Amazonia during the last millenia (see Chapter 8). Research workers today face a serious problem in trying to separate these from natural ones arising from human activity. Even in the Americas it is difficult to establish the actual influence of colonisation (deforestation and agriculture). There are no data available on the primeval conditions before European activity started in the region. In some places, such information is unavailable, even today.

The colonisation of the north, west and southwest regions of the State of Paraná, Brazil, is a typical example. Within a few decades, practically all forests in the region, including large stands of araucaria, were replaced by agricultural systems (coffee, soybeans, wheat and pastures). However, there were no meteorological records for this region, and even the existing ones are obtained using imprecise methods. Data is available only for the last two decades, when the primary ecosystem was already practically completely altered. Similarly, it is difficult to obtain long-term meteorological and hydrological records which are susceptible to reliable statistical analysis to identify the modifications in the regions of the humid tropics which are today being actively exploited for lumber and agriculture.

The same history is repeating itself in the Amazon region, where many basic data will only be obtained after the ecosystem has been totally modified. In this region alone, three million hectares of land are probably changed annually, in the absence of basic ecosystem information. It will consequently be difficult to detect anthropogenic modifications to the biogeochemical cycles, the water cycle and the energy balance.

Since 1970, there have been attempts to develop direct and indirect research which would permit evaluation of some parameters of Amazonian ecosystem, especially to quantify the components of the hydrological cycle. This chapter summarises some of the information obtained and considers some aspects of possible ecological alterations.

More detailed information can be found in the chapter on 'Climatologia da Amazônia' (Salati, E. and Marques, J.) in a book edited by Harold Sioli (1984).

2.2. GENERAL CONSIDERATIONS

The climatological and hydrological characteristics of Amazonia are strongly linked with the geomorphology and geographic conditions of the region. As can be seen in Fig. 2.1, Amazonia is situated between 5°N and 10°S and its upper third is cut by the Equator. The Andean barrier (which limits the Amazon region to the west with a closed semicircle), and the Central Plateau with a maximum slope of 100 m for almost 4,000 km give the region special characteristics which are not found anywhere else in the world. The central plateau is limited to the north and to the south by moderate slopes (an average of about 800 m) giving the Amazon Basin the form of a 'U' opening to the east where it receives hot and humid winds from the Atlantic.

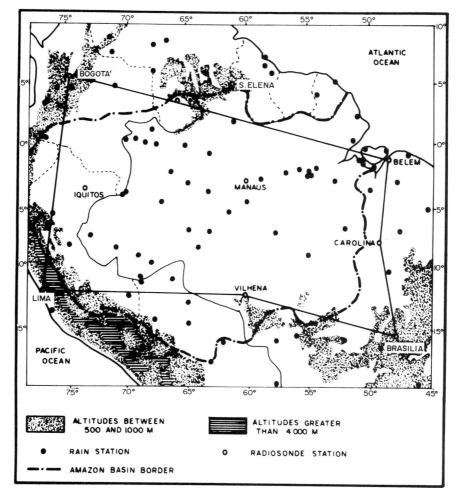

Fig. 2.1. The network of rain stations and radio sounding stations used for this study.

2.3. SOLAR ENERGY

As a result of its position between latitude 5°N and 10°S the Amazon Basin has a day-length which varies very little during the year. Theoretically, the maximum variation of sunshine at latitude 5°N is 11 hours and 50 minutes, in December, and 12 hours and 24 minutes, in June, and at latitude 10°S, 12 hours and 42 minutes and 11 hours and 32 minutes, respectively. In the central east — west strip of the basin, the duration of the day remains practically constant throughout the year.

In the city of Manaus, situated at 3°08'S latitude, practically in the centre of Amazonia, the solar energy at the limit of the earth's atmosphere, varies from a maximum of 885 calories per cm²/day in January to a minimum of 767 calories per cm²/day in June. Figure 2.2a shows the insolation ratio (n/N number of sunshine hours divided by the number of theoretical maximum shining), the solar radiation reaching the highest part of the atmosphere (Qo), and the solar energy which reaches the top of the trees

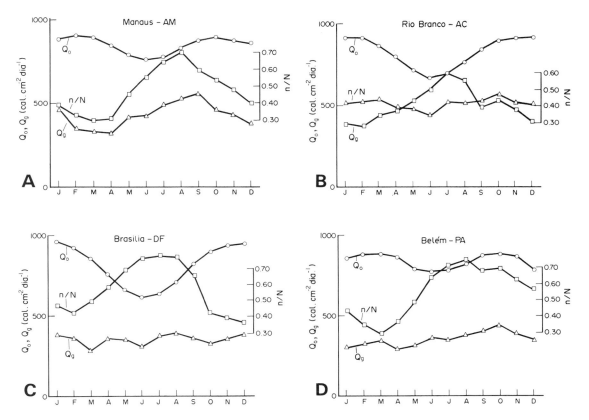

Fig. 2.2. Average monthly values for insolation (n/N), solar energy at the outer edge of the atmosphere (Qo) and total radiation at soil level
(Qg).
(a) Manaus, Amazonas (3° 08'S; 60° 2'W).
(b) Rio Branco, Acre (9° 58'S; 67° 48'W).
(c) Brasília, DF (15° 47'S; 47° 56'W).
(d) Belém, Pará (1° 28'S; 48° 29'W).

(Qg) in Manaus (Villa Nova *et al.*, 1978). What really limits the hours of insolation and the energy available at plant level is the cloud cover, which is relatively high in the region although variable throughout the year.

Similar measurements are available for Belém (Pará), Rio Branco (Acre) and Brasília (Federal District) (Figs. 2.2b, 2.2c and 2.2d). These show that there is a variation, both in cloud cover and in total energy, for the different regions of Amazonia. The annual average insolation ratio in Amazonia is around 50%, again indicating that the amount of cloud cover is considerable, although varying throughout the year.

There are few precise measurements of solar energy in Amazonia. Only recently instruments (Eppley pyrometer), permitting highly reliable measurement, have been installed at some meteorological stations in Amazonia. The only published data are those of Ribeiro *et al.* (1982) and Villa Nova *et al.* (1976) in Manaus, which indicate an average energy incidence on the region of 400 calories cm²/day.

Both insolation and the available energy are strongly dependent on cloud formation in the region. These, in turn, are directly influenced by air humidity and the mechanism of cloud production.

The spectral distribution of the solar radiation on a cloudless day (Almeida *et al.*, 1979), are shown in Fig. 2.3 together with the results obtained for the spectral distribution of global radiation.

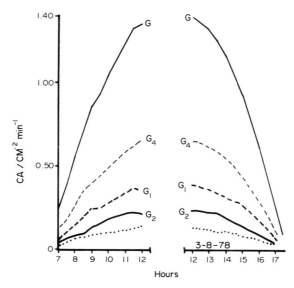

Fig. 2.3. Total spectral distribution of radiation at grand scale in Manaus. G. total; Gl violet-blue; G2 green-yellow; G3 red; G4 infrared.

2.4. TEMPERATURE

The average monthly temperature varies very little throughout practically the entire Amazon region. On the coast at Belém, the highest monthly average temperature, 26.9°C, occurs in November and the lowest in March, 24.5°C. The annual variation of average temperature is very small in the central strip of the basin in part because there are no relief effects, and in part because of the position of the region. In Manaus, the highest average monthly temperature, 27.9°C, occurs in September and the lowest, 25.8°C, between February and April, with a variation of only 2.1°C. In the city of Iquitos the highest average monthly temperature, 32°C occurs in November and the lowest, 30°C in July.

This situation is valid for the whole Amazonian plain. However, toward the border regions of Amazonia the situation begins to change. Thus, to the west, at the Andean border the temperature falls, and in the highest parts the most significant precipitation is in the form of snow.

To the north and south towards the Guyana Plateau or the Central Brazilian Plateau, thermal conditions change. In the northern and southern limits of the Amazon region there is a tendency towards continentality, with well-defined dry periods and lower temperatures as can be seen (Figs. 2.4a-d).

An important phenomenon which causes significant temperature variations, sometimes with ecological consequences, is the 'friagem' (cold spell). This occurs when masses of cold south polar air reach the central and western parts of Amazonia. This can cause the minimum temperature to fall as low as 14°C.

2.5. WINDS

As elsewhere, but in Amazonia in particular, knowledge of the water vapour origin and distribution is fundamental for explaining the influence of the forest on conditions in the region. It is important to know the winds not only at surface level, but especially in relation to the altitude profile (at least to the

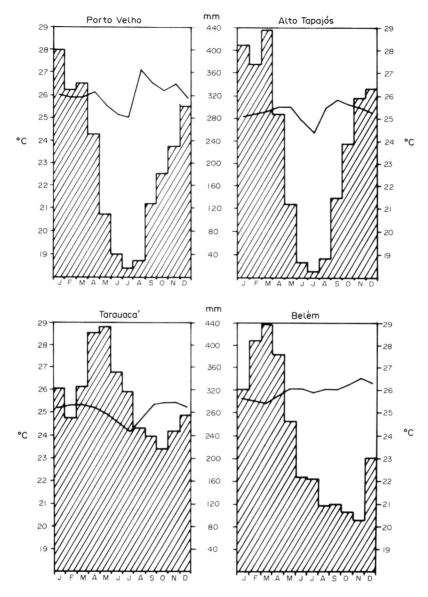

Fig. 2.4. Climate diagrams for rainfall and temperature in some Brazilian Amazon towns:
(a) Porto Velho, Alto Tapajós, Tarauacá, Belém.

500 mb level). Above that level the quantity of water vapour in the atmosphere is small and has little significance in the calculation of water vapour flow deviation. Radiosonde data from a network of aircraft flight control stations (Marques *et al.*, 1979) (Fig. 2.1) provide general information on air movement.

In general, the prevailing winds in the region come from the east as part of the trade winds of the general atmospheric circulation. To the north of the Equator, these are the northeastern and to the south, the southeastern trade winds.

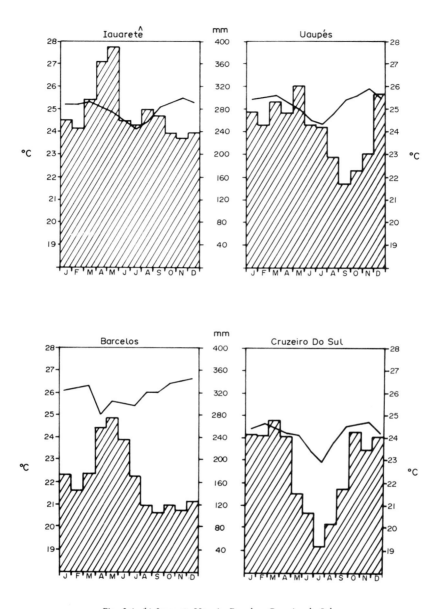

Fig. 2.4. (b) Iauaretê, Uaupés, Barcelos, Cruzeiro do Sul.

Which of these winds predominates in the region depends on the displacement of the belt of the intertropical convergence zone that swings to the north or to the south depending on the displacement of the thermal Equator from the annual variation in the sun declination.

The intertropical convergence zone (which is well defined over the ocean) becomes increasingly diffuse in December to February as it penetrates the continent. The influence of the movement of air masses can be clearly observed by an analysis of cloud formation using meteorological satellite

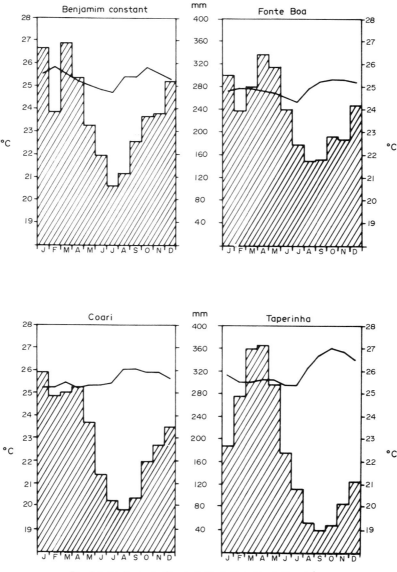

Fig. 2.4. (c) Benjamin Constant, Fonte Boa, Coari, Taperinha.

photography (Figs. 2.5a-d show some characteristic situations, while Figs. 2.6a,b show the structure of the winds in Belém and Manaus : data from Marques *et al.*, 1978). More detailed information is available in Marques (1978).

2.6. WATER VAPOUR

Atmospheric water vapour has a fundamental importance in the characteristics of climate. Our studies have therefore given special attention to the understanding of its origin and its spatial and temporal distributions as well as to its involvement in the dynamics of cloud formation, whether of local or frontal origin.

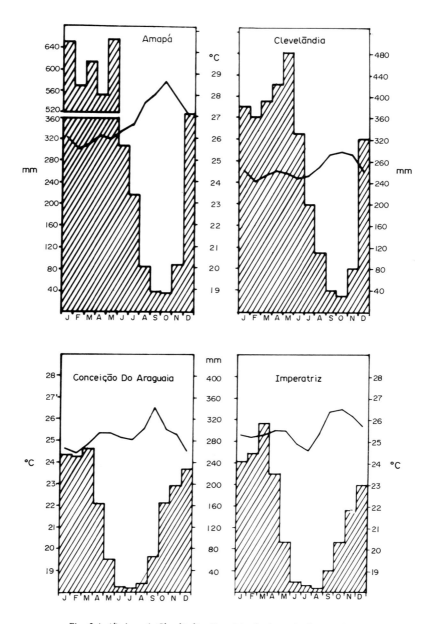

Fig. 2.4. (d) Amapá, Clevelândia, Conceição do Araguaia, Imperatriz.

Water vapour controls the balance of energy, limits the rates of evaporation and transpiration and determines the predominant cloud systems in the region. Although the Amazon region may be defined as having a hot humid climate there are variations in the quantity of water vapour in the atmosphere, both in the central strip and in regions with higher altitude.

In our studies we have always tried to identify the origin of the water vapour, and thus to differentiate between that coming from the ocean (primary vapour) from that arising from transpiration

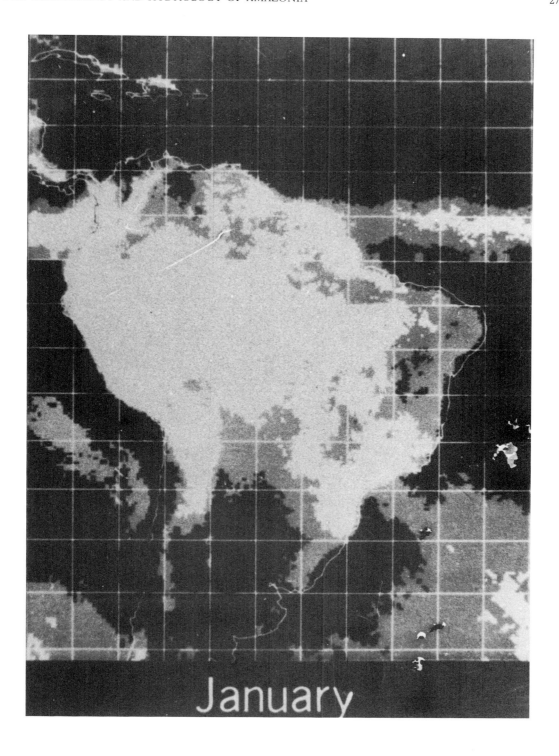

Fig. 2.5a. Cloud cover for 4 years for the month of January from stationary satellite data (courtesy of INPE).

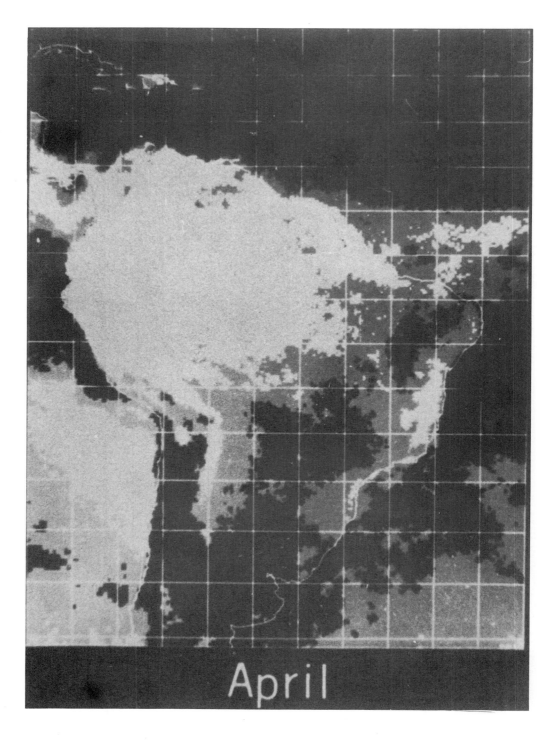

Fig. 2.5b. Average cloud cover for 4 years for the month of April from stationary satellite data (courtesy of INPE).

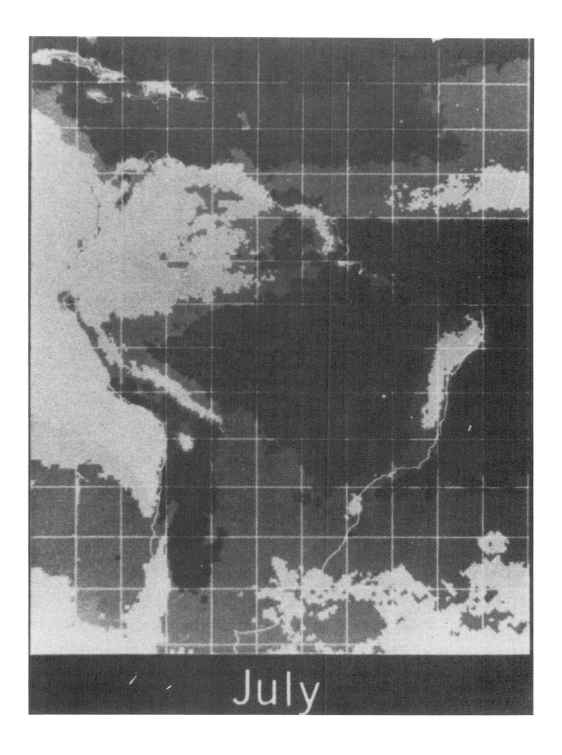

Fig. 2.5c. Average cloud cover for 4 years for the month of July from stationary satellite data (courtesy of INPE).

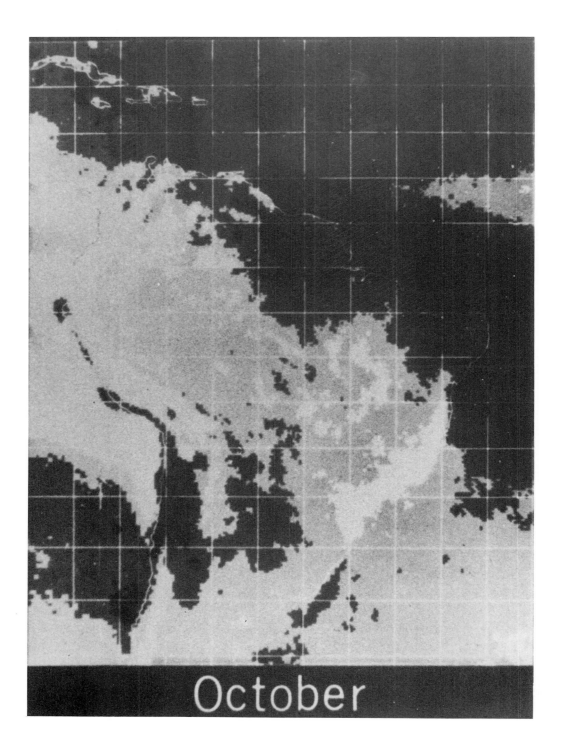

Fig. 2.5d. Average cloud cover for 4 years for the month of October from stationary satellite data (courtesy of INPE).

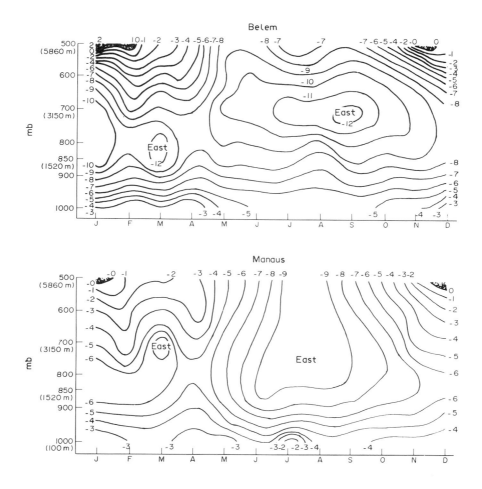

Fig. 2.6a. Monthly wind variation in each layer in Belém and Manaus. Isolines in m/s. The negative values indicate east.

and evaporation (secondary vapour). For many areas of the world the secondary vapour is negligible or very little in comparison with that from the ocean. In contrast in the Amazon region, the secondary vapour is of the same magnitude as the primary vapour.

The consequences of the interaction between the forest and the present dynamic equilibrium of water in the region, should be carefully analysed to determine the possible climatic modifications due to deforestation.

The quantities of precipitable water vapour found in the Amazon region are shown in Fig. 2.7 (Marques et al., 1979), the average being of the order of 40 mm. This indicates that there is a mass of water in the form of vapour over the Amazon region corresponding to 24×10^{10} tons.

If one knows the flux of water vapour it is possible to calculate the net flow through a closed polygon enclosing the hydrographic basin, and this value should be equal to the water outflow from the system for a certain period. The deviation of the water vapour flow in the Amazon Basin was estimated by Marques et al. (1980) and corresponds to 172,616 m^3/s.

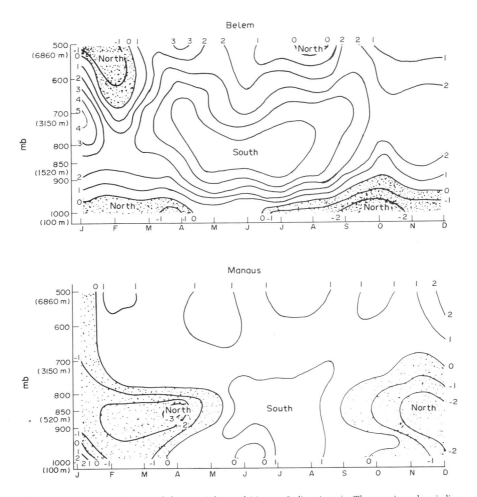

Fig. 2.6b. Monthly wind variation in each layer in Belém and Manaus. Isolines in m/s. The negative values indicate north.

2.7. PRECIPITATION

If the deforestation brings climatic modifications, one of the main expected variations would be in the levels and distribution of precipitation. Thus a detailed knowledge of its distribution (measured in isohyets) is basic to identifying subsequent fluctuations caused by ecological alterations. Not only is the total rainfall important, but so also is its distribution during the year and the frequency of various types of rain. It is very common at certain times of the year to get local rains from precipitation of cumulonimbus clouds, or, sometimes, drizzle from cumulocongestus clouds. These rains are important in the regional ecological equilibrium: often during periods of least precipitation, water from these sporadic rains can reactivate the vegetative growth system, dynamizing biological processes in general.

In the central region of Amazonia near Manaus, where there is a fairly well defined dry season from June to November, trees begin to lose their leaves after a dry period of 10 − 15 days, indicating a deficit of water in the soil. Consequently a relatively long drought period could be important in modifying the ecological equilibrium.

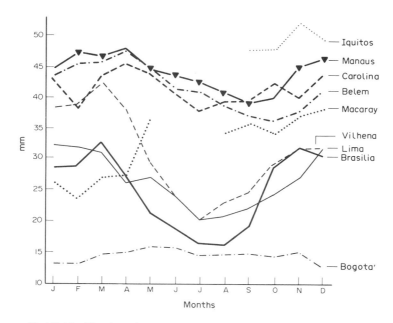

Fig.2.7. Monthly values of precipitable water in various Amazonian and nearby cities.

On Marajó Island the distribution of rain defines distinct botanical landscapes of different vegetation types. Here, close to oceanic sources of water vapour, there is minimal effect on precipitation patterns from recycling of water. Total precipitation (an average of 3,000 mm) varies little on the island but there is variation in distribution as can be seen in Fig. 2.8. In the forested regions (half of the northwest of the island) the minimum precipitation (150 mm) occurs in October, and the maximum (470 mm) in March. In the pasture regions the minimum falls to zero in March (IDESP, 1977).

In other regions of the world, where deforestation has modified the landscape, and the forests have been replaced by human activities linked with agriculture and animal husbandry, it has been impossible to quantify the changes in the water regime either as far as quantities or distribution of precipitation are concerned.

In Amazonia, although the current meteorological data are insufficient, some stations distributed throughout the region have a series of readings which will probably make possible more detailed observations of the changes possibly resulting from human modification of the landscape.

2.7.1 Distribution of rainfall

Figure 2.9 shows the isohyets for the Amazon region and the total precipitation varying within the basin from 1,500 mm to over 3,000 mm (IBGE, 1977). The annual totals of precipitation are greater in the north coast, with values over 3,250 mm. These values decrease towards the Central Amazon region, and increase in more western regions, especially in the Northwest. Extremes of precipitation reaching above 5,000 mm occur in some places influenced by the Andes. Figure 2.10 describes rainfall distribution in some characteristic points of the region. Generally there is a large variation in the seasons and a 6 month displacement between maximum precipitation rates to the north and south of the Equator. To the west of the basin the distribution becomes more uniform, and there is precipitation practically throughout the year.

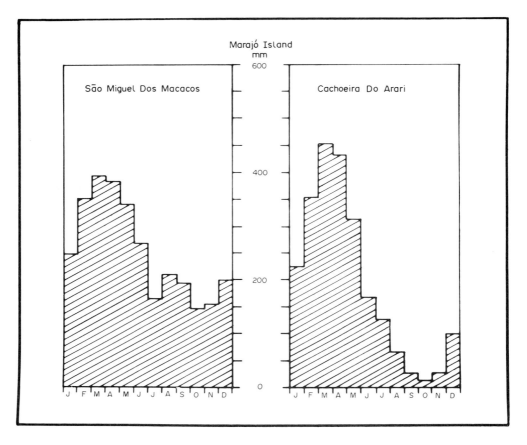

Fig. 2.8. Precipitation for two places on Marajó Island in the Amazon delta: S. Miguel dos Macacos (1° 11'S; 50° 28'W) in forested area; Cachoeira do Arari (1° 01'S; 48° 58'W) in savannah.

2.8. WATER AND ENERGY BALANCE

Many papers have been published in the last few years which attempt to evaluate the components of the water balance for Amazonia. Some authors have tried to study the components of the water balance by direct measure of the water flow, particularly plant transpiration (Jordan *et al.*, 1981).

Other authors have attempted to evaluate the water balance for representative hydrographic basins (Leopoldo *et al.*, 1982a,b), and others for the Amazon Basin as a whole (Marques *et al.*, 1980b; Molion, 1975; Lettau *et al.*, 1979 and Villa Nova *et al.*, 1976).

2.8.1. Water balance in a model basin

In 1979 a special programme was established between INPA, CENA and WMO to study the water balance in a 'model' basin. The site chosen was 60 km north of Manaus on the road linking Manaus to Caracarai. The model basin is 25 km^2 and is covered with a dense forest typical of the region (Fig. 2.11a-c give an idea of the region). The trees are up to 50 m tall. Dra. Maria Nazaré Goes Ribeiro (INPA) was put in charge of the project.

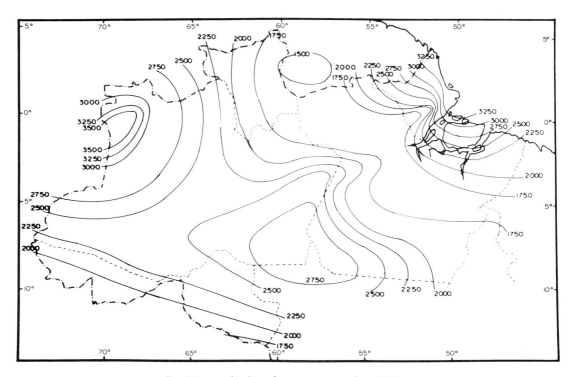

Fig. 2.9. Annual isohyets for Amazonia (data from IBGE).

Pluviometers were installed above the tree tops to measure total precipitation, and at ground level for interception and measurements of stemflow. Limnimeters were installed and conventional meteorological measurements also made, including measurements of evaporation in a 20 m^2 tank. Specific studies were directed to measuring the movement of groundwater using heavy rains with their low concentration of ^{18}0 and D as tracers. There is a series of publications containing these data (Leopoldo *et al.*, 1981, 1982b).

Annually, 25.6% of precipitation is intercepted by the vegetation and returns to the atmosphere by direct evaporation, 45.5% is transpired by plants and 25.9% is drained through the igarapé. Figure 2.12 (Leopoldo *et al.*, 1982a), illustrates results obtained from February 1980 to February 1981, in which about 74% of the precipitation returns to the atmosphere in the form of vapour through evapotranspiration.

The results also indicate that the interception depends on the intensity of the rain. Figure 2.13 (Leopoldo *et al.*, 1982a) shows the interception values as a function of rain intensity. It can be seen that for 0 − 2 mm rain the interception is 28%, stemflow 0.1% and throughfall 71.9%. For 20 − 40 mm rain the interception is 23.7%, stemflow 0.2% and throughfall 76.1%. For 40 − 60 mm rain interception is 23.7%, stemflow 0.4% and throughfall 80.8%. The average for the period studied (1 year) was interception 22.0%, stemflow 0.3% and throughfall 77.7%. The amounts of interception in Figs. 2.12 and 2.13 while not identical (because they were measured differently) are nevertheless of similar magnitude.

The readings show about 75% of the precipitation returns to the atmosphere in the form of water vapour through the action of plants (25% is due to interception and direct evaporation and 50% to transpiration of the trees) indicating the importance of the type of vegetation cover for the components

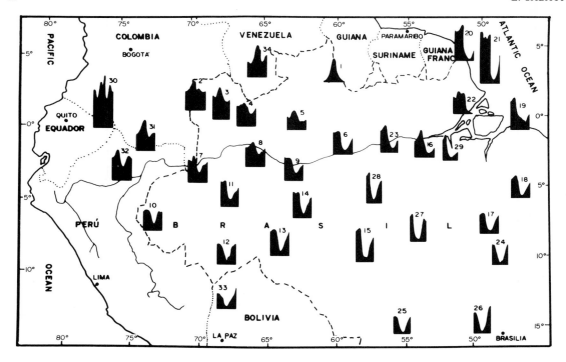

Fig. 2.10. Rainfall distribution in Amazonia 1. Boa Vista, 2 etc. (from original).

of the water budget. Other types of vegetation cover could lead to two types of change: first, different values for the components of the hydrological cycle and secondly, an alteration in the quantity of water vapour in the atmosphere which, in turn, affects energy balance and cloud formation.

As there is an appreciable amount of water vapour (more than 50% of precipitation) which returns to the atmosphere, the latter could be an important fact or in either energy balance or cloud generation effects.

2.8.2. Water balance in the Amazon Basin

Water balance in the Amazon Basin as a whole has been established by two different methods: first, using meteorological data (Villa Nova *et al.*, 1976; Molion, 1975 and Lettau *et al.*, 1979) and secondly, using radiosonde data (Marques *et al.*, 1980b). The basic problem is the estimate of evapotranspiration which has been made using different methods.

Water balance estimates are possible because measurements of Amazon water flow (Oltman *et al.*, 1967) make it possible to assess average run-off. A summary of the values obtained can be found in Table 2.1 where estimates of actual and potential evapotranspiration are shown. There is a variation depending on the method and combination of values used, however, a general average of these measures suggests that evapotranspiration is equal to 48.4% and run-off 51.6%. The average values for evapotranspiration are less than those obtained in the model basin because the model basin has a vegetation density and soil characteristics not uniform across Amazonia.

Fig. 2.11a. View of forest of model watershed, 60 km north of Manaus, taken from the tower shown in 11b.

The general conclusion is that the Amazon Basin receives $11.87 \times 10^{12} m^3$/year of rainwater, loses $6.43 \times 10^{12} m^3$ through evapotranspiration and $5.45 \times 10^{12} m^3$/year through the Amazon River discharge. The average mass of water vapour in the region is 24×10^{10} tons. Figure 2.14 gives a chart of these values.

2.9. EVIDENCE OF WATER RECYCLING

Is there any likelihood of climatic modification due to deforestation? This question can be analysed in various ways depending upon the subsequent changes. For example, it will vary if the deforested area is re-covered with other forest types, or if there is regeneration of the original forest, or if the deforested area is used for other agricultural activities (perennial agriculture, annual crops or pastures). The capacity of the ecosystem to regenerate itself, and the degree of modification in each of them, for each kind of activity to be introduced must therefore be considered.

The next step is to forecast, with mathematical models, how the changes in land use could influence climatic changes. This is not an easily solved problem, and, so far, there is no complete work on the subject. What can be done, is to understand, using simple hypotheses, the mechanisms which determine the present levels of precipitation and their distribution.

As a first approximation, an attempt was made to ascertain the dependence, within the present dynamic equilibrium, between the atmosphere, the forest and the precipitation. To analyse this interdependent relationship, we have tried to discover if there is any water vapour recycling which orginates in the Amazon Basin itself, and whether or not this is significant in relation to the water vapour from the ocean. Molion (1975) divided recycling into two types. The first involves more rapid circulation than would occur in the lower layers of the atmosphere and the other a greater residence time of the water vapour in the atmosphere (involving an interaction of the higher layers of atmosphere and water vapour generated at the surface).

Fig. 2.11b. Observation tower in model watershed area.

Fig. 2.11c Meteorological station of model watershed with typical forest in background.

Two distinct methods have been used to evaluate the problems related to the water vapour recycling (Salati *et al.*, 1978; Marques, 1976 and Dall'olio, 1976). As, on average, 50% (and in some cases up to 75%) of the precipitated water returns to the atmosphere through evapotranspiration, about 6.43×10^{12} tons of water vapour are generated within the Amazon basin as a whole through the direct action of plants in interception, evaporation and transpiration. This is the same magnitude as water vapour coming from the ocean, Marques *et al.* (1980a). The calculation of water vapour from the ocean was obtained by methods and data independent of evapotranspiration estimates.

Is the mass of vapour generated by the forest significant in the production of precipitation in the region, and can it influence rainfall levels in adjacent regions? In the simplest case, the generated vapour would leave the Amazon region towards the west, and would be substituted by primary vapour, also generated in the ocean. According to this hypothesis, there would be a vapour flow from the Atlantic Ocean in the direction of the Amazon region and an equivalent vapour flow from the Amazon Basin to the Pacific Ocean. A second possibility would involve vapour flow from the Atlantic Ocean and an equivalent vapour flow divided partly toward the Pacific Ocean and partly toward the neighbouring regions of the Atlantic Basin, at higher latitudes.

These hypotheses are only partially acceptable because of the geomorphology of the Amazon Basin. The Andean Mountains form a natural barrier to the west 4,000 m, and effectively prevent the exit of water vapour to the Pacific Ocean (as is shown by the higher levels of precipitation in the Andean region). Water vapour flow to the north and south are possible, bearing in mind the relatively low altitudes (on average $700 - 800$ m) in the Central Plateau of Brazil and the Guyana Plateau.

Recent data (Marques *et al.*, 1980a) indicate that a water vapour flow to the south occurs in almost every month of the year, but at much lower amounts than the flow from the Atlantic Ocean. These observations indicate that there must be a recycling of the water vapour in the Amazon region. Radiosonde data obtained in the polygons shown in Fig. 2.1, are convergent to the river outflow measured by independent methods (Marques, 1976). Another independent method to assess the extent of water vapour recycling, used ^{18}O and D concentrations in rain and river waters of different regions (Salati *et al.*, 1979). This isotopic method is simple in principle, gives a deeper insight and also estimates how much water vapour leaves the region and its isotopic concentration.

Water in general has various molecule types depending on the hydrogen and oxygen isotopes of which it is composed. The stable hydrogen isotopes are ^{1}H and ^{2}H or D. The stable oxygen isotopes are ^{16}O, ^{17}O, ^{18}O. Different species of water molecules are formed by the combination of these various isotopes, e.g. $HH^{16}O$, $HH^{18}O$, $HH^{17}O$, $HD^{16}O$, etc. Of these molecules the most important because of their abundance and relevance to our work are $HH^{16}O$ and $HH^{18}O$.

In the process of evaporation of water in the ocean, molecules of the type $HH^{16}O$, which have a molecular mass equal to 18, are evaporated before molecules of the type $HH^{18}O$ which have a molecular mass of 20. During evaporation there is, therefore, an isotopic fractionation and the vapour from the seawater has an ^{18}O concentration about 8% less than the ocean concentration. As this water vapour enters the continent it will condense and probably become rain and then soil and river waters. Since heavier molecules condense first, the process of cloud formation and precipitation leads to isotope depletion of residual water vapour, so that water vapour of the westerly regions has lower concentrations of ^{18}O.

When systematic measurements of the isotopic composition of the Amazon region rainwater were made, the decrease in ^{18}O concentration was less than that expected in a process of continuous removal of water vapour through precipitation. This could be the consequence of water vapour produced by evapotranspiration mixing with the oceanic vapour such that rain in a certain place is formed by mixture

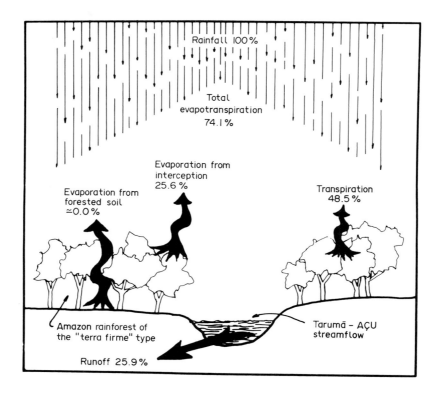

Fig. 2.12. Hydrological balance in model watershed.

Interception as a function of rainfall classes

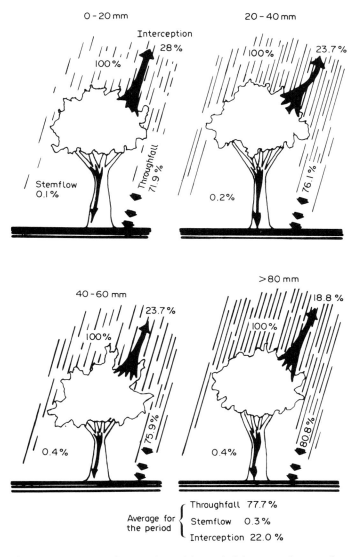

Fig. 2.13. Interception of water by the crowns of trees in the model watershed shown as a function of precipitation intensity.

of the two. Models have been developed to estimate the isotope composition of rain at different longitudes as a function of known values of precipitation, evapotranspiration and isotope composition of rain and water vapour in a more easterly region (Dall'olio *et al.*, 1979).

Figures 2.15 and 2.16 summarise the two models used in these calculations. Salati *et al.* (1979) analysed the problem. The hypothesis of water vapour recycling leads to [18]O values which are closer to those observed in nature.

In view of the above lines of evidence, water vapour recycling in the atmosphere within the Amazon Basin must exist, and be relevant to the existing water budget.

TABLE 2.1. Summary of the results obtained by different researchers on the hydrological cycle of the Amazon Region

Research	Rainfall mm	Transpiration mm	Transpiration %	Transpiration mm/day	Evapotranspiration mm	Evapotranspiration %	Evapotranspiration mm/day	Runoff mm	Runoff %
MARQUES et al 1980	2328 (1)	—	—	—	1260 (r)	54,2	3,5	1068	45,8
	2328 (2)	—	—	—	1000 (r)	43,0	2,7	1328	57,0
	2328 (3)	—	—	—	1330 (p)	57,1	3,6	998	42,9
VILLA NOVA et al 1976	2000 (4)	—	—	—	1460 (p)	73,0	4,0	540	27,0
		—	—	—	1168 (r)	58,4	3,2	832	41,6
	2101 (5)	—	—	—	1569 (p)	73,4	4,3	532	26,6
MOLION 1975	2379 (6)	—	—	—	1146 (r)	48,2	3,1	1233	51,8
RIBEIRO et al 1979	2478 (7)	—	—	—	1536 (p)	62,0	4,2	942	38,0
		—	—	—	1508 (r)	60,8	4,1	970	39,2
IPEAN 1972	2179 (8)	—	—	—	1475 (r)	67,5	4,0	704	32,5
		—	—	—	1320 (r)	60,6	3,6	859	39,4
DMET, 1978	2207 (9)	—	—	—	1452 (p)	65,8	4,0	755	34,2
		—	—	—	1306 (r)	59,2	3,6	901	40,8
JORDAN et al 1981	3664 (10)	1722	47,0	4,7	1905 (r)	52,0	5,2	1759	48,0
LEOPOLDO et al 1981	2089 (11)	1014	48,5	2,7	1542 (r)	74,1	4,1	541	25,9
LEOPOLDO et al 1982	2075 (12)	1287	62,0	3,5	1675 (r)	80,7	4,6	400	19,3

OBSERVATIONS: (r) = real evapotranspiration; (p) = potential evap.; (1) aerological method, applied for all Amazon Basin, period 1972/1975; (2) idem, for the region between Belém and Manaus; (3) by Thornthwaite method, for the region between Belém and Manaus; (4) Penman method, mean for the period 1931/1960: (5)idem, for Manaus Region; (6) climatonomic method, for all Amazon Region, mean for the period 1931/1960; (7) water balance by Thornthwaite and Mather method for the Ducke Forest Reserve, mean for the period 1965/1973; (8) Thornthwaite method for all Amazon Region and estimated for a period over 10 years; (9) idem, for various periods; (10) water balance, with transpiration estimated by class A pan-evaporation for San Carlos Region; (11) "Model Basin" water balance and (12) "Barro-Branco" water balance (Ducke Forest Reserve).

Fig. 2.14. Hydrological balance and store of water vapour in the Amazon Basin.

2.10. DEFORESTATION AND CLIMATIC CHANGES

It is difficult, if not impossible, to separate the effect of deforestation on the climate from its influence on the water and biogeochemical cycles. This is because it will be necessary to analyse the existing equilibrium and the transient periods necessary for the disturbed ecosystem to reach other states of equilibrium.

Two distinct situations can be considered: the forest can regenerate and reach a state similar, or close to, the present one or the disturbance to the system can be permanent and lead to a final equilibrium state, which is completely different from the original — as with the establishment of annual crops and pastures.

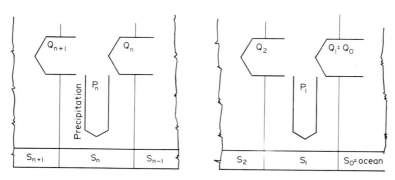

Fig. 2.15. Model of precipitation of Amazonia allowing only one source of water vapour. The water vapour coming from the ocean (Qo) which will be removed by rainfall (P).

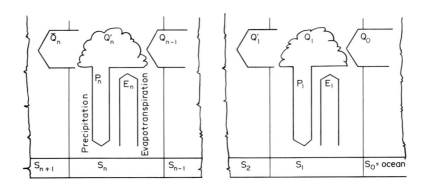

Fig. 2.16. Model to explain the distribution of rainfall (P) in Amazonia allowing two sources of water vapour; oceanic (Q) and evapotranspiration (E).

Autoregeneration of the forest (i.e. the capacity of the ecosystem to re-establish itself and to be replaced by a forest similar or identical to the original) is a forest management long employed by shifting agriculturalists (Indians and indigenous peoples). After deforestation, an area is immediately planted with small subsistence crops (e.g. rice, beans, corn and manioc). After 2 or 3 years, and a decrease in soil fertility, the site is abandoned, and a new one prepared for subsistence agriculture. In the deserted location a regeneration of forest begins with a secondary forest called 'capoeira'.

In this type of forest, small clearings are formed in the middle of the forest. All have the genetic potential for regeneration of the original forest. The time for final recovery of the forest from this shifting agriculture in the Amazon is still undetermined. After some decades, the 'capoeira', when viewed from above, has the appearance of a continuous forest but the trees are of lesser girth than in the original forest. Direct observation shows that some trees need at least 100 years to reach the dimensions in which they are naturally found. While there is no precise calculation of the exact time needed for total renovation, an estimate of two or three hundred years is not out of the question.

Deforestation of large areas is quite different from that of shifting agriculture and natural regeneration is problematic. First, some species may be totally destroyed and with no chance of the remaining trees assisting in the regeneration of the vegetation. Secondly, there may be a high level of erosion with very great disturbance in the biogeochemical cycles hampering vegetation growth. In the case of large-scale deforestation the time of regeneration is even more uncertain, but in some systems, particularly in poorer soils, this time could range from 300 to 1000 years depending on the size of the deforested area and the soil type (the data are based on an estimated time of 200 − 300 years for total recycling of the ecosystem).

When permanent agriculture is established, there is a total modification of the ecosystem (Fearnside, Chapter 21). There is no recycling of nutrients and productivity will only be maintained through continuous application of fertilizers. Water and energy cycles will also be affected.

2.11. THE PRESENT WATER BALANCE DEPENDS ON THE FOREST

Water balance is intimately related to the energy balance. Any modification in the water cycle will influence the energy cycle and *vice versa*. The fundamental problem is to know how deforestation could change these and other meteorological cycles. This is a complex problem without simple answers due to the diversity of possible interactions under conditions different from the present.

We shall attempt to analyse the problem which indicates the tendencies of the modifications based on known empirical data (already quantified in the previous sections), through successive approximations, stressing the tendencies of the parameters most directly linked with the subject of this section.

Let us consider the modifications which might occur if deforestation was carried out in a small experimental hydrographic basin, such as the model basin, mentioned in section 2.8. The present equilibrium shows that 75% of precipitation returns to the atmosphere in the form of vapour through evaporation of the water retained by the leaves (25%) and through transpiration of the plants (50%).

The area of this experimental basin is about 25 km^2. Obviously, in the case of total deforestation, such as is carried out in many colonisation schemes, there will be changes. If an annual crop (maize, beans, sugar cane, etc.) is planted, we will have one or two plant species to replace the thousands existing in the primary forest. This change in the flora will in turn imply an alteration of the fauna and of the microflora and microfauna of the soil. Thus the biogeochemical cycles will inevitably be altered from the beginning.

As far as the water cycle is concerned, the tendency will be for a greater surface run-off, with much less water retained by the plants. On the other hand, unless the agriculture is highly advanced (including contour ploughing, grading and terracing) the water loss from surface run-off will be much greater. Even with these techniques, the forest cleared soil tends towards compaction, which lessens permeability. The same total precipitation will then be divided into the same fractions but with an increase in the amount of water drained off through the streams during rainfall, especially heavier rains and a decrease in the amount of water available for evaporation and transpiration.

This will modify the water cycle and the energy cycle. As there will be less water available for evapotranspiration there will be a decrease in relative air-humidity, which will alter the energy balance. The incident solar energy instead of being used for water evaporation will be used for heating the air as was noted by Ribeiro et al. (1975) in an area of 'campina' near Manaus, where temperatures were higher than in the forest. Thus, the effect of deforestation on air temperature can be noted in small deforested areas. Also the influence of deforestation on the water balance on an hydrographic basin is easily detected with water transit time in the forest different from where annual crops have been established.

In addition, the change in vegetation cover involves a change in albedo (the power of light reflected on the surface under consideration). Change in albedo also involves changes in the energy balance. Modifications of small areas, surrounded by forest, should not influence the energy and water balance or the regional climate as a whole. Yet can the small clearings, annual agriculture and cattle raising, influence the regional climate?

The earlier sections show that 50% of precipitation returns to the atmosphere through evaporation and transpiration processes. In the course of this approximately 50% of the incident solar energy is transformed into latent heat and the other 50% is used for heating the air, photosynthesis and other processes (Fig. 2.17).

Deforestation or replacement of the forest by other types of soil cover, will modify and thus heat water balance. Such changes occurring in small areas gradually add up to produce a large change, with final consequences difficult to analyse because of complex interactions related to general movement of air masses.

It is also important to consider, in a larger scale study, the effect of the variation in the quantity of vapour condensing in the higher parts of the atmosphere. During evaporation solar energy is transformed into latent heat which is released in the highest layers of the atmosphere where the water vapour condenses to form clouds. This energy is partially responsible for the circulation movements of the upper atmosphere. Part of this vapour is transferred to the polar regions and upon condensation releases energy; this is one form of energy transfer from equatorial to the polar regions. While it is difficult to measure how much deforestation of Amazonia might influence atmospheric general circulation, it is clear some changes will be introduced.

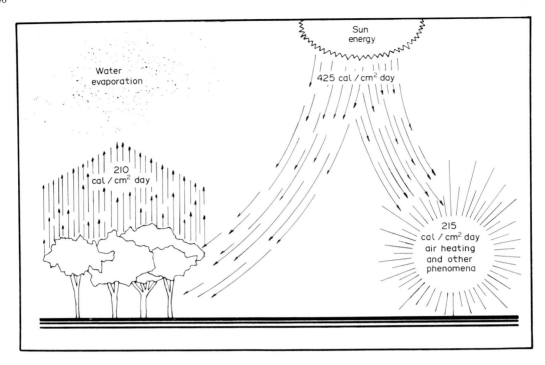

Fig. 2.17. Daily average energy balance for the Amazon Basin.

Attention must also be drawn to the evidence of water vapour recycling. Besides controlling the energy balance the large quantity of water vapour in the atmosphere in the Amazon Basin and which of course is partly due to forest activity, permits cloud formation and therefore some rainfall. Thus a decrease in the forested area will possibly involve a decrease in the water vapour in the atmosphere and a consequent decrease in precipitation. At least in a first approximation the quantity of vapour coming from the ocean, and which tends to form rain in the region will not be changed. However, it is probable that rain distribution, which is in part due to water vapour recycling, will be changed and that total precipitation will also be different from present levels. The extent of change will depend upon the level of the disturbance which will take place.

It is important to stress that, in addition to changes to the energy balance, the transformation of the forest into agricultural areas will lead to changes in the chemical composite of the atmosphere. Woodwell *et al.* (1983) estimate that the carbon dioxide in the atmosphere is increasing at a rate of 1.5 ppm/year, being at present equal to 340 ppm. It is estimated that about 5.2×10^{15}g carbon a year are released into the atmosphere by the burning of fossil fuel, and that a similar amount is released by deforestation. This deforestation is especially significant in the humid tropics because stocks of carbon in agricultural ecosystems are much smaller than that of the original forest. If the present level of fossil fuel consumption and deforestation are maintained, the estimated increase of carbon dioxide may lead to a rise in average atmospheric temperature, with the greater effects towards the poles. The detailed consequences of this temperature rise on climate in general and on the ecosystems of the earth are beyond the scope of the chapter. However, within the limited information available, unless the causes which lead to the increase in atmospheric carbon dioxide are altered, the situation predicted above will be reached in the next few decades.

The following strategies would minimise the effects of deforestation on the present Amazon meteorology:

1. Use of the most fertile soils for agriculture leading to smaller modifications of the biogeochemical cycles.

2. Plan land use within hydrographic basins, always leaving strips of forest at the same level of the surrounding area of development. This will tend to diminish effects of deforestation on water transit time and energy balance.

3. Use of soil conservation techniques will avoid erosion and run-off as much as possible and ensure replenishment of groundwaters, and diminish effects on the biogeochemical cycles.

4. In areas of very poor soils and especially in the central strip of Amazonia, forestry will maintain existing water, energy and nutrient equilibria including maintenance of a great supply of carbon in the ecosystem.

5. In areas of plantation forests using exotic species, always leave strips of primary forest. This will protect the germplasm and flora and fauna of the original forest, as well as diminish the effects on the water, energy and nutrient cycles.

REFERENCES

Almeida, R., Salati, E. and Villa Nova, N. A. (1979) Distribuição espectral e coeficiente de transmissão da radiação solar para condições de céu limpo em Manaus. *Acta Amazonica* 9(2), 279 – 285.

Dall'olio, A. (1976) A composição isotópica das precipitações do Brasil: modelos isotérmicos e a influência da evapotranspiração na bacia Amazônica. MS Thesis, ESALQ. University of São Paulo.

Dall'olio, A., Salati, E., Azevedo, C. I. and Matsui, E. (1979) Modelo de fracionamento isotópico da água na Bacia Amazônica. *Acta Amazonica* 9(4), 675 – 687.

Franken, W., Leopoldo, P. R., Matsui, E. and Ribeiro, M. N. G. (1982) Interceptação das precipitações em floresta Amazônica de terra firme. *Acta Amazonica* 12(3), supplemento, 15 – 22.

IBGE (1977) Geografia do Brasil. 1: Região Norte. I.B.G.E., Rio de Janeiro.

IDESP (1977) *Estudos hidrológicos da Ilha de Marajó.* IDESP.

Jordan, C. F. and Heuneldop, J. (1981) The water budget of an Amazonian rain forest. *Acta Amazonica* 11(1), 87 – 92.

Leopoldo, P. R., Franken, W., Matsui, E. and Salati, E. (1982a) Estimativa da evapotranspiração de foresta Amazônica de terra firme. *Acta Amazonica* 12(3), 23 – 28.

Leopoldo, P. R., Matsui, E., Salati, E., Franken, W. and Ribeiro, M. N. G. (1982b) Composição isotópica das precipitações e da água do solo em floresta Amazônica do tipo terra firme na região de Manaus. *Acta Amazonica* 12(3), 7 – 13.

Lettau, H., Lettau, K. and Molion, L. C. B. (1979) Amazonia's hydrologic cycle and the role of atmosphere recycling in assessing deforestation effects. *Monthly Weather Review* 107(3), 227 – 238.

Marques, J. (1976) Contribuição ao estudo hidrológico da bacia Amazônica. MS Thesis, ESALQ. University of São Paulo.

Marques, J. (1978) A transferência horizontal de vapor d'água na troposfera e a hidrologia de bacia Amazônica. Doctoral Thesis, ESALQ. University of São Paulo.

Marques, J., Salati, E. and Santos, J. M. (1980a) A divergência do campo do fluxo de vapor d'água e as chuvas na região Amazônica. *Acta Amazonica* 10(1), 133 – 140.

Marques, J., Salati, E. and Santos, J. M. (1980b) Calculo de evapotranspiração real na bacia Amazônica através do metodo aerológico. *Acta Amazonica* 10(2), 357 – 361.

Marques, J., Santos, J. M. and Salati, E. (1978) Considerações sobre os ventos na região Amazônica. *Acta Amazonica* 8(1), 110 – 113.

Marques, J., Santos, J. M. and Salati, E. (1979) O armazenamento atmosférico de vapor d'água sobre a região Amazônica. *Acta Amazonica* 9(4), 715 – 721.

Molion, L.C.B. (1975) A climatonomic study of the energy and moisture fluxes of the Amazonas basin with consideration of deforestation effects. Doctoral Thesis, 133 pages.

Oltman, R.E. (1967) Reconnaissance investigations of the discharge and water quality of the Amazon. In *Atas do Simpósio sobre a Biota Amazônica. 3. Limnologia.* Ed. Herman Lent, pp. 163 – 185. CNPq, Rio de Janeiro.

Ribeiro, M.N.G. and Santos, A. (1975) Observações microclimáticas no ecossistema Campina Amazônica. *Acta Amazonica* 5(2), 183 – 189.

Ribeiro, M.N.G., Salati, E., Villa Nova, N.A. and Demetrio, C.g.b. (1982) Radiação solar disponível em Manaus (AM) e sua relação com a duração do brilho solar. *Acta Amazonica* 12(2), 339 – 346.

Salati, E., Dall'olio, A., Matsui, E. and Gat, J.R. (1979) Recycling of water in the Amazon basin: An isotopic study. *Wat. resources Res.* 15(5), 1250 – 1258.

Salati, E., and Marques, J. (1984) Climatology of the Amazon region. In. The Amazon, limnology and landscape ecology of a mighty tropical river and its basin. Ed. H. Sioli. pp. 85 – 126. W. Junk, Dordrecht.

Salati, E., Marques, J. and Molion, L.C. (1978) Origem e distribuição das chuvas na Amazônia. *Interciencia* 3(4), 209 − 222.

Villa Nova, N.A., Salati, E. and Matsui, E. (1976) Estimativa da evapotranspiração na bacia Amazônica. *Acta Amazonica* 6(2), 215 − 228.

Villa Nova, N.A. and Salati, E. (1978) Radiação solar no Brasil. In *Simpósio Anual da Academia de Ciências do Estado de S. Paulo.* São Paulo, 17 − 18 de novembro de 1977. Anais, S. Paulo ACIESP. pp. 27 − 33.

Woodwell, G.M., Hobble, J.E., Houghton, R.A., Melillo, J.M., Moore, B, Petersen, B.J. and Shaver, G.R. (1983) Global deforestation: Contribution to atmospheric carbon dioxide. Science 222: 1081 − 1086.

CHAPTER 3

Amazonian Geology and the Pleistocene and the Cenozoic Environments and Paleoclimates

JOÃO JOSÉ BIGARELLA* and ANTONIA M.M. FERREIRA**

* Universidade Federal do Paraná, Brazil, ** Universidade do Estado do Rio de Janeiro, Brazil

CONTENTS

3.1. INTRODUCTION

To understand the environmental problems of the Amazon Pleistocene reliable knowledge of the basic geologic and geomorphologic features of the landscape is essential. However, this is not easily acquired because of the enormous area of the region, its thick forest cover and the scarcity of systematic studies integrating available information. For our discussion of the Amazonian Pleistocene we have used for comparison a schematic model (Bigarella, Mousinho and Silva, 1965) representing the Quaternary events from other better known areas, especially from southern and northeastern Brazil. This model has been tested in several places, and was improved and worked out in more detail after the work done in the Serra do Mar (Bigarella *et al.*, 1978) and in the metropolitan region of Curitiba (Bigarella *et al.*, 1979; Passos and Costa, unpublished data).

To prepare this account we made a broad survey of the available literature. The data are very inconsistent, being mostly preliminary, with the notable exception of a few papers which are more consistent and objective. Thus, it is almost impossible to establish a Cenozoic stratigraphic column. The stratigraphic position of the several geologic formations described in the literature is frequently confusing giving different, often contradictory, opinions.

Nevertheless, we will attempt to outline a tentative model for the region. We hope, however, to contribute to a new approach which will solve some of the problems of paleoenvironmental interpretation. The main purpose of this paper is to discuss the Pleistocene and Cenozoic paleoclimates. However, we must begin even earlier with the description of the development of an erosion surface (pediplane Pd_3) that probably occurred in the late Oligocene.

Our statements are based on the principle that the Cenozoic paleoclimatic changes were of a global nature since they resulted from extra-terrestrial causes. These were determined by the periodic cyclical variations due to gravitational perturbations inherent in the planetary system, which in turn influenced the intensity of solar radiation on the earth's surface. With this principle in mind we presume that the paleoclimatic events which occurred elsewhere in northeastern Brazil (Bigarella and Andrade, 1964; Bigarella, 1975) and in southeastern and southern Brazil (Bigarella and Ab'Sáber, 1964; Bigarella, Mousinho and Silva, 1965) also affected Amazonia. We tentatively accept this correlation because it is supported by the few field observations which we have made in Amazonia where we have found a few deposits which allow us to apply our model. Nevertheless, much further work is still needed in Amazonia.

The preparation of this summary of the situation has emphasised the importance of finding new research areas to resolve the details of Amazonian geoscience. More appropriate new techniques are needed to replace the usual descriptive procedure which lacks chronostratigraphic support and has not provided enough data for adequate paleoenvironmental interpreting.

Amazonia as a whole belongs to the equatorial belt. Most of the region is lowland and has a humid, warm climate. Both north and south of the lowland terrain there are reliefs whose elevations reach $600-800$ m in the south and more than 3000 m in the north. In the higher elevations the temperatures are lower as would be expected. In this way, Amazonia is not a homogeneous climatic region because it already contains important climatic diversity in temperature, precipitation and seasonality of the rainfall. Although these features cannot be discussed in detail here they contribute to the interpretation of the paleoclimatic events, and suggest the position of refuge areas where the forest remained intact (*see* Chapter 8). The present day forested areas, with annual markedly dry periods (usually quite short), are potential areas for environmental deterioration where drier climates could form characteristic semiarid conditions. In Amazonia there is a system of approximately two corridors in which the present day precipitation is somewhat less than in the surrounding regions. In the past these corridors became much drier and the aridification of Amazonia could have started and spread from them.

Several authors have discussed the existence of enclaves of various open vegetation types inside the Amazonian forest as evidence and remnants of a more severe paleoclimate. They are relicts which are maintained by poor edaphic conditions. The distribution of these open areas allows us to visualise which regions were drier or remained longer under displuvial climatic conditions.

The present day precipitation and air moisture conditions are quite different from those of the displuvial times. Today Amazonia is under the influence of four large circulation systems. The trade-wind system from NE and E is linked to the semimobile anticyclones of the northern and southern Atlantic. The westerly wind system is tied to the equatorial continental air mass (tropical instability). The other systems of influence, the northerly winds (intertropical convergence) and the southerly winds related to the mobile anticyclones (polar front). These four main atmospheric circulation systems must have undergone considerable changes in the geologic past and caused climatic changes leading to retraction of forest cover and expansion of open vegetation formations. The changes resulted mainly from the displacement of the semimobile Atlantic anticyclones towards the equator. With decreased oceanic temperatures the winds entered the continent with much less moisture. In addition, the action of the dry polar air mass reaching lower latitudes than usual would contribute to the aridification of the intertropical region. This over-simplification of the events does not explain all the problems inherent in the phenomena that occurred during the glacial epochs of the Quaternary, and data provided by the literature are extremely scarce. At this time it is difficult to establish a more comprehensive panorama of the Pleistocene events and of the mechanisms involved in the evolution of the landscape.

3.2. THE GEOLOGICAL SETTING

The Amazon Basin is located between the Guiana and Brazilian shields and contains a thick sequence of Paleozoic, Mesozoic and Cenozoic rocks. The area occupied by sediments is about 1,250,000 km^2. The basin is elongate in shape, tending to lie in an east-northeast direction from the Peruvian and Columbian Andes to the mouth of the Amazon river. The basin is about 3,000 km long and 300 km wide in the eastern part and 600 − 800 km wide in the western region.

The geology of the Amazon Basin is known in a broad sense, but is poorly surveyed in detail. The Amazonas sedimentary basin developed on the large Brazilian craton and is regarded as an intercratonic basin by most geologists. The Guiana shield is an old cratonic area which underwent an orogenic cycle around 2,000 million years ago (m.y.). Part of the shield is covered by subhorizontal sediments of the Roraima Foundation intruded by dolerite sills dated about 1,700 m.y. (Cordani et al., 1968). The absence of metamorphism and folding indicates that the area has been tectonically stable, at least since that time. Older tectonic and metamorphic events were recorded at 3,000 − 2,700 m.y. (Singh, 1972) and at 4,400 m.y. (Amaral, 1974) among other references. The southern part of the Guiana shield is overlain by Paleozoic and extensive Tertiary deposits and towards the Atlantic coast by Tertiary and Quaternary sequences. On the southern margin of the Amazon Basin another old cratonic area extends between the Madeira and Tocantins rivers. The last orogenic event to affect the Amazon Basin region is indicated by the locally slightly metamorphasised and folded pre-Silurian Uatumã Formation. The whole cratonic and intercratonic regions may be considered tectonically undisturbed since the Silurian, except for epeirogenic movements, deep-seated folding and warping, and the reactivation of the main fault lines (Bigarella, 1973). In addition to its existing Tertiary deposits, the northern part of the Brazilian shield is also overlain by Paleozoic sediments of Silurian, Devonian, Carboniferous and Permian age, which outcrop in a relatively restricted area. The Mesozoic rocks are represented by basic intrusions (dykes and sills) and also by Cretaceous sedimentary sequences.

In the Amazon Basin, two main periods of tectonic activities can be recognised from epeirogenic disturbances. During the Silurian − Devonian time general subsidence occurred everywhere within the Amazon Basin, followed by marine transgressions apparently coming from two opposite directions. Epeirogenic movements during the Carboniferous followed the same pattern as in Silurian and Devonian. Differential movements lasted during the development of the whole sedimentary sequence especially in Permian and Cretaceous times.

As a rule, all over the Brazilian territory the extensive sedimentation usually ends with the deposition of the Cretaceous sequences. Frequently these rocks spread over the limit of the Paleozoic sedimentary basins into the cratonic areas. Most of the Cretaceous deposits are continental, but some are marine.

The enormous Amazon Basin which, superficially, seems to be so uniform, is in fact, the result of the coalescence of several large sedimentary units deposited more recently during the Cenozoic. The upper Amazon (west from Manaus) probably drained to the west before the uplift of the Andes. In the Miocene part of this area was a vast, brackish basin changing slowly into a freshwater environment (Beurlen, 1970).

3.3. GEOMORPHOLOGICAL FEATURES

The morphology of Amazonia was well-surveyed by the RADAMBRASIL Radar Project. The main objective of the project was to identify the morphoclimatic units and eventually to give an idea of the evolution of the relief through the radar images and low flying air reconnaissance. However, the project did not attempt to establish a chronology related to the correlative sedimentary succession, which would help elaborate part of the Cenozoic stratigraphic column.

From the Amazon river northward and southward one can distinguish four bands of distinct relief forms all of less than 300 m in elevation: (1) wide alluvial terrains; (2) low Tertiary plains, or low plateau (tabuleiros); (3) hilly landforms corresponding to the paleozoic areas; (4) crystalline terrains downcut by pediplanation processes (Ab'Sáber, 1967). Inside this landscape one can find discontinuous terrace levels and remains of pediments developed during Upper Pleistocene. Every one of the above relief forms have characteristic features in their morphostructural development, morphoclimatology and pedology.

The present morphological development started in Tertiary times. From the Upper Cretaceous onward, the margins of the Amazonian region became uplifted, while Amazonia itself remained depressed and subjected to some important areal subsidence such as that of the Marajó or Nova Olinda areas. The uplifted areas became a complex series of bevelled surfaces. The detrital material produced during the erosive periods seems to have been evacuated both to the west (Acre Basin) and to the east (Marajó Basin).

During the Miocene extensive areas from the Paleozoic basin and the Precambrian shields were subjected to successive erosive phases and became lowered in elevation. This long-lasting erosive episode before the Pliocene prepared the pre-Barreiras erosion surface (Howard, 1965). The main epoch of bevelling occurred during the deposition of the Barreiras Group, which was tied to a basin with an axis dipping slightly eastward. This axis was subsequently followed by the Amazon river during the Quaternary (Ab'Sáber, 1967).

The discrete regional subsidence occurring at the end of the Tertiary followed the reactivation of the former axis of the Paleozoic basin, especially in western Amazonia. This subsidence was responsible for the thickening of the sediments (mostly lacustrine in origin), which in some areas reached several hundred metres (600 m).

The origin of the Barreiras sequence in the Amazonas region is linked with the neogenic denudational lowering of the landscape as well as with the moderate subsidence rate, which occurred at the end of the Tertiary in association with intensive erosive phases. The majority of the neogenic sediments were derived from the Brazilian and Guiana shields weathering mantles and originated by the chemical decomposition of the crystalline rocks.

The retention of the sediments in the basin is supposed to be related to fault tectonics, which started in the Miocene with the development of the Marajó Graben. These movements continued during the Pliocene, as an extensive regional subsidence, still related to the reactivation of the fault lines (Ab'Sáber, 1967). Besides the possibility of fault tectonics events, the presence of deep-seated folding movements could also be responsible for the differential subsidence displacements inside the basin.

The reactivation of former fault lines seem to have continued in post-Barreiras times as a late and residual phenomenon represented by a generalised ortogonal joint pattern affecting the poorly consolidated Barreiras sediments (Sternberg, 1950). The rivers have to some extent adapted to this pattern.

In spite of the intensive pre-Barreiras erosive episode, the development of the modern landscape is due mainly to the general pediplanation event, which was penecontemporaneous to the sedimentation of the Barreiras sequence which considerably enlarged the erosion surface. A new cycle of pediplanation was responsible for the development of the most recent erosion surface represented by the pediplane Pd_1.

Amazonia is a domain of equatorial lowlands covered by rainforests. It represents a combination of different physiographic units including flood plains, *tabuleiros* (plains) and hills. This landscape contrasts with the savannah-like plateau of Central Brazil which are covered by *cerrados* and interspersed occasionally with gallery forests along the rivers. It also contrasts with the semiarid northeastern *caatingas* and with the tropical pluvial forests of the Paraná river.

The Amazonian region is characterised by extensive lowlands drained by giant rivers. An extensive forest covers the region but is occasionally interrupted by open vegetation islands, relicts of former drier climates. These enclaves consist of *cerrados*, *cerradões*, open woods and dry woods. They depend on edaphic factors restricting the ecological conditions which favour forest development.

The present climatic conditions indicate that some parameters are relatively homogeneous. Annual average temperatures are high and the thermal variation small. Cloudy skies are rather frequent and the air humidity high. Rainfall is high and relatively well distributed.

Although the whole region seems homogeneous, there are slight differences in the regional topographic features of the various geologic units. There are also different types of soils (*see* Chapter 5). The waters flowing in the rivers and streams are also of several different types. Even the forest itself is not homogeneous. The Amazonian region is therefore not composed of a monotonous landscape of extensive lowlands covered by equatorial forests, but it actually conceals remarkable differences in soil and forest distribution, as well as its geomorphological contrasts.

The study of Amazonian geomorphology is handicapped by many problems. Because of the small differences in elevation it is difficult to characterise the different levels of terraces and of erosion surfaces. Up to now, there has been no precise information on the question. New surveys, like the one performed by Project RADAMBRASIL contributed much to the understanding of the Amazonian morphology.

The Marajó level between Belém and Macapá is represented by terraces (5 to 12 m) maintained by laterites (Marbut and Manifold, 1925). Terraces at 6 to 15 m above mean sea level were considered Pleistocene by Moura (1943). In the Rio Branco basin, Paiva (1939) identified a bevelled and lowered region referred to as the 'crystalline peneplane.' This concept was generalised by Moura (1943) for all the Precambrian areas to the north and to the south of the Amazon sedimentary basin. The Marajó terrace and the crystalline peneplane levels were accepted by Gourou (1949). This author also described the Santar + M = 1em terrace and mentioned the importance of the lateritic material in the maintenance of the Barreiras 'plateau'.

The inset character of the different levels of the Amazonian relief was referred to by Sakamoto (1957). This author considered that the erosive and sedimentary processes in this region were controlled by the glacio-eustatic changes of sea level. In Amazonia there are hills or other topographic features which stand a hundred metres or even more above the surrounding plains covered with forests. Some of the elevations are sugar loaf-like representing former inselbergs from the pedimentation times.

In the upper Rio Branco basin the pediplane and the correlative semiarid deposits are of Quaternary age (Beigbeder, 1956, 1959; Ramos, 1956, 1958; Ruellan, 1957; Barbosa, 1958; Barbosa and Ramos, 1959, 1961). They indicated that the climate at that time was completely different from today. In this region in some areas the sediments may be 30 m thick.

3.4. EROSION SURFACES AND CORRELATIVE DEPOSITS

The end of the Cretaceous continental sedimentation (mostly under semiarid conditions) possibly coincides with the development of an extensive erosion surface (pediplane). Local remnants of this surface were mentioned for Minas Gerais (King, 1956). However, as a rule, no remnants of this surface were left elsewhere in the present day topography. Inhumate evidences of this surface could eventually be found at the contact between Cretaceous and Early Tertiary beds.

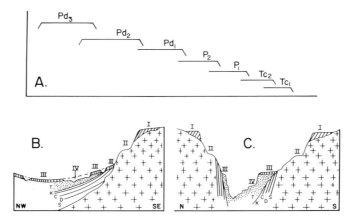

Fig. 3.1. Geomorphologic sketches and transversal profiles through the Amazon region. A — Schematic representation of the main erosional features represented elsewhere by three erosion surfaces (Pd$_3$, Pd$_2$ and Pd$_1$) and two inset pediments (P$_2$ and P$_1$) plus two lower grand terraces, as well as younger floodplain terraces. This model is tentatively applied to the Amazon region and should be further tested and adapted to the local conditions. B and C — Upper and Middle Amazon Basins respectively (modified from Sombroek, 1966). I — Surface with elevations from 400 to 600 m considered by Sombroek as the Cretaceous surface corresponds to the pediplane Pd$_3$. II — Surface (250 — 400 m in elevation) referred by the same author as the Lower Tertiary surface is considered by us as the pediplane Pd$_2$. III — This surface (50 — 200 m) is considered as the Plio-Pleistocene one which corresponds to the pediplane Pd$_1$. IV — The pleistocenic terraces would be related to the terraces corresponding to the development of the pediments P$_2$ and P$_1$. Actually these surfaces split in one or more components, therefore being a group of erosional features.
S. Silurian D. Devonian C. Carboniferous K. Cretaceous T. Tertiary.

In Amazonia a Pre-Cretaceous erosion surface (pediplane) is referred to by the RADAMBRASIL team on the summits of the Tumucumaque and Roraima orographic systems. This conclusion is questionable and actually there is no evidence to prove it. This region seems to have been considerably uplifted, especially after Mid-Tertiary times. Pre-Cretaceous topography was completely eroded. The same also seems to be true for the Cretaceous relief. Remnants of the oldest erosion surface occurring as summit features are usually considered to have developed in Mid-Tertiary times (Oligocene). This surface is referred to as the pediplane Pd$_3$. During Lower Miocene the sea covered part of this surface depositing the Pirabas Formation.

Available information indicates that during the Cenozic, the Brazilian landscape was characterised by intensive erosive processes. They gave rise to three main erosion surfaces as shown by the remnants (Bigarella and Ab'Sáber, 1964; Bigarella and Andrade, 1964). There are no remains in the present-day relief of features developed before Mid-Tertiary times. Towards the end of the Oligocene the landscape of most of the continent was well plannated (bevelled) and topographically low, even in the Andean region (pediplane Pd$_3$). From that time on, epeirogenic movements accompanied by fault tectonics disturbed the pediplane. This surface became slightly folded and faulted (e.g. in the Marajó Graben area). In some regions strong uplift movements brought this surface to high elevations (e.g. in the Roraima and in the high plateau areas of Mato Grosso).

Inset in the Pd$_3$ level there are two other pediplanes (Pd$_2$ and Pd$_1$), developed respectively in the Upper Miocene — Lower Pliocene and in the Upper Pliocene — Lower Pleistocene times. The preliminary studies made in the Amazonian region confirm the observations gathered in the eastern part of Brazil (Fig. 3.1). In Amazonia there are evidences of these two very widespread erosion surfaces. Remnants of the older one are found in Amapá, in the Serra do Navio, Iratapuru and Ipitinga at 300 — 350 m elevation (Barbosa et al., 1973; Journaux, 1975). This surface is actually the pediplane Pd$_2$ maintained by ferruginous and manganiferous crusts. In southern Amazonia there are low remnants of this surface represented by domic forms, some appalachian crest lines and inselbergs which are above the lower erosion surface. The Barreiras sediments corresponding to the Guararapes Formation were deposited as correlative deposits of the processes which culminated with the elaboration of the pediplane Pd_2. According to the authors mentioned above this surface is referred to as the Pliocene erosion surface.

In the lower Amazon region the Pd_2 consists of a set of residual tabular forms and crest lines, which cut Paleozoic rocks at elevations between $300 - 600$ m (Serra Maraconai and Maracanaquara plateau). The correlative deposits of this erosion surface is represented by the Barreiras Group sediments (lower formation in the sense of Bigarella and Andrade, 1964), made up by a complex variety of facies. These include material deposited in an environment of differentiated climatic energy. The elaboration of the Pd_2 surface took a long time, under semiarid conditions with fluctuations toward humidity, including savannah type climates for the formation of laterite.

There is evidence which favours the idea that after the subsidence, which contributed to the retention of the Barreiras sediments, there was a period of positive epeirogenesis which established the $W - E$ drainage pattern of the present Amazon river. The Amazon is, in fact, a post-Barreiras river, and is younger than the upper sections of the tributaries flowing away from the Mato Grosso and Goiás plateau (Barbosa, 1958; Ab'Sáber, 1964).

The most extensive erosion surface in Amazonia is represented by the pediplane Pd_1 which developed as a post-Guararapes Formation event during the Upper Pliocene to Lower Pleistocene time. This surface is well preserved in the interfluvium of the Xingu and Tapajós rivers. It also occurs in Amapá at the elevation of about 200 m. In the lower Amazon region it forms the low plateau relief areas. The pediplane Pd_1 cuts different lithologies, like the Precambrian rocks and the correlated Tertiary deposits of the pediplane Pd_2 represented by the lower part of the Barreiras Group. The pediplane Pd_1 dips slightly toward the coastline, from elevations of about 200 m to around 50 m near the coast. The continuation of the pediplane Pd_1 somewhere offshore is overlain by reworked marine deposits. This pediplane has also been affected by laterisation processes operating during a time of savannah-like climate. The correlative deposits of the Pd_1 along the coastal plain are composed of fluvio-lacustrine sediments. In the Marajó area they have been referred to as the Tucunaré Formation (Barbosa, Renno and Franco, 1974).

The presence of an intermediate surface inset in the Barreiras sediments at 25 to 40 m in elevation indicates the existence of an epoch of pedimentation. The terraces situated at $25 - 30$ m and the ones of $30 - 40$ m are actually remnants of well-developed pediments (Ab'Sáber, 1967). Penecontemporaneously to the development of the intermediate pediment level the drainage pattern of the Amazon river probably would have been braided with sand and gravel deposits. At this time the vegetation was open savannah type (cerrado).

According to Sakamoto (1957) the regional bevelling of the terrain was pre-Pleistocene, while the downcutting insetting the fluvial system is identified as Pleistocene. After the initial dissection of the Barreiras sediments the erosion of the talwege was attenuated and a climatic change provided conditions for pedimentation. The more important incisions of the topography were initiated following the development of the Santarém level. After the occurrence of deep downcuttings, the glacio-eustatic movements permitted fast alternations between flooding (drowning) and renewed erosion (incision). Epeirogenic movements continued or even became accelerated after the Santarém level was developed, causing an uplift of the Amazon Basin (Ab'Sáber, 1967). The pedimentation surfaces originated during episodes when the sea level was below the present one. At that time the forest retreated into refuge areas and the open vegetation spread over the region (see Chapter 8). Humid climates corresponded to periods of rising sea level.

The seasonal climates responsible for savannah-like vegetation seem to have favoured the formation of laterites, which play an important role in the regional morphology. There are several levels and ages of the laterisation phenomena.

In the middle Amazon region there are sequences of colluvial deposits separated by gravel material which form stone lines. They represent slope deposits which are in erosive unconformity over laterite. The gravel lag deposits are rather immature. Upward the colluvial material becomes finer grained (Meis, 1968; Ventura et al., 1975). These interpretations were also accepted by Journaux (1975).

Ventura et al. (1975) considered the above-mentioned deposits as correlative of the Pd_1 surface. However they seem to be much younger, as they are inset in the pediplane level. They were deposited after the dissection cutting the laterite belonging to the pediplane Pd_1 surface.

The coarser material was deposited in a drier climate. Afterwards this climate became progressively more humid until the time when the forest reached its greatest development. The deposition of the colluvial material and the formation of the stone lines do not agree with the present-day conditions of forest cover. Evidently the sheet wash processes can only be effective without the forest protection of the soil and stabilisation of the slopes. The sediments reaching the sea today consist exclusively of clayey muds, which are deposited near the river mouth (Millimann et al., 1975).

The occurrence of coarse alluvial deposits including gravel material indicate a former greater energy capacity of transport, when the river profile was graded to a base level below present-day sea level. During the last glaciation, with the lowering of the sea level, the Amazon river incised its channel deeply to about 2,000 km up stream from its mouth (Tricart, 1977). With sea level dropping below -100 m the river's sediment load was carried through what is now a submarine canyon and deposited as a deep-sea fan, known as the Amazon cone (Millimann et al., 1975; Damuth, 1977). The glacial-aged sediments of this fan are composed of arkosic sands, suggesting semiarid conditions in the Brazilian and Guiana shields and in the Amazon Basin (Damuth and Fairbridge, 1970).

3.5. CENOZOIC SEQUENCES

The processes operating during the Cenozoic led to the development of the modern environment of today's Amazon. The Cenozoic sequences are widespread and less deformed and their study provides more geoscientific information than those of the older sedimentary sequences. The Cenozoic was an age of exceptional tectonic instability between the Laramide and the Cascadian-Alpine revolutions. The first one closed the Mesozoic Era and the second was active not very long ago. In the Cenozoic large tectonic movements gave rise to very important mountain chains. Before the Cenozoic, the Andes did not exist to the west of the Amazon Basin. This mountain chain developed during and after the middle Tertiary, completely changing the South American equatorial belt, including the Amazon region.

The Cenozoic Era apparently represents an anomalous time with very widespread land masses, extensive high plateaus and mountains higher than in former geologic times. This situation provided for intensive erosional activity accompanied by formation of extensive sedimentation, like the one in the Amazon Basin.

The Tertiary sequence of the Amazon Basin is one of the most important in the world. Some geologists refer to the Tertiary beds under the generic name of Alter do Chão Formation. In the eastern and western parts of the Amazon Basin several stratigraphical units have been described, such as the Pebas, Pirabas, Rio Branco, Manaus, Barreiras and Alter do Chão formations.

The Cenozoic sequences in Brazil occur along the coast from the southern to the northern part of the country, and elsewhere. In the Amazon region they spread inland extensively over large areas. The Amazonian Cenozoic deposits rest nonconformably on older beds and are generally transgressive, passing over Mesozoic and Paleozoic rocks on to the Precambrian shields. They consist of poorly consolidated, sandy, silty and clayey sediments often with a basal conglomerate. These sediments may reach 600 m in Nova Olinda and even more elsewhere.

During the Cenozoic epeirogenic movements were important. Mesozoic faulting displacements continued during part of the Cenozoic. The middle Tertiary erosion surface (Pd$_3$) was disturbed and uplifted in some cases up to 2,000 m in elevation. In a general way the whole continent became uplifted and consequently the erosive processes increased in intensity. In several areas, especially that of Manaus, recent tectonic movements of small magnitude can be seen in road cuts with stone lines of Upper Pleistocene deposits.

The majority of the Cenozoic sediments were laid down in a continental environment, although important marine successions are known from the Marajó Graben and from the Pirabas Formation. In the Marajó sub-basin the Tertiary sequence begins with the Lower Tertiary (Eocene?) beds followed by a well-developed Miocene sequence. The lower part of the Cenozoic sequence was deposited in marginal lagoons or in marine swamps with poor circulation. According to Petri (1954) the marine environment became dominant in the upper part of the sequence. Above it there are 245 m of Quaternary deposits of fluvial origin. Presumably Early Eocene continental beds from Acre contain fossil remains of reptiles and petrified woods.

The Pirabas Formation occurs in the coastal area of the State of Pará. The formation consists of limestones, sandy and clayey sediments. It also contains a rich marine pelecypod and gastropod fauna, as well as a fauna of bryozoans, crustaceans, coelenterates and foraminifera (Maury, 1924; Ferreira, 1960; Petri, 1954). A Lower Miocene age was suggested by Maury (1924), while Petri (1954) referred to it as Middle Miocene. The Pirabas Formation was deposited over the pediplane Pd$_3$ surface in a warm and limpid marine environment (Petri, 1957). Together with the marine fossils there are reptile bones (crocodile and turtle), hydrophyte and some mesophyte plants suggesting the presence of a hydrophytic forest adjacent to the area of sedimentation.

The Barreiras Group occurs along the Brazilian coast especially north from Rio de Janeiro. This group is subdivided into two formations: Guararapes and Riacho Morno (type locality and section near Recife, PE). The first one is supposed to be Late Miocene to Lower Pliocene in age and correlated with the pediplanation of the pediplane Pd$_2$, while the second would be Upper Pliocene to Pleistocene being correlated with the pediplane Pd$_1$ and the pediments P$_2$ and P$_1$ (Bigarella, 1975). The sediments of both formations were deposited under semiarid climatic conditions characterised by concentrated rainfalls. The sediments seem to contain no fossils. In some areas the sediments are well cross-bedded suggesting a braided stream environment; in others the stratification indicates a lacustrine environment. In the Amazon Basin the Barreiras Group includes sandy and silty-clayey deposits showing distinct features when compared to the ones located along the coast (Goés, 1980).

The Belterra deposits usually occur in the upper part of the exposed sequences of the Barreiras sediments. According to Truckenbrodt and Kotschoubey (1981) the Belterra clay is kaolinitic in nature, and is coloured yellowish. Visible stratification is apparently lacking. The Belterra deposits, with a maximum thickness of 20 m, form the extensive coverage of the lowland plateau. The clay was derived from outside and within the Amazonian bauxite belt, and transported as mud flow or sheet flood in a semiarid environment (Truckenbrodt and Kotschoubey, 1981). A lacustrine or fluvio-lacustrine environment has been postulated as well (Sombroek, 1966; Klammer, 1971) for the Belterra deposits, which are considered as the upper part of the Barreiras Group. The age of the Belterra clay is still controversial; Miocene-Pliocene (Truckenbrodt and Kotschoubey, 1981); Pliocene (Klammer, 1971) and Plio-Pleistocene (Sombroek, 1966). The laterites connected with the Belterra deposits have been considered Upper Tertiary to Quaternary (Grubb, 1979; Dennen and Norton, 1977; Wolf and Silva, 1973) or older as Eocene/Oligocene (Krook, 1979). The Belterra sediments as they have been mentioned in the literature must be related to more than one sedimentary cycle. They are found in the Pd$_2$ level and as well in the Pd$_1$. In the last case they would correspond to the Riacho Morno Formation. In Amazonia the sequence of Cenozoic events seems to be the same or at least somewhat equivalent to those known from other areas of Brazil where they have been better surveyed.

3.6. THE BARREIRAS GROUP

Older references about the Tertiary sediments of the Amazon Basin are found in Branner (1915). This author described these sequences along the Brazilian coast from the neighbourhood of Vitoria (Espírito Santo) northward to the Amazon valley. Albuquerque (1922) pointed out that the Tertiary beds in the Amazon river are well exposed along the margin of the river. According to Moura (1938) the fossil barren pliocenic beds of the lower Amazon are identical to the ones of the 'Barreiras Series' outcropping along the Brazilian coast. The distinction between Pliocene and Pleistocene sequences is not an easy task due to their lithologic similarities (Moura, 1938).

The Barreiras sequence outcrops are not only in the lower Amazon, but also in the lower and middle Solimões valleys and along most of the tributaries from the mouth up to the Colombian and Peruvian borders, where the Barreiras is replaced by the underlain Pebas Formation. The absence of fossils in the sequence does not allow the establishment of a correct chronology (Matoso and Robertson, 1959). The Barreiras sequence was revised and redefined in Pernambuco by Bigarella and Andrade (1964), as the Barreiras Group subdivided into two formations: Guararapes and Riacho Morno, both apparently fossilless and of continental origin.

The term Barreiras Group was used as well by Francisco et al. (1971) in the Amazonian region for the sediments stratigraphically above the Pirabas Formation, or above older rocks. However, many other authors working in the Amazon region still use the concept 'Barreiras' in the broad sense, including several distinct units which may or may not be correlated to the Barreiras Group, as described from elsewhere in Pernambuco.

The term Barreiras has also been used improperly to describe the whole Tertiary Amazonian succession. In this way the Pirabas, the Ipixuna and other formations have been considered as faciologic variations of the Barreiras sequence (Nunes et al., 1973; Santos et al., 1975). However, there are important stratigraphic principles to be considered. The Pirabas and the Barreiras beds are completely distinct units, and are not contemporaneous. Moreover, between them there is an hiatus representing a non-deposition and, possibly, an erosive episode.

The stratigraphy of the Amazonian Tertiary sequence especially from the Barreiras Group is still poorly known and controversial. Some formations like the Pirabas are better known from the paleontological point of view, but on the whole the scientific knowledge of the regional Cenozoic is still chaotic and far from resolved. Actually, more field work and new approaches to the problem are necessary in order to reach a systematic revision of the whole succession.

3.7. TERRACES

The several authors who have studied the terraces of the Amazon region have contradictory opinions about how many there are, their sequence and elevations. According to Klammer (1971) there are Pliocene and Pleistocene terraces, which differ in sedimentary nature, physiography and structure.

The 'Pliocene' terraces of the Belterra Plateau have elevations between 135 and 194 m. Apparently they represent only one surface, which according to Klammer (1971) was tectonically disturbed. However, there is a possibility that the differences in elevations of this surface is due to natural dipping or grading at the time of development of the surface, and is actually a pediplane (Pd_1).

The Belterra plateau was considered to be formed by lacustrine clayey sequences, which contain a single horizon of concretionary iron hydroxide at about $10 - 15$ m below the surface (Klammer, 1971). The plateau is almost flat, and lacks a surface drainage without gullies established on fractures and joints.

The Belterra plateau is formed by the Barreiras succession. The lower part is probably equivalent to the Guararapes Formation including sequences of poorly consolidated sandstone, multicoloured, fine-

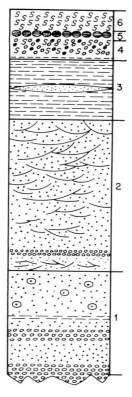

Fig. 3.2. Schematic section of the upper 200 m of the Barreiras group in the Santa Mônica hill (Jari River). 1 — Sandstone poorly consolidated, coarse-grained and partially conglomeratic; 2 — Sandstone poorly consolidated, multicoloured, fine-grained with some granule horizons, frequently cross-bedded; 3 — Kaolinitic clay; 4 — Mottled kaolinitic clay; 5 — Iron concentrations; 6 — Bauxitic clay (modified from Klammer, 1971).

grained with some granule horizons. The sandstone can also be coarse-grained and partially conglomeratic (Klammer, 1971). The sandstones are frequently cross-bedded and overlaid with clay deposits (Fig. 3.2). Eastward from the Belterra Plateau the Barreiras sediments rest on the Lower Miocene Pirabas Formation, both being successions separated by an unconformity. The upper part of the Belterra plateau sequence differs greatly from the lower one, since it is clayey and deposited in a different environment. Klammer (1971) considers that the upper clay sequence of the Barreiras Group was deposited in a freshwater lake, while the sandstone represents a fluvial-lacustrine environment. The complete sequence of the Barreiras Group in the Serra da Paranaquara is more than 250 m (Hartt, 1874) and about 700 m in the Marajó Graben.

The Pliocene and Pleistocene levels studied by Klammer (1971) occur in the lower Amazon region along the Tapajós, Amazon, Paru and Jari rivers (Figs. 3.3 and 3.4).

3.7.1. Pleistocene terraces

(1) *The 88 — 101 m terrace* (Monte Alegre) is the oldest level in the area studied by Klammer (1971). It represents an aggradational level composed of about 50 m of pleistocenic sediments.

(2) *The 68 — 74 m terrace* (Monte Dourado) is also composed of Pleistocene sediments.

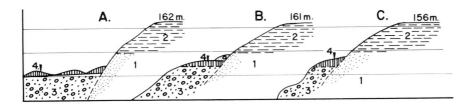

Fig. 3.3. Pliocene levels and inset pleistocenic terraces (modified from Klammer, 1971). A — Almeirin, Amazon river, B — Monte Santa Mônica, Jari river, C — Monte Felipe, Jari river. 1 — Barreiras multicoloured sandstone, 2 — Belterra kaolinitic clay, 3 — coarse sand with pebbles, poorly stratified, 4 — iron cemented sandstone. 1 and 2 — Pliocene; 3 and 4 — Pleistocene.

(3) *The 28 — 31 m terrace* (Santarém) has been referred to as the Santarém surface.

(4) *The 19 — 23 m terrace* (Almeirim) has been identified on Marajó Island (Guerra, 1959) and elsewhere in the lower Amazon region. The sediments of this terrace are widely distributed.

(5) *The 8 — 11 m terrace* (Marajó) was described by Marbut and Manifold (1925) and is referred to as the Marajó level. It is conspicuous in the lower Amazon river, and is apparent upstream as far as the Madeira river.

3.7.2. Pleistocene sediments

The Pleistocene deposits are composed of unconsolidated mud, sand and gravel materials. Besides some structureless sediments there are stratified ones and sometimes cross-bedding is present. The sands are frequently muddy and poorly sorted. Everywhere the unconsolidated sediments show some evidences of laterisation or of hardpan formation. The sand may change into a ferrugineous sandstone which is largely exposed.

The lateritic material indicates the past presence of a savannah-like type of climate. The poor sorting and the cross-bedding indicate that the sediments were transported by a fluctuating stream regime with a high capacity of transport typical of seasonal climates unlike the present pluvial one.

3.7.3. Origin of the terraces according to Klammer

The Late Tertiary and the Quaternary relief of the alluvial Amazon Basin originated through successive alternating periods of erosion and sedimentation. The alternations were probably due to climatic changes which greatly affected the ocean level (Klammer, 1978).

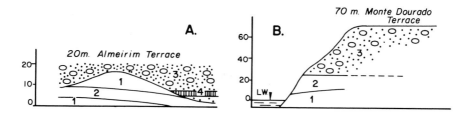

Fig. 3.4. Pleistocene valley filling relative to the Almeirim and Monte Dourado terraces (modified from Klammer, 1971). 1 — Dolmitic limestone, 2 — Cross-bedded sandstone, 3 — Coarse sand with pebbles, poorly sorted, 4 — Iron cemented sandstone. 1 and 2 — Upper carboniferous; 3 and 4 — Pleistocene.

Sea level rose in Late Pliocene times during the terrestrial sedimentation of parts of the Barreiras Group to about 180 m above the present sea level (Klammer, 1978) and remained for a long time at this level. Subsequently it fell during a time of uniform, non-oscillatory regression to close to 90 m, to the formation of a gently undulating relief.

When the regression ended the sea level was again lowered to about 55 m and with subsequent transgression the sea level then rose to 80 m. After this transgression there were nine alternating positive and negative movements between the 80 m level and the present day sea level.

The sea level changes have been considered as eustatic in origin (Klammer, 1978). The data from the Amazon Basin, when compared with the record established for other regions (including paleoclimatic, paleomagnetic, stratigraphic and pedologic evidences), show great similarities in the climatic and eustatic rhythms in the Brunhes Period and below the Sicilian sea level, which would suggest a glacial eustatic origin for the Amazonian sedimentary sequence.

Beginning at a time shortly before the Sicilian, the glacial eustatic oscillations were superimposed on a tecto-eustatic regression from the Calabrian level which began in the vicinity of the Olduvai event.

Journaux (1975) and the staff of the RADAMBRASIL project believe that the Belterra surface is an erosive one. Nascimento et al. (1976), Ventura (1975), Barbosa (1974) and others consider this surface as developed under more arid conditions. The Belterra surface is considered as formed in Late Pliocene to Early Pleistocene (Klammer, 1978). There is a question whether this surface is aggradational or erosional. However, this surface corresponds to the clayey sedimentation of the Barreiras Group. It is possible to differentiate in the outcrop the Late Barreiras sediments from the Quaternary ones although both are fluvial-lacustrine in origin. In the Quaternary there is a greater heterogeneity of facies variation which is lacking in the Barreiras. The Barreiras sediments are 180 m thick with the upper part consisting of clay deposits of 40 to 50 m.

There is a similarity between the origin of the Barreiras and the Quaternary sediments, as well as in their mineralogic composition. The more recent 20 m terrace in the Trombetas river is somewhat similar in grain size composition to the 65 m terrace of the Jari river, although the later one is coarser.

Two types of Pleistocene deposits may be recognised. The oldest one representing the filling of depressions is composed of fine-grained sediments derived from the slopes of the Belterra plateau. The other constitutes the inset terraces. After Early Pleistocene time it is possible to recognise 7 to 9 erosive and sedimentary cycles which according to Klammer correspond to the eustatic movements.

3.7.4. Age of the terraces according to Klammer

The development of the Quaternary morphology according to Klammer (1976) was due to post-Tertiary fall of the sea level and the superimposed glacio-eustatic oscillations. The glacial regression, the interglacial and some interstadial transgressions can be recognised by their erosional and depositional features. The elevation of fossil floodplains can be related to high interglacial sea level stands. The rhythm of alternating aggradational and degradational events in Amazonia can be tentatively correlated with the stratigraphy of the Late Quaternary.

(1) The 20 m terrace is correlated with the Main Monastirian (Mindel/Riss). Warm climate (about 2°C above the present day average temperature).

(2) Regression (dissection) during Riss time. Cooler temperature (up to 4°C below the present one).

(3) The 9 – 10 m terrace is referred to as the Late Monastirian (Riss/Würm I). Warm climate.

(4) Regression (Riss/Würm I/II). Mild temperature.

(5) The 5 – 6 terrace is correlated to the Epimonas terrain (Riss/Würm II). Warm climate.

(6) Regression (Würm I). Cold climate.

(7) The − 2 to 3 m terrace represents the old várzea. Warm climate.

(8) Regression (Wúrm II). Cold climate.

(9) Present day alluvium.

3.8. PALEOCLIMATIC CHANGES

During the Cenozoic the climatic belts of the earth were characterised by the alternation of two main groups of processes. One of them was responsible for extensive slope erosion accompanied either by lateral degradation or vertical dissection of the terrain (Bigarella and Mousinho, 1966), referred to as bio-rhexistasic (Erhart, 1955) or morphodynamic activity (Rohdenburg, 1970). The other, responsible for extensive pedogenetic activities, was referred to as biostasic (Erhart, 1955) or morphodynamic stability (Rohdenburg, 1970).

In the Brazilian tropical and subtropical regions the landscape development and evolution resulted from the alternation of: (a) epochs of active lateral degradation (semiaridity); (b) epochs of vertical dissection, gullying with extensive chemical weathering and pedogenesis (humid climatic conditions) (Bigarella, Mousinho and Silva, 1965).

The lateral degradation processes with development of pediments (or slope deposits) occurred under a regime of concentrated heavy rainfall representing severe semiarid climatic conditions. The correlative deposits formed during these epochs show the evidences of climatic fluctuations toward humidity, i.e. with phases of more evenly distributed precipitation which favoured chemical weathering and pedogenesis (Bigarella, Mousinho and Silva, 1965).

During humid epochs chemical weathering and pedogenesis prevailed. The forest cover protected the soil against mechanical erosion. Solifluction (*sensu lato*) or colluviation was present in the steep slopes. Leaching seems to have been important. The humid epoch was characterised by short climatic fluctuations toward dryness, which caused the retreat of the forest and expansion of the open vegetation cover. These fluctuations favoured the fast removal of the unprotected soils by sheet and rill wash originated by the concentration of the rainfall distribution (Bigarella, Mousinho and Silva, 1965).

During the Cenozoic and especially in the Pleistocene the paleoclimatic conditions were strongly differentiated. In the Pleistocene the environmental alternations were almost extreme between glacial and interglacial epochs in higher latitude regions, and between humid and semiarid conditions in subtropical to tropical regions.

Up to the Mesozoic the paleoclimates are recognisable in a general way. From the Tertiary onward more details became available especially because both fossil flora and fauna allow better comparisons with recent vegetation and fauna. Deduction of paleoclimatic conditions becomes more effective once angiosperms appear.

During the Tertiary the climate was warmer than today. From the beginning of this period the temperature decreased slowly until about one million years ago when climatic conditions were very similar to the present (Schwarzbach, 1963). While Pliocene temperatures were higher than today, climatic changes similar to those from the Pleistocene began although they were less prominent.

During the Tertiary there are evidences of pluvial and semiarid episodes all over the world. An accentuated tendency for generalised aridification happened in Upper Eocene to Lower Oligocene times and as well in the Upper Miocene (Schwarzbach, 1963).

In the temperate regions a lowering of $8° − 13°C$ or even more in annual mean temperature is suggested for the pleistocenic glacial epochs (Schwarzbach, 1963). During the glaciations, the entire earth became cooler and in the equatorial region the snowline in the mountains lowered 500 to 1500 m below the present position.

According to Flohn (1952) in the tropics there was a decrease in the annual average temperature of about 4°C in comparison with the present situation. During glaciation the temperature in the equatorial region could have been around 23°C as compared to present annual mean temperature in Manaus and Belém of about 26°C.

During glaciation the average annual temperature in the warmer regions of the oceans was not below 20°C, otherwise the coral reefs could not have survived (Schwarzbach, 1963).

During the glacial times the arid regions of the world became semiarid with increasing precipitation. These episodes have been called 'pluvial' phases. They are more properly termed displuvial episodes because at the same time the tropical and equatorial pluvial or rainforest climate (isopluvial) became displuvial as well. Under the new conditions the forest cover changed to open vegetation of the savannah or caatinga type.

The climate conditions during the interglacial epochs were generally similar to the present ones. However, there were warmer and cooler phases evident from pollen analysis.

The old concept that during the Pleistocene glacial epochs the climate was humid in the intertropical regions was criticised by Bigarella and Salamuni (1961) and by Bigarella and Ab'Sáber (1964). These authors concluded that semiarid conditions prevailed in the tropics at that time. This conclusion was based on geomorphologic, stratigraphic and sedimentologic evidences, besides other evidences based on palynology, paleobotany, lake-level fluctuations and deep-sea core data. Moreover the colluvial and alluvial deposits indicate environmental changes which occurred during the Quaternary.

Evidence to date clearly shows arid conditions spread periodically over the continent during the Late Cenozoic times. These conditions were closely connected with cosmic phenomena which affected the distribution of the air systems and the circulation patterns. Consequently changes occurred as well in the ocean current pattern.

The oscillations inside the glacial activity represented either by ice-advances or ice-retreats influenced the moisture conditions of the intertropical belt, causing minor changes in the environment. These are represented by variations in the textural and structural properties of the sediments, and by hydrodynamic change favouring either downcutting or sedimentation.

All the paleoclimatic changes caused large impacts in the Amazonian environments. During the alternations of the main climatic types the vegetation changed from pluvial forest (isopluvial climate) to open vegetation landscape (displuvial climate), represented by savannah-like features. Simultaneously changes occurred in slope development and also in fluvial channel processes.

Street (1981) refers to the last 127,000 years as a phase of interglacial conditions followed by a long period of greater ice cover in which there occurred two major ice-advances. The interglacial phase was characterised by fluctuations responsible for a series of high sea levels in contrast to the low sea levels of glacial episodes.

Although there were small temperature changes in low latitude regions during the Late Quaternary, there were major climatic changes caused by water balance, leading to fluctuations between pluvial or semiarid environmental conditions.

In addition to physical evidence for great climatic and environmental changes which could have affected the Amazonian biogeographic distributions, there have been several studies dealing with the faunistic and floristic problems of the centres of dispersion and refuge areas (Haffer, 1969; Vanzolini, 1970; Müller, 1970, 1971; Müller and Schmithusen, 1970; Prance, 1973, 1982; Avila-Pires, 1974; van der Hammen, 1974, 1982; Bigarella, Andrade-Lima and Riehs, 1975; Brown, 1977; Ab'Sáber, 1977, 1979; Simpson and Haffer, 1978; Brown and Ab'Sáber, 1979; Castro, 1981; Bigarella and Andrade-Lima, 1982). These are discussed further in Chapter 8 of this volume.

The physical interpretations are based mostly on geological, geomorphological, pedologic and palynologic evidences (*see* Chapter 4). The biological data are inferred from the modern distribution of animals and plants. Evidence indicates that during the semiarid climatic periods the forests were restricted to relatively small enclaves or refugia. The aridity epochs seem to have occurred during and after the Pleistocene glacial maxima.

The refuge areas were restricted to areas where the availability of water was enough to maintain the vital processes of the flora and fauna, and to prevent environmental degradation. The available water resources were restricted to relatively high ground-water levels, to the location of springs, and to the condensation of air moisture in areas where the relief is somewhat elevated. The occasional rainfalls were enough to replenish the underground water sources.

Temperature changes in the Amazonian region were too small to produce much impact on the life conditions of the refugium itself, when compared to the effect either in higher latitude regions or in mountainous areas. In this way water would have been the most important factor for preservation of the minimum environmental conditions for the survival of species.

3.9. EVOLUTION OF THE CENOZOIC LANDSCAPES

The following tentative reconstruction of the evolution of the Amazonian landscape is based on physical evidence from different sources, and especially from our observations in other Brazilian regions. The work performed by the RADAMBRASIL Project including the mapping of the morphologic features, the investigations on palynology (van der Hammen, 1974; Absy, this volume) and the lithostratigraphic information (Meis, 1968; Klammer, 1971, 1975, 1978; Tricart, 1974, 1977; Journaux, 1975) make possible the establishment of the relative sequence of the Cenozoic events. Nevertheless, an absolute chronology has not been possible up to now due to the scarcity of paleontologic and radiometric dating. The following paragraphs are based on the above-mentioned data complemented with other information, especially from northeastern Brazil (Bigarella, 1975).

In the evolution of the regional landscape several large episodes were recognised and are briefly discussed:

(1) The oldest episode considered in our discussion is represented by a long lasting semiarid period originating with topographic inversion of the high structural reliefs of the Roraima region. During this episode the pediplane Pd_2 was formed spreading extensively around and off the inselberg areas. In the northern Amazonian region (Guiana Shield) the main erosive processes cut the Roraima and Vila Nova groups of the Middle Precambrian age (RADAMBRASIL Project). Within this semiarid period there are evidences of more humid phases like the ones referred to by Bigarella and Ab'Sáber (1964), Bigarella and Andrade (1964) and Bigarella, Mousinho and Silva (1965).

The semiarid period was characterised by intense erosive processes causing lateral degradation of the landscape. During this episode the diamond bearing conglomerates of the Roraima group were reworked. In this region there are no correlative deposits of the Pd_2 surface, but in the Middle and Lower Amazon regions this pediplane is correlated with the lower sequence of the Barreiras Group, often referred to in the literature as the Barreiras Formation. This climatic episode is considered Upper-Miocene to Lower-Pliocene in age.

(2) After the development of the Pd_2 surface under semiarid conditions the climate changed to a tropical seasonal one with characteristic dry and wet seasons, favouring development of savannah-like vegetation and formation of laterite below the surface in the zone of ground water fluctuations. The remnants of the Pd_2 occurring both in the northern and southern regions of Amazonia have always had lateritic crusts, which may be ferriferous, manganiferous or bauxitic in nature (for example, Serra do Navio in Amapá; Serras da Prata and Mucajai in Roraima Territory; Altamira in Amazonas; and Serra de Maraconaí in Pará).

The laterites are post-depositional features of the sedimentation of the lower sequence of the Barreiras Group. They were formed at a time of non-deposition, i.e. during a time of intensification of the pedogenetic processes and slight erosion. The laterite itself, however, is a hydrogeological phenomenon independent of the local soil profile development. The age of these lateritic crusts would probably be Lower Pliocene.

(3) In a third episode (in the Pliocene) the climatic conditions became humid and forest cover spread. Dissection of the terrain was intensified during small climatic fluctuations toward dry conditions, which exposed the soils to vertical downcutting. In this stage the Boa Vista and Pirarucu formations, from Roraima and the lower Amazonas region respectively were deposited but are considered to be younger in age (Lower Pleistocene) by the RADAMBRASIL team. Still in the third main episode, according to this project an intermediate level between Pd_2 and Pd_1 was developed consisting of well-rounded half-orange topography.

Toward the end of this third humid episode transition into a fourth episode began. Aridification increased, the forests retreated into refuge areas and savannah-type vegetation (seasonal climate) expanded. Although this transition was rather short, theoretically there were possibilities of formation of new lateritic horizons, reworkable by the subsequent erosion cycle. With increasing aridification the climate again became semiarid with the intensification of the lateral degradation processes (rhesistasic or morphodynamic activity).

(4) In the fourth episode semiaridity returned providing conditions for a new cycle of pediplanation. The new pediplane (Pd_1) developed inset in the Pd_2 surface, cutting not only the Precambrian and Paleozoic rocks but also the Barreiras sediments (lower formation) formed during Pd_2 times. The pediplane Pd_1 was possibly formed in Upper Pliocene − Lower Pleistocene time, but it was certainly formed by the beginning of the Pleistocene. During the pediplanation processes, in addition to the material already deposited during the climatic transition from humidity into semiaridity, further detrital material was available for sedimentation. Theoretically all these sediments would have been deposited unconformably over the lower part of the Barreiras Group sequence. Unfortunately there have been no systematic studies in the region to prove the above speculation. The formations described in the literature are not tied to geomorphological levels, which would be necessary for establishment of an Amazonian Quaternary stratigraphy. During Pd_1 times the fluviatile system became largely braided with deposits of sandy and gravel sediments along the drainage zones.

Some of the so-called Belterra sediments, which are predominantly argilaceous at the base and became arenaceous toward the top, are related to the later phase of the pediplane Pd_1 correlative deposition. The Solimões Formation in the Acre region is also considered to be correlative of the Pd_1 surface. The same supposition is made for the Tucunaré Formation in Pará (Barbosa et al., 1973; RADAMBRASIL Project). Nevertheless, the stratigraphic position of these sequences are still unresolved problems. The Belterra clay deposits are attributed to a humid climate (Truckenbrodt and Kotschoubey, 1981). Actually it could represent a humid phase inside the semiarid epoch which accentuated the chemical weathering of the basement rocks, but a displuvial climate would be required for the transportation and deposition of the argilaceous sequence. The terraces of about 200 m described by Klammer (1971) could eventually be attributed to the Pd_1 level.

Toward the end of the semiarid conditions there was an amelioration of the climate. The open vegetation of the caatinga-like formations started to be replaced by cerrado vegetation adapted to seasonal climate. At the same time laterite developed by the action of the groundwater table fluctuations. This phenomenon gave origin to the extensive lateritic crusts connected with the Pd_1 surface.

(5) The fifth episode corresponds to the extensive return of humid conditions all over the region. In this stage processes related to biostasic or morphodynamic stability prevailed. Chemical activity became intense giving rise to deep weathering mantles. The cerrado retreated and was replaced by the forest. Fluctuations toward dryness speeded the dissection of the landscape. Apparently the downcutting of the terrain continued during the climatic transition to the next semiarid epoch, when the sea started to be

lowered by glacio-eustatic phenomena, because the next sequence has an erosive nonconformity deeply inset in the Pd_1 level.

(6) The sixth episode is characterised by the return of semiarid conditions responsible for the development of the pediment P_2 and the sandy and gravel terraces (Tp_2) inset in the Pd_1 surface. The colluvia deposited during P_2 times are usually reddish in colour. At this time the forest retreated into the refuge areas and the open vegetation spread over the region. From the data described in the Amazonian literature it is by now impossible to define which deposit would correspond to this level, which is well characterised in other regions of Brazil.

Inside the P_2 epoch there were climatic fluctuations toward humidity responsible for chemical weathering and for a relatively small amount of downcutting. Towards the end of P_2 time the climate started again to change to prevailing humid conditions. During the transition an episode of seasonal climate contributed to the development of the cerrado vegetation cover and the formation of a new level of laterite crust by groundwater activity.

(7) In the seventh episode the humid climate conditions prevailed and the forest returned. Chemical weathering prevailed and downcutting was accelerated by fluctuations toward dryness. During this episode brownish-yellowish colluvia were formed. Toward the end of the humid stage the climate changed into a semiarid one accompanied by the lowering of sea level by glacio-eustatism and the valley floor became lowered even below its present day level. The lateritic crusts which eventually developed during this last climatic transition were mostly eroded in the next stage.

(8) In the eighth episode the semiarid conditions returned, and were responsible for an important new retreat of forest cover and the spread of open vegetation exposing soils to fast removal by the lateral degradational erosive processes. This led to development of the P_1 pediment and a new sequence of sandy and gravelly fluvial terraces (Tp_1) with deposits formed in a braided stream environment. Again it is difficult to establish from the literature which deposits correspond to P_1 events, as the work performed in the Amazon has not been properly correlated with the geomorphologic history of the region.

At the end of the P_1 episode a transition in the next humid epoch brought back a seasonal climatic phase with development of cerrado vegetation and the formation of a new lateritic crust or a mottle horizon.

(9) The ninth episode was characterised by a new long lasting humid epoch with the usual fluctuations toward dryness. Again chemical weathering prevailed and downcutting was prominent producing yellowish colluvium. Toward the end of this stage, in the transition to a semiarid epoch a short phase of seasonal climate led to expansion of cerrado vegetation and ferrification of the groundwater fluctuation zone. Most of these features were destroyed however, by the subsequent erosive stage.

(10) The tenth episode included a semiarid epoch separated by an important humid phase. In other regions of Brazil, especially in the Lower Itajai-Mirim valley (SC), two low gravel terraces (Tc_2) and Tc_1) were formed (Bigarella, Mousinho and Silva, 1965). These terraces were supposed to have been formed during the main glacial episodes of the Wisconsin glaciation or to the Würm I and II times.

There is little chronologic information concerning the Upper Pleistocene of Amazonia. During the last glaciation, however, the climatic changes are better known. During the period between 90,000 and 21,000 B.P. the South American climate was more humid than in the Holocene (van der Hammen, 1974). The paleoecologic changes from the Upper Pleistocene of South American tropical regions were tentatively summarised by van der Hammen (1974). He concluded that in the period between 21,000 and 12,500 B.P. there was a lowering of temperature of 6 to 7°C in the high elevations of the Andean Mountains, and of about 3°C in the low regions, with a more significant temperature gradient than at present. From palynological studies, van der Hammen (1974) showed this cooler period was drier as well, with a maximum dryness phase at 18,000 B.P. At this time the tree line in the Andes was 1,200 to 1,500 m below the present one, and the herbaceous savannahs were widespread in Colombia, Guiana,

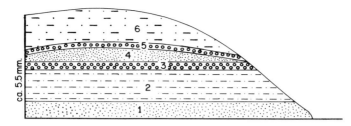

Fig. 3.5. Schematic section in a level at 35 m above the river high water. Manaus-Itacoatiara highway (216.1 km). 1 — Sandy sediments with granules and small angular quartz pebbles; 2 — sandy-silty-clayey sediments with granules and small quartz pebbles. In the lower part of this layer laterite fragments are present; 3 — rudaceous reddish material composed by the lateric pebbles up to 15 cm in diameter; 4 — brownish sand scattered with lateritic fragments; 5 — same as in item 3; 6 — yellowish sandy material (modified from Meis, 1968).

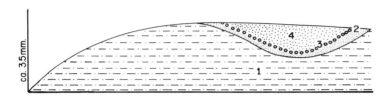

Fig. 3.6. Schematic section in a 55 m high level above the Rio Negro water table. Manaus — Caracarai road (20.5 km after the junction to Itacoatiara. 1 — Whitish sandy-silty-clayey sediments with quartz granules; 2 — yellowish sand with quartz granules; 3 — stone line made up of laterite fragments up to 2 cm in diameter; 4 — yellowish sandy sediments (modified from Meis, 1968).

Suriname and Rondônia. Pollen diagrams indicate that the frequency of herb pollen increased from 5% to 95% in relationship with the tree pollen. Ab'Sáber (1977, 1979, 1982) in several papers agreed with the postulations of van der Hammen (1974) and prepared a paleoenvironmental map for the entire South American continent (see also Absy, this volume).

Corresponding to the Upper Pleistocene (Tc_2 and Tc_1 times) there are a sequence of yellowish colluvia and rudaceous paleopavements (stonelines) rich in limonitic fragments, occurring in the Middle and Lower Amazon valley (Meis, 1968; Journaux, 1975) (Figs. 3.5, 3.6, 3.7). The yellowish colluvium of the terrace slope dips toward the river and continues below the water line indicating that at the time of colluviation the river was at a lower position (Meis, 1968). There are possibly several colluvium units. The colluviation processes in humid episodes were accentuated during the fluctuations toward dryness, which seem to correspond to lower sea levels.

On slopes of higher relief in the Amazonian region there are coarse colluvium sequences enclosing large boulders. Elsewhere the RADAMBRASIL Project refers to the presence of colluvium units without more details.

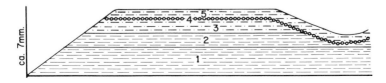

Fig. 3.7. Schematic section of an intermediate level in the Manaus — Itacoatiara highway (km 238). 1 — Clayey sediments; 2 — mottled clay deposits with incipient ferrugineous concretions; 3 — yellowish silty-sandy sediments; 4 — stone line composed of lateritic fragments; 5 — yellowish sandy-silty deposits (modified from Meis, 1968).

The Landsat and SLAR (radar) imagery show stabilised gullies in the present day forest area, which were supposedly developed previously to the Flandrian transgression at a time when the landscape was covered by open vegetation formation (dry episode) and the weather was characterised by intensive showers (Tricart, 1974; Journaux, 1975). The relict nature of this drainage network is clear. During the Holocene transgression the drainage was blocked by the levees of the trunk streams and are now occupied by fluviatile *rias* and '*terra-firme*' lakes which show little sign of infilling by sediments (Meis, 1968; Tricart, 1975, 1977).

Outside the Amazonian region there are more radiometric datings available. The low terrace in Falcon State (Venezuela) is related to the penultimate transgression which occurred during the last interstadial period between 35,000 – 30,000 B.P. (Ochsenius, 1979). In the semiarid period between 18,000 – 14,000 B.P. the Maracaibo lake was much smaller (Ochsenius, 1980). Lake Valencia became dry at 13,000 B.P. when the climate was very dry (Salgado-Labouriau, 1982). At the Pleistocene – Holocene boundary there was a shift toward more humid climate. At about 10,000 B.P. the lake was formed again, with development of a vegetation adapted to a more humid climate.

The change of semiarid conditions to humid ones marks the boundary between the Pleistocene and the Holocene. There are several datings from different regions of Brazil indicating that this change occurred about 10,200 B.P. for the Pirabeiraba terrace (Bigarella, 1971) and for the Doce river valley lacustrine deposits (Meis and Monteiro, 1979). This is also backed by evidence from Lake Valencia in Venezuela (Salgado-Labouriau, 1982).

In the Doce river valley there was a climatic oscillation slightly toward dryness between 10,220 and 7,840 B.P., causing intensification of erosive processes on slopes (Meis and Monteiro, 1979). Afterwards, from 7,840 B.P. on, the climate became humid. In the Holocene, the glaciers of the Serra Nevada de Merida (Venezuela) became reduced to about one-fifth of the previous pleistocenic extension (Schubert, 1972 and Salgado-Labouriau, 1976, 1977). According to Giegengack and Grauch (1973) the biggest ice retreat in Mucuchache was about 12,700 B.P. A brief cooling oscillation happened in the Venezuelan Andes between 6,000 and 5,000 B.P.

Oscillations of oceanic level in the coastal plain of Paraná indicate the presence of high sea level stands at about 5,700 B.P. and 2,675 B.P. (Bigarella and Becker, 1975). The 5,700 B.P. level corresponds to the maximum retreat of the ice-sheets and possibly to the warmest temperature in the Holocene as well as to a general increase in humidity creating conditions for the maximum expansion of the vegetation. At this time there were conditions for the Amazonian forest and some of its species to expand along the coast into the northeastern and eastern Brazilian coastal plain regions. In the Atlantic forests of these regions there are over 400 species of trees from the Amazonian forest, as well as many species of animals now isolated in the forest refuge areas. The possible connections between the Amazonian and Atlantic forests could only have been made during the interglacial times.

In southern Brazil at about 2,400 – 2,700 B.P. there was a climatic oscillation toward dryness which exposed the soils to erosion in the Pirai-Mirim valley (Joinville, SC) filling it with a sequence of 2 – 3 m of sandy and clayey sediments (Bigarella, 1971). The same event was registered in the Amazonian region by Absy (1982, and this volume) who dated it as being between 2,700 – 2,000 B.P.

REFERENCES

Ab'Sáber, A. N. (1967) Problemas geomorfológicos da Amazônia brasileira. *Atas do Simpósio sobre a Biota Amazônica*, Vol.1. pp. 35 – 68.

Ab'Sáber, A. N. (1977) Espaços ocupados pela expansão dos climas secos na América do Sul, por ocasião dos periodos glaciais quaternários. Inst. Geociên, Univ. São Paulo, *Paleoclimas* 3, 1 – 18.

Ab'Sáber, A. N. (1979) Os mecanismos da desintegração das paisagens tropicais no pleistoceno: efeitos paleoclimaticos do periodo Würm Wisconsin no Brasil. UNESP, *Interfacies* 4, 1 – 19.

Ab'Sáber, A. N. (1982) The paleoclimate and paleoecology of Brazilian Amazonia. In *Biological Diversification in the Tropics*, Ed. G.T. Prance, pp. 41 – 59. Columbia Univ. Press.

Absy, M. L. (1982) Quaternary Palynological studies in the Amazon basin. In *Biological Diversification in the Tropics*, Ed. G.T. Prance, pp. 67 – 73. Columbia Univ. Press.

Absy, M. L. and van der Hammen, T. (1976) Some paleoecological data from Rondônia, southern part of the Amazon Basin. *Acta Amazonica* 6(3), 293 – 299.

Albuquerque, O. P. (1922) Reconhecimentos geológicos no valle do Amazonas (Campanhas de 1918 and 1919). *Serviço Geol. Mineralógico, Bol.* 3, 1 – 84.

Amaral, G. (1974) Geologia pré-cambriana da região amazônica. S. Paulo, Univ. de S. Paulo, Inst. Geocien, 212 pp. *Tese de Livre-Docência.*

Avila-Pires, T. D. de (1974) Caraterização zoogeográfica da provincia amazônica. I-Expedicões cientificas na Amazônia brasileira. *An. Acad. Bras. Cien.* 46(1), 133 – 158.

Barbosa, G. V., Renno, C. V. and Franco, E. M. S. (1974) Geomorfologia. In Brasil, DNPM, Projeto RADAMBRASIL, Folha S. A. 22 Belém. *Lev. Recurso Naturais*, Vol. 5.

Barbosa, O. (1958) Geomorfologia do Território do Rio Branco. *Not. Geomorf.* 1, 16 – 18.

Barbosa, O. and Ramos, J. R. A. (1959) Território do Rio Branco (Aspectos principais da Geomorfologia, da geologia e das possibilidades minerais de sua zona setentrional). DNPM, *Div. Geol. Min., Bol.* 196.

Barbosa, O. and Ramos, J. R. A. (1961) *Principal aspects of the geomorphology and geology in the Territory of the Rio Branco, Brazil.* 5th Int. Guiana Geol. Conf., Proc. pp. 33 – 36.

Beigbeder, Y. (1956) Etude preliminaire des aplanissements observés dans le Haut Rio Branco entre les rios Surumu, Cotingo et Maú, 15 au Nord et au Sud du 4° degré de latitude Nord. In: Premier Rapport de la Commission pour l'étude et la correlation des niveau d'erosion et des surfaces d'aplainissement autour de l'Atlantique. *Congres. Int. Geogr.* 5, 31 – 36.

Beigbeder, Y. (1959) La region moyenne de Haut Rio Branco (Brésil). Etude geomorphologique. Travaux et Memoires de l'Institut des Hautes Etudes de l'Amerique Latine, X-Université de Paris et Inst. Nac. Pesq. Amazônia.

Beurlen, K. (1970) *Geologie von Brasilien.* Gebruder Borntraeger, Berlin, Stuttgart, 414 pages.

Bigarella, J. J. (1973) Geology of the Amazon and Parnaiba basins. In *The Ocean Basins and Margins*, Eds. A.E.M. Nairn and F.G. Stehli, Vol. 1, pp. 25 – 86. Plenum Publ. Corp., New York.

Bigarella, J. J. (1975) The Barreiras Group in Northeastern Brazil. *Anais Acad. Bras. Cien.* 47 (Supplement), 365 – 394.

Bigarella, J. J. *et al.* (1978) A Serra do Mar e a porção oriental do Estado do Paraná. 249 pages. *Secretaria do Planejamento do Estado do Parana e ADEA. Curitiba.*

Bigarella, J. J. *et al.* (1979) Ouro Fino: recursos naturais. 30 pages. COMEN e ADEA. Curitiba.

Bigarella, J. J. and Ab'Sáber, A. N. (1964) Palaeogeographiche und Palaeoklimatische Aspekte des Kainozoikum in Suedbrasilien. *Zeit. f. Geomorph. N.F.* 8(3), 286 – 312.

Bigarella, J. J. and Andrade, G. O. (1964) Considerações sobre a estratigrafia dos sedimentos cenozoicos de Pernambuco (Grupo Barreiras). *Arq. Inst. Cien. Cien. Terra* 2, 2 – 14.

Bigarella, J. J. and Andrade-Lima, D. (1982) Paleoenvironmental changes in Brazil. In *Biological Diversification in the Tropics*, Ed. G.T. Prance, pp. 27 – 40, Columbia Univ. Press.

Bigarella, J. J., Andrade-Lima, D. and Riehs, P. J. (1975) Considerações a respeito das mudanças paleoambientais na distribuição de algumas espécies vegetais e animais no Brasil. *An. Acad. Bras. Cien.* Vol 47 (Suplemento), 411 – 464.

Bigarella, J. J. and Mousinho, M. R. (1966) Slope development in southern and southeastern Brazil. *Zeit. f. Geomorph.* 10(2), 150 – 160.

Bigarella, J. J., Mousinho, R. M. and Silva, J. X. (1965) *Processes and Environments of the Brazilian Quaternary.* Curitiba Univ. Fed. Paraná.

Bigarella, J. J. and Salamuni, R. (1961) Ocorrência de sedimentos continentais na região litorânea de Santa Catarina e sua significação paleoclimática. *Biol. Paran. Geogr.* 4/5, 179 – 187.

Branner, J. C. (1915) *Geologia elementar.* ed. 2, Rio de Janeiro, F. Alves, 396 pages.

Brown Jr., K. S. (1977) Centros de evolução. Refúgios quaternários e conservação de patrimonios genéticos na região neotropical: padrões de diferencição em *Ithomiinae* (Lepidoptera-Nymphalidae). *Acta Amazonica* 7, 75 – 134.

Brown Jr., K. S. and Ab'Sáber, A. N. (1979) Ice age forest refuges and evolution in the neotropics: correlation of paleoclimatological, geomorphological and pedological data with modern biological endemism. Univ. S. Paulo, Inst. Geogr., *Paleoclimas* 5, 1 – 30.

Buisonje, P. de (1974) Neogene and Quaternary geology of Aruba, Curacao and Bonaire. In *Natuurwetwnschafpelyke Studiekrung voor Suriname en de Nederlandse Antillen* Ed. Vitgaven, 291 pages. Utrecht.

Castro, M. P. de (1981) A complexidade da vegetação amazônica. *Rev. Bras. Geogr.* 43(2), 283 – 300.

Cordani, U. G., Melcher, G. C. and Almeida, F. F. M. de (1968) Outline of the Precambrian geochronology of South America. *Can. J. Earth Sci.* 5, 629 – 632.

Damuth, J. E. (1977) Late Quaternary sedimentation in the western equatorial Atlantic. *Geol. Soc. Am. Bull.* 99, 695 – 710.

Damuth, J. E. and Fairbridge, R. W. (1970) Equatorial Atlantic deep sea arkosic sands and ice-age aridity in tropical South America. *Geol. Soc. Am. Bull.* 81, 189 – 206.

Dennen, W. H. and Norton, H. A. (1977) Geology and geochemistry of bauxite deposits in the Lower Amazon basin. *Econ. Geol.* 72, 82 – 89.

Erhart, H. (1955) Biostasie et rhesistasie: esquisse d'une théorie sur le rôle de la pedogenèse en taut que phenoméne geologique. *C.R. Acad. Sci. (France)* 241, 1218 – 1220.

Ferreira, C. S. (1960) Contribuição a paleontologia do Estado do Pará. Revisão da familia Pectinidae da Formação Pirabas VI (Mollusca-Pelecypoda). *Arq. Mus. Nac.* 50, 135 – 166.

Flohn, H. (1952) Algemeine atmosphärische Zirkulation and Paläoklimatologie. *Geol. Rundscheun* 40.

Francisco, B. H. R. *et al.* (1971) Contribuição a geologia da folha São Luis (SA 23) no Estado do Pará. Belém. *Museu Paraense Emílio Goeldi, Bol.* 17 1 – 40.

Giegengack, R. and Grauch, R. J. (1973) Quaternary geology of the Central Andes, Venezuela: a preliminary assessment. *Excursion no. I, Cordillera de los Andes. II Congreso Latinoamericano de geologia*, Venezuela, pp. 38 – 39.

Goés, A. M. (1980) Caracterização faciológica e interpretação ambiental dos sedimentos Barreiras da região bragantina, nordeste do Pará. *Anais do XXXI Congr. Bras. Geol.* v. 2, 766 – 771.

Gourou, P. (1949) Amazonie (Problèmes geographiques). *Les Chiers d'Outre Mer* 2(5), Bordeaux.

Grubb, P. L. C. (1979) Genesis of bauxite deposits in the Amazon Basin and Guianas coastal plains. *Econ. Geol.* 74, 735 – 750.

Guerra, A. T. (1959) Geografia do Brasil, grande região Norte. *IBGE, CNG Bibl. Geo. Brasileira 1.* Rio de Janeiro.

Haffer, J. (1969) Speciation in Amazonian forest birds. *Science* 165, 131 – 137.

Hartt, C. F. (1847) Contributions to the geology and physical geography of the Lower Amazonas. *Buffalo Soc. Nat. Sci. Bull.* 1.

Howard, A. D. (1965) Photogeologic interpretation of structure in the Amazon Basin: A test study. *Geol. Soc. Am. Bull.* 76, 395 – 406.

Journaux, A. (1975) Recherches geomorphologiques en Amazonie, *C.N.R.S.* 28, 1 – 68.

King, L. G. (1956) Geomorfologia do Brasil Oriental, *Rev. Bras. Geogr.* 18, 147 – 265.

Klammer, G. (1971) Über plio-pleistozäne Terrasen und ihre Sedimente im uteren Amazonasgebiet. *Z. Geomorph. N.F.* 15(1), 62 – 106.

Klammer, G. (1975) Beobachtungen an Hängen im tropischen Regenwald des uteren Amazonas. *Z. Geomorph. N.F.* 19(3), 273 – 286.

Klammer, G. (1976) Zur jungqutären Reliefgeschichte des Amazonastales. *Z. Geomorph. N.F.* 20(2), 149 – 170.

Klammer, G. (1978) Reliefentwicklung im Amazonasbecken und plio-pleistozäne Bewegungen des Meeresspiegels. *Z. Geomorph. N.F.* 22(4), 390 – 416.

Klinge, H. (1965) Podzol soils in the Amazon Basin. *J. Soil Sci.* 16(1), 95 – 103.

Kotschoubey, B. and Truckenbrodt, W. (1981) Evolução poligenética das bauxitas do distrito de Paragominas Açailândia (Estados do Pará e Maranhão). *Rev. Bras. Geociências* 11(3), 193 – 202.

Krook, L. (1979) *Sedimentpetrographical Studies in Northern Suriname.* Academish Proefschrift, Amsterdam, 154 pages.

Kuhlmann, E. (1977) Vegetação. In *Geografia do Brasil: Região Norte,* Fund. Inst. Bras. Geogr. Estat. Brasil, pp. 59 – 94.

Marbut, C. F. and Manifold, C. B. (1925) The topography of the Amazon valley. *Geograph. Rev.* 15.

Matoso, S. O. and Robertson, F. S. (1959) Uso geológico do termo 'Barreiras.' *Bol. Tecn. Petrobras* 2(3), 37 – 43.

Maury, C. (1942) Fosseis terciários do Pará. *Serv. Geol. Min. Brasil, Monogr.* 4, 46 – 389.

Meis, M. R. M. (1968) Considerações geomorfológicas sobre o Médio Amazonas. *Rev. Bras. Geogr.* 30(2), 3 – 20.

Meis, M. R. M. and Monteiro, A. M. F. (1979) Upper Quaternary "rampas" Doce river valley, Southeastern Brazilian Plateau. *Zeit für Geomorphologie.* 23, 132 – 151.

Milliman, J. D., Summerhayes, C. P. and Barretto, H. T. (1975) Quaternary sedimentation on the Amazon continental margin. A model. *Geol. Soc. Am. Bull.* 86(5), 61 – 614.

Moura, R. de (1938) Geologia do Baixo Amazonas. *Serv. Geol. Mineral Bol.* 91, 1 – 94, Rio de Janeiro.

Müller, P. (1970) Vertebratenfaunen brasilianischer Inselnals indikatoren für Glaziale und Postglaziale Vegetations fluktuationen. *Verhdl. Dt. Zool. Ges. Würsburg.*

Müller, P. (1971) Ausbreitungszentren und Evolution in der Neotropics. *Mitteilungen 1* (1 – 911971) aus der Biogeographischen Abteilung der Geogr. Inst. Univ. Saarlandes, 20 pages.

Müller, P. and Schmithusen, J. (1970) Problem der Genese. Süd-amerikanischer Biota. In *Deutsche Geographische Forschung in der Welt von Heute. Festschrift fur Erwin Gentz,* pp. 109 – 122. Verlag Ferdinand Hirt, Kiel.

Nascimento, D. A. do, Mauro, C. A. de, and Garcia, M das G. (1976) Geomorfologia da Folha SA 21. Santarém. Projeto Radambrasil 10:131 – 131. Rio de Janeiro.

Nunes, A. B., Burros Fo., C. N. and Lima, R. F. (1973) Geologia das Folhas SC 23, São Francisco e SC 24, Aracaju. In *Brasil, D.N.P.M., Projeto RADAM, Levant. de Rec. Naturais 1.*

Ochsenius, C. (1979) Ancient beaches and biogeographic landbridges resulting from Pleistocene neotectonism and glacioeustatism. Quarternary ecology in the peri-Caribbean arid belt, Corian region, Northernmost South America. *Scient. Monogr. no. 2.*

Ochsenius, C. (1980) Quaternario en Venezuela. Introducción a la paleoecologia en el Norte de Sudamerica. *Cuadernos Falconianos* 3, 1 – 68.

Oliveira, A. I. and Leonardos, O. H. (1943) Geologia do Brasil. 2nd ed. rev. atual. Rio de Janeiro. *Serv. Inf. Agricola,* 813 pages. *Serie Didatica* No.2.

Paiva, G. (1939) Alto Rio Branco. Brasil. *Serv. Geol. Mineral, Bol.* 99.

Petri, S. (1954) Foraminiferos fosseis da Bacia Marajó. Univ. S. Paulo, *Fac. Fil. Ci. Letr. Bol. 176, Geol.* 11, 1 – 172.

Petri, S. (1957) Foraminiferos miocenicos da Formação Pirabas, Univ. S. Paulo. *Bol. Fac. Fil. Ci. Letr. 216, Geol.* 16, 1 – 79.

Prance, G. T. (1973) Phytogeographic support for the theory of Pleistocene forest refuges in the Amazon Basin, based on evidence from distribution patterns in Caryocaraceae, Chrysobalanaceae, Dichapetalaceae and Lecythidaceae. *Acta Amazonica* 3(3), 5 – 26.

Projeto RADAMBRASIL (1974, 1978) Geomorfologia. *Geologia Vols. 4, 5, 6, 7, 8, 10, 11, 18.* (several authors).

Ramos, J. R. A. (1956) Reconhecimento geológico no Território do Rio Branco, Brasil, *D.N.P.M., Relatório Anual*, pp. 58 – 62.

Ramos, J. R. A. (1961) Reconhecimento geológico Brasília-Belém. Brasil. *D.N.P.M., Div. Geol. Mineral, Relatório Anual*, pp. 80 – 90.

Rohdenburg, H. (1970) Morphodynamische Akttivitäts und Stabilität-zeiten statt Pluvial und Interpluvial-zeiten. *Eiszeitalter und Gegenw*. 21, 81 – 96.

Ruellan, F. (1957) Expedições geomorfológicas no Território do Rio Branco. *Inst. Nac. Pesq. Amazonica INPA*.

Sakamoto, S. (1957) Trabalhos sedimentológicos, geomorfológicos e pedogenéticos referentes a Amazônia. *Missão FAO-UNESCO junto a SPVEA* (mimeograph).

Salgado-Labouriau, M. L. (1976) Historia de la vegetacion de los Andes en los ultimos ocho mil años. *Rev. Lineas* 232, 6 – 11.

Salgado-Labouriau, M. L. (1982) Climatic change at the Pleistocene-Holocene boundary. In *Biological diversification in the tropics*, Ed. G.T. Prance, pp. 74 – 77. Columbia Univ. Press.

Salgado-Labouriau, M. L. and Schubert, C. (1977) Pollen analysis of a peat bog from Laguna Victoria (Venezuelan Andes). *Acta Cient. Venezolana* 28, 328 – 332.

Sanchez, P. A., Bandy, D. E., Villachica, J. H. and Nichdaides, J. J. (1982) Amazon Basin: Management for continuous crop production. *Science* 216 (4548), 821 – 827.

Santos, *et al*. (1975) Geologia da Folha SB21, Tapajós. Brasil. *D.N.P.M., Projeto RADAM, Lev. Rec. Nat*. 7, 23 – 99.

Schubert, C. (1972) Geomorphology and glacier retreat in the Pico Bolívar area, Sierra Nevada de Merida, Venezuela. *Zeit. für Gletscherkunde und Glazialgeologie* 8(1/2), 189 – 202.

Schubert, C. and Sifontes, R. S. (1970) Bocanó fault, Venezuelan Andes: Evidence of postglacial movement. *Science* 170, 66 – 69.

Schwarzbach, M. (1963) *Climates of the past: An introduction to paleoclimatology*. Van Nostrand, London, 328 pages.

Simpson, B. B. and Haffer, J. (1978) Speciation patterns in the Amazon forest biota. *Ann. Rev. Ecol. & Systematics* 9, 497 – 518.

Singh, S. (1972) The tectonic evolution of that portion of the Guyana Shield represented in Guyana. An evaluation of the present status of investigations and correlation across Guyana Shield. Georgetown. *Geol. Surv. Min. Dept*., 10 pages.

Sombroeck, W. G. (1966) Amazon soils. A reconnaissance of the soils of the Brazilian Amazon region. *Wageningen, Center for Agric. Publ. Document* 292 pages.

Sternberg, H. O'R. (1950) Vales tectônicos na planície amazônica? *Rev. Bras. Geogr*. 12(4), 513 – 533.

Street, F. A. (1981) Tropical paleoenvironments. *Prog. Physical Geogr*. 5(2), 157 – 185.

Tricart, J. (1974) Existence de périodes sèches au Quaternaire en Amazonie et dans les regions voisines. *Rev. Geom. Dyn*. 23, 145 – 158.

Tricart, J. (1975) Influence des oscillations climatiques récentes sur le modèle en Amazonie orientale (Region de Santarém) après les images de radar latéral. *Zeit. fur Geomorph*. 19, 140 – 463.

Tricart, J. (1977) Types et lits fluciaux en Amazonie brésiliene. *Ann. Geogr*. 473 IXXX VI, 1 – 53.

Truckenbrodt, W. and Kotschoubey, B. (1981) Argila de Belterra Cobetura terciaria das bauxitas amazonicas. *Rev. Bras. Geociencias* 11(3), 203 – 208.

Truckenbrodt, W. and Kotschoubey, B. (1982) Alguns aspectos microfaciológicos das bauxitas na parte leste da região amazônica. *Anais XXXII Congr. Bras. Geol*. v.2, 695 – 700.

Truckenbrodt, W., Kotschoubey, B. and Goés, A. M. (1982) Considerações a respeito da idade das bauxitas na parte leste da região amazônica. *Anais do I Simp. Geol. da Amazônia*, 201 – 209.

Van der Hammen, T. (1974) The Pleistocene changes of vegetation and climate in tropical South America. *J. Biogeogr*. 1, 3 – 26.

Van der Hammen, T. (1982) Paleoecology of tropical South America. In *Biological Diversification in the Tropics*, Ed. G.T. Prance, pp. 60 – 66. Columbia University Press.

Vanzolini, P. E. (1970) Zoologia sistemática, geografia e a origem das espécies. *Univ. S. Paulo, Geogr., Série Teses e Monografias* 3, 1 – 56.

Ventura, L. M., D'Avila, L. M. and Barbosa, G. V. (1975) Geomorfologia. Brasil. *D.N.P.M., Projeto RADAM. Folha SB 21, Tapajós Lev. Rec. Nat*. 7, 119 – 149.

Wolf, F. A. M. and Silva, J. M. R. (1973) Provincia bauxitifera da Amazônia. *D.N.P.M. 5° Distrito, Belém*, 35 pages (unpublished report).

CHAPTER 4

Palynology of Amazonia: The History of the Forests as Revealed by the Palynological Record

MARIA LÚCIA ABSY

Instituto Nacional de Pesquisas da Amazônia, Manaus, Brazil

CONTENTS

4.1. INTRODUCTION

The great diversity of species of the Amazon forest contributes to a rich variety of pollen and spore types. Both pollen and spores are produced by plants from all the different habitats in the region, so that each habitat has a characteristic pollen spectrum.

The term 'palynology' was coined by Hyde and Williams in 1945 to designate the morphological study of pollen grains and spores, as well as the applications of such study.

Palynology has developed rapidly in the past few decades. Studies of fossil pollen and modern pollen are of great importance in various fields of research. Taxonomists have used morphological pollen studies as an auxiliary character in the classification of some plant families. Pollen studies also include analysis of the pollen in bee honey (melitopalynology), and pollen and spore distribution through the air (aeropalynology).

In 1916, Lennart von Post, a Swedish geologist, recognised pollen analysis as an excellent tool for interpreting vegetational and climatic history. This branch of pollen study relies on the identification of fossil pollen grains preserved in areas where sediments accumulate, such as lake bottoms. Since the time of von Post, pollen analysis of sediments has expanded greatly, especially for Quaternary-age sediments. Palynology has also become an important auxiliary science for archaeology, aiming at dating artifacts

72

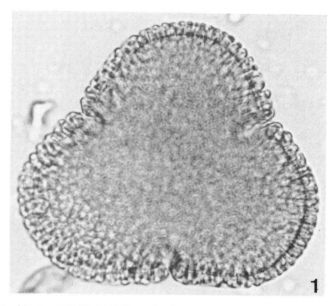

Fig. 4.1. *Pseudobombax* (BOMBACACEAE): pollen from Costa da Terra Nova section, depth: 12 m.

and the establishment of human cultures because pollen history reveals the presence of the pollen of crop plants and weeds.

With increasing knowledge of the significant events which took place during the Quaternary in several parts of the world, palynological evidence has become an essential adjunct for the explanation of the vegetational changes in light of climatic history.

An example of the application of pollen analysis is found in the extensive work of Thomas van der Hammen in Colombia, South America. Van der Hammen, a Dutch geologist, has been working since 1951 on the Quaternary history of Colombia. He introduced students of several countries to palynology, including the author, who was one of his students at Hugo de Vries-Laboratorium in Amsterdam. By means of pollen analysis and radioactive carbon (^{14}C) dating of sediment samples, van der Hammen demonstrated correlation between climatic changes in tropical latitudes and those of the northern temperate regions. When combined with ^{14}C dating and stratigraphic studies, van der Hammen's palynological investigations documented Quaternary age-level changes in northern South America.

The series of publications by van der Hammen and collaborators on Quaternary history of Colombia, which includes studies in palynology, archaeology, and prehistory, vertebrate paleontology, paleopedology, geomorphology, among others, give us an idea of the wide scope of palynology.

4.2. INTERRELATIONS BETWEEN SEDIMENTS AND POLLEN CONTENT

The pollen grains of wind pollinated species are the most important group for study of sediment pollen content. The wind pollinated species generally produce very great quantities of pollen, which are liberated and dispersed into the atmosphere as 'pollen rain' (Faegri and Iversen, 1966) and then fall slowly to the earth's surface.

Many of the pollen grains (Figs. 4.1 and 4.2) and pteridophyte spores (Figs. 4.3 and 4.4) are blown into lakes and bogs, or carried in by streams, rills or slope-wash (Livingstone, 1969). When conditions

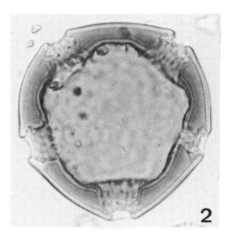

Fig. 4.2 .*Symphonia* (GUTTIFERAE): pollen from Costa da Terra Nova section, depth: 8.10 m.

are favourable for pollen and spore preservation, for example, if they are not exposed for a long period to the atmosphere, they are generally well preserved especially in such places as peat and sediments. This is due to the resistant outer wall, or exine, of the pollen grains. Other microfossils could also be preserved, such as algae — like *Botryococcus* (Fig. 4.5), foraminifers, and diatoms.

Faegri and Iversen (1966) distinguished between peat and sediment. Peat is mainly autochthonous, consisting of remains of vegetation that once lived in that particular place where the sample was recovered. Sediments, on the other hand, are mainly allochthonous, consisting of material that has originated elsewhere and been deposited or redeposited in the place where it is recovered.

Clay and peat are also found intercalated with layers of sand. However, sand is not of much interest for pollen analysis because it is very poor or barren of pollen.

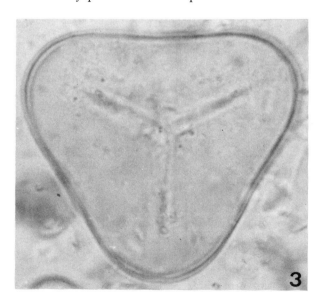

Fig. 4.3. *Trilete psilate:* Lago Arari section, depth: 4 m.

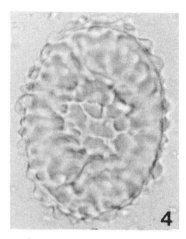

Fig. 4.4. *Monolete verrucate:* Lago Arari section, depth: 4.50 m.

Lake deposits are generally preferred for pollen analysis. For each site that is investigated, general information is also required, such as: a precise map reference, a locality description with photographs or sketches, geologic aspects, a list of local and surrounding vegetation, and samples of the present day pollen rain (Kummel and Raup, 1965). The relation between pollen rain and the local vegetation types is of considerable importance for a better interpretation of the fossil pollen spectra and pollen diagrams.

After a sampling site has been chosen the collecting of samples for palynological investigation varies from hand-operated corers (Fig. 4.6) to more complex boring or well-drilling equipment (Fig. 4.7). The latter two types of equipment are used for sampling at deeper levels and need a working platform. Samples for pollen analysis should be taken at regular depths. In routine work they are taken at 5 cm or 10 cm intervals.

After collecting samples, they must be transported to the laboratory, and prepared in conditions that avoid contamination by fresh pollen and spores or by sediments of another age.

The first step in studying pollen for microscopic analysis is the preparation of sediment samples and the preparation of recent pollen for comparison with one another. The purpose of preparation of the sediment samples is to separate and concentrate the pollen and spore types found in the sample.

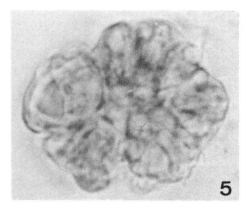

Fig. 4.5. *Botryococcus* (algae): Lago Arari section, depth: 4.80 m.

Fig. 4.6. Collecting pollen samples with hand-operated corer.

There are several methods of preparation of sediment samples for microscopic analysis. The choice of method to be used is important because some pollen grain walls are delicate and easily damaged.

A common method of preparation of a sediment sample involves treatment of the sediment with ten per cent potassium hydroxide (KOH) aqueous solution to remove 'humic acids' (Faegri and Iversen, 1966) followed by acetolysis (Erdtman, 1960) which also destroys the cellular content of recent pollen grains. After acetolysis the exine becomes more distinct permitting a more detailed examination.

A gravity separation by use of heavy liquid (e.g. Bromoform-alcohol mixture) is required. The density of this is such that mineral fragments sink, whereas pollen and other organic constituents float (Faegri and Iversen, 1966).

After preparation, the residue containing pollen is mounted in glycerin jelly on a slide for microscopic analysis.

The pollen grains found on the slides are identified and counted. The identification is made with the aid of published descriptions, keys and comparisons with a collection of recent pollen slides.

4.3. POLLEN DIAGRAM

For a better understanding of the most important fluctuations of pollen belonging to different species of plants, a pollen diagram is made based on results of pollen analysis of individual core sites.

A standard diagram may be composed of two parts: (1) a general diagram illustrating pollen percentages of indicator plant associations, and (2) individual curves representing the pollen percentages of each taxon (Figs. 4.8,9).

Fig. 4.7. Collecting pollen samples with well-drilling equipment.

Indicator associations are selected on the basis of modern plant distributions. For example, *Byrsonima* and *Curatella* are characteristic plants of Neotropical savannah and their presence in a pollen diagram is taken to represent a typical savannah plant association.

Abrupt changes in pollen frequency in the core delineate the boundaries between 'pollen zones', where one plant association may have been replaced by another. Such changes may be due to changes in rainfall, hydrology, sea level, or other environmental factors. By this means the pollen diagram is divided into local, provisional pollen zones, according to the fluctuations of pollen percentages thought to be significant. These zones are indicated by a letter (A,B,C, etc.).

To the left of a standard general pollen diagram we find the stratigraphic column showing sediment types and ^{14}C dates of core samples. The radiocarbon dates are given in years before present (B.P.), which is delimited to be 1950 AD.

4.4. PALYNOLOGICAL RECORDS FOR AMAZONIA AND NEIGHBOURING REGIONS

In order to discuss the most important events that occurred during the Quaternary-age in Amazonia we may consider the history of the vegetation as revealed by pollen analysis.

In the beginning of the Quaternary, about 2.5 million years ago, a remarkable series of worldwide changes of climate, the Pleistocene ice age, began (Livingstone and van der Hammen, 1978). Pleistocene glacial and interglacial periods changed the face of the earth in the northern and southern temperate latitudes. It caused extinction, speciation and marked changes in the geographical distribution of plants and animals (van der Hammen, 1974). However, it was realised only comparatively recently that these

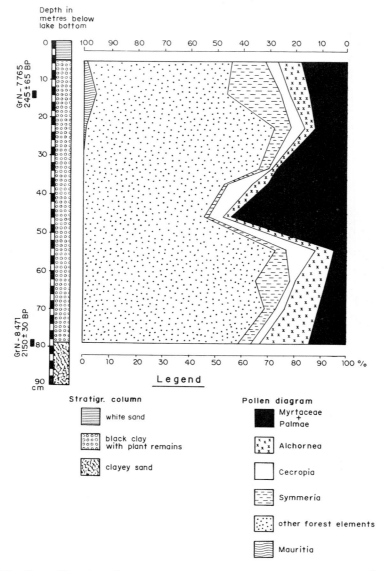

Fig. 4.8. Pollen diagram illustrating pollen percentages of indicator plant associations for Caju lake, Amazonas, Brazil.

climate changes had a profound effect on the tropical regions, and recently an increasing number of studies have been published concerning the climatic and vegetational changes in tropical South America.

Palynological studies and ^{14}C datings in the sediments of the coastal plain near Georgetown (Guyana), have shown the history of this area during the last interglacial, the last glacial and the Holocene (van der Hammen, 1963). van der Hammen presented evidence of profound vegetational changes in this area from forest or woodland to savannah. A grass savannah must have been the predominant vegetation type during the last period of glaciation, in areas where nowadays a tropical lowland forest is found.

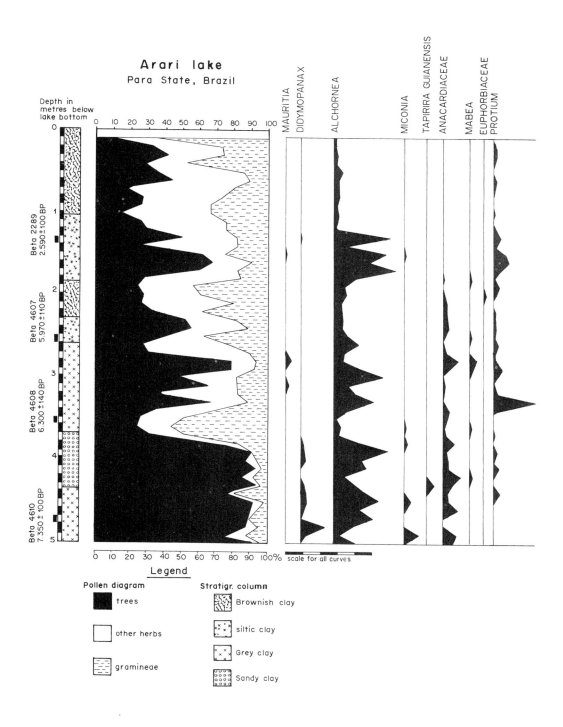

Fig. 4.9. Complete pollen diagram for Arari lake, Para, Brazil, showing percentages of indicator plant associations (left) and part of the individual curves of pollen percentages of the taxa.

A significant extension of savannahs during glacial periods has also been recorded in the studies of Plio-Pleistocene deposits from coastal lowlands of Suriname by Wijmstra (1969, 1971). Pollen diagrams of this area show that phases of savannah alternated with phases of mangrove and swamp forest. In both coastal lowlands of Guyana and Suriname the dominance of savannah vegetation occurred during periods of low sea level.

In the Rupununi savannahs of Guyana, near the Brazilian border, pollen data and ^{14}C analyses of sediments from Lake Moreiru, have shown a major expansion of open savannah which coincided with a very low lake level. During part of the Holocene at least 5000 B.P. and particularly in the last 3000 years, palynological evidence indicates that open savannah dominated in this area (Wijmstra and van der Hammen, 1966).

Palynological studies in coastal Suriname show changes in vegetation during the last 2000 years (Laeyendecker-Roosenburg, 1966). The marked changes in the vegetation of this area were possibly caused by minor transgressions and regressions of the sea.

Changes of the vegetation caused by incursion of the sea during the post-glacial rise of sea level were revealed by pollen diagrams of the young coastal plain of Suriname (Roeleveld, 1969). The savannah and marsh vegetation was slowly replaced by a mangrove forest as the environment became more brackish.

In the Venezuelan Andes, palynological study of sediments from Lake Valencia by Salgado-Labouriau (1980, 1982) showed that at the end of the Pleistocene c. 13,000 B.P. the climate was very dry and the region was occupied by semiarid vegetation. Pollen diagrams show that there was no rainforest at the end of the Pleistocene until c. 11,500 B.P. and that the humid tropical forest that occurs today in the area, did not exist during this interval.

4.5. POLLEN DATA FROM THE AMAZON BASIN

There is still a paucity of palynological evidence for the interpretation of the Quaternary vegetational history of the Amazon Basin. Biogeographers have pointed out that more palynological studies are needed to provide more concrete data relating the climatic and vegetational changes in this region during the Quarternary. Nonetheless, pollen data from a number of Amazonian lakes have brought to light interesting information on changes in the vegetation and climate of this region.

Preliminary palynological investigation of a series of Upper Cenozoic sediments from Rondônia, in the southern part of the Amazon Basin, indicate that the tropical forest was temporarily replaced by open savannah vegetation, possibly during a part of the Pleistocene (van der Hammen, 1972, 1974).

Pollen diagrams presented in later studies by Absy and van der Hammen (1976), based partially on the same material studied earlier by van der Hammen, showed that at least this currently forested part of Rondônia was covered by a grass savannah during at least some intervals of the Late Cenozoic (Quaternary). The dominance of open vegetation with mainly grasses, *Cuphea* and Cyperaceae suggests that savannah existed in this area. Apparently the climatic changes during several intervals of the Late Cenozoic (Quaternary) caused the development of savannahs in this region, which is now covered in tropical forest.

Palynological investigation of lake sediments in the savannah area of Boa Vista, Territory of Roraima has shown a complete dominance of grass, with surprisingly few trees. One of the few trees represented in the pollen diagram is the palm *Mauritia*. This is in agreement with the modern vegetation of the area (Absy, 1979).

Pollen analytical studies of a 20 m core from Costa da Terra Nova, on the margin of the Amazon river, show a high percentage of grasses. It seems, however, more probable that most of the grass pollen of this section was produced by 'floating meadows' (Absy, 1979), which are an important component of the flora of the modern flood plain and river margin.

Pollen diagrams show fluctuations in this area that might be explained by local changes in the extension of open water, floating meadows, *Cecropia* 'forest', and várzea forest. The lower part of the diagram, dated c. 2840 B.P. shows a relatively high percentage of grass pollen. There seems to be one major successional trend, namely from a predominance of open water to a predominance of várzea forest (Absy, 1979).

In the sediments of Terra Nova, pollen of alder (*Alnus*), an Andean plant, was regularly found in low frequencies. These allochthonous pollens were probably carried down from the Andes by the river and not by air-currents, since they do not occur in the sediments of the lakes (Absy, 1979). This shows the need for caution in the interpretation of pollen diagrams especially in seasonally flooded areas.

Pollen data from sediments of Lago do Cajú (Absy, 1979) a lake near Manaus which is surrounded by sandy beaches of the Rio Negro, have shown changes from a rather savannah-like vegetation to várzea (Fig. 4.8). The pollen content of the uppermost sediments may reflect wetter local conditions. A dry phase was found at 2150 B.P. and it is striking that this is also the date for the dry period in Terra Nova and elsewhere in tropical South America.

The sandy beach of the Rio Negro is covered today by open vegetation with blackwater igapó-forest behind it.

The study of 9 m of sediment samples of Lago Surara, about 175 km southwest of Manaus, along the lower Purus River, provided a pollen diagram that shows in the lowermost part, dated at 5240±100 B.P., the presence in the area of a vegetation type rich in *Ouratea* which indicates that it may have been a relatively dry period. A várzea type of vegetation with *Symmeria* existed at the same time. Soon *Ouratea* disappeared completely, and the next phase contained a local abundance of *Cecropia*. The later part of the diagram shows an increase of Gramineae.

The area of Lago Surara today has a blackwater igapó forest, and only in more recent time may some whitewater of the Purus river have entered the area (Absy, 1979).

The pollen diagram of Lago Cuminã, about 181 km northeast of Santarém, along the Trombetas River, reflects strong local changes in the extension of persistent open water, floating meadows and várzea forest. In the lower part of the diagram, Gramineae are well represented. This represents a relatively dry phase and is dated at 3980 B.P. (Absy, 1979). This date corresponds with the low lake level period in the Colombian Llanos Orientales (Wijmstra and van der Hammen, 1966) and in the lower Magdalena valley (unpublished, oral communication, van der Hammen). The surrounding area of Lago Cuminã is nowadays covered with forest.

The changes in the várzea and igapó forests reflected in the pollen diagrams include successions in which *Alchornea*, *Symmeria*, Myrtaceae, and *Miconia* play an important role; other successions seem to be from open water via floating meadows (mainly of grasses) and *Cecropia* stands to várzea forest (Terra Nova diagram).

The changes of vegetation in the diagrams of Costa da Terra Nova, Lago do Cajú, Lago Surara, Lago Cuminã and Lago Galheiro apparently were due mainly to local successions induced by relative changes of water level. The contemporaneity of certain phases of local low water level over a large area suggests strongly that they are of regional importance, induced by regional or even continental changes in effective rainfall caused relatively low water levels in the Amazon Basin around 4000 B.P.: c. 2100 B.P., and around 700 B.P. (A.D. 1200).

ACKNOWLEDGEMENTS

The author thanks Dr. Thomas van der Hammen for valuable suggestions and reviewing the manuscript. Dr. Bruce W. Nelson and Dr. Norman D. Penny for revision of the English text and Aurea A. Pessôa for kindly typing the manuscript.

REFERENCES

Absy, M. L. (1979) A palynological study of holocene sediments in the Amazon basin. Thesis. University of Amsterdam.

Absy, M. L. and van der Hammen, T. (1976) Some palaeoecological data from Rondônia, southern part of the Amazon basin. *Acta Amazonica* 6(3), 293 – 299.

Erdtman, G. (1960) The acetolysis method in a revised description. *Sv. Bot. Tidsk Lund.* 54(4), 561 – 564.

Faegri, K. and Iversen, J. (1966) *Textbook of Pollen Analysis.* 2nd ed. Munksgaard, Copenhagen.

Hyde, H. A. and Williams, D. A. (1945) The pollen of lime (*Tilia* spp.). *Nature* 155, 457.

Kummel, B. and Raup, D. (1965) *Handbook of Paleontological Techniques.* Freeman, San Francisco.

Laeyendecker-Roosenburg, D. M. (1966) A palynological investigation of some archaeologically interesting sections in northwestern Surinam. *Leidse Geol. Meded.* 38, 31 – 36.

Livingstone, D. A. (1969) Communities of the past. In *Essays in Plant Geography and Ecology.* Ed. K. N. H. Greenidge, pp. 82 – 104. The Nova Scotia Museum, Halifax, N.S.

Livingstone, D. A. and van der Hammen, T. (1978) Palaeogeography and palaeoclimatology. In *Tropical Forest Ecosystems.* Ed. UNESCO/UNEP/FAO, pp. 61 – 90. UNESCO, Paris.

Roeleveld, W. (1969) Pollen analysis of two sections in the young coastal plain of Surinam. *Geol. en Mijnbouw.* 48(2), 215 – 224.

Salgado-Labouriau, M. L. (1980) A pollen diagram of the Pleistocene – Holocene boundary of Lake Valencia, Venezuela. *Rev. Paleob. Palynol.* 30, 297 – 312.

Salgado-Labouriau, M. L. (1982) Climatic change at the Pleistocene – Holocene Boundary. In *Biological Diversification in the Tropics.* Ed. G. T. Prance, pp. 74 – 77. Columbia University Press, New York.

van der Hammen, T. (1963) A palynological study on the Quaternary of British Guiana. *Leidse Geol. Meded.* 29, 125 – 180.

van der Hammen, T. (1972) Changes in vegetation and climate in the Amazon basin and surrounding areas during the Pleistocene. *Geol. en Mijnbouw.* 51, 641 – 643.

van der Hammen, T. (1974) The Pleistocene changes of vegetation and climate in tropical South America. *J. Biogeogr.* 1, 3 – 26.

von Post, L. (1916) Om skogsträdpollen i sydsvenska torfmosslagerföljder. *Geol. för. Stockholm förhdl.* 38 – 384.

Wijmstra, T. A. (1969) Palynology of the Alliance Well. *Geol. en Mijnbouw* 48, 125 – 133.

Wijmstra, T. A. (1971) The palynology of the Guiana coastal basin. Thesis. University of Amsterdam.

Wijmstra, T. A. and van der Hammen, T. (1966) Palynological data on the history of tropical savannas in northern South America. *Leidse Geol. Meded.* 38, 71 – 83.

CHAPTER 5

Soils of the Amazon Rainforest

CARL F. JORDAN

Institute of Ecology, University of Georgia, U.S.A

CONTENTS

5.1. INTRODUCTION

Most of the soils of Amazon rainforests have a low potential for supplying nutrients such as calcium and potassium to plants. The low potential is due to effects of high temperatures and heavy rains as well as the geological history of the region. Intense weathering and leaching over millions of years have removed the nutrients from the minerals which form the parent materials of the soil. Nutrients lost through leaching or erosion usually cannot be replaced through weathering of the subsoil as they are in many other regions of the world.

Amazonian soils also have a low capacity for retaining any nutrients which leach down from decomposing organic matter. The low capacity is due partly to high concentrations of aluminium and hydrogen which occupy the sites where nutrients could be retained. Aluminium comprises a high percentage of the minerals from which the soil is formed. Hydrogen comes from organic acids formed in the litter layer above the soil.

Despite the inability of the soil to retain and supply nutrients, the survival of the undisturbed forest growing on these soils is not endangered. This is because the tree species of the Amazon Basin have adapted to the highly leached and weathered soils of the region. The adaptations enable the trees to conserve nutrients, thereby reducing nutrient demand from the highly leached soils. One of the most important adaptations is a concentration of roots near the surface of the soil (Fig. 5.1A) instead of a distribution over a greater depth as occurs in richer soils (Fig. 5.1B). High concentrations of roots near the soil surface increase the efficiency with which nutrients are cycled from decomposing organic matter

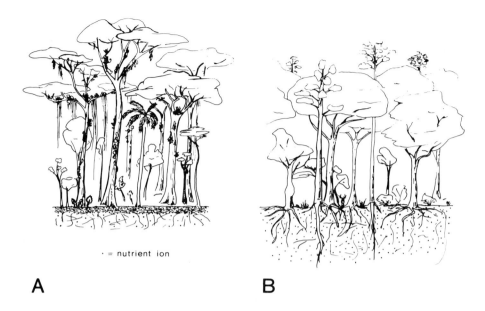

· = nutrient ion

A   B

Fig. 5.1. Distribution of roots and nutrient ions in the soil of a typical Amazon rainforest (A) contrasted with a forest in a more nutrient rich environment (B).

Fig. 5.2. Soil pit in sandy, podsol soil in Río Negro region. Notice the thick mat of humus and roots on top of the mineral soil.

into roots. In this tight recycling system, fewer nutrients can be leached beneath the rooting zone and lost from the ecosystem.

The adaptation of root concentration on or near the soil surface is most pronounced in the most nutrient poor soil. In forest communities on coarse sands, the roots are heavily concentrated in a thick mat above the soil surface (Fig. 5.2). The humus in the mat is intimately mixed with the roots, and mycorrhizal fungi are important in the transfer of nutrients from the humus to the roots (Herrera *et al.*, 1978). This nutrient recycling mechanism can be extremely efficient. Stark and Jordan (1978) simulated nutrient input into the root mat by sprinkling radioactive phosphorus and calcium on the surface. They found that almost all of the radioisotopes were taken up by the surface mat.

One useful way to evaluate the efficiency of nutrient recycling is to calculate the Cycling Index (Finn, 1976). This index gives the proportion of nutrients moving through the soil that are recycled within the ecosystem compared to the amount that move straight through, that is, that are not recycled. For example, a cycling index of 1.0 means that all the nutrients entering the soil are recycled through the vegetation and eventually return to the soil. An index of 0.5 means that only half are cycled and the other half are leached away to nearby streams. The cycling index of a forest in the Amazon Territory of Venezuela ranged between 0.6 and 0.8 depending on the nutrient (Jordan, 1982). This is the same range as the cycling index for forests on soils where the capacity for holding nutrients is much higher (Finn, 1978). The conclusion is, the mechanisms of recycling within the surface roots of the forests of the Amazon Basin are as efficient as the recycling through the mineral soil in other regions.

There are also other adaptations of the Amazon forest which help to conserve nutrients. One is the sclerophyllous nature of many of the leaves. The tough, leathery texture discourages attacks by insects and other herbivores, and also reduces leaching by the rain passing through the canopy. The leaves are long lived and leaf fall is less than in other tropical forests on richer soil. The leaves and stems support many plants such as algae and lichens which adsorb nutrients from the rainwater running over their surfaces. Larger plants such as bromeliads are attached to the surfaces of the branches and stems of trees. Some rainforest trees sprout roots directly from their branches and leaves to take advantage of this nutrient source (Nadkarni, 1981).

In regions where the mineral soil is important in recycling, such as often occur in the temperate zone, the destruction of the forest does not result in important nutrient loss, and the soil can be cultivated for decades without significant fertilisation. In contrast, in central Amazonian forests when the living forest is cut and burned, the nutrient conserving mechanisms are destroyed, and the nutrients which are released by burning and decomposition are quickly leached away. Within a few years, the productive capacity of the soil is greatly diminished.

Despite these characteristics of Amazon rainforests, there have been reports that cutting and burning of the primary Amazon forest actually increases the nutrient content of Amazon soils. These reports have been from agencies interested in developing pastures in the Amazon Basin. However, there is no apparent explanation for such enrichment (Fearnside, 1980). The question of whether deforestation increases or decreases nutrients in Amazonian soils has been clarified by an intensive study of nutrient dynamics during slash and burn agriculture in the Amazon Basin (Jordan, 1985). As a result of cutting and burning the forest, the total amount of nutrients in the soil actually does increase over a short period of time (Fig. 5.3). Due to the burning, the soil receives in one fast pulse the nutrients accumulated over hundreds of years by the primary forest. Nutrient input to the soil continues for a few years due to release from decomposing slash not consumed by the burn. But after the ash is leached away and the decomposing slash is gone, the level of nutrients in the soil decreases below the level in the undisturbed forest (Fig. 5.3).

Why are the soils of the Amazon rainforests unable to retain nutrients effectively? Why can't the parent material below the soils supply nutrients as it does in many temperate zone systems? The reason lies in the nature of the parent material of Amazonian soils.

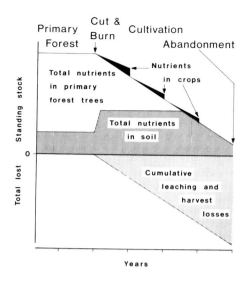

Fig. 5.3. Standing stocks of nutrients as a function of time in a slash and burn plot in the Amazon Basin (above abscissa) and cumulative losses from the soil (below abscissa) beginning at the time the plot was cut and burned. Adapted from Jordan, 1985.

5.2. ORIGINS OF AMAZONIAN SOILS

There are three major geological regions in the drainage area of the Amazon river. One region is the Pre-Cambrian Shield comprised of the Guiana Shield in the northern portion and the Brazilian Shield in the southern portion. Between the two shields is the Central Amazon Basin, a depression formed in the Paleozoic. Of much more recent geologic origin are the Andes to the west of the Amazon Basin which also form part of the drainage basin, but which constitute a relatively small proportion of the drainage area.

In the late Tertiary period, sediments were eroded from the highlands surrounding the Central Amazon Basin and deposited in the Basin forming what is sometimes called the Amazon Planalto, a relatively flat surface throughout the Amazon Basin extending up to 250 m above sea level in the western end of the Basin (Beek and Bramao, 1968). The surface of the Planalto consists of a layer of kaolinitic clay, 10 – 20 m thickness. Kaolinite is one of the most highly weathered minerals and consequently lacks the nutrients necessary for plant growth. Kaolinite consists of silicon, aluminium, hydrogen, and oxygen.

Dissection of the Amazon Planalto during the Pleistocene and the reworking and sedimentation of the older deposits has resulted in a series of terraces at various levels. Topography is gentle to steep. The additional erosion and leaching has reduced even further the fertility of the soils of these terraces. As on the Planalto, most of the soils are deeply weathered. Toward the eastern part of the Basin, texture becomes more sandy. In places depositions of coarse, acid sands and subsequent leaching has resulted in the formation of soils characterised by a humic 'B' or lower horizon. These soils support the characteristic heath-like forest which is called Amazon caatinga or campina in Brazil.

In some parts of the Amazon Basin, there occur patches of black soil developed by prehistoric Indian tribes for intensive cultivation by addition of organic matter. These patches of soil still maintain high levels of fertility.

Along the floodplains of several of the main branches of the Amazon which carry high loads of sediment, the annual rising and falling of the river level results in deposition, erosion, and redeposition of sediments of relatively recent geologic origin in the Andes. These depositions are known in Brazil as várzeas, and some of the better crop production in the Amazon Basin occurs on these soils.

5.3. PHYSICAL PROPERTIES OF SOILS

While intense weathering and leaching over millions of years in the Amazon Basin has resulted in upland soils very low in nutrient content, the resultant physical properties are generally very good. Soils of the Planalto and surrounding uplands are deep, well-drained, and have excellent granular structure. The granular structures are usually composed of clay bound into stable aggregates. The high stability is associated with a coating or cementing of amorphous iron and aluminium oxides (Sanchez, 1976). This structure results in two very favourable properties for root growth. First, the clay aggregates are efficient at retaining water after the soil horizon as a whole has drained following a rainstorm. This lessens water deficits during dry periods (Chauvel, 1981). Second, the voids between the aggregates permit rapid drainage, thus preventing water-logging. These voids or 'drainage channels' also may result in nutrient conservation. Most of the water which passes through the soil during a rainstorm passes through these channels and thus is not able to leach nutrients held inside the aggregates (Nortcliff and Thornes, 1978).

The stability of the aggregates is one of the factors determining whether laterization will occur. Laterization, that is, the formation of concretions or pavement of iron and aluminium oxides, occurs as a result of continued wetting and drying of clay with a high content of these elements. It was once believed that laterization would occur following any clearing of the Amazon forests. However, it has been shown that clearing alone will not cause laterization. Breaking of the aggregates by compaction and several cycles of wetting and drying also are necessary. Following clearing, weedy vegetation normally becomes established within a few months and prevents compaction and the cycles of wetting and extreme drying necessary for laterite formation. Cultivation of crops also protects the soil from laterization.

However, when surface vegetation is continually removed and the soil compacted, laterization will occur. Use of laterite for construction of roads and air strips is a common practice in the Amazon Basin, when a hard surface is needed but where importation of asphalt or cement is not practical (Fig. 5.4).

5.4. SOIL CLASSIFICATION

More than three quarters of the soils of the Amazon Basin consist primarily of mixtures of kaolinite, iron oxides, and quartz very low in nutrient-supplying ability (Sanchez, 1976). In the U.S. soil taxonomy system, these soils fall under three soil orders — Oxisols, Ultisols, and Alfisols. The Oxisols are the most nutrient poor, while the Alfisols have the highest amount of nutrients. However, even the Alfisols are relatively infertile compared to major soil groups in other parts of the world. The reason that the soils are so low in nutrients and nutrient-supplying power is because they have been subjected to the intense weathering of the tropical climate for many millions of years.

The classification of soils based on their genesis, as on the FAO Soil Map of the World (FAO, 1971), results in a close correlation between soil type and geologic origin (Fig. 5.5). The sediments weathered from the highlands surrounding the central Amazon Basin and deposited in the central depression are classified on the FAO map as Xanthic Ferralsols and as kaolinitic yellow latasols on earlier genetic maps

Fig. 5.4. Road built from laterite on the Jari plantation, Pará, Brazil.

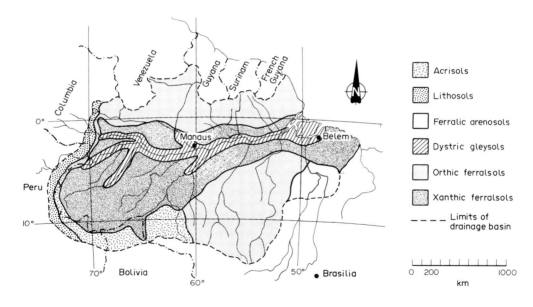

Fig. 5.5. Soils map of the Amazon Basin. Adapted and simplified from FAO-UNESCO Soil Map of South America (1971).

(Beek and Bramao, 1968). Towards the mouth of the Amazon and to the south of the central Basin, the depositions are more sandy and are classified as Ferralic Arenosols or Regesols. The alluvial clays and silts carried down the main branches of the Amazon and deposited during periods of falling river level were previously called Humic Gleys and now are classified as Dystric Gleysols.

TABLE 5.1. Approximate correlation of the FAO, U.S., and Brazilian soil classification systems. (Simplified from Sanchez, 1976 and Aubert and Tavernier, 1972)

FAO Classification	U.S. Soil Taxonomy Classification	Brazilian Classification
Ferralsols	Oxisols	Latasols
Acrisols	Ultisols	Red-yellow podzolic
Ferralic Arenosols	Psamments	Red and yellow sands
Dystric Gleysols	Tropaquepts	Hydromorphic soils
Lithosols	Lithic subgroups	—

The soils weathered in place from the formations both to the north and south of the central depression are classified as Orthic Ferralsols or previously, red-yellow latasols. In the southwest portion of the Basin, where the transition from lowland rainforest to mountains is more gradual, Orthic Acrisols or red-yellow podzolic soils are important. In the extreme western portion of the Basin, where the altitudinal gradient is much steeper, Lithosols derived from rocks of the Andes Mountains are important.

While for regional classifications, as in Fig. 5.5, the FAO system is useful, on a smaller scale classification by other criteria may be preferable. For example, on a tree plantation in the eastern Amazon Basin, gmelina, (*Gmelina arborea*) a broad-leafed species imported from the far East was initially planted throughout the plantation. However, only in certain areas was the growth of this species satisfactory. After a soil survey, the better growing stands of gmelina were found to be on Ultisols, higher in nutrient content, while the poorer growing stands were on Oxisols, with a very low nutrient content. Consequently, for the second series of plantings, gmelina was planted only on the Ultisols, while pine was planted on the Oxisols. Despite different criteria for classifying soils, there is a very approximate correlation between the FAO, the U.S., and the Brazilian soil classification systems (Table 5.1).

Moran (1981) has pointed out that although on regional soil maps most of the Amazon Basin is shown as having Ferralsols or Oxisols very low in nutrients, on a local scale there are often micro-patches of better soil sometimes only a few hundred metres in extent. Moran has attributed success of some farmers in the Amazon to their ability to recognise these micro-patches.

5.5. VEGETATION AND SOILS

In temperate zones, certain forest communities are known to occur on certain soil types. But because of the unfamiliarity of the average person with the Amazon Basin, the region is often thought of simply as a homogeneous 'tropical rainforest'. Viewed from the air, the Amazon forest, with mile after mile of unending green carpet does look quite homogeneous, but this is a misleading impression (*see also* Pires, Chapter 7). Detailed studies of the forest have shown that actually the forest is extremely heterogeneous.

The Amazon forest is heterogeneous in two ways. It is heterogeneous in the sense that there are a large number of species within each community type. It is also heterogeneous in the sense that there are a large number of community types in a given area. The large number of community types results from very fine adaptations of each community to subtle differences in the soil. A very slight difference in soil quality within an area is reflected in an entirely different forest community. For example, Fig. 5.6 shows a forest and soil profile which commonly occurs in the upper Río Negro region of the Amazon Basin, in the Amazon Territory of Venezuela. Within a distance of 500 m and an elevational span of less than 8 m, six distinct communities and associated soils occur.

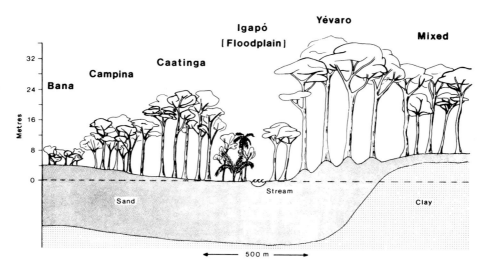

Fig. 5.6. Cross-sectional transect of a forested area near San Carlos de Río Negro, Venezuela showing the relationship between soil conditions and vegetation type.

Underlying the soil is granitic bedrock, weathered into clay for a depth of several metres below the soil surface. The bedrock and clay cap have been eroded into gently rolling topography. In the depressions between the rolling hills, sand has been deposited, possibly carried there from the Guiana Shield to the northeast. On top of the hills, where the clay is close to the surface, a mixed forest occurs (Fig. 5.6). This community is the most species rich of the region, with over 80 species per hectare (Uhl and Murphy, 1981) and no one species clearly dominant. Size of the forest is not large, possibly because the roots are restricted to the soil surface and the layer of sand overlying the clay.

Closer to the streams, where the underlying clay dips to a greater depth, a community dominated by *Eperua purpurea* or 'Yevaro' occurs (Klinge, 1978). This community is the most productive of the region. The large biomass and high growth rates probably result from soil and terrain conditions. The topography consists of hummocks, 1 − 2 m high and several metres across separated by twisted drainage streams. These hummocks provide opportunity for deep rooting, yet the drainage streams prevent anaerobic conditions in the root zone.

Along the small streams or caños, near the major rivers, the 'igapó' (Anderson, 1981) or flooded forest occurs. The rise of the Río Negro in the rainy season blocks the drainage of the caños and they rise above their banks, inundating the forests along the edge for 6 months or more each year. The igapó community has adapted to this stress. Despite the flooding, the trees keep their leaves throughout the year.

'Amazon caatinga' (Klinge and Medina, 1978) occurs where bedrock is very deep and the parent material for the soil is coarse sand. Podsolization is the dominant soil forming process, and a 'B' soil horizon enriched in organic matter, iron, and aluminium often occurs at a metre or more in depth. Local names and dominant species for this vegetation type vary throughout the Amazon Basin (Anderson, 1981), but regardless of the region in the Amazon Basin, vegetation on podsol soils usually has thick, leathery leaves and is reduced in stature. In the Amazon Territory of Venezuela, near the Río Negro, three types of communities occur on the coarse podsolized sands within an elevational gradient of 2 m or less.

Near streams, but above the level of seasonal flooding occurs the 'high caatinga' dominated by trees 20 to 30 m in height (Klinge and Medina, 1978). Because of the coarseness of the sand, lateral drainage occurs quickly following storms and within a few days after a storm, communities on soils which are only a metre or two above those of the 'high caatinga' can begin to experience water stress. The stress is reflected in a change in community type from high caatinga through a more reduced type of vegetation sometimes called 'campina' (Klinge and Medina, 1978). At 2 m above the stream level, the stress between rain storms becomes severe, and the vegetation is reduced to low shrubs called 'bana' (Klinge and Medina, 1978). The rapid drainage of water from the bana and campina may result in a nutrient as well as a water stress. Nutrient stress could be an additional factor causing the reduced stature of this vegetation.

The sandy podsol soils give rise to the so-called 'blackwater' rivers which are common in the Río Negro region of the Amazon Basin, but also occur elsewhere. The black colour comes from plant compounds such as tannins leached from leaf litter. Waters draining mixed forest do not have this black colour. In mixed forests on soil high in clay content, the compounds leached from the litter are adsorbed on the clay and are decomposed, whereas on the sandy soils, the compounds are rapidly carried through the soil into the rivers.

Throughout the Amazon Basin there are many other distinct community types. One occurs on 'terra roxa', red-coloured soil derived from basic parent rock such as limestone, and consequently relatively rich in certain nutrients such as calcium (Camargo and Falesi, 1975). Even though the soil type is limited in extent, and sometimes occurs in patches of only a few hundred metres, the soil is important because of its high agricultural potential (Moran, 1981).

Another unusual soil — vegetation type in the Amazon region are savannahs caused by poor drainage, resulting in permanent shallow flooding (Anderson, 1981).

5.6. USE OF AMAZON SOILS

One of the most striking results of the Amazon slash and burn study (Jordan, 1985) is the fact that only a very small percentage of the nutrients in the primary forest are actually incorporated into the crops. Only 3% of the nitrogen was incorporated into crop plants, and less than 1% was in the edible portion. For calcium the percentages were 12 and 1, for potassium 24 and 4, and for phosphorus 5 and 1 (Jordan, 1985).

Cations such as calcium, potassium, and magnesium are quickly leached out of the soil following burning of the slash. Only 18% of the original standing crop of potassium remained at the time of abandonment of the plot 3 years after burning (Jordan, 1985).

The problem with phosphorus in many Amazonian soils is not leaching but availability. There is usually a relatively large quantity of phosphorus held in the soil, complexed with iron and aluminium. However, because of the stability of these compounds at the low acidities normally found in Amazonian soils, phosphorus is only very slightly available.

When the forest is cut and burned, the cations decrease the acidity of the soil. This in turn, results in release of phosphorus from the iron and aluminium compounds. Consequently, crops have an adequate supply of phosphorus for the first year or two of cultivation. However, as the cations are leached away by heavy rains, the acidity again begins to increase, and phosphorus becomes less and less available for crop uptake. In the slash and burn plot of the Amazon Territory of Venezuela, it appeared that phosphorus was the first element to become limiting to crop production.

Nitrogen does not disappear from the ecosystem as fast as the cations following cutting and burning and thus does not seem at first to be as critical. However, rate of replenishment of nitrogen via nitrogen fixation is slow relative to the total amount needed. Under long-term exploitation, nitrogen could be more of a problem.

Fig. 5.7. Proposed harvest rotation scheme to minimise nutrient losses. Year interval indicates number of years since strip was cut.

Does the low fertility and low nutrient retaining power of the soils over most of the Amazon Basin mean that it is not possible to use the Amazon forest for economic gain? Not necessarily, if exploitation is carried out so as not to destroy the nutrient recycling mechanisms of the entire forest, or so as to restore the cycles as quickly as possible after harvest.

Sioli (1973) has suggested that export crops such as Brazil nut, rubber, cocoa, and palm fruits can be harvested and exported without destroying the long-term productivity capacity of the region, because the amount of nutrients removed from the forest when these crops are harvested is only a small proportion of the total amount in the entire ecosystem. Further, since the trees are left intact following harvest, the erosive force of the heavy Amazon rains is broken by the intact canopy.

It also may be possible to carry out limited timber harvests in such a way as to preserve the system's ability to recover. Ideally, a logging system should be a selective harvest of logs, carried out in such a way that basic structure of the forest is not destroyed and the nutrient recycling mechanisms are left intact. However, such a scheme often is not practical because the cost of putting in a road requires that more than just a few trees be harvested. In addition, species or crops other than native forest species are often desired.

However, there are ways of harvesting and utilising the forest that are practical yet that will not permanently destroy the productive capacity. For simplicity, let us begin with an illustration of a harvest scheme for native hardwoods. Although the terrain of the Amazon Basin is not generally rugged, throughout most of the region it is rolling and there are usually well-defined slopes and drainage streams. A strip is harvested on the contour of a slope, parallel to the stream (Fig. 5.7). After harvest the area is left for a few years until saplings begin to regenerate in the cut area. Then the loggers come back and clear-cut another strip above the first strip. There are several big advantages of this system. First, the nutrients from the freshly cut area wash downslope into the rapidly regenerating strip where the trees can quickly take-up the nutrients. Secondly, seeds from the strip of mature forest above the cut will roll down into the recently cut strip. In contrast, in clear cutting there are no saplings with well-developed roots capable of retaining nutrients in the system as there are in strip cutting. Also, in clear cuts, there is no source of seed for regeneration of the forest.

Admittedly, there are economic problems with this scheme. There is not a well-developed market for many native tropical species. Many of the extremely hard tropical species are not useful to the paper and pulp industries or even to furniture manufacturers. However, the market could be developed. For example, the harder species are generally highly resistant and can be used for things like railroad ties and pilings.

The concept developed in Fig. 5.7 need not be limited to production of native trees. The important point is that only a small proportion of an area be disturbed at one time and that for most of an area, roots are present to recycle nutrients that are leached from the disturbed portion. For example, a clear-cut strip could be planted with an annual crop for a few years and interspersed with fruit trees. When the annual crop begins to decline, the fruit trees would begin to bear. Once a network of roots is re-established in a strip, another upslope strip can be cut, the timber used, and the newly cut strip used for another crop.

A small amount of cutting and cultivation is not permanently harmful to Amazonian forests, because there is a small but continuous replenishment of nutrients into the ecosystem from the atmosphere and in the rainfall. When the forest is harvested moderately and in such a way as to minimise wasteful nutrient leaching into streams, the Amazon can sustain production indefinitely.

For the Amazon to be productive in future generations, man must use the forest in ways that will conserve the scarce nutrient capital. He must figure out how to use what the forest can produce naturally, not to try to make the forest produce things demanded by an economic system. Most important, man must not be greedy. He must be content with what the forest can give without destroying the forest's ability to regenerate. Destroying the forest for greater riches now only leads to greater poverty in the future.

REFERENCES

Anderson, A. (1981) White-sand vegetation of Brazilian Amazonia. *Biotropica* 13, 199 – 210.

Aubert, G. and Tavernier, R. (1972) Soil survey. In *Soils of the Humid Tropics*, pp. 14 – 17. National Academy of Sciences, Washington, D.C.

Baver, L. D. (1972) Physical Properties of Soils. In *Soils of the Humid Tropics*, pp. 50 – 62. National Academy of Sciences, Washington, D.C.

Beek, K. J. and Bramao, D. L. (1968) Nature and geography of South American soils. In *Biogeography and Ecology in South America*, Vol. 1, Eds. E.J. Fittkau, J. Illies, H. Klinge, G.H. Schwabe and H. Sioli, pp. 82 – 112. Junk, The Hague.

Camargo, M. N. and Falesi, I. C. (1975) Soils of the Central Plateau and Transamazonic Highway of Brazil. In *Soil Management in Tropical America*, Eds. E. Bornemiza and A. Alvardao, pp. 25 – 45. Soil Science Department, North Carolina State University, Raleigh, North Carolina.

Chauvel, A. (1981) Contribuição para o estudo da evolução dos latossolos amarelos, distroficos, argilosos na borda do plato, na região de Manaus: mecanismos da gibbsitização. *Acta Amazônica* 11, 227 – 245.

FAO-UNESCO (1971) *Soil Map of the World*, Vol. IV South America. UNESCO-Paris.

Fearnside, P. M. (1980) The effects of cattle pasture on soil fertility in the Brazilian Amazon: consequences for beef production and sustainability. *Tropical Ecology* 21, 125 – 137.

Finn, J. T. (1976) Measures of ecosystem structure and function derived from analysis of flows. *J. Theoret. Biol.* 56, 363 – 380.

Finn, J. T. (1978) Cycling index: a general definition for cycling in compartment models. In *Environmental Chemistry and Cycling Processes*. Eds. D. C. Adriano and I. L. Brisbin, pp. 138 – 164. CONF-760-429, Technical Information Center, U.S. Dept. of Energy, Washington, D.C.

Herrera, R., Merida, T., Stark, N. and Jordan, C. F. (1978) Direct phosphorus transfer from leaf litter to roots. *Naturwissenschaften* 65, 208 – 209.

Jordan, C. F. (1982) Nutrient cycling index of an Amazonian rain forest. *Acta Oecologica*, Oecologia Generalis. 3, 393 – 400.

Jordan, C. F. (1985) An Amazonian ecosystem. Manuscript submitted.

Klinge, H. (1978) Studies on the ecology of Amazon caatinga forest in southern Venezuela. *Acta Cientifica Venezolana* 29, 258 – 262.

Klinge, H. and Medina, E. (1978) Rio Negro caatingas and campinas, Amazonas states of Venezuela and Brazil. In *Ecosystems of the World*, Vol. 9, Ed. R. L. Specht, pp. 483 – 488. Elsevier, Amsterdam.

Moran, E. F. (1981) *Developing the Amazon*. Indiana University Press, Bloomington.

Nadkarni, N. M. (1981) Canopy roots: convergent evolution in rainforest nutrient cycles. *Science* 214, 1023-1024.

Nortcliff, S. and Thornes, J. B. (1978) Water and cation movement in a tropical rainforest environment. *Acta Amazônica* 8, 245 – 258.

Sanchez, P. A. (1976) *Properties and Management of Soils in the Tropics*. Wiley, New York.
Sioli, H. (1973) Recent human activities in the Brazilian Amazon region and their ecological effects. In *Tropical Forest Ecosystems in Africa and South America: A Comparative Review*. Eds. B. J. Meggers, E. S. Ayensu and W. D. Duckworth, pp. 321 – 334. Smithsonian Institution Press, Washington, D.C.
Stark, N. and Jordan, C. F. (1978) Nutrient retention by the root mat of an Amazonian rain forest. *Ecology* 59, 434 – 437.
Uhl, C. and Murphy, P. G. (1981) Composition, structure, and regeneration of a terra firme forest in the Amazon Basin of Venezuela. *Tropical Ecology* 22, 219 – 237.

CHAPTER 6

Nutrient Cycling in Amazonian Forests

RAFAEL HERRERA

Centro de Ecología, Instituto Venezolano de Investigaciones Científicas, Apartado 1827,
Caracas 1010A, Venezuela

CONTENTS

6.1. INTRODUCTION

The Amazon Basin is covered by the largest remaining tropical forest domain on Earth. These forests, collectively known as Hylaea are a large array of forest types growing on different substrata and occupying various geomorphological positions. The 'terra firme' forest type occupies the vast non-flooded interfluvial plains on the slightly elevated rolling terrain with very mature, deeply weathered soils, usually oxisols or ultisols. Other forest types grow on the seasonally flooded lowlands and are classified according to whether the river is white or black. There are also various types of forests growing on deep quartz sandy soils or on freatic podsols. Some of these grade into very open 'campinas' or into 'banas' of low stature.

Only a few examples of these forest types have been studied from the point of view of nutrient cycling although it has long been thought that tropical forests growing on low fertility soils should depend for their existence on the efficient recycling of mineral nutrients (Walter, 1936; Hardy, 1936; Nye and Greenland, 1960). For the purpose of this publication we can define nutrient cycling as the distribution of a given mineral nutrient among the various compartments usually distinguishable in a forest (i.e. stems, roots, leaves, fruits, flowers, soil, microorganisms, herbivores and carnivores) and the amounts

95

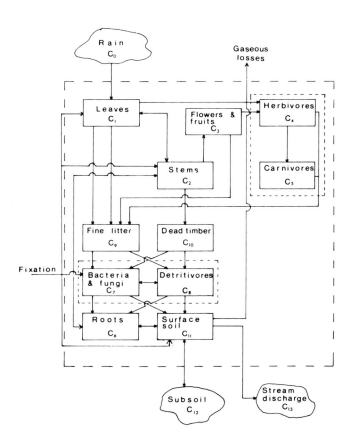

Fig. 6.1. Schematic model of nutrient cycling, including nitrogen biological fixation and gaseous losses. Rectangles represent compartments within the ecosystem. Flows are represented by arrows. Sources of input or output sinks are represented by irregular shapes. (Taken from Herrera and Jordan, 1981).

of the same element that moves in and out of the same compartments per unit time. It is common to represent nutrient cycles as block and arrow diagrams in which blocks represent compartment content and arrows represent fluxes between compartments (Fig. 6.1).

6.2. TWO MAIN TYPES OF CYCLES

Some chemical elements such as calcium, magnesium and potassium present cycles that are called sedimentary because they are bound to the soil and water phases while other groups of elements such as oxygen, carbon, sulphur and nitrogen have important parts of their cycles in the atmosphere. The cycle of each element shows its own peculiarities. Nitrogen, for example, while very often being a limiting nutrient in agriculture, can be fixed from the atmosphere by microorganisms and thus made available to plants and animals. By the same token, nitrogen can also be lost back to the atmosphere. Plants exert a relatively strong control over this element in their metabolism while other elements are recycled in a more passive way.

Although most nutrient cycling studies include the elements nitrogen, phosphorus, potassium, calcium and magnesium, for the purpose of this publication we shall draw information mainly from data on nitrogen and calcium. Nitrogen is often limiting for cultivated plants and its cycle has received much attention both from the processes point of view and from the ecosystem approach. Salati *et al.* (1982) have made some calculations for the overall nitrogen cycle of the Amazon Basin, considering the different forest types. They have calculated that a weighted mean of 120×10^5 tonnes N/yr are biologically fixed; about 84×10^5 tonnes N/yr are lost to the atmosphere by denitrification, the remaining 36×10^5 tonnes N/yr are lost to the ocean in river discharge. Additionally some 36×10^5 tonnes N/yr are recirculated to the atmosphere as ammonium/ammonia which are washed down again by rain.

As for the elements showing sedimentary cycles, the Amazon Basin presents some peculiarities. Sioli (1964), Furch *et al.* (1982) and Herrera *et al.* (1978) have shown that in general Amazonian surface waters are extremely low in alkali-earth metals, particularly in calcium when compared to rivers elsewhere. Fittkau (1971) has proposed a geochemical division of Amazonia which partially explains this phenomenon in terms of geologic history. He points out that northern and southern peripheral Amazonia are geochemically depleted in these elements because these areas correspond to the geologically ancient Guiana and Brazil shields. Central Amazonia has been exposed to several cycles of meteorisation, erosion and sedimentation. As a consequence the sediments have been depleted of these elements. Only western Amazonia, receiving younger sediments from the Andean foothills, and the seasonally flooded 'várzeas' are richer in alkali earth metals.

One aspect which deserves much attention is the role tropical rainforests play in the CO_2 balance (Lugo, 1982). Little is known about the sulphur balance in tropical rainforests and their possible role in injecting sulphur into the atmosphere. This issue is of special importance to understand the problem of acid rain. Clark *et al.* (1980) and Galloway *et al.* (1982) have reported acid rain from Amazon forested areas very distant from industrial sources of pollution. Only a few forest types have been the subjects of nutrient cycling studies in Amazonas. A 'terra firme' forest near Manaus was studied by Klinge and Rodrigues (1968). Other forests on oxisols in the upper Río Negro Region of Southern Venezuela have been studied in greater detail by Jordan and Herrera (1981) and Herrera *et al.* (1981). A few studies deal with the seasonally flooded 'igapó' forests of Central Amazonia (Irmler, 1982) in relation to nutrient dynamics. The poorest sites in which tropical rainforests are known to grow are the podzolised quartz sands which, in the Río Negro region, occupy intermediate positions between the flooded forests and the 'terra firme'. These soils are very wet and present a fluctuating water table. Nutrient cycles of these forests are thought to be very revealing of the various nutrient conserving mechanisms time and again proposed to explain the relative efficiency of nutrient use under stress conditions. Herrera (1979), Herrera and Jordan (1981) and Klinge and Herrera (1983) have studied an 'Amazon caatinga' forest in the upper Río Negro on freatic podzols.

Went and Stark (1968) after working in Amazon forests hypothesised that a direct nutrient cycle should exist in very poor sites in which mycorrhiza should play an important role in reutilising the nutrients held in the organic litter of the forest. Very slowly, the evidence to support such views has been growing, although still conflicting views arise as to whether 'special' mechanisms should be invoked to explain the existing closed nutrient cycles (Herrera *et al.*, 1978; Cuevas and Medina, 1983). The existing evidence for Amazonian forests does point towards a quantitative if not also qualitative difference in nutrient cycling patterns when compared to those in richer sites elsewhere. Jordan and Herrera (1981) have tried to visualise these differences in the light of a continuum of nutritional conditions between the extremes of eutrophy and oligotrophy. More recently Vitousek (1982) has expanded the range of forests analysed and explored the possibility of finding a common expression for nutrient use efficiency in nutrient cycling.

6.3. TERRA FIRME FOREST

Of the Amazon forests, the case best studied regarding nutrient cycling is a 'terra firme' forest growing on oxisols near San Carlos de Río Negro, T.F. Amazonas, Venezuela. The forest occupies the elevated portions of the rolling hills in a general peneplain landscape. This forest is a species-rich mixed vegetation 25 − 30 m high. A peculiar feature of some forests which is very well developed in this example is the existence of a root mat composed of a tangled net of fine, hairless roots growing outside the soil; the root tips grow strongly attached to fallen leaves, branches, fruits etc. The nitrogen cycle of this forest has been recently reported by Jordan *et al.* (1982) and compared to the nitrogen cycle of an Amazon caatinga forest growing adjacent to the terra firme forest on lower podzolised sand site (Herrera and Jordan, 1981). Table 6.1 shows the distribution of nitrogen and calcium in this forest.

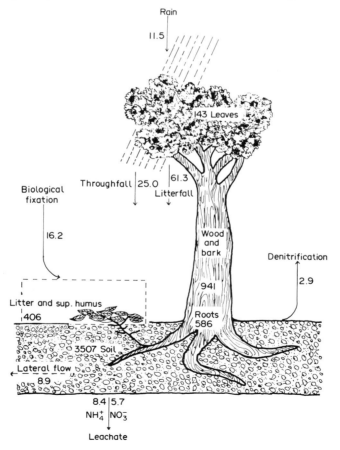

Fig. 6.2. Schematic representation of some parameters of nitrogen cycling in terra firme forest. Figures inside ecosystem parts or boxes represent stocks in kg N/ha. Figures accompanying arrows indicate fluxes in kg/ha/yr. (Data from Jordan *et al.*, 1982).

TABLE 6.1. Distribution of Nitrogen and Calcium in a 'terra firme' forest on oxisol near San Carlos de Río Negro, T.F. Amazonas, Venezuela

Compartment	N, kg/ha	%	Ca, kg/ha	%
Leaves	143	2.6	10.7	3.3
Wood	941	16.9	202	62.2
Roots	586	10.5	45.4	14.0
Litter and superficial humus	406	7.3	10.0	3.1
Soil	3507	62.8	56.4	17.4
Total	5583	100.0	324.5	100.0

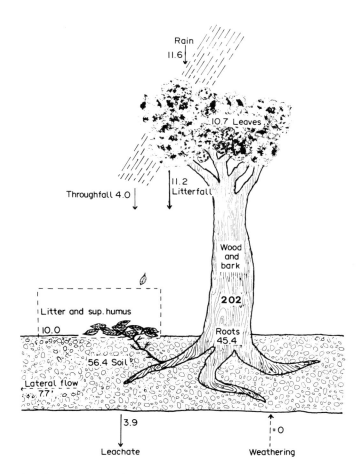

Fig. 6.3. Schematic representation of some parameters of calcium cycling in terra firme forest. Conventions as in Fig. 6.2. (Data from Jordan and Herrera, in press).

The total amount of nitrogen in the system is comparable to other forest growing on medium-rich sites in the tropics and in the temperate areas of the world. About two thirds of total nitrogen in this ecosystem is in the soil organic matter and the root system contains about one tenth of total nitrogen or 35% of that in the vegetation. When compared with the Amazon caatinga (see below) growing adjacent to this forest, it is remarkable that the latter contains only one third of the total amount of nitrogen. The situation regarding calcium is however reversed. The terra firme forest contains substantially less calcium than other tropical forests or even the Amazon caatinga down slope. Almost 80% of total ecosystem calcium is in the vegetation, the largest store of this element is in branches, boles and bark which accounts for over 60% of calcium in the vegetation. Figure 6.2 shows a schematic nitrogen cycle for this forest including the fluxes which were estimated or calculated. We can calculate a total throughflow of 26 kg/N/ha/yr, a stock of 5583. The ratio of stock to throughflow can be considered a measure of turnover of this element. This value is 215 years for nitrogen while the same calculation yields 28 years for calcium (Fig. 6.3). Under these circumstances, the low capacity of the soil to retain calcium as well as the extremely low proportion of weatherable calcium minerals are expressed in a very tight calcium cycle with the higher proportion of this element in the living parts. Stark and Jordan (1978) have found that surface root mat of this terra firme forest was able to retain over 99.9% of a radioactive isotope of calcium in water applied to the surface. In unilateral Ca-fertiliser experiments Cuevas (1983) found that root growth was enhanced in this forest. She also found that root growth inside litter decomposition bags was positively correlated with calcium content in the litter.

In studying the dynamics of nitrogen during conversion of the same terra firme forest to slash and burn agriculture Jordan et al. (1983) have found that while the total amount of soil nitrogen did not decrease during the normal three-year slash and burn rotation, a net loss of 7% of the original forest stock per year is due to leaching, harvesting and denitrification. The soil compartment was recharged with nitrogen coming from decomposing slash. Nitrogen fixation decreased markedly during conversion to agriculture and the rates of denitrification increased more than ten times.

6.4. AMAZON CAATINGA

These forests, growing on very poor quartzic sandy freatic podzols, although covering only a small proportion of the Amazon Basin, are however, quite abundant in coexistence with 'terra firme' forests in the Río Negro region (Klinge et al., 1972). Related forest types such as the Wallaba forests (Richards, 1952) are common in the Guiana region. The Amazon caatinga forests are lower than the adjacent 'terra firme' forests reaching heights of 20 − 25 m but grading into much shorter heath-like 'bana' in better drained areas. It is very revealing to study the nutrient cycles of a forest growing under very limiting fertility conditions because it can shed light on the mechanisms which are responsible for the efficient use of available nutrients. The total standing stock of nitrogen in Amazon caatinga is much lower than in the 'terra firme' forest. Not only the soil shows much lower amounts of total nitrogen but the standing stock in vegetation is very low. Figure 6.4 shows the distribution and cycling of nitrogen in the Amazon caatinga of Upper Río Negro. Note that while the total amounts of nitrogen in leaves and woody parts are less than half those in 'terra firme' forest, the amount in roots is considerably higher, mainly due to the extraordinarily high root biomass of this forest (Klinge and Herrera, 1978). Over one half of total nitrogen in the ecosystem is in the living vegetation, the soil being poor in this element. A contrasting situation is found when calcium is considered. Almost double the amount found in 'terra firme' is present in Amazon caatinga (Fig. 6.5). While only 15% of total ecosystem calcium was present in the oxisol under 'terra firme' forest, the spodosol under Amazon caatinga contains 30% of total ecosystem calcium, mostly in the organic matter of the surface horizon. Another important store of calcium is the decomposing wood and litter. The relative abundance of these two elements in the two contrasting forests presented, makes itself very evident in several features related to the fluxes. Biological nitrogen fixation seems to be higher in Amazon caatinga. Scavenging of nitrogen input by rainfall as it passes through the canopy is very pronounced in Amazon caatinga where of the incoming 14 kg/ha/yr only 9 reach the ground with throughfall water: the rest remains in the canopy and probably appears as

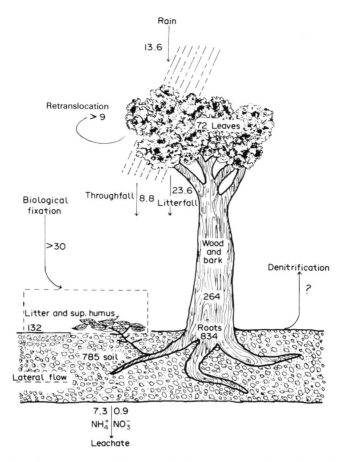

Fig. 6.4. Schematic representation of some parameters of nitrogen cycling in Amazon caatinga forest. Conventions as in Fig. 6.2. (Data from Herrera and Jordan, 1981).

litter nitrogen. In the 'terra firme' forest the opposite effect was observed: more nitrogen reaches the ground with throughfall than comes by rainfall. Much higher fluxes of nitrogen are involved in litterfall of 'terra firme' forest than in Amazon caatinga.

The Amazon caatinga forest functions with a low nitrogen budget, as shown by the absolute amounts in the various living compartments. A large proportion of nitrogen is held in the root biomass, and the relative proportion of nitrogen in litter is the highest reported for a tropical forest. The overall balance of input versus output seems to indicate that, if the system is in a steady state, important losses of N should occur to the atmosphere by denitrification. Ammonia or NH_4^+ losses are less probable owing to the low pH of the soil. The turnover of nitrogen through the litter pathway is of the same order as the input by rainfall. Retranslocation of nitrogen from leaves before senescence accounts for about one-third of all nitrogen in litter fall. Some of the nitrogen coming with rain is trapped as it passes through the canopy, probably by the abundant epiphyllous organisms. The surface of leaves covered by these organisms is a minor but significant, site for biological nitrogen fixation. More important, however, are the bark — lichen surfaces and the soil and root compartments.

In the soil the predominant soluble form is NH_4^+, as it is in throughfall. Jordan *et al.* (1979) found the number of nitrifying bacteria to be very low, possibly owing to the low pH and the high tannin content of roots and litter. This inhibition favours the NH_4^+ form and can be considered to act as a nitrogen-conserving mechanism by preventing leaching losses. Inhibition of nitrification and the ability to use NH_4^+ as the main source of nitrogen were suggested by Rice and Pancholy (1972) as advantageous characteristics of climax ecosystems. Jordan *et al.* (1979) showed that increasing the pH of the soil by liming at the experimental site increases N losses, but virtually all of the losses were in the form of NH_4^+.

Amazon caatinga forests on low-fertility sandy spodosols represent an extreme case where, owing to nutritional stress, a very tight nitrogen cycle exists. Several nutrient-conserving mechanisms seem to be operative both at the ecophysiological level and at the structural organisation level. A low nitrogen budget owing to low concentration in living parts, and long-lived sclerophyllous leaves where retranslocation before senescence returns a sizeable amount of nitrogen and other nutrients into the tree, are considered to be among the nutrient-conserving mechanisms. A highly-developed root biomass consisting mostly of fine roots that are predominantly mycorrhizal is another important characteristic which would serve to enhance nutrient absorption. The development of a very superficial root mat that is capable of becoming attached to decomposing litter through mycorrhizal hyphae was shown by

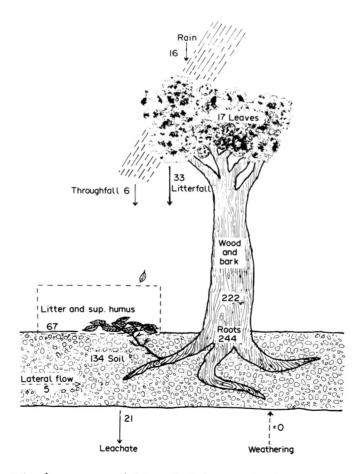

Fig. 6.5. Schematic representation of some parameters of calcium cycling in Amazon caatinga Forest. Conventions as in Fig. 6.2. (Data from Herrera, 1979).

Herrera *et al.* (1978) to act as a bypass for P litter by direct transfer through the external hyphae to the roots. Ectotrophic mycorrhiza may have the ability, lacking in higher plants to absorb and utilise organic nitrogen forms taken directly from decaying organic matter (Mallock *et al.*, 1980). In a study of ecosystem recovery following various forms of disturbance of Amazon caatinga forest, Uhl *et al.* (1982) found that of the 336 kg N/ha in the biomass only 55, 33 and 3 kg N/ha were present 3 years after cutting, cutting and burning, and bulldozing treatments. For calcium the corresponding stocks were 239, 64, 96 and 2 for the control forest, cut, cut and burned, and bulldozed areas after the same period. These authors suggest that if the observed biomass accumulation continues the original standing stocks could be built up after some 100 years for the cut and cut and burn treatments but it would take more than a thousand years in the case of the bulldozed site.

6.5. INUNDATION FORESTS

The valleys of the Amazonian rivers are seasonally inundated. Water levels and inundation periods which average about 6 months, change gradually from the river bank towards the elevated sites away from them. The 'várzeas' of the Solimões, Amazon and other white rivers receive sediment loads with

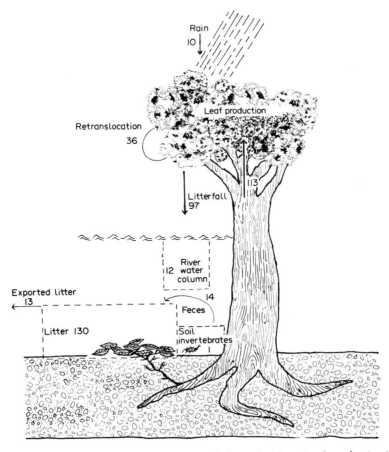

Fig. 6.6. Schematic representation of some parameters of the nitrogen cycle during the submersion phase of an igapó forest in Lower Río Negro. (Figure redrawn from Irmler, 1982).

the seasonal floods while in the blackwater tributaries, sediment load is almost negligible and thus no silting of the floodplain occurs. Irmler (1982) and Irmler and Furch (1980) report on the nitrogen cycle of an 'igapó' forest in the blackwater Tarumã-Mirim river a tributary of the lower Rio Negro in Brazil. A major part of the system's nitrogen content is probably in the soil organic matter and the standing vegetation. The litter on the soil on average contains 130 kg N/ha. The rate of nitrogen mineralisation amounts to 95% of the original content in litter in 4.7 years. This slow rate of nitrogen release, by tropical standards, is due to the fact that litter is submerged during half of the year. An important pathway of nitrogen cycling in this system is the flow through the litter animals which although containing only about 1 kg N/ha in their biomass, they recycle through their digestive tracts 13 kg N/ha/yr. The same author also observes that litter arthropods may play an important role in redistributing nitrogen in litter, thus lowering the C:N ratio. Figure 6.6 shows some parameters of nitrogen cycling in the 'igapó' forest studied by Irmler (1982). Part of the litter is lost during the submersion phase dragged by the water (13 kg N/ha/yr). A slightly lower amount of nitrogen (10 kg/ha/yr) enters the ecosystem with rainfall. Part of the nitrogen in leaves is retranslocated before leaves are shed (about 36 kg/ha/yr) and therefore does not appear in litterfall. The water column during the submersion phase contains an average of 12 kg/ha. The overall balance probably depends on biological nitrogen fixation in the above-water parts occurring during the immersion phase. These complex inundation forests need more detailed studies in order to understand better the role they play in the transference of both dissolved and particulate carbon and other elements from the terrestrial ecosystems to the aquatic environment. Nutrient cycles of the richer 'várzea' sites are little understood. Especially interesting is the annual fertilisation effect brought about by the sediment load. An additional source of enrichment of these systems is the high potential for nitrogen fixation in várzea sites which can reach values of some 200 kg/ha/yr (Salati et al., 1982). Since these Amazonian valleys represent richer soil enclaves in the Amazon Basin, they have been the subject of historical and present human intervention. Accordingly they should be given priority for general ecosystem studies as well as nutrient cycling investigations.

REFERENCES

Clark, H. L., Clark, K. E. and Haines, B. L. (1980) Acid rain in the Venezuelan Amazon. In *Tropical Ecology and Development*, Ed. J. Furtado, pp. 683 – 685. Kuala Lumpur.

·Cuevas, E. and Medina, E. (1983) Root production and organic matter decomposition in a terra firme forest of the Upper Río Negro basin. In *Wurzelökologie und ihre Nutzanwendung*. Int. Symp. Gumpenstein Irdning, Austria, pp. 653 – 666.

Cuevas, E. (1983) Crecimiento de raices finas y su relación con los procesos de descomposición de materia orgánica y liberación de nutrientes en bosques del alto Río Negro en el T.F. Amazonas. Ph. Sc. Thesis IVIC, Caracas, 178pp.

Fittkau, E. J. (1971) Oekologische Gliederung des Amazonas-Gebietes auf geochemischer Grundlage. *Münsterische Forschl. Geol. u. Paläont* 20/21, 35 – 50.

Furch, K., Junk, W. J. and Klinge, H. (1982) Unusual chemistry of natural waters from the Amazon region. *Acta Cient. Venez.* 33, 269 – 273.

Galloway, J. N., Likens, G. E., Keene, W. C. and Miller, J. M. (1982) The composition of precipitation in remote areas of the world. *J. Geophys. Res.* 87, 8771 – 8786.

Hardy, F. (1936) Some aspects of cacao soil fertility. *Trinidad Trop. Agric.* 13, 315 – 317.

Herrera, R., Jordan, C. F., Klinge, H. and Medina, E. (1978) Amazon ecosystems. Their structure and function with particular emphasis on nutrients. *Interciencia* 3, 223 – 232.

Herrera, R., Merida, T., Stark, N. and Jordan, C. (1978) Direct phosphorus transfer from leaf litter to roots. *Naturwissenschaften* 65, 208 – 209.

Herrera, R. (1979) Nutrient distribution and cycling in an Amazon Caatinga forest on spodosols in Southern Venezuela. Ph.D. Thesis, Univ. Reading, U.K., 241pp.

Herrera, R. Jordan, C. F., Medina, E. and Klinge, H. (1981) How human activities disturb the nutrient cycles of a tropical rainforest in Amazonia. *Ambio* 10, 109 – 114.

Herrera, R. and Jordan, C. F. (1981) Nitrogen cycle of a tropical rainforest of Amazonia. The case of low mineral nutrient Amazon Caatinga. *Ecol. Bull. (Stockholm)* 33, 493 – 506.

Irmler, U. and Furch, U. (1980) Weight, energy and nutrient changes during the decomposition of leaves during immersion phase of Central Amazonian inundation forests. *Pedobiologia* 20, 118 – 130.

Irmler, U. (1982) Litterfall and nitrogen turnover in an Amazonian inundation forest. *Plant and Soil* 67, 355 – 358.

Jordan, C. F., Todd, R. and Escalante, G. (1979) Nitrogen conservation in a tropical rainforest. *Oecologia* 39, 123 – 128.

Jordan, C. F. and Herrera, R. (1981) Tropical rainforests. Are nutrients really critical? *Amer. Natur.* 117, 167 – 179.

Jordan, C. F., Caskey, W., Escalante, G., Herrera, R., Montangini, F., Todd, R. and Uhl, C. (1982) The nitrogen cycle in a 'terra firme' rainforest on oxisol in the Amazon territory of Venezuela. *Plant and Soil* 67, 325 – 332.

Jordan, C. F., Caskey, W., Escalante, G., Herrera, R., Montangini, F., Todd, R. and Uhl, C. (1983) Nitrogen dynamics during conversion of primary Amazonian rainforest to slash and burn agriculture. *Oikos* 40, 131 – 139.

Klinge, H. and Rodrigues, W. (1958) Litter production in an area of Amazonian terra firme forest. I. Litterfall, organic carbon and total nitrogen contents of litter. *Amazoniana* 1, 287 – 302.

Klinge, H., Medina, E. and Herrera, R. (1972) Studies on the ecology of Amazon Caatinga Forest in Southern Venezuela. I. General features. *Acta Cient. Venez.* 28, 270 – 276.

Klinge, H. and Herrera, R. (1978) Biomass studies in Amazon Caatinga forest in southern Venezuela. I. Standing crop of composite root mass in selected stands. *Trop. Ecol.* 19, 93-110.

Klinge, H. and Herrera, R. (1983) Phytomass structure of natural plant communities on spodsols in southern Venezuela: The tall Amazon Caatinga forest. *Vegetatio* 53, 65 – 84.

Lugo, A. (1982) Are tropical forest ecosystems sources or sinks of carbon? In *Role of Tropical Forests of the World Carbon Cycle*, Eds. S. Brown and A. Lugo. U.S. Dept. Energy, Univ. Florida, Gainesville.

Mallock, D. W., Pirozynski, K. A. and Raven, P. H. (1980) Ecological and evolutionary significance of mycorrhizal symbiosis in vascular plants (a review). *Proc. Natl. Acad. Sci. USA* 77, 2113 – 2118.

Nye, P. H. and Greenland, D. J. (1960) *The Soil Under Shifting Cultivation*, Tecn. Comm. N°51 Commonwealth Bureau of Soils, Harpenden.

Rice, E. and Pancholy, S. (1972) Inhibition of nitrification by climax ecosystems. *Amer. J. Bot.* 59, 1033 – 1040.

Richards, P. W. (1952) *The Tropical Rain Forest*. Cambridge Univ. Press.

Salati, E., Sylvester-Bradley, R. and Victoria, R. L. (1982) Regional gains and losses of nitrogen in the Amazon Basin. *Plant and Soil* 67, 367 – 376.

Sioli, H. (1964) General features of the limnology of Amazonia. *Verh. Int. Ver. Limnol.* 15, 1053 – 1058.

Stark, N. and Jordan, C. F. (1978) Nutrient retention by the root mat of an Amazonian rainforest. *Ecology* 59, 434 – 437.

Uhl, C., Jordan, C. F., Clark, K., Clark, H. and Herrera R. (1982) Ecosystem recovery in Amazon Caatinga forest after cutting, cutting and burning and bulldozer treatment. *Oikos* 38, 313 – 320.

Vitousek, P. (1982) Nutrient cycling and nutrient use efficiency. *Amer. Natur.* 119, 553 – 571.

Walter, H. (1936) Nährstoffgehalt des Bodens und natürliche Waldbestände. *Forstl. Wshcr. Silva* 24, 201 – 214.

Went, F. and Stark, N. (1968) Mycorrhiza. *BioScience* 18, 1035 – 1038.

PART II

The Biology

CHAPTER 7

The Vegetation Types of the Brazilian Amazon

JOÃO MURÇA PIRES* and GHILLEAN T. PRANCE**

*Museu Paraense Emílio Goeldi

**The New York Botanical Garden, New York, U.S.A.

CONTENTS

7.1. INTRODUCTION

In this chapter we try to analyse the principal variations in the forms of vegetation in the Brazilian Amazon, and the practical ways in which the inhabitants of the region classify and name these variations. Because more than half of the Amazon region is situated in Brazilian territory, the concepts analysed here can be, for the most part, extrapolated for all of Amazonia.

7.2. THE AMAZONIAN VEGETATION AND ITS PHYSIOGNOMIC CHARACTERISTICS

The Amazon region is a physiographic and biological entity which is well-defined and distinct from most of the rest of South America by its dense forest, and large biomass. It should be emphasised that this broad physiognomic view is not based on a superficial, or purely scenic interpretation but rather on one from the origin and evolution of the region as a single unit. The relief for example, is very important because it is related to the division of the region into older and younger areas, it has geological implications, hydrological implications and is closely related to the origin of the region.

The hydrographic basins are very important in relation to the flora. Physiognomically the forest is uniform, but, when analysed in detail, the composition varies a great deal from place to place and there is a very evident correlation between the similar forest types and the hydrographic basins. Adolfo Ducke, one of the botanical experts of the region, believed that the floristic division of the Hylaea is linked to the rivers. The opinions of renowned zoologists and limnologists corroborate this from faunal evidence.

Another important factor in the floristic and vegetational diversity of the area is the effect of the ocean level which has, in the past, caused erosion and sedimentation. Recently much discussion has arisen about the climatic variation (particularly the climatic fluctuations of the Pleistocene) which has affected the vegetation, and is discussed separately in Chapter 8 of this volume.

Amazonia occupies a vast area of South America, nearly 6,000,000 km^2, with more than half of this in Brazilian territory. The enormous area of dense forest is continuous around its perimeter, while in the interior there can be interruptions, or places where small or relatively large non-forest formations occur. The forest region usually appears physiognomically uniform; however, when examined in detail, considerable local variations of vegetation and floristic composition are encountered.

The term 'vegetation' refers to the life-forms which are associated, in various ways, in each area, or are the result of the adaptations which better adjust it to environmental variations. Ecological and environmental variations always exist, even in areas which are relatively close to one another, creating a large number of niches for the different species. The vegetation types are therefore physiognomic or landscape patterns which are practically differentiated and named by the local people. The floristic differentiation is somewhat more subjective and depends on the species found in association with one another. We intend to outline the former types of vegetation which are easily recognised by local people, yet make good sense botanically.

The detailed study of the variations which occur in the vegetation and flora is a complex issue. However, in an overview, major groups of physiognomic variation patterns can be established. The practical classification which is used regionally in Amazonia is based primarily on the relief, and it recognised two principal types of vegetation: terra firme and inundated formations (várzea and igapó). As Amazonia is basically a forest region, the terra firme and várzea forests are of primary importance, the non-forest types of vegetation are more restricted in area and of less importance.

Before giving a detailed analysis of Amazonian vegetation, it is necessary to take a general and superficial look at the vegetation of the tropics as a whole. Because Amazonia is part of a larger universe, vegetation of the humid tropics, there are many worldwide physiognomic and functional similarities.

7.3. GENERAL NOTIONS ABOUT TROPICAL VEGETATION

It is generally accepted that the colonisation of the earth by plants had a point of origin and an evolutionary development, but there is little to document this history. However, even today certain areas occasionally open up for new colonisation and provide evidence of how plants occupy new areas. This occurs, for example, in clearings caused by storms, natural changes in river courses, and new lands arising from volcanoes. In tropical areas, clearings tend to be invaded by plants in such ways that the biomass gradually increases until it reaches a climax. In this evolutionary process there is a time when competition begins between these species, and at this point natural selection begins to play a more important role.

When the whole globe is analysed in terms of vegetational cover and their variations, two principal areas become evident: the tropical region and the temperate or cold region. The tropical region is that in which natural selection is primarily governed by competition to capture and use light and water. In cold regions, a third factor enters into play, temperature. In the case of the lowland tropics, plants do not need to develop specialised mechanisms to adapt to temperature variations because, by definition, the temperature is elevated and uniform for the whole year. For this reason, the protection of buds which serve as the base for the classification of life-forms by Raunkiaer is not as important for the humid tropics.

Theoretically, the tropical region is the region up to 23° 27' north and south of the equator. This belt, however, can vary a lot depending upon the climate, altitude and other factors. The humid tropics (mainly forest vegetation) are differentiated from the arid tropics (with largely non-forest vegetation) by their humidity.

In the tropics, natural selection depends mainly on competition for either light or water, but usually not on both at the same time. This is because under optimal conditions (when there is no lack of water) the biomass tends to be high and the plants tall, and the plants use cover (which produces shade) as a means of eliminating competitors since there is no competition for water. When there is a shortage of water, the plants cannot form a large biomass, and are unable to cover all of the three-dimensional space which is available. Consequently, the sun penetrates to the ground and light is, therefore, not an object of competition. This is an important aspect in order to understand tropical vegetation. The structure and function of the vegetation is dependent on this, as are the association of small, medium and large sized species, the distribution of individuals by size categories, by age classifications, by means of reproduction, by growth increments and their position in successions.

The only other factor of such importance as light and water is that of the avoidance of predators, which abound in tropical forest. However, this does not express itself so much in the form of the forest, but rather in the chemistry of the plants (*see* Janzen, Chapter 11, this volume) or in special adaptations such as ant associations (*see* Benson, Chapter 13, this volume).

One characteristic of the humid tropics is the large number of associated species in any area. This leads to complex interrelations among themselves, with the fauna, and with the physical environment which fosters competition, symbiosis, commensalism and parasitism. In some places, restrictions on plants' lives may arise through limiting stress factors. In this case the plant species must specialise. This affects the floral composition of the area and can give rise to specially adapted endemic species, and it generally causes decreased biomass.

The difficulties or restrictions to development which affect tropical plants, are usually related to the lack of or excess of water. The lack of water is often seasonal. For example, in rocky and shallow soils a short drought can have serious consequences. In the case of an excess of water such as when the water table is near the surface, it can rise to the surface in the rainy season and the aeration of the soil is disturbed, impeding root respiration.

Also, it is important to emphasise that the quantity of biomass of a particular vegetation type is not necessarily correlated with soil fertility. Massive forests can develop on soils of a very low fertility, by the developmental process of a slow gradual increase. This ultimately results in a closed ecosystem, in which the nutrients are stored in the plants themselves, and thanks to a good system of retention, the insignificant loss caused by leaching, is compensated for by nutrients which come with rainwater. In such a complicated ecosystem, primary production depends on secondary production (decomposition), on the live parts which die and disintegrate and are recycled back into the system.

7.4. REGIONAL NAMES FOR PRINCIPAL TYPES OF VEGETATION OF BRAZILIAN AMAZONIA

Amazonia falls within the humid tropical region and is largely covered by climatically controlled vegetation which extends over a vast area. Since relief plays an important role on the vegetation type, the vegetation is divided into two principal groups, the terra firme vegetation and the inundated vegetation (várzea and igapó). Inundated vegetation is defined as all the flood plains (Moura, 1943) and any areas which become flooded by the rise of the water table on a seasonal or permanent basis.

Within Amazonia there has been much confusion over the local terms for inundated vegetation: várzea and igapó. In lower Amazonia igapó is used for the areas where flooding is more pronounced, but in upper Amazonia it is used for blackwater flooded areas. Here we have adopted the terms as defined in Prance (1979) where várzea is used for areas flooded by muddy or whitewaters and igapó for areas flooded by black and clearwaters.

A practical way to express the differences between vegetation types is to correlate the differences with the index of biomass. Similar types of vegetation have approximately the same biomass. Biomass can be expressed by the basal area of trees per hectare, using individuals of 30 cm or more in circumference. On this basis, the exceptionally large forests can exceed 40 m^2 of basal area. The open forests or vine forests usually are between 18 and 24 m^2, and open grass savannahs will register zero.

The estimate of the biomass can be expressed in several ways. The weight is difficult to obtain and the volume involves estimates of height which vary from person to person. For practical purposes, the basal area is very useful and is easily obtained.

The principal vegetation types as they are locally known are shown in the following summary:
1a. Widely distributed vegetation formations
  2a. Forest formations of relatively dense biomass
    3a. Forest on terra firme (*mata densa*)

4a. Dense forest
4b. Open forest formations (*mata aberta*)
  5a. w/o vines and palms
  5b. w/palms
  5c. w/vines (Liana Forests)
  5d. Dry forest
  5e. Montane forest
3b. Várzeas and igapós, seasonal and permanent swamp
  6a. Forest on clay soil (muddy river water)
    7a. Várzea forest of Upper Amazonia
    7b. Várzea forest of Lower Amazonia
    7c. Estuarine Várzea forest
    7d. Lower Rio Branco Swamps (*chavascal or pantanal de Rio Branco*)
  6b. Seasonal igapó forest on white sand
2b. Savannah and other low biomass non-forest vegetation
  8a. Terra Firme Savannah
    9a. Open Savannah
    9b. Orchard Savannah (*campo coberto*)
    9c. Roraima Savannah
    9d. Rock Outcrop formations (*campo rupestre*)
    9e. Coastal Savannah
  8b. Várzea Savannah
2c. Amazonian Caatinga and Campina, oligotrophic formations on white sand
1b. Vegetation covering restricted areas
10a. Mangrove swamp
10b. Restinga
10c. Buritizal (*Mauritia* formations)
10d. Pirizal or cariazal

7.5. GENERALISATIONS ABOUT FOREST FORMATIONS

Forest as defined here is dense vegetation which develops in the places where conditions allow the formation of an appreciable quantity of biomass (depending on the humidity of the area), thus allowing associated species to compete for light. This occurs when the basal area reaches something above 10 m^2 per hectare. Forests are characterised by their lack of grasses and sedges (Poaceae and Cyperaceae) between the trees. The denser the forests, the cleaner the forest floor, with the decrease of shrub like plants, herbaceous plants and vines. Lianas climb directly to the crown and do not block the area between the trees.

In the forest the orientation of the branches becomes important, the plants must adapt themselves to positions where they will receive enough light. Consequently the architecture of the branches plays an important role. For this reason, the physiognomy of forest plants is unique. This can be seen when the forest trees are isolated and survive in man-made clearings. These trees have very irregular asymmetrical crowns and expand their branches in directions which in the forest have more light. For this reason it is very difficult to present an adequate picture in a forest profile diagram, as used by various authors to illustrate the supposed stratification of crowns in the forest (Fig. 7.1).

A very interesting subject is the analysis of the lianas of a forest to understand how they reach the crown. There are vines which climb straight up looking like a normal plant initially, and only entwine

Fig. 7.1. A profile of dense terra firme forest near Altamira, Pará, Brazil.

Fig. 7.2. The cord-like roots of epiphytes which eventually reach the soil hang down from plants on the high branches of trees.

when they reach the canopy. Some species of liana begin their growth as an erect tree-like plant and only later turn into a vine, for example, Krukoff (1942: 253) refers to some species of *Strychnos* with this growth habit. Other species have a marked dimorphism between the young and adult stages. Some Araceae and Bignoniaceae when young are slender climbers which grow up the trunks of large trees, pressed firmly against the bark. When they reach a certain height the leaves and stem change completely so that an uninitiated person would never associate the two together because of their completely different appearance.

There are also semiepiphytes which begin their growth as epiphytes, i.e. they germinate in the trees and in their juvenile stage are epiphytes which obtain enough light, and are adapted to conserve and to

Fig. 7.3. Robust woody lianas are a characteristic of dense Amazon forest.

capture water. However, they then produce pendant cord-like roots that can be seen swinging in the wind (Fig. 7.2). In time these roots grasp the trunks of their host trees and when the roots reach the soil and plentiful water they lignify and change the plant into an independent individual.

Strangling plants (Pires and Dobzhansky, 1956) are a variation of this habit. These plants begin as epiphytes and after the roots reach the soil they enlarge and rapidly increase in number. They also fuse with other roots to form a column which completely surrounds the trunk of the host tree which disappears inside this jacket and generally dies. However, in some cases both crowns survive as is

Fig. 7.4. Lianas have many interesting growth forms such as the *Bauhinia* locally called 'turtle ladder'.

frequent with strangling *Clusias*. With strangling figs (*Ficus*) the host tree usually dies. In this case the roots turn into the trunk. In non-forest formations climbers are not abundant and when they exist they are slender herbaceous vines. Robust woody lianas are a phenomenon of the forests (Figs. 7.3, 7.4). The abundance of epiphytes on the branches and trunks of the trees including mosses and tiny ferns is an indication of high humidity and the absence of a prolonged dry season. High relative air humidity also encourages the presence of epiphytes.

In the tropical forest it is common to find plants with specific ant associations (Ducke and Black, 1954, page 6 and *see* Benson, Chapter 13, this volume). These ant cavities, hollow stems, modified petioles, stipules and leaf bases are described in Chapter 13. The myrmecodomatia appear even when the plants are cultivated in the absence of ants. The quantity of ant plants shows the importance of defence mechanisms against predators in the Amazon forest.

The roots of the Amazon forest trees are generally rather shallow even where the soil is deep. There is a greater quantity of organic material in the process of decomposition in the upper layers of the soil because the greater part of the nutrients are in the plants themselves and in the decomposing plant parts. Since roots are shallow, tree falls are rather frequent.

When the seeds of light-demanding species germinate, they produce seedlings that are not able to reach the adult stage in the dark forest. These species need natural clearings to develop further. Examples include the Brazil nut (*Bertholletia excelsa*), piquiá (*Caryocar villosum*), angelim (*Dinizia excelsa*). With these species small individuals are not found in mature forests.

The maximum age of a tree varies from species to species. As a general rule species which grow rapidly die more quickly. The incidence of death, based on our own data, tends to be more or less uniform by percentage in the different classes of trunk diameter. In mature forests there is much variation in the growth of the trunk diameter, and this is not necessarily correlated with age. There are trees of the same species and the same diameter class that show very different growth patterns. Zero growth over an extended period is common. Light is so important for plants that are poorly located and receive very little light, that it reduces or completely stops growth. Natural clearings play a very important role, allowing light demanding species the possibility of growth and regeneration. Natural clearings are caused by winds, storms, lightning, and the natural fall of large mature trees which are often entwined by lianas and may consequently uproot several other trees when they fall.

There are many other causes for the death of trees, but the main ones include having reached their maximum age, strangling lianas, lightning, fungal attack, and trunk boring insects. Attack by these insects is very important and there are many special adaptations by trees to survive this attack. There are trees that can renew damaged bark with great facility. Others produce thin roots below the dead bark, which thicken and fuse, finally forming a type of bridge that reunites the dead bark. *Ormosia nobilis* is an example. An interesting adaptation to survive damage is found in various palms (*Astrocaryum, Bactris*) which have an extremely hard part of the wood on the outside and soft interior equivalent to a trunk with the heart wood outside and the soft wood within.

Another important characteristic of dense tropical forests is that they are fireproof, even when attempts are made to set fire within the standing forest.

As a general rule, there is great species diversity in tropical forests, which indicates the large number of ways in which the plants can make use of the environment. This is adaptation to many niches.

Since there are large numbers of plant and animal species and microorganisms, interacting among themselves, variation within a species is extremely important. Therefore there is a tendency in plant species towards unisexuality. Even many species whose flowers are morphologically hermaphrodite, actually function as unisexual. There are also many examples of self sterility.

One of the most curious adaptations is monocarpy. In *Tachigalia myrmecophila*, for example, we have a tree species which takes many years to attain maturity and flowering. It produces its abundant crop of wind dispersed fruits once, and then dies. It is difficult to say what is the adaptive advantage for a species with this mechanism. Perhaps it can be explained because the death of the tree opens a clearing for its offspring which develop under its crown and these light demanding seedlings can then quickly replace the parent tree.

There are many species which, in order to survive, use both sexual reproduction and vegetative reproduction. For example in *Goupia glabra*, *Caryocar villosum*, and *Platonia insignis*, when the tree falls or is cut down, many sprouts occur from the roots and these may form new trees. Apomixis can also occur. For example, Maguire (1976) took seeds of a species of *Clusia* to greenhouses in New York and obtained fertile seedlings of this dioecious plant.

In the Amazon forest where there are large numbers of species growing together, true dominance of one species does not occur. However, there are generally a number of species, five or ten or even sometimes up to thirty, whose total number of individuals is more than 50% of the total number of trees. These are the most important trees in the forest and the rest are rare and are represented only sporadically.

Certain authors have discussed sample plots of vegetation as if they represented uniform vegetation formation. However, in practice our extensive sampling has shown that there is always a variation of floristic composition from one area to another if it is a little apart. For this reason, when one samples an increased number of plots, the species number always increases gradually because of the number of species represented by a single individual. In other words, when one plots a graph of area against number of species, the curve never truly reaches the asymptote, because one always comes across new species found for the first time. Because of the rarity of some individuals, in order to include all the species one would have to continue the sampling process indefinitely until it included the entire forest.

Theoretically, each species has an area of distribution which can be mapped and on this map the density of these species varies considerably from one locality to another. Thus, the floristic composition of a certain area or sample corresponds to the superimposition of all the distribution maps of the different species represented there, and it will vary more between the more distant samples than between samples close together.

There are some species which are much more important in their definition of the landscape. For example, the *Parkias* have a curious type of branching. Some species have extremely striking flowers, such as members of the Vochysiaceae and the genus *Tabebuia*. Certain groups can be readily recognised by the form of the plant, as in the palms, which are always quite striking.

The forest on terra firme dominates the largest percentage of the area of Amazonia. Most of it consists of undulating terrain at low altitudes, rarely rising above 200 m, and most of it below 100 m. As one moves away from the Amazon river, up the tributaries, one reaches a point where rapids begin. This is where one reaches the crystalline shields both to the north and to the south.

Both the vegetation types and floristics show that there is a strong correlation between these formations and the different river basins. Certain river basins are associated with certain vegetation types and certain groups of species. This has been shown from both botanical and zoological data, and limnologists are now studying the associated physical environment.

7.6. TERRA FIRME FORESTS

7.6.1. Dense forest

Dense forest is the formation with the greatest biomass, with a clear understory, and occurs where environmental conditions are optimal and there are no limiting factors such as a scarcity or an excess of water. It has been described in general terms above.

7.6.2. Open forest without palms

This is a variation of the forest landscape where the biomass is considerably lower and is generally slightly above 20 m^2 basal area per hectare, and the trees are lower. Since there is a greater penetration of light, there is a tendency for shrub and liana species to develop well, and the forest floor is much more densely covered by vegetation. In this forest, even though it is much lower, occasional scattered individuals of very large trees occur. The lower biomass can be caused by a lower water table, by the impermeability of the soil, by poor drainage or by conditions which do not permit good root penetration, or by the occurrence of relatively long dry seasons and a lower relative humidity. Aridity, whether it is seasonal or not, causes diminution in the abundance of epiphytes. These forests are not notably seasonally deciduous and they are also not affected by fire.

7.6.3. Open forest with palms

This formation is similar to the preceding, with trees of about the same height in the same density and of a similar floristic composition (Fig. 7.5). It occurs more frequently than the forest without palms. The most frequent palms are *Orbignya barbosiana* (babaçu), *Oenocarpus distichus* and other species of the genus (bacaba); *Jessenia bataua* (patauá), *Euterpe precatoria* (açaí da mata), and *Maximiliana regia* (inajá). One of these species may dominate or they may occur mixed together. In this type of forest, there are

Fig. 7.5. Open forest with palms near the Xingu river in Pará. The dominant palm here is babaçu (*Orbignya*).

frequently a large number of Brazil nut trees (*Bertholletia excelsa*). Sometimes there are concentrations of *Phenakospermum guianense* (sororoca), which looks banana-like, but, when seen in aerial photographs, is quite similar to palm trees.

7.6.4. Liana forest

This is a variety of open forest which generally has an abundance of lianas (Figs. 7.6, 7.7). In many places it also contains babaçu palm and the Brazil nut, either together or separately. It is a variation of the Amazon vegetation that is of special importance because of the vast area which it occupies, covering

Fig. 7.6. A tree draped in lianas, typical of liana forest, Rio Itacaiunas, Pará.

hundreds of square miles. However, liana forests are generally not continuous. They are usually intermeshed with dense forests without lianas forming a complex mosaic. This type of forest occurs in abundance along the Trans-Amazon highway from Marabá up to the Xingu River with less frequency as far as the Tapajós River. To the south it extends to the southern limit of Amazonia to the boundary of the cerrado of Central Brazil. Small patches of liana forest occur scattered well into the region of Sararé.

A particular river where liana forest dominates is the Rio Itacaiunas, which runs from west to east joining the Tocantins in Marabá. The region of Serra Norte and Serra dos Carajás, with one of the richest iron deposits in the world, is also rich in liana forest.

Liana forest characteristically occurs on geologically ancient terrain with a somewhat elevated altitude with rich mineral deposits such as iron, aluminium, manganese, nickel, gold and many others. The liana families that are characteristic of this region and most important in this formation are Leguminosae,

Fig. 7.7. The floor of liana forest is often impenetrable because of the quantity of liana stems.

Bignoniaceae, Malpighiaceae, Dilleniaceae and Menispermaceae. An interesting genus is *Bauhinia* which has both lianas and trees in this formation, whereas in the rest of Amazonia, only liana species of *Bauhinia* occur. In this formation most trees are *Bauhinia* spinous except *B. bombaciflora* which has enormous flowers, hence its name.

Falesi (1972) studied the soils along the Transamazon and did not find any correlation between the types of soil and the vegetation. For example where he found terra roxa (Nitosols of the FAO/UNESCO soil classification) of good fertility, many types of vegetation occurred: dense forest, open forest, with or without lianas or palms. In this area of terra roxa, the vegetation is quite variable between each of these different types. Falesi did his analysis at the highest level of soil divisions. For a better study and more detailed correlation between soil and vegetation, greater soil details are needed, especially about the depth of the water table and the drainage characteristics (*see* Jordan, Chapter 5).

The various forms of open forest are quite similar both in size and density of trees and their floristic composition. The major differences are in the presence or absence of lianas and of palms. The most frequent palm is the babaçu, the oil yielding seeds of which are used economically in the state of Maranhão, but not in the rest of Amazonia, because of the lack of a tradition and because there are other less strenuous sources of employment in the rest of the region.

It is important to note that in these types of open forest, gigantic trees occur sporadically spread throughout the forest. These very tall trees are principally: *Bertholletia excelsa*, *Hymenaea parvifolia*, *Bagassa guianensis*, *Tetragastris altissima*, *Astronium gracile* and *Ampuleia molaris*. In low and more humid places near the streams, *Swietenia macrophylla* occurs quite frequently. This is the much sought after mahogany or mogno and it is now threatened with extinction. Other common species are *Acacia* polyphylla, Sapium marmieri, Castilla ulei, and Myrocarpus frondosus. Castilla ulei was much exploited during World War II for its rubber latex. The wood of Myrocarpus frondosus, is excellent and is being exported under the name conduru de sangue or roxinho. Although the liana forests are generally located in southern Amazonia, there are patches also north of the river. For example, in the Rio Jari basin and principally in Roraima territory.

7.6.5. Dry forest

This is a formation of transition forest that is occasionally found in the southeastern part of Amazonia on the border between Amazonia and Central Brazil. In this region, the climate is much more seasonal and dryer with lower relative humidity, with the result that in the dry season, the trees lose some of their leaves. There is therefore, a tendency towards semideciduous forest, and a seasonal influence on the vegetation landscape is apparent. Dry forest occurs in small clusters that do not occupy large areas. There are also dry forests in Roraima territory where they are more abundant.

Throughout Amazonia there are some trees that lose their leaves but are not truly synchronised, either with the season or with each other and so cannot be considered part of a deciduous vegetation type. The dry forests are different and leaf fall occurs at a time determined by the season.

Along the rivers and the streams in the flooded areas, the vegetation is typical of that of the Amazonian várzeas and is not deciduous. Some species common in the dry forests are: Geissospermum sericeum, Cenostigma macrophyllum, Physocalymma scaberrimum, Lafoensia pacari, Magonia glabrescens, Sterculia striata, Erythrina ulei, Vochysia haenkeana, V. pyramidata; Orbignya barbosiana, Combretum leprosum, Bowdichia virgilioides. This region is not rich in endemic species. One of the common trees of the flooded areas is the blue-flowered Qualea ingens.

Dry forests physiognomically very similar, but with very different floras, are found in Roraima territory where the following species are common: Centrolobium paraense, Mimosa schomburgkii, Richardella surumuensis and Cassia moschata.

The analysis of the distribution of the babaçu palm is most important in understanding the forest that used to exist in the "Meio Norte" region through the states of Maranhão and part of Piauí. Babaçu is common throughout this large region bordering Eastern Amazonia, which today is not forested. It is a transition between the Amazonian hylaea and the cerrado of Central Brazil.

Before its destruction by man, all this babaçu region was forested with open and dry forest types. But the climate in this eastern part is seasonally drier with a lower relative air humidity. Thus, when man cut down these forests and burned them, the vegetation was gradually transformed into pure stands of babaçu without any other type of tree.

In 1943, the senior author had the opportunity to study areas of these forest types, which existed between Santa Filomena and Itapicuru, along the railroad from São Luiz to Terezina, places where today there is no forest left and are typically covered by pure stands of babaçu. This is largely because the babaçu palm is well adapted to fire resistance.

There is a certain similarity between the dry forests and the cerradão of Central Brazil, but the cerradão is taller cerrado as its name would indicate, with typical cerrado species and cerrado physiognomy with a greater amount of xeromorphism, thick barks, tortuous branches with short internodes, while the dry forest has a physiognomy affected by the arrangement of the branches on the trees which are arranged in adaptation to the penetration of light. Ratter et al. (1973) studied some examples of dry forest in Mato Grosso between Serra Roncador and the headwaters of the Xingu River.

7.6.6. Montane forests

Montane forests, as the name indicates, are forest formations which are differentiated by their altitude and rocky soil types. Most of the Amazon region can be classified as a plain, which although quite undulating in certain areas, is generally below 200 m above sea level. Mountainous regions occur only at the extremities of Amazonia. To the north, at the boundary between Venezuela and Guyana, there is a mountain region of exceptional botanical interest. This region, which is known by American authors as Guayana, has a fascinating flora (Fig. 7.8). Biological interest in the region was stimulated by the Tate expedition which made spectacular collections. Since then, various groups have studied these mountains, above all, the group of Basset Maguire, who has published much of his studies under the title 'Botany of the Guayana Highlands', published in the Memoirs of the New York Botanical Garden.

The montane vegetation of Amazonia is closely related to the vegetation of rocky places and can either be forests or open formations (Fig. 7.9). Shallow soils and rocky places, even in regions of high rainfall, suffer extreme drought, even in the short dry periods of the year, since there is no retention of water in the soil.

Humidity increases with altitude in the montane regions, and because the air is saturated with humidity, there is a great deal of mist, exemplified by the name of Brazil's tallest mountain, Pico da Neblina (the mountain of mist). As a consequence, the mountains have a large number of mosses, lichens, small pteridophytes, which form carpets over rocks and cover the trunks and branches of woody vegetation. It is not rare to find a carpet of lichen over rocky soils, giving a most spectacular landscape.

The steeper slopes have a tendency towards sparser vegetation because of their reduced water retention capacity. On the less steep slopes, much denser forest usually develops. As altitude increases,

Fig. 7.8. The montane forest formations are well developed in the table top mountains of tepuis of the Guayana Highland of Venezuela, here seen in Canaima National Park.

Fig. 7.9. Aerial view of Serra Araca and isolated Sandstone mountains in Amazonian Brazil.

biomass usually diminishes and the trees become smaller until eventually there is no longer a forest of any type. On Serra Neblina the tree line is about 2600 m, and this occurs throughout Guayana. In the Andean region, according to Livingstone and Van der Hammen (1978) the forests extend higher to about 3200 or 3500 m.

On the top of the mountains, the vegetation is sparse and trailing and often confined to the crevices between the rocks. In a habitat like this, on the top of Serra Neblina, the small unusual plant, *Saccifolium bandeirae* in a monotypic family, with sack-like leaves, was collected.

Physiognomy and floristic composition of the vegetation also become special with increase in altitude. The family Theaceae (*Bonnetia*, *Archytaea*, *Ternstroemia*), become much more important, and also certain Guttiferae (*Clusia*, *Tovomita*), and large Bromeliaceae such as *Brocchinia* or the smaller *Dyckia*, as well as robust members of the Eriocaulaceae and Poaceae. Various plant families which are rarely represented or absent from the lowland hylaea become frequent: Ericaceae (*Psammisia*), Cunoniaceae (*Weinmannia*), Cyrillaceae (*Cyrilla*), Winteraceae (*Drymys*), Podocarpaceae (several species), Dipterocarpaceae (*Pakaraimaea*) and Sarraceniaceae (*Heliamphora*, which has leaves adapted to trap insects).

The mountains of Guayana that lie to the west are in a much more humid region and do not suffer the effects of fires. But this is not so to the east in Roraima where the mountains have been considerably altered by the effects of fire.

In the Andes there are much higher mountains than those of Guayana, with other types of montane vegetation — Yungas, Punas, and Páramos, which are not described here because they are not truly Amazonian. Summary information about those types of vegetation can be found in Cabrera and Willink (1973) and Hueck (1972).

7.7. INUNDATED FORESTS (VÁRZEAS AND IGAPÓS)

Várzeas and igapós are regional terms applied both to types of soil and vegetation, denoting excess humidity or swampy conditions, or in other words, any ground that is not terra firme. Igapó is applied here to black and clearwater areas and várzea to muddy water inundation. Várzeas are formed by sedimentary ground that during its formation was influenced by fluctuation in sea levels.

The two principal types of inundation forests also differ in their soil. Várzea is formed by flooding with muddy water rivers, such as the Amazonas and the Madeira, and igapós by flooding with clear- and blackwater rivers without sediments, such as the Rio Negro, the Tapajós and the Arapiuns.

Because of this difference in water property the clay soil várzeas, as a general rule, have higher river banks (natural levees), since the larger and heavier particles are deposited first. In the várzeas and igapós on sandy soil and clearwater, this tendency to deposit new material does not exist and the soil is at a much lower level along the margin of the river. Thus, in this black and clearwater type of flooded area it is common to find in the dry season sandy beaches with trees on them, which in the rainy season are transformed into a type of inundated forest where the lower part of the trunk is completely under water. This is the typical landscape that one finds along the clearwater river. The subject of the difference between inundated forests was explained in great detail in Sioli (1951).

The várzeas have soils that are much more fertile than is usual in Amazonia because the soils originate from the fertile soils of the Andean region. However, until recently, the várzeas have been little used by people of the interior because traditional Amazonian agriculture is based on cassava, the roots of which rot even in the presence of the slightest flooding.

Pierre Gourou (1950) estimated that the inundated forests cover 2% of the surface of the Brazilian Amazonia excluding the water surface. However, more recent data show that they cover a considerably larger area. For example, in the region of the lower Rio Branco from Caracaraí to the confluence with the Rio Negro, including the basins of its tributaries Xeruini, Catrimani, Univini, Ajarani, Anauá, and also as far as the Jauaperi, there is an extraordinarily large region on low ground in which these rivers only flow independently in the dry season since the flooding is continuous between them in the rainy season. The region is covered with a low type of igapó forest. There are a few places where terra firme reaches right to the margin of the rivers and in these areas it is called *barrancos*, the term for high river banks. The few inhabitants of the region have their houses on these high river banks because in the other areas in the flood season the entire riverside area is inundated. In this region streams with crystalline or transparent water and blackwater are common. These rivers, which are practically without sediments, form a peculiar environment where it is common to find the boats of fishermen seeking ornamental fish. There are many very attractive little fish, some of which it has not been possible to raise in captivity or even in other streams, so they are caught in that region for export to aquaria.

Some typical plants of the flooded forest are *Sclerolobium aureum* (tachi), *Couma utilis* (sorva, the latex of which is coagulated to form chewing gum), *Exellodendron coriaceum*, *Parinari campestris*, *Euphronia hirtelloides*, *Chaunochiton loranthoides*, *Ambelania laxa* (molongo, a tree with extremely light wood) and *Leopoldinia piassaba* (which yields the much used piassaba fibre). In non-forested clearings *Lagenocarpus guianensis*, *Micropapyrus viviparoides*, *Dichromena* ssp., *Fimbristylis* ssp. and other Cyperaceae occur. On the river margin *Euterpe oleracea* is common but terra firme trees such as the Brazil nut, *Bertholletia excelsa*, are found only on the high river banks above flooding. Throughout Roraima territory, this vegetation type, as well as any other physiognomically similar (low and rhachitic) vegetation, is called by the collective term 'chavascal', whether forest, non-forest, terra firme or várzea. However, chavascal is a confusing term, and like igapó, it is not used consistently throughout the region, since there are also chavascals both on terra firme and marshy grounds and the term as applied locally covers woody through herbaceous vegetation types.

There are three principal types of clay soil várzeas: (a) those of the Upper Amazon which are not associated with fields of Canarana (grass meadows), (b) those of Lower Amazonia associated with robust grass meadows, (c) estuarine várzeas subject to flooding from the influence of tidal backup.

7.7.1. Clay soil várzeas without robust grass meadows

These are the várzeas that are found in the Upper Amazonas (Rio Solimões), from Manaus above and also along the major muddy water rivers such as the Madeira (Fig. 7.10). The forest is continuous, or is broken up by lakes only, and is not associated with areas of thick robust grassland. The várzeas have rich vegetation in the understory especially in the region of the upper Solimões, where there are abundant members of the Scitamineae (the ginger, maranta and heliconia families). Huber (1909), pointed out with good reason that the várzeas of the Upper Amazon are much richer than those lower down. Between the rivers Japurá and Içá there is a large area of these várzeas which is intersected with branches of the rivers locally called paranás, igarapés, and furos, as well as a large number of lakes that are linked to the principal river in such a way that in the flood season the Amazon river is extremely wide at this point.

In the rainy season the main river and its tributaries rise considerably during the floods which last for 5 months. At this time a large number of whole trees and tree trunks can be seen floating in the river, because large areas of the river banks are torn off as the water level rises. The lakes are very rich in large fishes and the numerous streams have an extraordinary variety of small fishes, some of which look most unusual, for example, one exactly like a cigar or one which always remains upsidedown or another which mimics a dead leaf.

Fig. 7.10. Clay soil várzea forest.

Ducke and Black (1945) pointed out that várzea species tend to have a softer wood than those of the terra firme. Lateral expansion of the trunk into buttresses is frequent in the várzea. Seeds are often light and have many different mechanisms to cause flotation such as spongy tissue or hollow areas or a light mesocarp. In some cases it is the seed that floats; for example in *Hevea brasiliensis*, the rubber tree. In others the entire fruit floats; for example in *Montrichardia*, a riverside Araceae.

Some of these floating seeds are collected commercially, for example the seeds of the andiroba (*Carapa guianensis*) and the ucuuba (*Iryanthera surinamensis*), which both contain an oil. There are several examples of well-known seeds used commercially, yet for many years without botanical names because

Fig. 7.11. The banks of the Rio Xingu.

Fig. 7.12. Canarana (robust grassland) várzea of the lower Amazon near Uaça, Pará.

they were collected entirely from floating masses in the river. For example *Acioa edulis* was finally described by Prance in 1973 and *Curupira tefeënsis*, was described by Black in 1948. Both of these are important oil yielding seeds, which had been used by local people for many years before they were described botanically.

7.7.2 Clay soil várzeas with grasslands of canarana

These are the typical várzeas of lower Amazonia (Fig. 7.12). They exist in the region where the Amazon river is very broad, especially between Monte Alegre and Itacoatiara and the lower part of the Madeira River. They cover the area of lower Amazonia from the mouth of the Rio Negro down to the mouth of the Xingu River. The lower Amazon várzeas are characterised by narrow stretches of forest on the higher ground beside the principal rivers and their tributaries, both paranás and igarapés. Behind the forests are meadows of robust grass known as canarana. These grass meadows tend to be lower and more flooded the further they are away from the river margins and they go right up to the edge of the terra firme. The lowest parts of all are open lakes. These lakes vary greatly in their size and can be very large in the rainy season and become smaller in the dry season. When the waters recede the open ground that appears quickly becomes covered with grass, augmenting the area of the meadows. Some of these lakes can cover tens of kilometres such as Lago de Maicurú and Lago Grande, in the region of Monte Alegre.

The arboreal species, which are most common are *Crataeva benthamii* (capitari), *Cordia tetrandra* (uruá), *Trichilia singularis*, *Pithecelobium multiflorum*, *Muntingia calabura*, *Bombax munguba* (munguba), *Hura crepitans* (açacu), *Cecropia paraënsis* and other species of *Cecropia* (imbaúba), *Calycophyllum spruceanum* (pau mulato), and *Salix martiana* var. *humboldtiana* (salgueiro, oeirana, which occurs mainly on the muddy beaches that are in the process of deposition). The grasses that form the meadowlands and which are associated with this type of várzea are described under the várzea meadows.

7.7.3. Estuarine várzea

The estuarine region is defined as that which occurs below the confluence of the Rio Xingu, and it includes the enormous Marajó Island which is about 40,000 square kilometres.

The estuarine várzeas (Fig. 7.13) are on clay soil formed by muddy water and they have an extraordinary abundance of palms (of relatively few species) and their flooding is caused by tidal movements rather than the annual river cycle. The other two types of várzea described above are flooded for about 5 months by the rise of the rivers during the rainy season. The estuarine várzeas are flooded by tidal backup twice a day. The seasonal rain has little effect on flood level in this region because the river is so extraordinarily broad and so close to the sea. The highest tides which cause the greatest flooding, happen twice a year; in September during the dry season and March to April in the rainy season. Some of the estuarine várzea forests have an extremely high biomass and consequently areas where there is much exploitation of timber, for example around Breves and Curralinho. The southwest portion of Marajó Island is largely várzea forest, apart from the areas that are upland and on terra firme.

The most abundant palms in estuarine várzea are murumurú (*Astrocaryum murumuru*), jupati (*Raphia taedigera*), açaí (*Euterpe oleracea*), Inajá (*Maximiliana regia*), bacaba (*Oenocarpus distichus*), patauá (*Jessenia bataua*), caraná (*Mauritia martiana*), buriti or miriti (*Mauritia flexuosa*), as well as other smaller species such as ubim (*Geonoma* ssp.).

Fig. 7.13. Estuarine, tidal várzea at Aurá, Belém, showing the pneumatophores (air breathing roots) *Symphonia globulifera*.

7.7.4. Igapós on white sand areas

These are riverside forests along certain parts of the clearwater rivers such as the Tapajós and the Arapiuns. They are white sand margins that are covered by trees (Fig. 7.14). In the dry season the trees are growing on pure white sand. In the flood season their trunks are underwater so that one is able to pass through the crowns of the trees in a canoe. These are the true igapós, or temporary igapós.

It is also a curious fact that the parts of this forest nearer to the rivers are the parts that are most flooded, in contrast to the clay soil várzeas with their natural levees.

Among the most common igapó trees are various members of the Myrtaceae, *Triplaris surinamensis* ('tachi', whose hollow branches are occupied by an ant, of the same name, that is very aggressive with a nasty sting), *Piranhea trifoliata* (piranheira), *Copaifera martii* (copaiba), *Alchornea castaniifolia* (oeirana). On one of these beaches, near to Maués, the very interesting plant *Polygonanthus amazonicus* (Rhizophoraceae) was collected. This plant has been much discussed in the literature because of its uncertain systematic position. It is one of the rare examples of an extremely local endemic in this type of habitat.

The area occupied by igapó is small along most rivers. However, as mentioned above, in the lower Rio Branco it can cover an extremely large area linking the basins of the Rios Xeruini, Catrimani, Univini and the igapó of the Anauá and Jauaperi.

7.8. SAVANNAH VEGETATION

As can be seen from the above, forest vegetation types cover the majority of the Amazon Basin. However, there are many interesting open savannah areas. No accurate estimate of the amount of forest versus savannah has been made, but with present remote imagery it should be possible.

Fig. 7.14. White sand igapó, beside Rio Negro near Manaus showing one of the characteristic palms *Leopoldinia pulchra*.

In Amazonian Brazil the general term for non-forest vegetation types is campo. In order to make an important distinction here, the patches of open vegetation areas of washed out white sand will be described separately under the names caatinga and campina. They represent a completely different vegetation form that is a transition between the forest and non-forest vegetation type.

The savannah formations that are not on white sand are classified into two main types, those on terra firme and those on várzea. The savannahs on terra firme may either be open grassland areas without woody vegetation, dominated by grasses with the basal area of $0 - 2 \, m^2$ per hectare or they may be more woody savannah types with a strong representation of woody plants, however generally not exceeding 5

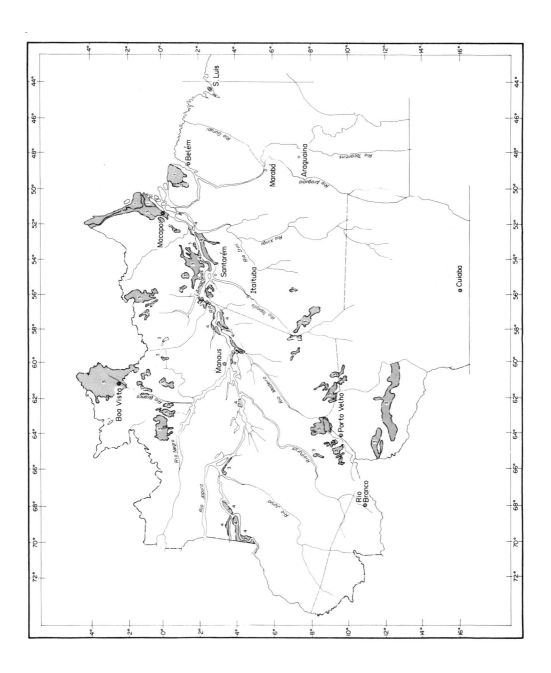

Fig. 7.15. Map of Amazonian Brazil, showing the principal areas of savannah and open vegetation: 1, littoral savannah; 2, Marajó terra firme savannah; 3, Amazon terra firme savannahs; 4, riverine flooded savannah.

Fig. 7.16. The cerrado of central Brazil.

m^2 per hectare (measuring trunks of 30 cm in circumference and above). The soil types of terra firme savannahs are varied. They may be on rocky soil such as the campos rupestres or they may be on deep soils which retain water much better, as in the majority of savannahs on terra firme.

7.8.1. Savannahs on terra firme

Apart from the generalisations made above, there are little data available separating and defining true savannahs on terra firme and savannahs on rocky soil (campos rupestres). Therefore, there is much confusion between these two vegetation types, and we do not have an accurate idea of the proportion of each vegetation type. The two types can exist side by side as they do in the cerrados of Central Brazil (Fig. 7.16), where there are many campos rupestres.

Beard (1946), Richards (1966) and other well-known authors, have proposed that there were no tropical grassland savannahs that were a true climatic climax. It was suggested that they were produced through human action helped by fire. However, there is no doubt that the grassland savannahs existed long before the arrival of man in Tropical America. This is supported with floristic, geologic, geomorphologic, and palynological data (Wijmstra and van der Hammen, 1966; Livingstone and van der Hammen, 1978). The area occupied by these formations however, may have increased through the action of man and fire.

Various authors have used the term 'cerrado' for the savannahs that exist within Amazonia, including Projeto RADAMBRASIL. This term is of recent introduction and is not used by the locals in the region. Also the Amazon savannahs are rather different formations from the central Brazilian cerrado.

Some Amazonian savannahs are physiognomically very similar to the cerrados of Central Brazil. For example, some of the savannahs of Marajó Island, especially those around Joanes or Curralinho. They have some species in common, but they are quite different in soil and climate. In Central Brazil there is a well-defined dry season and the air humidity can be very low and the soils are also very deep. Consequently, roots are also deep and specialised to reach water at considerable depth, when the upper part of the soil is dry. There is also a much greater incidence of plants with vegetative reproduction and organs that are fire resistant such as subterranean trunks, xylopodia, for example, *Anacardium humile* (the dwarf cashew), *Parinari obtusifolia*, *Andira humilis* and *Chrysophyllum suboliferum*. In the cerrados of Central Brazil when the soil is scraped off by a tractor, there immediately is a large amount of sprouting from vegetative organs, previously under the soil. In the Amazonian savannahs, the situation is quite different, and the roots are much more superficial and there are not so many vegetative parts that guarantee asexual reproduction. In addition, the climate is more humid and the relative air humidity higher, generally above 80%. Also in the Amazonian savannahs, there is never such a dense arboreal cover in the more closed type of savannah, whereas in the cerrados the dense cerrado is common and is quite similar to the dry forest.

The non-forested areas of Amazonia are located principally in the northeastern half of Marajó Island, the Atlantic coast of Amapá, in the middle and upper Trombetas River, and in Roraima territory. To the south of the Amazon river there are much smaller open areas such as the savannahs of Puciari-Humaitá (*see* Braun and Ramos, 1959) in the lower Purus region and the campos rupestres of Serra do Cachimbo, which has been estimated to be 16,000 km^2 (Soares, 1948). In addition there are various small patches of open vegetation scattered throughout the region. In total, the savannahs on terra firme, cover between $100-150,000$ km^2 or between $3-4$% of Brazilian Amazonia. In addition to some species that are common to all areas, there are some of restricted range and groups of endemic species vary from one location to another. Some patches of savannah are floristically poor (such as in Amapá), others are quite rich such as on the Rio Trombetas (Ariramba and Tiriós and in Roraima).

The term savannah, which according to Lanjouw, is of Carib origin, is a rather vague and imprecise term that includes all types of non-forest vegetation, not only in Tropical America but in all the world. The savannahs of the Trombetas, described by Egler (1960), Cruls (1950) and Sampaio (1933), reach Suriname in the region of the Tiriós. Following Cruls (1950), General Rondon estimated that the area of the Trombetas savannahs is $40-50,000$ km^2.

The terra firme savannahs have some species that are typical of the cerrados: *Curatella americana* (caimbê), *Anacardium microcarpum* (caju-i), *Salvertia convallariodora*, *Hancornia speciosa*, *Qualea grandiflora*, *Byrsonima crassifolia* (murici), *B. verbascifolia*, *Antonia ovata*, *Tabebuia caraiba*, and some grasses of the genus *Trachypogon* (various species), *Leptocoryphium lanatum*, and *Rottboellia*.

As well as those species common to Amazonian savannahs and cerrados of Central Brazil, there are local variations and groups of species endemic to each region. Thus, the different savannahs are quite distinct from each other.

7.8.2. Littoral savannahs

These savannahs occur in the coastal part of Marajó and in the Bragança region of Pará and are characterised by a cover of creeping grasses and shallow soil and frequent lakes. The commonest grass is *Paratheria prostrata*. In the lakes there are common aquatic plants, including some floating grasses of the várzea savannahs of lower Amazonia, *Cyperus giganteum*, *Thalia geniculata*. Various Pontederiaceae are common including in Bragança, the striking floating Scrophulariaceae, *Benjaminea utricularioides*. The babaçu palm is common in the savannahs of Bragança. The savannahs of Perizes and Jatuba and Anajatuba in Maranhão, are similar to the littoral savannahs of Pará (campos de Bragança).

7.8.3. Savannahs of Roraima

The Roraima savannahs (Fig. 7.17) are considered separately here because there are some differences from the rest of the Amazon savannahs on terra firme. Almost throughout the region they are open savannahs with few trees. They have numerous swampy places, which form either lakes or patches of swamp, where a large concentration of buriti palm (*Mauritia flexuosa*) occurs.

In the radar images of this region, the clumps of buriti palm appear as characteristic white lines, a feature that is not found either in the Amazon savannahs or in the cerrados of Central Brazil. In the classification of RADAMBRASIL, they are the areas called steppe savannah.

The typical species of the arboreal cerrado also occur in this region with the exception of *Hancornia*, and *Salvertia*, but in addition there is a considerable amount of endemism.

The Roraima savannahs are species rich and they reach into Guyana, in the region of the Rupununi River, where they have the same physiognomy as in Brazil. According to the Savannah Report of the McGill University (1966), the Roraima — Rupununi savannahs cover 54,000 km² with 41,000 in Roraima territory and 13,000 in Guyana. The Venezuelan and Colombian llanos are quite similar to the Roraima savannahs. For a definition of the Venezuelan savannah types see Huber (1982) who distinguished clearly between the llanos type savannah and Amazonian savannah.

The Roraima savannahs are not completely uniform. To the south they are much flatter, to the north they are more undulating and lie between various hills. They also have a more sandy soil and there are patches of white sand in this region. In low places, there are swamps of the vereda or varjão type, as it is called in Central Brazil, where the water table reaches the surface and *Mauritia* palms dominate. Also in these areas which are very acid, are *Xyris*, Eriocaulaceae (*Paepalanthus* and *Syngonanthus*), *Cephalostemon*, *Abolboda*, *Rapatea* and sometimes small species of the carnivorous *Drosera*.

7.8.4. Campo rupestre

The campos rupestres or open formations on rocks, are generally confused with open savannah and the orchard savannah on terra firme, but they are quite different physiognomically and floristically. They develop on rocks and in rocky terrain, because they suffer drought in the dry season despite the

Fig. 7.17. General view of the Roraima Savannah.

Fig. 7.18. Campo rupestre at Rio Cururu showing *Vellozia* a characteristic genus of this formation.

equatorial humid climate, and because there is no possibility for water retention and all rainfall runs off immediately.

Typical species of orchard savannah and cerrados do not occur here, such as *Curatella americana*, *Hancornia speciosa*, *Salvertia convallariodora*, and *Qualea grandiflora*. As substitutions there are various species of *Byrsonima*, *Clusia*, *Norantea*, *Vellozia*, certain Bromeliaceae (*Bromelia*, *Dyckea*, etc.) and many Eriocaulaceae (*Paepalanthus* and *Syngonanthus*). Lichens are also frequent and cover many of the rocks.

Campos rupestres are quite common also in Central Brazil where they have been much confused with cerrados (Eiten, 1982). For example, Serra do Cipó, in Minas Gerais, much cited in the literature because of its interesting landscape with a large number of Velloziaceae (Fig. 7.18), is mostly campo rupestre and not cerrado.

In Amazonia, Serra do Cachimbo, in the southwest of Pará, has an area of campo rupestre which covers a considerable area, estimated at about 16,000 km^2 (Soares, 1948). Another large patch is the Campos of the Rio Cururú, in the Tapajós River basin. At Ariramba, on the River Trombetas, both conventional savannah and campos rupestres (Fig. 7.19) occur (Egler, 1960).

The Canga or ironstone vegetation, which occurs on Serra dos Carajás (see Secco and Mesquita, 1983), over the iron deposit, is a special form of campo rupestre. On this formation, various extra-Amazonian species are common such as, *Pilocarpus microphyllus*, which occurs also in Piauí and Maranhâo in the north central region, the extra-Amazonian genus *Callisthene* is represented by *C. microphyllus* of Central Brazil, which only occurs within Amazonia on Serra Carajás. Also on Carajás, the curious and beautiful treelet *Norantea goyasensis* occurs. The branches of this thick barked treelet sometimes lengthen and turn it into a vine.

Fig. 7.19. Campo rupestre at Ariramba, Pará.

A detailed and accurate analysis of the amount of terra firme savannahs (both open and orchard types) would show that there is actually much less than current estimates indicated because they have included campo rupestre in that category. The same is true for the cerrado region of Central Brazil.

The Amazonian montane forests also show a strong affinity to campo rupestre and some could even be classified as floresta rupestre (i.e. forest on rock). In the mountain areas there has been a great accumulation of organic matter because although they sometimes endure short dry periods, the forest is maintained because of the high air humidity and mist.

7.8.5. Inundated savannah of lower Amazonia

In order to understand inundated savannah it is necessary to recall what was said above about the várzea forests of lower Amazonia (Sections 7.6.2 and 7.6.3). In this alluvial region between the Rios Negro and Xingu and especially between the Rio Madeira and the city of Monte Alegre, there are many large channels of the river and also small ones between islands (paranás, igarapés and furos). In this area sediments are deposited by the muddy river and the large particles filter out near the margins, building them up into várzea forests on levees. Beyond these margins the area is covered by grassland meadows and many lakes. In the five month rainy season the area of water shrinks considerably. The exposed ground is soon colonised by grasses which greatly enlarges the area of meadows.

There are various large grasses which are generally called canarana or false cane; *Echinochloa polystachya* (canarana peluda). *E. spectabilis* (canarana erecta), *Hymenachne amplexicaulis* and *H. donacifolia* (rabo de rato), *Leersia hexandra* (andrequicé), *Paspalum platyaxis* (taripucú), *Luziola spruceana* (uamá), *Panicum elephantipes*, *Paspalum fasciculatum* (muri), wild species of rice (*Oryza perennis*, *O. alta*, *O. latifolia*, *O. grandiglumis*). Other common species of grass are *Eragrostis hypnoides*, *E. glomerata*, *Paspalum orbiculatum*, *P. guianense*, and in the Cyperaceae: *Scirpus cubensis*, *Cyperus luzulae*, *C. ferax*, and *Scleria geniculata* (see Black, 1950).

Shrubs and small vines: *Artemisia artemisiifolia* (artemija), a very common shrub which becomes more frequent when there is excessive grazing and which can sometimes completely dominate areas: *Ipomoea fistulosa*, (manjorana or algodão bravo), a shrub that invades pastures and with sap toxic to cattle, *Polygonum punctatum* (erva de bicho), *Justicia obtusifolia*, *Alternanthera philoxeroides*, *Capironia fistulosa*, *Sesbania exasperata*, *Thalia geniculata*, *Hyptis mutabilis*, *Aeschynomene sensitiva*, *Mimosa pigra*, *Montrichardia linifolia*, *Sphenoclea zeylanica*, *Clematis aculeata*, *Cassia reticulata* (mata pasto), *Phaseolus lineatus*, *Rhabdadenia macrostoma*, and *Clitoria triquetum*.

Floating species: *Ceratopteris pteridioides*, *Eichhornia azurea*, *Salvinia radula*, *Neptunia oleracea*, *Pistia stratiotes*, *Lemna* sp. Also some of the grasses already cited may float: *Leersia hexandra*, *Luziola spruceana* and the various species of *Oryza* (Black, 1950).

A large number of the grasses detach and float freely and are seen descending the Amazon river together with trees that have separated. These floating islands may also contain various animals, including the manatee, an animal actually in danger of extinction. The rivers that have lakes and flooded grass are also very rich in their fish fauna.

These open areas of canarana exist only in the lower Amazon between the mouth of the Xingu river and the mouth of the Amazon and also in some of the rivers of the Amapá that flow into the Rio Oiapoque, Rio Uaçá, Caripi and Urucauá. They also exist in a low lying region in the headwaters of the Xingu river or its tributaries the Rios Culiseu, Jatobá and Ronuro between 12 and 13° and 53 − 54°W. The majestic marsh deer are common in this region because although there are Indian tribes there, they do not hunt them because of their religious taboos. These are all muddy rivers that are subject to the tidal bore and are rich in fish and turtles (Pires, 1964).

The fields of canarana are much used as pastures but the ranches of the region lose many head of cattle annually in the flooded season because the entire region is inundated and there is little terra firme. The soils are fertile, are used for jute plantations, and have much potential for the mechanised cultivation of rice during the dry seasons. These are areas that have their fertility renewed each year by the deposit of sediments. They are an Amazonian resource of great value which has not yet been fully exploited.

7.9. CAATINGAS AND OTHER OLIGOTROPHIC SERAL VEGETATION

Amazonian caatinga, campina, campinarana, chavascal, charravascal are words that are used to signify the same vegetation or small variations of a group of vegetation types that are well defined and are characterised because they grow over pure leached white sand. The name caatinga is also used in Northeastern Brazil but there it is a term for a completely different type of arid vegetation. In this report Amazonian caatinga is treated separately from other open formations because it ranges from completely open through to closed vegetation types. It is difficult to separate these into specific associations because there is complete continuity from the open types to the closed forest formation on white sand.

Fig. 7.20. Campina on white sand at Serra do Cachimbo, Pará.

The caatinga is characterised as a form of vegetation that develops in a climate suitable for forest, but limiting factors restrict the vegetation cover and the species have adapted to the various stress factors. These are the nutrient poor soil and the seasonality caused either by the flooding of the soil which removes the air necessary for root respiration, or extreme drought caused by the excessive porosity of the sand not permitting ascent of water by capillarity. In the first case, since the soil is shallow, the water table is near the surface and can rise above the surface in the rainy season. In the second case, the water table is deep and the deep area of pure sand causes periodic drought. Since these factors vary over a gradient from forest soil to the soils with extreme stress, the plants will increase their biomass to an extent dependent on local conditions. If it is possible to accumulate a large amount of biomass, the plants may also use the factor of shade as part of their adaptation, shading other individuals.

The caatingas are a special type of vegetation (Fig. 7.20). They have a peculiar flora that is reflected in their different physiognomy. The number of species per unit area is generally less, but since the caatingas offer a great variety of different habitats from one location to the next, the sum total is an extremely rich flora that is very interesting and poorly known.

There are a certain genera of plants that are characteristic of caatingas: *Clusia*, *Tovomita*, certain genera of Ericaceae, *Lissocarpa*, *Byrsonima*, *Sipapoa*, *Pagamea*, *Retyniphyllum*, *Zamia*, *Barcella*, *Platycarpum*, *Henriquesia*, genera of Rapateaceae, Xyridaceae, Haemodoraceae, some characteristic species such as *Hevea rigidifolia*, *Compsoneura debilis*, *Hevea camporum*, and *Phyllanthus atabapoensis*. Some Amazonian caatingas do not have grasses or sedges, such as those of the Rio Uaupés, *see* Pires and Rodrigues (1964); Rodrigues (1961); Ferri (1960); Vieira *et al.* (1962). Some caatingas, such as those of the Rio Anauá, a tributary of the Rio Branco are rich in grasses and especially Cyperaceae. An important genus of Cyperaceae in this formation is *Lagenocarpus*.

Fig. 7.21. Lichens covering the ground of a white sand campina near Manaus.

The caatingas have a xeromorphic aspect, thick leaves, thick bark, and an abundance of lichens and mosses on the branches and on the soil surface. Sometimes the soil surface is covered with a spongy mat of *Cladonia* (Fig. 7.21). *Sphagnum* is less frequent.

The caatingas of the Rio Negro were the first to be described and have been much cited in the literature since the time of Spruce (1908), but caatinga exists in large or small patches scattered throughout all of Amazonia (Fig. 7.22). In each region they are slightly different, and tend to have different local names. In Roraima, the common name is chavascal, and there are arboreal chavascais and also shrubby and herbaceous ones. The Dutch authors who have worked in Suriname use the term White Sand savannahs, and for the arboreal caatinga, White Sand Savannah Forest.

7.10. VEGETATION COVERING SMALL SPECIALISED AREAS

There are some vegetation types that cover small areas, but are quite distinct. They are less important, but four types should be mentioned here. Mangrove forest, Restinga, *Mauritia* swamp (Buritizal) and Pirizal.

7.10.1. Mangrove forest

The mangroves occupy a small area of Amazonian Brazil in a narrow littoral belt that is subject to salt water inundation. It is a vegetation type poor in species number, and is quite uniform. The principal species, almost always present in Brazilian mangrove are *Rhizophora mangle* (mange, mangue verdadeiro,

Fig. 7.22. Campina forest with epiphyte laden trees near Manaus.

mangue vermelho), *Avicennia nitida* (siriuba, mangue branco), *Laguncularia racemosa*, *Conocarpus erecta*. Beside these species, a few others are occasionally encountered: *Pterocarpus officinalis*, *Hibiscus tiliaceus*, *Annona palustris*, and *Pithecelobium cochleatum*. In areas of extreme clay salt beaches, the small grass, *Spartina brasiliensis* (paraturá, capim estrepe) occurs. This can form carpets which bind the soil. The prostrate vegetation that covers certain areas of mud is generally called *apicum* (Huber, 1909).

Rhizophora mangle is quite variable as a species and some authors have described varieties. Lindeman and Mennega (1963) treat these varieties as three different species: *Rhizophora mangle*, *R. harrisonii* and *R. racemosa*. According to Huber (1909), variety *typica* is abundant in the Costa de Salgado, going up the rivers as far as 20 km from their mouths, whereas variety *racemosa* is much more local in the coast of Marajó Island and extending from there up to Guiana. The Siriuba, *Avicennia* or white mangrove, penetrates inland for a considerable distance up the zone of fresh water, high into the estuary, whereas the true mangrove (*Rhizophora*) only extends as far as the influence of salt water. Areas of mangroves are more common on the west part of the coast between Ilha Maracá and the Rio Oiapoque. In this part, the region is all muddy. There are no sandy beaches, such as occur further to the east. This is caused by the effect of the marine current which pushes the sediments to the west (Pires, 1964).

Because of the small area that is occupied, mangrove is not of great economical importance in Brazil. Up to 1945, thermo-electricity in São Luis in the state of Maranhão was generated from mangrove wood, but today, little use is made of the wood.

7.10.2. Pirizal

This is a form of vegetation that occurs in small restricted areas (Fig. 7.23). They are shallow lakes or puddles with stagnant water that is dark and transparent, with a large quantity of rooted plants with upper parts out of the water. The most frequent plants are *Cyperus giganteus* and *Thalia geniculata* as well

Fig. 7.23. A pirizal near Mazagão Velho, Amapá.

as floating aquatics or plants with floating leaves. For example, *Salvinia*, *Eichhornia*, *Sagittaria*, *Cabomba*, *Nymphaea*, *Limnanthemum*, *Eleocharis*, and other species of Cyperaceae. The mauritia palm may grow around the margins. These pirizais are common in Amapá, in an area along the coast, in the region of Mazagão and Mazagão Velho. They occur as enclaves in the midst of dense forest. In the grassy meadows in the Rio Uaçá, Caripi and Uracauá, at the mouth of the Rio Oiapoque, there are also enclaves in the grassland, which are called Cariazal. Cariá is the indigenous name for *Diplasia karataefolia* and other robust Cyperaceae. On the Island of Marajó, also in the Savannah, there are similar formations which are called Mondongo.

It is interesting to note that in these peculiar lakes, there is a small species of turtle known as Muçuã, which is much cherished as a food in regional dishes. When the waters recede, a large part of the area becomes dry. The local residents often set fire to the vegetation causing the turtles to flee and then they can be hunted in large quantities. Even though trade in turtles is currently prohibited, this predatory hunting continues, threatening the extinction of this species.

In Amapá, they are removing sand from the bottom of these lakes, which indicates the nature of the soil. These pirizais seem to be unique to the estuarine area of Amazonia.

7.10.3. Buritizal (*Mauritia* formation)

In various parts of the estuary, in low várzeas which are formed in the middle of the river, one finds dense, practically pure stands of *Mauritia flexuosa* (locally called buriti, Fig. 7.24). The rather large area covered by these stands, justifies separating this as a special type of várzea. There are other places in

Fig. 7.24. *Mauritia flexuosa*, the dominant palm of the Burutizal formation.

Amazonia where buriti is present, but the vegetation is quite different. For example, the buritizais of the Roraima savannahs discussed above form narrow corridors within the savannahs and should be classified differently (*see* the section on the Roraima savannahs).

7.10.4. Restinga (coastal sand dune)

Restinga is the vegetation that develops in sand dunes. It has a xeromorphic aspect and resembles the physiognomy of the Amazonian caatingas.

In Amazonia, the restingas are of minor importance with few species, but in Bahia there are restingas that extend over large areas and are very interesting, having a rich flora with endemics. They have as yet been poorly studied. A good example is the restinga of Maraú.

From Amazonia to Rio de Janeiro, the restingas are morphologically very similar. Common species are *Chrysobalanus icaco*, *Hisbiscus tiliaceus*, *Byrsonima crassifolia*, *Ipomoea pes-caprae*, *I. asarifolia*, and *Manilkara triflora*.

REFERENCES

Beard, J. S.(1946) *The natural vegetation of Trinidad*. Oxford Forestry. Mem. 20.
Black, G. A. (1950) Os capins aquáticos da Amazônia. *Bol.Tecn.IAN* (Belém) 19, 53 – 94.
Braun, E. H. and Ramos, J. R. A. (1959) Estudo agroecológico dos campos Puciari-Humaitá. *Rev. Bras. Geogr. (Rio de Janeiro)* 21(4), 443 – 497.

Cabrera, A. L. and Willink, A. (1973) Biogeografia da América Latina. *OEA, Série Biologia, Monogr.* 13, 1 – 120.

Cruls, G. (1950) *A Amazónia que eu vi.* Rio de Janeiro (s. ed.) 362 pages.

Ducke, A. and Black, G. A. (1954) Notas sobre a fitogeografia da Amazônia Brasileira. *Bol. Tecn. IAN (Belém)* 29, 1 – 62.

Egler, W. A. (1960) Os campos de Ariramba. *Bol. Mus. Par. Emílio Goeldi (Belém)* 4, 1 – 40.

Eiten, G. (1982) Brazilian 'Savannas'. In *Ecology of Tropical Savannas*. Eds. H. B. Huntley and B. H. Walker, pp. 25 – 47. Springer-Verlag.

Falesi, I. C. (1972) Os solos da rodovia Transamazônica. *Bol. Tecn. IPEAN (Belém)* 55, 1 – 196.

Ferri, M. G. (1960) Contribution to the knowledge of the ecology of the Rio Negro caatinga (Amazon). *Bull. Research Council of Israel (Jerusalem)* 80(3 – 4), 171 – 350.

Gourou, P. (1950) Observações geográficas na Amazônia. *Rev. Bras. Geogr.* 12(2), 171 – 350.

Huber, J. (1909) Matas e madeiras amazônicas. *Bol. Mus. Par. Emílio Goeldi (Belém)* 6, 91 – 225.

Huber, O. (1982) Significance of savanna vegetation in the Amazon territory of Venezuela. In *Biological Diversification in the Tropics*. Ed. G. T. Prance, pp. 221 – 224. Columbia University Press, New York.

Hueck, K. (1972) *As florestas da América do sul.* Editora Univ. Brasília, 466 pages translated by Hans Reichardt.

Krukoff, B. A. (1942) The American species of *Strychnos. Brittonia* 4, 248 – 322.

Lindeman, J. C. and Mennega, A. M. W. (1963) *Bomenbock voor Suriname.* Mededel. Bot. Mus. Herb. Rijksuniv., Utrecht 200.

Livingstone, D. A. and Hammen, T. van der (1978) Palaeogeography and palaeoclimatology. In *Tropical Forest Ecosystems*. Ed. UNESCO/UNEP/FAO, Nat. Resources Research (Paris) 15, 61 – 90.

Maguire, B. (1976) Apomixis in the genus *Clusia* (Clusiaceae) a preliminary report. *Taxon* 25(2 – 3), 241 – 244.

McGill University (1966) Savanna Research Project. *Technical Report 5.*

Moura, P. (1943) O relevo da Amazônia. *Rev. Bras. Geogr. (Rio de Janeiro)* 5(3), 3 – 38.

Pires, J. M. (1964) Exploração no Território de Amapá (Rio Oiapoque). *Anais 13° Congr. Soc. Bot. Brasil (Recife 1962)*, 164 – 199.

Pires, J. M. and Dobzhansky, T. (1954) Strangler trees. *Sci. American* 190(1), 78 – 80.

Pires, J. M. and Rodrigues, J. S. (1964) Sobre a flora das caatingas do rio Negro. In *Anais 13° Congr. Soc. Bot. Brasil (Recife 1962)*, 242 – 262.

Prance, G. T. (1979) Notes on the vegetation of Amazonia III. The terminology of Amazon forest types subject to inundation. *Brittonia* 31, 26 – 38.

Ratter, J. H., Argent, G. A. and Gifford, D. R. (1973) The woody vegetation types of the Xavantina – Cachimbo expedition area. *Phil. Trans. Roy. Soc. Lond., Biological Science* 266(866), 449 – 492.

Richards, P. W. (1966) *The Tropical Rain Forest*. Cambridge University Press.

Rodrigues, W. A. (1961) Aspects phytosociologiques des pseudo-caatingas et forêts de varzea du rio Negro. In *Etude ecologique des principales formations végétables du Brésil*. Ed. A. Aubréville, pp. 109 – 265. Nogent-sur-Marne.

Sampaio, A. J. (1933) A flora do rio Cuminá. *Arch. Mus. Nac. Rio de Janeiro* 35, 9 – 206.

Secco, R. S. and Mesquita, A. L. (1983) Notas sobre a vegetação de Canga da Serra Norte-I. *Bol. Mus. Par. Emílio Goeldi* 59, 1 – 13.

Sioli, H. (1951) Alguns resultados e problemas da limnologia amazônica. *Bol. Tecn. IAN (Belém)* 24, 3 – 4.

Soares, L. C. (1948) Delimitação da Amazônia para fins de planejamento econômico. *Rev. Bras. Geogr. (Rio de Janeiro)* 10(2), 163 – 210.

Spruce, R. (1908) *Notes of a Botanist on the Amazon and Andes*, 2 vols. Ed. A. R. Wallace, Macmillan, London.

Vieira, L. S. and Oliveira Filho, P. S. (1962) As caatingas de Rio Negro. *Bol. Tecn. IAN (Belém)* 42, 7 – 32.

Wijmstra, T. A. and Hammen, T. van der (1966) Palynological data on the history of tropical savannas in northern South America. *Leidse Geol. Meded.* 38, 71 – 90.

CHAPTER 8

The Changing Forests

GHILLEAN T. PRANCE

The New York Botanical Garden, New York, U.S.A.

CONTENTS

8.1. INTRODUCTION

Many books and papers about Amazonia comment that the rainforest is so diverse because it has been stable for many millions of years, and that this is the main reason for its amazing species diversity (e.g. Federov, 1966; Richards, 1969). The previous two chapters on geology, paleoclimate and palynology in Amazonia, show that this presumed stability is a fallacy, and that there have been many changes in climate and consequently in the vegetation cover, especially during the Pleistocene and early Holocene epochs. These changes have profoundly affected the evolution and biology of the plants and animals of the region. Because these changes in the forest cover have at times led to a reduced amount of forest surrounded by other vegetation types, they create refugia or isolated patches of the original forest. This has led to much debate about the refuge theory which discusses the biological role of these refugia.

At the time, in the Pleistocene, when the temperate region was undergoing a series of ice-ages or glaciations, the world climate was fluctuating between wet and dry periods. In the colder regions of both hemispheres and in tropical mountains the cool periods led to vast glaciations. Since much water was tied up as ice, there were also considerable changes in the worldwide sea levels (*see* Donn *et al.*, 1962; Fairbridge, 1962; and Batchelor, 1979 for reviews of sea level changes). The profound effect of these worldwide climate fluctuations on the tropical regions has only recently been realised. In the Amazon region the climate was cooler and drier during the glacial periods and warmer and more humid during the interglacial phases. This changing cycle of cool and warm periods led to changes in the vegetation cover since the tropical rainforest was able to persist intact only in certain places where local climate variations maintained a warm humid climate suitable for forest. These refugia were due largely to the local topography where conditions encouraged greater rainfall. The intervening drier areas were filled by savannah, caatinga and species of poor transition forest rather than true rainforest. At least three major dry periods occurred during the Pleistocene and so there was a constant change in the forest cover. This means that fluctuations of the forest have been more important than stability as an evolutionary influence.

8.2. THE EFFECT OF REFUGIA

The reductions of the rainforest into small patches or refugia had a profound effect on the biology of the region. When the forest that covered most of Amazonia was reduced to isolated refugia, one of three things can happen to the organisms that inhabit the region. They can become extinct because of the changes, they can survive without any evolutionary changes or they can begin to differentiate in the different refugia. Local conditions could differ between the refugia, and adaptive selection would begin to cause differences between the two populations isolated in different refugia. This diversification would continue until the forest coalesced and the refugia were again united. In some cases the separation of refugia caused minor differentiation of subspecies of common organisms, but in others the separation was long enough for two reproductively isolated populations to evolve and consequently the establishment of two closely related but distinct species. This is one of the reasons why there are often two or more closely related species of the same genus growing side by side in the same habitat in Amazonia. The establishment of refugia would increase the species diversity of the forest if more new species evolved through isolation than became extinct by the loss of forest area. Refuge theory and its effect on various groups of organisms has been discussed by many biologists and we will look at a few of these studies after we have reviewed briefly some of the physical evidence for climate changes in the Amazon region.

8.3. THE EVIDENCES FOR PLEISTOCENE CLIMATE CHANGES IN AMAZONIA

8.3.1. Pollen

One of the best evidences for fluctuations between forest and savannah is the study of fossil pollen. This has been reviewed elsewhere in this volume by Absy (Chapter 4) and in the many papers of Van der Hammen and associates (e.g. 1972, 1974, 1982) and so there is no need to discuss it further here. However, there is increasing evidence from pollen that areas which are now covered by forest were formerly occupied by savannah and dated sequences have been worked out especially around the periphery of Amazonia.

8.3.2. Geomorphology

The Brazilian geomorphologist Aziz Ab'Sáber has provided much evidence for climate fluctuations in the Pleistocene (Ab'Sáber, 1977, 1982). His evidence is based on the occurrence of the stone lines in different areas now forest covered, especially in the interfluvial areas of the margins of Amazonia; that the way in which the slopes are dissected could only have happened through fluctuations of changing climates; that the strata laid down in alluvial forms and terraces in the process of transformation into pediments occurs in significant locations in the low tablelands and plateaus; that fluvial gravel occurs in elevated locations and gravel terraces in lower topographic levels; from the study of the geomorphic features associated with deposits of laterite and limonite; and from the occurrence of patches of white sand on divides between river valleys, fossil stream channels, river terraces, sand backswamps and former riverbeds. In summary, from the morphology of the landscape, Ab'Sáber, and others (e.g. Barbosa, 1958 and Cole, 1960) conclude that many climate changes have taken place over the last million years. Garner (1959) also observed that the characteristic landforms along some of the Andean slopes were the result of climate fluctuation. He also concluded that the landscape of the Río Caroni region of Amazonian Venezuela was caused by the alternating climate phases.

Mousinho (1971), working near to Manaus in the centre of Brazilian Amazonia, found variations in the sediments from the upper Pleistocene and Holocene that correlated well with the temperate glacial and interglacial periods. Bakker (1970) also studied terracing and terrace deposits in Suriname and found evidence of dry climate in what are now forest areas. There is therefore a growing body of geomorphological evidence to back up both the climate and vegetation changes. Many of the geomorphologic effects are the result of the changes to other vegetation types that do not protect the landscape in the way that the forest does. A summary of Ab'Sáber's interpretation of the Amazonian vegetation 18,000 years ago is given in Fig. 8.1. The chapter by Bigarella and Ferreira in this volume, gives considerable details of the geological and paleoclimatic history which led to the Amazonian climate changes.

8.3.3. Marine studies

Damuth and Fairbridge (1970) studied marine sediments and concluded that the large deposits of arkosic sands off northeastern South America in the Guiana Basin originated from an arid period during the last part of the Wisconsin — Würm glaciation. Twenty-three cores were examined and showed that cores of the latest Wisconsin glaciation contained 25 — 60% feldspar while a sample of the Holocene sand at the mouth of the Amazon contained only 17 — 20% feldspar. The arid climate periods together with a eustatic drop in sea level caused the degradation of the principal river valleys near the coast. At the time unweathered feldspars, chlorite and other relatively coarse clastics were transported into the ocean instead of the usual lateritic clays of gibbsite and kaolinite, characteristic of the interglacial periods.

From a study of fossil Foraminifera, Emiliani (1970) also demonstrated Pleistocene climate changes which affected sea temperatures and consequently the distribution of various species of the minute Protozoan animals. A graph of paleotemperatures was produced based on oxygen isotopic analysis of the Foraminifera from deep-sea cores and demonstrated the many temperature fluctuations over the last 175,000 years corresponding to climate changes.

There are many well established lines of data to demonstrate that the climate changes took place in South America during the Pleistocene and early Holocene, and that the fluctuations correspond closely

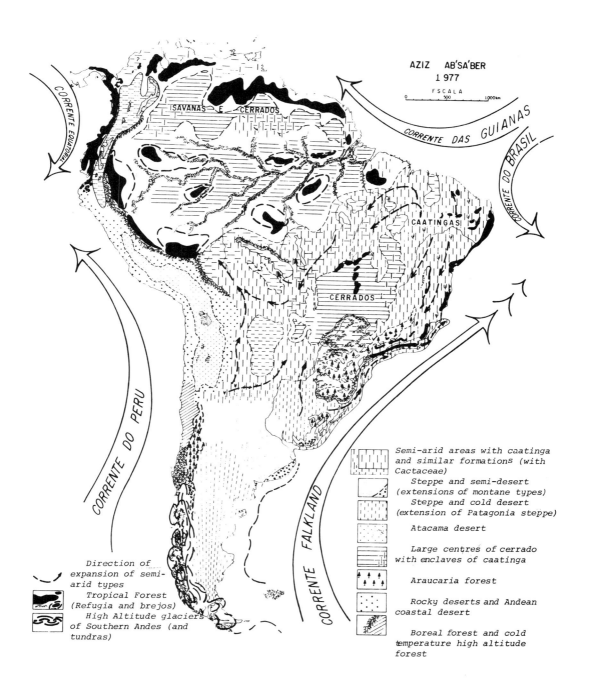

Fig. 8.1. The Amazon vegetation of 18,000 years ago according to geomorphologist Ab'Sáber (1977).

in time with the temperate glacial and interglacial periods. Since Chapters 3 and 4 have given full details of geological, paleoclimatic and palynological evidences for the formation of refugia, it is the purpose of this chapter to concentrate more on the biological evidence and the biological effect of this situation.

8.4. BIOLOGICAL EVIDENCE FROM LIVING ORGANISMS

Many different biologists have now commented on the Pleistocene climate changes and its effect on the particular group of organisms which they study. A few of the most important examples that refer directly to Amazonia will be given below. Many papers about the biological effect of climate and the occurrence of refugia have been published with examples from Mexico to Argentina, as well as extensive similar work on African organisms (e.g. Grubb, 1982; Moreau, 1963).

8.4.1. Birds

The example from birds must come first because it was the first group to be studied in both Africa (Moreau, 1963) and South America (Haffer, 1969). The latter was the first biological paper to apply refuge theory in detail to any group of Amazonian organisms. He studied the speciation patterns of the toucans (Rhamphastidae), and as a result of distribution patterns and the locations of hybrid zones between subspecies he produced the first map of the location of the postulated refugia (Fig. 8.2). This map indicated the areas where, on the basis of the evidence from toucans, it was most probable that the forest had remained intact.

The evidences which Haffer (1969, 1974) used were threefold: 1. current rainfall patterns; 2. current distribution patterns of Amazonian birds; and 3. the location of secondary contact zones between species that had differentiated.

There is much variation in rainfall over the Amazon Basin (*see* Fig. 8.3), and especially noticeable is a drier more seasonal belt that goes from the Llanos in Colombia through Venezuela, Roraima Territory Brazil, the Tapajós River region of Brazil to the south. Haffer postulated that refugia are more likely to be located in the areas of higher present-day rainfall with a less seasonal climate, where rainfall remained higher and enough to permit continued forest cover throughout the Pleistocene dry periods.

The current bird distribution patterns show various centres of distribution that coincide with the climate data such as the upper Amazon from the Andes to the Rio Negro, part of the Guianas, and the Rio Tapajós region eastwards. Haffer worked out the location of these distribution centres using information from various bird superspecies that form assemblages of allopatric species. For example, Fig. 8.4 shows the distribution of the toucanet superspecies, *Selenidera maculirostris*. The separation of the different allopatric elements is obvious. By putting together a larger number of similar distributions many of which closely coincide, Haffer was able to define the distribution centres.

With the return of a humid climate, the expanding forest from two neighbouring refugia would eventually come together and lead to renewed contact between the plants and animals from each refugium. These areas of secondary contact between the forest refugia, can be located for birds by the occurrence of hybrids, and by the mutual exclusion of ecologically incompatible species which were no longer able to interbreed. Based on his large sample of bird species, Haffer was able to define the nine refugia that are given in Fig. 8.3.

8.4.2. Lizards

Vanzolini (1970) and Vanzolini and Williams (1970) studied the geographic variation of the *Anolis chrysolepis* complex of anoline lizards. This group of four South American species was analysed numerically for the regional variation of various characters (16 quantitative and 2 qualitative characters).

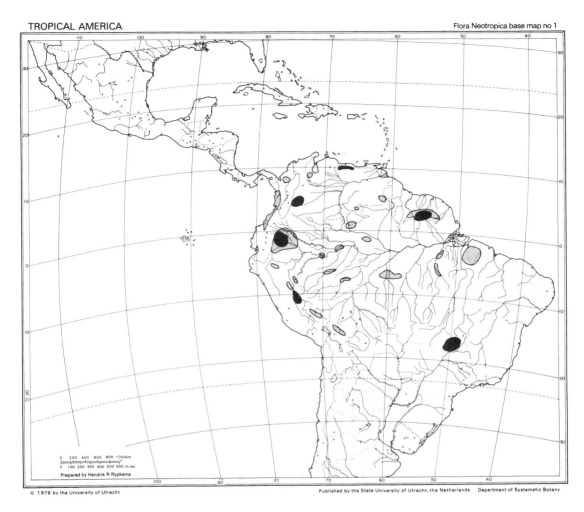

Fig. 8.2. The proposed forest refugia of Haffer (1969) based on data from toucans (lighter areas), and of Vanzolini (1970) based on lizards.

Over some areas they found gradual and clinal changes, but in others they found no character variation, but in both types of areas certain character complexes consistently occurred together. In some places the character complexes broke down and the individual characters exhibited a large amount of variation. They concluded that the areas where there was little variation in characters indicated areas where populations had remained stable for long periods of time, and in contrast, areas of high variation were where formerly separated forms came together with the coalescence of forest to form contact zones. The area of stable characters were their refugia. All six areas which they proposed were upland refugia around the fringes of the Amazon Basin (*see* Fig. 8.2). Vanzolini and Williams' refugia are the least in number and the most drastic reduction of the Amazon forest proposed by any author. All later authors have tended to increase rather than reduce the area and number of forest refugia proposed by Haffer. However, those of Vanzolini and Williams do correspond with refuge areas of most other authors.

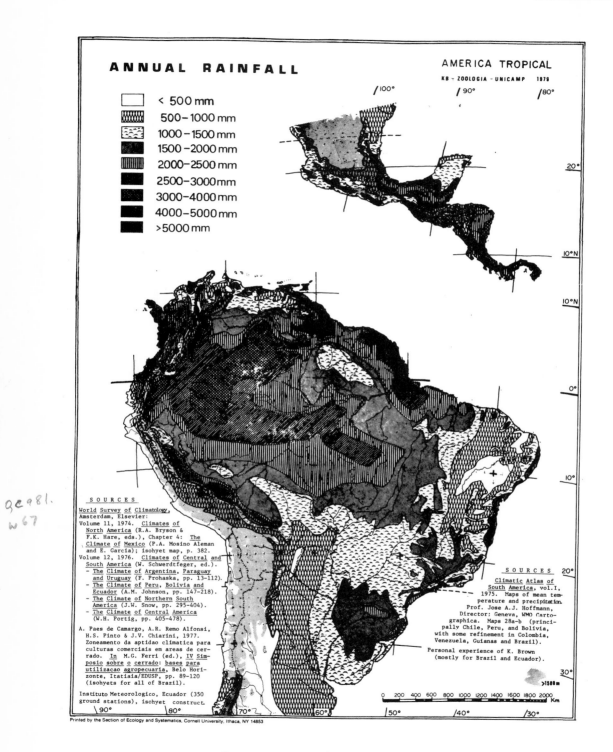

Fig. 8.3. Amazonian rainfall (from Brown, 1979).

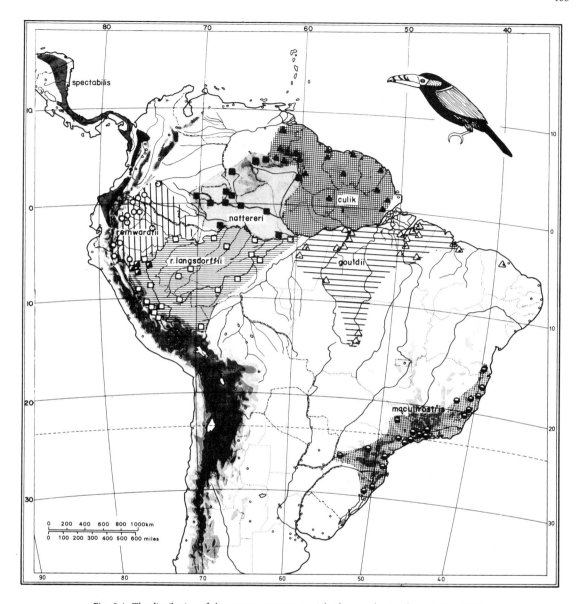

Fig. 8.4. The distribution of the toucanet superspecies *Selenidera maculirostris* (from Haffer, 1974).

8.4.3. Butterflies

By far the most extensive study of forest refugia has been that of Keith Brown based on his work on Heliconiini or passion flower butterflies (Brown *et al.*, 1974; Brown 1976a, 1976b, 1977, 1979, 1982). He studied the regional patterns of differentiation of wing-colour patterns in two groups of Nymphalidae, the Heliconiini and Ithomiinae (Fig. 8.5). In many ways these organisms are an ideal study model because of the large quantity of information available about them and their preference for

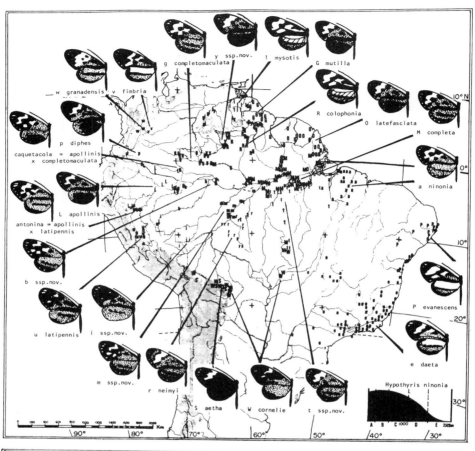

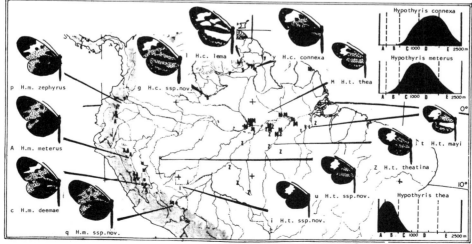

Fig. 8.5. Wing pattern and geographical distribution of species of butterflies (from Brown, 1979).

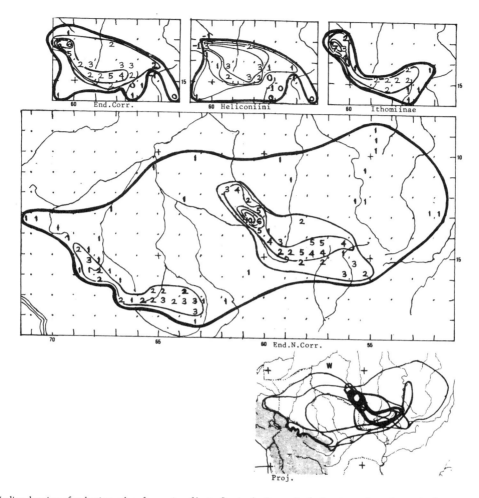

Fig. 8.6. Isoline drawing of endemism values for species of butterflies in the Guaporé refugium in southern Amazonia (from Brown, 1979).

restricted areas of rainforest, and their short generation span. Brown made a biogeographical analysis of 123 species, superimposed their differentiation patterns, and prepared isoline maps of the endemism (*see* Fig. 8.6 as examples). This led to the recognition of 44 centres of endemism in tropical America. Each of these centres is characterised by the presence of a number of associated subspecies (10 for 41 centres and more than 5 in the other three more isolated areas). The isoline diagrams are drawn from corrected endemism values, determined from the subspecies present in each grid square. Figure 8.6 is an example of an isoline drawing based on the species of the Guaporé refuge and vicinity in southern Amazonia.

Brown also correlated his data closely with data from present-day rainfall maps, satellite cloud cover maps, seasonal variation throughout the region, vegetation and soil types and geomorphological evidence (Brown and Ab'Sáber, 1979). The 44 centres of endemism that were most likely to have remained stable during the Pleistocene dry periods are given in Fig. 8.7. Brown's work covered the area from Mexico to Southern Brazil which in part accounts for the greater number of centres, but he divided the Amazonian region more finely than Haffer. This is to be expected using such different organisms with a much shorter generation time than birds. It is interesting to see the close

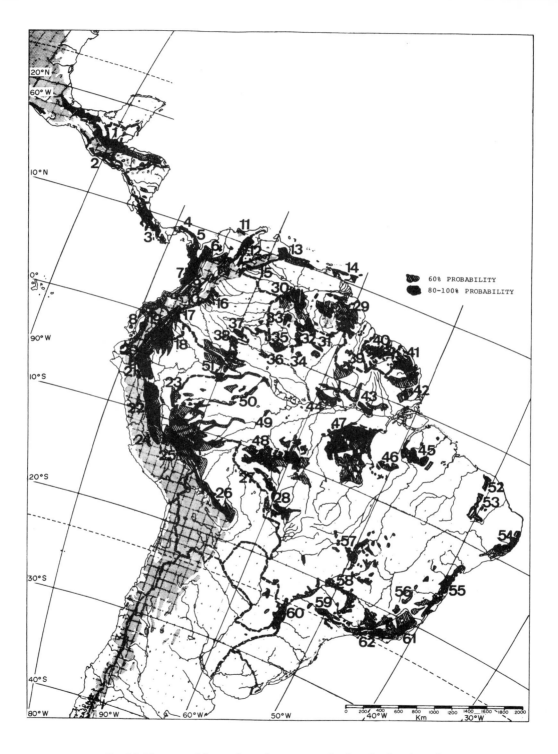

Fig. 8.7. The proposed forest refugia of Brown (1979) based on data from butterflies.

correspondence between the areas of Haffer and Brown. Brown's work is really a refinement of the Haffer system.

Other authors have presented evidence for forest refugia based on insects, some also on the Nymphalidae butterflies (e.g. Turner, 1977).

8.4.4. Plants

Prance (1973, 1982) studied the distribution of woody predominantly rainforest plant families, Caryocaraceae, Chrysobalanaceae, Dichapetalaceae, and Lecythidaceae and presented maps of lowland endemism centres of tropical South America based on the distribution of over 500 species (Fig. 8.8). The 26 centres include 14 in Amazonia, 8 in Colombia and Venezuela and 4 in eastern Brazil.

The botanical evidences for refugia, as is the case in zoology, are based primarily on the study of current distribution patterns of rainforest species, but there are also a number of other interesting correlations with the expanding and contracting forest that are discussed below. The analysis of distribution patterns of Amazonian woody species studied by Prance (1973, 1982) showed a number of clusters of rainforest endemics similar to those found in the Heliconiini butterflies, and many of these areas coincided with the refugia of Haffer. In addition refugia were proposed at Paria and Imataca in Eastern Venezuela, Olivença and Tefé in the western part of Brazilian Amazonia, and north of Manaus in Central Amazonia (see Fig. 8.8).

One of the most important evidences for refugia from botanical studies is that of the number of disjunct distributions of rainforest species that occur between different parts of Amazonia and other rainforest regions of South America. A few examples of common disjunct patterns are given in Fig. 8.9. It is hard to explain the gap in the distribution of *Mouriri oligantha* Pilg. (Fig. 8.9) without changes in the forest cover. The species that have a disjunct distribution are examples where differentiation did not take place when they were isolated in refugia. Other pairs of closely related species that occur in different centres are examples where differentiation occurred.

Other botanists have used evidence from savannah species to draw conclusions about the spread of savannah during the drier periods. For example, Sastre (1976) made a study of open vegetation areas in the Guianas in savannahs and mountain tops. He discussed species isolated on mountain top savannahs which are often divided into separate populations separated by 300 km or more of forest. Although long distance dispersal by birds answers some of this disjunct distribution, many were caused by the spread of savannah in the dry periods. He also found that the Guiana mountains are a centre of species differentiation for species of open habitats because of their subsequent isolation as small islands of vegetation where differentiation between islands took place.

De Granville (1982) also discussed remnants of an arid flora of French Guiana in today's humid climate. The arid vegetation is now separated into discrete isolated sites acting as refugia for the arid species. The arid vegetation type of the coastal savannahs is of limited use for refuge study because it was flooded as recently as 6,000 years B.P. However, the rock outcrops (inselbergs) and emergent rocks in rivers are much older refugia for arid region species. De Granville provided further data about the vegetation outcrops of the Tumac—Humac region studied by Sastre (1976) and Descamps *et al.* (1978). Some of the arid adapted species are equally saxicolous, savannicolous and of the coastal savannahs, e.g. *Borreria latifolia* (Aubl.) K. Schum., *Stylosanthes hispida* Rich. and *Xyris fallax* Malme. Other species are confined to one of these arid vegetation types.

Descamps *et al.* (1978) in part of the same study as Sastre (1976) worked on the plants and animals of savannahs and rock outcrops of French Guiana. They divided the Guianas into three biogeographic subregions based on the distributions of various forest species. They concluded that speciation of forest

SOUTH AMERICA

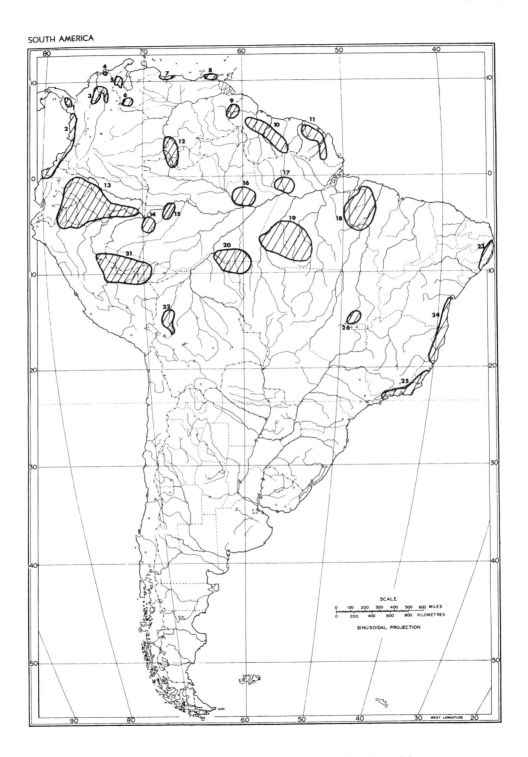

Fig. 8.8. The proposed forest refugia of Prance (1982) based on botanical data.

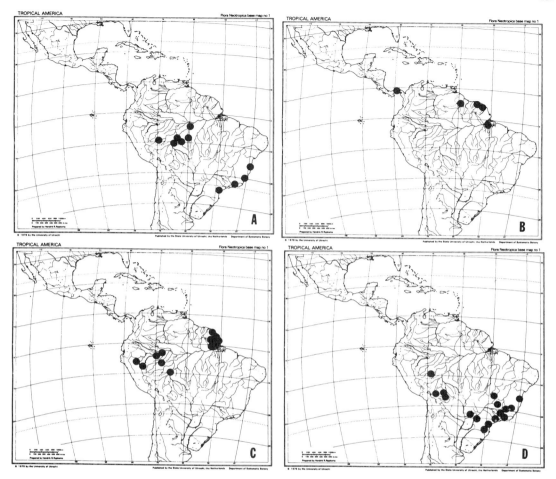

Fig. 8.9. Example of disjunct distribution of rainforest plant species. A, *Couratari macrosperma* A.C. Smith; B, *Licania affinis* Fritsch; C, *Mouriri oligantha* Pilg.; D, *Cariniana estrellensis* (Raddi) Kuntze.

species in the Guianas took place in more than one centre and that during the times of dry climate the Guianas were broken up into at least three refugia rather than the single one proposed by Haffer (1969) and Prance (1973). They suggested that the easternmost refugium is located north of the Tumac — Humac mountains between Tampoc and Camopi rivers around Saül and between the Comté and the Appronaque. This is farther northwest of the Oiapoque refugium of Brown (1976).

Both Simpson (1972) and Toledo (1976, 1982) studied the distribution of xerophytic elements in tropical rainforest areas. That is plants now belonging to the rainforest that still retain some adaptations that are characteristic of plants of drier regions such as thick scleromorphic leaves. They consider these as evidences of former dry periods since the xeromorphic leaves evolved in a drier xerophytic climate.

Evidence from the periphery of Amazonia is also important to demonstrate the regional climate changes. Simpson (1975) presented botanical evidences for Pleistocene climate changes in the high tropical Andean region. She described the changes of the flora at altitudes of over 3000 m in the páramo of the northern Andes, the puna of the Altiplano, the upper Andean forests and the dry desert scrub of the high intermontane valleys. Since most of these habitats have become available primarily in the

Quaternary or only the late Tertiary after the uplift of the Andes, they are intimately connected with the vegetation of the lowlands. Simpson found an altitudinal and latitudinal variation in the way plant species moved into the Andean habitats, the manner of differentiation during the Pleistocene, and the time of immigration into their habitat. Speciation appears to have taken place mainly through geographic isolation caused by the various changes in vegetation distribution during the Pleistocene and Holocene. With the exception of the Altiplano most species expanded their ranges when lowering of the high altitude habitats occurred during the Pleistocene cool periods. For example, in the northern páramos the greatest colonisation was during the glacial periods in a manner similar to Oceanic islands. At the lower elevation in the northern Andes of the eastern cordillera direct migration was possible. The interglacial periods, which occurred several times, were times of isolation and differentiation. In contrast, in the Altiplano the glacial periods were times of population fragmentation accompanied by differentiation and/or speciation.

Simpson distinguished two elements in the Páramo flora: (1) species groups which are not closely related to lowland groups, and (2) species groups which are closely related to lowland groups. It is the latter that are of interest for the study of the history of the lowland Amazon flora. An analysis of the high Andean flora shows that it was colonised in a way analagous to oceanic islands because there are significant correlations between areas of páramo and their distances from source areas and the number of plant taxa which now inhabit them. There is an even stronger correlation with glacial period parameters and páramo size which suggests that the majority of colonisation occurred in glacial periods when plant propagules were able to disperse more easily because of increased size of the páramos.

These highland Andean data together with much palynological work have proved undisputably that there were considerable changes in the highland South American flora during the glacial periods. The changes in páramo in the extreme highlands meant changes in cloud forest and mountain slope forest at lower altitudes. The importance of the slope forest as a possible migration route for plant species must be considered in a discussion of the lowland forest. The details of the lowland flora have not worked out so thoroughly as those of the highlands. An interesting part of the highland work is the comparison with and use of some of the concepts of island biogeography which are an integral part of the refuge theory.

Another most interesting study was that of Andrade-Lima (1982) who investigated the little known present-day forest refugia of the periodically arid northeastern region of Brazil. Most of the area is covered by the xeric caatinga vegetation. However, forest has persisted on some hills which attract cloud moisture and therefore also have a cooler climate than the surrounding caatinga. These forest patches on hills, termed *brejos* in Brazil, are in a refuge situation. Andrade-Lima listed over twenty such brejos which can extend to as low as 500 m (Fig. 8.10). The species composition of the *brejos* with many Amazonian forest species indicates that they are forest remnants rather than forest formed from easily dispersed colonisers. Such Amazon species as *Manilkara rufula* Mig., *Apeiba tibourbou* Aubl., *Orbignya martiana* B. Rodr., *Parkia platycephala* Benth. and *Virola surinamensis* (Rol.) Warb. are typical of the *brejos*. The *brejos* also contain some forest species of the southern forests of Brazil indicating that they are a most interesting relict with a mixture of isolated species. Southern elements include such species as *Caesalpinia peltophoroides* Benth., *Phyllostyllon brasiliensis* Capanema and *Myrocarpus fastigiatus* Fr. All. Another species of *Myrocarpus* was mentioned by Steyermark (1982) as a species which has become isolated in the northern coastal cordillera refugia of Venezuela.

Andrade-Lima also mentioned the reverse phenomenon of northeastern arid species which are markedly disjunct having now become isolated by extensive forest or cerrados between their populations. Such species include *Anadenanthera macrocarpa* (Benth.) Brenan, *Amburana cearensis* (Fr. All.) A.C. Smith, *Prosopis ruscifolia* Griseb. and *Schinopsis brasiliensis* Engl.

Studies of northeastern Brazil with its arid caatinga vegetation and of the savannah areas such as the cerrado of Central Brazil give us some idea of the possible landscape in parts of Amazonia. In most

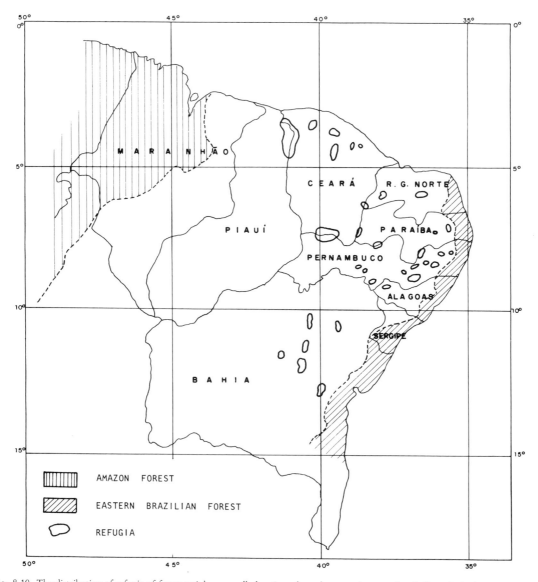

Fig. 8.10. The distribution of refugia of forest mainly on small elevations throughout northeastern Brazil (from Andrade-Lima, 1982).

contemporary savannah areas there are islands of forest, transition forests on the boundaries with rainforest areas and most important of all gallery forests along the rivers. Gallery forests tend to be flooded less than the seasonally flooded forests of lowland Amazonia. They are flash flooded from time to time and dry out even in the rainy season. This enables some upland Amazon species to survive in the gallery regions. This means that gallery forests and forest islands were most important in the Pleistocene and that not every species was confined to the small pure rainforest refugia. The distribution of *Cariniana estrellensis* (Raddi) Kuntze (Fig. 8.9D) shows a forest species that persists today in the Central Brazilian cerrado region in the gallery forests. The importance of gallery forests as refugia was emphasised in Prance (1982).

Fig. 8.11. Data used by Wetterberg on endemism centres to make a conservation plan. The shaded areas are areas where the refugia of two or more authors coincide. The lines divide Amazonia into various phytogeographic regions following Prance (1977).

The above review shows that there is now a lot of direct palynological, geomorphological, and indirect biological evidence for the fluctuation of the Amazonian forest, rather than its continuous stability. The effect of this changing forest cover has varied considerably from one group of organisms to another, but it has tended to increase the diversity of the forest rather than decrease it. There are many reasons for the diversity of the Amazon forest, such as the defence it gives from predators (*see* Janzen, Chapter 11 this volume), and refuge theory, another cause of diversity. There tends to have been more differentiation in refugia in organisms with a relatively short life-cycle and rapid generation time such as insects and birds. In contrast, generation time in trees is long and there was comparatively little time between the dry periods for diversification to occur. That is why there is so much evidence of differentiation, hybrid contact zones and the effect of refugia in insects and birds.

8.5. THE PRACTICAL SIDE: CONSERVATION

The refuge theory has been useful to explain one of the methods of species evolution in Amazonia. It is also of great practical interest to people studying conservation. In Brazil, Wetterberg *et al.* (1976) did an analysis of the areas of endemism pinpointed as refugia by Haffer (1969), Vanzolini (1970), Prance (1973) and Brown (1976). The centres of endemism of each author were superimposed on a map and also compared with the phytogeographic subdivisions of Amazonia of Prance (1977). The areas where the centres of endemism of more than one author coincided (Fig. 8.11) were pinpointed as priority areas for conservation and then a policy statement for the planning of national parks was produced based on this analysis and taking care that adequate areas existed in each phytogeographic region. This report recommended that each phytogeographic region should contain an average of six protected areas to be adequately conserved. Other considerations, such as the minimum size (*see* Lovejoy, 1982) and shape of reserves was also reviewed in Wetterberg's analysis, and the result was a recommendation for 30 conservation units in Amazonia. Subsequently this report was widely circulated in government and private circles and the Brazilian part was incorporated in the country's 'National System Plan for Conservation Units' approved by President João Figueiredo on June 5, 1979. After field studies and the involvement of many Brazilian conservation agencies, by mid 1981 Amazonian national parks and biological reserves of more than 8 million hectares had been set aside. Most of these areas coincide with areas recommended in the analysis based on refugia. While there is still a lot to do to have adequate protection of the Amazon biome, this is an encouraging start, and it is good that the conservation planning has been based on scientific data. A full report of this process in Brazil is given in Wetterberg *et al.* (1981).

The refuge theory has been and will continue to be useful for conservation planning, but it is only a part of the evidence needed for conservation. It is based on changes in the primary rainforest cover, and the designation of reserves based on refugia is likely to pick out some of the most important areas of that forest type. However, as we see in Pires' chapter (Chapter 7, this volume) the Amazon has many different types of vegetation. It is therefore also most important to produce conservation policies that cover all habitats. In addition there is a danger that planners will think that the forest can safely be reduced to areas the size of the postulated refugia. However, the serious modification of climate precipitated by removal of forest (*see* Salati, Chapter 2 this volume) also indicate that this would be highly dangerous. Refugia have already been an important part of conservation planning, but are not the only answer.

REFERENCES

Ab'Sáber, A. N. (1977) Espacos ocupados pela expansão dos climas secos na América do Sul, por ocasião dos períodes glaciais quaternarios. *Paleoclimas* Univ. São Paulo, Inst. de Geografia 3, 1 – 19.

Ab'Sáber, A. N. (1982) The paleoclimate and paleoecology of Brazilian Amazonia. In *Biological Diversification in the Tropics*, Ed. G. T. Prance, pp. 41 – 59. Columbia University Press, New York.

Andrade-Lima, D. (1982) Present day forest refugia in Northeastern Brazil. In *Biological Diversification in the Tropics*, Ed. G. T. Prance, pp. 245 – 254. Columbia University Press, New York.

Bakker, J. P. (1970) Differential tectonic movements and climatic changes in the mountain area of Surinam (Guyana) during the Quaternary period. *Acta Geogr. Lodziensia* 24, 43 – 60.

Barbosa, O. (1958) Geomorfologia do Território do Rio Branco. *Resumo de conferência Notícia Geomorfológica (Campinas)* 1, 16 – 18.

Batchelor, B. C. (1979) Discontinuously rising late caimozoic eustatic sea levels with special reference to Sundaland, Southeast Asia. *Geologie em Mijnbouw* 58, 1 – 20.

Brown, Jr., K. S. (1976a) Geographical patterns of evolution in Neotropical Lepidoptera. Systematics and derivation of known and new Heliconiini (Nymphalidae: Nymphalinae). *J. Ent. B.* 44, 201 – 242.

Brown, Jr., K. S. (1976b) Geographical patterns of evolution in Neotropical forest Lepidoptera (Nymphalidae: Ithomiinae and Nymphalinae-Heliconiini). Ed. H. Descimon. Biogéographie et Evolution en Amerique tropicale. *Publ. Lab. Zool. Ecole Normale Sup.* 9, 118 – 160.

Brown, Jr., K. S. (1977) Centros de evolução, refúgios quaternários e conservação de patrimônios genéticos na região neotropical: padrões de diferenciação em Ithomiinae (Lepidoptera-Nymphalidae). *Acta Amazônica* 7, 75-137.

Brown, Jr., K. S. (1979) Ecologia geográfica e evolução nas florestas Neotropicais. Thesis. Univ. Estadual de Campinas, São Paulo, 265 pp.

Brown, Jr., K. S. (1982) Paleoecology and regional patterns of evolution in Neotropical forest butterflies. In *Biological Diversification in the Tropics*, Ed. G. T. Prance, pp. 255 – 308, Columbia University Press, New York.

Brown, Jr., K. S. and A. N. Ab'Sáber (1979) Ice age forest refuges and evolution in the neotropics: correlation of paleoclimatological, geomorphological and pedilogical data with modern biological endemism. *Paleoclimas (São Paulo)* 5, 1 – 30.

Brown, Jr., K. S. *et al.* (1974) Quaternary refugia in tropical America: evidence from race formation in Heliconius butterflies. *Proc. Roy. Soc. Lond.* B 187, 369 – 378.

Cole, M. M. (1960) Cerrado, caatinga and pantanal: the distribution and origin of the savanna vegetation of Brazil. *Geogr. J.* 126, 166 – 179.

Damuth, J. E. and Fairbridge, R. W. (1970) Equatorial Atlantic deep-sea arkosic sands and Ice-Age aridity in tropical South America. *Bull. Geol. Soc. Amer.* 81, 189 – 206.

Descamps, M. *et al.* (1978) Etude des écosystemes guyanais. II. Donnees biogéographiques sur la partie orientale des Guyanes. *Compt. Rend. Seances Soc. de Biogéographie* 467, 55 – 82 (1976).

Donn, W. L. *et al.* (1970) Pleistocene ice volumes and sea-level lowering. *J. Geol.* 70, 206 – 214.

Emiliani, C. (1970) Pleistocene Paleotemperatures. *Science* 168, 822-824.

Fairbridge, R. W. (1962) World sea-level and climatic changes. *Quaternaria* 6, 111-134.

Federov, A. A. (1966) The structure of the tropical rain forest and speciation in the humid tropics. *J. Ecol.* 54, 1 – 11.

Garner, H. F. (1959) Stratigraphic-sedimentary significance of contemporary climate and relief in four regions of the Andes mountains. *Bull. Geol. Soc. Amer.* 70, 1327-1368.

Granville, J. J. de (1982) Rain forest flora and xeric flora refuges in French Guiana during the late Pleistocene and Holocene. In *Biological Diversification in the Tropics*, Ed. G. T. Prance, pp. 159 – 181, Columbia University Press, New York.

Grubb, P. (1982) Refuges and dispersal in the speciation of African forest mammals. In *Biological Diversification in the Tropics*, Ed. G. T. Prance, pp. 537 – 553, Columbia University Press, New York.

Haffer, J. (1969) Speciation in Amazonian forest birds. *Science* 165, 131-137.

Haffer, J. (1974) Avian speciation in tropical South America. *Nuttall Ornith. Club No. 14*, Cambridge, Mass.

Lovejoy, T. E. (1982) Designing refugia for tomorrow. In *Biological Diversification in the Tropics*, Ed. G. T. Prance, pp. 673 – 680, Columbia University Press, New York.

Moreau, R. E. (1963) Vicissitudes of the African biomes in the late Pleistocene. *Proc. Zool. Soc. Lond.* 141, 395 – 421.

Mousinho, M. R. (1971) Upper Quaternary process changes of the middle Amazon area. *Bull. Geol. Soc. Amer.* 82, 1073 – 1078.

Prance, G. T. (1973) Phytogeographic support for the theory of Pleistocene forest refuges in the Amazon Basin, based on evidence from distribution patterns in Caryocaraceae, Chrysobalanaceae, Dichapetalaceae and Lecythidaceae. *Acta Amazonica* 3(1), 5 – 28.

Prance, G. T. (1977) The phytogeographic subdivisions of Amazonia and their influence on the selection of biological reserves. In *Extinction is Forever*, Eds. G. T. Prance and T. S. Elias, pp. 195 – 212, New York Botanical Garden.

Prance, G. T. (1982) Forest refuges: evidence from woody angiosperms. In *Biological Diversification in the Tropics*, Ed. G. T. Prance, pp. 137 – 158, Columbia University Press, New York.

Richards, P. W. (1969) Speciation in the tropical rain forest and the concept of the niche. *Biol. J. Linn.* 1, 149 – 153.

Sastre, C. (1976) Quelques aspects de la phytogéographie des mileaux ouverts guyanais. Ed. H. Descimon. Biogéographie et evolution en Amerique Tropicale. *Laboratoire de l'Ecole Normale Supérieure, Paris, Publication No. 9*, 67 – 74.

Simpson, B. B. (1975) Pleistocene changes in the flora of the high tropical Andes. *Paleobiology* 1, 273 – 294.

Simpson, D. (1972) Especiación en las plantas leñosas de la Amazonia peruana relacionada a las fluctuaciones climaticas durante el Pleistoceno. *Resumos do I Congresso Latinamericano de Botanica, Mexico*, 117. Steyermark (1981).

Steyermark, J. A. (1982) Relationships of some Venezuelan forest refuges with lowland tropical floras. In *Biological Diversification in the Tropics*, Ed. G. T. Prance, pp. 182 – 220, Columbia University Press, New York.

Toledo, V. M. (1976) Los cambios climaticos del Pleistoceno y sus efectos sobre la vegetación tropical calida y humeda de México. Thesis, Univ. Nac. Autonoma de México, 73 pages.

Toledo, V. M. (1982) Pleistocene changes of vegetation in Tropical Mexico. In *Biological Diversification in the Tropics*, Ed. G. T. Prance, pp. 93 – 111, Columbia University Press, New York.

Turner, J. R. G. (1977) Forest refuges as ecological islands: disorderly extinction and the adaptive radiation of muellerian mimics. Ed. H. Descimon. Biogéographie et evolution en Amerique Tropicale. *Laboratoire de l'Ecole Normale Supérieure, Paris, Publication No. 9*, 98 – 117.

Wetterberg, G. B. *et al.* (1976) Uma análise de prioridades em conservação da natureza na Amazônia. *PNUD/FAO/IBDF/BRA-45, Serie Tecnica No. 8*, 62 pages.

Wetterberg, G. B. *et al.* (1981) Conservation programs in Amazonia. A structural review. *Parks* (2), 5 – 10.

Van der Hammen, T. (1972) Changes in vegetation and climate in the Amazon basin and surrounding areas during the Pleistocene. *Geologia en Mijnbouw* 51, 641 – 643.

Van der Hammen, T. (1974) The Pleistocene changes of vegetation and climate in tropical South America. *J. Biogeography* 1, 3 – 26.

Van der Hammen, T. (1982) Paleoecology of tropical South America. In *Biological Diversification in the Tropics*, Ed. G. T. Prance, pp. 60 – 66, Columbia University Press, New York.

Vanzolini, P. E. (1970) Zoologia sistemática geografia e a origem das espécies. *Inst. Geográfico São Paulo. Série teses e monografias* 3, 1 – 56.

Vanzolini, P. E. and Williams, E. E. (1970) South American anoles: geographic differentiation and evolution of the *Anolis chrysolepis* species group (Sauria, Iguanidae). *Arq. Zool. São Paulo* 19, 1 – 298.

CHAPTER 9

The Pollination of Amazonian Plants

GHILLEAN T. PRANCE

The New York Botanical Garden, New York, U.S.A.

CONTENTS

9.1. INTRODUCTION

One of the most important aspects of ecological studies in any forest is the understanding of its pollination and floral biology mechanisms. Pollination is one of the many ways in which the plants and animals of the forest are closely linked; and there has been close coevolution between pollinators and the plants that they visit. The species diversity of the Amazon forest is accompanied by a great diversity of pollination mechanisms. It is therefore surprising that there is a lack of data about the pollination of many important groups of Amazonian plants. The information already collected indicates that there is a need for many more detailed experimental studies. One of the greatest deterrents to pollination observations, and especially to experimental work, is the size of the trees. Many of the interesting pollination events are taking place at 30 m or more above the forest floor, and can only be observed by climbing the trees or building towers and platforms into the crowns of the trees. The diversity of the forest also impedes pollination studies. For many trees the nearest individual of the same species may be

400 m distant, so it is almost impossible to follow the pollinators' movements from one tree to another. However, it is this very fact that makes the study of pollination in the region interesting and challenging.

Early botanists assumed that self-fertilisation must be a common feature of rainforests because the individual trees of each species are so widely spaced apart and, therefore, it seemed unlikely that pollen could be reliably transferred for cross pollination. However, more recent studies of rainforest trees show that the vast majority are obligate out-crossers (e.g. Bawa, 1974). What is remarkable is that mechanisms have evolved whereby the pollen is transferred faithfully by various animals from tree to tree over the long distances that are involved. In temperate forests wind pollination is very common. There, catkins are produced before the leaves and bear copious pollen, and as the forest is uniform in its composition, the wind is an effective method of pollen transfer. In the diverse and evergreen tropical forest wind pollination is much rarer and would not be effective within the closed evergreen canopy. In the tropics wind pollination occurs only in a few special cases such as in a few epiphytes, in open grass covered savannahs and in secondary forests where one often gets pure stands of trees such as *Cecropia*. In the Amazonian primary forest there is a tendency for pollination to depend on large strong flying pollinators that are capable of travelling the long distances involved. Therefore, pollination by euglossine and carpenter bees, birds and bats is very common.

In order to give an idea of the spectrum of pollinators at work in the Amazon I will give some specific examples that cover the major groups of pollinators that occur in the region. Since bees are probably the single most important group of pollinators let us begin with them.

9.2. THE BEES

Janzen (1971) was one of the first people to emphasise the importance of long distance foraging by female euglossine bees. He found that certain bees travel over distances of several kilometres in the course of their normal day. Released bees of *Euplusia surinamensis* returned 23 km to their nest. He also pointed out that other large bee genera such as *Xylocopa* (carpenter bees) and *Bombus* (bumble bees) are capable of such long distance foraging. These 'traplining' bees as they are called, make a regular route from flowering tree to flowering tree and are responsible for pollination of a large number of Amazonian tree species. Few experimental studies have been made in Amazonia to show the definite transfer of pollen from tree to tree, but this can be inferred from studies made in Central America and elsewhere. For example, Frankie *et al.* (1976) showed the transfer of pollen in Costa Rica from tree to tree of *Andira inermis* (Swartz) H.B.K. (Leguminosae) by using coloured powder. The trees were visited by 70 different species of bees belonging to the common genera of New World forest bees such as *Euglossa*, *Melipona*, *Trigona* and *Xylocopa* all of which are abundant in Amazonia. Since *Andira inermis* is also a common Amazonian species, we can infer that a similar pattern of pollen transfer takes place there. It is certainly much visited by bees in Amazonia.

Some groups of bees, especially some of the solitary ones, have very precise relationships with specific groups of plants and have coevolved closely with them (monolectic and oligolectic bees). Others are generalists that visit a large number of different plant taxa during the course of the year, these are termed polylectic. However, even if they visit many species, they tend to be rather specific in any particular forage. For example, data for a single species of *Trigona*, *T. seminigra merrillae* Cock. collected in the vicinity of Manaus in Central Amazonia showed that the bees from one hive visited 33 species of plants in 21 different plant families during the course of a year (Absy and Kerr, 1977). However, 60.7% of the bees examined were carrying pollen of a single species when captured and another 23.3% carried pollen of only two plants. Only 15.9% of the bees carried pollen of three or more species of plants.

Hence, this example of a polylectic species of bee, shows that bees exhibit a high degree of constancy to a particular plant taxon during an individual flight. This constancy, characteristic of many species of bees, enhances their value as pollinators.

Plants too have evolved different phenological strategies to cope with the different types of bees. I remember well a tree of *Tapirira guianensis* Aubl. outside my office in Manaus. Early one morning my attention was drawn to that tree by the sound of buzzing as well as a very sweet scent in the air. The small insignificant flowers had opened simultaneously. The tree was alive with thousands of bees, especially of the genera *Trigona* and *Melipona*. The next morning there were only a few flowers left, attended by very few bees. The tree was using what has been termed by Gentry (1974) as the 'big bang' phenological strategy whereby the whole tree bursts into flower simultaneously. This big show attracts pollinators visually or by scent, as in the case of *Tapirira*, a large number of bees for a short time. In contrast there are many Amazonian trees that produce one or two flowers on each inflorescence per day and have an extended flowering period such as the *Gurania* vines described as an example of butterfly pollination by *Heliconius*. These long-flowering plants are generally the ones that are pollinated by the long-distance solitary traplining bees such as *Euglossa* and *Xylocopa*. This type of phenology was termed 'steady state' by Gentry.

Good examples of various types of bee pollination are found in the Brazil nut family (Lecythidaceae) which is one of the most abundant plant families in the forests of Amazonia (for full details *see* Mori and Kallunki, 1976; Mori *et al.*, 1978; Prance, 1976). The Lecythidaceae exhibit a series of different morphological types and pollinator rewards which correspond to a series of bee pollinators in size, food preferences and diversity. The more primitive genera of the family, *Gustavia* and *Grias*, have regular or symmetrical flowers with the androecium consisting of a circle of numerous stamens united only at their base (Fig. 9.1).   The stamens are curved inwards and there is a strong sweet smell produced inside the circle. The anthers produce an abundance of pollen. The large white or pink flowers of *Gustavia* attract a wide range of small and medium-sized pollen gathering bees (e.g. *Trigona*, *Melipona* and *Bombus*). These enter the central cavity formed by the androecium and they forage for the copious pollen available. The stigmatic surface at the centre of the circle is touched frequently by the foraging bees who consequently leave pollen from another tree in the correct place. At the same time they become thoroughly dusted with pollen to carry to another flower. Our experiments have also shown, in at least two species of *Gustavia*, that they are allogamous, that is they are out-crossing species that cannot self-fertilise.

There are other genera of Lecythidaceae such as *Cariniana* with slightly one-sided androecium that also attract the small pollen gathering bees. The genus *Couroupita* and most species of *Lecythis* are quite different because the androecium is highly zygomorphic (Figs. 9.1, 9.2). It consists of a basal circle of stamens surrounding the usually conical stigmatic surface and one-sided lateral strap or ligule that is curved over 180° to arch above the basal ring. The apex or hood of the ligule which is directly above the staminal ring contains another group of numerous stamens. The most interesting discovery is that whereas the pollen of the staminal ring germinates normally in a sugar solution, that of the hood is sterile. Bees, usually much larger than those that visit *Gustavia*, such as *Xylocopa* and *Bombus*, land on the hood and enter into the gap between the hood and the staminal ring to forage for pollen in the hood stamens. However, at the same time, their backs rub against both the stigmatic surface and the basal stamens to effect pollination. *Couroupita* and *Lecythis* produce a sterile feed pollen for their pollinators as occurs also in some species of *Cassia* (Caesalpiniaceae). Since the androecium is open small bees such as *Trigona* can also enter the androecium without effecting pollination.

The next step in the evolutionary progression of the Lecythidaceae is found in the Brazil nut genus *Bertholletia* and in the largest genus in the family, *Eschweilera*, that contains over 100 species. In these genera, the hood of the androecium is tightly closed over the staminal ring, and the hood stamens are substituted by sterile staminodes (Fig. 9.1). Nectar is produced at the base of the staminodes. Since the hood is firmly coiled over the staminal ring, the ligule acts like a spring, and only a strong bee can lift it

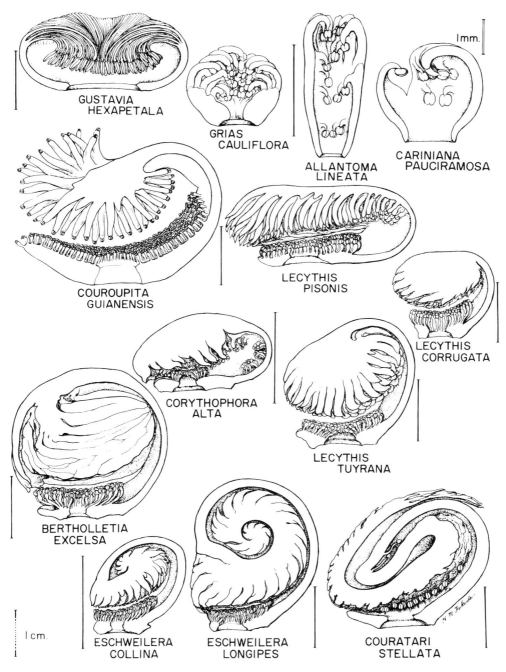

Fig. 9.1. The androecium structure of the Lecythidaceae showing the different arrangements of the stamens which occur for different pollinators, varying from the actinomorphic regular structure of *Gustavia* with no nectar, but open for pollen-gathering bees, to the highly coiled structure of *Couratari* which has nectar in the centre of the coil that can be reached only by long-tongued euglossine bees.

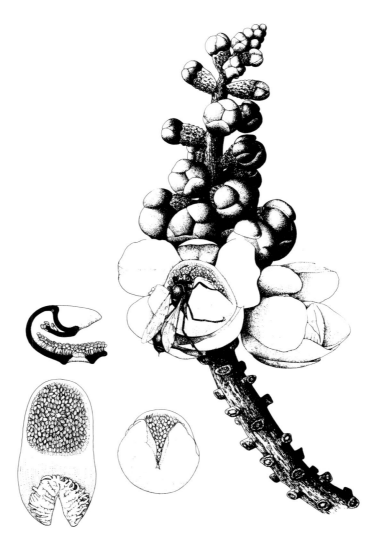

Fig. 9.2. Wasp entering the androecium of *Couroupita subsessilis* Pilg. It lands on the V-shaped platform of the androecium hood then turns upside down as it enters the flower to forage for pollen in the infertile stamens on the inner surface of the hood. At the same time its back touches the fertile stamens of the ring.

up to gain access to the nectar. The large pollinators of *Eschweilera* are usually carpenter bees (*Xylocopa*) and female euglossine bees. Other smaller bees and also other flower predators are excluded by the pressure of the hood. The correct pollinators also land on the hood as in *Lecythis* then push their way into the slit between the staminal ring and the hood. As they widen this opening so that they can enter, the spring of the ligule strongly pushes their back against the staminal ring, thus guaranteeing the bees are well dusted with pollen. The Brazil nut and its nearest relatives such as *Eschweilera* have evolved a highly specialised relationship with certain large nectar gathering bees. The specialisation gives the floral organs greater protection, but also greatly limits the number of possible pollinators.

The most advanced genus of Lecythidaceae in terms of floral evolution is *Couratari* which has most of its 18 species confined to Amazonia. In this genus the hood of the androecium has an extra coil (Fig. 9.1). The effect is that the nectar-producing staminodes are hidden right inside a long coil about 3 − 5 cm from the opening where the bees enter when they lift the hood. This means that only long-tongued bees have access to the nectar, which limits the number of potential pollinators. *Couratari* appears to be pollinated exclusively by female euglossine bees. In *Couratari atrovinosa* Prance which is known only from the vicinity of Manaus, Brazil, the pollinator is *Eulaema meriana* (Oliver) a large euglossine bee. We built a ladder into the crown of this tree to observe pollinators, but passed an entire day and night without observing any floral visitors that succeeded in lifting the androphore hood. However, our patience was rewarded at the Amazonian dawn at 5.45 a.m. when two bees of *E. meriana* visited the few open flowers on the tree. This happened three days in a row confirming other observations about the habits of female traplining euglossine bees that make regular foraging journeys visiting the same flowering trees day after day. It is interesting to note that trees of *Couratari atrovinosa* produce only a few flowers each day rather than the 'big bang' strategy of *Tapirira*. This is much more in accord with the foraging habits of its highly specialised pollinator. Not only has the flower structure evolved appropriately for the pollinator, but also the phenology.

The Brazil nuts then show a progression from the more unspecialised genera that attract many species of generalist pollen gathering bees, to the more advanced genera that attract a few species of large nectar feeding bees, and the evolutionary progression culminates in the most advanced, *Couratari*, where only a long-tongued bee is effective.

The behaviour of the male euglossine bees is as fascinating as that of the female bees but quite different. When the males leave the hive they become solitary wandering bees and they have evolved a relationship with a complete group of plants, the Orchids.

The male euglossine bees display the lek phenomenon in which certain species of animals have evolved gaudy colouring and demonstrative behaviour which they display to attract the females for mating. The brightly-coloured male euglossine bees never return to the nest once they leave. They feed on nectar-producing plants and sleep on leaf undersurfaces. They are also attracted by highly aromatic compounds produced by many species of neotropical orchids. The male bees brush the surface of the odour producing parts of the flowers with special pads on their front feet. They then fly off and while they are airborne they squeeze the contents of the pads into the cavities of their swollen hind legs. This process is repeated many times until the cavities are full. The fragrances do not attract the female bees, but attract other males so that a small swarm is formed. The swarm of brightly-coloured bees performs a series of complicated flight and buzz rituals that attract the females and mating then takes place. The orchids benefit by this curious behaviour since the male bees carry their pollinia from flower to flower. The fragrance chemicals also help to prolong the life of the bees which are extraordinarily long-lived (about 6 months). Many people have worked on this unique coevolution between orchids and male euglossine bees, most notably Van der Pijl and Dodson (1966), Dodson (1966, 1967), and Dressler (1967, 1968a,b). It is possible to attract these bees to lures using the orchid scent compounds such as eugenol and cineole, and many experiments with these attractants have been carried out mainly in Central America by Dodson and Dressler.

Braga (1976a) carried out similar experiments in three different Amazonian vegetation types (campina, campinarana and forest on terra firme, *see* Chapter 7). He used the attractants eugenol, vanilline, cineole, and methyl salycilate, and collected ten species of euglossine bees including the male of *Eulaema meriana*, the female of which pollinates *Couratari* in the Lecythidaceae. *Eulaema meriana* was collected by using cineole in the forest on terra firme, also the habitat of *Couratari*. This species is an important orchid pollinator in the vicinity of Manaus. Braga collected bees in the genera *Euglossa*, *Euplusia*, *Eulaema*, *Efriesea* and *Exaerete* and this helped to show their importance as orchid pollinators. All species of bees studied by Braga are active in the three different habitats in which he worked.

In addition to attracting bees, Braga also observed directly the pollination of several Amazonian orchids by these odour-gathering bees. For example, in the vicinity of Manaus, the attractive large-flowered orchid *Stanhopea candida* Barb. Rodr. is pollinated by *Eulaema mocsaryi* Friese (Braga, 1976b). The pendulous flowers of *Stanhopea* attract the *Eulaema mocsaryi* bees (Fig. 9.3F) which begin to scrape the central part of the labellum of the flower where the odours are produced. When the bee takes off from the labellum it must descend and its scutellum brushes the retinaculum and the orchids' pollinia becomes firmly attached to the bee. When the bee visits another flower after scraping the odour and leaving the labellum it brushes the new flower and deposits the pollinia in the stigmatic cavity. Another species of *Eulaema*, *E. ignita* Smith, also visits the same species to collect odour but does not brush the flower as it leaves, and is thus a robber of odour, rather than a pollinator. It is not the correct size for the flower which has coevolved with *E. mocsaryi* to fit exactly the size of the bee. This type of pollination where the bee lets go of a pendulous flower and brushes the correct part in its initial drop was termed 'fall-through' pollination by Dressler (1968b) in contrast to other orchids including other species of *Stanhopea* with conchiform or 'gullet flowers' and others with tubular flowers with 'back out' pollination. These two examples in orchids and Brazil nuts serve to show the importance of the long distance flying euglossine bees in the Amazon forest.

Bees are also attracted to some flowers by their alimentary oils, a phenomenon which was elucidated as recently as 1974 by Vogel. It is common in Amazonia because several of the plant families produce oil instead of nectar or pollen as the pollinator reward, especially in the family of vines and trees Malpighiaceae and the tribe Memecylaeae of the Melastomataceae (*see* Buchmann and Buchmann, 1981). These groups of plants have oil-producing glands or elaeophores instead of nectar. They attract bees of the family Anthophoridae especially the genus *Centris* in the Centridini which have legs that are especially adapted for the collection of the oil. The bees collect the oil which is full of glycerides and take it to their hives where it is mixed with pollen to make the larval food in which the female bees will deposit their eggs and the larvae develop. This oil production is the way in which the common Amazonian genus *Mouriri* attracts its pollinators. However, the bees also collect pollen which is difficult to obtain from the short apical slits of the anthers of *Mouriri*. To extract pollen, the bees use what is termed 'buzz pollination' (Buchmann *et al.*, 1977) whereby they land on the flowers and produce a vibration by shivering their indirect flight muscles. This produces an audible buzz, but more important the vibrations propel a cloud of the small pollen grains out of the small terminal opening of the anthers. The pollen lands directly on the venters of the bees and is collected also for use to provide food for the larval cells.

Buzz pollination occurs in at least 71 plant families (Buchmann and Buchmann, 1981) and is common among Amazonian plants. The Melastomataceae for example, is a family common in the region. The Amazonian genera, other than *Mouriri*, belong to other tribes of the family and have poricidal anthers (that is, anthers with only a small apical opening). These plants are all pollinated by the buzz method, which is the only way the pollen can be extracted from them in any quantity. A recent, but as yet unpublished, study of the pollination of several Amazonian species of Melastomataceae by Suzanne Renner (pers. comm.) will provide much more data about the floral biology of that family. The Solanaceae or nightshade family is another common group in Amazonia in which buzz pollination occurs.

9.3. THE FLIES

The large group of insects, the Diptera or flies, although known for their association with animals, are also important flower visitors and myophily or fly pollination is quite important to the plant kingdom in general. There are several groups of flies with special adaptations for flower visiting. In

Fig. 9.3. Amazonian flowers and their pollinators: A – D, *Victoria amazonica* (Poepp. and Endl.) Sowerby. A, white first day flower; B, purple second day flower; C, flower section showing cavity where beetles enter; D, pollen-loaded beetle emerging.

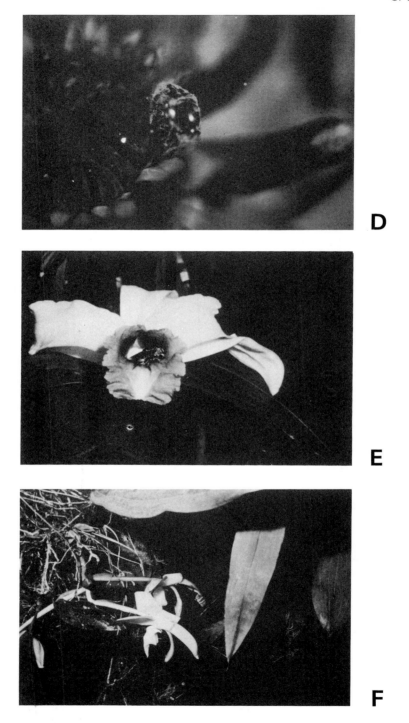

Fig. 9.3. (cont.) Amazonian flowers and their pollinators: E, orchid with green euglossine bee pollinator (photo P.I.S. Braga); F, *Stanhopea candida* Barb. Rodr. with its bee pollinator, *Eulaema mocsaryi* Friese (photo P.I.S. Braga); G – H, three red bird-pollinated flowers with different structures to attract birds.

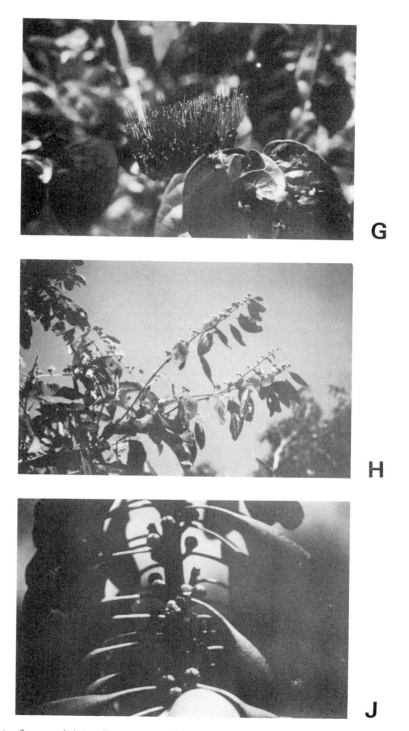

Fig. 9.3. (cont.) Amazonian flowers and their pollinators: G, *Combretum* vine with mass of flowers and erect brush type stamens; H, *Warszewiczia coccinea* (Vahl) Klotzch with brightly coloured bracts and small flowers. J, *Norantea guianensis* Aubl. with bright red nectar glands and small flowers (photo D. Daly).

Amazonia fly pollination has not been well studied, but this does not mean that it is not an important pollination mechanism in the region. There are several groups of Amazonian plants that are well adapted to flies as their floral visitors, for example, the *Aristolochias*, large woody vines of the tall forest. The trumpet-like flowers of *Aristolochia* (Figs. 9.4D, E) often have mottled, shiny red, fleshy lobes at the opening of the trumpet. They attract carrion flies by this fleshy appearance and by a foul smell of rotting protein. The flies enter the tube and pass a barrage of reflexed hairs, finally reaching the central cavity below. The flies are then trapped inside because they cannot reverse their direction against the reflexed hairs. They fly around inside and land on the stamens and style and become dusted with pollen. Later the hairs at the entrance wilt and the flies are free to continue on to another flower.

Braga (pers. comm.) has observed flies visiting several species of small flowered Amazonian orchids and he has captured flies bearing the pollinia of orchids. It is generally some of the small, inconspicuously coloured orchids with small pollinia that are pollinated by flies. South of Amazonia, Sazima (1978) has made a detailed study of the pollination of the orchid *Bulbophyllum warmingianum* Cogn. by small females of *Pholeongia* sp. in the Milichiidae. Again in this case the flowers are greenish with purple spots and stripes.

One of the most important of all Amazonian plants *Theobroma cacao* L. or the cocoa plant is fly pollinated. The small flies that visit the flowers, which are produced on the trunk and branches of the tree, breed mainly in the decaying fruit pods on the ground (*see* Dessart, 1961). This means that clearing of plantations will jeopardise pollination of the crop. In the flowers of cocoa, the anthers are hidden in pouch-like petals, and a ring of staminodes hinders access to the stigma which means that the flowers can only be pollinated by an insect that can gain access. Cocoa is pollinated mainly by small certapogonid midges that are attracted by and feed on the purple staminode tissue. In foraging their backs touch the stigma, style and pollen, and pollination takes place.

Apparently many relatives of the cocoa in the family Sterculiaceae are fly-pollinated. Taroda and Gibbs (1982) have recently shown that the Brazilian species *Sterculia chicha* St. Hil. is pollinated by some of the sapromyophilous genera of flies. They also showed that *S. chicha* is self-incompatible. Pollen tube growth, however, occurs following both compatible and incompatible self-pollination showing that, as in the cocoa plant, the incompatibility mechanism is based on the nonfusion of gametes in the embryo sac. There are several species of *Sterculia* present in the Amazon forest and since this type of mechanism occurs in both *Theobroma* and *Sterculia* it is likely that it is widespread in the family.

9.4. THE BEETLES

The beetles or coleoptera are another insect group that are common in the region and important pollinators of many interesting plants. Beetles are an ancient group of animals that existed before the flowering plants evolved, and were therefore around to pollinate the earliest angiosperms. Today we find that many of the beetle-pollinated plants of Amazonia, such as members of the Annonaceae and the Nymphaeaceae, belong to the plant families that are considered to be more primitive in evolutionary terms. Beetles are clumsy, awkward flying insects that generally land on flowers and eat much of the floral parts. Most beetle pollinated flowers do not have many complicated adaptations and pollination tends to be fortuitous.

The Amazon water-lilies are a good example of beetle pollination, where a greater degree of specialisation has evolved. There are several species of *Nymphaea* in the lakes of Amazonia, for example *N. rudgeana* G.F.W. Meyer and *N. amazonum* Mart. & Zucc. These two species have been studied (Prance and Anderson, 1976; Prance, 1980a) and it has been clearly shown that they are visited abundantly by scarab beetles of the genus *Cyclocephala* (Dynastinae).

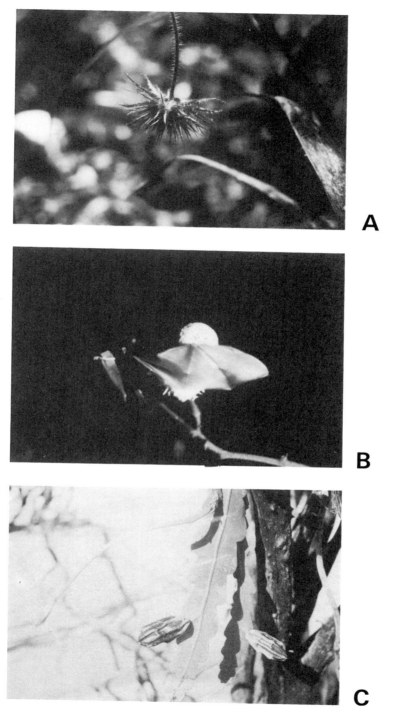

Fig. 9.4. Amazonian flowers and their pollinators: A, *Gurania* in the cucumber family, see text; B, flower head of *Parkia nitida* Miq. being visited by a bat (photo M. and H. Hopkins); C, an *Epiphyllum* cactus at Tefé, Brazil with 12 cm long corolla tube, pollinated by a hawk-moth with an equally long tongue to reach the nectar.

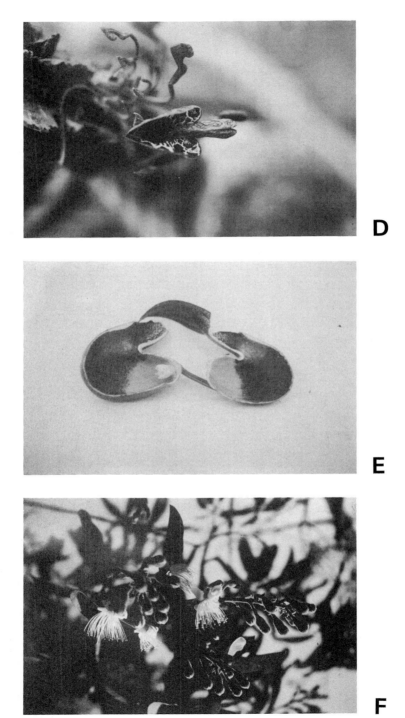

Fig. 9.4. (cont.) Amazonian flowers and their pollinators: D, *Aristolochia* sp. with fleshy glossy appearance to attract flies. E, inside of *Aristolochia* flower showing reflexed hairs at mouth which trap pollinating flies; F, *Couepia grandiflora* (Mart. & Zucc.) Benth., with erect brush-like flowers and further exerted style to touch pollinating hawk-moths.

Fig. 9.4. (cont.) Amazonian flowers and their pollinators: G – H, the two morphs of the heterostylous *Turnera ulmifolia* L., G, long style, H, short style. J, a *Mandevilla* vine with clear central nectar guide to attract pollinators.

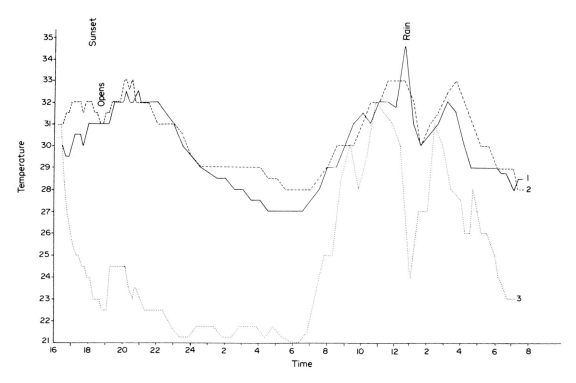

Fig. 9.5. Graph of the temperature of two flowers of *Victoria amazonica* (Poepp. & Endl.) Sowerby (lines 1 & 2) compared with air temperature (dotted line 3), showing the large temperature difference of 9.5°C in the early evening of the first day when the white flowers open.

The flowers of both species open at night as soon as darkness falls. They are white and emit a strong fruity scent akin to ripe pineapple. Soon after the flowers open beetles begin to arrive. They push their way into the centre of the flowers where they eat sterile staminodes that are starchy feeding tissue. The flowers are protogynous, meaning that the stigma is receptive before the pollen is shed. The first night that they open no pollen is released, but on the second night abundant pollen is released. So a beetle moving from a second day flower to a first day flower will effect cross-pollination. In case this does not happen self-fertilisation can take place on the second day. *Nymphaea rudgeana* is visited by the beetles *Cyclocephala castanea* Oliv. and *C. verticalis* Burm. and *N. amazonum* by the smaller beetle for the smaller flowers *C. mollis* Endrodi. There are other species of *Nymphaea* which are day flowering such as *N. ampla*. These species are pollinated by bees, such as species of *Trigona*.

The pollination of the Royal water lily, *Victoria amazonica* (Poepp.) Sowerby, also of the Nymphaeaceae, is one of the most sophisticated examples of beetle pollination that has been recorded (*see* Prance and Arias, 1975). It is a coevolved mechanism that compares in elegance and complexity to any of the bee mechanisms described above (*see* Fig. 9.3A – D).

The large flower buds of *Victoria* emerge from below water and once the receptacle is completely above water they are ready to open. Like *Nymphaea* the flowers open at dusk, controlled by the phytochrome system of the plant. The opening of the flower is directly correlated with light intensity. There is a dramatic beauty when within a 15 minute period all the buds which are ready to open transform themselves into large white star-like flowers. When the flowers first open the petals are white

(Fig. 9.3A), and the temperature inside the flower can be as much as 11°C above air temperature (Fig. 9.5). As the flower temperature rises the flowers also emit a strong fruity odour. As soon as the flowers start to open there is much beetle activity and large dynastid beetles, *Cyclocephala hardyi* Endrodi and *C. castanea* Oliv. begin to arrive. The commonest beetle is *C. hardyi*, but two other beetles are occasional visitors to these flowers, *C. verticalis* Burm. and *Ligyrus similis* Endrodi.

The beetles, attracted by the odour and white colour of the flowers, immediately begin to enter the flowers and push their way into the central cavity (Fig. 9.3C). At this stage the stigma is receptive to pollen, but the stamens are tightly closed and although the beetles pass by them as they enter the flower they receive no pollen. *Victoria* is therefore also protogynous like its cousins in *Nymphaea*. The beetles remain in the warm central cavity where they feed on a row of knob-like carpellary appendages called paracarpels (Fig. 9.3C) that are full of starches and sugars. The flower temperature drops towards dawn, the fruity scent gradually disappears and the flower closes tightly shut, trapping the beetles inside. Beetles were found in 94% of the 500 flowers that we opened. There was an average of 7 beetles per flower and the most we ever counted in 1 flower was 47.

During the next day the petals of the flower gradually change colour to a dark purplish-red (Fig. 9.3B). Then in the afternoon the sepals and petals open and during the early evening the flowers reopen completely to release the beetles. Because the carpellary appendages have been eaten away by the beetles, both the stamens and inner staminodes fall loosely inwards. At this time the anthers have already dehisced and pollen is scattered all over the beetles. It adheres to their bodies because they are now very sticky from all the juices of the interior of the flower (Fig. 9.3D). The beetles climb up and out of the flower and take off to fly to another first day flower. It is guaranteed that they will not return to a second day flower because these are red, scentless and at ambient temperature. Each plant produces flowers every other day so that the beetles are sure to fly on to a different plant and thereby ensure xenogamy.

This type of sophisticated relationship with beetles is rare in plants. Other Amazonian plant families in which beetle pollination is common are the Annonaceae, a common forest family of trees, and the Araceae or arum-lily family. The Araceae are well known for the highly elevated flower temperatures as the flowers open.

The first observations of pollination in an Amazonian species of Annonaceae was made recently by Webber (1981), for *Annona sericea* Dun., although the family has been studied in southern Brazil (Gottsberger, 1970). There are many similarities between *Victoria amazonica* and *A. sericea*. *Annona sericea* has three thick fleshy petals that never fully open, that enclose the conical central knob that bears the stigma and stamens (Fig. 9.6). At about 7 p.m. at night the flower temperature begins to rise until it is 6°C above the ambient, and at the same time an intensive odour reminiscent of a mixture of chloroform and ether is produced. As the aroma intensifies the nocturnal visitors arrive. They are small chrysomelid beetles as well as flies of the family Sciaricae. The beetles push their way in through the petals and at this time the stigmas are receptive, but the pollen is still enclosed, so this is another example of protogyny.

After the flowers open just enough to let the insects in, they go through an interesting progression of events (Fig. 9.6C, D). First is the rise in temperature and production of odour. Next the stigmas which are at the top of the central cone fall off, ending the possibility for further pollination. The loss of the stigmas causes the anthers below to assume an erect position and then the pollen is released. After this the stamens drop off and finally, one by one, the petals drop off and release the insects. The beetles usually remain inside the flowers until the petals drop off although there is no actual trapping mechanism in this plant. The beetles eat the basal portion of the petals. They frequently copulate inside the flowers, resulting in further contact with the stigmas and stamens. The small flies walk all around the interior of the flowers and sometimes oviposit on the sepals, but the primary pollinators of this and many other Amazonian Annonaceae are beetles.

9.5. THE BUTTERFLIES

Another group of Amazonian pollinators are the butterflies which both flit about in the canopy of the forest and also through its lower levels. The heliconiid butterflies are very common in the lower levels of the forest.

One of the best examples of butterfly pollination in Amazonia is found in the two genera of Cucurbitaceae vines, *Anguria* and *Gurania* (Fig. 9.4A), that are pollinated by various species of *Heliconius* (Gilbert, 1972, 1975). These vines have dense clusters of visually attractive flowers that usually have a mixture of red and yellow colours that is characteristic of many butterfly plants of the tropics. The *Anguria* vines are dioecious, that is male and female flowers are produced on separate vines. The male flowers are produced in inflorescences and last only one day after which they fall. Many more male flowers than female are produced and the inflorescences continue to produce flowers for extended periods. The vines are well spaced out in the forest (an average of 100 − 500 m, Gilbert, 1975) and so the long-lived *Heliconius* butterflies trapline like bees when they are foraging for pollen. It has been shown experimentally that they quickly learn the routes between the scattered plants in the forest. The *Heliconius* butterflies have obviously coevolved closely with the cucurbit vines that they visit. The butterflies benefit from the nitrogen rich pollen that enables them to increase their egg production. In the dioecious vine-like *Anguria* or *Gurania* the need for a reliable pollen vector is obvious. Seed-set requires that an animal bring pollen from male to female plants. The large supply of male flowers assures that the butterflies obtain adequate pollen for their needs. Since the female flowers do not produce pollen for the pollen-gathering visitors, they are actually mimicking the male flowers. The pollen collecting butterflies are deceived to visit the pollenless flowers by the similar appearance of the female flowers that

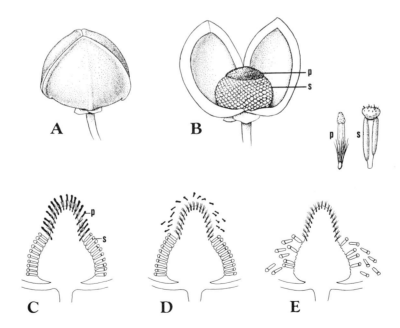

Fig. 9.6. The beetle-pollinated flower of *Annona sericea* Dun. A, flower in normal state of anthesis when beetles push their way into the centre; B, opened flower to show the pistil (p) and the stamens (s); C − D, the sequence of loss of floral organs during the life of the flower. C, intact column with stamens and styles intact; D, the fall of the styles after pollination, with stamens remaining intact; E, later the stamens also fall (adapted from Webber, 1981).

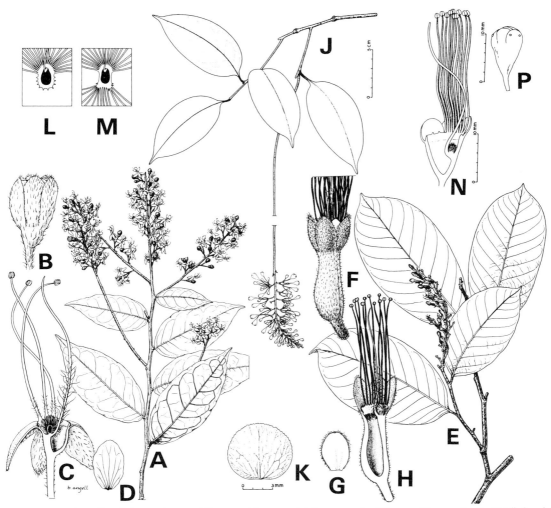

Fig. 9.7. Species of *Hirtella* and *Couepia* showing differences of flowers and inflorescences for different pollinators. A – D, *Hirtella barnebyi* Prance, butterfly pollinated with few stamens and purple flowers with many open together; A, habit X 0.45; B, flower bud X 4; C, flower section X 4; D, petal, X 4; E – H, *Couepia bernardii* Prance, moth-pollinated and with many stamens, white flowers with few open at any time; E, habit X 0.45; F, flower X 3; G, petal X 3; H, flower section X 3; J – P, *Couepia dolichopoda* Prance, bat-pollinated with long pendulous flagelliflorous inflorescence; J, habit X 0.25; K, petal X 3; L, staminal base X 8; M, staminal base of related *C. longipendula* Pilg.; N, flower X 1.5; P, flower bud X 1.5.

have a stigmatic surface covered with pollen-sized bumps that the butterflies confuse with pollen. One mistake visit like this of a pollen-laden butterfly is usually enough to pollinate the female flower so it does not have to be part of the regular trapline.

Hirtella a large genus of the Chrysobalanaceae, is another butterfly-pollinated genus. The purple flowers have long protruding stamens and a single exserted style (Fig. 9.7A – D). Butterflies of many sorts alight on the flowers to collect the abundant nectar produced from the disc that lines the inside of the floral cavity, the hypanthium. The flowers of *Hirtella* are well adapted to butterflies, providing a landing place for them, and a nutrient rich nectar. It is also well designed to ensure that the butterflies brush the stamens and the style.

9.6. THE MOTHS

The evolutionary change from butterfly to moth pollination is slight, but plants adapted to moth pollination require certain modifications, for example they will tend to be nocturnal rather than diurnal. *Couepia*, another large Amazonian genus of Chrysobalanaceae and the closest relative of *Hirtella*, is pollinated mostly by moths. Some of the differences between these two genera are given below.

Couepia (Fig. 9.7E — H)	*Hirtella* (Fig. 9.7A — D)
Flowers open at night	Flowers open during the day
Few flowers/inflorescence each day	Many flowers open each day giving a showy appearance
Flowers always white	Flowers pink or purple (rarely white)
Stamens numerous (10 — 300)	Stamens few (3 — 8)
Stamens often appearing tangled	Stamens separate not tangled
Copious nectar	Nectar less abundant

These are some of the many taxonomic characters of the flower that have been used by botanists to separate these two closely related genera. What systematists use as important taxonomic characters are often linked to differences in the pollination syndrome as in the case of *Hirtella* and *Couepia*. *Couepia* has many more stamens that form a brush-like mass when the flowers first open. The long exserted style protrudes slightly beyond the stamens in the centre of the flower (Fig. 9.7E — H). *Couepia* flowers are visited by many different moths, but the most regular and efficient pollinators are the large hawk moths (Sphingidae). I have observed hawk moths pollinating *Couepia grandiflora* (Mart. & Zucc.) Benth. ex Hook.f. (Fig. 9.4F) (*see also* Gottsberger and Gottsberger, 1975), *C. paraensis* (Mart. & Zucc.) Benth. and *C. robusta* Huber, all Amazonian species. The moths brush firmly against the stamens as they hover and forage for nectar. This explains why the erect, orderly, freshly-opened stamens of *Couepia* are a tangled and bent mass in the morning. They have performed their function and are thus expendable. Each inflorescence of *C. paraensis* or *C. robusta* will produce one or two open flowers the next night ready for the next visit of the moths. These moths visit the flowers mainly at dusk and dawn. Before they wilt entirely the old flowers are often visited by other animals that are not well adapted for *Couepia*, and that come to steal nectar and pollen. In the early morning it is common to see small bees gathering the remaining pollen, but they usually do not touch the stigma and so are not pollinators. Other frequent visitors are hummingbirds, that collect any nectar left by the moths. Although *Couepia* flowers receive these extraneous visitors they are clearly adapted to hawk-moths. In studies of pollination it is never enough to state that an animal pollinates because it visits the flower. Detailed observations of its behaviour and capture to collect pollen from it are a necessity.

9.7. THE BATS

Two Amazonian species of *Couepia* are quite different from the rest, *C. dolichopoda* Prance from the Peruvian Amazon (Fig. 9.7J — P) and *C. longipendula* Pilg. from Central Amazonian Brazil. Both species exhibit what is termed flagelliflory. That is the inflorescences hang down, pendent, on exceptionally long stalks. The flowers of these two species are also red, not white like other species of *Couepia*, and nectar is even more abundant. These species are typical of many other bat-pollinated species of the tropics. Bat-pollinated flowers must be easily accessible to the bats which navigate by a sonar system. As bats cannot fly into the intricate web of the crown branches of the tree, long pendent inflorescences as in *Couepia* is one way of making flowers accessible to them. I have observed numerous bats visiting a flowering tree of *Couepia longipendula*. They fly up to the inflorescence, alight for a few seconds to grasp it while they feed, and thereby brush the mass of stamens on to their chests which are dusted with pollen. The changes from moth pollinated flowers of the other species of *Couepia* are few, apart from flagelliflory. *Couepia longipendula* has the same brush-like flowers that open at night, produce copious nectar, and inflorescences in which only a few flowers open each night. If a single tree had too many open flowers on a particular night the bats would be satiated, and they would not carry pollen to another tree. The pollination of *C. longipendula* and other bat-pollinated Amazonian trees was described in detail by Vogel (1968, 1969).

Many other Amazonian trees have pendulous inflorescences, such as *Eperua falcata* Aubl., a species that dominates the white sand communities of northern Amazonia and the Guianas. One of the most beautiful and best known flagelliflorous trees is *Parkia pendula* (Willd.) Benth. ex Walp. in the Mimosaceae (Fig. 9.8F). This tree has a remarkable flat spreading crown and the globular bright red inflorescence hangs down from long stalks like a mass of Christmas decorations. Each inflorescence is a globose cluster of numerous flowers with protruding stamens and stigmas. The uppermost flowers at the top of the globe are sterile and secrete copious nectar. Bats visit and alight for a few seconds, embracing the flower and becoming dusted with pollen. The floral biology of the Amazonian species of *Parkia* is well known after a recent study of them by Dr. Helen Hopkins.

In *Parkia* the flowers begin to open in midmorning, starting with the basal ones, and by midafternoon they are all open. Anthesis and nectar production begin at dusk and the nectar flow ceases by early morning. By daylight of the second day there is no nectar left and the flowers have faded and the filaments wilted. The flowers therefore last only a single night. The timing is perfect for the nocturnal bat pollinators.

Parkia flower clusters, which look like pom-poms when they open, have the ideal structure for bat-pollination. When the bat alights to get nectar from the top of the ball, it cannot avoid being well dusted with pollen from the numerous exserted stamens that protrude from the inflorescence cluster. The commonest bat visitors to *Parkia* are those of the genus *Phyllostomus* and other Phyllostomatinae, but Stenoderminae bats are quite common in *Parkia pendula*. It is interesting that in the studies of Hopkins most of the bats caught in *Parkia* trees had pollen of *Parkia* on their fur or in their stomachs, indicating that during a particular night the bats concentrate on a single species of tree, thereby increasing the probability of effective pollination.

Another strategy to make the flowers available to bats is to have them project above the crown of the trees. There are also several species of *Parkia*, such as *P. decussata* Ducke (Fig. 9.8), *P. igneiflora* Ducke and *P. nitida* Miq. (Fig. 9.4B) which have upright inflorescences. One predominantly Amazonian plant family, the Caryocaraceae, is entirely bat-pollinated. The species of *Caryocar* all have erect inflorescences with numerous brush-like stamens and abundant nectar produced by a row of staminoides at their base. *Caryocar microcarpum* Ducke is a riverside tree and the flowers always attract many bats. Other species such as *C. glabrum* (Aubl.) Pers. and *C. villosum* (Aubl.) Pers. are giants of the upland terra firme forest, and *C. brasiliense* Camb. is a savannah tree of the southern savannahs. All of them regardless of their habitat are visited by bats.

The last way in which tropical trees make their flowers available to bats is through cauliflory, or the production of flowers on the trunk and woody branches. A good example of a bat-pollinated tree of this sort is the calabash or *Crescentia cujete* L. This species produces numerous green, open tubular flowers. Bats can frequently be seen pollinating this plant, the fruit of which is the calabash, an important utensil that serves as soup bowls, canoe bailers, water jars, etc. for Amazon natives.

9.8. THE BIRDS

The other important large flying Amazonian pollinators are birds, principally hummingbirds or Trochilidae. These attractive hovering birds with long fine beaks tailored to fit the tubes of many flowers are common in Amazonia. Hummingbird-pollinated flowers are usually but not always red, the colour which these birds see best. Red is also a good bird colour because it is not conspicuous to most groups of insects with the notable exception of the butterflies which also see red well. These flowers produce large quantities of nectar needed by hummingbirds which have a high rate of metabolism to sustain their buzzing, bee-like flight pattern of over 3000 wing beats per minute. The flowers are also usually tubular matching the length of the birds' beaks. The beaks are often curved and are well

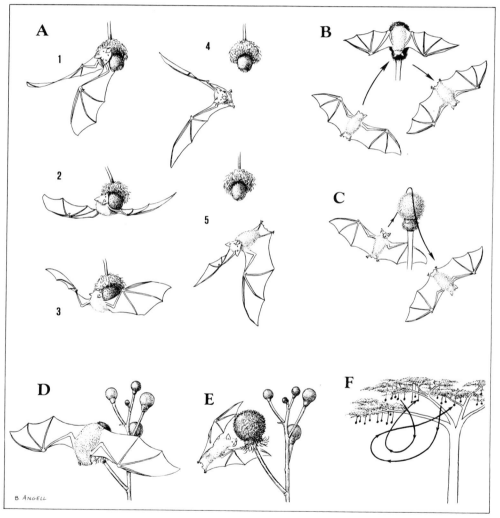

Fig. 9.8 *Phyllostomus* bats and their method of visiting *Parkia* flowers. A, series showing visits to *P. discolor* Spruce ex Benth. probably by *Phyllostomus discolor* (Wagner); 1 – 3 bats land briefly upside down with their heads close to the nectar-secreting flowers and the sides of their bodies in contact with fertile pollen-bearing flowers, 4 – 5 bats taking off by dropping after a visit; B, C, bats visiting *P. decussata* Ducke showing schematic flight paths; B, the bat approaches the flower-head from below and twists to grab the uppermost part with its feet, and then takes off downwards; C, the bat approaches from below but flies over the top of the flower-head, grasps the uppermost part with its feet, lands briefly and takes off downwards. This method is only possible in species with erect flower heads; D, large bat, probably *Phyllostomus hastatus* (Pallus) taking nectar by landing upside down on a capitulum of *Parkia cachimboensis* H.C. Hopkins; E, unidentified bat taking nectar on the wing without contacting the fertile flowers of *P. cachimboensis*; F, bat activity in *P. pendula* (Willd.) Benth. ex Walp. is almost exclusively below the crown, where the pendulous inflorescences hang. (Drawings all adapted from Hopkins, 1981).

modified for nectar sucking. The two halves form an airtight tube from which the long vermiform tongue can be stuck out for a considerable distance.

One of the most important Amazonian groups of bird pollinated flowers are the *Heliconias* (Heliconiaceae), closely related to the bird-of-paradise or *Strelitzia* and to the banana family, Musaceae. *Heliconia* plants have been made famous by the well-known Brazilian landscape artist Roberto Burle-Marx, who uses them extensively in his gardens on account of their attractive bright colours, the same thing that attracts their hummingbird pollinators. The showy parts of the *Heliconia* inflorescence are the bracts and behind them are the flowers which are touched by the nectar-gathering birds. Many of the bird-pollinated flowers are tubular such as the brightly-coloured red flowers of some of the mistletoes (Loranthaceae). In this case the birds insert their beaks into the tube and are dusted with pollen on their heads and chests. However, some bird-pollinated flowers are of the brush type, similar to bat-pollinated flowers. A good example in Amazonia is *Calliandra* in the Mimosaceae that has several bird-pollinated species. The flowers are borne in dense clusters which give the effect of a mass or brush of stamens, although there are only a few on each individual flower. While obtaining the nectar from the base of the stamens the birds are brushed all over their lower side, and are dusted with pollen. There are a few very large bright red papilionaceous flowers, that is, sweet pea-like flowers, which are bird pollinated. Among them are two spectacular genera of the Papilionaceae, *Mucuna* and *Erythrina*. These have strong, thick, wiry stamens that are not easily broken by the birds' activity.

In a few bird-pollinated flowers the birds trigger an explosion mechanism to release the pollen. This has recently been described in a mint, *Hyptis pauliana* Epling (Brantjes and de Vos, 1981), but it also occurs in some Marantaceae and tropical Asian Loranthaceae. These explosive mechanisms attack their pollinators with a large dusting of pollen.

An important Amazonian plant family in which many species are bird-pollinated is the pineapple family, Bromeliaceae. These plants, with bright red bracts and often contrasting blue flowers, have tubular corollas with nectar at the base. The protruding stamens and styles touch the birds as they gather nectar. Many Bromeliads are epiphytes in Amazonia and there are bird-pollinated examples amongst both the epiphytic and terrestrial species.

Bird-pollinated flowers produce the most abundant quantity of nectar of any flowers but they are often scentless, because of birds' poor sense of smell. Since birds can easily damage flowers, bird visited flowers frequently have ingenious devices to protect the floral parts, especially the ovary. For example, in the common Amazonian family Marcgraviaceae, nectar is isolated in a spur that is away from the flowers. The birds forage in the spur, touch the stamens and style, but do not harm the essential organs of the flower. One of the most attractive vines of the Amazon forest has this mechanism, *Norantea guianensis* (Aubl.) (Fig. 9.3J). The brightly-coloured nectar spurs look like red fruit to the uninitiated. They are in fact the only bright part of the flower, and the small inconspicuous flowers are well removed from the spur. All that is necessary is that the spur is in a position which ensures that the bird will brush into the stamens and style.

9.9. NON-FLYING MAMMALS

There has been much recent discussion about the role of non-flying animals in pollination. Most reports of this came from places other than Amazonia such as for honey possums in Australia, desert rats in South Africa, and most recently rice-rats in the cloud forests of Costa Rica (Lumer, 1980). It is probable that non-flying animals are incidental pollinators in quite a number of Amazonian plants, but that they do not play a major role. There have been at least two recent reports of *Cebus* monkeys visiting and carrying pollen of species of *Combretum* (Prance, 1980b) and *Mabea fistulifera* Benth. (Torres de

Assumpção, 1981). In this case the monkeys are also floral predators eating perhaps two-thirds of the flowers for the nectar. However, those that remain stand an excellent chance of being pollinated by the monkeys, who have so much coloured pollen on their fur that it is visible through binoculars.

Lecythis poiteauii Berg is the only species of the Brazil nut family in which we have observed bat pollination (Mori *et al.*, 1978). Hundreds of bats visit the pendulous flowers of this species and there is no doubt that bats are the principal pollinators. However, observations made by Mori and Bolten showed that an opossum (*Marmosa* sp.) visited the flowers of *Lecythis poiteauii*. The opossum grasped the hood in its front paws and stuck its head into the flowers to drink nectar. The same authors observed visits to the pendulous flowers of *Eperua falcata* Aubl. (Caesalpiniaceae) by a mixed group *Cebus apella* L. and squirrel monkeys (*Saimiri sciureus* L.). The monkeys pull up the long flagelliform inflorescences hand over hand and drink nectar from the flowers. Although pollination by opossum in *L. poiteau* and by monkeys in *E. falcata* is possible, they are certainly not the main pollinators of either species both of which have all the usual features of bat-pollinated flowers. Many more observations are needed to determine the role of non-volant mammals in the pollination of Amazonian plants.

9.10 HETEROSTYLY

The phenomenon of heterostyly is quite frequent in Amazonia. This is the breeding system where there is floral polymorphy with the stamens and styles being inserted at two or three different levels accompanied by a strong self-incompatibility between similar morphs. It is therefore another system of ensuring out-crossing. Several plant families that are common in Amazonia are known for their heterostyly, for example, the Rubiaceae, Turneraceae (Fig. 9.4G, H) and Erythroxylaceae.

The family of the water hyacinth, Pontederiaceae, is a good example of an Amazonian plant where heterostyly has been worked out (*see* Barrett, 1977; Francois, 1964; Hazan, 1918; Mulcahy, 1975 and Ornduff, 1966). The water hyacinth (*Eichhornia crassipes* (Mart.) Solms.) and many of its relatives such as the common species *Pontederia cordata* L. are tristylous a phenomenon that occurs in only three plant families. That is there are three types of plants.
1. Flowers with long styles and anthers at two levels below the stigma.
2. Flowers with mid-length styles and one set of anthers above the stigmas and the other set below.
3. Flowers with short styles and the anthers at two levels above the stigmas.

Experiments by Ornduff (1966) showed that the short-styled form has strong self-incompatibility, the long-styled slightly weaker, and the mid-styled a much weaker incompatibility.

All field studies have shown that in any population the three morphs are not evenly distributed, but seed set is much greater when pollination occurs between any two dissimilar morphs. The water hyacinth is largely pollinated by Hymenoptera (Hazan, 1918; Lovell, 1918) but it is also visited by Lepidoptera. The biological importance of heterostyly is that the differences in anther and stigma positions in the three floral forms is such that they encourage cross-pollination between anthers of one floral morph with the stigmas at the same height of another floral form. These were termed 'legitimate' pollinations by Darwin (1877) who wrote a book on floral variations. Pollinations between different style/stigma lengths is termed illegitimate. The illegitimate pollination in heterostylous plants usually produced fewer seeds, and in the case of the Pontederiaceae this has proved true (Ornduff, 1966; Barrett, 1977).

Distyly is much commoner in the plant kingdom and occurs in Amazonian Rubiaceae and in the coca or cocaine plant *Erythroxylum coca* Lam. (Ganders, 1979), an important stimulatory plant of many Indian tribes of western Amazonia. *Erythroxylum coca* is distylous with a strong self-incompatibility system. In this case there are long-styled or so called 'pin' flowers and short-styled or 'thrum' flowers. The anthers and stigmas are reciprocally positioned in the flowers of the two morphs, thus encouraging legitimate pollination.

Heterostyly is probably more frequent in Amazonia, but there is still a lack of adequate observations in the region and it is yet another aspect that needs further study by naturalists.

9.11. THE RECENTLY ARRIVED VILLAIN — THE AFRICAN BEE

The advance of the African variety of honey bee (*Apis melifera* L.) or so-called killer bees has drawn much over-exaggerated attention from the popular press. Nevertheless, it is true that they escaped from a research laboratory in São Paulo in southern Brazil and they have subsequently advanced over 200 km a year. These bees, which produce much more honey than the normal bees, are also being hived quite successfully by many apiarists. Currently (1982) the bees are crossing Colombia thousands of miles north of the point of origin, so they have now crossed Amazonia and are well established in the region. The trait that has made these bees famous is their aggression. They are not only aggressive to humans but also to their fellow insects, including the pollinators of many Amazonian plants.

In 1973 I observed the pollination of one of the Amazon species of Lecythidaceae, *Couroupita subsessilis* Pilg. This tree was much visited by wasps and a few native bees which carried out pollination effectively as described above. However, observation in 1974 showed that the only floral visitor to these plants in the vicinity of Manaus was *Apis melifera*. The study coincided with the arrival of the African bee. In the case of *Couroupita*, the bees are about the same size as the pollinators, and they are an adequate substitute for the wasps. However, there will be many other cases where this is not true and the pollination of native plants will be affected adversely by the presence of the African bee in the region. Future pollination studies in Amazonia should monitor the effect of these new bees. This is one of the disturbing examples of the rapid invasion of a species introduced by people to a new region.

9.12. CONCLUSION

This account of the pollination of just a few Amazonian plants demonstrates the diverse strategies by which Amazonian plants achieve their pollination. The plants and animals have evolved together over a very long time. From the ancient beetles to the much more recently evolved hummingbirds, plants have been able to make use of this faunistic diversity for their benefit.

The study of pollination is an essential part of the understanding and use of the Amazon forest. New still unexploited plants of economic potential cannot be grown as crops unless we understand how they are pollinated and many other aspects of their biology. Until it was discovered that the South American native orchid *Vanilla* could be manually pollinated it was not possible to grow it outside its native range (a range which corresponds with that of its pollinator). Today Madagascar is the major producer of *Vanilla* where it is entirely artificially pollinated. Even within its native Amazonia greater production of cocoa beans (*Theobroma cacau* L.) occurs if manual pollination techniques are used. In many cases the destruction of a pollinator will also mean the destruction of the plant species. Conservation planners have to take into consideration how the different components of the forest are linked, and formulate their policies based on this integrated biological knowledge. More work is needed on the pollination of Amazonian flora. The studies cited here are only a beginning of what we can find out about Amazonian pollination. Other studies are underway, or have recently been completed but not yet published such as studies of the floral biology of Amazonian laurels (Lauraceae) in the vicinity of Manaus by Holger Kurz, and the study of some members of the large Melastome family of the same region by Suzanne Renner.

Pollination study is an important part of the future rational development of plants of economic importance. Such facts as the obligatorily out-crossing Brazil nut will not produce its valuable harvest without the work of the large euglossine and carpenter bees, and that the important Amazonian crop of *Guaraná* (*Paullinia cupana* HBK var. *sorbilis*) is dependent on the smaller *Trigona* and *Melipona* bees should stimulate further pollination studies.

REFERENCES

Absy, M. L. and Kerr, W. E. (1977) Algumas plantas visitados para obtenção de pólen por operarios de *Melipona seminigra merrillae* em Manaus. *Acta Amazônica* 7, 309 – 315.

Barrett, S. C. H. (1977) The breeding system of *Pontederia rotundifolia* L., a tristylous species. *New Phytol.* 78, 209 – 220.

Bawa, K. S. (1974) Breeding systems of tree species of a lowland tropical community. *Evolution* 28, 85 – 92.

Braga, P. I. S. (1976a) Atração de abelhas polinizadores de Orchidaceae com auxílio de iscas-odores na campina, campinarana e floresta tropical úmida da região de Manaus. *Ciência e Cultura* 28, 767 – 773.

Braga, P. I. S. (1976b) Estudos da flora orquidológico do Estado do Amazonas. 1. Descrição e observação da biologia floral de *Stanhopea candida* Barb. Rodr. *Acta Amazônica* 6, 433 – 438.

Brantjes, N. B. M. and de Vos, O. C. (1981) The explosive release of pollen in flowers of *Hyptis* (Lamiaceae). *New Phytol.* 87, 425 – 430.

Buchmann, S. L., Jones, C. E. and Colin, L. J. (1977) Vibratile pollination of *Solanum douglassii* and *S. xanti* (Solanaceae) in southern California. *Wasmann J. Biol.* 35(1), 1 – 25.

Buchmann, S. L. and Buchmann, M. D. (1981) Anthecology of *Mouriri myrtilloides* (Melastomataceae: Memecyleae), an oil flower in Panama. *Reproductive Botany 1981*, 7 – 24.

Darwin, C. (1877) *The Different Forms of Flowers on Plants of the Same Species.* Murray, London, 352 pages.

Dessart, P. (1961) Contribution a l'étude des Ceratopogonidae (Diptera). *Bull. Agric. Congo Belge* 52, 525 – 540.

Dodson, C. H. (1966) Ethology of some Euglossine bees. *J. Kansas Entomol. Soc.* 39, 607 – 629.

Dodson, C. H. (1967) Relationship between pollinators and orchid flowers. *Atas. Simp. Biota Amazônica* 5 (Zoologica), 1 – 72.

Dressler, R. L. (1967) Why do Euglossine bees visit orchid flowers? *Atas. Simp. Biota Amazônica* 5 (Zoologica), 171 – 180.

Dressler, R. L. (1968a) Observations on orchids and Euglossine bees in Panama and Costa Rica. *Rev. Biol. Trop.* 15, 143 – 183.

Dressler, R. L. (1968b) Pollination by Euglossine bees. *Evolution* 22, 202 – 210.

François, J. (1964) Observations sur l'heterostylie chez *Eichhornia crassipes* (Mart.) Solms. *Acad. Roy. Sci. d'Outre-Mer, Bull. Seances 1964*, 501 –

Frankie, G. W., Opler, P. A. and Bawa, K. S. (1976) Foraging behaviour of solitary bees: implications for out-crossing of a neotropical forest tree species. *J. Ecol.* 64, 1049 – 1057.

Ganders, F. R. (1979) Heterostyly in *Erythroxylum coca* (Erythroxylaceae). *Bot. J. Linn. Soc. London* 78, 11 – 20.

Gentry, A. H. (1974) Coevolutionary patterns in Central American Bignoniaceae. *Ann. Missouri Bot. Gard.* 61, 728 – 759.

Gilbert, L. E. (1972) Pollen feeding and reproductive biology of Heliconius butterflies. *Proc. Nat. Acad. Sci.* 69, 1403 – 1407.

Gilbert, L. E. (1975) Ecological consequences of a coevolved mutualism between butterflies and plants. In *Coevolution of Animals and Plants*, Eds. L. E. Gilbert and P. H. Raven, pp. 210 – 240, University of Texas Press, Austin.

Gottsberger, G. (1970) Beiträge zur Biologie von Annonaceen.-Blüten. *Osterr. Bot. 2* 118, 237 – 279.

Gottsberger, I. S. and Gottsberger, G. (1975) Über sphingophile Angiospermen Brasiliens. *Pl. Syst. Evol.* 123, 157 – 184.

Hazan, T. (1918) The trimorphism and insect visitors of *Pontederia*. *Mem. Torr. Bot. Club* 17, 459 –

Janzen, D. H. (1971) Euglossine bees as long-distance pollinators of tropical plants. *Science* 171, 203 – 205.

Lovell, J. H. (1918) *The Flower and the Bee.* Charles Scribner's Sons, New York.

Lumer, C. (1980) Rodent pollination of *Blakea* (Melastomataceae) in a Costa Rican cloud forest. *Brittonia* 32(4), 512 – 517.

Mori, S. and Kallunki, J. (1976) Phenology and floral biology of *Gustavia superba* (Lecythidaceae) in Central Panama. *Biotropica* 8, 184 – 192.

Mori, S., Prance, G. T. and Bolten, A. (1978) Additional notes on the floral biology of neotropical Lecythidaceae. *Brittonia* 30, 113 – 130.

Mulcahy, D. L. (1975) The reproductive biology of *Eichhornia crassipes* (Pontederiaceae). *Bull. Torr. Bot. Club* 102, 18 – 21.

Ornduff, R. (1966) The breeding system of *Pontederia cordata* L. *Bull. Torr. Bot. Club* 93, 407 – 416.

Prance, G. T. (1976) The pollination and androphore structure of some Amazonian Lecythidaceae. *Biotropica* 8, 235 – 241.

Prance, G. T. (1980a) A note on the pollination of *Nymphaea amazonum* Mart. & Zucc. (Nymphaeaceae). *Brittonia* 32, 505 – 507.

Prance, G. T. (1980b) A note on the probable pollination of *Combretum* by Cebus monkeys. *Biotropica* 12, 239.

Prance, G. T. and Arias, J. R. (1975) A study of the floral biology of *Victoria amazonica* (Poepp.) Sowerby (Nymphaeaceae). *Acta Amazônica* 5, 109 – 139.

Prance, G. T. and Anderson, A. B. (1976) Studies of the floral biology of neotropical Nymphaeaceae 3. *Acta Amazônica* 6, 163 – 170.

Sazima, M. (1978) Polinização por moscos em *Bulbophyllum warmingianum* Cogn. (Orchidaceae), na serra do cipó, Minas Gerais, Brasil. *Rev. Bras. Bot.* 1, 133 – 138.

Taroda, N. and Gibbs, P. E. (1982) Floral biology and breeding system of *Sterculia chicha* St. Hil. (Sterculiaceae). *New Phytol.* 90, 735 – 743.

Torres de Assumpção, C. (1981) *Cebus apella* and *Brachyteles arachnoides* (Cebidae) as potential pollinators of *Mabea fistulifera* (Euphorbiaceae). *J. Mamm.* 62, 386 – 388.

Van der Pijl, L. and Dodson, C. H. (1966) *Orchid Flowers their Pollination and Evolution*. University of Miami Press, Coral Gables.

Vogel, S. (1968, 1969) Chiropterophilie in der Neotropischen. *Flor* 157, 562 – 602; 158, 195 – 202, 289 – 323.

Vogel, S. (1974) *Olblumen und Olsammelade Bienen*. Wiesbader, Steiner.

Webber, A.C. (1981) Alguns aspectos da biologia floral de *Annona sericea* Dun. (Annonaceae). *Acta Amazonica* 11, 61 – 65.

CHAPTER 10

The Dispersal of Forest Plants

KLAUS KUBITZKI

Institut für Allgemeine Botanik und Botanischer Garten, Universität Hamburg, Ohnhorststr. 18, 2000 Hamburg 52, Federal Republic of Germany

CONTENTS

10.1. INTRODUCTION

Integration of plant and animal life reaches its climax in the humid tropics. It is there that biologists have been unveiling the complex interactions between different components of the ecosystem, for example, between flowers and their visitors (in part pollinators), or between fruits and their eaters (in part dispersers). Besides a lot of antagonism between species, there are innumerable adaptations that have evolved during a long process, in which alterations in one kind of organism stimulated the selection of changes in the organisation or behaviour of another kind of organism, to be followed by a return influence on the first kind of organism: processes that have been named coadaptation, reciprocal evolution or coevolution.

There is little doubt that the high degree of coevolutionary relationship in the tropical forest is one of the main factors causing its immense richness of different kinds of plants and animals (Burger, 1981). In the forests of northern temperate zones there are usually only 10 to 15 tree species growing together on one hectare. However, in the humid tropical forest usually at least 100 to 200 occur, and in Central Amazonia occasionally more than 500 species of trees and shrubs can be found in an area of the same size. This implies an extremely low population density for many species and often about half of all tree species are only represented by a single individual on one hectare. This diversity could never be maintained if trees were eventually replaced by their own progeny that had germinated below them. It is believed that dispersal contributes to the retention of the mixed composition of the forest. There are indications that diversity as such is of an adaptive nature, and the theoretical framework available (*see* section 10.5) supports this suggestion.

While the process of dispersal can be studied directly in the field, if the observer is sufficiently patient and willing to observe what is happening, dispersal that contributes to the range extension of a given species is a process that can often be better assessed indirectly. It has often been observed by biogeographers that hardly any species of plant or animal in the world occupies all places in the biosphere where it could live judging from environmental requirements. Thus the area occupied by most species are examples of incomplete dispersion and when considering this, one should bear in mind that range extension depends not only on transport of seeds to an appropriate site, but also on a complex interaction of other factors and processes (*see* section 10.4). Due to this complexity, range extension as the result of a historical process is much more difficult to define than the process of dispersal.

The following account will focus on the adaptive relationships between plants and animals for seed dispersal in the Amazonian forest. In addition, the consequences of dispersal to the composition and dynamics of the community will be discussed.

There is a vast literature available about these topics, which has been summarised in the monumental book by Ridley (1930), while more modern aspects are dealt with by van der Pijl (1982) and Kubitzki (1983). The only comprehensive treatment for the Amazon region is the vivid account of the biology of the forest by Huber (1910) which is still readable today. In the decades following the time of Huber, studies in natural history fell into disrepute, and interest in plant-animal relationships has only recently been revived.

10.2. EVOLUTIONARY RELATIONSHIPS BETWEEN PLANTS AND THEIR DISPERSAL AGENTS

10.2.1. Dispersal by water and wind (Abiotic dispersal)

There is no other region in the world in which water is more omnipresent and at the same time important for the shaping of the landscape than in Amazonia. Its rivers with their different types of water — white, black and clear (*see* Chapter 1) — are tied up with the physical and biotic environment, soils and forest, but at the same time they each create quite different scenarios for their biota.

The water levels of the Amazonian rivers are subjected to annual fluctuations between 7 and 13 m that occur with remarkable regularity from year to year. This regularity has allowed the evolution of flooded forests that grow along the rivers and are highly adapted to withstand partial or complete submersion during part of the year. Here we find a high proportion of tree species whose fruits or seeds remain afloat on the surface of the rivers and are thus dispersed. Palms and legumes, which abound in the flooded forests, are the most important families with fruits which are dispersed by water; among the first, *Mauritia flexuosa* and *Euterpe oleracea* (the latter otherwise zoochorous) are good examples, while legumes are represented by species of the following genera: *Macrolobium*, *Crudia*, *Pterocarpus*, *Pithecellobium*, *Peltogyne*, *Dalbergia* and *Cynometra*. Many of these fruits have visible traits that keep them afloat, such as spongy pericarps; Ducke (1949) gave a list of them. The seeds of the large aroid herb *Montrichardia arborescens*, which is so characteristic of Amazon river margins, are dispersed by water.

The seeds of the rubber tree *Hevea brasiliensis* (Euphorbiaceae) which grows predominantly in the forests on alluvial flood plains of whitewater rivers have been observed to remain afloat for at least 2 months, and like those of the riverine tree *Pachira aquatica* (Bombacaceae) they often start to germinate when still floating.

Hernandia guianensis, a riverine tree distributed from coastal Guyana to the mouth of the Amazon, has drupes surrounded by a tender, creamy envelope which permits it to float on rivers. However, this seems to be a curiosity rather than an efficient dispersal method since this tree has such a restricted area of distribution.

Another curiosity is provided by rain ballists, a group of plants that grows on the forest floor where their seeds are dispersed by heavy rain drops that drip from wet foliage and make diaspores jump over some distance. The melastomaceous herb *Monolena* is an example of this category.

It must be emphasised that the problem with aquatic dispersal is that it operates almost exclusively in a downstream direction. Upstream dispersal requires other agents, such as fish (*see* Chapter 14), turtles, other reptiles, or wind. The Podostemonaceae, interesting plants that only grow on the rocks of the rapids, have to rely on dispersal by wind for directions other than downstream (Grubert, 1974).

It is not surprising that at the margin of the immense Amazonian rivers and lakes wind is an important dispersal agent. Riverine trees with pronounced adaptations for wind dispersal include *Triplaris surinamensis* with alate drupes, *Couratari oligantha* with winged seeds, *Calycophyllum spruceanum* with minute seeds, and *Pseudobombax munguba*. Also two species of willows, *Salix martiana* and *S. humboldtiana*, and the silk cotton tree, *Ceiba pentandra*, are good examples of wind dispersed riverine trees because their seeds are equipped with cotton-like hairs, which enable them to float in the air.

In the high forest, three groups of plants characteristically show a preponderance of adaptations for dispersal by wind. First of all, the trees of the uppermost storey of the forest, especially the emergent trees, must be mentioned. Examples include many species of the Bombacaceae (seeds surrounded with hairs), Bignoniaceae (with broadly winged lightweight seeds), legumes (with one-seeded, alate pods) and Vochysiaceae (with small, winged seeds). Lianas, which climb up the canopy of the forest, form the second important group of wind dispersed plants, and many members of this group of plants (Malpighiaceae, Bignoniaceae, Polygalaceae, and many others) have winged seeds or fruits. Wind, however, is only one of the methods of dispersal adopted by lianas; many of them are dispersed by birds. Although fierce storms in Amazonia may not be too rare, dispersal by wind is mostly over small distances (up to a few hundred metres), and it contributes to the retention of the population rather than to an extension of the area of distribution.

The third group in which wind dispersal is prominent are epiphytes, i.e. plants that live on others with or without parasitising them; here again, another part of this group is adapted for bird dispersal. The majority of the non-parasitic epiphytes is formed by orchids, ferns and Bromeliads. The orchids are characterised by seeds of an extremely low weight (0.003 mg), the so-called dust seeds; the ferns propagate by equally lightweight spores, and the Bromeliaceae have specialised flight adaptations in the form of feathery or tailed appendages that are present also in the rubiaceous epiphytic shrub *Hillia*. Other members of the Bromeliaceae produce berries whose seeds are bird dispersed.

These epiphytes, which are too weak as competitors to be able to grow on the floor of the forest, depend on appropriate sites that are relatively rare and can only be reached either with the aid of frugivorous animals that rest on trees, or by producing the enormous 'rain' of dispersal units that reaches all potentially suitable sites. This explains the need for the small size and enormous quantity of the propagules. The complete absence of storage tissue from the seeds of the orchids is compensated by their obligate mutualistic relationship with fungi (mycorrhiza, *see* Chapter 15).

Dispersal by water and wind have their limitations: the first can only be operative in aquatic, or amphibious vegetation and normally functions only in the direction determined by the flow of the water. Wind dispersal is possible only for lightweight fruits or seeds or spores, and can only operate at the edges and in the canopy of the forest. Wind currents are not strong enough in the sheltered interior of the forest. It is interesting that nature indeed makes use of these abiotic agents for dispersal as far as these are available and wherever these are practical. The advantage of abiotic dispersal for the plant is that it is less costly than dispersal by animals.

10.2.2. Dispersal by animals (Biotic dispersal)

Animals are not actually interested in dispersing plant propagules but only in eating the fruits and seeds. Therefore, a plant-animal interaction in which the animal carries away ripe fruits and seeds, consumes the pericarp, aril and other soft parts and rejects the seeds or discharges them via its digestive tract undamaged, is but one extreme in the possible range of plant-animal relationships. The other extreme is represented by animals that eat fruits primarily in order to digest the seeds. From the viewpoint of dispersal it is important to make a distinction between frugivores and seed dispersers. For the disperser the seed is only ballast which it gets rid of as quickly as it can. There is much evidence of the surprising rapidity with which some birds can remove the edible parts of a fruit and regurgitate the seed, and this is clearly an important part of their adaptation to such diet.

Bound up with the whole subject of dispersal are the energetics involved. Dispersers need energy in order to carry away fruits; therefore, the amount of energy offered by the edible part of the fruit must not be too small, so that the animal becomes frustrated and stops feeding on the fruits. On the other hand, for effective dispersal it must not be too high so that the animal would already be satiated after eating a small number of fruits.

Another important aspect is the plant's need for defence against seed predators. This may be accomplished by different means, such as the production of hard mechanical tissue; the small size of the seeds so that they escape from mechanical destruction by the predator; synchronised ripening of several plants within a population, or even a community, by which satiation of predators is attained; and by chemical defence (*see* Chapter 11).

Bats, birds, rodents, and monkeys are the more important dispersers in present-day Amazonian forests. Due to the differences in the sensory capacities of these animals, during the process of coadaptation different traits have evolved in the fruits that act as signals to attract the dispersers. These differences are due to the fact that birds have a weak sense of smell, if any at all, and are visual animals, while mammals have a well-developed sense of smell, are mostly night-feeders and are often colour-blind.

10.2.2.1. Birds and bats

Accidental transport by birds takes place with small, unadapted fruits or seeds which are present in the mud and stick to the feet of waterfowl. Even if transport of this kind over wider distances is a rare event, it cannot be ignored because many water plants have obviously attained a wide, transcontinental distribution through this method of dispersal. Accidental and incidental dispersal also results when fruit-eating birds that normally destroy the fruits cache part of their food or place it somewhere to be pecked, but forget to eat it. While this is mainly known as an important means of dispersal in temperate forests, it may also be present in the tropical rainforest. Granivorous birds may also be important dispersers in Amazonia, but again little is known about them. Even if in the majority of cases the grain is bitten up, or is completely destroyed by the digestive processes, as to be nongerminable, a few grains may survive and be dispersed.

Such cases may be important for the plant population even if leading to successful dispersal only occasionally. In these cases, however, no visible adaptations have evolved in the fruits or seeds, which makes study of this type of dispersal harder.

In contrast to this, fruits adapted to dispersal by birds possess optical lures in the form of a vivid colouration often of contrasting colours in which red is the most frequent colour. For the same reason red is also typical of bird pollinated flowers (see Chapter 9), and seems to be a highly efficient attractant for birds, because red and orange are conspicuous neither to insects (except butterflies) nor (probably) to monkeys. Even if birds appear to have no intrinsic preference for red, they apparently learn to recognise it as a 'signal' for a high caloric reward, which invariably is connected with this optical lure.

It is interesting that some legumes (*Ormosia*, *Pithecellobium*, *Rhynchosia* spp.) imitate the possession of an aril by mere colouration. Such mimetic seeds profit from the conditioning of the dispersers without investing anything in the formation of nutritive tissue.

From the viewpoint of dispersal, two different classes of birds have to be distinguished: *Unspecialised*, or *opportunistic*, *frugivores*, that utilise fruits primarily as a source of carbohydrate and water; otherwise they are more or less insectivorous. Birds belonging to this group are mostly smaller than those of the second group, the *specialised frugivores*. These cover their demand for carbohydrates, lipids and proteins from fruits that are relatively large (McKey, 1975; Snow, 1971); they do not eat anything except fruit. The favourite fruits of the unspecialised frugivores are berries that have a rather watery flesh and a large number of small seeds; they are mostly blue, black or red. Good examples are many members of the plant families Melastomataceae, Myrtaceae and Rubiaceae. Such plants are typically understorey trees or shrubs often occurring in secondary vegetation like edge habitats or recently cleared ground. For this type of colonising plant it is advantageous to attract as many kinds of different frugivores as possible and thus to scatter widely many seeds.

Migrant wood warblers (Parulidae) like many other primarily insectivorous birds are often observed visiting fruiting trees in tropical areas. In Central America, they have been found to act as important dispersal agents of the meliaceous understorey tree *Guarea glabra*. In Barro Colorado Island, the trees *Lindackeria laurina*, *Casearia* spp. (Flacourtiaceae) and *Miconia* spp. (Melastomataceae) are dispersed nearly exclusively by migrant warblers (Greenberg, 1981).

Fruits adapted for dispersal by *specialised frugivorous birds* are typically different. They are large, because they are mostly produced by trees of the primary forest and therefore need large seeds, frequently only one per fruit, with ample food reserves so that the seedlings have a chance to establish themselves on the forest floor. The fruits generally have a firm, dense flesh that is rich in fats and proteins. A characteristic feature of many specialised frugivores is the little muscularised, thin-walled, often small stomach. This reflects the relatively small amount of mechanical breakdown necessary for the digestion of the fruit flesh. Another feature of these animals is their habit of regurgitating larger seeds immediately after the surrounding fruit flesh has been removed in the stomach, before the seed can enter the rest of the digestive tract. This explains why the seeds of many Lauraceae, which are much consumed by specialised frugivores, are comparatively soft, and why these large, seemingly vulnerable seeds remain totally unharmed in the stomachs of the Oilbird (*Steatornis caripensis*) and some cotingids in Trinidad (Snow, 1962, 1971).

Specialised frugivorous birds reach an upper size limit that is much the same in all tropical countries. This is exemplified by the large toucans and the largest cotingas in the neotropics. The upper size limit of these birds presumably has determined the upper size limit of the fruits adapted for avian dispersal. Alternatively, the process may have been mutual, the selection for large fruits leading to selection for increased size in the birds. An upper size limit of 70 by 40 mm for oval fruits seems to be the general rule, as is shown by the fruits of the Lauraceae, Burseraceae, Myristicaceae, Araliaceae and palms, families which are predominantly dispersed by large frugivorous birds and produce fruits of the kind described here. Fruits that exceed this size limit may be expected to be dispersed by other agents, and concomitant modifications are likely to have occurred.

The fruit of the Greenheart, *Ocotea rodiaei*, belonging to the otherwise invariably bird-dispersed Lauraceae, is larger than the rest; its pericarp is hard and woody, and the fact that it is unusual in growing semicolonially within a restricted area in Guiana suggests a limited facility for dispersal (Snow, 1981).

Bird dispersed epiphytes seem to have their own specialised dispersers, which is understandable because these plants have to be able to germinate and to establish themselves very quickly, before they can be washed from their perch or blown off by the wind. In mistletoes for instance (which are frequent in Amazonia) there are mucilaginous-seeded berries the seeds of which are void of a seed coat but surrounded by a sticky layer of viscin, which is impregnated by chemicals hastening the seed's passage through the bird's gut. In the neotropics, small tanagers of the genus *Euphonia* seem to be specialised for a diet of mistletoe berries. In Trinidad (and certainly elsewhere in the New World tropics) *Euphonia violacea* feeds regularly on the berries of different species of the Cactaceae (*Rhipsalis*), Araceae and Bromeliaceae, the fruits of which are somewhat similar to mistletoe berries. In *Rhipsalis*, a pendent epiphytic cactus, transcontinental dispersal from the New World to the Old has occurred, Madagascar being the secondary dispersal centre of the genus, from which tropical Africa and Ceylon have been reached (Barthlott, 1983).

Many fruits are eaten and dispersed by both birds and bats, such as those of the fig trees (*Ficus*) and the most important tree genus of secondary growth, *Cecropia*. However, bats are nocturnal and colour-blind so that colouration plays no part in attracting them. Moreover, bats — like all mammals — have a well-developed sense of smell, have teeth and can masticate much better than birds, so that the general syndrome of diaspores dispersed by bats differs from that of ornithochores. Typical bat dispersed fruits possess a hard skin, often a 'stable', musty, sometimes rancid odour, and drab colours. Often bats do not eat the fruits immediately on the tree where they grow, but have the habit of many frugivores of consuming them in one or several special locations, sometimes their roosting places. The reason for this behaviour may be to avoid competitors or predators. Only in the case of small seeded fruits are the seeds ingested; the bats usually consume the juice after intensive chewing. Thereafter the fruits are dropped or spat out in heaps on the ground where they are often destroyed by insects or rodents.

Bat dispersed seeds often hang outside the foliage because the bats, with their sonar navigation system, have difficulties in flying inside the foliage (Fig. 10.1). A fine example is the tree genus *Lecythis* (Lecythidaceae) the large woody capsules of which remain on the trees after opening. The seeds hang attached to a large funicle aril that is fleshy and sweet tasting. Bats have been observed entering the capsule and removing the arils and seeds together; later they drop them either in flight or at their roosts (Prance and Mori, 1983).

By radiotelemetry it could be shown that individuals of the bat *Carollia perspicillata* change their feeding area once every 1.5 hours and visit two to four different areas containing two or more fruit species per night. The passage time of small seeds through the gut of the bats is rapid (15 to 20 minutes), so that most of the seeds ingested will remain close to the parental source (Fleming and Heithaus, 1981). Bat dispersal is local and heterogeneous; at one of two studied trees of *Andira inermis* in Costa Rica an estimated 48% of the seed crop remained under the parent canopy, and from 0.002 to 35% of the seed crop accumulated under several roost trees located up to 100 m or more from the parent tree. Occasionally, transport over larger distances has been observed. Virtually all of the seeds that were

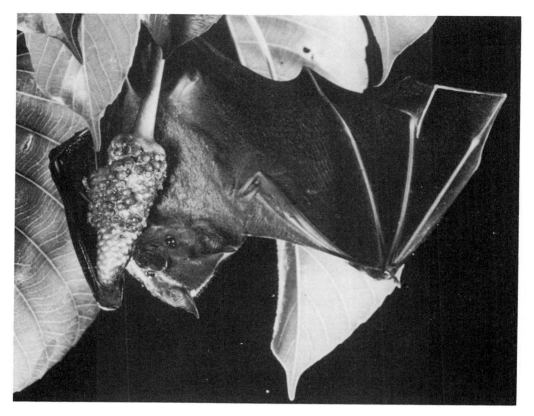

Fig. 10.1. The Jamaican fruit-eating bat *Artibeus jamaicensis* feeding on an euphorbiaceous tree in Panama. This is one of the most frequent and best studied fruit-eating bats of the neotropical realm (photo courtesy of Merlin D. Tuttle, Milwaukee Public Museum).

deposited under the parent tree were seriously destroyed or damaged by weevils (Janzen *et al.*, 1976). However, this does not automatically lead to clumped distribution because only an unpredictably small fraction of the seedlings will ultimately grow up in a clearing.

Three groups of plants can be considered to be especially well-adapted for bat dispersal: First, those with drupaceous, one-seeded fruits with a large and hard kernel. Examples include several legume genera, such as *Dipteryx* and *Andira*, and representatives of other families like *Licania*, *Parinari* and *Couepia* (Chrysobalanaceae), *Poraqueiba* (Icacinaceae), *Sacoglottis*, *Vantanea* and *Humiria* (Humiriaceae), *Spondias mombin* (Anacardiaceae) and *Calophyllum brasiliense* (Guttiferae).

The bat relationship with these plants is well-known to local people; 'andirá' means 'bat' in the 'lingua geral' of Brazil, and the Portuguese name for *Andira inermis* is 'morcegueiro' or bat tree (*see also* Chapter 9).

A second group has large, slippery seeds that are embedded in sweet, smooth tissue and fall easily to the ground; members of the Sapotaceae and Annonaceae belong here. A third category is formed by sweet and soft fruits or infructescences containing numerous tiny dispersal units exemplified by *Cecropia*, *Ficus* and *Piper*, *Solanum* spp. and *Muntingia calabura*. The latter species is a widespread tree of secondary vegetation. The genus *Piper*, which has numerous Amazonian species, is mostly dispersed by bats of the genus *Carollia* which may be a *Piper* specialist, just as manakins are specialists on shrub fruits (Fleming *et al.*, 1977).

10.2.2.2. Rodents and other mammals

Agoutis (genus *Dasyprocta*) are large, diurnal rodents and are found throughout the humid neotropical forest. Rodents usually destroy the seeds that they eat, but agoutis scatter hoard, that is, they carry individual seeds for a distance up to 50 m and bury them without damage just as squirrels bury acorns in the northern temperate region. Usually the animals bury the seeds near an object like a buttress, a fallen log or the base of a palm clump. Later, when there is scarcity of fresh fruit, they search at these places, but there is no evidence that they remember specifically where they have buried the seeds (Smythe, 1970).

There are several tree species with fruits too heavy for bats and monkeys that are dispersed on the forest floor by agoutis. They seem to be regular dispersers of palm fruits and have been observed to scatter hoard, for instance, fruits of the palms *Astrocaryum* and *Iriartea excelsa*. Huber (1910) who was fully aware of the role of agoutis, expressed the view that palms like the Royal Palm (*Maximiliana regia*) and the Pataua (*Oenocarpus bataua*) could not have attained their vast distribution without the activity of agoutis. Huber even observed that these animals, after eating the tasty mesocarp, scratched a hole with their forehands in which they buried the seeds.

It had long been a puzzle how the seeds of the Brazil nut tree *Bertholletia excelsa* are liberated from the hard, woody capsule that can be opened by man only with the aid of an axe. Huber (1910) showed that these capsules, after having fallen down to the ground, are opened by agoutis that eat some seeds but scatter hoard the rest. Later, when they fail to find some of the buried seeds these become available for germination.

Rodents are mostly destructive, but due to the peculiarities of their behaviour on the one hand, and the mechanical protection often developed in the fruits they handle on the other, they can be important dispersal agents. This seems to be even more true for monkeys which eat everything edible in the forest but have a preference for large, nutritious fruits. From a detailed study of the diet and feeding behaviour of the black spider monkey (*Ateles paniscus paniscus*, Fig. 10.4) in Surinam (van Roosmalen, 1980), it has become clear that spider monkeys are the most important dispersers of the larger fruits of the rainforest. Although these animals prefer fruits with an agreeable smell they also consume fruits that appear to have coevolved primarily with other animals. In Surinam, fruits of *Virola* (Fig. 10.7), normally dispersed by birds, are an important part of the diet of the spider monkey, and in Costa Rica, *Ateles geoffroyi* has been observed to eat unripe fruit of *Swartzia cubensis* (Boucher, 1981), a species also exhibiting the ornithochorous syndrome.

In Amazonia, monkey dispersed fruits have a sweet pulp that is enclosed in a firm pericarp which can be opened only with some effort. Fruits of wild cacao (*Theobroma*) and its relative *Herrania* (both Sterculiaceae), *Mammea* (Guttiferae) and some species of *Inga* (Leguminosae) are good examples. They share the peculiarity that the pulp forms part of the relatively large seeds that are sucked but not swallowed. The animals usually take the fruits to a safe place in order to open them and to feed on the contents.

Little is known about the impact of squirrels on dispersal but it may be assumed that these animals are primarily seed predators in Amazonia.

Among other mammals, white lipped peccaris (*Tayassu pecari*) and collared peccaris (*Tayassu tajacu*) forage extensively on the ground of the forest and eat everything edible. The latter species migrates in large herds that demand great amounts of food so that these animals have to be considered as potentially important dispersal agents. This may also be true for the tapir although in an experiment four-fifths of the seeds requiring about 15 days to pass the animal's gut were killed.

10.2.2.3. Ants

Although dispersal of seeds by ants may be far more common in tropical regions than previously suspected, there are only a few well documented cases from the humid tropics of the New World. In two species of the genus *Calathea* (Marantaceae), which are forest floor herbs, ants are attracted by the soft envelopes of the seeds (arils); they transport the seeds to their nests and remove the arils. There is evidence that seeds without arils germinate more readily than seeds with arils (Horovitz and Beattie, 1980). Also in the Central American/Andean terrestrial and epiphytic herb *Chrysothemis friedrichsthaliana* (Gesneriaceae) the seeds are provided with fleshy, white appendages called elaiosomes that attract ants of the genera *Azteca*, *Paratrichina* and *Pheidole*. Moreover, the genera *Renealmia* (Zingiberaceae), *Cryptochloa* (Gramineae) and the sedge *Dichromena radicans* may be ant-dispersed. The common weedy species of waste places in Amazonia, *Turnera ulmifolia* is also ant dispersed.

10.2.2.4. Anachronistic fruits

There are fruits of the Neotropics that are disregarded by all potential dispersers. Janzen and Martin (1981) have developed the hypothesis that their reproductive traits could have been moulded through evolutionary interaction with the Tertiary megafauna of Central and South America that, for reasons not yet understood, became extinct towards the end of the Pleistocene roughly 10,000 years ago. This megafauna included, among others, giant armadillos, gomphotheres and horses (Simpson, 1980). This hypothesis is supported by observations on the interaction between introduced large herbivores and the New World flora. The large, round, hard, ripe fruits of the Central American tree *Crescentia alata* (Bignoniaceae), for instance, are ignored by all native potential dispersers but eagerly eaten by introduced horses. Range cattle ignore the fruit of *C. alata* but avidly eat the fruits of the legume tree *Pithecellobium saman* which are in turn ignored by range horses. Both these reintroduced animals are effective dispersers for the seeds of the fruits they eat, and this makes it credible that the Pleistocene horses and cattle also functioned in the same way. After the extinction of the megafauna, the population density of the tree species which had lost their dispersal agents may have shrunk but not gone extinct because the tree-disperser interaction is not so tightly coevolved that the loss of one component leads to the immediate extinction of the other.

Among the trees and shrubs the seeds of which were probably dispersed by the extinct megafauna, Janzen and Martin (1981) list the following: *Spondias mombin*, *Hippomane mancinella*, *Andira inermis*, *Dioclea megacarpa*, *Hymenaea courbaril*, *Chlorophora tinctoria*, *Alibertia edulis*, *Genipa americana* and *Randia echinocarpa*, to which some others, such as *Crescentia cujete* and *Couroupita guianensis* might be added. These latter species have large, round, heavy fruits with a woody pericarp and the seeds are embedded in sweet smelling pulp. The fruits of *Couroupita*, the cannon ball tree, are often found in large numbers under mature trees where they rot. The seeds often begin to germinate without secondary dispersal by terrestrial animals having occurred (Prance and Mori, 1983). A single observation has been made where a herd of the white-lipped pecary was seen feeding on the fruit. Other fruits coevolved with extinct mammals may be found among those eaten by man and described by Cavalcante (1976) in his book on edible fruits of Amazonia.

10.2.3. Diversification of adaptations for dispersal

The riverine forests in Amazonia are composed of specialised, flood resistant tree species the congeners of which grow in the non-flooded forests on 'terra firme'. Many of the riverine species are known to possess indehiscent, often corky, spongy or otherwise buoyant fruits while their closely related species on 'terra firme' have dehiscent fruits usually with an animal relationship for dispersal. Ducke (1949) gave an impressive list of such plants.

There are also fine examples of an adaptive radiation with respect to dispersal in major plant groups. An especially wide array of relevant adaptations has evolved in the Brazil nut family, Lecythidaceae, a family of tropical trees well represented in Amazonia (Prance and Mori, 1983). The large, indehiscent fruits of the cannon ball tree *Couroupita* have already been mentioned as mammal dispersed (see p. 200), while the similar fruits of the riverine *Gustavia augusta* are not only rafted by water but their seeds have also been found to be dispersed by fish. In addition to indehiscent fruits, the Lecythidaceae have several genera with dehiscent fruits in which the capsules open by a peculiar circular lid or operculum. While the capsules of *Lecythis* contain seeds dispersed by bats, those of *Eschweilera* have a relationship with monkeys (e.g. *Chiropetes*). In the Brazil nut tree whose dispersal has been referred to on p. 199, the need for protection of the seeds has led to a secondarily indehiscent fruit. One species of *Eschweilera, E. tenuifolia*, and *Allantoma lineata* produce seeds dispersed by water; they have been observed to remain afloat for months. Finally the two genera *Couratari* and *Cariniana* have given up an animal relationship for dispersal of their seeds by wind; these trees are restricted to open habitats such as riversides and savannah edges or are unusually large trees emergent above the forest canopy.

There are also other plant families which show a comparable amount of radiation for dispersal. However, in other families a restricted number of dispersal methods or fixation of only one type is found. In order to understand the evolutionary switch-overs that must have occurred in the past it is important to recognise that coevolved plant-animal relationships are frequently not exclusive, but allow for considerable flexibility. The central American tree species *Stemmadenia donnell-smithii* (Apocynaceae) that displays the classical ornithochorous syndrome is reported to be dispersed by birds *and* monkeys; *Virola surinamensis*, although coevolved with birds, is water dispersed. Other examples where a *prima vista* relationship is broken have been referred to above (see p. 199). All this shows that in the whole process of dispersal a high degree of opportunism occurs. For this reason there are many starting points for selective changes of the respective adaptations.

10.3. DISPERSAL AND THE COMMUNITY

10.3.1. Frugivory in relation to plant diversity

The high number of species that exist today in some of the plant families that are important for frugivores, such as the Lauraceae (about 2,500 species) or the Melastomataceae (about 4,500 species) is presumably the result of a long evolutionary history. However, apart from the mere length of the interaction, plant speciation may well have been influenced by the special nature of the relationship. Dispersal by birds, but also by other animal vectors, should provide the opportunity for plant populations to establish themselves well beyond the range of the parental stock. This may be a stimulus for geographical differentiation of populations which is considered as the most widespread mechanism involved in the evolution of new species. If this dispersal and subsequent speciation is followed by migration back into the original area, a number of closely related species with overlapping areas of distribution will result. They can be expected to have rather similar fruits, because selection for dispersal by a common pool of frugivores will tend to standardise their size and shape (Snow, 1981). In such a situation, competition for dispersal agents may affect the fruiting seasons of the individual species and lead to sequential fruiting. This has been observed in bird dispersed Melastomataceae in Trinidad and elsewhere (*see* Fig. 10.2). Such differential fruiting, similar to differential flowering (*see* Chapter 9), serves the important function of contributing towards the sustenance of the dispersing fauna around the year. However, the explosive radiation leading to numerous species with overlapping areas appears to be restricted to the lower storeys of the forest and other evolutionary patterns may be typical of canopy trees (Gentry, 1983). Staggered fruiting is less likely to occur in canopy trees that produce mostly large seeds and have fruiting seasons which are often synchronised with the annual distribution of rainfall. Where such synchronised fruiting occurs within and between species, it has been interpreted as contributing to an oversatiation of the food requirements of dispersers and predators, especially in the cases where scatter hoarding rodents are involved, thus leaving a surplus of seeds for germination.

10.3.2. Dispersal and forest regeneration and succession

Many factors interact in determining the distribution patterns of tree species in humid tropical forests. Seed dispersal is but the first step in this process, followed by a critical phase of seedling establishment. Later on, the availability of light will be of utmost importance for the future development of forest tree seedlings, and it is especially the size of the light gap in the forest that will determine the reaction of the vegetation. Small light gaps which are caused by storms or by the falling of dead trees without the influence of man, will give an opportunity for growth to light demanding seedlings that may have been 'waiting' in the shade for years without showing growth. In this way, a continuous regeneration of the primary forest takes place. A peculiarity of the seeds of most of the trees of these primary humid tropical forests is that they are large and have only a short-term viability during which they have the potential to germinate. In larger clearings such as those that primitive people leave behind in the process of 'shifting cultivation', or the still larger ones that originate from modern forest destruction, the seeds and seedlings of the species of primary forest are destroyed. In this situation the large number of small seeds which are omnipresent in the upper layers of the forest soil germinate and form what is called a

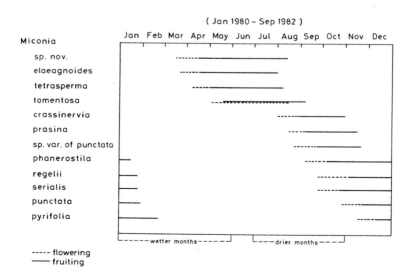

Fig. 10.2. Flowering and fruiting seasons of 12 species of *Miconia* (Melastomataceae) co-occurring in the middlestorey of a Central Amazonian rainforest north of Manaus. Because all species share a common pool of pollinators and dispersers, competition between them for the services of these insects and birds has led to sequential flowering and fruiting (based on doctoral thesis by Susanne Renner, 1984, Hamburg).

Fig. 10.3. A patch of secondary forest on a slope by a stream near Humaitá on the Rio Madeira, Brazil, formed by *Cecropia membranacea* (photo courtesy of G. Gottsberger, São Luis, Brazil).

'secondary forest'. This is composed of light demanding species in which initially the genus *Cecropia* (Fig. 10.3) plays the dominant role.

The omnipresence of *Cecropia* seeds and those of the other species of the secondary vegetation is due to dispersal by animals, primarily bats and birds which continually fill up the 'seed bank' in the upper layer of the forest soil. In the Surinam forests, for example, 76 species of birds, 12 of bats and 8 of monkeys were found to feed on *Cecropia* fruits (Holthuijzen and Boerboom, 1982). The seeds remain dormant as long as the environment prevents germination and react immediately to full daylight and in the case of *Cecropia* (but not of other species), also to fluctuations of temperature, which are the consequences of the clearing of the forest. Thus the seeds of pioneer plants 'wait' for the increased light intensity that accompanies disturbance. Over the years, if left undisturbed, the secondary vegetation will be gradually transformed into primary forest through the stepwise invasion of the elements of the latter. It is clear that this process is not possible if the size of the clearings exceeds an upper limit (*see* Chapter 18), and there is no source of seed parents of the primary forest species.

Thus bats and birds have an important role in influencing the dynamics of forest succession by introducing seeds of the secondary growth vegetation into the soil of the primary forest and *vice versa*.

In addition to providing mobility for seeds, frugivores can sometimes affect the germination probability of the seeds they defecate or regurgitate. Seeds of *Cecropia peltata*, for instance, have a higher germination probability when they pass through birds; monkey-passed seeds of *Miconia argenta*, *Carludovica palmata*, *Genipa americana* and *Trichilia cipo* germinate at a faster rate than the controls and bat-passed seeds of *Cecropia peltata* and *Solanum hazenii* have an increased germination rate.

Fig. 10.4. Two year-old individual of the spider monkey (*Ateles p. paniscus*) leaning on a *Phenakospermum* tree. This is one of the most important fruit dispersers in Surinam (photo courtesy of M.G.M. van Roosmalen, Utrecht).

Fig. 10.5. A day's diet for a subgroup of the spider monkey in the rainy season (16 Apr. 1978), showing *Clusia grandiflora* (largest fruit), *Bagassa guianensis* (green warty fruit), *Spondias mombin* (yellow fruit), *Virola surinamensis* (red striate fruit), *Clarisia racemosa* (greyish curved fruit), *Cayaponia rigida* (second largest fruit), *Tetragastris altissima* and *T. panamensis* (small and larger red fruit with white arils, respectively) (photo courtesy of M.G.M. van Roosmalen).

Fig. 10.6. Fruiting branch of the melastome *Leandra micropetala*, the berries of which are dispersed by unspecialised frugivorous birds. The contrasting colours (blue berries on red stalks) form part of the ornithochorous syndrome (photo courtesy of Susanne Renner, Hamburg).

Fig. 10.7. Fruits of the nutmeg related *Virola sebifera*. Colour contrast between red aril enveloping the seed and white inner side of the capsule valves. This fruit is coevolved with birds but also dispersed by other animals like monkeys and by running water (photo courtesy of G. Gottsberger, São Luis, Brazil).

10.4. DISPERSAL AND DISTRIBUTION

There are many obvious relationships between the type of diaspore, its dispersal agent and the range of distribution attained by a taxon. One generality is that species of primary forest that are endowed with heavy, few- to one-seeded, mostly mammal dispersed fruits tend to have restricted areas of distribution. The other extreme would be represented by the species of secondary growth forest all of which have fruits with numerous, minute seeds. Although many of these species have a wide distribution throughout tropical America, the small size of their diaspores seems to be primarily related to the need to produce a constant seed rain as part of their reproductive strategy. In general it seems as if all dispersal in the rainforest habitat, whether by mammal, bird, bat, wind, water, etc., serves the primary function of maintaining the population. In closed communities, wind or bird dispersed species very often have a relatively small range of distribution, which reflects the limited efficiency of their dispersal. However, in more open and in drier vegetation, wind and animal dispersal may have been much more efficient with respect to the area occupied by the species. In the case of bird dispersal this might be related to the differences in behaviour of the animals involved.

It would be foolish in the extreme to expect a clearcut relationship in a given plant taxon between the means of dispersal for which adaptations have evolved and its range of distribution. Similarly, the simplistic attempts of Willis (1922) to relate the size of the areas of distribution with the age of the taxa involved ('age and area hypothesis') have been discredited (Kubitzki, 1975). The reason for this is that dispersal is but one condition necessary for the successful range extension of a species. Others may be the survival of the vulnerable seedling stage; entering into an alien biocoenosis and building up of a population; and overcoming the reproductive constraints. Because of this, the possibilities for range extension of a given taxon are difficult to analyse and can hardly be predicted with any certainty.

10.5. CONCLUSION

Dispersal ecology has proven to be an important tool for an analysis of the structure and functioning of the neotropical rainforest communities. Although we are only beginning to understand the interdependencies of the components of tropical rainforest, it has become clear that these communities are highly integrated systems. Intense interactions may underly the biotic complexity of these tropical ecosystems. Probably the most interesting aspect of dispersal ecology is its relationship to plant community diversity. In the foregoing, some hints as to the evolutionary origin of this diversity have been given (p. 201). Another question is that of the maintenance of the species richness. Janzen (1973 and elsewhere) has put forward the hypothesis that diversity of tropical lowland forests is strongly influenced by the herbivore community, in which seed predators may play an important role. These consumers prevent the best competitors in a given life form from becoming common enough to competitively eliminate the other species of that life form from the community. Thus the herbivores are making space for the poorer competitors. This leads to the further question about the significance of diversity itself. An interesting suggestion is that given by Klinge (1973) and Fittkau (1973): that the highly structured stands of tropical rainforests with their abundance of species and life-forms (trees of various size, shrubs, lianas, epiphytes, epiphylles etc.) constitute a biological 'filter system' for nutrient scavenging of the rainfall, for which experimental proof has since been adduced (Jordan et al., 1980). Here dispersal comes in as a means of controlling and maintaining biotic diversity as a prerequisite for the continued existence of these tropical ecosystems.

ACKNOWLEDGEMENTS

This chapter has greatly profited from the comments given by St. Vogel, G. Gottsberger, G.T. Prance, H.-H. Poppendieck, U. Kühn and S. Renner, for which I am most grateful.

REFERENCES

Barthlott, W. (1983) Biogeography and evolution in neo- and paleotropical Rhipsalinae (Cactaceae). In *Dispersal and Distribution. A Symposium*. Ed. K. Kubitzki, pp. 241 – 248, Sonderbd. naturwiss. Ver. Hamburg 7.

Boucher, D. H. (1981) The 'real' disperser of *Swartzia cubensis*. *Reproductive Botany, Suppl. to Biotropica* 13(2), 77 – 78.

Burger, W. (1981) Why are there so many kinds of flowering plants? *Bioscience* 31, 572 – 581.

Cavalcante, P. B. (1976) *Frutas comestíveis da Amazônia*. 3rd ed. Falangola. Belém.

Ducke, A. (1949) Arvores amazônicas e sua propagação. *Bol. Museu Paraense E. Goeldi* 10, 81 – 92.

Fittkau, E. J. (1973) Artenmannigfaltigkeit amazonischer Lebensräume aus ökologischer Sicht. *Amazoniana* (Kiel) 4, 321 – 340.

Fleming, T. H., Heithaus, R. E. and Sawyer, W. B. (1977) An experimental analysis of the food location behavior of frugivorous bats. *Ecology* 58, 619 – 627.

Fleming, T. H. and Heithaus, E. R. (1981) Frugivorous bats, seed shadows, and the structure of tropical forests. *Reproductive Botany, Suppl. to Biotropica* 13(2), 45 – 53.

Gentry, A. H. (1983) Dispersal ecology and diversity in neotropical forest communities. In *Dispersal and Distribution. A Symposium*. Ed. K. Kubitzki, pp. 303 – 314, Sonderbd. naturwiss. Ver. Hamburg 7.

Greenberg, R. (1981) Frugivory in some tropical forest wood warblers. *Biotropica* 13, 215 – 223.

Grubert, M. (1974) Podostemonaceen-Studien I. Zur Ökologie einiger venezolanischer Podostemonaceen. *Beitr. Biol. Pflanzen* 50, 321 – 391.

Holthuijzen, A. M. A. and Boerboom, J. A. H. (1982) The *Cecropia* seedbank in the Surinam lowland forest. *Biotropica* 14, 62 – 68.

Horovitz, C. C. and Beattie, A. J. (1980) Ant dispersal of *Calathea* (Marantaceae) seeds by carnivorous ponerines (Formicidae) in a tropical rain forest. *Am. J. Bot.* 67, 321 – 326.

Huber, J. (1910) Mattas e madeiras amazonicas. *Bol. Museu Goeldi (Museu Paraense) hist. nat. ethnogr.* 6, 91 – 225.

Janzen, D. H. (1973) Comments on host-specificity of tropical herbivores and its relevance to species richness. In *Taxonomy and Ecology*. Ed. V. H. Heywood, pp. 201 – 211. Academic Press, London.

Janzen, D. H. and Martin, P. S. (1981) Neotropical anachronisms: The fruits the Gomphotheres ate. *Science* 215, 19 – 27.

Janzen, D. H., Miller, G. A., Hackforth Jones, J., Pond, C. M., Hooper, K. and Janos, D. P. (1976) Two Costa Rican bat-generated seed shadows of *Andira inermis* (Leguminosae). *Ecology* 57, 1068 – 1075.

Jordan, C., Golley, F., Hall, J. and Hall, J. (1980) Nutrient scavenging of rainfall by the canopy of an Amazonian rain forest. *Biotropica* 12, 61 – 66.

Klinge, H. (1973) Struktur und Artenreichtum des zentralamazonischen Waldes. *Amazoniana* (Kiel) 4, 283 – 292.

Kubitzki, K. (1975) Relationships between distribution and evolution in some heterobathmic tropical groups. *Bot. Jahrb.* 96, 212 – 230.

Kubitzki, K. (1983) *Dispersal and Distribution. A Symposium*. Sonderbd. naturwiss. Ver. Hamburg 7.

McKey, D. (1975) The ecology of coevolved seed dispersal systems. In *Coevolution of Animals and Plants*. Eds. L. E. Gilbert and P. H. Raven, pp. 159 – 191. University of Texas Press, Austin.

Prance, G. T. and Mori, S. A. (1983) Dispersal and distribution of Lecythidaceae and Chrysobalanaceae. In *Dispersal and Distribution. A Symposium*. Ed. K. Kubitzki, pp. 163 – 186, Sonderbd. naturwiss. Ver. Hamburg 7.

Ridley, H. N. (1930) *The Dispersal of Plants Throughout the World*. Reeve, Ashford.

Simpson, G. G. (1980) *Splendid Isolation. The Curious History of South American Mammals*. Yale University Press, New Haven.

Smythe, N. (1970) Relationships between fruiting seasons and seed dispersal methods in a neotropical forest. *Am. Natur.* 104, 25 – 35.

Snow, D. W. (1962) The natural history of the Oilbird, *Steatornis caripensis*, in Trinidad, W. I. II. Population, breeding, ecology and food. *Zoologica* 47, 199 – 221.

Snow, D. W. (1971) Evolutionary aspects of fruit-eating by birds. *Ibis* 113, 194 – 202.

Snow, D. W. (1981) Tropical frugivorous birds and their food plants: A World survey. *Biotropica* 13, 1 – 14.

Van der Pijl, L. (1982) *Principles of Dispersal in Higher Plants*. 3rd ed. Springer, Berlin.

Van Roosmalen, M. G. M. (1980) Habitat preferences, diet, feeding strategy and social organisation of the black spider monkey (*Ateles paniscus paniscus* Linnaeus 1758) in Surinam. RIN-Rapport Rijksinstituut voor Natuurbeheer, Leersum 1980.

Willis, J. C. (1922) *Age and Area*. Cambridge University Press, Cambridge.

CHAPTER 11

Plant Defences against Animals in the Amazonian Rainforest

DANIEL H. JANZEN

Department of Biology, University of Pennsylvania, U.S.A.

CONTENTS

11.1. INTRODUCTION

Plants stand still. This is as true in Amazonian rainforest as it is in boreal coniferous forest. As the architects of every medieval castle understood, if you are fixed in place, your past experiences (natural selection) lead you to develop (evolve) both intense standing defences and facultative ones. Furthermore, which defences are present at any given time reflect at least four quite different processes: how much resources you have to build and maintain, the traits of past and present attackers, and the structure of the entire edifice when a new defence is being considered. Finally, by the possession of ever more defences, the castle is rendered ever more immobile (physically, culturally), ever more a long-term investment, and ever more vulnerable if the defences are breached. Natural selection has generated the above pattern in plants just as it has done in humans, and in the lowland tropical rainforests of the world we find the epitome of the lesson. It is here that a plant stands against its herbivores with little or no help from cold winters, harsh droughts, irregular growing seasons, low species richness of herbivores or competitors, high quality population cueing systems, and all the other little ways (besides their intrinsic personal defences) that plants may use to defend themselves against animal herbivores or that may result in lower populations of herbivores.

However, I must at the outset emphasise that there is no single truly 'archetypical' lowland tropical rainforest. Many of the lowland tropical rainforests are covered by vegetation types which deviate in one or more ways in the direction of extra-tropical systems. Amazonian rainforests are no exception: seasonal flooding of the Amazonian riparian forests, vegetation expansion and contraction during moisture cycles (*see* Absy and Prance, Chapters 4 and 8 this volume), occupation of soils so poor in nutrients that they are as hard on the trophic pyramid as is any northern winter (Janzen, 1974) (e.g. the drainage basin of the Río Negro), dry seasons well-defined in the calendar year and dry seasons of highly irregular depth and extent, etc. Such deviations provide the circumstances for the evolution of a variety of behavioural and strategic herbivore avoidance traits also characteristic of extra-tropical forests and tropical forests outside the lowland rainforests (e.g. seed predator and new leaf herbivore satiation at the population and habitat level; timing of leaf flushes with times of year that are difficult for herbivores; seed escape by submersion in water; escape from herbivores that have not yet reached the plant in geographic space or evolutionary time; escape from herbivores by growing where the physical conditions are too difficult for them).

The focus of this book is on *Amazonian* rainforest, a particular habitat with which I have no direct personal experience. However, the Amazonian rainforest has quite enough in common with lowland rainforests (or rather, with what is left of lowland rainforests) in other parts of the globe that one can write about it without ever having seen it. Such a great leap into the dark is made further reasonable by the fact that individual herbivores by and large display consistency in desires and behaviours the world over; the rumen environments of an arctic musk ox (*Ovibos*) and an Amazonian brocket deer (*Mazama*) have much more in common than do either their gross morphology or the habitats in which they live; an aristolochia swallowtail caterpillar (*Battus* spp.) in Texas, U.S.A. (Rausher, 1978), probably deals with the aristolochic acid in the *Aristolochia* leaves it eats in exactly the same manner as does an aristolochia swallowtail caterpillar in Manaus; and the seeds of *Hymenaea* pods in Amazonia are attacked by *Rhinochenus* weevils that are sister species to those which attack *Hymenaea* seeds throughout Central America (Lewinsohn, 1980; Janzen, 1974, 1975, 1978; Whitehead, 1976). Most of the astounding animal – plant interactions to be found in Amazonia are also to be found (or were to be found) in other sites in different combinations. One does not have to examine Brazilian *Cecropia* trees to evaluate the recent report (Andrade and Carauta, 1982) suggesting that because Amazonian *Cecropia* trees occupied by *Azteca* ants sustain conspicuous herbivore damage, the ants are not protecting the *Cecropia* trees; Wheeler (1942) made the same kind of deduction and observations on Central American ant-acacias and was as wrong (Janzen, 1966) for the same reason. In Amazonia, just as in Central America, the effectiveness of ants as protectors of plants cannot be determined without experimentally removing the ants and *then* observing what the herbivores do to the plants (*see* Janzen, 1973; Janzen and McKey, 1977 on the subject of *Cecropia*). I hope that the reader will forgive the tendency for the remainder of this essay to be a more generalised statement about defences against herbivores in tropical rainforests, rather than a focus on the essentials of Amazonian defences against herbivores.

11.2. THE DEFENCES OF AMAZONIAN PLANTS AGAINST HERBIVORES: THE RUBBER CONNECTION

Perhaps the Amazonian defence best known to the general public is rubber, the congealed latex of a tree (*Hevea brasiliensis*, in the Euphorbiaceae, the poinsettia and castor bean family). The latex, so cleverly removed by cutting the bark only deep enough to sever the laticifers (latex-containing ducts external to the cambium and phloem), serves the double defence function of all latices. When a boring insect (termite, scolytid, cerambycid, moth caterpillar, weevil larva) drills into the bark of a healthy living rubber tree (or chews into one of its leaves), it gets a 'face-full' and 'lung-full' of sticky congealing liquid, which is probably enough to stop almost any insect not specialised at dealing with

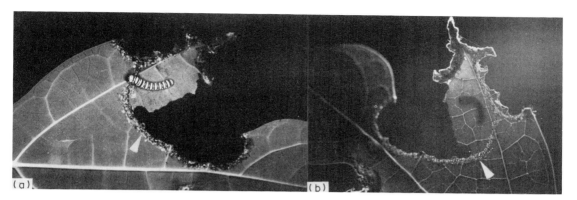

Fig. 11.1.a. Half-grown larva of *Lycorea cleobaea* resting on a portion of a leaf of *Carica papaya* that the larva has isolated by cutting a semicircular row of small holes through the leaf blade (arrow); following cutting the holes, latex flow is negligible from the isolated portion of the leaf as the caterpillar feeds.

Fig. 11.1.b. Same leaf as in a., but viewed from underside by transmitted light; row of small holes cut through the leaf (arrow) appears as small light dots. The remnants of other portions of isolated leaf segments are evident on both sides and the tip of the peninsular leaf projection.

latex (*see* below). Even if it can survive the mechanical effect of the latex there are also insecticidal chemicals in the latex. It is a striking commentary on the energy cost of this defence to the plant that once serious tapping of medium-sized rubber trees in a plantation begins, they increase in size at much slower rate and produce very few seeds, suggesting that their rubber production approaches the value of their net national product, so to speak. When the latex is not being removed at frequent regular intervals, the cost to the plant of maintaining this defence system is clearly much less but probably not trivial. Such an unchallenged 'standing defence is often thought of as a form of 'insurance' against herbivory, but the analogy is inappropriate. The cost of insurance purchases future recompensation for damages; the insurance does not deter the accident. A more appropriate and quite accurate analogy is the national defence budget. Just as in this budget, there are enormous costs not readily apparent in a cursory examination of the plant's phenotype. Furthermore, just as in national defence the real threat is extremely difficult to define and demonstrate unless the experiment of removing the defence system is conducted. In the same vein, the cost of maintaining the defence is generally much greater than the actual cost of the occasional losses when the defence system is penetrated; the true cost of herbivores clearly cannot be measured by just the amount of leaf they eat. Finally, just as in national defences, plant defences are rich in anachronisms and pleiotropisms.

Just as humans undoubtedly evolved the cultural trait of throwing a deadly projectile many times — the convergent evolution of biologists — latex is a defence trait that appears in many different quite unrelated families of tropical plants (Euphorbiaceae, Moraceae, Apocynaceae, Caricaceae, Asclepiadaceae, Guttiferae, Sapotaceae) and is itself very analogous to the convergent defence of resin and gum production in yet another set of tropical plant families. Not surprisingly then, a few herbivores have independently evolved quite similar ways to circumvent this defence (here is perhaps the place to remind the reader that *all* defences of plants have some species of herbivores that normally circumvent them). The striking black and white ringed caterpillar of the aposematic butterfly *Lycorea cleobaea* avoids the latex from the papaya (*Carica papaya*) leaves it eats by first cutting semicircled holes through them so as to isolate sections of the leaf blades (Fig. 11.1). The breaking of the laticifers causes the latex flow to the margin of the cut leaf to be halted and the caterpillar feeds without ingesting any latex. Since such a behavioural trait would work on any plant species whose defences include laticifers, it is not surprising to find this butterfly's caterpillar also feeding on the leaves of figs (*Ficus* spp.) and milkweed vines (*Matelea trianea*), and doing the same thing to these latex-rich leaves as it does to papaya leaves.

However, it is equally striking that *Lycorea* caterpillars do not feed on the latex-rich leaves of many other families and species of plants in the same rainforest habitats. The general statement is that each species of plant interacts with its potential herbivores through a characteristic set of defences that is in some way different from that of all other species of plants; secondary compound chemistry of each plant species is unique and distinctive in ways that matter to herbivores. The specific statement is that *Lycorea* may not be able to feed on other kinds of latex-rich leaves because (1) those leaves contain other secondary compounds besides those in latex and these compounds may be inimical to *Lycorea* caterpillars, and/or (2) the 'latex' of those leaves may be white and sticky like the latex of the leaves it eats but it is likely to contain quite different chemicals. It is at this point that thoroughness demands the addition of another factor which may be of equal importance but is both beyond the scope of this essay and is unfortunately traditionally left out of discussions of the defences of plants. *Lycorea* caterpillars may not be found on the leaves of the other latex-bearing species in the habitat because even if the butterfly puts its eggs there, the physical conditions and carnivore regimes (parasites and predators) of those species of plants eliminate the butterfly. Finally, we must not discount the possibility that the 'failure' of *Lycorea* to use these other plants as hosts may be a simple anachronism (e.g. Janzen and Martin, 1982). That is, they may be quite suitable hosts but the butterfly has not yet, if it ever will, come up with the appropriate mutations leading it to respond to those plants with oviposition.

In the usual ecologist's tradition, we have now discussed briefly the defence traits and latex properties of the rubber tree, and herbivore responses to them. But the rubber tree is good for more than that. It also allows us to examine the relationship of defences to resource availability and habitat-wide patterns in defences. It is no accident that rubber was a highly successful plantation crop growing on some of the worst tropical soils in the world — the sandy podzols of peninsular Malaya, generated by eons of leaching of granite with no periodic inundations of the sea. These soils are so poor that generally they were not farmed by shifting or fixed-field cultivators prior to rubber planting, nor is the pressure at present to turn them to this use. Further evidence is in the form of the consideration that the caloric value of the rubber generated by a sustained yield rubber plantation is pitifully small compared to, say, that of rice production on nearby alluvial bottomlands; rubber is a crop not because of its food value (its biological content or yield, so to speak) but because of its strategic value outside of the ecosystem. So why do rubber trees survive on poor soils? Because one of their native habitats is white-sand soils or similar podzols in the Amazon; it is a specialist at running its motors on low intake of low quality fuel. And the possession of a copious latex defence along with the numerous other nasty chemical defences characteristic of the Euphorbiaceae is not accidentally encountered in a tree that is a specialist on very poor soils. Rubber is a specific example of the general case that the worse the resource base for a plant, the better protected one expects the plants that grow there to be. In the tropics, without winter on the plant's side, this by and large means more protective chemistry.

The rationale is quite straightforward in theory (Janzen, 1974), and matches observations of places such as the vegetation of the Río Negro drainage moderately well. The harder it is for a plant to replace lost tissues (and their contained mineral ions) taken by an herbivore, the more intense should selection be for those traits that prevent herbivory. This might be termed the 'rich man spendthrift' hypothesis. And the worse the soil (or other resource base), the harder it is to replace a loss due to herbivory (note that losses due to defence budgets may be subject to the same kinds of selection, but the outcome may well be more recyclable defences and more clever defences rather than fewer of them). The outcome should be an increasing intensity of herbivore defences along a gradient of increasing soil sterility. I should be quite clear at this point that there is a severe herbivore threat in *all* Amazonian forest types, and that chemically well-defended plants likewise occur in *all* Amazonian forest types; it is the matter of degree that is under discussion.

But white-sand soils have more growing on them than just latex-rich (and resin-rich) plants. They are notorious the world over for producing blackwater rivers such as the Río Negro. These rivers derive their name from the large amounts of dark-coloured polyphenols (or tannins, the source of the colour of tea) in their water (and the absence of particulate erosive materials of latosol origin that would obscure the dark colour imparted by the tannin colloids). The tannins have only one origin — the foliage of the woody plants growing over the soil drained by blackwater rivers. But tannins are prominent among the foliage defences (as well as wood and bark defences) of many species of trees, including those growing on latosols and other kinds of lowland tropical soils more rich in nutrients than are white-sand podzols. Why do they end up in the streams in bulk when the vegetation grows on white-sand soils? There are clearly at least two answers. First, the vegetation itself appears to be richer in tannins on such sites than on latosols. Second, it appears that the soil — litter — microbe complex does not degrade tannins and tannin-rich foliage as fast on white-sands as on more fertile soils. This is likely due to (1) a lower nutrient content of the falling foliage (the worse the site, the more is extracted from a leaf before it falls), (2) a lower (slower) rain of partly processed material in the form of caterpillar dung (the worse the site, the lower the biomass of herbivores that it sustains), (3) a lower litter fall rate (the worse the site, the more intense the selection for evergreen leaves with more than a year lifespan), (4) a higher tannin content of the foliage that does fall, and (5) a lowered ability of soil microbes (including fungi) to degrade tannin-rich foliage residue as the availability of other nutrients declines.

And what do the tannins in leaves do to the herbivores that eat them? In the water of a blackwater river they chelate everything from themselves to calcium ions to the proteins on the oxygen-exchange surfaces of insect and fish gills. In the tanner's vat they bind with collagen to render the protein in a hide unavailable to bacterial enzymes — they 'tan' leather. The simple answer used to be that in the herbivore's gut they tanned the proteins of the gut wall, the bacteria in the gut lumen and the proteins released from the leaf by the herbivore's chewing (rendering them unavailable to the herbivore or its microbes). It is now becoming clear that the many different kinds of tannins respond differently to these three ecological groupings of substrate; at certain insect gut pH values, for example, a tannin may be quite inactive. To complicate the story even further, it is now clear that tannins are treated just like other defences by certain kinds of herbivores in that they may be actually used by the herbivore in its own metabolism (e.g. Bernays and Woodhead, 1982) and thereby become a nutrient from the herbivore's viewpoint.

11.3. HOST SPECIFICITY OF AMAZONIAN CATERPILLARS

As an educated guess, any square kilometre of Amazonian rainforest containing members of the populations of about 500 species of plants will be fed on by at least 2000 species of caterpillars of Lepidoptera (moths and butterflies). Two core questions leap to mind. How are these species spread over the various plant parts? That is to say, what fraction of the caterpillars are young leaf-eaters, old leaf-eaters, seed-eaters, stem-borers, etc. Second, how are these species spread over the various plant species? That is to say, do most of the species of caterpillars have only one species of host plant, many species, or some complex pattern of these two alternatives? Inherent in the latter question is the idea that it is the defences of the plants (and primarily their chemical defences) that produces the pattern observed through interactions with the ability of the insects to get around these defences. It is the latter question that I wish to address below, though the processes involved apply also to answers to the first-posed question.

First, even a small amount of collecting and rearing caterpillars will make it quite evident that there is no such thing as 'the caterpillar' or an 'average caterpillar' when it comes to host specificity. Different taxonomic groups display quite different patterns. It is a safe bet that in the Amazonian rainforest certain families of Lepidoptera will be quite different in their host specificity. For example, it is an easy prediction that for each of the 40 − 80 species of sphinx moth caterpillars (Sphingidae) there is only one or at most 3 − 4 (rarely) species of host plants. If there is more than one host for a species of caterpillar, the hosts will be closely related. Almost all of these host plants will belong to families that are famous for having members whose foliage is rich in toxic small molecules and/or latex, and none of the host plants will be in the Leguminosae. By way of striking contrast, for each of the 30 − 40 species of silk moth caterpillars (Saturniidae) there will usually be from 2 to many species of host plants, one species of caterpillar will feed on quite unrelated species of plants, many of the host plants will be species related to species notorious for high tannin content in foliage, and many of the host plants will be in the Leguminosae and Malvales (assuming that these families occur in the study plot). Additionally, there will be very little overlap in the list of sphingid hosts with the list of saturniid hosts (Janzen and Waterman 1984). Furthermore, it will be found that for a sphingid and saturniid larva of the same final body weight (weight just before pupation), the sphingid larva attains that weight in a significantly shorter period than does the saturniid.

Such a set of observations on the large caterpillars of two such widespread moth families leads to a characterisation of each that clearly relates to the impact that the chemical defences of their host plants have had on the moths' evolution. It appears that sphingid caterpillars are extreme specialists at, among other things, possessing the appropriate enzymes for degrading or otherwise avoiding the suite of specific small and quite toxic molecules to be found in a particular plant. They are therefore able to maximally use the nutrients in the relatively defenceless host plant, but able to feed only on the particular host plant for which they carry the appropriate enzymes. Since closely related plants are more likely to have similar defence fingerprints than are distantly related plants, if they have more than one host plant they are likely to be closely related. Such a way of doing things places a strong emphasis on the adult moth's ability to locate a host plant of the appropriate species and one with leaves at the appropriate stage of development so as to contain a defence profile which best complements the caterpillar's enzymatic abilities. Saturniid caterpillars appear to be extreme specialists at, among other things, possessing the appropriate gut milieu and growth rates to exist on a diet rich in tannins; the tannins would both lower the digestive efficiency of the gut process and render much of the protein in the leaf unavailable to the caterpillar. Here the answer appears to be able to grow slowly, process a lot of food, and get comparatively little out of each mouthful. Since tannins apparently show much less diversity in their chemistry than do such things as the alkaloids, cyanogenic glycosides, cardiac glycosides, etc. being dealt with by the sphingid larvae, and since the caterpillar is basically tolerating the tannin's effects rather than detoxifying it, such a caterpillar might be expected to be able to feed on many species of plants. The more the plant relies on a purely polyphenol defence system, the more it would appear to be susceptible to a saturniid caterpillar. Here, the ovipositing moth should have much more latitude in her choice of host plants, and the evolution of her choices should be determined in great part not so much by what kinds of polyphenol defences the plant has, as how much nutrient material is left over after the digestion-inhibiting processes have taken their toll. It will not now come as a surprise to the reader to find that sphinx moth adults are long-lived and feed at flowers through their adult life, developing a few eggs at a time. Saturniid adults do not feed as adults, live only a few days, and lay their entire clutch of several hundred eggs in 2 − 5 nights. As the caterpillars can feed on numerous species of plants, the females can be less specific in their choice of oviposition sites (and therefore can find them faster). Likewise, plants may be evolutionarily chosen through their abundance and nutrient content as much as through their defensive chemical traits (see Janzen 1984 for an elaboration).

In our hypothetical square kilometre of Amazonia there are more than sphingids and saturniids. A close look at the other families of caterpillars will reveal probably 1000 species of Noctuidae, Pyralidae and Notodontidae combined, acting largely like sphingids, and Lasiocampidae, Megalopygidae, Arctiidae, and Limacodidae acting largely like Saturniidae. Butterfly caterpillars (Nymphalidae,

Papilionidae, Pieridae, etc.) will act largely like sphingids in their host specificity.

Discussed above is the response of the animals that map their resource harvest onto a diverse array of plant defences. For each species of caterpillar there are one to a few species of plants where the chemical defences either make no difference or if responded to, it is often by *using* the very chemicals that deter all other herbivores as metabolic building blocks and signals to locate the plant. In a crude sense, the caterpillar may even evolutionarily view the defensive chemicals as important in keeping potential competitors from feeding on its host plant. At the other extreme, the caterpillar may view virtually all other species of plants that it encounters as simply unacceptable as food either because of direct perception of the secondary compounds as repellent or because the plant lacks the chemical fingerprint that tells the caterpillar to 'eat here'.

11.4. PATTERNS OF CHEMICAL DEFENCES AMONG PLANTS AND PLANT PARTS

The herbivores adjust their feeding in the vegetation according to their abilities, both evolved as part of that adjustment and ecological as part of the response to a new habitat that occurs when the herbivore first arrives. However, the pattern of defensive chemicals that any given herbivore or herbivore array interacts with is a combination of things evolved during the actual interaction and traits that are the result of other herbivore – plant evolutionary interactions. When a tapir (*Tapirus* spp.) picks and chooses among the many species of forest floor saplings to browse (Janzen, 1982), many of the chemicals that deter him were in fact probably evolved in response to selection by herbivorous insects, or if by browsing mammals, most of those that were responsible disappeared during the Pleistocene extinctions. The agouti sniffs and rejects a newly fallen soft legume seed; the lectins, alkaloids, protease inhibitors, cyanogenic glycosides and/or uncommon amino acids that render the seed inedible to this rodent constitute a defence repertoire whose traits have been selected by millenia of repelling parrots, climbing rats, bruchid beetles, monkeys, weevils, squirrels, agoutis, ground sloths, pyralid moth larvae, spiny rats, termites, fungi, bacteria, etc. The canavanine used by a bruchid as a major nutrient in a *Dioclea* seed (Rosenthal *et al.*, 1978) may well have been evolved in response to all or part of the other kinds of seed predators, and the bruchid simply adjusted its physiology to the changing defences as the centuries passed.

With the varied fluctuating selective pressures by herbivores on the one hand, and all the internal design and cost constraints on this or that defence on the other hand, it seems little short of a miracle that any pattern in chemical or secondary chemical defences would occur. However, such patterns do occur and I suspect that many more will appear as we map out the potential defence repertoires of tropical plants (a major stumbling block is the habit of searching for one class of compounds across many plant taxa, rather than taking the plants in a habitat and working out the distribution of all defensive compounds in those plants — largely because the work has been done as mining for organic chemicals, not as a search for biological understanding).

By some surveys, twice as many tropical plant species contain alkaloids as do extra-tropical ones (Levin, 1976). With the exception of certain resins and terpenes from conifers and a few odd sources of tannins for the tanning trade, tropical plants have been vastly more important in generating a variety of pharmacologically active compounds than have extra-tropical sources, and this resource is just beginning to be tapped. But what of our hypothetical square kilometre of species-rich Amazonian rainforest? If you want an edible seed (one low in defensive chemicals), pick something with the hardest indehiscent nut wall around it, one that is dispersed regularly by rodents that also survive on it, or one that is wind-dispersed with synchronous fruiting at greater than yearly intervals (it helps if the seeds are smaller than normal). Trees that produce very large crops of small seeds are much more likely to have seeds edible to humans than are trees with a small crop of large seeds (especially if they fruit annually). The other side of that coin is that if you are searching for seeds rich in exotic alkaloids, uncommon amino acids, lectins, etc., pick the largest soft seed you can find on the forest floor (if it was dispersed by being regurgitated by a large bird, so much the better). Likewise, if the tree occurs in nearly monospecific patches and fruits annually, its seeds are likely to be especially lethal.

Turning to the vegetative parts of plants, a best guess for food for a cow or tapir is a fast-growing deciduous sun-loving tree of riverbanks and other natural disturbed areas. An ant-plant without its ants is a sure bet for edibility to an enormous array of herbivores. At the other end, a truly evergreen tree with long-lived leaves growing in heavy shade is nearly guaranteed to generate stomachaches and worse for the 'generalist' herbivore. The same applies to the evergreen in full sun on white-sand soils. However, there are many ways that the particular capabilities of the vertebrate herbivore can render these generalisations ineffective in specific cases. A captive Costa Rican tapir accepted the foliage of virtually all species of early secondary succession vegetation except for *Trema micrantha* (Ulmaceae) a plant that by all reasoning should be highly edible; the same animal rejected the foliage of 42 species of woody legumes (ate one, *Pterocarpus rohrii*, in bulk) but ate about half of the species of legume vines that it was offered (Janzen, 1982).

Insects, with their gut specialisations to a small fraction of the total set of species in the habitat require a quite different perspective of chemical patterns. In the sphingid example mentioned above, caterpillars were commonly found on members of the Rubiaceae, yet Rubiaceae are well known for alkaloid-rich plant parts the world over; however, one of the rubiaceous food plants of two sphingid species, *Calycophyllum candidissimum* is also fed on by at least three species of saturniid caterpillars. Preliminary screening (P. Waterman, pers. comm.) shows this plant to have no alkaloids in the foliage and a moderate level of tannins.

The distribution of defensive compounds within the plant makes life difficult for the ecologist attempting to understand what physiological abilities are involved in various levels of host specificity. Growing tissues (cambium, ovules, apical meristems) characteristically have their chemical defences poorly developed and if an insect such as a sucking bug (Pentatomidae, Lygaeidae, Pyrrhocoridae) feeds on this plant part on a number of plant species, it may well not be at all versatile in its gut chemistry. On the other hand, a caterpillar that feeds on just one species of plant may well have to deal with several dozen quite different chemical defences as it consumes the blades and petioles of branches in the sun and shade, of old and young leaves, of leaves that have been fed on earlier in the season (and thereby carry induced defences as well as their standing defences). It is quite striking to watch a saturniid moth caterpillar eat all the old (mature) leaves from a branch and studiously avoid the new and expanding leaves (and shoot tip) at the branch end.

The tree trunk offers an especially visible example of heterogeneity of defences (Fig. 11.2). Starting at the outside, the bark is dead tissue thoroughly laced with secondary compounds in their most active, nonglucosylated forms (to avoid self-intoxication, many defence compounds in living tissues are stored attached to a sugar molecule, which renders them inactive until the appropriate enzyme in the animal or released by the broken cell splits off the sugar — e.g. cyanogenic glucosides, cardiac glycosides, alkaloid glycosides). Furthermore, it has virtually no nutrients in it to compensate for the damage potentially caused by its ingestion. Virtually no herbivores consume dead bark on the standing tree (except for some termites). Just below the bark lies an area of expanding and nutrient-rich tissues (bark cambium, phloem, cambium) which may be rich in defences but in a finely structured manner; the laticifers and resin ducts are missing from the cambial layers, the phloem may be rich in alkaloids that are quite missing from the cambium, etc. The defences are particularly active in this area, depending on a living and healthy tree. When a tree is stressed and the oleoresin or laticifer pressure falls (and the phloem flow to the active tissues ceases), this portion of the trunk is quickly invaded by a variety of boring beetles that were previously kept out by the active defences; they find a thin shell of very nutrient-rich tissues that they compete for with many other organisms. Moving into the xylem (sap wood), except for the

Fig. 11.2. Axe cut into trunk of 1 m diameter *Enterolobium cyclocarpum* (Leguminosae). The secondary compound-rich dead heartwood is bordered by the pale sapwood, which in turn has large drips of exuded gum from the gum vessels of the inner bark and phloem area. The bark and water-soluble gum are the outer defences of the living trunk, the heartwood the inner defences (Guanacaste Province, Costa Rica).

storage parenchyma (largely free of defensive compounds) we enter an area whose primary defence is its high water content, its largely indigestible (to an animal) cellulose structure, and its sandwiched position between the active defences of the bark-phloem area and the heartwood (*see* below). Once the outer defences are breached during tree death, the sapwood becomes the home and food of a great biomass and variety of animals that carry cellulose-degrading symbionts in their digestive systems or innoculate them as fungi. It is a striking characteristic of all of these animals that there can be no coevolution between them and their host plant, since the host plant is already dead or consigned to death when they enter (this does not apply to those much smaller number of species that may actually be the cause of tree weakening by massive attack, e.g. Scolytidae and sometimes Cerambycidae).

Finally, we reach the best protected portion of the tree, the heartwood — so prominent as the highly valued centre of a log that finds its way into beautiful furniture and veneers. This portion of the tree has died and as part of the senescence process, the cells were generally filled with tannins, terpenes, lactones, alkaloids, and a wide variety of other compounds in their most active unbound and unglucosylated state. When a rainforest tree falls, it is common for the sapwood and materials external to that to be degraded within a few months or a year, while the heartwood persists as a high quality log, degrading only very slowly as leaching by rainwater gradually removes the secondary compounds and allows fungi and termites to invade. Ironically, the tree sometimes appears to lay down less protective material in the centre of the heartwood, perhaps as a trait adaptive in that it results in the tree having a hollow ('rotted') core. This site becomes a haven for numerous animals which defecate and urinate in the cavity, thereby creating a small pocket of heavily fertilised soil that in fact may be mined by the tree responsible for it (Janzen, 1976). In other words, we have the herbivores to thank for the finest of the tropical hardwoods and those blemishes that bother the forester may be adaptive to the tree.

We have the herbivores to thank for more than latex, resin and tropical heartwoods (i.e. hardwoods of commerce, by and large). Fruits are perhaps the most complex of all the plant parts in the tropical rainforest, at least with respect to their chemistry. The biological function of a fruit is to get the seeds into the right place *and* keep them out of the wrong place. Since the entire herbivore array is a potential threat to immature fruits, and since nearly all the herbivores are a potential threat to ripe fruits (except for the very select few that actually disperse the seeds to a place that raises the fitness of the tree), it is the chemistry of that defence that is responsible for many of the different flavours (and other traits) that we enjoy (or dislike) in fruits. Of course, fruits have differentiated with respect to the (sometimes coevolved?) likes and dislikes of the proper dispersers as well. The striking absence of a bountiful harvest of commercial wild fruits from Amazonian rainforest (in contrast with the mangos, mangosteens, rambutans, lichees, durians, jackfruits, etc. of southeast Asian rainforests) is not coincidentally related to the fact that the Amazonian rainforest lacks a fauna of large primates with flavour preferences that could be expected to be similar to those of humans.

11.5. CONCLUSION

It may seem that I have not said much about *Amazonian* rainforest or even about *tropical* forests, since it is quite clear that much of what I have said applies to vegetation the world over. This is true, it does. What is unique about the Amazonian rainforest is not at the level of principles as I have dwelt on; it is at the level of the maximum variation on the many themes that I have briefly outlined. When a serious fruit chemist goes to work on a commercial fruit, 50 — 500 kinds of secondary compounds come to light (flavours, repellents, fungicides, antibiotics, odours, ripeners, hormones, colours, seed germination inhibitors, digestible structural agents, in addition to the varied vitamins, minerals, proteins, fats and carbohydrates put in the fruit as bait for this or that dispersal agent). Multiply that by the 2000 — 3000 species of plants whose seeds interact with animals in any Amazonian rainforest of several square kilometres in extent. Furthermore, it is a safe bet that each of those plants carries another 50-plus kinds of herbivore defence compounds in its leaves.

Plants are not the only organisms with multipliers like those above. It is a fair guess that there are more species of leaf-eating caterpillars in 10 km^2 of Amazonian rainforest on its better soils than occur in the eastern half of the United States. The possibility for fine-tuned interactions among these animals and their plants in one direction, and their carnivores in the other direction are simply beyond our wildest imagination.

However, to round out this all too brief essay, I should close by noting that there are some truly dramatic surprises in store, of which we have only an inkling. For example, there is evidence accumulating that despite the incredible increases in herbivore species richness that occur in moving from extra-tropical latitudes to lowland tropical rainforests, the carnivores that feed on them do not increase proportionately, at least with respect to the insects. It may turn out that the highest species richness of hymenopterous parasitoids per unit area are in mid-latitudes, rather than in the tropics (Janzen, 1981); a potential cause is easy to spot — the more species-rich the hosts, the fewer there are per average population, and the tougher life is for either a generalist or a specialist parasitoid. An Amazonian rainforest may then turn out to be the place where we can expect to witness just how herbivore populations are controlled when parasitoids become a relatively minor form of mortality.

The moths mentioned earlier offer another example of surprises. I work in a lowland tropical deciduous forest in Costa Rica, far ecologically and geographically from the Amazonian rainforest. Yet a very large number of the species of moths at my study site have distributions that include the lowland rainforests of Brazil; they also range up into Mexico. Yet the plants their caterpillars eat in Costa Rican deciduous forests are almost without doubt different species and genera from those they feed on in the Amazon; again, it is through the comparison of the Amazonian populations with the Costa Rican populations that we may come to understand what kinds of circumstances generate adults so similar that the taxonomists call them the same species, yet have larvae that differentiate among different host plants.

The ecology, physiology and biochemistry of plant defences impacts on far more than some lonely caterpillar looking for lunch. The caffeine, tannin and myriad of as yet chemically undefinable chemicals that give a Brazilian cup of coffee its value on the London market are there because of what African rainforest animals did to *Coffea arabica* seeds and fruits for millions of years.

ACKNOWLEDGEMENTS

This study was supported by NSF GB 80-11558, Servicio de Parques Nationales de Costa Rica, and the Museo Nacional de Costa Rica. The manuscript was constructively criticised by W. Hallwachs. It is dedicated to anyone with enough common sense to realise that the great-grandchildren of those who own the tropics at present are going to curse their great-grandparents for destroying their only chance to harvest from and enjoy tropical wilderness.

REFERENCES

Andrade, J. C. and Carauta, J. P. P. (1982) The *Cecropia – Azteca* association: a case of mutualism? *Biotropica* 14, 15.

Bernays, E. A. and Woodhead, S. (1982) Plant phenols utilized as nutrients by a phytophagous insect (*Anacridium melanorhodon*). *Science* 216, 201 – 203.

Janzen, D. H. (1966) Coevolution of mutualism between ants and acacias in Central America. *Evolution* 20, 249 – 275.

Janzen, D. H. (1973) Dissolution of mutualism between *Cecropia* and *Azteca* ants. *Biotropica* 5, 15 – 28.

Janzen, D. H. (1974) Tropical blackwater rivers, animals, and mast fruiting by the Dipterocarpaceae. *Biotropica* 6, 69 – 103.

Janzen, D. H. (1975) Behavior of *Hymenaea courbaril* when its predispersal seed predator is absent. *Science* 189, 145 – 147.

Janzen, D. H. (1976) Why tropical trees have rotten cores. *Biotropica* 8, 110.

Janzen, D. H. (1978) Seeding patterns in tropical trees. In *Tropical Trees as Living Systems*. Eds. P. B. Tomlinson and M. H. Zimmerman, pp. 83-128, Cambridge University Press, New York.

Janzen, D. H. (1981) The peak in North American ichneumonid species richness lies between 38° and 42° No. *Ecology* 62, 532 – 537.

Janzen, D. H. (1982) Wild plant acceptability to a captive Costa Rican Baird's tapir. *Brenesia* 19/20, 99 – 128.

Janzen, D. H. (1984) Two ways to be a tropical big moth: Santa Rosa saturniids and sphingids. *Oxford Surveys in Evolutionary Biology* 1, 85 – 140.

Janzen, D. H. and McKey, D. (1977) *Musanga cecropioides* is a *Cecropia* without its ants. *Biotropica* 9, 57.

Janzen, D. H. and Martin, P. S. (1982) Neotropical anachronisms: the fruits the gomphotheres ate. *Science* 215, 19 – 27.

Janzen, D. H. and Waterman, P. G. (1984) A seasonal census of phenolics, fibre and alkaloids in foliage of forest trees in Costa Rica: some factors influencing their distribution and relation to host selection by Sphingidae and Saturniidae. *Biol. J. Linn. Soc.* 21, 439 – 454.

Levin, D. A. (1976) Alkaloid-bearing plants: an ecogeographic perspective. *Amer. Nat.* 110, 261 – 284.

Lewinsohn, T. M. (1980) Predação de sementes em Hymenaea (Leguminosae: Caesalpinioideae): aspectos ecologicos e evolutivos. Ms. Thesis, Instituto de Biologia da Universidade Estadual de Campinas, Campinas, Brazil, 193 pages.

Rausher, M. D. (1978) Search image for leaf shape in a butterfly. *Science* 200, 1071 – 1073.

Rosenthal, G. A., Dahlman, D. L. and Janzen, D. H. (1978) L-canaline detoxification: a seed predator's biochemical mechanism. *Science* 202, 528 – 529.

Wheeler, W. M. (1942) Studies of neotropical ant-plants and their ants. *Bull. Mus. Comp. Zool., Harvard* 90, 1 – 262.

Whitehead, D. R. (1976) Classification and evolution of *Rhinochenus lucas* (Coleoptera: Curculionidae: Cryptorhynchinae), and Quaternary Middle American zoogeography. *Quaestiones Entomologicae* 12, 118 – 201.

CHAPTER 12

The Chemical Uses and Chemical Geography of Amazon Plants

OTTO R. GOTTLIEB

Instituto de Quimica, Universidade de São Paulo, Brazil

CONTENTS

12.1. INTRODUCTION

Chemical uses of Amazon plants are not exactly a new subject. In fact, they have been in the literature for close to 500 years as noted by Gottlieb and Mors (1978). It is nevertheless timely to recall these uses because they convey two important messages: an obvious one concerning the biological activity of organic compounds useful to mankind, and another concerned with the preservation of the remaining wildlife in the Neotropics. With respect to the first, how should we go about the quest for old and new compounds? With current methodology it is doubtful that even a few per cent more of the world's tropical organisms can be added to our woefully incomplete taxonomic, let alone chemical, inventories before a major portion becomes extinct (Raven *et al.*, 1971). Concerning the second, what part of the vegetation must be protected as 'genetic banks' in order to retain the structural diversity of its molecules? Current methodology for the investigation of conservation areas (e.g. Brown, Jr. and Ab'Sáber, 1979) certainly lacks the necessary chemical data.

12.2. THE QUEST FOR USEFUL NATURAL COMPOUNDS

Bannerman (1981) recently reaffirmed the importance in the acquisition of useful new information about medicinal and other useful plants of consultation with the traditional healers or medicine men. Prior to discussing this idea critically, let us examine briefly some of the more conspicuous chemical results of ethnobotanical investigations in the Neotropics (*see* Gottlieb and Mors, 1978, 1980, for refs. to the original literature) by looking at some compounds that have both traditional indigenous uses and modern uses by contemporary societies.

12.3. PLANT CONSTITUENTS WITH TRADITIONAL AND MODERN USES

12.3.1. Arrow poisons

Arrow poisons in Amazonia are generally called curare from the Indian name *uirari*. The true curares have a muscle relaxing and hence paralysing effect that is known as a curarising effect.

In Brazilian Amazonia curarising arrow poisons are derived from species either of *Chondodendron* in the family Menispermaceae or of the vine *Strychnos* in the unrelated family Loganiaceae, while in Venezuela products with similar action come from species of *Malouetia* (Apocynaceae). The curarising compounds from these three sources, although belonging to different structural types chemically, i.e. respectively the bis-benzylisoquinoline (12.1.1)[*], the bis-strychnine (12.1.2) and the di-trimethylammonium-5-α-pregnane (12.1.3) types, owe their common biological properties to the comparable distances between two quaternary nitrogen atoms. That the South American Indians discovered the value of these phyletically unrelated plants, with chemically different curarising compounds, is intriguing. In northwestern Amazonia arrow poisons are also derived from species of *Maquira* and *Naucleopsis* in the Moraceae or fig family. Their different action is due to cardenolides (12.1.4), as is the case for *Antiaris* spp., (also belonging to the Moraceae) used in Africa and Indonesia. In Africa, cardenolides from the Apocynaceae are also used in hunting. Although the Brazilian tree *Thevetia ahoai* (Apocynaceae) contains cardenolides, it does not seem to have come into practical use. A resin derived from the bark of *Virola theiodora* (Myristicaceae) is also used in arrow poisoning, especially by the Yanomamö Indians. Its action is due to a high concentration of tryptamines (12.1.5) and carbolines (12.1.6).

---

[*] The numbers following the chemical compounds refer not only to the formulas of Figs. 12.1.1 – 7, but also to their positions on Fig. 12.1.8.

1.1

1.2

1.3

1.4

1.5

1.6

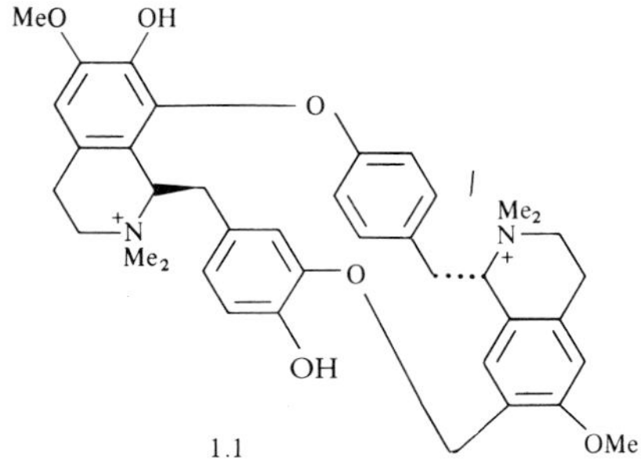

Fig. 12.1. Chemical constituents of arrow poisons.

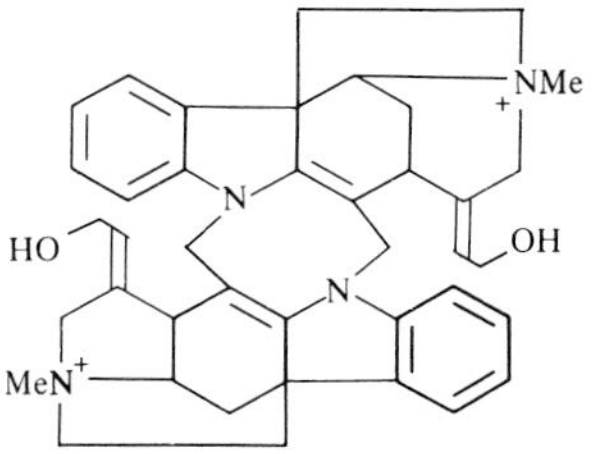

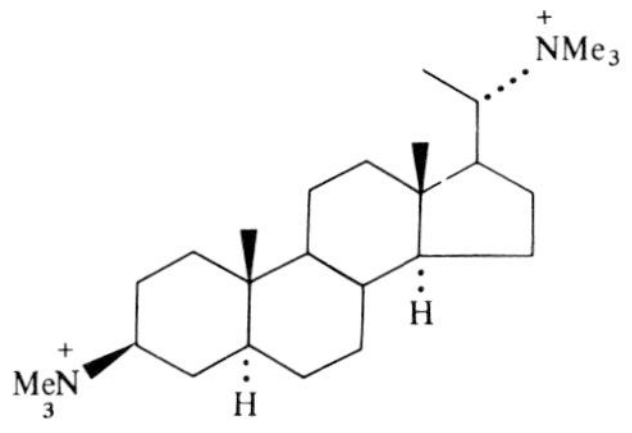

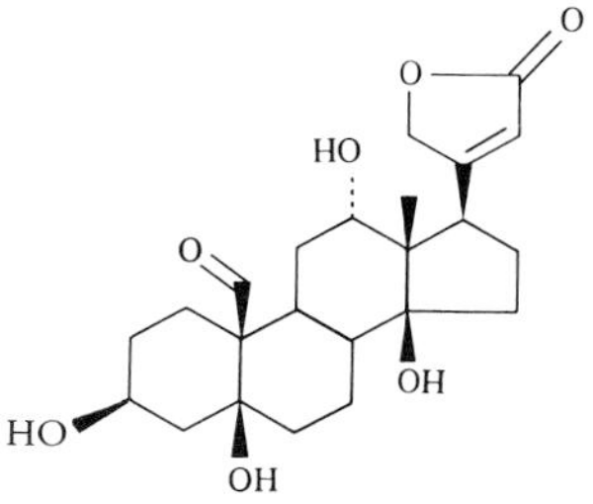

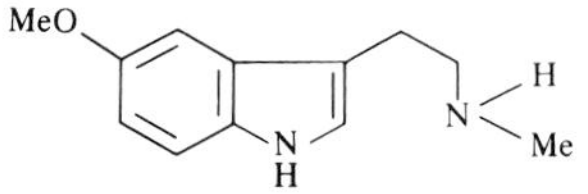

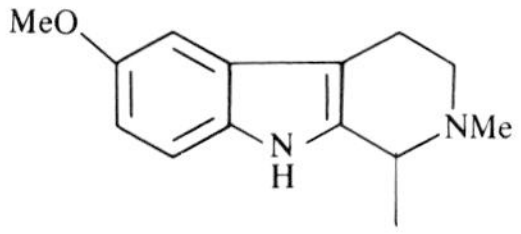

12.3.2 Hallucinogens

The Amazon Indians have found several products from a variety of plants which they use as hallucinogens. These are used in many of their traditional ceremonies and often by the Shamans as part of the healing rites.

The Indians who use *Virola* resin for hunting live in the dense forests covering the region where the frontiers of Brazil, Colombia and Venezuela converge. They employ resins with smaller concentrations of the active principles as hallucinogens. The same compounds (12.2.1, 12.2.2) are also found in the

2.1

2.2

2.3

2.4

2.5

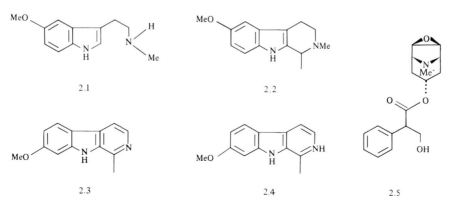

Fig. 12.2. Chemical constituents of hallucinogens.

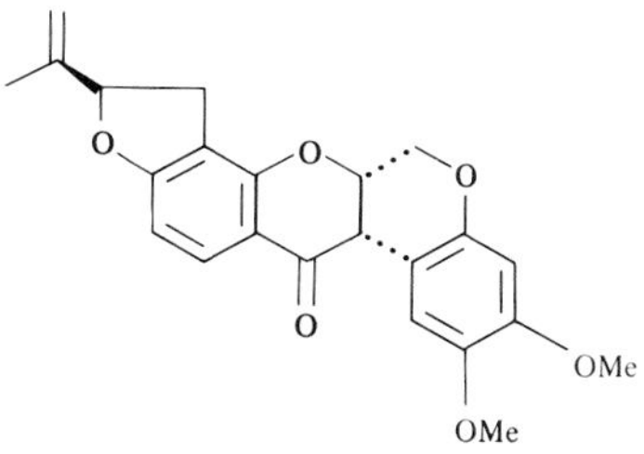

Fig. 12.3. Chemical constituents of fish poisons.

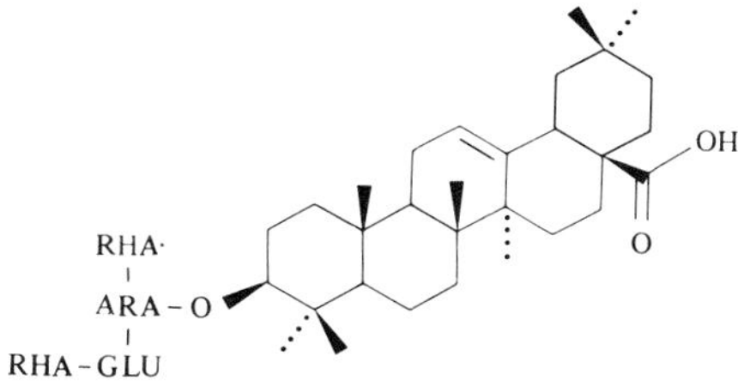

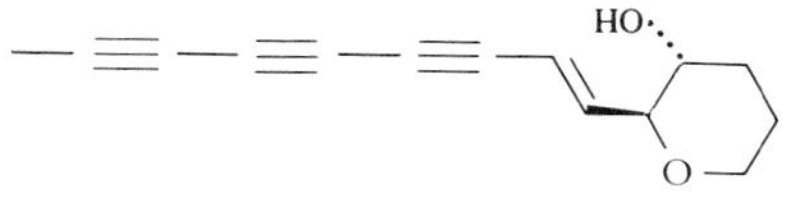

toasted and powdered seeds of *Anadenanthera peregrina*, a mimosaceous tree of the open Amazonian grasslands that is used in the rituals of other tribes. The powders derived from these products are blown into the nostrils of the participant through tubes made from the hollow stems of a Marantaceae or a hollow bone. Harmines (12.2.3) and carbolines (12.2.4) are the psychoactive ingredients of *Banisteriopsis caapi*, a malpighiaceous vine that forms the well-known hallucinogenic beverage Ayauasca of many tribes from northwestern Amazonia. Chemically very different sacred hallucinogens, tropane alkaloids (12.2.5), characterise *Brugmansia sanguinea* of the Solanaceae or nightshade family from western Amazonia and the Andes. *Brugmansia* is similar in composition and closely related to *Datura*, another genus of the Solanaceae, very widespread and used for the same purpose outside South America.

12.3.3. Fish poisons

Indigenous fishermen in Amazonia employ several methods which involve the use of plant compounds. One relies on a classical fish bait, which inebriates fish after ingestion. The bait is made from a herb, *Ichtyothere terminalis*, in the Asteraceae or daisy family, and contains polyacetylenes (12.3.1). In another method of chemical fishing the water is poisoned, either by soaking a mashed root of the vine *Lonchocarpus urucu* (Fabaceae) containing rotenoids in it (12.3.2), or by beating the stems of *Serjania caracasana* in the soapwort or Sapindaceae family, which contains serjanosides (12.3.3), into the water.

12.3.4. Drugs

Not all medically useful Brazilian plants were discovered by indigenous populations. For example, various *Rauvolfia* species (Apocynaceae) with useful hypotensive alkaloids (12.4.1), never seem to have attained practical importance in indigenous medicine although they grow all over tropical South America. Other widely used drug plants such as *Pilocarpus jaborandi* (Rutaceae) with the now widely used pilocarpine (12.4.2), *Tabebuia* species (Bignoniaceae) containing lapachol (12.4.3) patented as an anticancer agent by Pfizer, and *Ocotea glaziovii* (Lauraceae) containing glaziovine (12.4.4) patented as an ansiolytic by Simes, owe their discovery to modern scientific investigations. Good examples of the relatively few plants used by traditional healers which also yielded useful drugs when subjected to chemical and pharmacological testing are *Cephaelis ipecacuanha* (Rubiaceae) with the emetic and expectorant emitine (12.4.5); *Chenopodium ambrosioides* (Chenopodiaceae) with the vermifugal ascaridole (12.4.6); *Dialyanthera otoba* (Myristicaceae) with the fungistatic or fungicidal otobain (12.4.7); possibly *Maytenus illicifolia* (Celastraceae) with the antitumoral pristimerin (12.4.8); *Quassia amara* (Simaroubaceae) used against stomach disorders with quassin (12.4.9); *Carpotroche brasiliensis* (Flacourtiaceae) with esters of glycerol and hydnocarpic acid formerly used in the treatment of leprosy (12.4.10); *Stachytarpheta australis* (Verbenaceae) used as antithermic and sudorific (sweat inducing) with ipoliimide (12.4.11), and *Calea pinnatifida* (Asteraceae) used as an amoebicide with a polyacetylene (12.4.12) and a germacranolide (12.4.13).

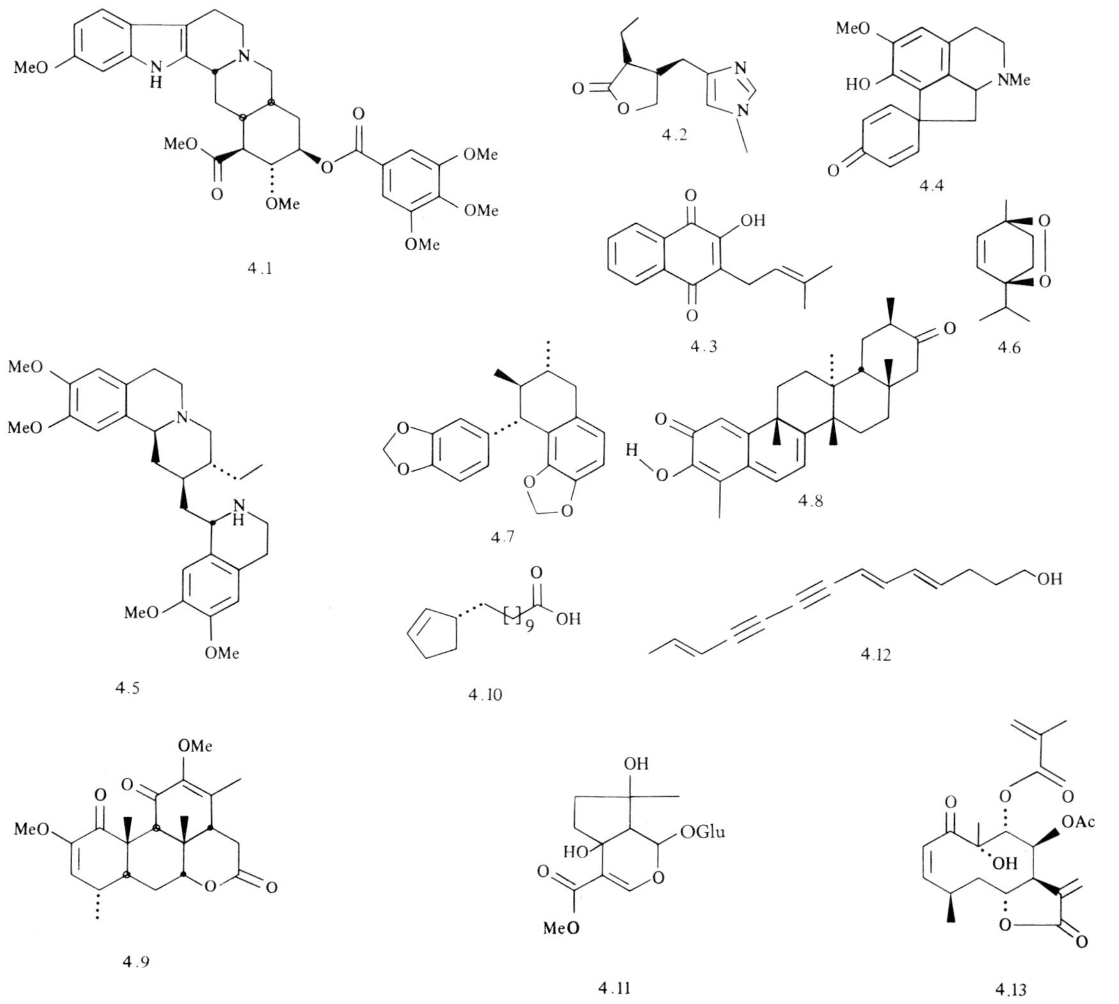

Fig. 12.4. Chemical constituents of some native drugs.

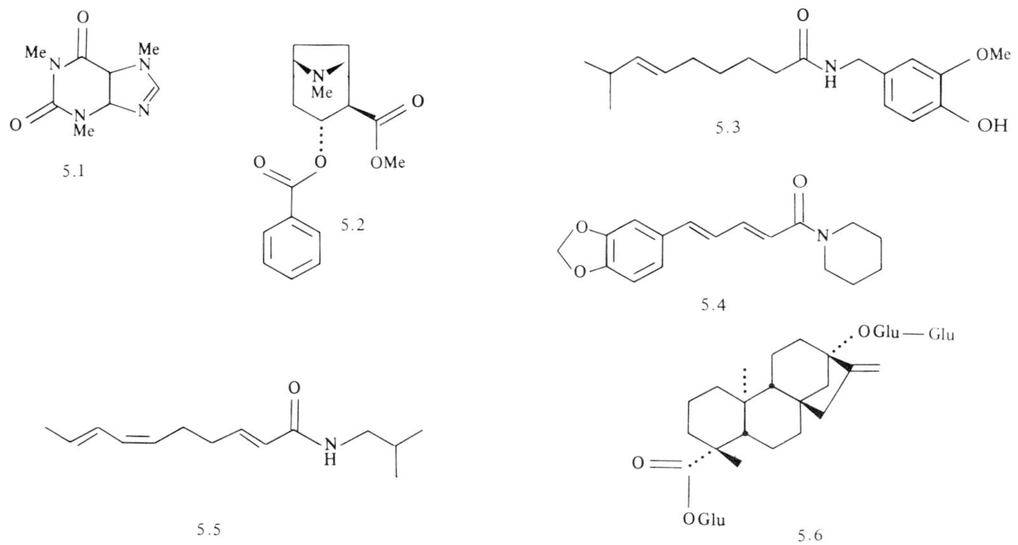

Fig. 12.5. Chemical constituents of some stimulants and spices.

12.3.5. Stimulants and spices

It is amazing how many independent populations incorporated plants containing the stimulant purines such as caffeine (12.5.1) into their living habits. In South America cacau (*Theobroma cacao*, Sterculiaceae), guaraná (*Paullinia cupana*, Sapindaceae) and yerba mate (*Ilex paraguariensis*, Aquifoliaceae) served as did African coffee (*Coffea arabica*, Rubiaceae) and Asian tea (*Camellia sinensis*, Theaceae) elsewhere. In Brazil the coca plant (*Erythroxylon coca*, Erythroxylaceae), widely cultivated in the Andean countries, is also used for its stimulating action due to the presence of cocaine, another type of stimulant (12.5.2). In Brazil *Capsicum brasilianum* (Solanaceae) and the unrelated *Xylopia brasiliensis* in the Annonaceae both provide pepper containing capsaicin (12.5.3) and piperine respectively (12.5.4). Similar amides with hot spicy flavour occur also in *Ottonia corcovadensis* (Piperaceae); its leaves and twigs are masticated by natives to relieve toothache as they have a numbing effect on the mucous membrane of the mouth. The leaves and flowers of *Spilanthes oleracea* (Asteraceae) are widely used in the seasoning of tacaca or of tucupi, typical Amazonian dishes. The constituent spilanthol, more commonly known as affinin (12.5.5), induces a tingling sensation of the tongue. Finally, the leaves of *Stevia rebaudiana* (Asteraceae) have long been used by people of Paraguay and the bordering region in the Brazilian State of Mato Grosso as a sweetening agent. Stevioside (12.5.6), the responsible compound, is 300 times sweeter than sucrose, and has become increasingly important with the removal of saccharin from food.

12.3.6. Essential oils

In the sixteenth century Amazonia was known as Cinnamon Country. Strangely enough nothing smells much like cinnamon in Amazonia except *Aniba canelilla* (Lauraceae), but this species, discovered by Humboldt and Bonpland in the Orinoco region, although quite widespread, is reasonably scarce. Its odoriferous principle is the natural product nitrophenylethane (12.6.1). The name Cinnamon Country is due to another species of Lauraceae *Ocotea quixos* which contains cinnamaldehyde (12.6.2) and other related compounds. Although this species is restricted in occurrence to the vicinity of Quito in the Ecuadorean Andes, it nonetheless inspired the fantastic voyage in 1514 during which Orellana and his Spanish soldiers believed they saw women warriors, which they called Amazonian, an episode which of course still lives on in the name of the river Amazon (Naranjo *et al.*, 1981). Other conspicuous examples of Brazilian aromatic plants include the much more important lauraceous species *Aniba rosaeodora*, the rosewood, rich in linalool (12.6.3), *Licaria puchury-major* and *Ocotea speciosa* with safrole (12.6.4) and the fabaceous tree *Myroxylon balsamum* with nerolidol (12.6.5). Except for puchury whose seeds are used in Amazonia as carminative and stomachic, all others are now being exploited industrially for their valuable essential oils. The wood of these trees is steam distilled to extract the oils that are used in cosmetics and perfumes. This requires felling of the trees, and they have become rare due to their over-exploitation.

12.3.7. Pigments

Not just Amazonas but Brazil also is a name with a chemical history. The sodium salt of brazilein, an oxidation product of brazilin (12.7.1) from the wood of the tree *Caesalpinia echinata* (Caesalpiniaceae) was widely used as purple pigment at the time of the colonisation of Brazil. The tree, named locally pau brasil eventually lent its name to the country because of the quantity of dye shipped to Portugal. *Chlorophora tinctoria* (Moraceae) was also shipped in colonial times to Portugal in large quantities. It still has small scale industrial use in the Amazon region furnishing a yellowish-brown dye which contains the flavonol morin (12.7.2) and the benzophenone maclurin (12.7.3). In much wider use is *Bixa orellana* (Bixaceae). Annatto, the fleshy pulp around the seeds of this plant, contains the carotenoid bixin (12.7.4) employed as food colorant, and is much used by the Indians as a body paint. The fruit juice of *Genipa americana* (Rubiaceae) blackens the skin due to the interaction of the iridoid genipin (12.7.5) with protein. Bixin, genipin and the flavan derivative carajurin (12.7.6) from *Arabidea chica* (Bignoniaceae) are in common use for skin painting by the Amazonian Indians.

The above story, as fascinating as it is in view of the uses of the mentioned chemicals, is rather perplexing. Is this all? Indeed, it seems absurd to believe that so few useful chemicals, from such a relatively insignificant number of species, should constitute the entire list of potentially interesting substances from Amazonian plants. The random search to extend the list while progressing routinely in several laboratories is, not surprisingly, neither representative nor highly successful, chiefly on account of the sheer enormity of the task. Faster results will be forthcoming if the predictive value of ethnobotanical information is used more than has often been the case.

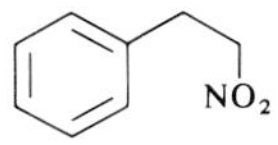

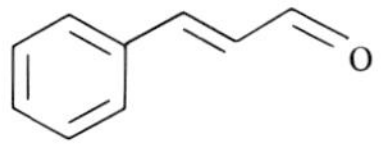

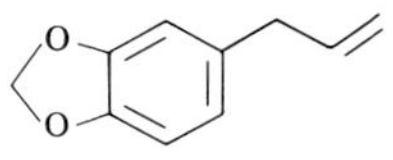

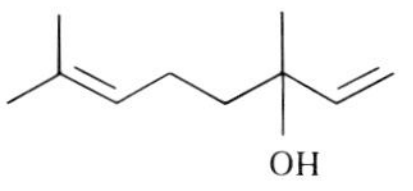

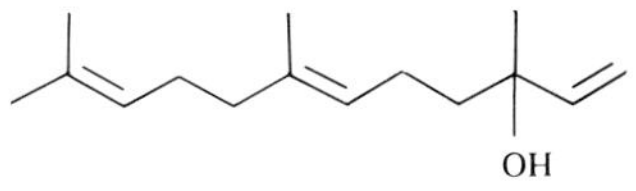

Fig. 12.6. Chemical constituents of essential oils.

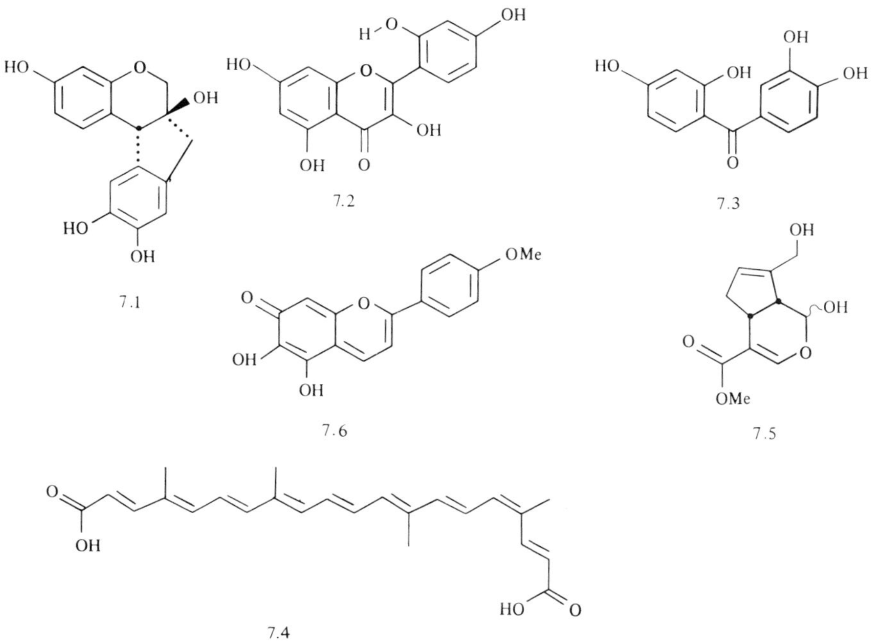

Fig. 12.7. Chemical constituents of pigments.

12.4. CHEMICALS AND THEIR SYSTEMATIC DISTRIBUTION

Is it feasible to extrapolate from existing information on useful chemicals from Brazilian plants to the search for further potentially useful compounds? To provide an answer to this question all chemicals mentioned in the last section (12.3) will be considered in the light of their systematic position. If the code numbers representing the compounds discussed above (12.3) are inserted on Dahlgren's (1980) representation of the orders within the superorders of the seed plants (Fig. 12.8), a markedly heterogeneous distribution is observed. These compounds occur mostly in species of the Magnoliiflorae and their entourage [Cronquist's (1968) subclass-Magnoliidae, left centre] and of the Gentianiflorae-Lamiiflorae-Solaniflorae-Asteriflorae (Cronquist's subclass Asteridae, lower right corner). There are two large areas in the diagram, one representing the monocotyledons [Cronquist's (1961) class Liliopsida, left periphery] and the other the Proteiflorae-Myrtiflorae-Podostemiflorae-Rosiflorae-Celastriflorae-Corniflorae-Theiflorae-Primuliflorae-Violiflorae-Malviflorae [broadly Cronquist's (1968) subclasses Rosidae-Hamamelidae-Dilleniidae, diagonal from right top to left bottom] where the absence of useful chemical products is rather conspicuous.

Such a result could arise from a differential distribution of plant families. Prance (1978) lists the occurrence of 126 families for Amazonia and Rizzini (pers. comm.) lists 130 families for Brazil, together over 30% of all angiosperm families recognised by Dahlgren (1980). If the number of Brazilian families is compared with the number of worldwide families for each of Dahlgren's orders, both monocotyledons and dicotyledons are well represented. The only exceptions are the dicot Rosiflorae and Corniflorae which occupy a central position on the diagonal of Dahlgren's diagram. This statistical result notwithstanding this diagonal includes some of the most widespread and best represented families in Amazonia, such as Rhizophoraceae (Myrtiflorae), Chrysobalanaceae (Rosiflorae), Lecythidaceae and

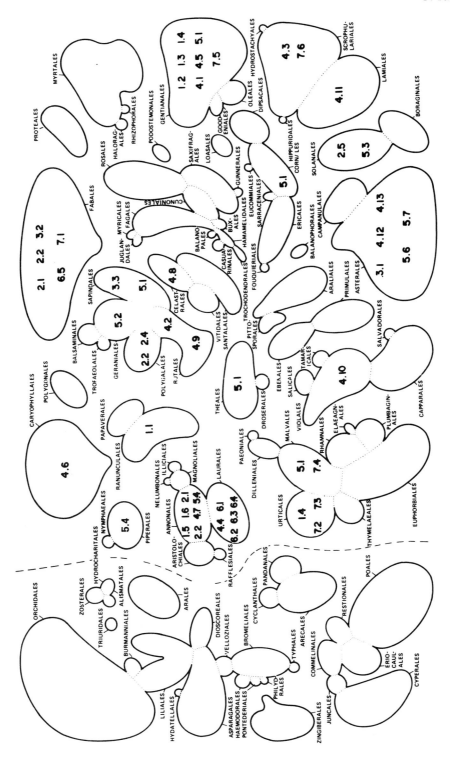

Fig. 12.8. Dahlgren's (1980) system of classification of angiosperms used to demonstrate the distribution of useful chemicals in Brazilian plants.

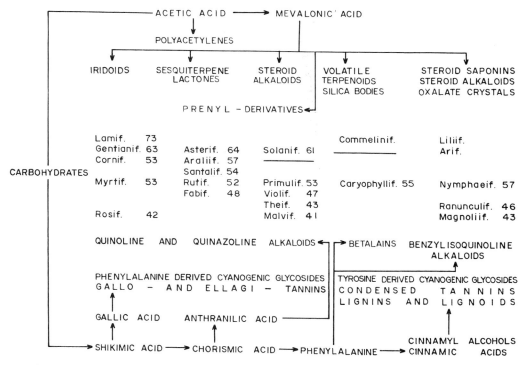

Fig. 12.9. Schematic representation of chemical evolution in angiosperm superorders characterised by the mean Sporne (1980) indices of their families; e.g. Araliif. ' (= Araliiflorae) : Pittosporaceae 63, Tremandraceae 50, Byblidaceae 60, Araliaceae 55, Apiaceae 57 $(63 + 50 + 60 + 55 + 57)/5 = 57$. The sub- and superscripts of columns refer to compound classes which show a trend towards replacement in the interposed superorders. Thus, from left to right, column 1 indicates gallic acid derivatives of Rosiflorae etc. to be supplemented by iridoids in Corniflorae and replaced by iridoids in Gentianiflorae and Lamiiflorae; column 2 indicates anthranilic acid derivatives of Rutiflorae etc. to be supplemented or replaced by sesquiterpene lactones and polyacetylenes in Araliiflorae and Asteriflorae; and column 5 indicates the phenylalanine derivatives of Magnoliiflorae etc. to be supplemented or replaced by steroid alkaloids and saponins in Liliiflorae. In columns 3 and 4 no chemical relationship is implied to exist between the superorders listed below and above the horizontal lines. With respect to the two basic stocks of the superorders mentioned in columns 1, 2 and 3 versus 4 and 5, the latter is considered more primitive, since its compound classes may also appear sporadically in the superorders of columns 1, 2 and 3, while in opposition the compound classes of the superorders of columns 1, 2 and 3 do not appear (or appear very rarely) in the superorders of columns 4 and 5. The outermost reaction sequences refer to primary metabolic routes common to all plants the shikimate pathway (bottom line) and the acetate pathway (top line).

Caryocaraceae (Theiflorae), as well as Dichapetalaceae (Malviflorae). Similarly, the Leguminosae, the dominant plant family of Amazonia, has a relatively modest known chemical use. The distribution and size of plant families in Amazonia may not therefore have great bearing on the importance of their chemical uses.

12.5. CHEMOSYSTEMATICS AND ITS EVOLUTIONARY RATIONALE

The clustering of useful chemicals in certain parts of the plant kingdom would nevertheless suggest that the systematic position of a species is of excellent predictive value concerning the existence of useful chemicals. These chemicals are useful to man precisely because they are synthesised by plants as allelochemics (Whittaker and Feeny, 1971), or chemical signals for the interaction with organisms other than the producer. These chemicals participate in the defence mechanisms of plants which have

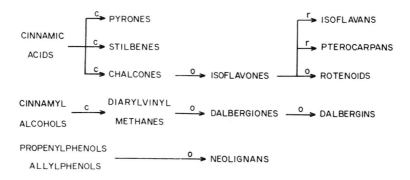

Fig. 12.10. Metabolic routes to biogenetic groups of micromolecules. Primary metabolites of the shikimate pathway (column 1, left; for previous stages see bottom line of Fig. 12.9) undergo condensation reactions (c) with acetate units to products (column 2) which suffer oxidative change (o) in primitive *Machaerium*, *Lonchocarpus* and *Aniba* species. Evolution to advanced species of these genera entails blocking of the oxidative pathways with consequent accumulation of or switch-over to condensation products and even enhancement of reductive pathways (r).

developed through a long process of interactive evolution. The constant battle between predator and prey to attack and defend (Janzen, 1978 and Chapter 11 this volume) has led to a close coevolution between animals (both insects and vertebrates) and plants. The evolution of chemical answers to ever more varied ecological demands could have led to a transition from general and quantitative, to specific and qualitative defence systems. I refer primarily to chemical rather than physical defence systems. With respect to the latter, depauperation of the shikimate pathway in angiosperms (*see* below) led to the replacement of lignins by oxalate crystals and silica bodies, which form a mechanical rather than chemical defence.

The systematic position of a species is of predictive value not only for the presence, but also for the type of useful chemicals. All primary metabolic routes (the carbohydrate and citric acids cycles, the acetate and shikimate pathways) existed already in the pre-angiosperms, or the ancestors of the seed plants. The use of metabolites of these routes for production of secondary metabolites, many of them allelochemics, is subject to a biosynthetic constraint: the evolution of catalysts for their formation and transformation. Being polypeptides, such enzymes have rules for construction encoded in nucleic acids of the organism's genome complex. Thus a 'usually primitive' chemical character may also appear sporadically in advanced taxa, while a character considered 'advanced' rarely appears in primitive taxa.

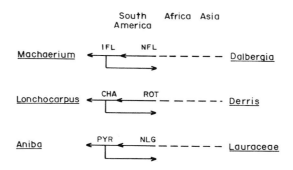

Fig. 12.11. Schematic representation of switch-overs of pantropical (neoflavonoid NFL, rotenoid ROT, neolignan NLG) chemistry to neotropical (isoflavonoid IFL, chalcone CHA, pyrone PYR) chemistry upon evolution of *Dalbergia* into *Machaerium*, *Derris* into *Lonchocarpus* and Lauraceae into *Aniba* respectively. Reversal of lineage extension, with consequent co-occurrence of morphologically related species in an identical habitat, may occur after the switch-over to a substantially different chemical composition.

Fig. 12.12. Jamamadi Indian scraping bark of a *Strychnos* stem for the preparation of curare (photo G.T. Prance).

Consequently the appearance of allelochemics is determined by both ecological demands and biosynthetic constraints. The efficiency with which plants are able to find answers to the demands within the limited flexibility of their genetic make-up determines their survival rate.

The angiosperms or flowering plants inherited from their primitive ancestors lignins and condensed tannins (in addition, possibly, to essential oils) which were replaced by gallo- and ellagi-tannins. This involved the contraction of steps of the shikimate pathway in the superorders listed from right to left in Fig. 12.9. In both major angiosperm groups, the one including the Magnoliiflorae (Fig. 12.9, columns 4 and 5 in the right) and the one including the Rosiflorae (Fig. 12.9, columns 1, 2 and 3 on the left), characterised by primitive bulk defence materials, evolution took a parallel course, that of replacement of these materials by specific chemicals via diversification of biosynthetic groups of secondary metabolites. These, while initially still derived from shikimic acid, were later replaced by derivatives of acetic acid. To give examples, benzylisoquinoline alkaloids gave way to steroidal saponins, and quinoline alkaloids gave way to polyacetylenes. The shikimate pathway lost importance in favour of the acetate pathway in the superorders listed from bottom to top of Fig. 12.9.

This general outline of chemical evolution in angiosperms shows scientific reasons for the heterogeneous distribution of compounds which man finds useful. Plant groups which derive natural protection by the massive presence of oxalate raphids or silica bodies such as the monocotyledons (Fig. 12.8: left periphery; Fig. 12.9: Ariflorae, Commeliniflorae, Liliiflorae), or of gallo- and ellagi-tannins (Fig. 12.8: diagonal from right top to left bottom), are unlikely candidates for the search of specific useful biologically active substances.

Micromolecular evolution, systematics and ecology (Gottlieb, 1982) are tools that can accelerate the pace of new discoveries of useful natural compounds. It is most important to recognise the predictive power of science in this field for three reasons. First, in South America, at least to me, the possibility of extracting additional information on medically or otherwise useful plants from indigenous populations appears slim. Many of the existing tribal customs have already been investigated, if not from the phytochemical, at least from the ethnobotanical point of view, and acculturation of primitive people is at present very rapid (Schultes, 1981). Second, in spite of all the near miraculous achievements and the fascinating history of traditional medicine, indigenous populations succeeded in discovering only a rather small proportion of all useful organisms. 'Higher plants continue an untapped and neglected source of potential drugs for use by man' (Farnsworth and Bingel, 1977). And last but not, the trial and error approach is limited because of the slowness inherent to chemical work and the enormous rate of extinction of organisms.

12.6. THE LOCALISATION OF ROUTES OF SPATIAL RADIATION

The geography of the occurrence of chemical compounds in plants is also a fascinating topic. By morphological evidence the modern Amazonian flora is most closely related to that of Africa. Indeed, according to Prance (1978), plate tectonics and the movement of continents explain that the floras of South America and Africa stayed linked via islands until 38 million years ago. Since the Amazonian flora stands, however, mostly on sediments deposited during the more recent Tertiary and Quaternary epochs, its precursors must have temporarily grown in the surrounding areas, before shifting into the

Fig. 12.13. Collecting the seeds of the legume tree *Anadenanthera peregrina* for use as an hallucinogen by the Yanomamo Indians (photo G.T. Prance).

Fig. 12.14. Preparation of the Paumari Indian hallucinogenic snuff by grinding *Virola* bark into a fine powder in Brazil nut shell (photo G.T. Prance).

present position in the central lowland. Even here, however, severe climatic changes caused repeated alternation between humid forest and dry savannah with forests reduced to refugia (*see* Chapter 8). The present forest continuum started to reform only 12,000 years ago. In spite of all these vicissitudes, close ties still exist between the Amazonian and the African floras.

Man-made destruction may also be reversible as long as the refugia with their concentrations of endemic species are located in time and extinction does not progress too far. The identification of refugia so far has involved mapping of spatial radiation of organisms, among which birds, butterflies, lizards and a few plant families have been used with conspicuous success (Brown, Jr. and Ab'Sáber, 1979; Prance, Chapter 8 this volume). Secondary metabolites are indicators of interaction of plants with many organisms, and the study of phytochemical specialisation itself thus may possibly serve as an indicator of spatial radiation. The number of cases which have so far been studied is ridiculously small, and this prediction can only be confirmed by much further chemical study.

12.7. SOME EXAMPLES OF PLANT RADIATION AND ACCOMPANYING CHEMICAL CHANGES

12.7.1. Neoflavonoids versus isoflavonoids

Dalbergia is a pantropical genus of the pea family (Fabaceae). Many of its species possess a characteristic and conspicuously uniform chemistry based on neoflavonoids and isoflavones. For example, *D. sissoo* from India, *D. melanoxylon* from Africa, as well as *D. spruceana*, *D. nigra* and *D.*

miscolobium from South America, all contain in their heartwoods highly-coloured dalbergiones (Fig. 12.10). The last three species, as is usual for species with similar composition, occur in three different phytogeographic regions, respectively the terra firme forest of Amazonia, the Atlantic coastal forest of southern Bahia to São Paulo and the wooded as well as grassy savannahs of central Brazil. In all these regions they co-occur not only with other *Dalbergia* species but also with the morphologically closely related *Machaerium* species, in which the emphasis of biosynthesis switched from neoflavonoids to isoflavonoids, chiefly pterocarpans and isoflavans (Fig. 12.10). *Machaerium* species are restricted to the American continent and must thus represent a relatively recent development (Oliveira *et al.*, 1971).

The chemistry of the primitive, paleotropical *Dalbergia* — *Machaerium* complex was dominated by oxidative reaction sequences leading to dalbergins and isoflavones (Fig. 12.10). The introduction of the chemistry of the more recent *Machaerium* taxa entailed not only the trend towards abandoning of the oxidative sequences, but also the introduction of reductive reactions leading to pterocarpans and isoflavans, as summarised in Fig. 12.11.

12.7.2. Rotenoids versus chalcones

Derris is a southeast Asian genus of the family Fabaceae. Its species are mainly tropical rainforest lianas with clustered flowers and contain characteristically the fish poisons, rotenoids. South American *Lonchocarpus* species are morphologically closely related and several Amazonian representatives can be described in precisely the same way. The spread of *Lonchocarpus* species from the Amazonian lowland

Fig. 12.15. Two Sanema Yanomamo Indians under the influence of their *Virola* based hallucinogen (photo G.T. Prance).

Fig. 12.16. Maku Indians catching fish with the use of fish poison from *Euphorbia cotinifolia*. The plant is placed on a long bridge over the river and the leaves pounded with sticks. Here they are throwing water over the beaten leaves to send the poisonous plant juices into the river (photo G.T. Prance).

into the contiguous savannahs is accompanied by a change to arboreal habit and contraction of the inflorescence, as well as by a trend towards the replacement of the isoflavonoid chemistry by a chalcone and stilbene chemistry.

This chemogeographical view of evolution in the *Derris — Lonchocarpus* complex (Gomes *et al.*, 1981) summarised in Fig. 12.11, shows that primitive pantropical chemistry is dominated by oxidative reaction sequences, leading in this case to isoflavonoids and rotenoids (Fig. 12.10). The more recent South American chemistry entailed blocking of oxygen requiring steps with consequent enhancement of the fundamental condensation steps leading to chalcones and stilbenes, as well as additional reduction to deoxychalcones.

12.7.3. Neolignans versus pyrones

Cinnamomum, *Eusideroxylon* and *Ocotea*, respectively Asian, African and American genera of the family Lauraceae, all characteristically contain neolignans. In *Aniba*, a related but exclusively South American genus, a neat dichotomy exists between neolignan versus pyrone containing species. Not once have both types of compounds yet been reported for a single species. Neolignans are all formed by oxidative coupling of allylphenols and propenylphenols (Fig. 12.10), while pyrones are formed by condensation reactions, sometimes supplemented by reduction. So here again, the general, and hence presumably primitive pantropical chemistry implies oxidative steps, while the specialised, more recent, exclusively South American chemistry is based on condensation and even reduction reactions (Fig. 12.11).

Chemogeographical relations of *Aniba* species have been reported (Gottlieb and Kubitzki, 1981a,b). All the known neolignan containing species are concentrated in Amazon lowland or adjacent Guiana while the pyrone containing species reach much farther north and south.

12.7.4. Chemogeography and its evolutionary rationale

The case studies given above suggest three conclusions: (1) In spite of the relatively recent origin of the Amazonian lowland forest, there is evidence that the chemical composition of its flora has close ties with the chemical composition of the pantropical rainforest flora. It is on the geologically very much older surrounding cerrados that a specifically South American chemistry is to be found. If correct, this hypothesis may bear on the chemically conservative nature of the arboreal tropical vegetation. (2) It may be anticipated that species of one genus growing side by side in the same Amazonian habitat (Prance, 1978) should have different allelochemical composition in order to resist pest pressure (Janzen, 1973). If the fragmentary evidence for this hypothesis is confirmed, this difference should be due to plant migrations caused by the frequent alternations of climatic conditions in Amazonia. (3) Last but not least, chemical variation within a lineage of plants not only follows the route of phylogenetic differentiation, but at the same time also conforms to a geographical continuity, reflecting its spatial evolution (Gottlieb and Kubitzki, 1982).

Fig. 12.17. Guaraná (*Paullinia cupana*): an important economic plant of Amazonia because of its high caffeine content (photo G.T. Prance).

Fig. 12.18. Maku Indians roasting the leaves of the coca plant (*Erythroxylum coca*) containing cocaine for use in the diet to alleviate hunger pains (photo G.T. Prance).

12.8. CONCLUSIONS

Chemical data have until now played rather a small role as markers in the search for new pharmacologically and otherwise useful natural products and in the mapping of spatial radiation of organisms. This is not due to their lack of relevance in these matters. Quite the contrary, chemosystematics could be a more thorough method than ethnopharmacology for the discovery of useful compounds and chemogeography could be a generally valid method for the identification of centres of dispersal. The lack of impact of chemical data is due to their relative scarcity. By the end of 1977 only 470 of the estimated 50,000 angiosperm species native to Brazil (a large proportion of the

Fig. 12.19. A rosewood factory near Manaus, Brazil. This plant steam distils the wood of *Aniba rosaeodora* to extract its essential oil (photo G.T. Prance).

entire neotropical flora) or 1%, had been examined for the existence of pure chemical compounds (Gomes and Gottlieb, 1977). Isolation and structural elucidation of compounds, on which such work is based, is just not fast enough by presently available methods given the number of species and their rate of extinction. Furthermore, such work requires highly specialised equipment with ever increasing acquisition, maintenance and actualisation costs. Chemosystematics and chemogeography will become as practicable as ethnological or biological work only when procedures of equivalent speed and cost become available.

Clearly, chemical tests, applicable by routine operations to a significant part of the entire flora of selected areas, are required. Even without departing from the basic philosophy and the standard methods of natural products chemistry, the work can be highly rewarding (Levin and York, 1978; McKey *et al.*, 1978). Such efforts have not led to relevant results in the present context simply because of the diversity of naturally occurring chemical compounds which cannot be identified by practical field tests for alkaloids, phenols, tannins and other substances.

According to the evidence reported in the above case studies and elsewhere (Gottlieb, 1982) structural specialisation and oxidation level of natural compounds may be useful indicators of their evolutionary status, whatever the biogenetic group to which they belong. Such a unifying theory of micromolecular evolution would be useful in the evaluation of the phylogenetic position of the taxon characterised by the compounds, somewhat in the sense in which mutation of amino acids reveals the trend of macromolecular (protein) evolution (Dayhoff, 1969). Clearly, the prerequisite for structural diversity and for a particular oxidation state of micromolecules is the evolution of enzyme systems capable of producing both phenomena. Large quantities and many kinds of secondary compounds may require large quantities and many kinds of coenzymes for proper synthesis (Janzen, 1979). Coenzymes normally contain so-called trace elements, some of which are transition metals with variable oxidation states and involved in enzymatic electron transfer processes (Nicholas, 1975). The qualitative and quantitative determination of inorganic elements and ions is a speedy, easily automised, analytical operation. Using this comparatively simple analysis combined with deductions about chemistry made from the taxonomic position of the plant under study, it should be possible to predict its approximate chemical composition with some degree of accuracy. When judged sufficiently novel or interesting these preliminary data can then be supplemented by the traditional isolation and work on elucidation of structure. It is my hope that this will stimulate work necessary to discover the many chemical substances hidden in Amazonian plants which have uses beneficial to mankind.

12.9. RECOMMENDATIONS

If the social impact of the relatively few compounds of Amazon plants already in use is representative, and there is no reason to believe the contrary, one is entitled to speculate how many more wonder drugs lie hidden in the wilderness, waiting to be discovered and used for the benefit of humanity. Already drugs derived from higher plants represent at least a 3 billion dollar annual market in the U.S.A. alone (Farnsworth and Bingel, 1977) and are by far the most widely used remedies by the massive population of China. However, the amount of private and governmental financial support of programs designed to uncover new drugs from higher plants is lamentably negligible (Farnsworth and Bingel, 1977).

Large financial support is needed for basic natural products chemistry, especially where it aims at isolation and structural elucidation of compounds following the phylogenetic and ecogeographic guidelines discussed above. Further, in the case of Amazonia rapid action is required. Within a few more years no amount of money will bring back the chemical treasures lost in the annihilation of the region's flora we witness today.

This chapter also shows that there is more to naturally occurring chemical compounds than we might suspect. They are markers of phylogenetic evolution and of ecogeographic radiation of species. Once enough data are available to consolidate the scientific bases for these concepts it will become possible to trace the spatial history of lineages and hence determine their centre of irradiation from where they might arise again when the present trend towards the destruction of nature is halted. It follows logically that joint efforts of multidisciplinary groups will be necessary to elucidate the causes of natural diversity, including of course, chemical diversity. New methods must be developed for rapid chemical analysis of plants which can be applied to organisms within selected geographic areas. I believe that chemistry is fundamental to the understanding of ecological interactions, and will furnish much new invaluable information for the planning and execution of conservation programs.

REFERENCES

Bannerman, R. H. (1982) Traditional medicine in modern health care. *World Health Forum* 3(1), 8 – 26.
Brown, Jr., K. S. and Ab'Sáber, A. N. (1979) Ice-age forest refuges and evolution in the Neotropics: correlation of paleoclimatological, geomorphological and pedological data with modern biological endemism. *Paleoclimas* No. 5, Instituto de Geografia da Universidade de São Paulo.
Cronquist, A. (1961) *Basic Botany*. Harper & Row, New York.

Cronquist, A. (1968) *The Evolution and Classification of Flowering Plants*. Nelson, London.

Dahlgren, R. (1980) A revised system of classification of the angiosperms. *Bot. J. Lin. Soc.* 80, 91 – 124.

Dayhoff, M. O. (1969) Computer analysis of protein evolution in *Facets Genetics*. Readings from *Scientific American*, selected and introduced by A. M. Srb, R. D. Owen and R. S. Edgar, pp. 265 – 274, Freeman, San Francisco.

Farnsworth, N. R. and Bingel, A. S. (1977) Problems and prospects of discovering new drugs from higher plants by pharmacological screening. In *New Natural Products and Plant Drugs with Pharmacological, Biological or Therapeutical Activity*. Eds. H. Wagner and P. Wolff, pp. 1 – 22, Springer, Heidelberg.

Gomes, C. M. R. and Gottlieb, O. R. (1977) *Cadastro Fitoquímico Brasileiro*. Universidade de São Paulo.

Gomes, C. M. R., Gottlieb, O. R., Marini-Bettòlo, G. B., Delle Monache, F. and Polhill, R. (1981) Systematic significance of flavonoids in *Derris* and *Lonchocarpus* (Tephrosieae). *Biochem. Syst. Ecol.* 9, 129 – 148.

Gottlieb, O. R. and Mors, W. B. (1978) Fitoquímica amazônica: uma apreciação em perspectiva. *Interciencia* 3, 252 – 263.

Gottlieb, O. R. and Mors, W. B. (1980) Potential utilisation of Brazilian wood extractives. *J. Agric. Food Chem.* 28, 196 – 215.

Gottlieb, O. R. and Kubitzki, K. (1981a) Chemosystematics of *Aniba* (Lauraceae). *Biochem. Syst. Ecol.* 9, 5 – 12.

Gottlieb, O. R. and Kubitzki, K. (1981b) Chemogeography of *Aniba* (Lauraceae). *Plant Syst. Ecol.* 137, 281 – 289.

Gottlieb, O. R. (1982) *Micromolecular Evolution, Systematics and Ecology*. Springer, Heidelberg.

Gottlieb, O. R. and Kubitzki, K. (1983) Ecogeographical phytochemistry. A novel approach to the study of plant evolution and distribution. *Naturwissenschaften* 70, 119 – 126.

Janzen, D. H. (1978) The ecology and evolutionary biology of seed chemistry as relates to seed predation. In *Biochemical Aspects of Plant and Animal Coevolution*. Ed. J. B. Harborne, pp. 163 – 206, Academic Press, New York.

Janzen, D. H. (1979) New horizons in the biology of plant defenses. In *Herbivores: Their Interaction with Secondary Plant Metabolites*. Eds. G. A. Rosenthal and D. H. Janzen, pp. 331 – 350, Academic Press, New York.

Levin, D. A. and York, Jr., B. M. (1978) The toxicity of plant alkaloids: an ecogeographic perspective. *Biochem. Syst. Ecol.* 6, 61 – 76.

McKey, D., Waterman, P. G., Mbi, C. N., Gartlan, J. S. and Struhsaker, T. T. (1978) Phenolic content of vegetation in two African rain forests: ecological implications. *Science* 202, 61 – 67.

Naranjo, P., Kijjoa, A., Giesbrecht, A. M. and Gottlieb, O. R. (1981) *Ocotea quixos*, American cinnamon. *J. Ethnopharm.* 4, 233 – 236.

Nicholas, D. J. D. (1975) The function of trace elements in plants. In *Trace Elements in Soil Plant-Animal-Systems*. Eds. D. J. D. Nicholas and A. B. Egan, pp. 181 – 198, Academic Press, New York.

Oliveira, A. B. de, Gottlieb, O. R., Ollis, W. D. and Rizzini, C. T. (1971) A phylogenetic correlation of the genera *Dalbergia* and *Machaerium*. *Phytochemistry* 10, 1863 – 1876.

Prance, G. T. (1978) The origin and evolution of the Amazon flora. *Interciencia* 3, 207 – 222.

Raven, P. H., Berlin, B. and Breedlove, D. E. (1971) The origin of taxonomy. *Science* 174, 1210 – 1213.

Schultes, R. E. (1981) Phytochemical gaps in our knowledge of hallucinogens. In *Progress in Phytochemistry*. Eds. L. Reinhold, J. B. Harborne and T. Swain, Vol.7, pp. 301 – 331, Pergamon Press, Oxford.

Sporne, K. R. (1980) A re-investigation of character correlations among dicotyledons. *New Phytol.* 85, 419 – 449.

Whittaker, R. H. and Feeny, P. P. (1971) Allelochemics: chemical interaction between species. *Science* 171, 757 – 777.

CHAPTER 13

Amazon Ant-Plants

WOODRUFF W. BENSON

Departamento de Zoologia, Universidade Estadual de Campinas, Campinas, São Paulo, Brazil

CONTENTS

'Being unacquainted with the . . . tree and its formidable [ant] inhabitants, and ignoring the warning gesticulations of my Waraus, I was trying to break off one of its boughs, when thousands of these insects rushed out of the small round openings in the internodes, completely covered me and in the greatest fury seized my skin with their jaws and, vomiting a white liquid, buried their terrible stings in my muscles. But not only had the ants from the severed portion of the bough fallen into our corial, but thousands more poured out of the openings in the stump and rained down into the boat since the whole colony had been aroused by the shaking of the tree. A few powerful strokes of the oars carried the boat out of the neighborhood of the tree and in the twinkling of an eye the whole crew was in the water, for only thus could we escape from the savage onslaughts of the ants. Even a few tame [monkeys] and parrots were not spared. The former with wild leaps freed themselves from their tethers and jumped into the river after us, although few animals are more averse to water. . . . . . . I must confess that thereafter a secret horror crept over me whenever we passed one of the trees.' (Richard Schomburgk, 1848, transl. Wheeler, 1942: 44).

13.1. INTRODUCTION

During the Age of Exploration, visitors to tropical America sent back reports of many extraordinary plants and animals. Among the most curious were the hordes of ferocious ants that regularly occupied certain 'ant-plants'. No less curious were the myrmecophytes themselves, with their specialised hollow myrmecodomatia (i.e. 'ant-houses') and other modifications seemingly designed to favour their ant colonists. With time botanists discovered and named several hundred species of these unusual plants, with a disproportionate fraction coming from tropical America and particularly the Amazon.

These plants have proved to be structurally and taxonomically the most diverse imaginable. They occur in 16 plant families and 35 genera in America alone, and in his now out of date monograph,

Bequaert (1922) recognised a total of 116 Neotropical species, whereas 109 were indicated for the East Indies and Australasia and only 40 for Africa. The species total for America now stands near 200, 150 for the Far East and some 65, including doubtfuls, for Africa.

Although myrmecophytes are conspicuous elements of much tropical vegetation, they rarely occur outside the tropics, possibly because ants cannot resist cold weather in thin-walled plant cavities. The ant species that colonise ant-plants are almost as numerous as the plants themselves, although, in contrast to the ants that caught Schomburgk's attention, most are innocuous as far as people are concerned.

In addition to the domatia-bearing ant-plants, many epiphytes grow preferentially on ants' nests, and when several species of these ant-epiphytes grow associated on the same nest, visually pleasing 'ant-gardens' (Ule, 1901) result. Most South American ant-epiphytes, including ant-garden plants, lack the domatia of true myrmecophytes, although in the Far East epiphytic ant-plants are plentiful (Huxley, 1980).

South American myrmecophytes are typically bushes and small trees of the forest interior, although some such as *Tachigali* trees may become giant canopy emergents and others like the fern *Solanopteris* are inconspicuous epiphytes. The trumpet-trees (*Cecropia* spp.), recognised by their distinctive candelabra-like growth form, are abundant in disturbed vegetation all over the American tropics, and the 'Long-John', the name given to *Triplaris* spp. by the inhabitants of Guyana and so vividly described in the opening paragraph, grows to a handsome medium-sized tree in floodplain forest.

Despite their intrinsic interest, Amazon ant-plants have received little attention since the classic studies of Schimper (1888), Schumann (1888), Forel (1904), Ule (1907, 1908), Spruce (1908) and Wheeler and Bequaert (1929), and only now with refined concepts and increased accessibility of the Amazon region have new studies become possible.

13.2. THE STRUCTURAL AND TAXONOMIC DIVERSITY OF AMAZON ANT-PLANTS

The ant-inhabited domatia of myrmecophytes vary greatly in their location and morphological development in different plants, although they seem to share the property of being natural structures of a plant and develop without the interference of ants or other organisms. The tropical American plant genera known to have species with ant domatia are given in Table 13.1, along with estimates of the number of myrmecophytic species and the general regions where these occur. As recognised by Warburg in 1892, myrmecodomatia of these plants can either be derived from normal cavities, such as hollow stems, or be produced from pouches, folds or internal embryonic buds that have no counterpart in other types of plants. Primary domatia, those produced from hollow or hollowed-out plant parts, are not simply cavities that ants use opportunistically to nest: either they demonstrate a series of traits which facilitate their use by ants or the ants which use them are highly specialised, or both. Most tropical American myrmecophytes do in fact present conspicuous adaptations which suggest that evolution has designed their cavities to house ants.

The ant-Cecropias (Moraceae), first described by Müller (1880), provide particularly good examples of plants with specialised primary domatia (Fig. 13.1). *Cecropia* stems are naturally hollow — their soft pith tissue stops growing well before a stem reaches its full diameter — although, like bamboo, the internal cavity is partitioned by a thin septum at each stem node. To establish a colony in *Cecropia*, a queen ant must find an unoccupied plant and gnaw through the stem wall to gain access to the central cavity. However, the wood is full of vascular tissue and, if damaged, exudes a gelatinous sap which may deter the ant or fill the stem cavity with liquid. This problem is overcome by the plant's providing a thin unvascularised membrane, the prostoma, at the top of each internode where the ant can safely and

TABLE 13.1. New World Ant-Plants and their Geographic Distributions

Family/Genus	Type of Ant Domatia	Number of Ant-Plant Species/ Species in Genus	SE Brazil & Parana Basin	Amazon Lowlands	Amazon Region Guiana & Venezuela	E Andean Slopes	W Andes & Central America
POLYPODIACEAE (fern family)							
Polypodium?	primary	1?/150		(X)			X
Solanopteris	secondary	4/4					X
ARACEAE (arum family)							
Anthurium	secondary	1/500		X	X	X	X
ORCHIDACEAE (orchid family)							
Caularthron?	primary	1?/2		(X)	(X)	(X)	(X)
Schomburgkia?	primary	1?17					(X)
BROMELIACEAE (pineapple family)							
Tillandsia	secondary	6 – 12/500		X	X	X	X
PIPERACEAE (pepper family)							
Piper	secondary	7/700					X
MORACEAE (mulberry family)							
Pourouma	secondary	3 – 4/50		X			
Coussapoa	primary	1 – 2/50		X			
Cecropia	primary	±40/50	X	X	X	X	X
POLYGONACEAE (buckwheat family)							
Ruprechtia	primary	1 – 3/20		(X)			
Triplaris	primary	±20/25	X(north)	X	X	X	X
MONIMIACEAE (monimia family)							
Siparuna	primary	1/150		X			
LAURACEAE (laurel family)							
Ocotea	primary	1/300		X			
Pleurothyrium	primary	5 – 10/30		X	X	X	X
CHRYSOBALANACEAE (tropical rose family)							
Hirtella	secondary	6/88		X	X		
LEGUMINOSAE (pea family)							
Acacia	primary	15/100	(X)(Chaco)	X	X		
Sclerolobium	primary	2/30		X	X		
Tachigali	primary	20/23		X			
Platymiscium	primary	1 – 2/30		X		(X)	
Ormosia	primary	1/30		X		(X)	
SIMAROUBACEAE (quassia family)							
Picrolemma	primary	2 – 3/3		X			
EUPHORBIACEAE (spurge family)							
Mabea?	primary	1 – 2?/50		(X)			
Sapium ?	primary	1 – 2?/50		(X)			

Taxon	Habit	Species ratio					
MELASTOMATACEAE (melastome family)*							
Allomaieta	secondary	1/1					
Blakea	secondary	1/100		X			
Clidemia	secondary	30 – 35/165	X	X	X	X	
Conostegia	secondary	2/50	X				
Henriettella	secondary	1/40					
Maieta	secondary	3/3	(X)	(X)	X	X	
Micoania	primary	4/1000	X	X	X	X	
Myrmidone	secondary	2/2			X	X	
Ossaea	secondary	1 – 2/80			X	X	
Tococa	secondary	30 – 35/50	X	X	X	X	X
GENTIANACEAE (gentian family)							
Tachia?	primary	1?/4		(X)	(X)	(X)	
BORAGINACEAE (borage family)							
Cordia	secondary / primary	2 – 3/100	X	X	X	X	X(north)
SOLANACEAE (nightshade family)							
Markea	unknown	4 – 5/20		X	X	X	
GESNERIACEAE (gesneria family)							
Besleria	secondary	1/150	X		X	X	
RUBIACEAE (madder family)							
Duroia	secondary	2 – 3/20	X	X	X	X	
Hoffmannia	secondary	1/100					
Patima?	primary	1?/4		(X)	(X)	X	
Remijia	secondary / primary?	1 – 3/35	X	X	X	X	
Number of ant-plant species:		223 – 258					
Number of ant-plant genera:		35	16	13	16	23	4

Amazon region: 27 genera

X: Myrmecophytic species present in region
(X): Myrmecophytic species possibly present in region
?: Doubtful Myrmecophyte
* Species data for the Melastomataceae provided by J. J. Wurdack (pers. com.)

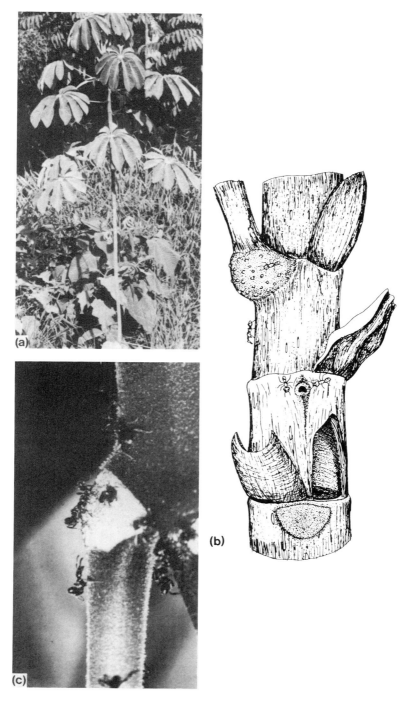

Fig. 13.1. *Cecropia* from the Central Amazon. (A) Young 2 m tall *Cecropia concolor* Willd. occupied by an active colony of *Azteca alfari* in roadside second growth. (B) Upper trunk and petiole base of *Cecropia purpurascens* showing a trichilium with Muellerian bodies and its relation to a nest entrance hole excavated at a prostoma and the hollow stem domatia (schematic cutaway). (C) Ants (*Azteca* aff. *isthmica*) aggregated around trichilium of a young *Cecropia distachya* leaf. The trichilium is almost completely white due to the closely packed Muellerian bodies which in the course of a few hours will expand beyond the adjacent hairs and be harvested by the ants.

easily bite a hole. The eight species of obligate *Cecropia*-ants of the genus *Azteca* always cut their entrance holes at this point, whereas most other ants ignore the shallow pit which marks the location of the prostoma.

After invading the stem, the *Azteca* queen closes up the entrance hole with pith material and begins laying eggs. The ant larvae feed upon secretions provided by the queen and perhaps the spongy pith remnants lining the stem cavity. As the colony grows, worker ants take over brood care, chew holes in the stem septa to expand nest space and kill or wall off other queen ants until the entire plant is colonised.

Worker ants are also responsible for gathering food for the colony. The *Cecropia* plant provides this in the form of modified hairs called bead bodies located on the leaf blades, and as globular swellings (Muellerian bodies) continually produced from trichilia, velvety pads borne singly near the base of each leaf petiole (Fig. 13.1B,C). The bead bodies are especially rich in oil (Rickson, 1976) and Muellerian bodies contain large quantities of carbohydrate in the form of animal glycogen rather than starch (Rickson, 1971). Muellerian bodies may therefore be viewed as imitation animal prey provided by the plants for their essentially predacious ants.

The surfaces of *Cecropia* plants seem well adapted to aid ant movement. The undersides of leaves and sometimes other surfaces are covered with a cottony network of twisted hairs, and the erect hairs on stems and petioles are slanted upwards and frequently possess hooked tips. All of these furnish excellent footholds for *Azteca* and provide traction when the ants attack and subdue other animals intruding on a plant. In addition some *Cecropia* have minute upward-angled spines inside the stems which may help anchor cardboard-like brood platforms and masses of refuse material fastened to the domatia walls by the ant.

The few species of *Cecropia* that are not ant-plants lack a number of the peculiar traits of the ant-Cecropias. *Cecropia sciadophylla* Mart., the only myrmecophobic species in the Amazon lowlands (Berg, 1978), besides being noticeably less hairy than ant-Cecropias, does not develop trichilia, and the stem, although hollow, lacks the unvascularised prostoma and spongy layer of pith remnant. Populations of the common Central American myrmecophyte *Cecropia peltata* L. that are native to the West Indies where its *Azteca* ants do not occur tend to have their trichilia reduced or wanting (Janzen, 1973).

The stem domatia of *Triplaris* (Polygonaceae), normally occupied by slender ants of the genus *Pseudomyrmex*, are similar to those of *Cecropia*, but the cavities are much narrower and the stems crack open at an unvascularised point below each node (Fig. 13.2). To enter a stem, an ant needs but enlarge this natural groove. Herbarium specimens of *Picrolemma* (Simaroubaceae) possess almost identically split branch-tips together with exit holes and other signs of ant occupancy.

The structurally simplest ant domatia are little more than solid swellings filled with soft pith that ants can cut into and hollow out. *Cordia alliodora* (R. & P.)Oken (Boraginaceae), a widespread tree of drier regions, has stem domatia of this type that are regularly colonised by a diversity of ants, some specialised and some not (Wheeler, 1942). Similar plants of the humid Amazonian forest seem to harbour ant specialists. In the only known species of myrmecophilic *Siparuna* (Monimiaceae), its unnamed *Pseudomyrmex* occupants invariably tunnel into stems just below the nodes where they remove the soft internodal pith. Since many ant-plants have never been observed without ants living in them, it is not known for certain whether they are naturally hollow or if the ants excavate the cavities. The few species of *Miconia* (Melastomataceae) colonised by ants, in this case *Myrmelachista* (Forel, 1904), have a single exit hole cut by the ants below each node. In *Pleurothyrium* (Lauraceae) and *Ormosia* (Leguminosae) the otherwise smooth stems are covered with lenticels, fissures that expose underlying tissue, which may break through to an inner cavity as happens in *Triplaris* (Schumann, 1888; pers. obs.). The scattered ant exit holes in *Ocotea* (Lauraceae) correspond to thin spots in the stem wall (Janzen, 1974).

A few plant groups produce primary domatia in structures other than stems. The petiole base of the large compound leaves of myrmecophilic *Tachigali* (called *Tachigalia* in older works) and *Sclerolobium*

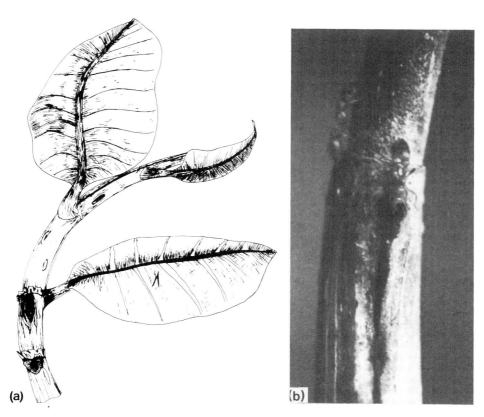

Fig. 13.2. *Triplaris* sp. native to the Pantanal of Mato Grosso, Brazil. (A) Natural orifice on branch of an antless tree growing in south Brazil. (B) Obligate *Triplaris*-ants (*Pseudomyrmex triplarinus*) patrolling the stem of a plant in its natural habitat near Cuiabá, MT, Brazil.

(Leguminosae) develop cavities that are penetrated by specialised *Azteca* and *Pseudomyrmex* (Bailey, 1923; pers. obs.). In the Bull's-Horn Acacias of Central America, and perhaps *Acacia cavenia* H. & A. of the Paraguaian Chaco, enlarged stipular thorns are hollowed out and occupied by specialised *Pseudomyrmex* (Fig. 13.3). The thorn pith is said to be sweet-tasting and may be eaten by the ants (Janzen, 1966). The *Acacia* also provides sugar secretions from nectar glands on the petioles and, in Central America, Beltian bodies, modified leaflet tips that the ants harvest for food. Finally, the swollen rhizomes of *Solanopteris* ant-ferns and perhaps those of *Markea* (Solanaceae), epiphytes related to the potato, degenerate internally, and ants gain access to a chamber by chewing through a localised thin spot in its outer wall (Wagner, 1972).

Some ant-plants possess a far stranger method of providing ant shelters. These produce secondary domatia, or ant pouches, which represent new, qualitatively distinct organs of ant-plant derived through drastic modification of pre-existing structures. All the many ant domatia developed on leaf blades are of secondary origin. Melastomes, in particular species of *Tococa*, *Maieta*, *Myrmidone*, *Clidemia*, *Conostegia*, *Ossaea*, *Henriettella*, *Allomaieta*, and *Blakea*, often have a pair of adjacent ant pouches embedded in each leaf base. Each chamber opens through a more or less constricted passageway and pore to the underside of the leaf at the junction of the mid-vein and a major lateral nerve (Fig. 13.4A). The pouches develop during leaf growth by the invagination of the leaf undersurface at the point of the pore,

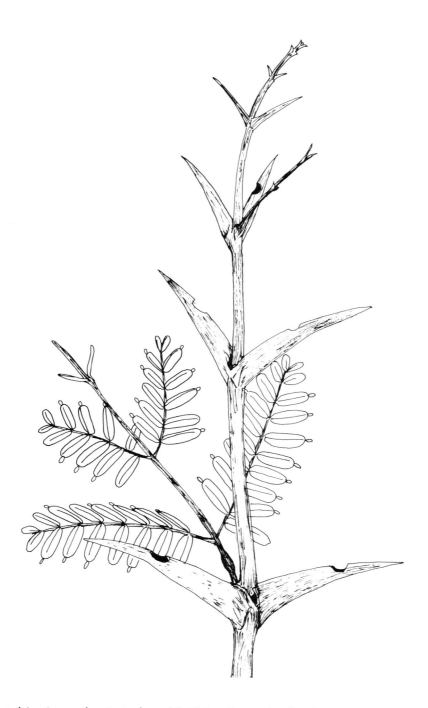

Fig. 13.3. The Central American ant-plant *Acacia sphaerocephala* Schul. & Cham. with perforated stipular thorns tenanted by *Pseudomyrmex*, modified leaflet tips (Beltian bodies) harvested and eaten by the ants, and the ant nectary borne near the base of the petiole (after Schimper, 1888).

and the cavities are therefore extensions of the ventral leaf surface which are manifested dorsally as a biconvex dome near or on top of the petiole. The pouches frequently share a common medial wall, although they do not interconnect.

The genera possessing these peculiarly melastome-type domatia are not necessarily closely related, and a number (*Henriettella, Blakea, Conostegia, Ossaea, Clidemia*), although rich in species, are relatively poor in myrmecophytes. This suggests that the domatia of many genera are not homologous, but rather they have evolved independently on several occasions. Interestingly, plants of the two genera of African Sterculiaceae, *Cola*, and *Scaphopetalum*, have developed leaf domatia structurally similar to those found in melastomes (Bequaert, 1922).

A second type of leaf domatium, demonstrated only by the Amazonian plants *Duroia saccifera* Benth. & Hook., *Remijia physophora* Benth., both Rubiaceae, and half a dozen species of *Hirtella* (Chrysobalanaceae), results from the curling up (*Duroia*) or under (*Remijia* and *Hirtella*) of the leaf margin on the side of the petiolar insertion (Fig. 13.5). Two small myrmecophilic shrubs from Panama, *Hoffmannia vesciculifera* Standl. (Rubiaceae) and *Besleria formicaria* Nowicke (Gesneriaceae), also have paired leaf domatia; however, it is not known how these are formed.

True petiolar ant pouches are known in three tropical American plant genera. In three species of Central American *Piper* (Piperaceae) studied by Rische *et al.* (1977), the domatia are produced by petiolar sheaths which fold over to form a tube on top of each petiole. The ants of these plants also burrow into the stem at the base of each leaf and hollow out branches. A second type of petiolar ant pouch is exemplified by *Clidemia ferox* Gleason and several species of *Pourouma* (Moraceae) (Fig. 13.6). In these Amazonian plants the petiole is deeply cupped on its upper surface near its contact with the stem, and the sides of the depression project upwards and converge to form a lip-like groove. Although the upward directed opening is partially blocked by dense networks of long hairs, the small ants which colonise these plants have little trouble in entering or leaving a pouch. *Clidemia killipii* Gleason, a species from the Pacific lowlands of Colombia, has a curious highly perforated domatium that appears to be slung from the underside of the petiole. Nothing is known about its mode of development.

Pouches can grow into stems and rhizomes, giving rise to secondary ant domatia. Several species of *Clidemia* produce paired pendent pouches on stems just below the nodes with their entrance pores to the side of a petiole (Fig. 13.4B). These domatia are superficial and do not invade the solid cylindrical stem of the plant. In contrast, the stem domatia of *Cordia nodosa* Lam., *Duroia hirsuta* (Poepp. & Endl.) Schum. and perhaps other related South American species go right into the wood. In *Cordia* the growing shoot-tip invaginates through a subapical pore and develops into an ice-cream-cone-shaped cavity (Bailey, 1924), (Fig. 13.7). The hollow spindle-shaped swellings of *Duroia* stems develop as lateral longitudinal fissures immediately below certain stem nodes. In both *Cordia* and *Duroia* the pore closes over in the mature domatium, and plant-ants must reopen the chambers.

In a number of ant-epiphytes in the far East, domatia develop secondarily from germinal buds within the tubers (Huxley, 1978, 1980). A similar process may occur in Amazonian *Markea* which Spruce (1908) reported to have hollow ant-inhabited tubers the size of a small melon.

In all the myrmecophytes considered up to now the plant must produce a suitable domatium before it can be colonised by its typical ants. In the ant-epiphyte *Anthurium gracile* (Rudge) Lindl. (Araceae) this is not the case. Mature plants grow on thin branches exposed to full sunlight and produce large spherical root-balls from which a few roots depart to anchor the plant to its branch (Fig. 13.8A). In forests near Manaus, root masses of healthy plants are almost invariably inhabited by ants, in particular the fiercely stinging *Pachycondyla goeldii* (For.). After the mating flight, young queens of this ant do not seek out host plants but rather build shelters from plant fibres and other material on the undersides of leaves of forest bushes. They probably also collect *Anthurium* seed, perhaps voided in the droppings of birds, for seedlings germinate from the detritus (Fig. 13.8C) and apparently continue to grow into mature plants. The ants build chambers and galleries of detritus and refuse within the cavity formed by the roots, and

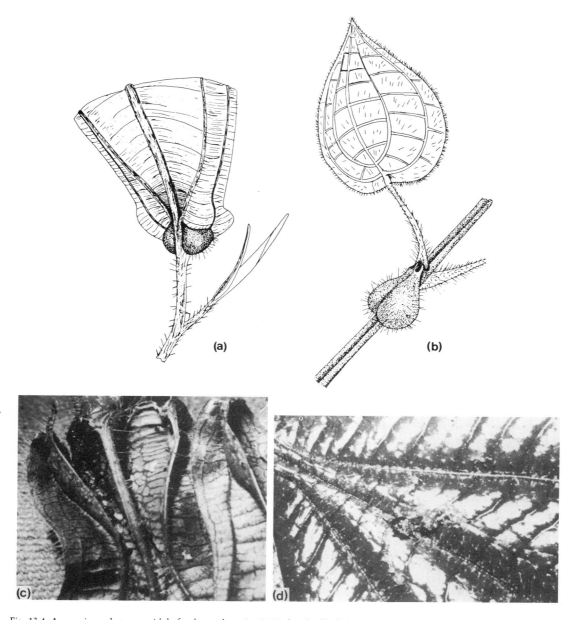

Fig. 13.4. Amazonian melastomes with leaf and stem domatia. (A) Underside of leaf of *Tococa coronata* Benth. with entrance pores to the paired ant pouches situated at the junctions of the major lateral veins with the mid-vein. This plant has larger globular leaf pouches that are usually occupied by a species of *Azteca*. (B) *clidemia tococoidea* (DC.) Gleason with paired stem domatia used by *Azteca*. (C) Ventral aspect of a leaf of *Maieta guianensis* inhabited by *Pheidole* cf. *minutula*, with the ant domatia cut open. The left pouch is filled with trash consisting of food leftovers and excreta deposited by the ants and dead ants and the right one contains ant brood, scale insects and their attendant worker ants. At the far right is a second brood chamber from another leaf. (D) Worker and soldier ants of *Pheidole* cf. *minutula* dismembering a dead insect. (*clidemia* after Schumann, 1888).

this is penetrated and reinforced by rootlets from the host (Fig. 13.8B). The worker ants forage on vegetation at night and return to the nest with insect prey and animal droppings (S.G. Egler, pers. comm.).

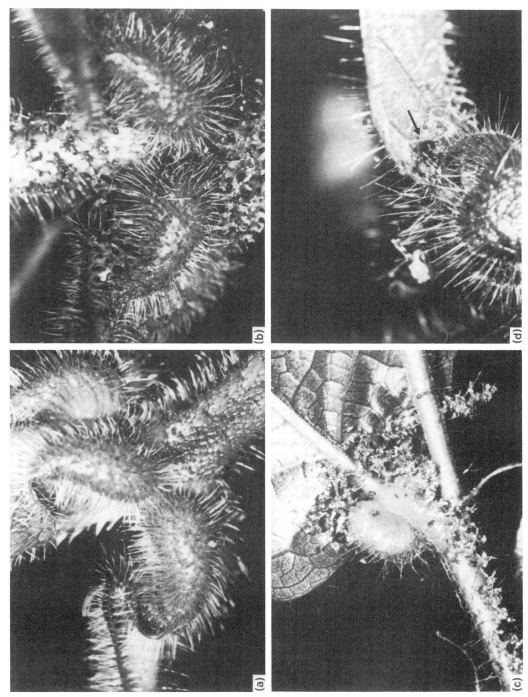

Fig. 13.5. Ant domatia derived from curled leaf margins. (A) Ventro-lateral view of ant-domatia on two young leaves of *Duroia saccifera*, and (B) an older leaf pair on the same plant covered with spongy-appearing detritus deposited by *Allomerus* ants. (C) Underside of leaf domatia of *Hirtella* cf. *physophora* colonised by *Allomerus*. Note that the *Allomerus* of this plant build detritus covered walkways (partially removed to expose the leaf pouches). (D) Side view of *Hirtella* leaf base with *Allomerus* ants hauling a dead (killed?) cephalotine ant (arrow) into a leaf pouch. Both *Duroia* and *Hirtella* are small trees of undisturbed Amazonian forest.

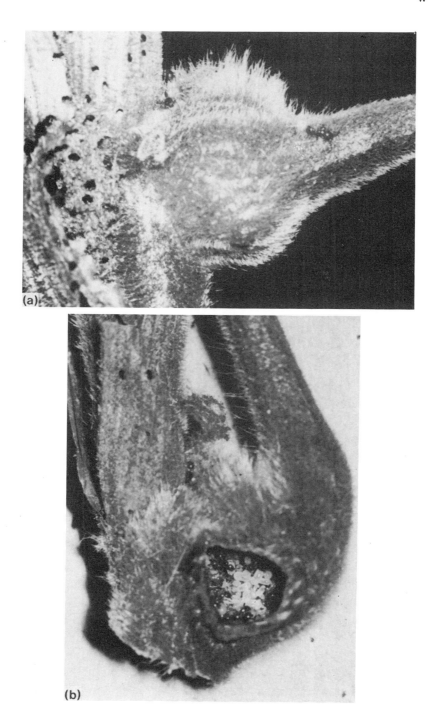

Fig. 13.6. Inflated ant pouch at the petiole base of *Pourouma heterophylla* Mart., a small understorey tree of the Hyleia. (A) A narrow slit bordered by long densely packed golden hairs on the upper surface of the petiole opens into the ant domatia. The *Allomerus* ants that colonise *Pourouma* honeycomb the persistent bud sheaths with access holes. (B) Ant chamber of young leaf with its side cut open to expose the ants and brood inside. The rough inner wall of the domatium produces an abundant supply of Muellerian bodies that are presumably eaten by the ants.

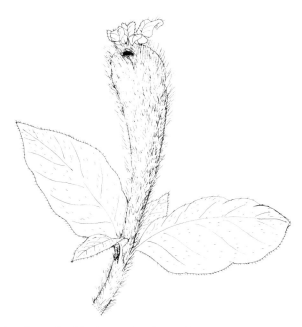

Fig. 13.7. Ant domatia of *Cordia nodosa* produced by the inward pocketing of a stem tip. The branches of these Amazonian forest bushes are usually colonised by one of several obligate *Azteca* ants (after Schimper, 1888).

13.3 HOW ANTS BENEFIT MYRMECOPHYTES

The repeated evolution by plants of complex structures seemingly designed for the well-being of ants points strongly to the idea that many ants must be beneficial to plants. Students of plant × ant interactions have identified two plausible and mutually compatible ways in which ants can be generally helpful to plants, and both have been repeatedly borne out by well-conducted observations. First, through normal nest construction activities and refuse disposal ants may accumulate nutrient-rich organic material from which plants can obtain scarce nutrients and rooting substrate (Miehe, 1911; Janzen, 1974). Also, ants may kill or ward off plant enemies during normal foraging and defensive activities (Belt, 1874).

The nutrient hypothesis is best documented for ant-epiphytes which grow, sometimes exclusively, on ant nests. Plants such as the gesneriad *Codonanthe crassifolia* (Focke) Morton grow better when ants nest among their roots (Kleinfeldt, 1978), and Malesian *Hydnophytum* and *Myrmecodia* directly absorb nutrients deposited on hollow tuber walls by their ants (Huxley, 1978; Rickson, 1979). The New World ant-epiphyte, *Tillandsia caput-medusae* E. Morren, can absorb calcium and probably other nutrients through their bulbous leaf sheaths where ants typically construct nests (Benzing, 1970). In ant-epiphytes such as *Solanopteris* and *Dischidia* (Asclepiadaceae), this latter from the Far East, roots produced near openings of ant domatia extensively invade the ants' detritus deposits within (Wagner, 1972; Janzen, 1974).

Non-epiphytic myrmecophytes no doubt similarly benefit from their ants. Many plant-ants deposit refuse inside domatia, and the decomposition products are at least potentially available to the plants. It is known that hollow-stemmed plants can make effective use of internal carbon dioxide in photosynthesis (Billings and Godfrey, 1967), and even atmospheric ammonia can be directly absorbed by leaves to

Fig. 13.8. The ant-epiphyte *Anthurium gracile*. (A) General aspect of a plant with a colony of *Pachycondyla goeldii* living in its hollow root-ball. (B) A sectioned root-ball showing the detritus lined galleries built by the ants and reinforced by fine roots growing from the epiphytes (a bromeliad is growing from the side of the Anthurium). (C) Nest initiation by *Pachycondyla goeldii*: detritus hut constructed by a young queen ant on the underside of a leaf. *Anthurium* seeds incorporated into the detritus have germinated giving rise to an incipient ant domatium.

provide a significant fraction of a plant's nitrogen demand (Hutchinson *et al.*, 1972). Lenticels have been implicated in water and nutrient uptake in certain ant-epiphytes (Huxley, 1980), and these structures are prominent on detritus covered stems of ant-plants such as *Hirtella physophora* Mart. & Zucc. (Prance, 1972).

Since Amazonian soils are frequently poor in nutrients, the use of ant-provided compost could give considerable benefit to an ant-plant. Although this possibility has not been directly investigated, Stark (1970) found markedly more calcium, nitrogen and phosphorus in the tissues of *Cecropia* occupied by ants than in plants without ant inhabitants.

The defence of plants by ants is well-documented for both myrmecophytes and non-myrmecophytes. At one extreme, the *Pseudomyrmex* ants of *Acacia* studied by Janzen (1966) are hyperaggressive and rapidly drive off or remove insect intruders and may effectively deter vertebrate herbivores from eating their host-plants. These ants additionally attack and kill plants rooted around the host *Acacia* and vines which start growing on it. Plants from which the ants have been removed are much more susceptible to injury and death from pest attack, vine overgrowth and being burned up by brush fires in their seasonally wet-dry habitats (Janzen, 1966, 1967). The *Pseudomyrmex* of Amazonian *Tachigali* and *Triplaris* seem equally aggressive, and the ants of the latter may also maul and kill competing vegetation around their nest trees (Ule, 1907).

The *Azteca* ants of *Cecropia* similarly attack and repel many pests of this plant, and they are especially effective in reducing insect damage to the photosynthetically important young leaves (Downhower, 1975). These ants also bite and kill vines that come in contact with the *Cecropia* (Janzen, 1969).

Contrary to much opinion, an ant need not be aggressive and painful in its bites and stings to provide significant protection for its host. Many species of small and apparently docile ants may be very effective predators of mites and insect eggs, and even slow clumsy species can through numbers profitably harass large insect herbivores. Admittedly, small plant-ants such as *Pheidole* and *Allomerus* would not be very effective against vertebrates, but browsing mammals have probably never been very abundant in Amazonian forests where the plants inhabited by these ants seem most frequently to have evolved.

Since colonies of specialised plant-ants depend upon their hosts for survival, it is not surprising that they adapt to forward their own well-being by caring for the plant. These beneficial actions may therefore be more a result of an ant's dependence upon a plant than a true expression of the conditions which prompted an ant-plant's evolution. To find clues to how myrmecophytes evolve we must look at how unspecialised ants act to favour typical tropical plants.

13.4. HOW ANTS BENEFIT NON-MYRMECOPHYTES

Hundreds of species of relatively unspecialised Amazonian ants nest in or habitually forage upon plants. Some, such as the leaf-cutting ants (*Atta* and its close relatives), are outright harmful to plants. Others may tend certain caterpillars and plant-sucking bugs for their sugary 'honeydew' secretions and thereby have important indirect effects on vegetation.

A good way to examine the effect of ants on plants is to lure ants to certain plants and see if these are benefited by a greater ant density. Bentley (1976) did this experiment using drops of sugar water placed on bean seedlings transplanted into a tropical forest. At sites with high ant abundances the 'sweet' plants suffered much less insect damage than untreated ones, whereas where ants were rarer either there was no difference or plants with sugar suffered more.

Many plants have developed their own ant-lures in the form of nectar-secreting glands located on leaves, stems and other places accessible to ants but unrelated to pollinator attraction (Fig. 13.9A). When ants are for some reason absent from such plants, or are barred from stems by means of sticky barriers, herbivore damage generally increases. Thus, when Schemske (1980) blocked the access of ants to their ant-nectaries on the bracts of *Costus woodsonii* Maas (Zingiberaceae) in Panamá, seed production fell by two-thirds due to increased seed predation by fly larvae. Moreover, the two species of ant implicated in the protection of *Costus* differed in their manner and effectiveness of plant defence. The medium-sized (5 mm) *Camponotus planatus* (Roger) chased adult flies from around developing fruit, but unlike the minute (1.2 mm) *Wasmannia auripunctata* (Roger), it was unable to forage and capture prey under the appressed bracts where fly larvae fed. Also, ovipositing female flies seemed to avoid plants

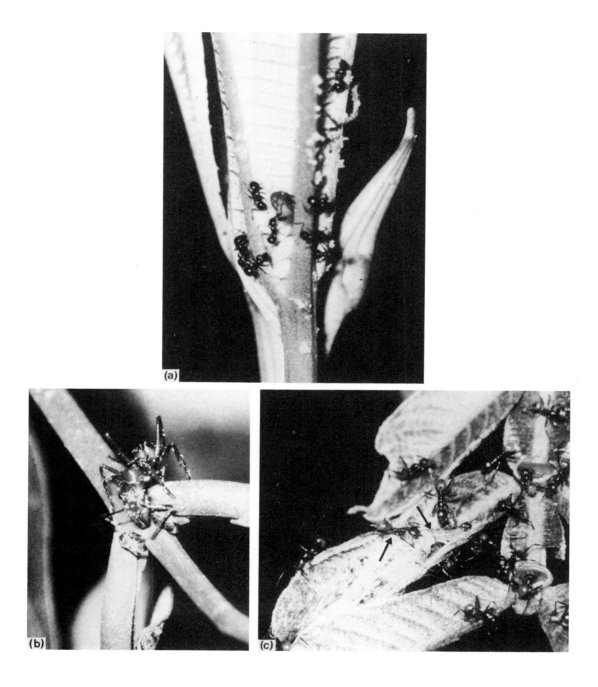

Fig. 13.9. Permanent and facultative ant-nectaries of Amazonian plants. (A) *Pheidole* sp. collecting honeydew from treehopper (membracid) nymphs lodged in the depressions formed by major secondary veins on the underside of a young *Miconia* leaf. (Compare with Fig. 4A). (B) The ant *Ectatomma tuberculatum* (Fabr.) tending treehoppers feeding petiole bases of an unidentified plant. (Compare with Fig. 4B). (C) The abundant and aggressive soil-nesting ant *Pheidole biconstricta* visiting petiolar ant-nectaries of a trailside legume (? *Inga* sp.) and predating defoliating caterpillars on the same leaf (arrows indicate ant and caterpillar near the middle of the centre leaflet).

with *Wasmannia* without having to be chased, thereby making this improbable ant an important plant ally.

Similar studies conducted principally in temperate regions show that ants attracted to nectaries notably reduce herbivory and its negative influence on reproduction in a variety of plants: *Catalpa* (Stephenson, 1982), *Helianthella* (Inouye and Taylor, 1979), *Ipomoea* (Keeler, 1980), *Mentzelia* (Keeler, 1981), *Opuntia* (Pickett and Clark, 1979), *Prunus* (Tilman, 1978), *Aphelandra* (Deuth, 1977), and *Bixa* (Bentley, 1977a). The fact that so many plants, especially tropical species that grow in habitats where ants are abundant, have evolved ant nectaries (Bentley, 1976, 1977b) suggests that nectar-feeding ants as a whole benefit their plant hosts.

Besides nectar, non-myrmecophytes also attract ants with bead bodies, also of frequent occurrence in ant-plants. These swollen plant hairs have much the appearance of insect eggs and are easily detached from plant surfaces. O'Dowd (1982) has recently reviewed much of what is known of their biology. Like nectar glands, they are eagerly sought out by ants, but whereas ant-nectar is predominantly a mixture of sugars and amino acids (Baker *et al.*, 1978), bead bodies generally contain more oil and protein. Since bead bodies are principally known from tropical plants grown in temperate greenhouses, presumably because ants rapidly remove them from plants growing in nature, it seems surprising that fifty plant genera have already been reported to produce them (O'Dowd, 1982). Bead bodies, like ant nectaries, are probably plant adaptations to improve ant defence and perhaps permit plants to attract selectively ants that are likely to eat the eggs of pest insects.

Independent of specific plant adaptations to attract ants, a number of aggressive tropical ants form very large colonies and, with the expulsion of other ant species, come to dominate large patches of vegetation. The resulting 'ant mosaics' (Leston, 1973) in otherwise uniform groves of tropical crop trees have been very instructive of the effects of arboreal ants on vegetation. In Africa these influences have been especially well studied in cacao plantations, and two canopy ants, *Oecophylla longinoda* (Latr.) and *Macromischoides aculeatus* (Mayr.) may actually be managed to take advantage of their controlling action on pests (Majer, 1976). Free-living *Azteca* ants seem to have the same action in South America. Large colonies of these ants may protect citrus groves and other trees from defoliation by leaf-cutter ants (*Atta* spp.) and this can more than compensate for their stimulation of populations of scale insects (Jutsum *et al.*, 1981). These types of effects are not limited to tropical forests; ground nesting *Formica* ants of temperate forests climb into trees where they can prey on a variety of pest insects, and trees without ants can suffer eight times more leaf damage than plants to which ants are allowed access (Skinner and Whittaker, 1981).

Thus, a growing body of data increasingly supports the idea that many ants of tropical as well as temperate vegetation can provide net benefits to plants they associate with. These effects could serve as potent selective forces in the evolution of ant-plants.

13.5. THE EVOLUTION OF ANT DOMATIA

The evolutionary development of primary ant domatia does not present any especially difficult conceptual problems. Ant nests were probably initially established in damaged or weakly protected plant structures, and, when the ants proved of benefit to a plant, plants with even more favourable nesting sites were produced as genetic variants among the progeny of these successful individuals.

Secondarily produced ant pouches are another story. Thus, although it may be highly advantageous for a plant to produce fully formed ant pouches, these must evolve over many generations from the incipient structure to the fully functional plant organ. For this to occur, the intermediate phases must also be beneficial to the plant. However, no one to my knowledge has ever identified an advantage for such structures too small for ants to colonise. I believe that incipient ant domatia, in many cases, functioned as feeding sites for sucking homopterans, in particular scale insects (coccids) and treehoppers (membracids). Although at first sight this may seem outlandish, in fact the hypothesis is supported by a number of lines of evidence, much of which has been presented by Way (1963) in his review of mutualisms between ants and homopterans.

Scale insects and similar homopterans live on plant sap which they tap by inserting their syringe-like mouthparts into vascular tissue. Heavy attack can inhibit plant growth, and virus transmitted by these bugs may sometimes kill plants. However, these small insects suffer greatly from their own predators and parasites, and plant adaptations such as hairs, bark and ducts containing latex and resin considerably reduce their access to natural vegetation. By attracting protective ants with their honeydew secretions, homopterans can gain protection from natural enemies, and many have become so dependent upon ants that they hardly survive in their absence (Way, 1963).

On woody plants homopterans frequently seek out crevices, particularly around major leaf nerves, petiole bases and the scars at stem nodes, presumably because of the greater accessibility of sap conducting tissues and the added protection from natural enemies. Many tropical ants further protect their honeydew sources by building plant-fibre shelters over them. These also provide protection for the ants during periods of rain and permit them to shepherd their homopterans continuously.

By enticing ants, honeydew secreting bugs are analogous to ant nectaries, and if the increased ant protection against chewing insects is greater than the damage caused by the bugs, it may be a distinct advantage for a plant to have sucking insects feeding upon it. Indeed, this sometimes is the case. Pugnacious ants (*Formica rufa*) attracted to treehopper nymphs (*Publilia concava*) feeding on goldenrod (*Solidago altissima*) repel and prevent devastating defoliation by leaf beetles (Messina, 1981). Plants with the membracids both have many ants and end up growing much taller and producing many more seeds than ones without them. I have observed similar situations in Amazonia: the ant *Pheidole biconstricta* Mayr (see Fig. 13.9C) is attracted in great numbers to plants with homopterans, and leaves of *Miconia* with both insects are much less damaged by alticine leaf beetles than leaves on adjacent stems with few or no membracids.

Since many homopterans have trouble surviving in the absence of attending ants, they may actually be more economical for a plant than ant nectaries. Nectar production has a fixed cost whether or not protective ants are present to make use of it, whereas outlays for honeydew producing homopterans may only be required when ants are in fact present. They would act as facultative ant nectaries, with the advantage that when a plant invests in ant protection, ants will be present to provide it.

The secondary domatia of ant-plants generally develop at points where membracids and scale insects prefer to feed on related species. In South American melastomes such as *Miconia* the favourite homopteran feeding site is in the angle between the mid-vein and a major lateral vein (Fig. 13.9A), in exactly the same position as the opening of the leaf domatia of melastome ant-plants (Fig. 13.4A). In some species of *Miconia* a more or less deep depression exists in this angle, and at least one species near Manaus has a membrane partially covering the space. Similar small chambers, classified as pouches, crypts, pits, hair tufts and pleats (at leaf margins) and generally referred to as acarodomatia (i.e. 'mite-houses'), exist on the leaves of a wide variety of woody plants, especially in the tropics (Schnell, 1963). These chambers have been assumed to house scavenging mites, and some apparently do. I suspect that many of these are really ant-coccid chambers and that this adaptive linkage has gone unrecognised because homopterans are thought of as intractable pests and mites are common opportunistic invaders of plant cavities. Young coccid nymphs, called crawlers, may have been occasionally mistaken for mites. A possible transitional situation between coccid and ant pouches is demonstrated by *Blakea formicaria* Wurdack. In this rare Ecuadorian melastome the leaf pockets are wide and deep, and their apertures are criss-crossed by stiff plant bristles. The type collection of this *Blakea* has white material in the interior of chambers which resembles wax from scale insects.

The two African Sterculiaceae mentioned earlier have well-developed leaf domatia, although ants do not seem regularly to colonise them. The paired chambers of *Cola marsupium* K. Schum. are small and seemingly adapted as shelters for coccids and aphids (Kohl, 1909, cited by Bequaert, 1922), and the single asymmetrical pouch of *Scaphopetalum thonneri* DeWild. & Dur. can contain both ants and scale insects. I have not examined close relatives of myrmecophytes with secondary domatia on petioles and stems, although homopterans select these places for feeding in unrelated plants (compare Figs. 13.9B and 13.4B).

Even the smallest ant domatia are much larger than needed to house just scale insects. I suppose that before the plants become ant-plants the extra space allows inactive ants, that might be aroused and unwittingly come to the plant's defence, to rest. (The fable of the diligent worker ant does not correspond to reality: only about 10% of the ants in a colony are normally active outside the nest (Petal, 1978) and loitering seems to be frequent).

Despite the fact that practically all South American ant-plants have coccids tended by their ants, I have never observed a plant heavily infested by these insects. *Pseudomyrmex* and *Azteca* plant-ants eat some of their scale insects (Wheeler, 1942; Carroll and Janzen, 1973) and may in this way obtain a protein supply as well as control scale insect populations on their hosts. Canopy nesting *Oecophylla* clearly limit coccids by harvesting those in excess of their honeydew needs (Way, 1963). Plant-ants have surely adopted a similar behaviour to guarantee sustained colony and plant growth.

If ant-coccid domatia have indeed been important precursors of ant pouches, such ant-plants should not have evolved from plants with functionally redundant ant nectaries. It is therefore not surprising that very few true ant-plants possess ant nectaries and those that do bear primary domatia (e.g. *Acacia*, *Macaranga*, and *Barteria*).

Large chambers to house coccids tended by ants have probably evolved more often in plants of the forest interior and in other places of low productivity where plant-foraging ants are relatively uncommon and ant nectaries relatively inefficient. Here, inexpensive plant options to attract and aggregate ants would be especially advantageous. In such habitats the ants themselves probably have considerable difficulty in finding enough food, and it is not much of a jump for a rare, food-limited ant to start nesting, and preferring to nest, in ant-coccid domatia with their assured food supplies.

The great majority of ant-plants with pouch domatia are bushes and small trees of the forest interior, as expected, and the few that are not grow in flooded areas (*Remijia*, some *Tococa*, and some *Clidemia*). None, so far as is known, is typical of ant-infested habitats such as vigorous second growth or the forest canopy (with the possible exception of some ant-epiphytes).

Why have nectary plants not evolved pouch domatia? There seem to be two basic reasons: nectary plants occur and presumably evolve in habitats associated with abundant aggressive ants, making it difficult for rare ants to establish specialised associations with these plants, and ant nectaries rarely need protection for they are seldom left unattended by the abundant ants and are not subject to predation when ants are not present. *Conceveibastrum martiana* (Baill.) Pax & Hoffman. (Euphorbiaceae), a small tree frequent in bottomland clearings of the Amazon, gives the strong impression of being on the verge of becoming a myrmecophyte, although this will probably never happen. Its leaves bear large ant nectaries in deep depressions to each side of the mid-vein, and the large persistent stipules are rolled inward to form semienclosed cavities lined with nectar glands. The trees I have examined have always been occupied by common unspecialised aggressive ants such as *Pheidole biconstricta* and *Crematogaster* sp. Even though it might be possible for some ant to nest in the stipular enclosures of this plant, it would be unlikely to resist unspecialised invaders or even find a plant not already occupied by these. With the ant protection apparently already received by *Conceveibastrum*, any additional adaptations to accommodate ants would seem superfluous.

13.6. THE EVOLUTION OF MYRMECOPHYTES IN ANT-RICH HABITATS

Cecropia is the only ant-plant characteristic of ant-infested second growth habitats in the Amazon. Like *Conceveibastrum*, *Cecropia* trees start out as perfectly erect 'beanpole' plants. This growth form limits ant access to the lower trunk of a plant, and were it not for the ant-food provided, neither would normally attract many foraging ants. By the same token, the restricted access route makes these plants easy to defend from other ants after the same food sources. In the case of *Cecropia*, the closed, hollow stems ensure that only specialised plant-ants capable of penetrating the trunk cavity will establish a hold in a tree's crown and from this strategic position be able to intercept and expulse competitors which must climb up the trunk. In contrast, ant-plants with either more accessible domatia or spreading growth forms may be overrun by abundant unspecialised ants, thereby eliminating many of the nesting and feeding opportunities of specialised plant-ants. In this regard, it is significant that in the Eastern Tropics the typical second growth *Macaranga* ant-plants also have erect, little-branched trunks and require specialised plant-ants to open their hollow stems (Rickson, 1980).

The hollow-branched bush *Remijia glomerata* Huber of disturbed marshy forest in the Central Amazon provides an especially good example of the difficulties second growth plants have in becoming myrmecophytes. Plants in young second growth harbour a number of unspecialised *Camponotus* and *Azteca* ants in the hollows of damaged branches, and these chew passageways through stem septa and cut exit holes in the stem walls, especially at weak points under the leaf scars. Inside older secondary forest where vegetation is less dense and stem-nesting ants are uncommon, the more isolated *Remijia* plants are colonised by an undescribed apparently specialised *Azteca* which defends itself in much the same way as species specialised upon *Cecropia*, *Tococa* and other ant-plants. The plant has no specialised structures to permit the colonisation of this or other ants, and a queen of the forest *Azteca* must initially invade a pathologically swollen branch tip through the hole left by a stem-boring caterpillar. As the *Azteca* colony grows, it occupies the entire plant, and the ants may build cardboard-like satellite nests in neighbouring vegetation. However, it does not seem likely that this ant could defend its plant and an exclusive foraging space around it in ant-infested second growth and therefore, either by preference or elimination, does not occur there.

These observations suggest that one critical factor in the evolution of ant-plants is the balance of the advantage to the ants, and that ant-plants have not evolved more often because ants would not benefit by specialising upon them. This may also be the reason why forest ant-plants found growing in open areas are almost always occupied by second growth ants rather than their characteristic plant-ants.

13.7. PLANT-ANTS AND THE COEVOLUTION OF PLANT AND ANT TRAITS

Different ants and ant groups vary greatly in their ecological characteristics, and this has been responsible for many conspicuous patterns in the association between ants and ant-plants. Of the six subfamilies of Amazonian ants, only four are regularly found in ant-plants (Table 13.2). Of the two that are not, the army ants (Dorylinae) are always on the move and could probably never establish specific relations with plants, and the morphologically primitive Ponerinae are highly predacious and tend to produce small colonies, perhaps because their dependence upon selected prey limits their food supply. A number of ponerines do nest opportunistically in epiphytes, and one, *Pachycondyla goeldii*, is a specialised inhabitant of the ant-epiphyte *Anthurium gracile*.

The two additional subfamilies of stinging ants, the Pseudomyrmecinae and Myrmicinae, do frequently inhabit ant-plants. *Pseudomyrmex*, the only pseudomyrmecine genus in the New World, is endemic to the region, and practically all of the approximately 150 species of these agile slender ants nest

TABLE 13.2. Ant genera regularly associated with Neotropical ant-plants, ant-epiphytes and ant-gardens (based on Wheeler, 1942, references cited in the text and personal observations).

Subfamily (number of neotropical genera)	Genus	Number of neotropical species*	Aggressive plant defence	Effective sting	Number of species in		Ant-plant genera colonized**
					Ant-gardens & epiphytes	Ant-plants	
PONERINAE (27)	Pachycondyla	50	+	+	few	1	Anthurium
	Odontomachus	25	+	+	few	0	
	Anochetus	20	+	+	1	0	
MYRMICINAE (80)	Pheidole	250	−	±	few	30/40	Piper, Clidemia, Conostegia, Maieta, Tococa, Cordia, Besleria
	Crematogaster	100	±	−	few	few	Clidemia, Maieta, Myrmidone, Ossaea, Tococa, Tachia?
	Allomerus	15/30	−	±	0	15/30	Pourouma, Hirtella, Clidemia, Myrmidone, Tococa, Cordia, Duroia
	Solenopsis	150	−	±	few	few	Besleria, Hoffmannia
	Zacryptocerus	80	−	−	few	1?	Platymiscium
PSEUDOMYRMECINAE (1)	Pseudomyrmex	150	+(−)	+(±)	0	30/40	Ruprechtia, Triplaris, Siparuna, Acacia, Platymiscium, Tachigali, Sclerolobium, Cordia, Sapium?, Mabea?, Coussapoa?
DOLICHODERINAE (13)	Hypoclinea	20	+	−	few	0	
	Monacis	20	+	−	few	0	
	Iridomyrmex	15	−	−	few	0	
	Azteca	150	+	−	10/20	30/50	Cecropia, Coussapoa, Triplaris, Hirtella, Pleurothyrium, Clidemia, Ossaea, Tococa, Solanopteris, Tachigali, Ormosia, Cordia, Duroia, Remijia?, Markea?
	Tapinoma	12	−	−	1	0	
FORMICINAE (13)	Nylanderia	25	−	−	1	0	Ocotea, Maieta, Clidemia, Miconia, Tococa, Duroia, Tachigali
	Myrmelachista	30/60	±	−	few	10/20	
	Camponotus	300	±	−	few	1	Cecropia

* Estimates based on Kempf (1972) and personal observations.
** Tillandsia is considered here as an ant-epiphyte.
? Plant may not be a myrmecophyte
Note: Ants have not been examined from Picrolemma, Allomaieta, Blakea or Henriettella.

in twigs and other hollow plant cavities. The colonies of free-living species are small, and the ants are diurnal and forage as solitary hunter-gatherers. Food consists of small living prey, scavenged spores and animal material and sweet plant and animal secretions. Despite possessing a formidable sting, used primarily to subdue prey, free-living *Pseudomyrmex* do not defend nectar sources or nest sites, nor is there evidence that much debris that might serve as plant food is accumulated in nests. It is somewhat surprising that these cowardly ants have produced the most ferocious and feared plant-ants, and even Schomburgk's *Pseudomyrmex* seems mild when compared with the African *Pachysima aethiops* (Em.) which inhabits *Barteria fistulosa* Mast. (Passifloraceae). Or as one experienced ant ecologist affirms: 'While hundreds of stings of *Pseudomyrmex* can be tolerated . . . 1 − 5 *Pachysima* stings were enough to drive me away from a tree, leaving me very reluctant to return' (Janzen, 1972: 890).

Besides their aggressiveness, *Pseudomyrmex* plant-ants usually depart from their relatives in that they maul non-host plants, are active 24 hours a day, produce large colonies that sometimes have multiple queens (Janzen, 1966) and discard trash that falls on leaves of the nest plant. These behaviours are not invariable, and notable exceptions exist such as the small timid *Pseudomyrmex* of *Siparuna*.

The passive nature of free-living pseudomyrmecines, together with the fact that ant-plant species always inhabit plants with primary domatia (Table 13.2), indicates that these ants start out by giving little benefit to their hosts, and only later evolve strongly beneficial behaviour as they lose their capacity to abandon and live away from their preferred plants.

Pseudomyrmex plant-ants have evolved from free-living ancestors on at least seven and probably many more occasions, and with subsequent rounds of speciation have produced as many as 30 or 40 species (Table 13.2). The *Pseudomyrmex* of the *latinodus*-group have radiated to occupy *Triplaris* [*Ps. triplaridis* (For.) and *triplarinus* (Wedd.)], *Tachigali* and *Sclerolobium* [*Ps. latinodus* (Mayr) and *malignus* (Wheeler)] and perhaps *Coussapoa* [*Ps. ulei* (For.)] and *Sapium* [*Ps. caroli* (For.)]. Ants of this group possess a number of peculiar traits, including unusually small eyes, suggesting a long specialised association with ant-plants. Some species of the *sericeus*-group have also adapted to occupy *Tachigali* and *Sclerolobium* as well as *Platymiscium stipulare* Benth. and *Cordia alliodora*. In the central Amazon *Ps. latinodus* and *malignus* tenant the petioles of saplings of two distinct species of *Tachigali*, while in the adult trees these tend to be replaced by a *Pseudomyrmex* of the *sericeus*-group. *Tachigali* and *Triplaris* are also colonised by *Azteca*; these cases will be treated with the latter genus.

The remaining major radiation of *Pseudomyrmex* on to ant-plants involves the Bull's Horn Acacias of Central America. Only *Pseudomyrmex* ants have established obligate associations with New World *Acacia*, and they seem to represent several unrelated evolutionary lines of the ants. Janzen (1975) reported eleven distinct species of specialised *Pseudomyrmex* inhabiting the Central American Bull's Horn Acacias, and from botanical evidence believes (Janzen, 1966) that these plants have evolved on at least five separate occasions from non-myrmecophytic ancestors. The most atypical of the *Acacia* ants is *Ps. nigropilosus* (Em.). This species is a parasite of the ant × plant mutualism; it refuses to protect its host and spends its time collecting nectar and Beltian bodies to raise a large brood of fertile daughters before the plant dies or is invaded by an aggressive ant (Janzen, 1975). The Paraguaian *Acacia cavenia* is said to have hollow thorns occupied by *Ps. fiebrigi* (For.) (see Wheeler, 1942), although it is not known if this is an obligate ant × plant symbiosis.

Although the pseudomyrmecine fauna of the Old World is comparable in size to that of South America, only three species seem to have evolved obligate relations with plants, and all of these are in Africa (Bequaert, 1922; Janzen, 1972).

The remaining group of stinging ants, the Myrmicinae, is extremely diversified. Of the 80 genera and more than one thousand species in tropical America (Kempf, 1972) well under one hundred species distributed among 5 genera seem to be obligate plant-ants (Table 13.2). *Crematogaster*, *Solenopsis* (fire ants) and *Zacryptocerus* (turtle ants), although having a large number of species, are poorly represented among the plant-ants. In the Amazon Region ants of these genera are rare colonists of a number of myrmecophytes which themselves more frequently host other ants. Thus, the widespread Amazonian *Crematogaster* aff. *laevis* Mayr lives occasionally in species of *Tococa*, *Maieta*, *Clidemia* and *Myrmidone* without being characteristic of any (Wheeler, 1942; pers. obs.). However, in Panamá, myrmecophytic *Hoffmannia* and *Besleria* typically house *Solenopsis*. The sporadic occurrence of plant-ants in these genera suggests that they are for the most part late-comers and have played little role in the evolution of Amazonian ant-plants.

Many species of *Pheidole* and all *Allomerus* (a relative of *Solenopsis*) are obligate plant-ants specialised, with the exception of a few *Pheidole*, on plants with secondary domatia. The ants of both genera are small and not notably aggressive, in contrast to many free-living *Pheidole* and *Solenopsis* which have quite effective bites and stings and use them without hesitation. The plant-*Pheidole* are predominantly and *Allomerus* entirely Amazonian in distribution, and both tend to live in myrmecophytes of the shady forest interior.

The worker ants of both *Allomerus* and *Pheidole* resemble in many respects the small *Wasmannia* ants studied by Schemske (1980) that were so effective in reducing seed destruction in *Costus*. These plant-ants forage over leaves and stems of their hosts (Figs. 13.4D, 13.5A − D, 13.6A) where they scavenge a variety of small items. If a leaf is rasped, simulating the disturbance of a chewing insect, more ants leave the associated domatia and wander more extensively on the leaf surface. The few caterpillars I have seen on their plants roll ant-proof cylinders from leaf-margins or weave silken walkways suspended by plant hairs above the leaf surface. In contrast, very small plants without active ant colonies frequently harbour caterpillars, some of which even seek refuge in the ant domatia when not feeding. Activity of these ants, and indeed practically all plant-ants, is especially intense at the tips of growing branches (Fig. 13.5A) where they may be removing newly produced bead bodies from leaves (O'Dowd, 1982) and the inner walls of domatia (Roth, 1976).

In addition to their possible protective role, many *Pheidole* and *Allomerus* gather and accumulate detritus of both plant and animal origin which they deposit on stems and leaves and inside domatia. *Allomerus* typically build spongy-appearing canopy-ways over leaf bases and stems, employing the stiff plant hairs for supporting framework (Fig. 13.5B,C). In *Clidemia juruensis* (Pilger) Gleason and *Tococa* aff. *capitata* Trail ex Cogn. of the southwest Amazonian lowlands, stems and leaf bases can hardly be seen for the great masses of ant trash. The detritus deposited externally on plants by *Pheidole* is stacked rather haphazardly, generally in the vicinity of domatia entrances. In addition at least some *Pheidole* store refuse directly in domatia. The *P.* cf. *minutula* Mayr of *Maieta guianensis* Aubl. use one pouch on each leaf for ants, brood and scale insects while the other is filled with a mixture of dead ants, insect parts and an amorphous dark material probably consisting of ant excreta (L.F.L. Duarte, pers. comm.; pers. obs.). *Azteca* and *Myrmelachista* (*see* below) produce similar 'latrines' in plant domatia (Wheeler, 1942; Vogel cited in Dumpert, 1981: 220; pers. obs.).

It is not unreasonable to suppose that inorganic nutrients released from decomposing ant detritus and refuse serve to nourish these ant-plants. Indeed, it is of utmost importance to an ant colony that its host-plant grows as rapidly as possible, for a colony is subject to many risks and must reach a certain critical size, determined in part by the size and health of its host, before it can produce queen ants to breed new colonies. For example, the colonies of *Pheidole* cf. *minutula* in forests near Manaus start reproduction with about 100 worker ants, and thereafter a colony will contain approximately 14 additional winged reproductives for every 100 workers added (Duarte and Benson, unpubl.). Moreover, the size of a colony is directly proportional to the number of leaves on its *Maieta*: about 45 worker ants for each leaf. It is easy to see that if a plant grows slowly, its ant inhabitant may forfeit a considerable fraction of its reproductive potential over the colony lifetime.

Pheidole cf. *minutula*, like all *Pheidole*, produces a soldier caste that presumably participates in colony defence. These big-headed ants mount guard over the domatia entrances and apparently leave only to help subdue larger food items (Fig. 13.4D). The number of soldiers in a colony increases asymptotically from zero in new colonies to a maximum of approximately 230 in plants with 30 or more leaves. Most leaves have from 2 − 5 soldiers, but the leaf pouch adjacent to that of the colony queen typically possesses a 'palace guard' of well over 50 (Duarte and Benson, unpubl.).

Both *Pheidole* and *Allomerus* contain a large number of morphologically similar plant-ant species. This has led to serious problems in naming the ants and determining their degree of specialisation on different hosts. From ants collected from many specimens of pressed plants deposited in museum harbaria, I have found that many superficially similar *Pheidole* are in fact distinct species restricted to different plant hosts. Those few which do inhabit more than one plant species colonise similar plants that occur in the same geographic region. For example, *Maieta guianensis* and *M. poeppigii* Mart. ex Cogn., both widely distributed in the Amazon Basin, are almost always used by *P.* cf. *minutula*. In northwest Colombia four plants from three genera (*Tococa spadiciflora* Triana, *Clidemia killipii*, *Conostegia setosa* Triana and *C. dentata* Triana) are tenanted by what appears to be a single species of *Pheidole*. What is curious and unique about these melastomes is that all four have domatia pierced by small exit pores. Since the density of pores varies with plant species, I presume that these are innate plant structures convergently acquired by different plants in response to selection pressures exerted by their shared *Pheidole*. The three ant-*Piper* studied by Risch *et al.* (1977) provide a somewhat analogous situation.

Most *Allomerus* ants of the Amazonian lowlands are so similar that it has not yet been possible to determine their patterns of host preference. However, four quite distinct species from the border region of Brazil and Venezuela are apparently all specialised to particular hosts, these being *Maieta neblinensis* Wurdack, *Tococa pachystachya* Wurdack *T. hirta* Berg, and *Myrmidone macrosperma* (Mart.) Mart. Although the latter is a widespread Amazonian plant, *Allomerus vogeli* Kempf is restricted to plants of the upper Río Negro, and other *Allomerus* colonise it in other regions.

Tropical American ants of the subfamilies Dolichoderinae and Formicinae do not sting, although they possess strong mandibles and irritating chemical secretions that serve both for attack and defence. In each subfamily only one of its 13 native genera has specialised to any great extent for life in myrmecophytes. The formicine genus *Myrmelachista*, particularly well represented in a wide variety of plants from the eastern slopes of the Andes where it seems to replace *Pheidole* and *Allomerus*, presents so many taxonomic problems that no generalisations can be made concerning host-plant specificity. Stout (1979) in the only field study of a *Myrmelachista* plant-ant found it colonising hollowed out stems and trunk of the small understorey tree *Ocotea pedalifolia* Mez where it foraged on leaves and buds and tended scale insects inside stems. Surprisingly, very few species of the large and diversified formicine genus *Camponotus* have adapted to Amazonian myrmecophytes. I have only observed one species regularly nesting in *Cecropia* and another, *Camponotus femoratus* (Fabr.), typically associates with ant-gardens.

Together with *Pseudomyrmex*, the dolichoderine *Azteca* is the most notable group of Amazonian plant-ants. Although these ants are rather small (2 − 4 mm long) and delicate, most have large colonies and even free-living species spare no effort in defending their nests and food sources from disturbance. Queens of different species establish nests in live and dead twigs, rot holes and the chambers of a wide variety of ant-plants, and depending upon the species, the colony foraging area can be very restricted or spread across a wide swath of vegetation with associated satellite nests constructed in or on branches or among the roots of epiphytes.

All the ant-Cecropias apparently host *Azteca* as do a majority of the species of *Tococa* and a good many *Tachigali*, and other species colonise plants in a wide range of genera. Recent studies indicate that the *Azteca* of ant-plants are predominantly specialists that occupy one or a few similar species of plants. The *Azteca* of *Cecropia* provide a particularly well documented case of this phenomenon (Harada, 1982). The most abundant *Cecropia*-ant, *Azteca alfari* Em., occurs overwhelmingly in second growth *Cecropia* from Mexico to Argentina. In the Amazon, certain *Cecropia* such as *C. distachya* Huber, *C. ficifolia* Snethl. and *C. purpurascens* Berg may also become established in undisturbed forest, in which case they are usually colonised by *A.* aff. *isthmica* (Wheeler). *C. ulei* Snethl. in the same forests is occupied by *Camponotus* sp. The riverside species *C. latiloba* Miq. may harbour *A. alfari* or *A. xanthochroa* (Roger). A fourth species *Azteca schimperi* Em. has been found exclusively in tall mature *Cecropia* plants where, in addition to colonising the hollow stems, it builds a globular cardboard-like nest which superficially resembles that of a hornet. This ant appears to specialise on mature trees that have lost the previous *Azteca* occupants.

In other regions within the range of *A. alfari*, different species of *Cecropia*-ants parallel the habitat shifts documented in the Amazon. In south Brazil there are but two common ant-Cecropias, *C. lyratiloba* Miq. of open marshy places with *A. alfari* and *C. adenopus* Mart. of wet forest with *A. muelleri* Em. However, the specialisation of each ant to a particular *Cecropia* is not absolute, for either may occupy the other's plant if this grows too near the 'wrong' habitat. A third ant of this region, *A. lanuginosa* Em., appears identical to *A. schimperi*. Microdistributional data are lacking for north of the Amazon where *Azteca constructor* Em., and for Central America where both it and *A. coeruleipennis* Em. are added to the *Cecropia*-ant fauna and *A. isthmica* drops out.

It therefore seems that the *Azteca* of *Cecropia* specialise more by habitat than in function of particular species of ant-*Cecropia*. This makes sense since the morphological variation among *Cecropia* species is not great whereas the physical and biological conditions likely to affect colony success diverge greatly among second growth, floodplain and the forest interior.

The *Azteca* that live in *Cecropia* have apparently evolved independently from separate ancestors on four or more occasions: *A. alfari* is very distinct and the species *muelleri/constructor*, *schimperi/lanuginosa* and perhaps *xanthochroa/isthmica/coeruleipennis* represent natural groups whose closest relatives do not inhabit *Cecropia*. The *Azteca* of *Tococa*, consisting of a yet undetermined number of species, appear to be more uniform among themselves, and as a group they are distinct from the *Cecropia* ants. The three *Azteca* I have found in *Cordia nodosa* have certainly been derived from different, perhaps free-living immediate ancestors. Finally, the one or more groups of *Azteca* which colonise *Tachigali* and *Triplaris* seem distinct from those of other plants.

Thus *Azteca* like *Pseudomyrmex* presents a picture of repeated adaptation to myrmecophytes from diverse lineages within the genus. Although the two genera have about the same number of species, many more *Azteca* seem to have established specific relationships with plants, presumably because they occur abundantly in a wider range of habitats and because these ants can be of great initial advantage to a plant through their effective defence of nest and food resources.

13.8. OVERVIEW

The picture given by Amazon ant-plants is one of repeated evolution of diverse levels of mutual coadaptation between ants and plants. The same pattern is largely mirrored in other tropical regions where completely different insects and plants have come together to create qualitatively identical relationships. Given the inherent properties, needs and adaptive potentials of ants, plants and sap-feeding homopterans, and tremendously long periods of favourable tropical conditions for their evolution, the appearance of ant-plants was no doubt inevitable.

Although the patterns presented by Amazon myrmecophytes have not yet told us why some plants house ants and others do not, they do give insights into the importance of ants to plants, the conditions, both for ants and for plants, which favour the evolution of specialised ant × plant relationships and some ideas as to why ant-plants are rare in some habitats and common in others. The potential of allying ants to tropical agriculture also cannot escape notice.

On a larger more general scale, the coevolved mutualisms represented by ant-plants help clarify the conditions and limits of complex biological adaptation. The relative paucity of ant-plants in Africa is paralleled by its reduced floral richness, and both are perhaps due to the reduced area of tropical rainforest on that continent and the severe climatic variation which it experienced during prehistory. While ant-epiphytes with domatia are common in the Far East, outside of tropical America non-epiphytic myrmecophytes with pouch domatia are not at all common and highly specialised plant-ants seem to be the exception.

The intricate complexion of the biota of the Amazon rainforest, considered by some to be advanced and modern in origin, is most probably due to the ancient isolation of the forest and its integrity over geological time. I suspect that this forest started early and has had fewer and less severe interruptions in its development than forests of other tropical regions. This has provided the time and environmental constancy necessary to develop a diversity of finely tuned coevolved interactions among its plants and animals. The stable conditions which have promoted highly integrated tropical forest ecosystems also seem necessary for their continued well-being, and this fact I believe in large part explains the devastating biotic consequences of large-scale perturbations in these forests. The coevolved systems of tropical forests are unique, as certainly are the forests which they compose, and unique and thoughtful conservation practices will be necessary for their continued existence.

ACKNOWLEDGEMENTS

Studies on ant-plants and their ants have been greatly aided by the Instituto Nacional de Pesquisas da Amazônia (INPA, Manaus), Missouri Botanical Garden (St. Louis), New York Botanical Garden (New York) and United States National Herbarium (Washington, D.C.) through their kind permission to examine ants from their extensive collections of Amazon myrmecophytes. I am especially grateful to John Wurdack, Ghillean Prance, John Dwyer, Alwyn Gentry, Laurence Skog and Charles Berg for the information and botanical insights so freely shared, and to William Rodrigues for plant identifications. William L. Brown, Jr. identified specimens of *Pachycondyla geoldii*, and Thomas Lewinsohn, John Wurdack, Ghillean Prance, Laurence Skog, Helena Morais and Paulo Oliveira provided invaluable comments on the manuscript. Work in the Amazon was aided through transport and field support furnished by INPA, the Força Aérea Brasileira (Brazilian Air Force) and World Wildlife Fund, for which I am most appreciative. The drawings were prepared by Luis Fernando Aguiar.

REFERENCES

Bailey, I. W. (1923) Notes on Neotropical ant-plants. II. *Tachigalia paniculata* Aubl. *Bot. Gazette* 75, 27 — 41.
Bailey, I. W. (1924) Notes on Neotropical ant-plants. III. *Cordia nodosa* Lam. *Bot. Gazette* 77, 39 — 49.
Baker, H. G., Opler, P. A. and Baker, I. (1978) A comparison of the amino acid complements of floral and extrafloral nectars. *Bot. Gazette* 139, 322-332.
Belt, T. (1874) *The Naturalist in Nicaragua*. Bumpus, London, 403 pages.
Bentley, B. L. (1976) Plants bearing extrafloral nectaries and the associated ant community: interhabitat differences in the reduction of herbivore damage. *Ecology* 57, 815 — 820.
Bentley, B. L. (1977a) The protective function of ants visiting the extrafloral nectaries of *Bixa orellana* (Bixaceae). *J. Ecol.* 65, 27-38.
Bentley, B. L. (1977b) Extrafloral nectaries and protection by pugnacious bodyguards. *Ann. Rev. Ecol. Syst.* 8, 407 — 428.
Benzing, D. H. (1970) An investigation of two bromeliad myrmecophytes: *Tillandsia butzii* Mez, *T. caput-medusae* E. Morren and their ants. *Bull. Torrey Bot. Club* 97, 109 — 115.
Bequaert, J. (1922) Ants in their diverse relations to the plant world. *Bull. Amer. Mus. Nat. Hist.* 45, 333 — 621.
Berg, C. C. (1978) Espécies de *Cecropia* da Amazonia brasileira. *Acta Amazonica* 8, 149 — 182.
Billings, W. D. and Godfrey, P. J. (1967) Photosynthetic utilization of internal carbon dioxide by hollow-stemmed plants. *Science* 158, 121 — 123.
Carroll, C. R. and Janzen, D. H. (1973) Ecology of foraging by ants. *Ann. Rev. Ecol. Syst.* 4, 231 — 257.

Deuth, D. (1977) The function of extra-floral nectaries in *Aphelandra deppeana* Sch. and Cham. (Acanthaceae). *Brenesia* 10, 135 – 145.

Downhower, J. F. (1975) The distribution of ants on *Cecropia* leaves. *Biotropica* 7, 59 – 62.

Dumpert, K. (1981) *The Social Biology of Ants*. (transl. C. Johnson). Pitman, London, 298 pages.

Forel, A. (1904) In und mit Pflanzen lebende Ameisen aus dem Amazonas-Gebiet und aus Peru. *Zool. Jahrb. Syst.* 20, 677 – 707.

Harada, A. Y. (1982) Contribuição ao conhecimento do gênero *Azteca* Forel, 1878 (Hymenoptera: Formicidae) e aspectos da interação com plantas do gênero *Cecropia* Loefling, 1758. Masters Thesis in Biological Sciences, INPA/FUA, Manaus, 181 pages.

Hutchinson, G. L., Millington, R. J. and Peters, D. B. (1972) Atmospheric ammonia: absorption by plant leaves. *Science* 175, 771-772.

Huxley, C. R. (1978) The ant plants *Myrmecodia* and *Hydnophytum* (Rubiaceae) and the relationships between their morphology, ant occupants, physiology and ecology. *New Phytol.* 80, 231 – 268.

Huxley, C. R. (1980) Symbiosis between ants and epiphytes. *Biol. Rev.* 55, 321 – 340.

Inouye, D. W. and Taylor, O. R. (1979) A temperate region plant-ant-seed predator system: consequences of extrafloral nectar secretion by *Helianthella quinquenervis*. *Ecology* 60, 1 – 7.

Janzen, D. H. (1966) Coevolution of mutualism between ants and acacias in Central America. *Evolution* 20, 249 – 275.

Janzen, D. H. (1967) Fire, vegetation structure, and the ant × *Acacia* interaction in Central America. *Ecology* 48, 26 – 35.

Janzen, D. H. (1969) Allelopathy by myrmecophytes: the ant *Azteca* as an allelopathic agent of *Cecropia*. *Ecology* 50, 147 – 153.

Janzen, D. H. (1972) Protection of *Barteria* (Passifloraceae) by *Pachysima* ants (Pseudomyrmecinae) in a Nigerian rain forest. *Ecology* 53, 885 – 892.

Janzen, D. H. (1973) Dissolution of the mutualism between *Cecropia* and its *Azteca* ants. *Biotropica* 5, 15 – 28.

Janzen, D. H. (1974) Epiphytic myrmecophytes in Sarawak: mutualism through the feeding of plants by ants. *Biotropica* 6, 237 – 259.

Janzen, D. H. (1975) *Pseudomyrmex nigropilosa*: a parasite of a mutualism. *Science* 188, 936 – 937.

Jutsum, A. R., Cherrett, J. M. and Fisher, M. (1981) Interactions between the fauna of citrus trees in Trinidad and the ants *Atta cephalotes* and *Azteca* sp. *J. Appl. Ecol.* 18, 187 – 195.

Keeler, K. H. (1980) The extrafloral nectaries of *Ipomoea leptophylla* (Convolvulaceae). *Amer. J. Bot.* 67, 216 – 222.

Keeler, K. H. (1981) Function of *Mentzelia nuda* (Loasaceae) postfloral nectaries in seed defense. *Amer. J. Bot.* 68, 295 – 299.

Kempf, W. W. (1972) Catálogo abreviado das formigas da Região Neotropical. *Studia Ent.* 15, 3 – 344.

Kleinfeldt, S. E. (1978) Ant-gardens: the interactions of *Codonanthe crassifolia* (Gesneriaceae) and *Crematogaster longispina* (Formicidae). *Ecology* 59, 449 – 456.

Kohl, H. (1909) Die Ameisenplanzen des tropischen Africa mit besonderer Berücksichtigung ihrer biologischen Verhältnisse. *Natur. u. Offenbarung* 55, 89-111, 148 – 175.

Leston, D. (1973) The ant mosaic — tropical tree crops and the limiting of pests and diseases. *Pest Articles and News Summaries* 19, 311 – 341.

Majer, J. D. (1976) The influence of ants and ant manipulation on the cocoa farm fauna. *J. Appl. Ecol.* 13, 157 – 175.

Messina, F. J. (1981) Plant protection as a consequence of an ant-membracid mutualism: interactions on goldenrod (*Solidago* sp.). *Ecology* 62, 1433 – 1440.

Miehe, H. (1911) Untersuchungen über die javanische *Myrmecodia*. *Abhandlungen der mathematisch-physischen Klasse der Königlich Sachsischen Gesellschaft der Wissenschaften* 32, 312 – 361.

Müller, F. (1880) Die Imbauba und ihr Beschützer. *Kosmos* 8, 850 – 856.

O'Dowd, D. J. (1982) Pearl bodies as ant food: an ecological role for some leaf emergences of tropical plants. *Biotropica* 14, 40 – 49.

Petal, J. (1978) The role of ants in ecosystems. In *Production Ecology of Ants and Termites*. Ed. M. V. Brian, pp. 293 – 331, Cambridge University Press, London, 409 pages.

Pickett, C. H. and Clark, W. D. (1979) The function of extrafloral nectaries on *Opuntia acanthocarpa* (Cactaceae). *Amer. J. Bot.* 66, 618 – 625.

Prance, G. T. (1972) Chrysobalanaceae. *Flora Neotropica, vol. 9*. Hafner, New York, 410 pages.

Rickson, F. R. (1971) Glycogen plastids in Müllerian body cells of *Cecropia peltata*, a higher green plant. *Science* 173, 344 – 347.

Rickson, F. R. (1976) Anatomical development of the leaf trichilium and Müllerian bodies of *Cecropia peltata*. *Amer. J. Bot.* 63, 1266 – 1271.

Rickson, F. R. (1979) Absorption of animal tissue breakdown products into a plants system — the feeding of a plant by ants. *Amer. J. Bot.* 66, 87 – 90.

Rickson, F. R. (1980) Developmental anatomy and ultrastructure of the ant-food bodies (Beccarian bodies) of *Macaranga triloba* and *M. hypoleuca* (Euphorbiaceae). *Amer. J. Bot.* 67, 285 – 292.

Rische, S., McClure, M., Vandermeer, J. and Waltz, S. (1977) Mutualism between three species of tropical *Piper* (Piperaceae) and their ant inhabitants. *Amer. Midl. Natur.* 98, 433 – 444.

Roth, I. (1976) Estrutura interna de los domacios foliares en *Tococa* (Melastomaceae). *Acta Biol. Venez.* 9, 227 – 258.

Schemske, D. W. (1980) The evolutionary significance of extrafloral nectar production by *Costus woodsonii* (Zingerberaceae): an experimental analysis of ant protection. *J. Ecol.* 68, 959 – 967.

Schimper, A. F. W. (1888) Die Wechselbeziehungen zwischen Pflanzen und Ameisen im tropischen Amerika. *Bot. Mitteil. aus den Tropen, Jena* 5, 1 – 95.

Schnell, R. (1963) Le problème des acarodomaties. *Marcellia* 31, 95 – 107.

Schomburgk, R. (1848) *Reisen in British-Guiana in dem Jahren 1840 – 1844*. Vols. 2 – 3, Leipzig, 1260 pages.

Schumann, K. (1888) Einige neue Ameisenpflanzen. *Jahrb. Wiss. Bot.* 19, 357 – 421.

Skinner, G. J. and Whittaker, J. B. (1981) An experimental investigation of inter-relationships between the wood-ant (*Formica rufa*) and some tree-canopy herbivores. *J. Anim. Ecol.* 50, 313 – 326.

Spruce, R. (1908) Ant-agency in plant structure. In *Notes of a Botanist on the Amazon and Andes*, pp. 384 – 412. Macmillan, London.

Stark, N. (1970) The nutrient content of plants and soils from Brazil and Surinam. *Biotropica* 2, 51 – 60.

Stephenson, A. G. (1982) The role of extrafloral nectaries of *Catalpa speciosa* in limiting herbivory and increasing fruit production. *Ecology* 63, 663 – 667.

Stout, J. (1979) An association of an ant, a mealy bug, and an understory tree from a Costa Rican rain forest. *Biotropica* 11, 309 – 311.

Tilman, D. (1978) Cherries, ants and tent caterpillars: timing of nectar production in relation to susceptibility of caterpillars to ant predation. *Ecology* 59, 686 – 692.

Ule, E. (1901) Ameisengärten in Amazonasgebiet. *Bot. Jahrb.* 30 (Beibl. 68), 45 – 52.

Ule, E. (1907) Die Pflanzenformationen des Amazonas-Gebietes. Pflanzengeographische Ergebnisse meinen in den Jahren 1900 – 1903 in Brasilien und Peru unternommenen Reisen. *Engl. Bot. Jahrb.* 40, 114 – 172.

Ule, E. (1908) Die Pflanzenformationen des Amazonas-Gebietes. II. Pflanzengeographische Ergebnisse meinen in den Jahren 1900 – 1903 in Brasilien und Peru unternommenen Reisen. *Engl. Bot. Jahrb.* 40, 398 – 443.

Wagner, W. H. (1972) *Solanopteris brunei*, a little known fern epiphyte with dimorphic stems. *Amer. Fern J.* 62, 33 – 43.

Warburg, O. (1892) Ueber Ameisenpflanzen. *Biol. Centralbl.* 12, 129 – 142.

Way, M. J. (1963) Mutualism between ants and honeydew producing Homoptera. *Ann. Rev. Ent.* 8, 307 – 344.

Wheeler, W. M. (1942) Studies of Neotropical ant-plants and their ants. *Bull. Mus. Comp. Zool.* 90, 1 – 262.

Wheeler, W. M. and Bequaert, J. (1929) Amazonian myrmecophytes and their ants. *Zool. Anz.* 82, 10 – 39.

CHAPTER 14

Forest Fishes of the Amazon

MICHAEL GOULDING

Museu Paraense Emílio Goeldi, Belém, Brazil

CONTENTS

14.1. INTRODUCTION

Rainforest is the principal plant community on Amazonian floodplains (Fig. 14.1). Unlike their upland counterparts, however, floodplain rainforests are semiaquatic communities adapted to withstand, and even take advantage of, periodic inundations. There is still no reliable estimate of the total amount of floodplain forest in the Amazon Basin, but a reasonable guess is that there are at least 100,000 km^2, or an area about the size of the state of Florida. Floodplain forests — or flooded forests as they will hereafter be called — are most conveniently classified by the temporal manner in which they are inundated. Four Amazonian types may be recognised.

14.2. INUNDATED FOREST TYPES

14.2.1. Seasonally flooded forest

All of the larger Amazonian rivers have their floodplains inundated seasonally. In most of the Amazon there is only one flood each year, and this occurs, depending on the exact area, between about January and July. In most years the floods are fairly predictable, though high water peaks in any particular system can deviate several metres from the recorded means. Most Amazonian rivers are bordered by high levees that have been built up from alluvial sediments. These first levees are higher than the floodplain areas in the back of them, and thus, to some extent, act as fringing dams to river channel waters. In most floodplain areas, however, there are breaks in the levees where stream-like waterbodies have excavated their ways through the soft sediments. Consequently, when the main river rises and falls, the floodplain is likewise filled or drained through the levee excavations. At the height of the floods some rivers rise above their levees and then inundate the floodplain with one massive onslaught of water.

The amount of time that seasonally flooded forest is inundated depends on the relative levels of the flood in any particular year and on the local floodplain topography. It is thus misleading to assume that total flooding time is correlated with the total annual river level fluctuation. For example, river level fluctuation in the upper Rio Madeira averages about 12.5 m annually, whereas the middle Rio Amazonas oscillation is only about 7.0 m; nevertheless, the Rio Amazonas floodplain is inundated for about 6 months annually, compared to only 2 to 5 months for the upper Rio Madeira (Goulding, 1980; Smith, 1981). This is because the Rio Amazonas floodplain is lower, relative to river level, than its counterpart in the upper Rio Madeira. Depending on floodplain topography and river level fluctuation in any particular year, Amazonian floodplains are inundated from about 2 to 10 months annually. Seasonally flooded forest accounts for at least 90% of the total flooded forest found on Amazonian floodplains.

Though seasonally flooded forest shares the common denominator of being inundated on a fairly regular basis each year, there are distinct vegetation types within this category that can be recognised by differences in species composition and physiognomy. These floristic and morphological differences are most closely correlated with water type, that is, with the so-called whitewater, blackwater and clearwater rivers that drain most of the Amazon Basin (Figs. 14.2, 14.3 and 14.4). Whitewater rivers are laden with silt transported out of the Andes. The alluvial soils that have formed on their floodplains are much richer in nutrients than those found in most of the lowlands. These better soils may in part help account for the fact that whitewater river flooded forests are high in stature (often reaching over 40 m) and biomass, and also rich in species (Prance, 1978). Blackwater rivers have minimum sediment loads because their headwater streams drain the Amazonian Lowlands where erosion is minimal. Their waters, however, are stained dark by organic compounds derived from the forest litter. The flooded forests of the Rio Negro, the largest blackwater river in the world, are relatively low in stature and biomass, but perhaps comparable in species diversity to their whitewater river counterparts. It is still unknown whether their lower stature and biomass are due to poor soils or to the high acidity (often below pH 4) of the waters that annually invade them, or perhaps to both factors. Clearwater rivers drain the Brazilian and Guianan Shields and the Amazonian lowlands where blackwaters are not produced. Like blackwater rivers, they have minimal sediment loads but, unlike them, they are not stained by humic acids and thus have relatively high transparencies. The flooded forests of clearwater rivers are usually high in stature but perhaps lower in biomass than their whitewater river counterparts. Floristically they appear to be between whitewater and blackwater rivers, but more study is needed.

14.2.2. Irregularly flooded forest

The Amazon Basin contains thousands of small streams that are subject to local inundation at any time of the year when there are heavy, but usually ephemeral, rains. Often a stream has seasonally and irregularly flooded forest along its course. This is due to the damming effect that the principal river may have on its affluent. In this case, the waters of the lower course of the stream are impounded by the

Fig. 14.1. Inside a flooded forest. The water depth is about 10 m.

Fig. 14.2. Floodplain forest of the whitewater Rio Madeira.

Fig. 14.3. Floodplain forest of the blackwater Rio Negro.

Fig. 14.4. Floodplain forest of the clearwater Rio Machado on Rondônia.

higher level of the principal river, and thus the former follows the latter's flooding regime. The upper course of the stream, which is usually higher topographically, will still only be affected by the local rains. There are no reliable estimates of the area occupied by irregularly flooded forest, but floristically and physiognomically it appears to resemble terra firme forest more than seasonally flooded forest.

14.2.3. Swamp flooded forest

In many interfluvial areas and on some floodplains there are low-lying swamps that remain waterlogged throughout the year. These are usually marked by the presence of palms (especially *Mauritia flexuosa*). Swamp forests are low in biomass and species diversity, and represent only a small percentage of the total flooded forest of the Amazon Basin.

14.2.4. Tidal flooded forest

The oceanic tides are felt in the lower Rio Amazonas and in the inferior reaches of its affluents. The floodplains of the lower Rio Amazonas region are relatively low in many cases, thus making them subject to inundation twice daily (but only by freshwater). The flooded forests of the lower Rio Amazonas have many of the same species associated with whitewater rivers.

14.3. FRUIT AND SEED EATING FISHES

Fruit and seed eating fishes are poorly represented outside of South America, though this in part may be due to floodplain modification, especially in the Asian tropics, but also to a paucity of studies reporting them. The carps are the most diverse fish group in the Asian tropics, but only one species (*Leptobarbus hoevenii*) has been reported to eat fruits (Smith, 1945). The walking catfish (*Clarius betrachus*) and ariid catfishes of the genus *Hemipimelodus* in southern Asia and New Guinea are also known to eat fleshy fruits (Whitmore, 1975; Roberts, 1978). In contrast to Asia and South America, no African fishes have been reported to eat fruits. Fossil fish teeth greatly resembling those of extant South American fruit eaters, however, have been found in African deposits, suggesting that the continent once supported frugivorous fishes (Greenwood and Howes, 1975). Ariid catfishes are also known to move into mangroves to feed on fruits, but they have been little studied in this context. The main centre of fruit and seed eating fishes is the Amazon Basin. This is due to both the fishes and the flooded forests available for this activity.

The Amazon has the richest freshwater fish fauna in the world. The total number of species can only be guessed — as many areas remain to be collected and even more groups await taxonomic revision — but there are probably somewhere between 2,500 and 3,000 species. The two great groups of Amazonian fishes are the characins and catfishes, each alone accounting for about 40% of the total described species. Nearly all of the fruit and seed eating fishes of the Amazon are also either characins or catfishes. The large electric eel (*Electrophorous electricus*) is widely reported in fishing folklore to eat fruits, but the habit has not yet been observed by naturalists. The oscar (*Astronotus ocellatus*) occasionally eats fleshy fruits, but it is the only cichlid known to do so.

Although the characins and catfishes are the main fruit and seed eating fishes of the Amazon Basin, they differ greatly from each other in morphological structure (though internal anatomical characteristics show clearly that they are related at higher taxonomical levels). Most of the fruit and seed eating characins have well developed dentition and strong jaws, whereas catfishes have small teeth that are not highly adapted for crushing but for grasping.

14.4. FISHES AS SEED PREDATORS

Characins are the main seed predators of Amazonian floodplain forests. They appear to take a much heavier toll on seeds than even birds, and perhaps even more than insects, fungi and bacteria (the last three when the seeds are on the ground) in the case of many plant species. To be a seed predator a fish

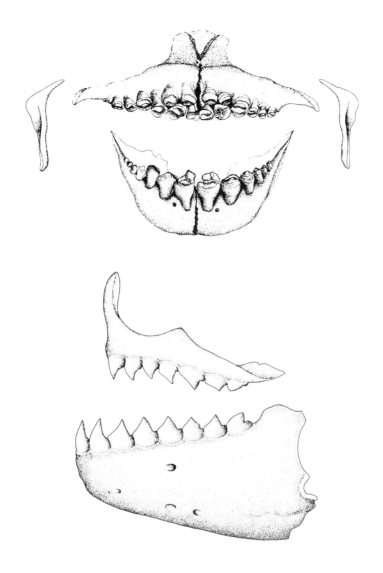

Fig. 14.5. *Above*: the molariform dentition of the tambaqui (*Colossoma macropomum*, Characidae). *Below*: the sharp dentition of a seed-eating piranha.

appears to require strong dentition that enables it to crush hard nut walls. Germination experiments have shown that nut walls are not destroyed by fishes' digestive processes. Seed predation by fishes, then, takes place in the mouth and not in the digestive tract.

The characins are the most morphologically diverse group of vertebrates on earth. Three groups of characins are adapted to crush seeds. Within this trio there are two main types of dentition (Fig. 14.5). The most common consists of relatively broadbased molariform-like teeth that are embedded in strong jaws; the individual teeth are usually multicusped and thus can cut as well as crush. Genera with this type of dentition include *Colossoma*, *Myleus*, *Mylosomma*, *Triportheus* and *Brycon*. The second type of

Fig. 14.6. The tambaqui (*Colossoma macropomum*, Characidae), a fruit and seed eater and the most important food fish species of the Central Amazon.

dentition is found in the piranhas, a diverse group of fishes that have been stereotyped as all being highly carnivorous, but which in fact display a variety of feeding habits. Piranha teeth have a single cutting edge, often razor sharp, and this character has led to the putative voraciousness of the group. The sharp teeth of piranhas, however, are also effective for crushing and masticating seeds.

Most of the seeds crushed by fishes are from dry fruits — usually capsules — and contain little or no fleshy material associated with them. To illustrate the manner in which fishes feed on flooded forest seeds — and destroy them — two examples will be cited here. Spruce's rubber tree (*Hevea spruceana*, Euphorbiaceae), a closely related species to the Pará rubber tree (*H. brasiliensis*) of latex fame, is a common element in many floodplain forests of the Amazon. It produces relatively large explosive capsules that usually contain three 4 – 5 cm seeds. The capsules begin maturing rapidly at the beginning of the floods and, about a month later, they begin bursting open on hot days. When the capsules explode they are able to eject their seeds for up to 20 m. This explosive activity lasts for about 2 to 3 months in most flooded forests. When Spruce's rubber tree seeds are falling into the water, the large characin called *tambaqui* (*Colossoma macropomum*) feeds on almost nothing else (Fig. 14.6). The fish finds rubber trees, the capsules of which are exploding, and waits nearby to snap up the seeds the second they hit the water. Because the seeds float they are an easy target for the large characins. The fishes appear to wait beneath a tree until its seed crop is depleted — or at least the mature part exploding — and then move on to another where the same behaviour is repeated. Rubber tree seeds have a hard nut wall but the large characin, with its strong dentition and massive jaws, easily crushes it. Ten to fifteen kg *tambaqui* often have 500 g to one kg of rubber tree seeds in their stomachs and intestines when they are feeding on this species. If a man weighing 70 kg were to eat a comparable quantity of, say, Brazil-nuts, then he would have to accommodate 7 kg (about 15 pounds) in his digestive system; an unlikely prospect indeed. When rubber tree seeds can no longer be found, then the *tambaqui* looks for other favourite species.

The masticated seeds found in piranha stomach contents often appear to have come prepackaged from a processing plant. Piranhas shell the nuts they eat and ingest only the soft seed contents, which are usually white in colour. After the nut wall is broken, the endosperm contents are removed and the shell is discarded. By doing this the piranha does not fill its stomach and intestines with material that cannot be digested but that will take up space. The sharp teeth of piranhas allow them to masticate the soft seed contents into small bits that are usually of nearly equal size. Very rarely do piranhas attack fleshy fruits or seeds with succulent attachments. They appear to be only interested in endosperm material. Most of the seeds eaten by piranhas are relatively small (less than about 1 cm in diameter when round or in thickness when flattened). In flooded forests, fishes appear to be the most important seed predators of many plant species. Next to fishes, birds play a relatively similar but less important role. Insects as flooded forest seed predators do not appear to be very important, at least when the fruit is still on the tree or when it is in the water. When the water level drops and the flooded forests are drained, colonising insects may be heavy seed predators but this is not yet known. There is no doubt that fishes are able to take a heavy — and in many cases the heaviest — toll on the seeds of many floodplain plant species. In general, fishes are facultatively host-specific, that is, a population of the same species tends to feed on the same seed species at the same time. When the seeds of favourite species can no longer be found, then the population seeks the next favourite, or favourites, within the sequence of fruit fall in any particular flooded forest. Several fish species often attack the same seed crops under the same tree. In fact, it is difficult to see how seeds escape their fish predators, but many obviously do, as the standing trees themselves testify. Water dispersal is the main escape mechanism for the seeds of dry fruits, and for many other types as well, as will be discussed below.

Fishes, as seed predators — and also as seed dispersers, as we shall see later — would appear to have played some role in the evolutionary ecology of Amazonian floodplain forests. Flooded forests fruit mostly during the inundation season and this would appear to favour dispersal by water for most of the plant species. Water can act not only as a dispersal agent but also as a defensive aquatic palisade against terrestrial seed predators during the most vulnerable period, that is, immediately after fruit fall. Water, in fact, plays this role in Amazonian flooded forests but, on the other hand, it allows large numbers of seed-eating fishes to enter these plant communities. Whether fishes, as a group, are less destructive as seed predators than are terrestrial insects and mammals, is unknown; the opinion of the author is that, because of the huge fish biomass that is able to move into flooded forests, they play more or less the same role as insects and mammals do in the terrestrial habitats. Because fruit-eating birds are volant and little or not at all affected by flooding, their role as dispersal agents in flooded and upland forests may be similar in both habitats.

14.5. FISHES AS SEED DISPERSAL AGENTS

Fishes were probably the first vertebrates to eat fleshy fruits, or more correctly, the pulpy outgrowths associated with some ancient gymnosperm seeds. For most of fish history there have been no real fruits, produced only by the flowering plants, or angiosperms. The gymnosperms were the first seed plants and, like fishes, appeared on earth for the first time in Palaeozoic times, more than 400 million years ago. During the Paleozoic and most of the Mesozoic Eras, the gymnosperms were the dominant seed plants. A few ancient gymnosperm groups produced seeds with attached or adjacent fleshy material, and it is reasonable to believe that some fishes may have been attracted to this supposedly sweet flesh. The fossil record, however, is silent on the matter, though gymnosperm seeds have been found with turtle and other reptile fossils from the Mesozoic. The rich Amazonian rainforest has few gymnosperms, but at least one group of these, vines of the genus *Gnetum*, produces seeds surrounded by fleshy material.

These seeds are occasionally eaten by fishes, and this is perhaps living testimony of a biological interaction that reaches back to Paleozoic gymnosperm swamps (though none of the Amazonian fruit-eating fish groups were present in the Paleozoic Era).

About 65 million years ago, in the Cretaceous, occurred that abominable mystery, as Charles Darwin referred to the sudden appearance of flowering plants and their conquest of most of the earth. Flowering plants became experts at dispersal, and their seeds flew and floated, hitchhiked on fur and feather, or took passage inside of animals' guts. The latter is of concern here. A seed's passage via avian, mammalian, reptilian or piscine transportation was paid in fleshy currency. Both the passenger (seeds) and the transportation lines (animals) greatly benefited and diversified because of this highly admirable relationship. When we bite into an orange or papaya, we owe more of a debt than we know to those early fruit-eating vertebrates that became seed disseminators. Birds are usually the first animals to come to mind, and indeed they are important seed disseminators in today's world. But so, too, are fishes, at least in the Amazon.

The fleshy fruits that attract fishes are also appreciated — or at least close relatives growing in nonflooded areas — by other animals as well. The principal means of seed dispersal in Amazonian flooded forests, however, appear to be water and fishes, and secondarily, birds and monkeys. Per given area of flooded forest, fishes undoubtedly have a much larger biomass than the monkeys, birds and bats in the canopies above. Fishes also feed more at night than do birds and monkeys — but perhaps not bats, though their importance in flooded forests is still unknown — and thus spend more time dispersing seeds. Finally, many Amazonian fruit-eating fishes are relatively large, and can accommodate much larger quantities of seeds than any bird or monkey. For example, a large catfish (*Phractocephalus hemiliopterus*, Pimelodidae), weighing between 15 and 30 kg, can pack over 60 large palm seeds, weighing in excess of 2 kg, into its stomach and intestines (Fig. 14.7).

Both catfishes and characins have many species that eat fleshy fruits. The most common fleshy fruits eaten are drupes (similar in structure to olives) and berries (usually small seeded with much fleshy material surrounding them). There are also special fleshy fruit types that contain a pulpy outgrowth, called an aril, on the seed. In addition to these, there are aggregate fruits, such as soursop (*Annona* spp.) and fig syconia (*Ficus* spp.). The fleshy fruits eaten by fishes have a wide variety of sizes, textures and shapes. In general, the fleshy material is either sweet or tart (Fig. 14.8).

Fig. 14.7. The pirarara (*Phractocephalus hemeliopterus*, Pimelodidae), one of the largest fruit-eating catfishes of the Amazon. (Photo by Barbara Gibbs).

Fig. 14.8. Fleshy fruits of *Simaba guianensis* (Simarubaceae), a much procured species of Amazonian fishes. The fruits are usually swallowed whole and the seeds dispersed after being defecated.

Catfishes are excellent seed dispersal agents because, with a couple of minor exceptions, they are unable to crush nut walls. Characins eat many of the same fleshy fruit species appreciated by catfishes. Unlike catfishes, however, characins can crush seeds, and do and do not, depending on the plant species. When the seeds are extremely small, such as in fig syconia, crushing is very difficult and the fruit is eaten for its fleshy material. In some groups, as for example in the families Lauraceae and Burseraceae, the medium to large sized seeds are usually ingested whole, although the characin eating them could easily crush the nut walls. This suggests that the seeds contain toxic compounds that discourage their destruction. Seed toxicity may be an important adaptation for dispersal because, though the fish may eat the fruit for the fleshy material, it does not destroy the seed lest its toxins be released into the intestinal system, and consequently, into the body in general.

14.6. FLOODED FOREST FISHES AND HUMANS

Amazonian soils and waters, viewed in general, are a double mirror reflecting the nutrient poverty of the world's largest rainforest ecosystem. The massive biomass of the Amazonian rainforest seems to contradict this fact, but the 'green mansions' are illusive. The rainforest's nutrient bankroll has been accumulated over millions of years, and cannot be replenished very rapidly from the underlying bedrock. The rainforest has especially adapted root systems that act as a nutrient sieve, thus not allowing precious ions to escape to the streams and rivers. The nutrients, then, are quickly recycled back into the living vegetation from the detritus. Because the soils are poor, so too are most of the waterbodies of lowland Amazonia. The floodplain rainforests, however, provide an alternative food chain — *vis-à-vis* the nutrient-poor rivers — that is able to sustain relatively large biomasses of aquatic animals, especially fishes.

For the past decade or so the most important commercial fish species in the Central Amazon has been the *tambaqui* (*Colossoma macropomum*), and in the late 1970s it alone accounted for about 45% of all fish consumed in Manaus, the region's largest city. As adults, *tambaqui* feed almost exclusively on fruits and seeds derived from flooded forests. Many of the other commercial fish species are also fruit and seed eaters, or insectivores or detritivores who feed mostly in flooded forests. Flooded forest feeding fishes, taken together, probably account for something like 75% of the total catch sold in Manaus and smaller cities of the central Amazon. It should also be pointed out that fish is the most important source of animal protein in the region, and thus it seems safe to say that the flooded forests play an important role in the human ecology of rural and urban Amazonia.

At present the forest fishes of the Amazon, especially the commercial species, are threatened on two fronts. First, the commercial fisheries are being overexploited and the frugivorous fishes are the most heavily attacked because of their large size and highly-prized flesh. Second, agricultural developers are eyeing the floodplains as potential rice paddies and cattle pastures. If large-scale agriculture is implemented, this will lead to floodplain deforestation and the use of insecticides and herbicides. The fish and fauna will be seriously affected by both of these activities if they reach the proportions desired by developers.

REFERENCES

Goulding, M. (1980) *The Fishes and the Forest: Explorations in Amazonian Natural History*. University of California Press, Berkeley.

Greenwood, P. H. and Howes, G. (1975) Neogene fossil fishes from L. Albert and L. Edward rift (Zaire). *Bull. Brit. Mus. Nat. Hist. (Geol.)* 26(3), 209 – 214.

Prance, G. T. (1978) The origin and evolution of the Amazonian flora. *Interciencia* 3(4), 207 – 222.

Roberts, T. R. (1978) An ichthylogical survey of the Fly River in Papua New Guinea with descriptions of new species. *Smithsonian Contr. Zool.* 281, 1 – 77.

Smith, H. M. (1945) The freshwater fishes of Siam, or Thailand. *Smithsonian Inst. Bull.* 188.

Smith, N. J. H. (1981) *Man, Fishes, and the Amazon*. Columbia University Press, New York.

Whitmore, T. C. (1975) *Tropical Rainforests of the Far East*. Clarendon Press, Oxford.

CHAPTER 15

Mycorrhizae

T. V. ST. JOHN

Natural Resource Ecology Laboratory, Colorado State University U.S.A.

CONTENTS

15.1. INTRODUCTION

The subject of this chapter will be the distribution and function of mycorrhizal fungi in the tropical forests of the Amazon region. After first providing the necessary background on the topic of mycorrhizae, I will specifically examine what is known of mycorrhizae in Amazonia. There are several divergent viewpoints on the function of mycorrhizae, and these will be discussed in the light of recent field and experimental work. After discussing the effect of disturbance on the fungi themselves and on the nutrient-transfer processes in which they take part, I will suggest management practices for conservation of the fungi and their functions in Amazonian ecosystems.

15.2. MYCORRHIZAE AND THEIR RELATION TO HOST PLANTS

The soils of the Amazon are for the most part rather poor in mineral nutrients. The lush growth of Amazonian forests is attributable to adaptations that maximise nutrient acquisition from the infertile soil and conserve the limited nutrient capital. Probably the most important single adaptation that aids in nutrient acquisition is the mycorrhizal symbiosis.

The word mycorrhiza refers to a composite organ that consists of both fungus and root. The fungus has both an internal and an external phase; that is a portion of the fungal tissue exists inside the root and another portion extends out into the soil. There are several types of mycorrhizae, and for a complete discussion of them I will refer you to the authoritative book by Dr. J.L. Harley (1969). The first of the two types to be considered is the Ecto or sheathing mycorrhiza (ECM) (Fig. 15.1). This is the common type of mycorrhiza of temperate zone forest trees such as pines and oaks, but is now also known from many parts of the tropics. ECM are characterised by internal hyphae that penetrate the cortex but do not enter the cells of the host plant. A sheath of fungal tissue envelops the tips of fine absorbing rootlets, and hyphae or mycelial strands extend from the sheath into the surrounding soil or litter. The fungi that form ECM are in large part mushroom-forming basidiomycetes. ECM host plants in the American tropics include several members of the families Caesalpiniaceae, Nyctaginaceae, Gnetaceae, and others. ECM have also been reported from the African tropics in the Caesalpiniaceae, and in Asia in the important family Dipterocarpaceae.

The second type of mycorrhiza, and by far the most widespread type, is the vesicular-arbuscular type (VAM) (Fig. 15.2). VAM are characterised by fungal hyphae that penetrate the cells of the root's cortex, where they form finely branched haustoria called arbuscules. Oil-storage organs called vesicles may form either in the cortex or on the external mycelium, and are the other characteristic structure that provides the name for this kind of mycorrhiza. VAM are not usually visible without special preparation of root tissues. They do not form macroscopic fruiting bodies like many of the ECM fungi, but form characteristic spores in the soil. These are the largest of all fungal spores and their morphology provides the basis for distinguishing fungal species. VAM fungi are remarkably nonspecific with regard to host plant: a fungal species that forms mycorrhizae with a fern may also form mycorrhizae with a grass and a forest tree. Host plants include most temperate and tropical crop species as well as the majority of herbaceous and woody native plants from both temperate and tropical environments. Some

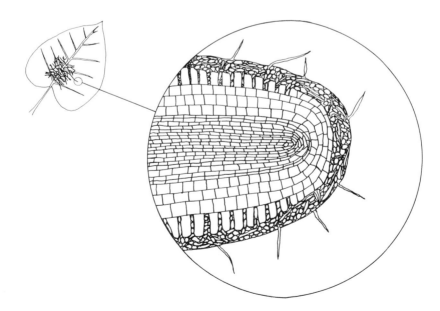

Fig. 15.1. Ectomycorrhizae are composite organs of a root and a higher fungus. In this illustration ectomycorrhizal roots are shown on the surface of a decomposing leaf, a sight common in Amazonian forests on nutrient-poor sandy soils. A longitudinal section of an ectomycorrhiza (enlarged) shows a rootlet with enlarged cortical cells. The fungal hyphae form a mantle around the rootlet. Some of the hyphae extend out into the surrounding litter. The internal hyphae pass between the cortical cells but do not enter the cells.

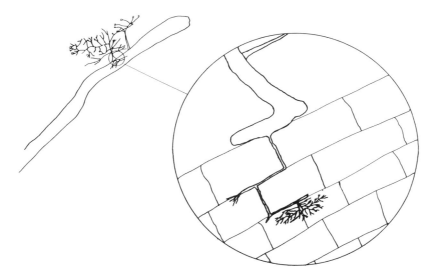

Fig. 15.2. Vesicular-arbuscular mycorrhizae are composite organs of a root and a fungus of the family Endogonaceae. The external phase of the fungus ramifies through surrounding soil or organic material. It may produce large spores that will be left in the soil to recolonise roots at a later time. The internal phase of the fungus enters individual cells of the cortex to form highly-branched arbuscules, the site of nutrient exchange between host and fungus. The morphology of the host root is not significantly modified by the formation of vesicular-arbuscular mycorrhizae.

examples of important Amazonian plant families in which most or all species form VAM are the legume families, Euphorbiaceae, Vochysiaceae, Rubiaceae, and Chrysobalanaceae.

There are some species that appear normally to be non-mycorrhizal. At present we know of no entirely non-mycorrhizal families of tropical trees, but there are non-mycorrhizal species within several important families such as Sapotaceae and Lecythidaceae.

Mycorrhizae have been shown in pot experiments to have a large effect on growth of a number of native and economic plants, with mycorrhizal plants reaching dry weights up to thirty times those of non-mycorrhizal plants. The growth response is primarily due to improved mineral uptake, and the element that is usually shown to be of primary importance is phosphorus. Some micronutrients have been implicated, but nitrogen is neither fixed by mycorrhizal fungi nor is its uptake improved except as a secondary effect of improved phosphorus nutrition (Bowen and Smith, 1981). It happens that Amazonian soils are often very low in available phosphorus and are exactly the kinds of soils in which mycorrhizal infection is most likely to be of great benefit to host plants.

The fungus obtains its energy from carbon compounds produced through photosynthesis of the host plant. In the case of VAM, the fungi may constitute about 1% of the total weight of an herbaceous plant, but require more than 1% of net photosynthetic production. The high carbon usage is due in part to the higher respiration rate of the fungi.

15.3. MYCORRHIZAE IN THE AMAZON REGION

Before we can understand the role that mycorrhizal fungi play in the mineral movement of the tropical forest, we have to examine the kinds and abundance of mycorrhizae in the Amazon region, their distribution within each environment, and their abundance in different vegetation types. Field observations on mycorrhizae in the tropics have been superficial and anecdotal until recently, and even now full documentation of mycorrhizal abundance in entire plant communities exists for only a few

Amazonian forests. Most of the information presented here is based on studies at a few primary and second-growth forest sites in Brazilian and Venezuelan Amazonia.

There are a number of different soils in the Amazon Basin (*see* Jordan, Chapter 5) each of which supports rather unique kinds of forests. The greatest abundance of mycorrhizae seems to be on non-flooded white-sand or on soils of other types where these are overlain by sand (Fig. 15.3). It is also on these sites where ECM reach their greatest development. Individual roots tend to be more heavily infected than on other soil types and there are few or no non-mycorrhizal species. Forests on the most common soil type in Brazilian Amazonia, the heavy clay oxisol, appear to support a great deal less mycorrhizal infection (Fig. 15.3). ECM plants are much less common, VAM infection in individual roots is lighter than on sandy soils, and non-mycorrhizal species are fairly common.

The second major factor that influences the distribution of mycorrhizal infection of forest roots is their depth in the soil. The deepest roots in the soil are rarely infected, but roots in the shallower layers are usually well infected with either VAM or ECM. In some forests there exists above the mineral soil a layer of organic debris permeated with fine roots of the forest trees; this has been termed the 'root mat' by some tropical ecologists. Most of the roots in the root mat become infected with either VAM or ECM.

15.4. THE ROLE OF MYCORRHIZAE IN THE TROPICAL FOREST

Mycorrhizae have been of great interest to tropical ecologists in the last few years, largely because of the direct cycling theory of Went and Stark (1968). According to the direct cycling theory, minerals contained in dead leaves and other organic remains are not released to the soil solution, as in the

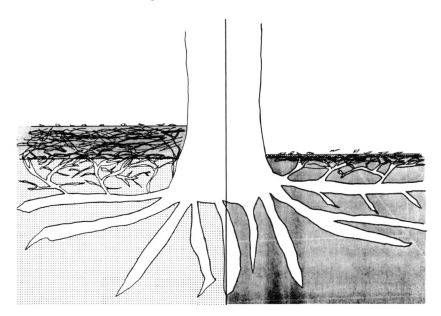

Fig. 15.3. Several distinctive types of soil support characteristic forests in Amazonia. Two kinds, discussed in the text, are illustrated here. The extremely nutrient-poor white-sand soils (left), some of which are seasonally flooded, often are overlain by a layer of humus and leaf litter. Most of the fine roots are found in the above ground layer, sometimes called a 'root mat.' In these forests almost all species are mycorrhizal; many of them ectomycorrhizal. In the most common soil type, heavy-textured oxisol that is not subject to seasonal inundation (right) there is little or no accumulation of humus at the soil surface. Most fine roots are found in the upper portion of the mineral soil. Mycorrhizal infection of all kinds is less intense than in sandy soils. Ectomycorrhizal species are relatively rare, and some species lack mycorrhizae altogether.

conventional view of nutrient movement, but are absorbed from the organic matter by mycorrhizal fungi and are then passed directly to the host plant. Some implications of the direct cycling theory are difficult to reconcile with the extensive literature on mycorrhizae, and experimental work in recent years is beginning to clarify some of the contradictions. The most difficult problem is the implication that the mycorrhizal fungi are actually carrying out some of the enzymatic processes in mineral release. Laboratory studies have shown that most ECM fungi grow poorly or not at all on resistant carbon compounds of the type found in plant structural materials. VAM fungi cannot yet be studied apart from a live host plant, but our best evidence indicates that they, too, have little or no ability to break down complex organic materials. However, new evidence continues to appear and an enzymatic role, at least for ECM fungi, may be documented in the future.

The role of mycorrhizal hyphae in the organic layer may be related to their proximity to the site of decomposition and nutrient release rather than to any enzymatic capabilities. Experimental work in Amazonia has shown that tropical forest roots branch profusely and soon fill test volumes of decomposing organic matter, but do not branch into control volumes of sand. VAM hyphae have responded to small organic particles in an analogous way. Since the slow diffusion of ions usually limits nutrient uptake by roots and hyphae, spatial proximity of nutrient-absorbing surfaces to the sources of ions materially improves uptake rate.

While decomposing organic matter may be somewhat richer in nutrient elements than the mineral soil, it is similar to soil in a number of ways: both have ion exchange capacities, both provide a physical support for root growth and both hold water and minerals. The simplest view of mycorrhizal function in Amazonia is that the benefits from mycorrhizal hyphae, whether in mineral soil or organic detritus, are essentially due to their physical placement. Tinker (1975) has explained how VAM hyphae exploit phosphorus in soil. Phosphate ions are held by the soil and are unable to diffuse more than a short distance. Hyphae exploit a volume of soil that the unaided roots cannot reach, but do not obtain chemical forms of phosphorus that would be unavailable to the root itself. To this we may add the further refinement that roots and hyphae place themselves in the most beneficial physical position by ramifying in the relatively nutrient-rich organic matter. The net effect is rapid and efficient absorption of minerals as they are released by decomposer organisms. The physical presence of roots and hyphae in the organic layers (where a root mat exists) or in the upper soil goes far toward explaining the efficient recovery of minerals in tropical forests.

Root hairs function in a manner similar to mycorrhizal hyphae, and Baylis (1975) has shown that plants that do not form the mycorrhizal symbiosis tend to have fine roots and well developed root hairs. This correlation holds true in Amazonia (St. John, 1980a). Root hair development is one way in which the non-mycorrhizal species of some forests survive. It is interesting that white-sand soils largely lack non-mycorrhizal species. Perhaps root hairs or other alternatives to mycorrhizae are not sufficiently effective to allow survival on the very poorest soils.

15.5. THE EFFECTS OF DISTURBANCE ON MYCORRHIZAL FUNGI AND MYCORRHIZAL FUNCTION

With clearing of tropical forests proceeding at a rapid pace, the fate of mycorrhizae after disturbance is an important question. In this regard it is fortunate that VAM fungi have such wide host ranges; the symbionts of the original forest trees can form mycorrhizae with successional plant species and with most crops that could be placed on the site. Thus while changes in host species and disturbance of the physical environment may modify the composition of the fungal flora, it is unlikely that all inoculum will be lost unless regrowth of plants is prevented. In the case of ECM, the outlook is less optimistic.

No tropical crops except some pulpwood and timber species are ectomycorrhizal, and the fungi are likely to be rather specific to the native host plants. Tropical ECM fungi can probably be conserved only by conserving their host plants.

A second, and perhaps more important side of the conservation question is the fate of the nutrient cycling processes in which mycorrhizae take part. We have said that mycorrhizae are essentially extensions of the host root system. The effects of disturbance on mycorrhizae parallel the effects on the host plants and on their natural environment. Where there is a surface organic layer, the loss of that layer may mean that some of the forest's stock of nutrient elements will be lost. Ions once held on exchange sites in the organic matter can be bound into unavailable complexes in the mineral soil or in the case of certain highly soluble ions, lost in drainage water. These effects are not directly attributable to the loss of mycorrhizal fungi, but to the loss of the environment in which they functioned.

15.6. OPTIMAL MANAGEMENT PRACTICES

When disturbance of an Amazonian forest must occur, some management practices will be more effective than others in maintaining the natural functions of mycorrhizal fungi. As pointed out above, VAM fungi will probably be conserved if secondary forest or crops are re-established quickly on the site. A partial list of mycorrhizal plants from Amazonia has been published (St. John, 1980b), and these are among the plants that should help preserve the native fungal flora. ECM fungi may be partially conserved by leaving ECM individuals as shade trees. Cacao and other tree crops may benefit from the shade of ECM trees of the Caesalpiniaceae and Nyctaginaceae.

The function of mycorrhizae can best be conserved by those practices that re-establish the kind of environment in which natural mineral cycling takes place. Roots grow back into the upper few centimetres of soil rather quickly when successional vegetation begins to cast a uniform shade on the ground, protecting the roots from extreme temperatures and drying. A similar growth of shallow roots, and even a humus layer and associated root mat, develops under some perennial crops soon after canopy closure. A 4-year-old plantation of cacao near Manaus, Brazil had a thicker organic layer and better developed root mat than a nearby old-growth forest on the same soil type. Other perennial crops also can produce surface root mats. Mixed plantations of tree crops, perhaps with some natives left as shade trees during the first few years, would be simple and probably effective ways to re-establish the kind of nutrient cycling processes that occur in the native forests.

15.7. CONCLUSIONS

In summary, two of the several kinds of mycorrhizal symbiosis are particularly important in Amazonian forests: ECM, found mostly in Caesalpiniaceae and Nyctaginaceae, and VAM, found in most other families. Non-mycorrhizal species are found in some forests but are rare on the poorest soils. The function of mycorrhizal fungi in Amazonian forests is probably very similar to their function in temperate habitats. Mycorrhizal fungi aid in uptake of nutrient elements, especially phosphorus, an effect brought about largely through the physical distribution of hyphae in soil or litter. The concentration of mycorrhizal roots in the upper soil or in a humus layer above the soil may account in large part for the efficient conservation of mineral elements in tropical forests. Destruction of the nutrient cycling process results from destruction of the soil or litter environment.

Fungi of the VAM type are unlikely to be lost in disturbance since successional vegetation and crop plants will form mycorrhizae with the fungi from the native forest. Some change of fungal species composition may result from changes in host species and the physical environment. ECM fungi will have to be conserved by preserving host trees, either in native forest stands or as part of a management scheme. The best management practice, from the viewpoint of conservation, would be one that would re-establish the environment in which mycorrhizal roots can form in the upper soil or in a humus layer above the soil.

REFERENCES

Baylis, G. T. S. (1975) The magnolioid mycorrhiza and mycotrophy in root systems derived from it. In *Endomycorrhizas*. Eds. F.E. Sanders, B. Mosse and P.B. Tinker, pp. 373 – 389. Academic Press, London.

Bowen, G. D. and Smith, S. E. (1981) The effects of mycorrhizas on nitrogen uptake by plants. In *Terrestrial Nitrogen Cycles. Processes, Ecosystem Strategies, and Management Impacts*. Eds. F.E. Clark and T. Rosswall, pp. 237 – 247. Ecol. Bull. (Stockholm).

Harley, J. L. (1969) *The Biology of Mycorrhiza*. 2nd ed. Leonard Hill, London.

St. John, T. V. (1980a) Root size, root hairs, and mycorrhizal infection: A re-examination of Baylis's hypothesis with tropical trees. *New Phytol.* 84, 483 – 487.

St. John, T. V. (1980b) Uma lista de espécies de plantas tropicais Brasileiras naturalmente infectadas com micorriza vesicular-arbuscular. *Acta Amazonica* 10, 229 – 234.

Went, F. W. and Stark, N. (1968) Mycorrhiza. *Bioscience* 18, 1035 – 1039.

CHAPTER 16

The Ecology of Amazonian Primates

JOHN TERBORGH

Princeton University, Princeton, New Jersey, U.S.A.

CONTENTS

16.1. INTRODUCTION

Of the 16 genera and 46 species of New World primates, all but 2 genera and 10 species occur within Amazonia, making this region the unequivocal centre of diversity for the group (Table 16.1). The highest diversities occur in central and western Amazonia where as many as 14 species of 12 genera can occur in sympatry (Freese *et al.*, 1982).

In spite of this great wealth of taxa and a strong worldwide interest in primates, very few field studies have been undertaken within the Amazonian region. This has not been because of a lack of interest on the part of investigators, but rather because of lack of adequately protected study sites. Monkeys are universally shot as game in the Neotropics (*see* Dourojeanni, Chapter 22, this volume) and the larger species especially have been decimated over vast areas of otherwise unexploited primary forest (Freese *et al.*, 1982). Some parks and reserves do exist, but in many of these furtive hunting continues to be a deterrent to research. Primate groups can be habituated to observation only where the animals are not terrified by the sight of a human being. This fact drastically limits the number of sites that are suitable for behavioural research, and at this writing there are fewer than a half-dozen locations in the entire Amazonian region where undisturbed primate populations could be studied under protected conditions.

This lamentable situation has served to perpetuate a near total ignorance of the structure and ecology of New World primate communities. Although detailed studies now exist for species in 9 of the 16

TABLE 16.1. Distribution of New World Primate Genera

Common name	Genus	No. of species in genus	Distribution of genus*
Pygmy Marmoset	Cebuella	1	W Amazonia from S Colombia to N Bolivia E to mouth of Rio Purús.
Marmosets	Callithrix	3	Cent. and E Brazil S of Amazon to E Bolivia and Rio Paraná.
Tamarins	Saguinus	10	Panama and NW Colombia; W and N Cent. Amazonia and Guianan region, S of Amazon in Pará; not in Orinoco basin. Does not overlap with Callithrix.
Lion Tamarins	Leontopithecus	1	Endemic to coastal forests of E and SE Brazil.
Goeldi's Monkey	Callimico	1	W Amazonia from S Colombia to N Bolivia E to mouth of Rio Japurá.
Night Monkey	Aotus	1	Panama to N Argentina; throughout Amazonia but absent from Guianan region and E Brazil; Pacific slope S to Ecuador.
Titi Monkey	Callicebus	3	From S Colombia to Bolivia and E to mouth of Amazon; an isolated species in the coastal forest of SE Brasil.
Squirrel Monkey	Saimiri	1	Costa Rica S through much of S America to Bolivia but absent from the Pacific slope of Colombia and Ecuador and from the coastal forest of SE Brazil.
Capuchin Monkeys	Cebus	4	Belize S through cent. and S America to Bolivia and Paraguay, including the Pacific slope of Colombia and Ecuador and SE Brazil.
Saki Monkeys	Pithecia	4	Cent. and W Amazonia S of the Orinoco; Guianan region; E only to Rio Tapajós S of Amazon.
Bearded Sakis	Chiropotes	2	The Guianan region and S of the Orinoco to Cent. Brazil but absent from W Amazonia W of the Rio Negro and Rio Madeira.
Uakaris	Cacajao	2	W and Cent. Amazonia E to Rio Aracá N of Amazon and Rio Juruá S of Amazon.
Howler Monkeys	Alouatta	6	S Mexico S through most of S America to N Argentina; Pacific slope S to N Peru.
Spider Monkeys	Ateles	4	From Lat. 23° in Mexico S through most of Cent. and S America to Bolivia and SW Brazil but not SE Brazil; Pacific slope S to Ecuador.
Woolly Monkeys	Lagothrix	2	W and Cent. Amazonia E to Rio Negro and Rio Tapajós; upper Orinoco drainage in Colombia; absent from Venezuela and Guianan region.
Woolly Spider Monkey	Brachyteles	1	Endemic to coastal forest of SE Brazil.

* Distributions compiled from information in Napier and Napier (1967), Walker (1975), Hershkovitz (1977), and Mittermeier and Coimbra-Filho (1981).

New World genera, community level investigations have been rare indeed. Prior to the results that will be described in this chapter, there existed only one thorough comparative study. This was of the 5 species that inhabit Barro Colorado Island in Panama (Hladik and Hladik, 1969; Hladik et al., 1971). More fragmentary accounts on the ecology of sympatric primates are available for a locality in Surinam (Mittermeier and van Roosmalen, 1981) and for two localities in Colombia (Klein and Klein, 1975, 1977; Izawa, 1975), but the only locality investigated to date which possesses a full complement of Amazonian species and genera is Cocha Cashu in Peru (Terborgh, 1983). This is located in southwestern Amazonia at Lat. 11°51'S and Long. 71°19'W in the Manu National Park. Within a few kilometres of the field station live 13 species representing 11 of the 14 Amazonian genera. This is the maximum number of species that has been reported from a New World locality, and it is matched only by the total of monkeys, apes and prosimians at some localities in equatorial Africa (Guatier-Hion *et al.*, 1980).

The remainder of this chapter consists of an account of the ecological relationships among the 13 primate species in the Cocha Cashu community.

16.2. THE PRIMATE COMMUNITY AT COCHA CASHU

Primate studies were initiated at Cocha Cashu in 1974 and are continuing at the present time. To date, 7 species have been intensively investigated for periods of 12 months or more, and another 4 have been studied for shorter periods. That leaves only 2 out of the total of 13 that have not been studied at all, but fortunately both of these (Goeldi's monkey and monk saki) have received some attention in other localities.

Some basic data on the 13 species are presented in Table 16.2. They are ordered in relation to size from the largest downward. The range in body size is quite remarkable, covering nearly two orders of magnitude. Size differences have proven the key to understanding ecological relationships in the community and will be stressed as the main organising theme for the ensuing discussion. Species of similar size are likely to be each others' closest competitors. To emphasise this, the species will be grouped into size classes and compared to other members of their class as their characteristics are described.

16.2.1. Large species (7 – 10 kg): spider, woolly and howler monkeys

Black spider monkey. This is the most conspicuous primate at Cocha Cashu, owing to its habit of living dispersed in small, flexible groupings rather than in aggregated groups. Any number of individuals from 1 to 30 or more may be encountered at a time. Groups, however, are strictly transitory, lasting from a

TABLE 16.2. Some characteristics of the primate species found in the vicinity of Cocha Cashu

Species Scientific name	English name	Mean weight (kg)	Group size	Population density (No./km^2)	No. groups per km^2	Biomass (kg/km^2)
Ateles paniscus	Black Spider Monkey	6.0	1 – 30	25	var.	175
Lagothrix lagotricha	Woolly Monkey	6.0	20?	?	?	?
Alouatta seniculus	Red Howler Monkey	6.0	4 – 6	30	6	180
Cebus apella	Brown or Tufted Capuchin	2.6	8 – 14	40	4	96
Cebus albifrons	White-fronted Capuchin	2.4	8 – 18	30	2	72
Pithecia monachus	Saki Monkey	1.0	5?	?	?	?
Saimiri sciureus	Squirrel Monkey	0.8	30 – 40	60	2	48
Aotus trivirgatus	Night Monkey	0.7	2 – 5	40	10	28
Callicebus moloch	Titi Monkey	0.7	2 – 5	24	6	17
Callimico goeldii	Goeldi's Monkey	0.5	4?	?	?	?
Saguinus imperator	Emperor Tamarin	0.4	2 – 10	12	3	5
Saguinus fuscicollis	Saddle-backed tamarin	0.3	2 – 10	16	3	5
Cebuella pygmaea	Pygmy marmoset	0.1	2 – 8	5	1	0.5

few minutes to a few hours. The only stable associations are those between females and their offspring. Individuals often travel alone, although several times a day they will meet or briefly join other individuals. Spider monkeys possess an extensive vocabulary of vocalisations, some of them loud enough to carry hundreds of metres over the forest. Dispersed individuals or small groups use these loud calls to keep track of each others' whereabouts, and perhaps to communicate the location of food sources. Even though the individuals seem to be autonomous in their movements, there is evidence of a higher level of spatial organisation. Klein and Klein (1975) found in their study of *A. belzebuth* that associations occurred freely within a subpopulation of 25 – 30 individuals, and that these individuals did not associate with other animals that lived in the vicinity. From this they concluded that spider monkeys are organised into loose, but mutually exclusive clans, rather reminiscent of those formed by chimpanzees (Wrangham, 1977). On many occasions we have observed apparently agonistic encounters in which two opposing groups of spider monkeys engaged in prolonged shouting matches from nearby treetops. Such observations are consistent with Kleins' suggestion of a clan based social system. However, it is not known at present whether the verbal clashes between groups take place at territorial boundaries or are simply related to temporary control of fruit resources.

Spider monkeys are inhabitants of the high canopy. They move with impressive speed and grace, traversing large crowns by walking swiftly along horizontal branches. Swinging or jumping to the next tree, they may then brachiate through the branches in a series of looping motions that carry them with impressive speed. At times they travel so rapidly that an observer on the ground has great difficulty keeping up. This extraordinary mobility enables them to patrol large areas for ripe fruit crops. Although home ranges have not been precisely determined for either individuals or clans, it seems certain from our limited observations that they must include a minimum of 100 – 200 ha.

Spider monkeys appear to be the most thoroughly frugivorous New World monkeys, if fruits are regarded as distinct from seeds. At Klein's study site in southeastern Colombia, fruit made up 83% of feeding observations (Klein and Klein, 1977). Data for other species of spider monkeys in Panama and Surinam closely corroborate this figure, nearly all observations referring to ripe fruit (Hladik and Hladik, 1969; Mittermeier and Van Roosmalen, 1981). Minor components of the diet include buds, young leaves, flowers, nectar, and dead wood.

Woolly monkey. Second in the triumverate of large primates. It closely resembles the spider monkey in both behaviour and diet, though the details of its habits are poorly known. Although woolly monkeys ostensibly have a broad distribution in Amazonia, they are curiously local in their occurrence, being found at widely scattered points and inexplicably absent from large areas in between. This hit-or-miss pattern holds true in the Manu region as well, for they are common both upstream and downstream but absent from the immediate vicinity of the research station itself. This seemingly capricious distribution, plus the fact that woolly monkeys are most favoured by hunters, must account for why a concerted study of this interesting and attractive species has not yet been done. The few data we have come from a two-month preliminary investigation at Pakitza, 30 km down the Manu from Cocha Cashu (Ramirez, 1980).

The social units of woolly monkeys contain about 15 individuals, including more than 1 adult male. Although the groups frequently break up into small feeding parties, they are considerably more cohesive than those of spider monkeys. The group observed by Ramirez covered more than 2 km^2 in just a few weeks, so it is likely that the annual range is still larger.

There is very little in the feeding data obtained by Ramirez to suggest that woolly monkeys are distinctive in their diets. A number of common fruits (e.g. *Ficus*, *Brosimum*) eaten by other monkeys formed the bulk of their intake. Such fruits provide mainly carbohydrate. Small amounts of young (flush) leaves may have supplied most of the required protein. The meagre data base available at present thus offers no basis for understanding why woolly monkeys are so patchily distributed over their range. Further study is clearly indicated.

Red howler monkey. The third and last of the large species. It has been studied briefly at Cocha Cashu by K. Milton (1980), and more extensively under very different environmental conditions in the llanos of Venezuela (Rudran, 1979). In the latter locality it attains the extraordinary population density of 150 per km^2, but at Cocha Cashu there are only about 30 per km^2. These live in small groups of 4 to 6 containing but a single adult male. Unlike spider and woolly monkeys, howlers are sedentary and lethargic, spending the major part of every day at repose in the branches of large trees.

Howlers are perhaps the most renowned of New World monkeys owing to the remarkable vocalisations of the males. The gruff, bass roaring conjures up images of some large, ferocious beast, and has startled many a naive traveller. The howling of the male is actually often accompanied by the females, but the vocal efforts of the latter are so feeble that they tend to get lost in the rush of sound. Howling is performed ritually at dawn, allowing the groups to take note of each others' positions. It may be triggered at other times of day by a chance encounter of two groups, whereupon a prolonged vocal contest may ensue until one of the groups withdraws.

Howlers possess the capacity to detoxify the defensive chemicals of many plants, thereby opening to themselves a large food supply that is indigestible to other New World monkeys (Milton, 1981). Leaves comprise between 40 and 60% of the diet of mantled howler monkeys in Panama (Milton, 1978). Young leaves are preferred, but mature leaves are consumed in small amounts, especially when young leaves are not available. Fruit makes up the remainder of the diet. Howlers generally feed on species of fruit that are consumed by other monkeys as well (especially figs), the difference being that howlers typically begin harvesting a crop several days before it is ripe enough to attract other species.

The capacity to feed on leaves and unripe fruit greatly increases the food supply of howlers relative to that of other monkeys. With little doubt, this is what accounts for their high biomass, which in many localities exceeds that of any other primate. Although howlers clearly prefer ripe fruit and young leaves, the ready availability of auxiliary food supplies in the form of mature leaves and unripe fruit, allows the groups to subsist within relatively small home ranges. At Cocha Cashu these average about 25 ha, with substantial overlap in the areas used by neighbouring groups, as has been found elsewhere (Milton, 1980).

The three large monkeys of the Manu region share a number of characteristics, and appear to differ mainly in the proportions of various kinds of plant materials included in the diet, though further investigation of their feeding habits is much needed. All are confined by their size to the upper stratum of the forest, where heavy horizontal branches provide pathways through the canopy. It is rare indeed to see one of these species in the understorey, partly because small shrubs and saplings will not support their weight, and partly because understorey plants are small and do not proffer enough fruit to be of interest to such large animals. Of the three species, only howlers regularly descend to the ground, which they do for the purpose of drinking and eating soil. The latter habit presumably provides minerals that are deficient in their diets. Another trait that the large species share in common is that they are all vegetarians. This might not seem noteworthy were it not for the fact that eight out of the ten smaller species in the community regularly hunt insects and other small prey, and appear to obtain most of their protein by this means. Later we shall see why large monkeys are at a severe disadvantage as predators, and for this reason are obliged to obtain their protein from plant material.

It is in the quest for protein that we find a probable basis for the ecological separation of the three species. The soft sweet fruits such as figs that are avidly eaten by all three contain abundant carbohydrate but very little protein. Spider monkeys must obtain protein from fruit for they eat little else, but without better information on the nutritional attributes of tropical fruits, one cannot conclude any more than this. The Klein's (1977) report that spider monkeys in Colombia consume quantities of palm fruits which are known to contain protein, but palms, although abundant, are virtually ignored by spider monkeys at Cocha Cashu. They do, however, eat a greater variety of fruits than other monkeys, including some (e.g. Lauraceae spp.) that are known to supply the protein requirements of certain frugivorous birds (Snow, 1981). Nothing definite can be said about how woolly monkeys obtain protein, though they appear to consume larger quantities of leaves than spider monkeys. As for howlers, there is no doubt that they obtain protein as well as a significant amount of energy from leaves. On the other hand, howlers do not consume such a wide variety of fruits as spider monkeys.

The diets of the three species thus seem to fit into a progression from a highly diverse collection of fruits and few leaves to a limited assortment of fruits and many leaves. Although the woolly monkey is clearly intermediate, just where it lies in the progression remains to be determined. Further information on its diet will surely clarify its ecological relationship with the other two species, and could even shed light on the causes of its unusual disjointed distribution.

16.2.2. Medium-sized species (3 – 5 kg): the capuchins

There are two species of capuchins in the Manu community, the brown and the white-fronted (Fig. 16.1). Their behaviour is similar in so many ways that their ecological roles do not at first appear to be well differentiated. For much of the year their lifestyles are nearly identical. It is mainly in the early dry season when fruit production by the forest dwindles to very low levels that important differences emerge. We will return to these differences after first discussing the many traits the two species share in common.

Capuchins are the jacks-of-all-trades among the New World monkeys. With the notable exception of leaves, they eat almost every conceivable type of plant material and spend nearly half of every day

Fig. 16.1. White fronted capuchin monkey (*Cebus albifrons*) in Manu National Park, Peru (photo by Charles Janson).

hunting arthropods and small vertebrates. They are, in other words, omnivores, *par excellence*. While all the vegetarians discussed above devote a great deal of time to digesting their bulky diets, capuchins are compelled by their search for prey to be almost continuously active. It is this high level of activity that makes them, of all New World monkeys, the most entertaining subjects of study.

The difference in activity levels between vegetarians and omnivores is quite profound. For vegetarians, especially folivores, the rate of passage of material through the gut is slow in relation to the rate at which food is consumed (Milton, 1981). Once an animal has filled its stomach, there is nothing for it to do but wait for the material to be processed. Digestion is slow because tough plant fibres must be broken down, frequently with the participation of symbiotic microorganisms. Because of the slow digestion of fibrous plant materials, howlers and titi monkeys, the two partial folivores in the community, spend more than half their time at rest. This situation can be contrasted with that of omnivores, which as a rule do not have special digestive adaptations for processing plant fibres. Omnivores are thus restricted to harvesting non-fibrous materials, of which the forest provides a wide selection: soft fruits, nuts, a few types of seeds, pith, meristematic tissues, some flowers, nectar, fungi and sap. Capuchins have been seen to eat all of these things, though of course, in greatly varying proportions. Such materials, while easily digested, are far less abundant than leaves and often are obtained in relatively small quantities. Ingestion is thus slower relative to digestion than it is in folivores so that the two processes are more nearly in balance. While howlers typically feed about three times a day, resting for long periods in between, capuchins remain on the move nearly all the time, feeding 10 to 20 or more times per day as fruit trees are encountered. Major feeding sessions can occur at any hour, though statistically feeding is more concentrated early and late in the day.

The soft, sweet fruits favoured by capuchins are generally low in protein. This fact obliges them to seek protein in some other form. Leaves are precluded, because the rapid progress of food through the gut does not allow time for the necessary break down of plant cell walls. The alternative is to seek protein in the form of animal matter, something capuchins do with an impressive single-mindedness. From the earliest glimmer of dawn to the last glow of sunset, capuchins occupy nearly every spare moment with foraging for prey. Throughout the year an average of nearly 50% of their time is devoted to this activity. The remainder of the day is mostly filled out with travel (ca. 20%) and feeding on plant material (ca. 20%), leaving only about 10% for rest. Omnivory thus calls for far higher levels of activity than a vegetarian mode of existence.

In their foraging behaviour capuchins display the same versatility they show in exploiting plant resources. Nearly every conceivable type of substrate is searched: live foliage, curled dead leaves, twigs and branches, even occasionally leaf litter on the ground. Their real forte, however, consists of activities that collectively can be termed destructive foraging. These include breaking myriads of dead and hollow twigs, stripping the bark from dead limbs, biting into and tearing open decaying wood, rummaging through dead leaves and debris in vine tangles and palm crowns, etc. Such searching actually destroys the retreats of their prey and would thus potentially be self-limiting if new hiding places were not regenerated by the forest at a rapid rate.

In view of their long canines and powerful builds, one might imagine that capuchins would concentrate on capturing large prey items. They are indeed capable of subduing large prey, but succeed in capturing them only on rare occasions. We have seen them take spiny rats, opposums, baby birds, large lizards, frogs, etc., but prize items such as these are mainly taken by adult males, and then only at long intervals separated by many hours of routine foraging. Normally their efforts are rewarded by a steady yield of small insects (one every 2 minutes, on average). Nearly half of the captures consist of the nests of hymenoptera (social insects), while the other half consists of a miscellaneous harvest of caterpillars, beetles, snails, grasshoppers, termites, spiders, and small vertebrates. Most of the latter types of prey are discovered in passing or as a result of superficial searches of leaves and branches. Destructive foraging, on the other hand, mainly results in exposing ant nests and termites. Capuchins do not seem to eat adult ants, but avidly consume the brood (eggs, larvae and pupae), which they lap up with their tongues, or pluck with pursed lips.

The two species of capuchins at Cocha Cashu are very similar in their foraging, the main differences being that the brown capuchin, which is conspicuously more burly, engages in heavier types of destructive foraging, and that the white-fronted capuchin displays a great fondness for wasp nests, apparently being protected from their stings by its noticeably fluffier fur.

It is hard to imagine that capuchins would be so dedicated to finding small beetles, caterpillars and ant eggs if there were good opportunities to catch larger prey. A single baby bird or moderate-sized lizard may weigh as much as scores of the minute arthropods that make up the usual harvest. Large prey are obviously favoured, for when one is captured by an adult, younger troop members typically crowd around whining and begging for scraps. Whenever a subordinate individual obtains an item that cannot be eaten in one bite, it generally has to flee from the group to retain control of its catch. Yet in spite of the obvious desire for large prey, only 1% of the items captured by brown capuchins were judged to be 1 cm or more in length. One thus infers that large prey are excessively rare or that capuchins are constitutionally inept at catching them. The latter proves to be the better answer, as will be shown later.

The many similarities of the two capuchins have been emphasised so far. There are, however, subtle differences in their morphology and behaviour that become crucial in separating their ecological roles during the annual period of fruit scarcity. Although the two species are nearly equal in length, the brown capuchin is more powerfully built, and possesses a heavier dentition and jaw musculature (Kinzey, 1974). The consequences of this become obvious when one compares their performances in opening palm nuts (*Astrocaryum*). These nuts are one of the few plentiful food resources available in the early dry season, and provide a staple for brown capuchins. Even juveniles open the nuts with ease, cracking them in a single bite. In the absence of other alternatives, white-fronted capuchins are sometimes obliged to feed on palm nuts as well, but their ability to exploit them is marginal. Many nuts are tested and rejected before one is found that is a little weaker than the rest and that can be broken. Instead of simply biting them as brown capuchins do, white-fronted capuchins often bash two together or bang one on a branch in the hope of initiating a crack that can then be extended by biting (Struhsaker and Leland, 1977). Each nut opened and eaten requires many minutes of effort, whereas for a brown capuchin the task is accomplished in a matter of seconds. The ability of white-fronted capuchins, especially young ones, to exploit palm nuts is so limited that other resources are almost certainly a necessity to sustain them through the dry season.

The other major resource available to omnivores at this time is the fruit of several species of figs. White-fronted capuchins make heavy use of these fruits throughout the year, but in the dry season figs account for about 90% of their fruit consumption. The total production of figs by the forest is evidently quite substantial, but the fruiting trees are widely scattered. This has important implications for understanding the ecology of the two capuchins. A brown capuchin troop may have access to more than 1,000 *Astrocaryum* palms within its home range of 50 − 80 ha. Fig trees, in contrast, are scarce, though they may be gigantic, some having crowns more than 40 m across and producing over a million fruits in a single crop. However, the entire three square kilometre study area supports only five mature individuals of the most important species, *Ficus perforata*. At this low density the average brown capuchin troop has only one tree within its home range. Consequently, figs are only intermittently available to this species, a matter that is of no great import, for the animals are able to subsist perfectly well on palm nuts. For the white-fronted capuchin, it is a different story. Palm nuts are exploited with difficulty and figs constitute the principal dry season resource. In order to be assured of a more or less continuous supply, groups of white-fronted capuchins must range over large areas of 150 ha or more. Since the density of troops is about 1.5 per km^2, neighbouring troops overlap a great deal in the course of a year, though they scrupulously avoid approaching one another. Large fruit trees are shared, however, in the sense that different troops commonly feed at different hours of the day.

In summary, ecological differences between the capuchins are minimal for much of the year but become conspicuous in the dry season when soft fruit is available only at highly scattered but very concentrated sources (fig trees). During this period, the respective ecological roles of the two species are defined by the greater ability of the heavy-jawed brown capuchin to open palm nuts and by the tendency of the white-fronted capuchin to search large areas for rare fruiting fig trees. Together, the capuchins differ from the larger vegetarian species considered above in travelling and feeding mainly in the middlestorey of the forest, in their use of palms (especially the brown capuchin), and in their ceaseless foraging for small prey.

16.2.3. Small species (0.8 – 3 kg): saki, squirrel, night and dusky titi monkeys

Although of similar size, these 4 species diverge radically in their habits. Two, the saki and dusky titi monkeys are basically vegetarians and two, the squirrel and night monkeys are omnivores. Three are diurnal and one is nocturnal, and three live in monogamous family groups while the squirrel monkey forms the largest social units of any species at Cocha Cashu. Major differences between the four are thus obvious at a glance and need not be expounded at length. Instead, as each species is characterised, its ecological role will be distinguished from those of trophically related species that are larger or smaller in size.

Saki monkey. This is the most enigmatic of the four. It has not been subjected to systematic study anywhere, though its range encompasses much of the Amazonian and Guyanan regions. Cryptic habits and an uneven distribution have no doubt helped to perpetuate ignorance of its ecology. Sakis have been seen at Cocha Cashu, but only on rare occasions, the most recent being 6 years ago. We suspect that they must have a restricted habitat in our area, but concrete information is lacking. The only quantitative data on saki ecology is based on groups of the related white-faced saki (*Pithecia pithecia*) observed in Surinam by Mittermeier and van Roosmalen (1981). They found sakis to be uncommon in the middle and lower-middle strata of several forest types. The diet was completely vegetarian, consisting 93% of fruit and 7% of flowers, though the number of observations (15) was scanty. Included in the list of fruits eaten are those of both soft and hard construction (Lecythidaceae). In half the observations of fruit use, the seeds were eaten. Monk sakis might thus prove to be seed predators, specialising on the immature fruits of Lecythidaceae (Brazil nuts, and related trees) and other large-seeded plants. While this is only conjectural, if true, it would differentiate their ecology from all other Cocha Cashu species in which seed eating is extremely rare, except for the use of *Astrocaryum* palm nuts by brown capuchins.

Squirrel monkey. At a population density of about 60 per km^2, this is the most common primate in the community. In its ecology, it is most closely related to capuchins with which the troops habitually associate. These associations are joined and broken off by the squirrel monkeys, the capuchins (of either species) playing a passive role. In our area the average squirrel monkey troop spends 90% of its time in mixed groups, and is alone principally during transits from one capuchin home range to another. The benefits of these associations accrue mainly to the squirrel monkeys, and appear to be twofold. Early warning of predator attacks is one. Capuchins are more watchful than squirrel monkeys and have better developed alarm calls. When an alarm is given, the reaction of the squirrel monkeys is as prompt and decisive as that of the capuchins themselves. Second, squirrel monkeys exploit capuchins as guides to lead them to fruit sources. It can be assumed that capuchins are in general better informed about the locations of fruiting trees because their home ranges are smaller and covered more frequently. This follows from the fact that squirrel monkey home ranges are extremely large, probably 3 to 5 km^2, large enough to encompass the ranges of many capuchin groups. While travelling with capuchins, squirrel monkeys exploit the same fruit trees, often running ahead in order to arrive first. So long as there are ample fruit resources in a capuchin home range, squirrel monkeys will usually continue an association. But if the resource level drops, they will quite promptly leave to look for another capuchin group.

Although squirrel monkeys consume much the same assortment of fleshy fruits that capuchins eat, they are more specialised in one sense. Their forte is locating what might be called resource 'hot spots'. Tropical forests, as already pointed out, contain many rare species of trees. Moreover, individual trees of a given species quite frequently fruit at somewhat different times. These two factors can result in a significant spatial heterogeneity of fruit abundance in a forest that is more or less homogeneous with respect to its tree species composition. Brown capuchins are versatile enough in their feeding habits to subsist on the resources produced in a relatively circumscribed area, but squirrel monkeys follow a different pattern in searching very large areas for ephemeral concentrations of fruit. White-fronted capuchins are intermediate in their behaviour, living in smaller and better defined home ranges than squirrel monkeys, covering ranges that are twice as large as those of brown capuchins.

These distinctions are especially pronounced during the dry season when figs provide the only major source of soft fruit. Squirrel monkeys are especially nomadic at this time, switching frequently from one capuchin troop to another if the ranges lack a fruiting fig. Through this behaviour several squirrel monkey troops will quickly converge on any major fruit source that may be in the vicinity. The groups then feed, simultaneously or sequentially, along with both capuchins, spider monkeys and howlers. Under such intense exploitation the crop of even a huge tree is exhausted in a few days. The groups then drift off in various directions to begin the search anew.

Squirrel monkeys are even more dependent on figs in the dry season than white-fronted capuchins, for they are unable to open palm nuts at all. Inevitably there are periods when no figs are available, and at such times we have seen groups go for as long as a week without finding a single fruit tree of any consequence. At such times the monkeys resort to non-stop insect foraging, an activity that occupies half their time under any circumstance. Squirrel monkeys are less versatile than capuchins in their foraging behaviour but forage at a higher rate. They are too small and light of build to engage effectively in destructive foraging, and so they specialise in searching foliage. Leaves in some form, alive or dead account for 89% of the substrates searched by squirrel monkeys at Cocha Cashu. Not surprisingly, the harvest consists mainly of folivorous insects: lepidopteran larvae and pupae — 50%, and orthoptera — 34%. Hymenoptera, which form the basic fare of capuchins, are almost missing from the diet of squirrel monkeys (4%), demonstrating that hunting technique largely determines the composition of the catch.

As insectivores, squirrel monkeys are highly proficient, making about one capture a minute (56 per hour) over the 5.9 hours they forage on an average day for a total of 330 prey. At this rate, they are matching the performance of insectivorous birds, many of which also make about one capture per minute. Squirrel monkeys, however, are much larger than any strictly insectivorous bird at Cocha Cashu, the very largest of which weigh around 200 g. For this reason it seems very doubtful that squirrel monkeys could survive indefinitely on the yield of their foraging efforts. They are small enough however, that they can sustain themselves for a time in this manner without starving. This is their gambit for getting through the dry season. There are often figs available, but their appearance is highly irregular in space and time. Privation must be endured in the in between periods, but foraging suffices to stave off rapid weight loss and exhaustion. Capuchins, at three times the weight of squirrel monkeys, are too large to get along without some form of plant food, but their very size gives them access to sources (i.e., palm nuts) that call for more strength than squirrel monkeys possess. There is thus a clear separation of the respective ecological roles of each species at the times of greatest stress.

Night monkey. A species that is unique in being the world's only nocturnal monkey. It is indeed truly nocturnal, for the family groups do not emerge from their well-concealed daytime roosts until a half-hour after sundown. The night monkey has been studied for a full year at Cocha Cashu by Patricia Wright, and the following account is based on her unpublished results.

Although virtually unknown in the natural state prior to Wright's study, the night monkey is actually a common species. At a density of 40 per km^2, it ties with the brown capuchin at Cocha Cashu as second in abundance after the squirrel monkey. The social units consist of a monogamous pair accompanied by up to three successive offspring. Families occupy well-defined territories, averaging 10 ha in extent that form a close-fitting checkerboard over most of the varied habitats included in the study area.

Night monkeys are omnivorous. Their insect catching propensities are known from observations by Wright on tame free-ranging animals. In the wild, however, even habituated groups are generally too high for close observation so their hunting activities have not been quantified. Dropped beetle elytra and orthopteran wings indicate that they capture members of at least these two orders, and Wright has seen them eat spiders, lepidopteran larvae and ants as well. The composition of their catch may not differ greatly from that of squirrel monkeys, which they resemble in their superficial searching of foliage. How much time they spend insect foraging, and the importance of prey in their diet have not yet been documented, however.

Night monkeys feed primarily on fruit species that are favoured by the larger monkeys. But instead of having to share the trees with crowds of capuchins, squirrel and spider monkeys, night monkey groups can feed unhampered, save for the occasional intruding kinkajou. By assuming a nocturnal mode of life the night monkey may have escaped the competition of diurnal species. This conjecture would gain plausibility if many of the fruit species eaten by night monkeys ripen at night as well as by day. Unfortunately, the data needed to test this possibility do not yet exist.

Remaining throughout the year within their 10-hectare territories, night monkeys do not have the same options open to them in the dry season as squirrel monkeys or capuchins. The presence of a large fruiting tree is by no means a certainty in so small an area, and palm nuts, due to their hardness, are out of the question. In lieu of other alternatives, the recourse of night monkeys is to exploit small crops, or scattered ripe fruits in trees that have not yet reached their fruiting peak, or that have passed it. Night monkeys can successfully survive on such meagre resources because they are small and live in small groups. The importance of these attributes can be illustrated by a hypothetical example. Consider a tree that contains only 12 fruits. If it is harvested by a group of four night monkeys, each animal can eat 3 fruits. If instead the tree is visited by a troop of 36 squirrel monkeys, at least 24 of them will go away hungry. If 12 capuchins come, each gets only one fruit, but a capuchin weighs more than three times as much as a night monkey, so in relation to its metabolic requirement, the capuchin harvests only one ninth as much. Harvesting small trees or sparse crops is therefore not adequately rewarding for a capuchin, but it can suffice for a night monkey or for that matter, any of the other lesser monkeys that live in small social units.

Dusky titi. The last of the four small monkeys to be discussed. In size, social habits and general appearance, titis are reminiscent of night monkeys, but they are far less active as a consequence of their vegetarian diets. Like night monkeys, they live in monogamous family units and occupy small, discrete territories. It is here that the resemblances end, for in other respects the two species are quite different.

Titis have received a good deal of attention at Cocha Cashu, especially from Patricia Wright whose unpublished results again constitute the greater part of our knowledge. Titis are not closely related ecologically to any of the other monkeys in their size class. Instead, they are diminutive counterparts of howlers, whose habit of chorusing at dawn they emulate. Their diet also consists of a seasonally varying blend of fruit and leaves, and in keeping with this about 60% of the day is spent at rest.

The major point of interest in comparing titis and howlers is that in detail their diets show surprisingly little overlap. The reasons for this provide a good deal of insight into the special role of titis. If the territories of the titi groups living in the vicinity of Cocha Cashu are plotted on a map, it is evident at a glance that the territories are located around edges — of swamps, lakes, streams, the main river and even large treefall openings in the interior of the forest. Although many of the territories include some area of high forest, none of them are confined to high forest.

What do edges offer that is essential? Edges in the tropics are typically festooned in vines, and vines, it appears, play a major role in the lifestyle of titis. Vines offer concealing cover, which is an important consideration for a small animal with many potential predators. Also, vines, unlike trees, tend to grow more or less continuously, and can thus provide a year round supply of fresh young leaves. Wright has found that most of the leaves eaten by titis are harvested from vines or from bamboo which also grows continuously. Perhaps most crucially, by eating vine leaves, titis avoid competition from howlers. The latter, by being 10 times the weight of titis, and living in larger groups, are obliged to exploit relatively concentrated resources. Howlers normally harvest leaves from the flushing crowns of sizeable canopy-level trees (Milton, 1980). In contrast, vine leaves come in very small quantities, a few at a time on the scattered ends of scrambling shoots. As a resource, vine leaves are analogous to the sparse fruit crops eaten by night monkeys — perfectly adequate for small monkeys, in small groups, but not for large monkeys. In unbroken high forest, where there are relatively few vines, titis would have to ascend into the canopy and compete with howlers for the leaf crops of large trees. But due to their larger size, howlers are capable of digesting poorer quality leaf material. They would therefore have a decisive advantage in such a competition. It is perhaps because of this that titis are confined to dense margins, situations where their small size is an asset rather than a handicap.

The small size of titis also helps them avoid the competition of howlers and other larger monkeys for fruit resources. Because the groups have a biomass of only 3 kg, equivalent to that of 1 capuchin, or half of a female howler, they can profitably exploit small trees, which is generally what they do. A number of the fruits they consume regularly are nominally bird dispersed, some of these being produced in large crops that are not much used by monkeys (e.g. Lauraceae spp.), and some being produced in crops that are made available a few fruits at a time over longer periods (e.g., *Trichilia* spp. — Meliaceae). Titis, like howlers, are also capable of exploiting a good many unripe fruits, some of which are apparently eaten for their immature seeds. They frequently pass up ripe fruit crops in large crowns, perhaps because they consistently try to avoid larger monkeys, particularly capuchins. Titis do eat figs whenever a crop ripens within their territories, but significantly, they visit the trees most consistently before the crop fully ripens, and then again after the larger monkeys have abandoned it. They seldom enter a fig tree during its ripening peak, another indication of their distaste for meeting other monkeys.

The fruit supply in a small area is bound to vary in an irregular fashion, even during parts of the year in which an ample quantity is generally available. It is thus hard to imagine that titis could survive within their six to eight hectare territories were it not for the fact that they are versatile enough to exploit opportunistically several classes of resources: large and small fruit crops, bird fruits, unripe fruits and young leaves. Of these, young leaves probably constitute the most reliable resource. In the dry season, titi territories may be altogether devoid of edible fruit, in which circumstances the groups show a remarkable change in behaviour. Instead of increasing the extent of their movements as capuchins and squirrel monkeys do, titis reduce their daily excursions from about 900 m to around 300 m (*fide* Patricia Wright). Evidently they 'know' that searching for fruit within the limited space of their territories is a futile proposition, and so they endeavour to conserve energy. The members of one group in such straits spent several hours a day patiently picking young bamboo leaf bases, virtually the only food available to them. This observation once again points to the dependency of titis on early successional vegetation, for bamboo is all but lacking in mature forest.

In concluding this section on the small monkeys at Manu, it is again appropriate to remark on the surprising heterogeneity of lifestyles represented by merely 4 species. There are differences in virtually every major aspect of their ecology and behaviour: in trophic position from vegetarian (saki, titi) to facultative insectivore (squirrel monkey); in fruit use from dependency on large ripe crops (squirrel monkey) to versatile opportunist (titi); in activity pattern from diurnal to nocturnal (night monkey); in habitat use from generalist (squirrel, night monkeys) to specialist (saki, titi), in territorial behaviour from extreme tolerance (squirrel monkey) to extreme intolerance (titi, night monkey); in group size from small (saki, titi, night monkeys) to very large (squirrel monkey), and in social system from monogamy (saki, titi, night monkeys), to competitive promiscuity (squirrel monkey). None of the 4 species is closely related ecologically to any of the others, and the closest potential competitors of each are species in the larger or smaller size classes.

It is interesting to consider whether, in an evolutionary sense, a greater range of lifestyles is potentially available to species in the small size class (around 1 kg). Large monkeys, as already pointed out, cannot harvest insects fast enough to be omnivores. Moreover, their need for firm support confines them to the heavy superstructure of the high canopy. Habitat specialisation is precluded by a level of metabolic demand that could not be satisfied by small patches of successional vegetation. Large arboreal monkeys are thus practically obliged to be vegetarians and to reside in the canopy of mature forest. At the other extreme, very small monkeys (less than 1 kg) are under a different set of restraints. They are too exposed to predation to spend much time in the open crowns of the canopy, and in any case are incapable of competing with larger species for the resources of the canopy. Small animals are metabolically at a disadvantage as vegetarians because they grow more rapidly than large animals and consequently require diets that are richer in protein. Young leaves could potentially supply the required protein, as they do for titis, but it is our impression that young leaves are not a reliable resource in the seasonal Amazonian forest, except perhaps in vine tangles and bamboo thickets. Seeds are another potential source of protein, but most primates lack the requisite dentition for exploiting them. Small prey remain as the only alternative protein source available to the smaller primates, thus explaining why nearly all of them are omnivores. It is only in the middle size range, evidently at body weights around 1 kg, that lifestyles representing both extremes are possible. While admittedly conjectural, this line of reasoning offers a plausible logic for the observed pattern. It may also help us to understand why there are so many species of small monkeys in the Amazonian forest.

16.2.4. Very small species (0.1 – 0.6 kg): the Callitrichids

We come now to the final size class to be considered, the very small monkeys. There are four of these in the Manu community, all of them members of the marmoset family. One of the distinguishing features of this family is the presence of claws on the digits instead of nails. While this may seem like a trivial distinction, it is actually a matter of decisive importance to the ecology of the group, for the possession of claws opens the possibility of vertical ascent and descent of trunks. The ability to cling on trunks opens to the marmosets as a group certain ways of life that are closed to the cebids, and explains the success of their radiation.

The 4 species of Callitrichids found in the Manu region represent 3 of the 5 genera in the family. Although quite distinct in some respects, the 4 species share a number of characteristics that help to distinguish them ecologically from larger primates. All of them are partial to certain types of successional vegetation and avoid unbroken tracts of mature forest. Within their chosen habitats, each of the species maintains discretely bounded and ardently defended territories. Group sizes throughout the family are characteristically low (less than 10), though one species (S. nigricollis) has been reported to travel in troops of 30 or more (Izawa, 1978). Mean group size for all the species in our area is in the range of four to six, though there is considerable variation around the mean values. The social units have conventionally been regarded as extended monogamous families, though accumulating evidence for several species indicates that this is an oversimplification. Groups sometimes contain more than one reproductively active male and/or female. At present, however, there is not enough information on any species in the wild to permit an unambiguous evaluation of its social system.

Regardless of the precise nature of the social system, the important ecological point is that group sizes are small for nearly all members of the marmoset family. Small body size coupled with small group size translates to a relatively low metabolic demand per group. This in turn opens the possibility of exploiting small and/or dispersed resources such as small fruit trees, nectar, sap and insects. We shall see in fact that these are just the sorts of resources that are used by the callitrichid species that have been observed at Cocha Cashu.

Goeldi's marmoset. The largest of the 4 species is this little-known marmoset, the largest member of the family at an adult weight of 600 g. Our limited experience with this interesting species consists of just two sightings, both of them in an area of dense swamp forest lying well beyond the limits of the regular study area. It is absent from high forest throughout the region and many local hunters are unaware of its existence. It must therefore be exceedingly rare, or more probably, confined to a very narrow range of habitats.

The little that is known of the behaviour of Goeldi's marmoset in the wild comes from two recent studies made in northwestern Bolivia (Pook and Pook, 1981; Masataka, 1981a,b). The habitat there is described as being variegated, as it is in the Manu region. Goeldi's marmosets were found in swamp forest and bamboo thickets, but not in the more commonplace forest types (Izawa and Yoneda, 1981). Thus, for whatever reason, the species appears only to use certain very dense types of vegetation where the groups are reported to travel and forage low, mostly within 5 m of the ground (Pook and Pook, 1981). To progress through the close stands of small diameter stems the animals employ what is known as cling-and-leap locomotion. In this, the movement is from stem to stem, in series of springing leaps from one vertical perch to another. Surprisingly rapid rates of travel can be achieved in this manner, especially in thick habitats of the kind favoured by Goeldi's marmoset. In high forest the trunks are much too far apart on the average and some other style of locomotion must be employed. Conversely, branch walking is not easily practised in dense stands of small trees where horizontal supports are not well developed. It thus appears that Goeldi's marmoset may be restricted to certain types of vegetation in which its peculiar style of locomotion gives it an advantage.

Tamarins. We come now to two members of the genus *Saguinus*, the species of which are known as tamarins to distinguish them from the members of *Callithrix* which are the true marmosets. The emperor tamarin is the larger of the species (Fig. 16.2), the adults weighing 500 − 550 g. With a grey body, orange rump and tail, black mask and long snow white mandarin moustaches, it is unquestionably one of the most exotic and colourful of all monkeys. Its smaller relative, the saddle-backed tamarin, is comparatively drab, being basically black with a dark red lower back and rump. A white muzzle provides the only relief in the otherwise sombre pattern.

The two tamarins are extremely similar in their ecology and will be discussed together. In fact it would not be convenient to do otherwise, for they have the remarkable custom of living together in permanent mixed associations. Most of the social units at Cocha Cashu consist of alliances composed of an extended family group of each species. Allied groups cohabit jointly held territories which are defended in concert against neighbouring mixed groups of similar composition. Such behaviour, which may be termed co-territoriality, has only recently been discovered in birds (Munn and Terborgh, 1980), and has not previously been recorded for primates. The adaptive basis for co-territoriality in tamarins is poorly understood at the present time.

The territories of tamarins at Cocha Cashu are comparatively enormous for such small animals. The combined weight of a mixed group is around 4 kg, only 25% more than the weight of a titi or night monkey group. Yet each of the several territories we have mapped contains at least 30 ha, and one was

Fig. 16.2. Emperor tamarin (*Saguinus imperator*) in Manu National Park, Peru (photo by Charles Janson).

found to have the astonishing area of 120 ha. The biomass of tamarins per unit area is thus much lower than that of the other species discussed so far, except for the rare monk saki and Goeldi's marmosets. Why the tamarins should maintain so low a biomass presents an interesting question that will be addressed at a later point.

One generalisation that can be made about the tamarin territories at Cocha Cashu, whether large or small, is that they contain a mosaic of vegetation types. The various types are: early and late successional forest, mature high forest, swamps, canebrakes, bamboo thickets, and flood disturbed areas near the river. No single territory would contain more than a few of these, but all seem to contain at least two. This apparent requirement for habitat heterogeneity may help to explain the large size of tamarin territories, and could also explain the total absence of tamarins from large homogeneous expanses of mature forest.

Tamarins display a penchant for concentrating on one major plant resource at a time, regardless of how many species may be in fruit within their territories. The troop that occupies the central part of our study area, for example, uses just six major resource species over the course of a year. Except during transition periods, 60 to 90% of feeding time is devoted to one of these resource species. When one considers the eclectic taste of most monkeys, this is seen as a most exceptional behaviour. It has nevertheless proven true of each of the several tamarin troops we have observed.

The main ecological distinction between the two tamarin species is based on contrasting locomotor patterns, and is manifested principally in their hunting techniques. The emperor tamarin, while capable of vertical movement up and down trunks, primarily travels along horizontal supports, either vines or branches. Its associate, the saddle-backed tamarin, frequently uses cling-and-leap locomotion, and is entirely at home on vertical surfaces, even resting on them at times. Nearly all of its hunting is carried out on vertical trunks, inclined limbs or hanging liane stems. The preferred substrates in these situations are bark crevices, flutings, junctures between vines and trunks, knotholes and tree cavities. Over 61% of all substrates searched were broadly classified as knotholes, while leaves accounted for only 9%. Knotholes were an exceedingly minor element (1 − 3%) in the foraging repertoires of other monkeys. Thus, by virtue of its great agility on vertical surfaces, the saddle-backed tamarin has a foraging niche all to itself. It is an exceptionally productive one as well, for the saddle-back catches a higher proportion of large prey (more than 1 cm in length: 42% vs 1% for the brown capuchin) and spends less time hunting (16%) than any other omnivore in the community.

The emperor tamarin hunts in an entirely different fashion. The groups select dense leafy areas in the understorey, particularly vine tangles. As they begin foraging, the individuals scatter along a loose front, moving slowly and quietly, pausing to scan intently at the leaf surfaces around them. (Leaves accounted for 88% of searches.) Captures are often made in sudden lunging strikes, suggesting highly mobile prey. In spite of the obvious differences in their hunting techniques, 60% of the identifiable catch of both tamarins consists of orthoptera. There is little potential for overlap in the species of orthoptera captured, however, since the saddleback mainly takes brown ones from tree cavities while the emperor takes green ones from leaves. The tamarins thus achieve their ecological distinction through differentiation of their hunting techniques as a concomitant of differing locomotor skills. For reasons that are still unclear, this permits them to live within shared territories on a common pool of plant resources.

In concluding the discussion of the two tamarins, it is interesting to note that their situation is almost diametrically opposite from that of the two capuchins. In the latter species, ecological separation entailed the differential use of plant resources resulting in part from distinct patterns of ranging behaviour. The differences in their hunting techniques on the other hand, were comparatively minor. In the case of the tamarins, the use of plant resources is virtually identical and it is the differences in their hunting behaviours that distinguish their ecological roles.

The final species in our roster is also the smallest, the pigmy marmoset. At a body weight of about 100 g, it is roughly the size of a hamster, and by all odds the smallest monkey in the world. In many ways, its behaviour is as extreme as its size.

Pygmy marmoset. A rare species at Cocha Cashu, it is restricted to the immediate vicinity of edges, generally along the exposed riverbank. In 10 years of field studies we have discovered the locations of only three groups. Though the animals themselves are extremely inconspicuous, their major activity, extracting sap from the trunks of certain trees, leaves obvious telltale signs. Thus it is unlikely that additional groups have gone undetected.

Knowledge of the species' ecology at Cocha Cashu is available from unpublished observations of Mariella Leo and Charles Janson. A study by Ramirez *et al.* (1977) at Iquitos in northern Peru provides some interesting contrasts.

The pygmy marmoset is most remarkable for its extreme dietary specialisation. Nearly all of its carbohydrate intake is in the form of sap which the animals actively mine from trunks by biting out shallow pits, one to two centimeters in diameter. The phloem vessels that supply the sap rather quickly become plugged, so new pits must be added every day. One *Inga mathewsiana* (Leguminosae) tree that had about 300 pits in December, 1976 had over 2,000 by June 1977 (Charles Janson, unpubl. obs.). To open and harvest the pits the animals clamber actively around on the trunks of their sap trees, often quite low to the ground. They move up or down with equal facility and often rest in the vertical position. When moving between trees, they generally do not use cling-and-leap locomotion, perhaps because they are too small. Instead, they dash quickly along horizontal branches and vinestems.

Harvesting sap from a fixed set of sources is inherently a sedentary occupation, and pygmy marmosets are consequently the most sedentary of all monkeys. The groups occupy tiny territories of less than 0.1 ha within which they tend from one to several sap trees (Castro and Soini, 1977; Ramirez *et al.*, 1977). The group observed at Cocha Cashu lived almost entirely in five neighbouring trees, three of which were exploited for sap. A fourth served as the night roost.

If a mere 0.1 ha can provide the resources for a family of these tiny monkeys, one inevitably wonders why the species is not incredibly abundant. There is obviously more to their needs than meets the eye. One eventuality faced by every group is that its sap trees will give out, if only because they become so covered by pits that there is no room to open more. The group observed most closely by us was discovered in November 1976, at which time it had only begun to exploit the set of trees it was using. It was still in the same location 9 months later in August 1977, but by July 1978, when we again returned to the field station, it had moved to a new location 200 m up the riverbank. It was still at the new site a year later in July 1979, but soon thereafter disappeared, presumably in another move to a spot we never discovered. Moves thus appear to occur at roughly yearly intervals in our area. A group must therefore have more space available to it than the 0.1 ha it actively exploits if it is to prosper over the long run.

A second non-obvious need for space by pygmy marmosets can develop in the dry season. Normally, if one uses a jacknife to excavate an artificial pit in an actively exploited sap tree, the pit will produce a copious flow of exudate for the next day or two. If, however, the experiment is repeated during a drought, the resulting sap flow can be too small to measure. Moreover, there may be no visible exudate in any of the hundreds of pits on the tree. We found that the marmosets vacate their territories at such times and travel up to 200 m to visit nectar sources, particularly *Combretum* vines.

The spatial needs of pygmy marmoset groups thus extended considerably beyond the limits of the tiny cluster of trees they use for sap. The additional spatial requirement may be especially large in southeastern Peru where prolonged periods of drought are a regular feature of the seasonal climate. Pygmy marmosets are considerably more common at Iquitos (lat. 4°S) than in the Manu region, perhaps because in the more equitable climate sap can be relied upon as a year-round resource (Ramirez *et al.*, 1977). If so, the groups would not be required to include emergency nectar sources within their territories and the average territory could then be smaller.

In concluding it should be mentioned that pygmy marmosets catch insects by slow stalking and pouncing, but there is no quantitative data to suggest how important animal matter is in their diet. We have no observations of fruit eating, and none are mentioned in the references cited above. In their near total specialisation on sap, pygmy marmosets enjoy a unique position in the Manu primate community, in which competition with other species is almost completely avoided except during the critical dry season.

16.3. CONCLUSIONS: THE ECOLOGICAL SIGNIFICANCE OF BODY SIZE

The recurrent theme in this chapter has been that an animal's body size influences its ecology in many important ways. This has been illustrated in a review of ecological relationships among the 13 sympatric primate species that inhabit the Manu National Park in southeastern Peru. The assemblage is the most diverse yet recorded for a New World locality, and includes 11 out of the 13 genera of monkeys that occur in the Amazonian rainforest.

The ecological correlates of body size include restraints on diet, resource concentration, prey search and capture techniques, vertical position in the forest, habitat use and locomotory patterns. The functional relationships between these ecological parameters and body size are most clearly discerned by sub-dividing the community into size classes and then comparing the species both within and between the classes.

Three canopy-dwelling vegetarians, the spider, woolly and howler monkeys, lie at the large end of the size scale (6 – 10 kg adult weight) and comprise the first class. These are restricted to the crowns of medium and large trees by their weight, which would not be supported by the slender saplings, vines and shrubs of the understorey. The requirement for stout supports at the same time restricts these species to relatively mature habitats. All three species are vegetarians, apparently because arboreal animals of such large size cannot catch small prey fast enough to meet their protein requirements. As vegetarians, their principal mode of ecological separation seems to relate to how protein is obtained. Spider monkeys, which are almost entirely frugivorous, consume a wide variety of fruit species. Some of these fruits, though it is not yet known which, provide much of their protein. Woolly monkeys are very poorly known in the wild, and little can be said about their diet in detail except that they appear to consume greater quantities of leaves than spider monkeys. Both spider and woolly monkeys range over areas of two to several square kilometres to exploit large, ephemeral concentrations of fruit. Howler monkeys diverge from this pattern in living within relatively small home ranges of ca. 25 ha and in consuming large quantities of (usually) young leaves. Leaves are thought to supply most of their protein requirement. By feeding on two abundant resources (leaves and fruit) instead of one (fruit), howlers are able to attain high biomass densities and to live in compact home ranges.

Of the ten smaller (less than 5 kg) primates in the Manu community, eight are omnivores, obtaining their protein requirements by consuming small prey rather than leaves or high protein fruit species. It is no coincidence that all the omnivores are small, because the major limitation in harvesting small prey is time. Interspecific comparisons of capture rates and the sizes of prey caught indicate that yields do not increase with the body size of the monkey. On the contrary, there is a surprising inverse relationship between body size and the average size of prey captured. The frequency of captures also declines with increasing body size, as 3 kg capuchins obtain prey only half as often as 800 g squirrel monkeys. The trend implies that it may not be worthwhile for species larger than capuchins to hunt for prey, but for smaller species hunting offers a reliable means of obtaining protein.

The brown and white-fronted capuchins comprise the second (medium) size class (2.5 kg). For most of the year the ecology of the two species is virtually identical: they eat the same fruits and forage for prey in ways that differ only in minor quantitative detail. Only in the dry season when fruit resources become relatively scarce do important differences develop. The brown capuchin then substitutes palm nuts (*Astrocaryum, Scheelea*) for most of the fruit that it normally prefers. Since palm nuts are abundant, this shift in diet is accomplished with only minor adjustments in the ranging pattern. The white-fronted capuchin opens palm nuts with the greatest difficulty and thus cannot take full advantage of the resource. Instead, the groups are obliged to travel large distances to exploit rare fruiting figs that provide the only major source of soft fruit in that season. There are thus two features that distinguish the ecology of the capuchins, a morphological one (jaw strength) that enables the brown capuchin to feed efficiently on palm nuts, and a behavioural one (large home range) that provides the white-fronted capuchin with a greater access to fig fruit.

The four small species (0.8 – 1.5 kg) are surprisingly diverse in their adaptations. Each appears to show more ecological overlap with species in other size classes than with any of those in the same class. One, the saki monkey, is a vegetarian that includes a high proportion of (usually immature) seeds in its diet; another, the squirrel monkey is a seminomadic fig specialist that can survive for brief periods as a facultative insectivore; the night monkey feeds on many of the same fruits as capuchins, but is nocturnal and territorial, and the titi monkey has a diet of fruit and leaves like the howler, but lives exclusively in edge environments where the vines it prefers for cover and food grow in profusion.

Three interrelated, size-dependent adaptations appear in this set of small monkeys that are not found in any of the larger species: specialised use of small and/or diffuse resources, territoriality and use of spatially restricted habitats. Exploitation of small, diffuse resources is often the critical condition that leads to territoriality and habitat specialisation. Small resources are here defined as foods that characteristically come in small quantities. Examples are: the fruit crops of small trees or vines, fruit crops that ripen bit by bit over prolonged periods, nectar, sap, insects, vine shoots, etc. Animals that are of large size, or that live in large groups cannot habitually exploit such resources because the amount of food available at any one stop is insignificant in relation to the metabolic demand of the individual or group. Resources of this kind are therefore the special province of small animals, especially ones that live in small social units. Seven out of the eight small or very small monkeys in the community are presumed to depend on such resources. The one exception is the squirrel monkey which lives in large social aggregations of 30 or 40 individuals and exploits resources of the very largest size — -the synchronously ripening crops of huge fig trees.

The habitual use of small resources often leads to territoriality, and six or seven of the eight small/very small primates at Manu are territorial, while none of the larger ones is (the exact number of territorial species is uncertain because the ranging habits of the saki monkey have not been studied). A strong correlation between use of small resources and territorial behaviour exists because such resources tend to have a strong continuity in time and/or space, thus justifying the defense of a delimited area. The fruit crops of common small trees, provide continuity in space, and the slow ripening of certain crops provides continuity in time. A few resources, such as the sap trees exploited by the pygmy marmoset display continuity in both space and time. Without exception, the territorial monkeys at Manu depend on such resources, particularly during the dry season when large fruit crops are widely scattered.

Habitat specialisation is another trait that is prevalent among the small and very small monkeys (6 out of 8 species), but not found among the larger ones. Small body size is a permissive condition for habitat selectivity. Spatially restricted habitats such as early successional patches, swamps, river margins, etc., with rare exceptions, do not supply resources in large enough quantities consistently throughout the year to support animals with large metabolic demands. Thus, small discrete patches of habitat can only be occupied by small animals. Even though this is inescapably true, it does not explain why so many of the small monkeys are absent from large tracts of mature high ground forest. The reason may again relate to resource size. Mature forest is dominated by large trees which capture most of the sunlight, and which therefore account for most of the primary productivity. Small trees, except those growing in gaps, are shaded and have insufficient energy budgets to produce good fruit crops. The larger monkeys exploit the resources of large trees, and since in general they can digest fruit at an earlier stage of ripening than small monkeys, they are better competitors. To obtain resources that are not sought by the larger species, the small monkeys may be forced into more open early successional habitats where small fruit crops abound. Patchy habitats and early successional vegetation may thus offer a refuge from the competition of large species. Such habitats may also provide havens from predation, in that dense viney cover affords far better protection from raptors than the high exposed crowns of the mature forest canopy.

The generalisations that have been drawn so far about small monkeys apply to all four of the species in the very small category (0.1 − 0.75 kg). They all depend on small resources that provide continuity of food supply in time and space, they are all territorial, and all are absent from unbroken tracts of mature high forest. The feature that most outstandingly differentiates the Callitrichids from all other New World monkeys is their capacity to climb with facility on vertical trunks and to engage in cling-and-leap locomotion. In the Goeldi's marmoset this is reflected in its ability to move rapidly from stem to stem through the dense understorey of its swamp forest habitat. The saddle-backed tamarin takes advantage of its agility on trunks to forage for prey in crevices, knotholes and tree cavities, sites that are virtually inaccessible to the other species of the community. The pygmy marmoset, while only rarely engaging in cling-and-leap progression, nevertheless spends much of its time on vertical bark surfaces, making and visiting the pits from which it harvests its specialised diet of sap. Of the 4 species only the emperor tamarin avoids frequent use of vertical perches, although it is fully capable of running up and down open trunks to gain access to high crowns. Its forte is hunting orthopterans and lepidopteran larvae in leafy branch tips and vine tangles where its small size and good balance, aided by a long tail, enable it to stalk prey on supports too supple and slender to sustain the weight of a larger animal. The distinctive ecological speciality of each of the Callitrichids in the community is thus made possible through a special ability in locomotion that provides access to a microenvironment that is not exploited by any other monkey. In this sense, the Callitrichids fit into the cracks of an ecological edifice that is structured by the larger species.

There are thus many ways in which differences in body size help to differentiate the ecological roles of New World primate species. Although we have been able to examine detailed results from just one locality, the main conclusions are of a general nature and can be expected to apply quite widely in Amazonia and elsewhere in the Neotropics. Many interesting questions nevertheless remain to be studied, such as, how do primate communities respond and adjust to different types of forest or selective modification of their habitat, why are some species mysteriously absent from regions that are well within the limits of their geographical ranges, and what factors determine the northern and southern latitudinal limits of each genus. At a more elementary level there remain genera for which field data are extremely scanty, such as *Pithecia*, *Chiropotes*, *Cacajao*, *Callithrix* and *Callimico*, as well as numerous unstudied species in the genera discussed in this report. Our understanding of the community ecology of New World primates is thus still very much in its infancy, and it is to be hoped that as additional parks and reserves are created more investigators will take advantage of them to expand our collective knowledge of these most interesting animals.

REFERENCES

Castro, R. and Soini, P. (1977) Field studies on *Saguinus mystax* and other callitrichids in Amazonian Peru. In *The Biology and Conservation of the Callitrichidae*. Ed. D. Kleiman. Smithsonian Institution Press, Washington, D.C.

Freese, C. H., Heltne, P. G., Castro, N. R. and Whitesides, G. (1982) Patterns and determinants of monkey densities in Peru and Bolivia, with notes on distributions. *Internat. J. Primatol.* 3, 53 – 90.

Gautier-Hion, A., Emmons, E. H. and Dubost, G. (1980) A comparison of the diets of three major groups of primary consumers of Gabon (primates, squirrels and ruminants). *Oecologia* 45, 182 – 189.

Hershkovitz, P. (1977) *Living New World Monkeys* (Platyrrhini). Vol. 1. University of Chicago Press, Chicago.

Hladik, A. and Hladik, C. M. (1969) Rapports trophiques entre vegetation et primates dans le foret de Barro Colorado (Panama). *La Terre et la Vie* 1, 25 – 117.

Hladik, C. M., Hladik, A., Bousset, J., Valdebouze, P., Viroben, G. and Delort-Laval, J. (1971) Le regime alimentaire des primates de l'ile de Barro Colorado (Panama). *Folia Primatologica* 16, 85 – 122.

Izawa, K. (1975) Foods and feeding behavior of monkeys in the upper Amazon basin. *Primates* 16, 295 – 316.

Izawa, K. (1978) A field study of the ecology and behavior of the black-mantle tamarin (*Saguinus nigricollis*). *Primates* 19, 241 – 274.

Izawa, K. and Yoneda, M. (1981) Habitat utilization of nonhuman primates in a forest of the Western Pando, Bolivia. Kyoto Univ. *Overseas Reports of New World Monkeys* (1981), Primate Research Inst., Kyoto Univ., pages 13 – 22.

Kinzey, W. G. (1974) Ceboid models for the evolution of hominoid dentition. *J. Human Evolution* 3, 193 – 203.

Kinzey, W. G. (1980) Distribution of some neotropical primates and the model of Pleistocene forest refugia. In *Biological Diversification in the Tropics*. Ed. G. T. Prance, Columbia University Press, New York.

Klein, L. L. and Klein, D. J. (1975) Social and ecological contrasts between four taxa of neotropical primates. In: *Sociobiology and Psychology of Primates*. Ed. R. Tuttle, pp. 59 – 85. World Anthropology, Mouton, The Hague.

Klein, L. L. and Klein, D. B. (1977) Feeding behavior of the Colombian spider monkey. In *Primate Ecology: Studies of Feeding and Ranging Behaviour in Lemurs, Monkeys and Apes*. Ed. T. H. Clutton-Brock. Academic Press, London.

Masataka, N. (1981a) A field study of the social behavior of Goeldi's monkeys (*Callimico goeldii*) in North Bolivia. I. Group composition, breeding cycle, and infant development. Kyoto Univ. *Overseas Reports of New World Monkeys* (1981), Primate Research Inst., Kyoto Univ., pages 23 – 32.

Masataka, N. (1981b) A field study of the social behavior of Goeldi's monkeys (*Callimico goeldii*) in North Bolivia. II. Grouping pattern and intragroup relationship. Kyoto Univ. *Overseas Reports of New World Monkeys* (1981), Primate Research Inst., Kyoto Univ., pages 33 – 41.

Milton, K. (1978) Behavioral adaptations to leaf-eating in the mantled howler monkey. In *The Ecology of Arboreal Folivores*. Ed. G. G. Montgomery, pp. 535 – 549. Smithsonian Institution Press, Washington, D.C.

Milton, K. (1980) *The Foraging Strategy of Howler Monkeys: a Study in Primate Economics*. Columbia Univ. Press, New York.

Milton, K. (1981) Food choice and digestive strategies of two sympatric primate species. *Amer. Natur.* 117, 496 – 505.

Mittermeier, R. A. and Coimbra-Filho, A. F. (1981) Systematics: species and subspecies. In *Ecology and Behavior of Neotropical Primates*. Eds. A. F. Coimbra-Filho and R. A. Mittermeier, pp. 29 – 109. Acad. Brasil. de Cien., Rio de Janeiro.

Mittermeier, R. A. and van Roosmalen, M. G. M. (1981) Preliminary observations on habitat utilization and diet in eight Surinam monkeys. *Folia Primatol.* 36, 1 – 39.

Munn, C. A. and Terborgh, J. (1980) Multi-species territoriality in Neotropical foraging flocks. *Condor* 81, 338 – 347.

Napier, J. R. and Napier, P. H. (1967) *A Handbook of Living Primates*. Academic Press, New York.

Pook, A. G. and Pook, G. (1981) A field study of the socio-ecology of the Goeldi's monkey (*Callimico goeldii*) in northern Bolivia. *Folia Primatol.* 35, 288 – 312.

Ramirez, M. (1980) Grouping patterns of the woolly monkey, *Lagothrix lagotricha*, at the Manu National Park, Peru. *Amer. J. Phys. Anthro.* 52, 269.

Ramirez, M. F., Freese, C. H. and Revilla, C. J. (1977) Feeding ecology of the pygmy marmoset, *Cebuella pygmaea*, in Northeastern Peru. In *The Biology and Conservation of the Callitrichidae*. Ed. D. Kleiman. Smithsonian Institution Press, Washington, D.C.

Rudran, R. (1979) The demography and social mobility of a red howler (*Alouatta seniculus*) population in Venezuela. In *Vertebrate Ecology in the Northern Neotropics*. Ed. J. F. Eisenberg, Smithsonian Institution Press, Washington, D.C.

Snow, D. W. (1981) Tropical frugivorous birds and their food plants: a world survey. *Biotropica* 13, 1 – 14.

Struhsaker, T. T. and Leland, L. (1977) Palm-nut smashing by *Cebus a. apella* in Colombia. *Biotropica* 9, 124 – 126.

Terborgh, J. (1983) *Five New World Primates: a Study in Comparative Ecology*. Princeton University Press, Princeton, N.J.

Wrangham, R. W. (1977) Feeding behavior of chimpanzees in Gombe National Park, Tanzania. In *Primate Ecology: Studies of Feeding and Ranging Behavior in Lemurs, Monkeys and Apes*. Ed. T. H. Clutton-Brock, pp. 503 – 538. Academic Press, London.

Walker, E. P. (1975) *Mammals of the World*. 3rd ed. Johns Hopkins University Press, Baltimore.

PART III

The Human Impact

CHAPTER 17

Aboriginal Adaptation to Amazonia

BETTY J. MEGGERS

Smithsonian Institution, Washington, D.C., U.S.A.

CONTENTS

17.1. INTRODUCTION

No species exploits or is affected equally by all aspects of its environment and humans are no exception. Differences in the kinds and abundances of local resources were less important for aboriginal groups than the infertile soil, high humidity, and warm temperature that limit the extent to which the ecosystem can be remade. Although the indigenous population did not achieve the degree of domination associated with the level of civilisation attained in the Andean region, their successful exploitation of an environment that has defied the expertise of Euroamerican technology is an equally remarkable accomplishment. The more we learn about the complexity of the Amazonian ecosystem, the better we can understand the function of cultural practices, including some that seem exotic or even cruel.

17.2. PREHISTORY

The effort to reconstruct Amazonian prehistory is frustrated by several kinds of obstacles. The paucity of stone suitable for manufacturing tools eliminates a major component of remains left by hunter-gatherers in other parts of the hemisphere. Wood, bone, tusk, and tortoise shell were common raw materials, all of them ephemeral in the climate of the tropical lowlands (Fig. 17.1). Plant and animal remains that provide clues to diet are similarly fugitive. Burials, when they can be found, seldom preserve skeletal parts that permit identifying age or sex. Consequently, the archaeological record is nearly blank prior to the introduction of pottery.

Although the presence of pottery identifies places once used for habitation or burial, encountering them is often difficult. Many sites along rivers and streams have been destroyed by erosion or concealed beneath sediment (Fig. 17.2). Remains in the forest are obscured by vegetation (Fig. 17.3). Accumulation of refuse is seldom sufficient to increase the elevation or change the colour of the soil to aid in detection. As a consequence, archaeologists depend heavily on the memories of local inhabitants, who encounter fragments of pottery when clearing land for agriculture, digging foundations for houses, and wandering through the forest in search of game.

To supplement the meagre direct evidence, archaeologists draw on various other sources of information. Data from the surrounding area, where conditions for preservation are better, provide a context for assessing certain kinds of interpretations. Surviving tropical forest groups whose indigenous ways of life remain intact suggest the kinds of subsistence, social, and settlement patterns potentially reflected in the locations, dimensions, thicknesses, and compositions of prehistoric habitation sites. Although languages leave no physical imprint on the landscape, their geographical distributions can reveal prehistoric migrations, whose routes and dates can be compared with those inferred from archaeological evidence. Another important category of information is the character of the natural sources relevant to human existence, including raw materials, wild plants and animals, soils, and climate. Although large tracts remain unexplored, these kinds of data are beginning to provide a general picture of the steps leading to the extraordinary adaptation that had been achieved by the time of European contact at the beginning of the sixteenth century.

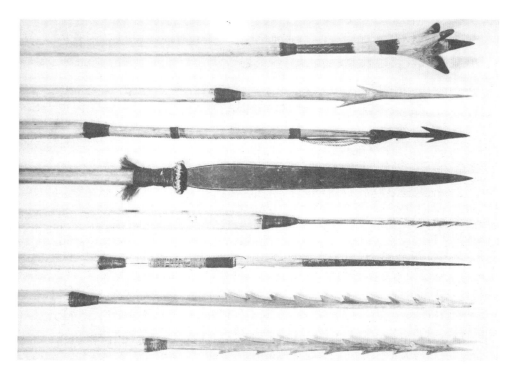

Fig. 17.1. Arrows with wooden heads of various shapes, each used for a particular category of game. The hard wood makes excellent projectiles, but leaves no trace in the archaeological record.

Fig. 17.2. Collecting fragments of pottery from the bed of a stream, where they were deposited during erosion of the adjacent bank, where an archaeological habitation site once existed.

Fig. 17.3. A prehistoric cemetery in a secluded part of the island of Caviana. The large burial urns were set on the surface of the ground, but have been broken and overgrown by roots, vines, and other vegetation.

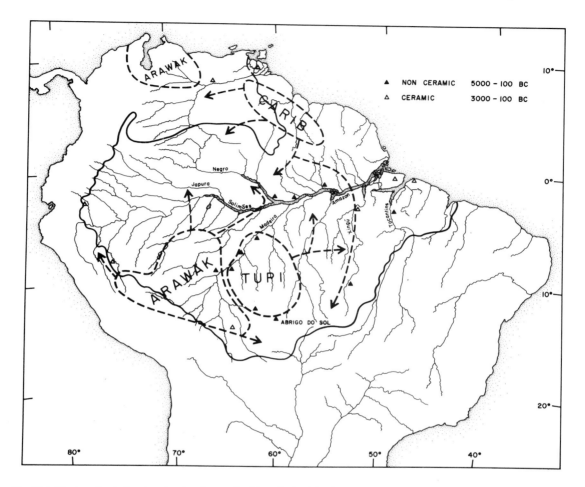

Fig. 17.4. Northern South America, showing the postulated homelands of the three major linguistic stocks, Carib, Arawak, and Tupí. The extent of the rainforest is indicated by the solid line. Dashed lines represent linguistic dispersals prior to the Christian era. Archaeological sites that have produced carbon-14 dates prior to the Christian era tend to correlate with these early centres and dispersals, suggesting they may represent camps of preceramic hunter-gatherers. Sites with pottery that date prior to the Christian era are confined to the margins of Amazonia.

17.2.1. Archaeological evidence

The antiquity of man's arrival in South America is still uncertain. Sites on the northern and western margins of the continent have produced carbon-14 dates between about 23,000 and 20,000 years before present, but their association with human activity is disputed. By 10,000 B.C., however, hunter-gatherers were living in the open environments east of Amazonia and had penetrated to the southern extreme of the continent. While no direct evidence is available from the central lowlands, Abrigo do Sol, a rockshelter in the south has produced a long series of dates indicating it was used from about 10,500 B.C. up to the present time (Fig. 17.4). Dates between 5400 and 3200 B.C. have been obtained from the base of refuse left by pottery-making groups on the middle Madeira, suggesting these locations were used by earlier people whose cultural inventory was completely perishable. The only other sites for

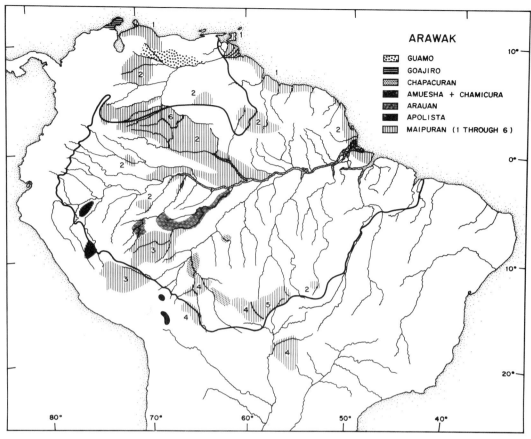

Fig. 17.5. The distribution of speakers of languages belonging to the Arawak stock suggests that strong ecological barriers restricted dispersal beyond the margins of the rainforest on the east and south. To the north, by contrast, speakers of several families settled along the Venezuelan coast and moved on to the Antilles. (After Migliazza, 1982, Fig. 27.6).

Fig. 17.6. A Waiwai communal house under construction. The high roof, dense thatch, and limitation of openings to two doors keep the temperature inside comfortable during the heat of the day and limit the level of illumination, discouraging entry of mosquitoes and flies.

Fig. 17.7. Waiwai villages consist of a single communal house inhabited by several related families. There are no partitions and each married couple is assigned space along the wall for hanging hammocks and storing possessions. A small fire is kept burning during the night to offset the chill. Waiwai custom dictates that the wife's hammock hangs beneath her husband's, where she can tend the fire. Arrows, baskets, and other articles are kept on platforms along the wall or inserted into the pole framework.

which similar antiquity has been established are shell middens on the Atlantic coast just east of the mouth of the Amazon. Dates prior to the Christian era from the lower Amazon, lower Tocantins, and upper Xingú may also be attributable to preceramic inhabitants.

17.2.2. Linguistic evidence

Language distributions also imply the existence of preceramic immigrants. Genetic relationships among languages can be reconstructed providing not only a relative chronology of diversification, but an absolute time scale. Criteria have also been established for inferring the 'homeland' or centre of emergence of a stock. Recent application of these procedures to the major families of Amazonia leads to identification of the Guianas as the homeland of Carib, the region east of the upper Madeira and Guaporé as the homeland of Tupí, and two widely separated homelands for Arawak, one on the Caribbean coast and the other west of the Tupí homeland (Fig. 17.5; Migliazza, 1982). These 'proto' stocks crystallised between about 3000 and 2500 B.C. and began to differentiate into families. Between

Fig. 17.8. Pottery characteristic of the Polychrome Tradition, which expanded along the várzea after the beginning of the Christian era. The technological excellence contrasts with the products of terra firme groups, such as the Waiwai (see Fig. 17.16), and implies manufacture by specialists. a. Incision on a white-slipped surface; the broader lines have been coloured red.

about 500 B.C. and the Christian era, widespread dispersals throughout the lowlands intermingled speakers of languages of these three affiliations with speakers of other languages. The distribution of Arawak speakers at the time of first reporting illustrates the magnitude of the distances travelled (Fig. 17.5).

The antiquity estimated for these origins and dispersals places them prior to the adoption of pottery over most of the lowlands, hampering archaeological confirmation. It is interesting to note, however, that sites on the upper Madeira and Guaporé that have produced the earliest carbon-14 dates fall within the region inferred to have been the homeland of Tupí (Fig. 17.5). Other sites dating prior to the Christian era are also in locations compatible with dispersals estimated to have occurred during the last millennium B.C.

17.2.3. Ceramic evidence

The earliest known pottery comes from the island of Marajó in the mouth of the Amazon. Here, globular bowls and jars occasionally decorated with patterns composed of broad incisions, either used alone or for defining zones filled with fine crosshachure, began to be made about 1500 B.C. The

Fig. 17.8. *cont.* b. Incision and excision executed on a red-slipped surface; the interior has painted decoration.

habitation sites are small, suggesting they correspond to a single communal house of the kind constructed by many surviving Indians (Fig. 17.6). Similarities in technique of decoration affiliate this pottery with complexes in Colombia and Ecuador but traces of its presence in the intervening area are rare. A few sherds with similar characteristics have been encountered on the middle Orinoco (Vargas, 1981; Roosevelt, 1980) and more closely related material was collected from a badly eroded site on the left bank of the lower Amazon (Hilbert, 1968). The long-distance migration implied by this distribution is consistent with the linguistic evidence for extreme displacements of people.

Around 1000 B.C., these initial colonists were assimilated by people who manufactured an equally simple but distinct kind of pottery, but their domination appears to have ended about a century later. There is no evidence for pottery-making groups on Marajó between about 900 B.C. and the Christian era, when the appearance of a third ceramic complex implies the arrival of new immigrants.

This hiatus equates with the period of major differentiation and initial dispersal of Arawak, Carib, and Tupí languages. People do not generally move long distances or abandon familiar territories without good reason, and there are indications that conditions were dryer during this interval than at present

Fig. 17.8. *cont.* c. Painting in red and black on a white-slipped surface.

Fig. 17.8. *cont.* d. Anthropomorphic vessel with painted decoration on the sides and back.

Fig. 17.8. *cont.* e. Painted decoration in red and black on a white slip and an elaborate treatment of the rim. a – c, Marajoara Phase, Marajó.
d – e, Napo Phase, eastern Ecuador.

(Prance, 1982). The devastating impact of drought on agricultural harvests is familiar and emigration is a typical response. The linguistic evidence that part of the population ranged to the farthest extremes of the lowlands may reflect search for more productive sources of food.

The paucity of archaeological sites prior to the Christian era contrasts with the situation thereafter. During the first two centuries A.D., a ceramic tradition characterised by painting, incision, and excision spread rapidly along the lower Amazon and up the Madeira (Fig. 17.8). Throughout most of this region, sites representing this Polychrome Tradition are the earliest reported, but distinct local complexes have been encountered near the mouth of the Trombetas and on the lower Xingú. Other kinds of pottery were also being made on the southern frontier of Amazonia and on the upper Solimões. Since pottery is generally associated with dependence on cultivated plants, this increase in the abundance and geographical distribution of sites may reflect a significant expansion in dependence on agriculture. Also, the termination of the arid interval may have created conditions more favourable for other kinds of human exploitation.

Fig. 17.9. Waiwai man burning a field cleared a few months earlier in primary forest.

Fig. 17.10. Waiwai man planting manioc between unburned stumps, trunks, and branches. A metal hoe has replaced the aboriginal digging
stick.

Fig. 17.11. The poison is removed from bitter manioc by grating the tubers and compressing the pulp in cylindrical stretchable baskets manufactured for this purpose. Two are suspended from the ridge of the lean-to. The tray at the left contains pulp that has been compacted during squeezing and is ready to be toasted; the buckets hold the poisonous juice.

Fig. 17.12. Waiwai woman toasting large circular wafers by spreading manioc flour on a hot griddle and compacting it. Pottery fragments from similar griddles in archaeological sites are indirect evidence for this method of preparing bitter manioc.

Fig. 17.13. Waiwai man carving stools. Metal tools have replaced the aboriginal implements of bone and tortoise shell. The finished stool is painted with black designs on a red background. Only men use stools; women sit on mats or on the ground.

Fig. 17.14. The Waiwai chief preparing fibres to be used in weaving baskets. Rectangular containers with patterns woven into their lids and feathers attached are used by men to hold cosmetics and small ornaments (14b).

Fig. 17.14. *cont.* Square flat trays usually have attractive woven designs (14c).

Fig. 17.15. Women's activities among the Waiwai include making manioc graters by inserting stone chips into boards carved by their husbands.

Whatever the cause, the numbers of archaeological sites continued to increase. By A.D. 1000, pottery-making groups were settled on the lower Tapajós, the lower and middle Negro, the Japurá, the upper Purus, and along the Solimões. By A.D. 1500, they predominated throughout the lowlands. In 1637, a Portuguese expedition that descended the Amazon reported 'the Indians so numberless that if a dart were to fall from the air, it would strike the head of an Indian and not fall on the ground' (Edmundson, 1920, 16). A century later, most of the floodplain population had vanished, the victim of slave raids, epidemics, and other detrimental by-products of European contact. Inhabitants of the vast tracts between major rivers were more fortunate and some have maintained their indigenous way of life little changed to the present time.

17.3. ECOLOGICAL BARRIERS AND HUMAN ADAPTATION

A strong correlation exists between the distributions of the principal language stocks and ceramic traditions and the region dominated by tropical rainforest. The spread of speakers of Arawak and Carib stopped at its eastern margin (Fig. 17.5; Migliazza, 1982) and prehistoric pottery-making groups living

Fig. 17.16. Waiwai woman preparing a coil of clay, which she will add to the vessel in front of her to increase the height of the wall. A carrying basket of the kind manufactured on the spot for transporting manioc tubers, firewood, and other heavy loads and discarded after use, lies beside her.

only a few kilometres apart maintained distinct Amazonian and Coastal ceramic traditions. Speakers of Tupí made the transition to the Atlantic coast, but did so in the south where environmental change was most gradual. Similarly little interchange took place on the southwest. To the north, where the ecological transition is more gradual, there is considerable linguistic and archaeological evidence for communication in both directions throughout the prehistoric period.

These patterns reflect the complexity of adaptation by human groups to the tropical forest environment. The heterogeneity of the vegetation is masked by uniformity in appearance, but survival depends on being able to distinguish plants potentially useful for food, tools, shelter, and other requirements, as well as those eaten by animals that were hunted. It was also important to know when fruits ripened and which were most prolific. Millennia of adaptation gave the indigenous population a remarkably intimate knowledge. For example, the Kuikuru of the upper Xingú can identify all trees, not only as adults but as seedlings or from dead leaves. They know the useful properties of bark, wood, leaves, fruits, seeds, saps, and resins; the animals that feed on each kind, and the quality of the soil in which each grows (Carneiro, 1978). The Tiriyó on the upper Paru de Oeste are familiar with the medicinal properties of at least 328 plants (Cavalcante and Frikel, 1973). Similarly extensive knowledge has been acquired of the fauna, whether aquatic, terrestrial, or arboreal.

Through processes not yet understood, this versatility led to the recognition that some plants could be made more reliable sources of food if they were propagated artificially. By the time of European contact, manioc (*Manihot esculenta*) was the staple crop throughout Amazonia and most groups grew several varieties. The Desana of eastern Colombia cultivate 40 (Kerr and Clement, 1980). Subtle morphological traits differentiate the deadly 'bitter' from the innocuous 'sweet' plants and their recognition is literally a matter of life or death. A diet based on manioc need not be monotonous. The Waiwai of Guiana, for example, prepare some 14 kinds of bread and 13 beverages in which it is the principal ingredient (Yde, 1965, 51). Multiple varieties of other tubers, such as sweet potatoes (*Ipomoea*

Fig. 17.17. Modern houses on the várzea of the lower Amazon at high water, when they are accessible only by canoe.

batatas) and yams (*Dioscorea* sp.), were commonly planted, as well as chili peppers, pineapples, papayas, peanuts, beans, maize, tobacco, medicines and hallucinogens.

The most significant aspect of the environment from the standpoint of cultural development is its subsistence potential. Where the supply of food can be concentrated and augmented, the size, density, and permanency of settlements can be increased. Where limits on productivity are set by environmental or technological factors, the population must stabilise at a level compatible with long-term exploitation. Using this criterion, two principal habitats can be distinguished in Amazonia. The terra firme, which comprises land above flood level or subject to inundation by blackwater and clearwater rivers, occupies about 98% of the area. Várzea, the term applied to floodplains of whitewater rivers, constitutes the remaining 2%. Distinct cultural configurations were associated with the terra firme and the várzea at the time of European contact.

17.4. CULTURAL ADAPTATION TO THE TERRA FIRME

Average population density on the terra firme has been estimated at about 0.2 persons per square kilometre (Denevan, 1976, 226). Villages consisting of one or more circular or oval multi-family houses had populations ranging from a dozen to several hundred. Social relations were based on kinship, which defined each individual's rights and obligations. The principal distinctions in status were based on age and sex. Puberty rites formalised passage from childhood to adult responsibility. Each village had a chief, but his influence depended on his knowledge and skill; he had neither power to command nor exemption from tasks assigned by tradition to men. Shamans, who performed cures, conducted ceremonies, and identified perpetrators of sorcery, were also part-time specialists.

Most tasks were allotted by sex. Hunting and clearing gardens were done by males, harvesting and preparing food by females (Figs. 17.9 – 17.12). Other activities were accomplished by either sex depending on the circumstances. When fishing was the major source of protein, it was a male responsibility; if it was supplementary, it was often done by females and children or by both sexes. Among crafts, the manufacture of bows and arrows, blowguns, clubs, paddles, stools, dugout canoes, and manioc grater boards was usually accomplished by men (Figs. 17.13, 17.14). Weaving baskets, hammocks, and cotton cloth were also usually assigned to males. Women always made pottery and generally spun cotton; they often completed the manioc graters by inserting the stone chips (Figs. 17.15, 17.16). Allocations were related to the proportions of time devoted by each sex to subsistence; where planting, weeding, harvesting, and preparing manioc were exclusively female activities, as among the Jívaro, all crafts except pottery making were assigned to males. Where men did most of the gardening, as among the Camayurá, non-subsistence tasks were more evenly distributed (Meggers, 1971, Table 3).

Strict adherence to sexual division of labour established the nuclear family as the minimal self-sufficient unit. Marriage consequently followed immediately after the puberty rites and loss of a spouse placed a man or woman at a serious disadvantage. The labour involved in processing bitter manioc made polygyny advantageous, and it was also favoured by the higher death rate among males in warfare.

Terra firme groups drew a large proportion of their food from cultivated plants. Although slash-and-burn or shifting cultivation appears sloppy and wasteful to temperate-zone observers, it is remarkably well suited to the infertile soils and hot, humid climate of Amazonia. Burning the felled trees removes leaves and small branches, providing a layer of ash that enhances the initial fertility of the soil. Decaying trunks protect the surface of the ground from erosion and contribute a continuous supply of nutrients to growing plants. Cultivars with differing requirements are interspersed, enhancing the recovery of nutrients and hampering the spread of insects and diseases. Rapid growth of both cultivars and seedlings of secondary vegetation minimises the length of exposure of the soil to sun and rain, both of which rapidly deplete fertility. Stumps left in place send up shoots that accelerate reforestation, as do the small size and wide spacing of clearings. During the first and second years, manioc cuttings are generally planted immediately after removal of mature tubers. In spite of these conservational measures, productivity drops by about half during the third year. To maintain a continuous food supply, a new field must be cleared annually. After abandonment, some 20 years or more are required for sufficient fertility to be restored to warrant reuse of a plot.

Manioc was the universal staple because of its high productivity and tolerance for poor soils and aridity. Another advantage is absence of seasonality; tubers can be removed as needed, eliminating problems of storage. Although manioc gives abundant and reliable yields of carbohydrates, and its nutritional value can be enhanced by methods of preparation such as fermentation, it is deficient in protein (Marinho and Arkcoll, 1981). This must be obtained from other plants or from game and fish. An immense variety of wild seeds, fruits, nuts, berries, sprouts, and roots are edible, and different kinds and amounts were consumed by most terra firme groups. Eggs, insects, and tortoises were usually eaten, but mammals, birds, and fish were the principal sources of meat. Their relative importance varied. At one extreme, the Sirionó of northeastern Bolivia considered all fauna edible except insects. At the other, the Camayurá of the upper Xingú avoided game in favour of fish. Most groups concentrated on a small proportion of the available resources and recent studies suggest that their choices optimised the return for effort invested (e.g. Hames and Vickers, 1982). The success with which the indigenous population assembled diets providing the essentials for good health is reflected in the absence of evidence for malnutrition, in contrast to its high incidence among modern rural inhabitants (Giugliano, Giugliano and Shrimpton, 1981).

The combination of declining productivity from hunting and exhaustion of suitable locations for fields within a convenient radius of the village made its relocation desirable after 5 to 7 years. Larger and more permanent settlements were maintained by some groups by separating into extended family bands during the dry season each year and subsisting on wild resources several days distant from the home base. Among cultural practices that offset any tendency to remain long enough in one place to inflict long-term damage on the environment was the requirement to abandon a village on the death of an adult resident.

Adaptive constraints appear to account for other kinds of behaviour, especially sorcery and warfare. Most Amazonian groups attribute the death of adults to sorcery, which must be avenged by killing the culprit. The significance of this concept for inhibiting increases in population size and concentration is evident from the manner in which its intensity fluctuates with changes in density. The larger the number of people with whom one comes into contact, the greater the risk of offending someone unintentionally. Even if the death rate remained constant, more people would die in a population of 60 than one of 20 adults, making the frequency appear higher. Two forms of response exist. One is retaliation with the purpose of eliminating the culprit or his or her entire village; the other is separating the population of the victims' village into two smaller settlements and thus reducing the size of the 'target'. The resulting declines in population concentration will normally be reflected in a decline in the perceived frequency of deaths and consequently in the intensity of sorcery and warfare. Raids were also undertaken to secure wives, to demonstrate prowess as a prerequisite for marriage, and to enhance prestige, but they were never for acquiring land and rarely involved acquisition of material goods. Indeed, the territory of the enemy was generally evacuated as speedily as possible to avoid retribution by unfriendly spirits.

17.5. CULTURAL ADAPTATION TO THE VÁRZEA

Along the Amazon floodplain or várzea, population density has been estimated at 14.6 persons per square kilometre (Denevan, 1976, 226). The riverbanks were lined with settlements, which were grouped into 'provinces' ruled by a chief who had the power to command and was obeyed 'with great submission' (Carvajal, 1934, 190). Although kinship governed many aspects of social relations, there was an incipient form of stratification. Chiefs, priests, and craftsmen were full-time specialists, exempted from labour in domestic and subsistence activities. Captives were not adopted, as among terra firme groups, but became slaves. Idols representing deities were kept in shrines, where they were entreated with offerings of food and wine, and sometimes with human sacrifices.

These features reflect the greater concentration of wild food resources and the potentiality for permanent cultivation on the várzea. The silt-laden water furnished nutrients to support an aquatic food-chain culminating in caimans, manatees, and tortoises, in addition to large and abundant fish. Sediments deposited during the annual rise and fall enriched the soil sufficiently for reliance on maize, although manioc also continued to be a staple food. Wild rice was harvested and made into wine; it and other aquatic grasses attracted large flocks of water birds, which constituted another abundant source of food.

Maximising these resources required careful management because of the regime of the river. Planting had to be timed so that crops matured before inundation. This was so skillfully executed that two harvests of maize were usually obtained. A variety of manioc that matured in 6 rather than 12 months was developed. Maize and manioc were stored or processed into beverages kept in large jars. Water turtles were kept alive in corrals, where they were available when needed. Turtle eggs were gathered by the thousands and processed into oil, which was used to preserve meat.

Subsistence activities had to be coordinated and completed prior to each inundation and provisions had to be sufficient to feed the population during about 3 months of high water. Although some supplies could be obtained during this period, the return for labour expended was low. Fish dispersed through flooded forest, where they were difficult to capture (Fig. 17.17). Resources of the terra firme offered only supplemental support for a large and concentrated population. Thus, when inundation occurred earlier than normal or continued longer, or the level was higher, the consequent loss of crops from fields on the várzea must have created severe hardship.

A number of cultural practices reported by early European explorers become intelligible as mechanisms for preventing growth of the population beyond the level sustainable during lean years. Infanticide was common, particularly for females (Meggers, 1971, 129). As among terra firme groups, adult deaths were attributed to sorcery and avenged by killing the culprit. Adultery by females was also punished by death. Warfare was chronic, particularly with neighbouring inland tribes.

A glimpse of the trial and error process that led to successful adaptation to the várzea is provided by the Marajoara Phase, a representative of the Polychrome Tradition that settled on Marajó about A.D. 400. Although the island lies in the mouth of the Amazon, it is inundated by local rainfall and does not receive a rejuvenating layer of sediment each year. The result is a combination of relatively rich aquatic resources and soils unsuitable for long-term cultivation. Archaeological evidence indicates that cultural complexity declined, culminating in a configuration similar to that characteristic of the terra firme (Meggers and Evans, 1957, 404).

Future archaeological investigations throughout Amazonia should produce other examples of unsuccessful as well as successful aboriginal adaptation, not only increasing our understanding of the prehistory of the region but creating a firmer foundation for assessing the options for intensified exploitation of its resources.

REFERENCES

Carneiro, R. L. (1978) The knowledge and use of rain forest trees by the Kuikuru Indians of central Brazil. In *The Nature and Status of Ethnobotany*. Ed. R. I. Ford, pp. 201–216. University of Michigan Anthropological Papers 67, Ann Arbor.

Carvajal, G. de (1934) *The Discovery of the Amazon, According to the Account of Friar Gaspar de Carvajal and Other Documents*. Compiled by J. T. Medina, ed. H. C. Heaton. Special Publications 17. American Geographical Society, New York.

Cavalcante, P. B. and Frikel, P. (1973) *A Farmacopéia Tiriyó*. Publicações Avulsas 24. Museu Paraense Emílio Goeldi, Belém.

Denevan, W. M. (1976) The aboriginal population of Amazonia. In *The Native Population of the Americas in 1492*. Ed. W. M. Denevan, pp. 205 – 233. University of Wisconsin Press, Madison.

Edmundson, G. (1920) The voyage of Pedro Teixeira on the Amazon from Pará to Quito and back, 1637 – 39. *Transactions of the Royal Historical Society*, 4th Series, Vol.3, pp. 52 – 71, London.

Giugliano, R., Giugliano, G. and Shrimpton, R. (1981) Estudos nutricionais das populações rurais da Amazônia. *Acta Amazônica* 11, 773 – 788.

Hames, R. B. and Vickers, W. T. (1982) Optimal diet breadth theory as a model to explain variability in Amazonian hunting. *American Ethnologist* 9, 358 – 378.

Hilbert, P. P. (1968) *Archäologische Untersuchungen am Mittleren Amazonas*. Marburger Studien zur Völkerkunde I. Dietrich Reimer, Berlin.

Kerr, W. E. and Clement, C. R. (1980) Práticas agrícolas de conseqüências genéticas que possibilitaram aos indios da Amazônia uma melhor adaptação às condições ecológicas da região. *Acta Amazônica* 10, 251 – 261.

Marinho, H. A. and Arkcoll, D. B. (1981) Estudos sobre o caroteno em algumas variedades amazônicas de mandioca (*Manihot esculenta* Crantz). *Acta Amazônica* 11, 71 – 75.

Meggers, B. J. (1971) *Amazonia; Man and Culture in a Counterfeit Paradise*. Aldine, Chicago.

Meggers, B. J. and Evans, C. (1957) *Archeological Investigations at the Mouth of the Amazon*. Bureau of American Ethnology Bulletin 167. Smithsonian Institution, Washington, D.C.

Migliazza, E. (1982) Linguistic prehistory and the refuge model in Amazonia. In *Biological Diversification in the Tropics*. Ed. G. T. Prance, pp. 497 – 519. Columbia University Press, New York.

Prance, G. T. (ed.) (1982) *Biological Diversification in the Tropics*. Columbia University Press, New York.

Roosevelt, A. C. (1980) *Parmana; Prehistoric Maize and Manioc Subsistence Along the Amazon and Orinoco*. Academic Press, New York.

Vargas Arenas, I. (1981) *Investigaciones Arqueológicas en Parmana*. Biblioteca de la Academia Nacional de la Historia 20, Caracas.

Yde, J. (1965) *Material Culture of the Waiwai*. Nationalmuseets Skrifter, Etnografisk, Roekke 10. Copenhagen.

CHAPTER 18

Amazonia, People and Today

THOMAS E. LOVEJOY

World Wildlife Fund-U.S., 1601 Connecticut Avenue, N.W., Washington, D.C. 20009, U.S.A.

CONTENTS

The relationship between people and the Amazonian environment is at a turning point. While not a situation beyond redress, care and intelligence must be exercised in large measure if major deleterious consequences — for Amazonia, Brazil, and the rest of the world — are to be avoided. Yet the Amazon is, at once, one of the most, if not the most, biologically important and promising places on Earth. Therein lies the great challenge of the Hylaea.

It is no secret that the Amazon is a focus of heightened interest socially, politically and, albeit frequently in error, economically. This is true for the eight nations and one French department having Amazonian or very similar vegetation within their domain. Peru envisions settlements in the high (altitude) forest. Ecuador permits colonisation in its oriente. But it was Brazil which signalled the beginning of a new era in the relationship between people and Amazonia, by the announcement of the TransAmazon highway and colonisation program. The capacity of modern technology and latter twentieth century governments to have an impact is orders of magnitude greater than ever before.

18.1. CLEARING SIZE

A major difference, and one with considerable, if not fully explored, implications, is the capacity to make much larger clearings than previously. Although historically, there have been a few exceptions, such as Mr. Ford's attempts to grow rubber on a large scale, the usual clearing consisted of what one person, perhaps aided by family, could do. Generally speaking, clearings were in the order of 1 or 2 ha. In such situations, a small amount of the ashes (nutrients) released by burning felled trees, goes into a crop (generally cassava). Most of the rest, while washed away by the rains, usually does not travel very far, and merely goes into the surrounding forest, to be taken up by the natural system.

When the clearing is abandoned by the agriculturalist, recovery starts with fast growing secondary succession plant species such as *Cecropia*. These light loving species usually have small seeds easily dispersed by wind or birds. Species of later stages of succession are shade tolerant; in many instances they may even require considerable shade for germination and growth. Many of these species have large seeds, often complete with a substantial nutrient store to get the sapling started under the low light and low nutrient conditions. These larger seeds do not disperse as widely, and are dependent on mammals to move them some distance. The distances involved in a clearing of a hectare or two are relatively easily accommodated by this system.

This slash and burn approach to agriculture in the Amazon forest appears to be a sustainable one on a long-term basis, even though the lifespan of a particular plot is very short. It is probably sustainable because such small clearings are not much larger than natural patches of second growth caused by windthrows. The natural recovery processes are in place and restore the ecosystem, building up over subsequent decades a nutrient store in the recovering vegetation, which then is available for a renewed period of agriculture.

Such a system can only work however, if there is a sufficient recovery period for any given location. This in turn implies a limit to population density for such a system to avoid degradation. Historical accounts of Amerindian population densities along the Amazon (Meggers, Chapter 17, this volume) would seem to indicate a relatively high population could be supported by this system. As those settlements were mostly along watercourses, the agriculture was able to depend on the more fertile alluvial soils (permitting in many instances a sustained if seasonal agriculture), and there was also a major protein supply available from the aquatic ecosystem (particularly fish and turtles). *Terra firme* slash and burn agriculture inevitably requires a lower population density.

That assumes of course that there are no additives to the agricultural system. There is in a sense no limit to the agricultural potential if fertiliser is applied *ad libidum*. Taking this to its logical extreme, the Amazon theoretically could be stripped of its forest and converted into a giant exercise in hydroponics, although this would not be without serious consequences. On a somewhat more realistic scale, the experimental work at Yurimaguas in Peru (Sanchez *et al.*, 1982) demonstrates the potential of a sustainable Amazonian agriculture, given no restraints on inputs. Social and economic realities, however, would suggest that such possibilities will be limited, and a prudent approach to development would seem best to avoid a heavy dependence of this sort. Further, heavy and forceful rainfall tends to shorten dramatically the residence time of agricultural chemicals, and hence to raise the expense.

There are certain to be, therefore, instances (perhaps even in the majority of cases) where fertiliser and pesticide additions will not be possible or highly limited. In such cases, the size of clearing may be of considerable importance. Certainly in the case of very large clearings, which in the case of some ranches range up to 100 km^2, recovery of the ecosystem and the vegetation will be retarded, almost to the point of no recovery, if only because of the limited dispersal capacities of some of the primary forest tree seeds. Although actual experience is so far lacking, or insufficiently studied, it is likely that large abandoned deforested areas will have very limited recovery: early successional plant species are likely to spring up uniformly across such areas, and succession is likely to halt at that stage, with further succession only minor and slow at the fringes.

This would indicate for conventional agriculture involving annual crops that clearing size should be very limited. This would at first appear contradictory to considerations arising from the need for at least some conservation areas to be large (millions of ha). The latter would seem to lead to concentrating forested areas into large blocks, and consequently concentrating agricultural areas likewise into large blocks. This does not, however, necessarily follow. It should be further noted that when clearing is followed by the planting of some form of tree cover, either for a cash crop (e.g. cacao) or for timber or pulp, these considerations change somewhat. In these instances the intent is to replace the forest with sustainable production, and recovery of the natural ecosystem is less of a concern. Nonetheless as any use of the land involves export of some product, and probably some nutrient in short supply, some additives may be necessary to maintain sustained production. It is no coincidence that the closer the land use is to the original vegetation, the more sustainable it is likely to be in the absence of additives.

Another factor which might impinge on ideal clearing size, has been raised by Stallard (pers. comm.), namely nutrients in aerosol flow from forest into cleared areas. This is no more than an hypothesis at this point. Aerosol flow has been neither measured nor its nutrient content analysed. Given the extremely tight nutrient cycling in these forests, and the resultant magnification of significance of what otherwise would seem minor flows (as in rainfall), it seems most important to investigate this possibility. If this is borne out, then it should be possible to identify a size below which there is significant nutrient flow into a clearing, and above which there would be rapidly diminishing returns for naturally sustainable agriculture.

18.2. FLOODPLAINS AND FISHERIES

As noted above, most of the settlement of Amazonia until very recently was concentrated along the watercourses which serve the region as a natural highway system. These várzea and igapó areas (Pires and Prance, Chapter 7, this volume) are a current focus of development interest by virtue of the annual replenishment of nutrients in the alluvium.

Nonetheless, the importance of these areas for the Amazon fishery dictates caution. That some of the fish feed on vegetable material has been known for some time. The recent detailed work of Goulding (1980; Chapter 14, this volume) has considerably amplified understanding and appreciation of this relationship whereby often the major component in the diet of a fish species is organic material (fruits, seeds, etc.) which falls into the water during high water times of year. Indeed this is commonplace knowledge among caboclos, and indigenous peoples such as the Tukano, the latter deliberately leaving forest at the water's edge to protect this relationship and thus the fishery (Chernela, pers. comm.).

Approximately 75% of the commercial fishes of Amazonia depend on this relationship. This is most remarkable biologically in that carnivory is the overwhelmingly dominant mode for fishes, and the Amazon fishes must have derived from carnivorous ones. An inkling of how the more elaborate adaptations, such as the molar-like crushing teeth (to attack palm nuts) of the tambaqui (*Colossoma macropomum*), came to be, can be seen in the switch by piranhas to a diet of rubber tree seeds at high water months of the year.

It is also important in providing a heightened yield from the Amazon fishery over that which the primary productivity of the Amazon waters would otherwise be able to support. Up to the present time, the fishery has been the single most important source of animal protein for the Amazon populace. In many locations fish provides almost the only source of animal protein. This may not, however, continue to be the case (Goulding, 1983) because the population is outstripping the fishery yield, and the yield is beginning to decline through mismanagement.

Some of that decline is recoverable through regulating the fishery to permit its recovery. The remainder may be recoverable, but this very much depends on land-use practices in the várzea. Widespread deforestation of the floodplains would cut this important nutrient flow link between the terrestrial and aquatic ecosystems, and impoverish the Amazon fishery permanently. No plans for the várzeas currently take this important factor into account.

If the yield of várzea lands in rice is compared with yield in fish, the grain harvest would dwarf the fish harvest probably by an order of magnitude in weight, but *not* in protein. The land-use choice does not have to and should not be made on such a simple basis. Rather certain areas can be designated for rice. Others can be set aside to provide fishery support, and could as well serve as sites for fish culture.

It will be very important to set aside some parks in the floodplain, with associated stretches of river and fish community. These will serve to protect the fundamental relationship and processes, as well as to provide a basis for comparing the relative success or failure of various management approaches for both the fishery and floodplain lands. In addition the protected system would provide stocks for restoring degraded portions of the floodplain and associated fisheries.

18.3. HYDROELECTRIC PROJECTS

A number of large hydroelectric projects are planned for Amazon tributaries (Caufield, 1983). The hydroelectric potential of the Amazon is indeed considerable, but it is not without difficult problems.

These derive in large part from the lack of major temperature variation during the year, which means that most tropical lakes do not experience a major mixing period when cooler waters sink. Rather, tropical lakes often develop permanent thermoclines, beneath which anoxic conditions develop. The flooded vegetation then becomes subject to anoxic decomposition, producing hydrogen sulphide, in certain instances to the point of reducing the pH of water to a sufficiently acid state where it can be corrosive to turbines.

This led in the instance of Tucurui dam on the Tocantins to the rather desperate notion of using defoliants on the thousands of square kilometres of forest involved, with a view to a major burn once the vegetation had dried out. It is likely that an adequate hydrological analysis of conditions that would follow closure of the dam, will reveal that anoxic decomposition may not be a concern in this case. In contrast to the shallow Curua Una dam, water flow is likely to be sufficiently strong as to maintain some mixing. A model is being developed to explore this possibility (Richey and Salati, in prep.) not only with respect to Tucurui, but for tropical hydroelectric projects generally. It should then be possible to predict in advance where anoxic decomposition is likely to be a problem (and hence where some preventive measures such as vegetation clearing should be considered).

Another major problem with tropical reservoirs is the likelihood of developing a major covering of floating aquatic plants. This has occurred in a number of tropical reservoirs including Curua Una. This virtually chokes off any other primary productivity, hence oxygen production and thus most animal life. A rather intriguing solution has been proposed by Best (1982), namely introduction of manatees. They are aquatic grazers which would both open up some stretches of water as well as return nutrients to the waters from the floating vegetation they consume, thus contributing doubly to an increase in productivity. This is being undertaken experimentally at Curua Una.

A remaining concern is the disruption of fish migratory patterns. Unfortunately these are very scantily known, so research is necessary even before it can be discerned as to whether such a problem exists with a particular project. Fish ladders have been used very successfully with some temperate zone migratory fishes such as salmon and shad, but hardly at all in tropical situations.

Of course a dominant concern in any hydroelectric project whether temperate or tropical is protection of the watershed. It is interesting to note that this became a matter of real concern to the government of Panama once it gained sovereignty over the Canal. This is a matter of the highest order in wet tropical latitudes where the capacity for erosion is so much greater due to both the greater quantity and greater intensity of rainfall. There is little sense, given there is a limited number of dam sites in the world, not to take all steps to guarantee maximum lifespans for them.

18.4. HYDROLOGICAL CYCLE

The research of Salati and colleagues (*see* Chapter 2, this volume) has elegantly demonstrated with a number of lines of converging evidence that the Amazon forest generates a significant fraction (ca. one half) of its own rainfall. This results from the combination of the capacity of forest to return water to the atmosphere through evapotranspiration and through direct evaporation, plus the capacity of soils beneath rainforest to absorb rainwater, then subsequently available in large degree for transport to the atmosphere through evapotranspiration. Bare soils as under pasture conditions absorb water at less than a tenth the rate, with consequent major runoff (and erosion) (Schubart, 1977). The water simply is not available under the deforested condition to be returned to the atmosphere.

This carries the serious implication that beyond a certain point deforestation in the Amazon would trigger an irreversible drying trend. Salati and Vose (1984) estimate that total deforestation of Amazonia would lead to a 600 mm reduction in annual average precipitation. In the central Amazon, as in the Manaus area, considerably lesser reduction in rainfall could have severe consequences on the local biology; it appears that rainfall in this area is sufficient but not in excess of the quantity necessary to support tropical rainforest. Obviously forest and tree cover in some combination and in some total area is necessary to maintain the integrity of the hydrological cycle. The amount necessary is not known, and will depend in part on the contributions (currently unknown) which various forms of land-use can make to the hydrological cycle.

There is undoubtedly a variety of combinations of land-uses of different sorts which would provide for this. This requires urgent study. It is also likely that a majority of the surface of the basin must be maintained in forest or tree cover. Again it is of interest that the forms of land-use most likely to sustain the hydrological cycle, are those that most closely approximate the natural vegetation.

18.5. RANCHING PROJECTS

In the last decade, a significant portion of the development beyond the Manaus economic free zone involved converting forest to pastureland. The experience has been largely unsuccessful, and probably would not have taken place were it not for both economic subsidies available from SUDAM, as well as economic incentives in terms of tax breaks.

A large proportion of the projects have been abandoned (Hecht, 1983) due to a number of adverse factors. These include soil compaction which is virtually unavoidable given that cattle have hooves. In addition the African savannah grasses (*Brachiaria*), even though carefully selected for the best possible species, experience a decline in productivity because of classic soil nutrient problems, and *Brachiaria* declines in digestibility at high temperatures (van Soest, 1982). Finally the invasion of the pasture by toxic weedy species requires expensive hand removal. In the last analysis, the yield per ha is low and declines.

There is some experimentation with other sorts of fodder, such as kudzu. It is not likely that all the problems can be avoided by using a different species. Many of the problems are ones that derive from using a vegetation form other than that natural to the region — again not a surprising result.

While there is no longer an official push for new cattle projects, the economic incentives and subsidies are still available for existing ranching projects, and for ones beyond the zone of dense forest. Most of the ranching has been in the southwestern quadrant, and the southern fringe of the Amazon forest. Ranching is also likely to occur in relation to large development projects such as Jari or Grande Carajás, simply to supply the workforce.

18.6. THE IMPACT OF FARMING

As noted earlier, the activities of the slash and burn agriculturalist are in harmony with the environment, as long as the population density remains low. Unfortunately the numbers of small scale agriculturalists are being rapidly supplemented by spontaneous settlement, made possible by the construction of roads, as in Rondônia and Roraima. In Rondônia, there is additional forest conversion for cooperatives formed by settlers from the south of Brazil, and subsidiaries of southern Brazilian corporations. In Rondônia, this kind of activity is fortunately focused on areas of better soils (terra roxa), and the construction of the road was predicated on this. In these areas there still are major logistic problems related to farming, particularly in getting crops to market in sufficient time.

Heretofore this has not been a problem for the caboclo, whose farming activities have been mostly a matter of self sufficiency, with residual needs being satisfied mainly through purchases with cash gained from a forest extraction crop such as Brazil nuts. At some point not too far distant, it will become necessary to encourage a shift by caboclos to a form of land-use which does not require constant moving to and clearing of new sites.

This is a task far easier described than achieved. By the very nature of their existence these people are widely dispersed, so even communicating and working with them will be difficult. A change from the shifting mode to permanent settlement, will involve a change in the type of crops they raise: most probably from an annual to a perennial (and most likely tree) crop, and from a subsistence crop to a cash crop. If that is the case, there will be a need for a system whereby the caboclo can market his cash crop, and spend the cash so gained on the necessities for his family. Further, there are likely to be some initial years before the cash crop is productive, during which some kind of subsistence will be requisite. This is a serious, large and complex problem, one that probably can only be tackled by large institutions such as the international development banks and bilateral aid agencies. Fortunately in the Amazon, the situation is not so urgent as in southeast Asia, and individual countries such as Haiti and Ruanda, but the time to start trying to do something is now.

In a number of tropical forest situations, there has been a flow of small farmers, of the caboclo *genre* into the cities, essentially depopulating the countryside. This has been the experience in Venezuela for example, and is responsible for the remarkable recovery of forest in Puerto Rico (where the cities serving as population magnets were on the mainland). To the extent that the light industry of Manaus is driving such migration it is worthwhile. What is worrisome is when cities attract the rural population for no particular purpose and their living conditions end up worse instead of better. Rarely in such situations is there a reverse migration.

The apparent flow of population from the countryside could be considered reason to allay concerns about Amazonian deforestation. Oddly enough, however, roads seem to continue to attract settlers. The move to urban situations seems to follow rather than divert. In either case, however, improving the lot of the subsistence agriculturalist is a matter of high priority, and part of the important goal to develop sustainable forms of land-use for Amazonia.

18.7. DEFORESTATION RATES

There has been considerable discussion, occasioned in turn by considerable uncertainty about the rate of deforestation in the Amazon. Flying over the basin in the daytime, it seems an almost endless stretch of green. Yet closer examination reveals signs of considerable recent deforestation activity. Landsat imagery of Rondônia shows the deforestation associated with recent settlement there. The smoke from deforested areas has been so great in the last year or two as to generate a haze which occasionally has proven to be an aircraft navigation problem.

The official Brazilian figures derived from satellite imagery by INPE, Brazil's space agency, estimated only 1.55% of legal Amazonia had been deforested by 1979. As the forested portion of legal Amazonia is only about 50%, the more representative figure would be about 3%. This figure must be low for a number of reasons. Historical deforestation, such as in the Zona Bragantina, adds up to a figure equal to a considerable proportion of the official figure (Fearnside, 1982).

More importantly, the analysis of the satellite imagery was unable to distinguish between secondary growth forest of more than a few years of age and primary forest. The difference between the two biologically is very great, and the difference in the natural potential of the land can also be considerable, depending on the particular previous history of the land beneath the secondary forest.

This distinction between total deforestation to a point of almost bare land, and modification of forest to the point where it is biologically quite different from primary forest, is often a source of confusion when deforestation is discussed. The term conversion (*sensu* Myers, 1980) encompasses both total deforestation and modification. From the point of view of sustainable landuse other than conservation areas (itself a form of sustainable land-use), the distinction can be important. Denuded lands as in the Zona Bragantina require considerable manipulation to restore to any form of productivity. Modified forest lands may or may not have potential depending on their previous history.

From the point of view of conservation areas, modified forest can differ tremendously from the primary vegetation with its wealth of species, without ever showing up differently in analysis of imagery. There are currently vast stretches of western Amazonian forest, long thought reasonably secure because of their remoteness, where hunters for the skin trade have removed most of the big mammals, particularly jaguar (Emmons, 1984). Even photography from low flying aircraft would reveal no difference. Where photography can detect a difference, the patch of secondary growth is likely to contain but a tiny fraction of primary forest species.

Consequently from the conservation point of view the extent of deforestation is considerably greater than the official 3%, with 10% probably being a conservative estimate. Others, including Ghillean Prance, estimate that forest modification approaches 25% of the total area.

It is also important to note that even by official statistics, the rate has been accelerating. Whether it will continue to accelerate as per Fearnside's model (1982) is open to question (Lugo and Brown, 1982), but it certainly is a possibility, and one to plan to avoid.

A further important consideration is the strong element of irreversibility in deforestation and conversion. This is often a point of confusion, when the developed nation experience, say in New England, is considered. If Americans were able to virtually deforest New England, and have that area heavily forested today, what then is the basis for concern about tropical deforestation?

There are fundamental differences in ecology. New England and indeed most temperate areas have relatively good soils in comparison to the average Amazonian soil (but not to deep prairie soils). Temperate plants have seeds with considerably greater viability; survival for centuries is possible in some instances, as compared to weeks for a tropical forest tree seed. Consequently there is a major seed bank in the soil which can produce forest recovery even in the absence of adult individuals. Further, the lower species numbers and simpler biological arrangements foster faster and more complete recovery. For example the dominance of wind pollination among temperate forest trees means that recovery need not depend on a series of insect pollinators. All this means that once a stretch of Amazon forest has been cut over, or heavily disturbed, the path to recovery is not easy and automatic. So each major increment of deforestation has, at least on a human historical time scale, some element of irreversibility.

18.8. CONSERVATION AREAS

It becomes critical, therefore, that attention be given to the question of establishment of conservation areas to safeguard the important fraction of this planet's biological diversity (most conservatively estimated at 10%) harboured by Amazonia. Fortunately, this matter has recently received increased attention in various, but not all, Amazonian countries (Wetterberg *et al.*, 1981), and most particularly in Brazil. Yet this is a considerably more difficult question than it might seem at first, because of the limited knowledge about this major segment of planetary biological diversity.

Very few groups of Amazonian organisms are well known, even to the point of the species actually being named, let alone anything else about their biology recorded. Birds which constitute the highest taxon considered well known, have about 1000 species known from the basin, yet almost yearly in the past decade a new species has been described from Peru, and some from the Amazon. Major range extensions continue to be recorded.

As there obviously is not time to await an exhaustive faunal and floral inventory, such as conveniently preceded national park planning in the United States, another approach must be taken. The current one (Wetterberg et al., 1976) agreed upon by all Amazon nations is based on distribution patterns of well-known organisms. Such organisms reveal clusters of endemic species. Many authors have accepted the interpretation that these represent sites where the Amazon forest was able to persist during the interpluvial periods of the Pleistocene, providing opportunities for speciation during these times of isolation. When the forest once again spread out to cover the basin some of these new species remained more restricted in distribution. Those accepting this interpretation believe these species indicate the sites of the isolated interpluvial forest tracts, and term these clusters of endemics Pleistocene refugia (Prance, 1982; Chapter 8, this volume).

This interpretation is not universally accepted (Brown, 1985), but acceptance is not necessary (Lovejoy, 1982) to accord these centres of endemism importance, from the point of view of conservation. Whatever their origin, these locations are, by definition, important to the conservation of the endemic species therein contained. Such refugia or centres have been defined for birds (Haffer, 1969, 1974, 1979), for two subfamilies of butterflies (Brown, 1977), for reptiles (Vanzolini, 1973), and four families of woody plants (Prance, 1973). The Amazon conservation plan is based on these, according priority to a site on the basis of the number of taxa for which refugia coincide.

The basic assumption here is that groups of organisms which are only sketchily known will be represented by endemics in these same locations, and hence will be swept up in the conservation units so defined. This clearly is a weak assumption, but one with no alternative in terms of present conservation action. Fortunately, it does not preclude simultaneously building a better data base where feasible, for subsequent analysis, and refinement of conservation plans.

Projeto Flora, the joint enterprise of INPA, the Museu Goeldi and the New York Botanical Garden, is just such an exercise. Organising, indeed validating, data from the literature and herbaria, and collecting new data from little studied areas, or ones newly opened to development, it will provide a basis for computer analysis which may well identify additional areas of conservation importance. Brazil's CNPq has established a Projeto Fauna in parallel, but the job is much bigger and more difficult. Nonetheless, some work is proceeding, largely funded by the World Bank and the Companhia do Vale do Rio Doce (CVRD), although computerisation is not part of the current plan.

So far, a number of parks have been established following this basis. The most important one, not yet established, is in the region of the Belém refugium, a focus of intense development activity, where the opportunity to create a park may soon vanish. A number of 'refugia' are not included in the present plan, because they do not coincide with ones defined for other taxa. It is important that such areas eventually be included in conservation plans. There is no reason (Lovejoy, 1982) to suppose that these centres should coincide for all groups; indeed there is every reason to expect that they should not.

Furthermore, isolated centres defined by smaller organisms might well turn out to be important centres for other small organisms, and, after all, the bulk of Amazonian diversity is made up of smaller bodied organisms. Curiously and sadly, if most of the Amazonian landscape outside of protected areas becomes highly modified landscape, we will never know if these protected areas were centres of endemism for groups currently poorly known. Such protected areas will a priori become centres of endemism, even if they are not so today.

As centres of endemism are based primarily on forest species, conservation plans based exclusively on them, would nonetheless, even if carried out to the fullest extent, be likely to miss certain key areas.

These would be areas of non-forest vegetation, such as campinas, and also areas of freshwater endemism. Although the latter may well coincide with centres defined on forest species, there may not be 100% coincidence. Further, plans for parks based on terrestrial species, may not have the proper configurations to protect aquatic ones. While certain aquatic habitat types merit conservation as discussed earlier, stream and river endemics will not necessarily be adequately protected by protecting one of each stream and river type. It is likely that headwater areas above cataracts where the shields rise both north and south of the floodplain harbour important endemics. The southern ones are currently being systematically examined by Michael Goulding of the Museu Goeldi.

As important as the question of location of reserves, is that of how big they should be. It is now widely known (Diamond, 1975, 1976; Lovejoy and Oren, 1981; Terborgh, 1974, 1975; Wilson and Willis, 1975), that isolated fragments of once continuous wilderness lose species after isolation. This has serious implications for national park design and management. Unfortunately, basic data about this species loss process are fragmentary themselves, and give us little guide, except that for Amazonian forest minimum reserve size (from the point of view of protecting a tract of forest capable of maintaining characteristic diversity) should be on the order of millions of hectares.

Fortunately, there has been a special opportunity to study this problem in a systematic, controlled experimental fashion. A joint INPA/WWF research program, 'The Minimum Critical Size of Ecosystems', is studying this problem on a long-term (20 + years) basis in the central Amazon, north of Manaus. The project takes advantage of the Brazilian requirement that 50% of the land of any development project must remain in forest. On four adjacent ranches, this 50% is being arranged geometrically to provide for a size series of forest patches, ranging from 1 to in excess of 10,000 ha. There are replicates in every size class except the largest.

These to-be-isolated reserves are picked out while the forest is still continuous, and studied in their pristine state. Then after isolation they are followed in great detail to document and understand the species loss process. The pre-isolation data and those from the largest tract provide scientific baseline controls against which to compare the data from isolated reserves. The small reserves provide quick and rough insights into the dynamics of species loss, while the larger reserves will provide deeper, more sophisticated understanding which is slower in coming. Results are analysed and published on a continuing basis, and have already provided some interesting views of changes induced by isolation (Lovejoy et al., 1983, 1984).

A final matter for concern with regard to parks and reserves, and to some degree to ecological stations (the reserves created by SEMA, the Special Secretariat of the Environment of Brazil, of which up to 10% of the area of each, may be used for manipulative research) is the need to develop an actual protection system. Many of these areas are in far remote portions of the basin, and so far have almost nothing in the way of a system for protection, including sufficient guards etc. At the moment most of these areas are relatively secure, but it would be good to develop their protection systems now before problems arise. So far it would appear that governments have found it easy to designate some areas for conservation, but that they are reluctant to put the financial resources behind them to protect them properly. This must be corrected in the near future, or there will be risk of having created aught but paper parks.

18.9. INDIAN RESERVATIONS

One important category of protected areas and land-use is the lands set aside for the remaining indigenous peoples of Amazonia. These are certainly important when considering how to meet the necessary minima for maintaining the integrity of the forest/hydrological cycle relationship. They are not necessarily important when considering at least some aspects of conservation, for though the forest in such areas is likely to remain intact, there is no guarantee that certain animal species will not be greatly diminished or exterminated locally by the indigens.

There is the further difficulty, arising from the impossibility, and probably even amorality, of shielding Indians from modern civilisation to complete exclusion. Gradually, most of the remaining tribes are likely to become acculturated, and with that is likely to come the use of modern means, such as guns, of hunting. At some point in this process, an Indian people will begin to exert a pressure on their environment and animal populations that must be considered to approach or be akin to that of technological Man. This is a very difficult point to define, and is enmeshed in difficulties when the indigenous people feel their ancient rights to take from their environment are being infringed.

This affects management of formally protected conservation units, because on occasion some of the habitats which most merit protection are ones in which some Indians are living. Technically in most nations national parks cannot be created in Indian areas, and yet in certain instances they are nonetheless. It is probably correct to do so, but the problem will remain to be resolved at some time in the future.

18.10. AMAZON FOREST POLICY

Brazil's President Figueiredo provided enormous encouragement when he established a commission in May 1979 to develop Amazon forest policy and legislation. A great deal of work went into developing policy and the scientific community was very much involved (INPA, 1979). Unfortunately the policy and legislation, which when last seen in public were quite sound from an environmental view, are still bottled up in the executive branch of the government. There have been periodic announcements that the legislation would be advanced to the Congress, but it has yet to happen.[1]

This would clearly be one of the most important things that could be done to achieve a sensible management of the Amazon forest and its great array of biological resources. It would also have considerable influence on other Amazon nations through the Amazon Pact, which was initiated by Brazil, and contains language about protection and wise use.

Otherwise development is likely to be an uncontrolled patchwork, of carefully managed projects, and ones which are very destructive. The great Carajás iron mine development being conducted by CVRD is a good example of the former. In contrast, the larger Grande Carajás project is lacking in general thoughtful planning, and appears, at least, to be no more than a collection of development schemes.

For the moment the general economic difficulties in Brazil are likely to slow development initiatives, and in essence buy time for more careful planning and setting the full protected area system in place in advance. Even without the general recession in the Brazilian economy and the difficult foreign debt situation, the economics of development in the Amazon is still often unattractive by virtue of the tremendous logistical problems and transportation costs. While the latter are likely to increase rather than decrease, there can be no certainty or comfort in the notion that demand curves will remain as they are, and not render certain development activities more attractive. Further the social pressures that lead the landless to try their luck in the Amazon wherever a road creates access are likely to increase under bad economic conditions. There is every reason to press ahead with sensible management, legislation, and establishment of an adequate reserve network.

---

[1] Legislation was forwarded to the Brasilian Congress by the executive branch in the waning days of the Figveredo administration.

REFERENCES

Best, R. (1982) A salvação de uma especie: novas perspetivas para o peixe-boi da Amazônia. *Revista IBM* 4(14), 6 — 15.

Brown, K. S., Jr. (1977) Centros de evolução, refugios quaternarios e conservação de patrimônios genéticos na região neotropical: padrões de diferenciação em Ithomiinae (Lepidoptera: Nymphalidae). *Acta Amazônica* 7, 75 — 137.

Brown, K. S., Jr. (1985) Butterflies. In *Biogeography and Quaternary History in Tropical America*. Eds. T. C. Whitmore and G. T. Prance. Oxford Monographs on Biogeography. Clarendon Press, Oxford.

Caulfield, C. (1983) Dam the Amazon: full speed ahead. *Nat. Hist.* 92(7), 60 — 670.

Diamond, J. M. (1975) The island dilemma: lessons for the design of natural reserves. *Biol. Conser.* 7, 129 — 146.

Diamond, J. M. (1976) Relaxation and differential extinction on landbridge islands: applications to natural preserves. *Proc. 16th Inter. Ornith. Cong.* 616 — 627. Australian Acad. of Sci. Canberra City, Australia.

Emmons, L. H. (1984) Geographic Variation in Densities and Diversities of Non-Flying Mammals in Amazonia. *Biotropica* 16, 210 — 222.

Fearnside, P. M. (1982) Deforestation in the Brazilian Amazon: how fast is it occurring? *Interciencia* 7(2), 82 — 88.

Goulding, M. (1980) *The Fishes and the Forest*. University of California Press, Berkeley.

Goulding, M. (1983) Amazonian fisheries. In *The Dilemma of Amazonian Development*. Ed. E. F. Moran, pp. 189 — 210. Westview Press, Boulder, Colorado.

Haffer, J. (1969) Speciation in Amazonian forest birds. *Science* 165, 131 — 137.

Haffer, J. (1974) Avian speciation in tropical South America. *Mass.: Publ. Nuttall Ornith. Club* 14.

Haffer, J. (1979) Quaternary biogeography of tropical lowland South America. In *The South American Herpetofauna: its Origin, Evolution and Dispersal*. Ed. W. E. Duellman, pp. 107 — 140. University of Kansas Nat. Hist. Monogr. 7.

Hecht, S. (1983) Cattle ranching in the Eastern Amazon: environmental and social implications. In *The Dilemma of Amazonian Development*. Ed. E. F. Moran, pp. 155 — 188. Westview Press, Boulder, Colorado.

INPA (1979) Estratégias para política florestal na Amazônia Brasileira. *Acta Amazônica* 9(4), 1 — 216.

Lovejoy, T. E. (1982) Designing refugia for tomorrow. In *Biological Diversification in the Tropics*. Ed. G. T. Prance, pp. 673 — 680. Columbia University Press, New York.

Lovejoy, T. E., Bierregaard, R. O., Rankin, J. M. and Schubart, H. O. R. (1983) Ecological dynamics of forest fragments. In *Tropical Rain Forest: Ecology and Management*. Eds. S. L. Sutton, T. C. Whitmore and A. C. Chadwick. pp. 377 — 384. Blackwell Scientific Publications, Oxford.

Lovejoy, T. E., Rankin, J. M., Bierregaard, R. O., Jr., Brown, K. S., Jr., Emmons, L. H. and Van der Voort, M. E. (1984) Ecosystem decay of Amazon forest remnants. In *Extinctions*. Ed. M. H. Nitecki, pp. 295 — 325. University of Chicago Press, Chicago.

Lugo, A. E. and Brown, S. (1982) Deforestation in the Brazilian Amazon. *Interciencia* 7(6), 361 — 362.

Myers, N. (1980) *Conversion of Tropical Moist Forest*. Rept. for Committee on Research Priorities in Tropical Biology of the National Research Council, National Academy of Science, Washington, D.C.

Prance, G. T. (1973) Phytogeographic support for the theory of Pleistocene forest refuges in the Amazon basin, based on evidence from distribution patterns in Caryocaraceae, Chrysobalanaceae, Dichapetalaceae and Lecythidaceae. *Acta Amazônica* 3, 5 — 28.

Prance, G. T. (1982) *Biological Diversification in the Tropics*. Columbia University Press, New York.

Richey, J. and Salati, E. A. (in prep.) *Projected Oxygen Concentrations in the Tucurui Reservior Under Varying Conditions of Vegetation and Discharge*.

Salati, E. A. and Vose, P. B. (1984) Amazon basın: a system in equilibrium. *Science* 225, 129 — 138.

Sanchez, P. A., Bandy, D. E., Villachica J. H. and Nicholaides, J. J. (1982) Amazon basin soils: management for continuous crop production. *Science* 216, 821 — 827.

Schubart, H. O. R. (1977) Critérios ecológicos para o desenvolvimento agrícola das terras-firmes na Amazônia. *Acta Amazônica* 7(4), 559 — 567.

Terborgh, J. (1974) Preservation of natural diversity: the problem of extinction prone species. *BioScience* 24, 715 — 722.

Terborgh, J. (1975) Faunal equilibria and the design of wildlife preserves. In *Tropical Ecological Systems: Trends in Terrestrial and Aquatic Research*. Eds. F. B. Golley and E. Medina, pp. 369 — 379. Springer Verlag, New York.

van Soest, P. (1982) *Nutritional Ecology of Ruminants*. O & B Books, Corvallis, Oregon.

Vanzolini, P. E. (1973) Paleoclimates, relief and species multiplication in equatorial forest. In *Tropical Forest Ecosystems in Africa and South America: A Comparative Review*. Eds. B. J. Meggers, E. S. Ayensu and W. D. Duckworth, pp. 255 — 258. Smithsonian Institution Press, Washington, D.C.

Wetterberg, G. B., Padua, M. T. J., de Castro C. S. and de Vasconcellos, J. M. C. (1976) *Uma Analise de Prioridades em Conservação da Natureza na Amazônia*. Programa do Desenvolvimento da Pesquisa Florestal (PRODEPEF Serie Tecnica No. 8), Brasilia.

Wetterberg, G. B., Prance, G. T. and Lovejoy, T. E. (1981) Conservation progress in Amazonia: a structural review. *Parks* 6(2), 5 — 10.

Wilson, E. O. and Willis, E. O. (1975) Applied biogeography. In *Ecology and Evolution of Communities*. Eds. M. L. Cody and J. M. Diamond, pp. 522 — 534. Harvard University Press, Cambridge, Mass.

CHAPTER 19

Useful Plants of Amazonia: A Resource of Global Importance*

MICHAEL J. BALICK

The New York Botanical Garden, New York, U.S.A.

CONTENTS

19.1. INTRODUCTION

Innumerable explorers and adventurers have searched the Amazon Valley in an intensive hunt for its treasures — minerals, oil, and precious metals were and are still the objects of this much publicised quest. Sometimes the results are successful. Brazil is currently developing a $60 billion project in the

* Contribution 83-1 of the New York Botanical Garden Institute of Economic Botany.

AMA-W

Amazon, 'Programa Grande Carajás' designed to, among other things, export 15 million tons of iron ore annually by 1985 and 35 million tons by 1987. In addition, some 14,000 kilos of gold have been mined from a nearby location (Ulman, 1982). However, upon the frustrating realisation that such treasures are not easily found and extracted, often man has taken out his anger on the forest itself — mechanically cutting and burning it, attempting to release the reservoir of nutrients contained within the forest ecosystem through their conversion to develop intensive agricultural activity. Once again when crop yields decrease after only a few harvests, people grasp the reality that a simple and expedient way of exploiting this green kingdom does not exist.

Indeed, the great treasure to be found within the Amazon is the most obvious — the vast biological array of living organisms. There are many tens of thousands of plant, insect, fish, and mammal species that inhabit this great tropical forest. Realistically accurate estimates of all the different kinds of organisms that live in the Amazon cannot be made, as many still remain to be discovered. Unfortunately, too few of us realise and appreciate this kind of wealth.

Numbering among its treasures, the Amazon forest contains a plethora of plants that have great promise for economic utilisation. Many of these plant species could be scientifically domesticated and used in agricultural programs within the Amazon Valley and elsewhere in the tropics. Some possess specific advantages for cultivation, such as the ability to grow under harsh conditions with minimal care, current acceptability as a food, construction, or fuel source by local peoples, and superior content or quality of oils, proteins, drugs, insecticides, waxes, or other products of importance to an industrialised society. Without such a verdant and diverse flora the ability of humans to survive and indeed flourish in the Amazon Valley would be greatly diminished.

The plants outlined in the following pages represent a selection of those Amazonian native species which were important in the past, are currently in use, or have much greater potential for future benefit. A complete treatise on the range of economic plants of the Amazon Valley would fill many volumes, and even then would be lacking. Thus, in this chapter, I will focus on only a few of the important species, to substantiate the theme that the Amazonian flora is a resource of global importance.

19.2. SOME ECONOMIC PLANTS OF AMAZONIA

19.2.1. *Astrocaryum aculeatum* Meyer; *A. murumuru* Mart.; *A. vulgare* Mart.

Regional names: 'Murumuru,' 'Tucumã,' 'Tucum' (Brazil) (Figs. 19.1 – 19.3).

Heavily spined trees, up to 20 m in height, these palms are common in many areas of lowland Amazonia, found in both moist and dry habitats. Among the commercial products obtained are palm heart and edible oil. One study of *Astrocaryum vulgare* reported the following proximate analysis of the fruit: water, 50%; carbohydrate, 19.1%; protein, 3.5%; fat, 16.6%; fibre, 3.5%; minerals, 1.3%; other, 6.0% (Chaves and Pechnik, 1947). This same study also reported that the Vitamin A content of 'Tucumã' is an astonishing 52,000 i.u./per 100 g of pulp, three times higher than that of the carrot, which is usually considered one of the best sources of Vitamin A. 'Tucumã' oil is calculated to have some 313,000 i.u. Vitamin A per 100 g. Analysis of the fatty acid composition of the oil reveals it to be similar to the coconut: Lauric acid, 48.9%; Myristic acid, 21.6%; Oleic acid, 13.2%; Palmitic acid, 6.4%; Capric acid, 4.4%; Linoleic acid, 2.5%; Stearic acid, 1.7% and Caprilic acid, 1.3%.

Fruits of these species are steamed and served in restaurants as appetizers in the major cities of the Amazon. Presently the entire crop is harvested from the wild stands. These stands are endangered due to the destructive nature of palm heart production as well as widespread habitat extinction.

Fig. 19.1. Seeds of *Astrocaryum vulgare* collected from the Peruvian Amazon. Collection shown is *Plowman 6945*.

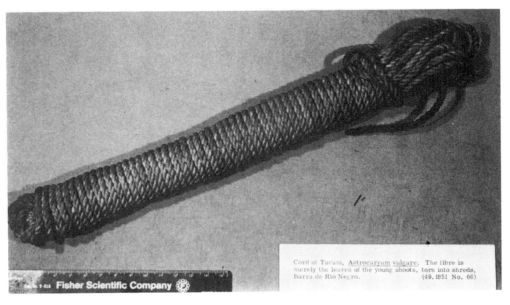

Fig. 19.2. Rope made from *Astrocaryum* fibre, collected by Richard Spruce in 1851. From the collections of the Economic Museum, Royal Botanic Garden, Kew.

Fig. 19.3. Fibre from two palm species was used to produce this hammock, the edge of which is shown here. The fringes are made from *Mauritia flexuosa* while the main section of the hammock is woven from *Astrocaryum chambira*. Reprinted from *Economic Botany* 33(4) 1980.

An excellent durable fibre is extracted from the young leaves of *Astrocaryum tucuma*, also referred to as *A. chambira* Burret. Individual leaf pinnae are selected, bent in half, and fibres peeled off. These are then crushed in water, cleaned and spun into cordage, for fish lines, bowstrings, nets, hammocks, ceremonial dress, and other products where strength and durability are of prime importance. An indigenous hammock made of *Astrocaryum* fibre is said to last many, many years, an impressive statement considering the humid environment of the Amazon Valley.

19.2.2. *Bactris gasipaes* H.B.& K.

Regional names: 'Cachipay' (Colombia); 'Pifuayo' (Peru); 'Pupunha' (Brazil): 'Tembé' (Bolivia) (Figs. 19.4, 19.5).

This species, known as the 'Peach palm' in English, is a caespitose palm of up to 20 m tall, with a crown of incurved crispate leaves, each about 2 m long. The stem and leaf are variably spined. Panicles of globose-rounded, glabrous fruits, to a maximum of up to 300 per inflorescence are produced just below the crown. This species yields up to 13 bunches of fruit annually (MacBride, 1960; National Academy of Sciences, 1975). The fruits are orange to red on the exterior, and inside contain a yellowish, somewhat mealy flesh and hard seed. The flesh, when boiled, tastes like 'something between a chestnut and potato in flavour and superior to either' (MacBride, 1960).

'Pupunha' is an extremely valuable palm which has not yet truly been documented in a wild state. It is commonly cultivated, and is a good indicator of a former habitation site.

Over time, a number of forms have been selected and domesticated by Amazonian Indians who utilise the palm to the fullest: the trunk for house construction, bows, and arrow points, fruits for human food

Fig. 19.4. A planting of *Bactris gasipaes* growing at the edge of a cultivated field.

and when fermented for 5 days as an alcoholic 'chicha,' dried mesocarp as an edible, storable carbohydrate product, and the entire fruit as an animal feed. This palm can also be cultivated for 'heart of palm' and will yield a marketable product in 2.5 – 4 years from seed. Success in cultivation with minimal spacing per tree at the Las Cruces Tropical Botanical Garden, San Vito, Costa Rica was reported by Balick (1976) who also noted that researchers at Turrialba Tropical Research and Training Center had planted 2,200 palms per hectare which could be expected to yield thousands of hearts for harvest. In addition, the 'pupunha' is a suckering palm which still offers the same advantage as the *Euterpe* species usually harvested from wild sources — multiple stems providing many 'hearts' per tree.

Fig. 19.5. Removing the 'heart' from *Bactris gasipaes* in an experimental planting in Costa Rica. Reprinted from *Principes* 20(1) 1976.

The fruit of this species has twice the protein content of banana, and in cultivation will produce more carbohydrate and protein per hectare than maize (National Academy of Sciences, 1975). One study of nutrient composition of the fruits revealed the following ranges in 100 g of fresh fruit: fat, 1.61 − 9.45 g; protein, 1.37 − 2.85 g; Carotene, 70 − 603 μg; Niacin, 0.07 − 0.19 μg; Vitamin C, 0.10 − 2.38 mg (Johannessen, 1967).

The future challenge of 'pupunha' is not only to promote its widespread use as a staple food and commercial crop, but to introduce into wider cultivation its special forms, such as spineless trees or those with large parthenocarpic fruits, traits known to exist in isolated areas of the Amazon Valley. Already one company has introduced tinned fruits in Costa Rica, and living collections of genetic variants are being developed. This is an ideal tree for sustainable agronomic systems in the lowland tropics.

Fig. 19.6. Experimental plantation of Brazil Nuts (*Bertholletia excelsa*) in the Bolivian Amazon.

Fig. 19.7. Fruits of Brazil Nuts as they appear on the trees. (Photo by G.T. Prance).

19.2.3. *Bertholletia excelsa* Humb. & Bonpl.

Common names: Brazil Nut; 'Almendra' (Venezuela); 'Castanha-do-Pará' (Brazil); 'Castana' (Peru) (Figs. 19.6 – 19.9).

The Brazil Nut is one of the larger trees of the Amazon rainforest, growing to 40 m or more. Its crown of leathery leaves supports a mantle of erect panicles of yellow flowers. The so-called 'nuts' are produced in globose woody fruits, each containing some 12 – 24 seeds. In much of the Amazon, the fruits ripen in December and January after a full year of development and fall from the tops of the trees, scattering around the base where they are harvested. The 'nuts' are an important product of Amazonian Brazil, Peru and Bolivia.

Collectors split open the fruits in the field and sell them to local factories. 'Nuts' are then inspected and either shelled or shipped with their hard brown coating. Largest export markets are the United States, England and West Germany. The 'nuts' can be consumed raw, roasted or employed in confectionery. A recent report of the nutritional composition of Brazil Nuts offered ranges as follows: oil, 65 – 70%; protein, 13.9 – 17.0%; ash, 3.0 – 4.0%; crude fibre, 0.9 – 3.21%; water, 2.0 – 5.94%; carbohydrate, 3.83 – 10.1% (Prance and Mori, 1979). Attempts at plantation cultivation have not been particularly successful to date, because of the period needed to first fruiting (8 – 16 years) and poor fruit set. Accelerated studies on the taxonomic variation and pollination mechanisms currently underway (G.T. Prance, pers. comm. 1982) should shed new light on plantation possibilities. Brazil Nut would seem an ideal tree for use in agroforestry, especially in regions where it is already native — where the surrounding vegetation can be thinned out and additional Brazil Nut trees planted for harvest.

19.2.4. *Erythroxylum coca* var. *ipadu* Plowman

Common names: 'Coca', 'Ipadu', 'Yapadu' (Bolivia, Colombia) (Fig. 19.10).

This slight shrub, some 2 – 3 m in height and often with a scraggly appearance, has become the focus of international attention and debate, primarily because it contains the alkaloid cocaine. Two species of coca are cultivated for their alkaloidal content, Bolivian or Huanuco coca, *E. coca* Lam. and Colombian coca, *E. novogranatense* (Morris) Hieron. These are primarily cultivated in the Andean regions. Plowman (1979) described a variety of the former species, *E. coca* var. *ipadu*, identifying it as the characteristic coca cultivated in the Amazon Valley. Unlike the other kinds, Amazonian coca is only known in cultivation, and rarely produces seed. Indigenous peoples throughout the Amazon Valley appreciate the importance of coca, employing it as a masticatory, medicine, food, and in ritual ceremony. One important use in the areas where it is grown is to suppress hunger and fatigue, serving to ameliorate the rigours of a subsistence life-style.

Recent studies have shown the nutritional value of coca to be quite high. Duke *et al.* (1975) noted that consumption of 100 g of Bolivian coca leaves would meet the recommended dietary allowance for calcium, iron, phosphorus, Vitamin A, Vitamin B_2 and Vitamin E. Plowman (1980) estimated that an Andean coca user might consume up to 60 g of leaves per day, which would represent an important contribution to a rather poor diet. Alkaloids present in coca include cocaine, cinnamoylcocaine, benzoylecgonine, and tropacocaine. By far the most important alkaloid is cocaine, present in quantities several times higher than the other alkaloids (Rivier, 1981). Burchard (1975) offered an interesting hypothesis linking coca-chewing to the control of blood glucose homeostasis and better carbohydrate utilisation.

The recent increased demand for cocaine has resulted in numerous illicit coca fields springing up throughout the Amazon Valley, along with 'factories' which produce a crude cocaine paste which is

Fig. 19.8. Once the fruits of Brazil Nuts are located, they are split open in the field and the 'nuts' removed. (Photo by G.T. Prance).

further refined elsewhere and smuggled into other countries for sale. It is unfortunate indeed that the many beneficial aspects of Amazonian coca will be overshadowed in the forseeable future by the intense controversy which surrounds it.

19.2.5. *Hevea brasiliensis* (Willd. ex Adr. de Juss.) Muell. Arg.

Common names: Rubber; 'Caucho' (Colombia); 'Seringueira' (Brazil) (Figs. 19.11 – 19.14).
One of the most important species of *Hevea* from a commercial standpoint, *H. brasiliensis*, produces about 99% of the world's natural rubber. This is a fast-growing tree native to the lowland forests of the

Fig. 19.9. Individual Brazil Nuts are cracked open with a small hand operated press, and the shells removed. (Photo by G.T. Prance).

Amazon Basin, common in seasonally inundated areas as well as in the drier uplands. In the wild, *Hevea* trees can reach to 40 m in height, but when in plantations the trees have a maximum height of 25 m. Whitish or yellow-whitish latex is obtained from the phloem cells which are tapped by cutting in as close to the cambium as possible without actually slicing through it. A knife with a V-shaped edge is used to cut channels into the tree at angles of 25 – 30°, beginning from the top left and extending to the bottom right. Increased yields and disease resistance are obtained by grafting bud wood on to nursery grown stock trees (Purseglove, 1974).

Some 9 species of *Hevea* are recognised. There are few comprehensive living collections of these species which could be used for breeding work — much fieldwork remains to be done. Incorporating genetic material of wild *Hevea* into currently existing agronomic stock would have important advantages. For example, certain interspecific hybrids between *Hevea brasiliensis* and *H. benthamiana* have shown resistance to *Phytopthora* leaf fall and die-back, as well as immunity to *Microcyclus ulei*, the South American Leaf Blight that has proven so fatal to New World plantations. Individual clones of *Hevea rigidifolia* have also shown resistance to leaf fall and die-back (Schultes, 1977). Other wild collections of *Hevea* have shown great promise for agronomic use. The forests of this region contain genetic material for an irreplaceable and unparalleled selection of variation in *Hevea* that must not be allowed to disappear. This important plant has not begun to reach the limits of its yields or cultural tolerance, and will do so only when the wide range of wild *Hevea* is properly collected, grown, analysed, and incorporated into existing stock. Although the great Amazonian empires based on the harvest of wild rubber collapsed with the introduction of cultivated rubber to the Old World at the beginning of this century, the harvest of this latex from wild and cultivated trees still is an important factor in the regional economy, especially in remote areas where so little else is produced. In addition, recent experiments in Venezuela cultivating *H. brasiliensis* in areas with a prolonged seasonal dry period have shown that incidences of disease are greatly reduced because the life cycle of the pathogen is interrupted and its ability to inflict injury to the trees is diminished (pers. obs.). Focusing on the agronomic manipulation of wild *Hevea* to better serve as a cultivated plant in its native range would seem a well-advised task of regional scientific and technical institutions throughout Amazonia.

Fig. 19.10. Field of *Erythroxylum coca* in the Northwest Amazon Valley of Colombia.

19.2.6. *Jessenia bataua* (Mart.) Burret

Regional names: 'Majo' (Bolivia), 'Milpesos', 'Patauá' (Brazil), 'Seje' (Colombia and Venezuela), 'Unghuaray' (Peru) (Figs. 19.15 – 19.18).

This stately palm with feathery leaves up to 8 m long grows to 20 m in height. It is restricted to lowland regions up to an altitude of 1,000 m. 'Patauá' is social in habit, and in swamplands may occur in pure stands of almost uncountable individuals. It is common throughout the Amazon Valley, and is highly esteemed by local inhabitants. Each year these trees produce large panicles of dark purple, ovoid fruits weighing 10 – 15 g each. The mesocarp of the fruit contain a high quality oil and nutritious pulp, both of which are exploited on a regional basis. The oil, light green or yellow in colour, is almost identical to olive oil in its physical and chemical properties (Table 19.1).

An amino acid analysis of *Jessenia bataua* protein, using the FAO/WHO provisional amino acid scoring pattern for comparison, has revealed that the protein of this plant is comparable to that of good animal protein and substantially better than most grain and legume sources of protein. In comparison with the biological value of soybean protein, *J. bataua* protein is almost 40% higher (Balick and Gershoff, 1981).

The closely related palm genus *Oenocarpus* is also used as a source of oil and protein-rich foodstuff. These palms, like many other potentially important species in the Amazon, have never been domesticated and cultivated. Basic biological and economic studies by Balick (1980) suggest that the *Jessenia — Oenocarpus* palm complex would be an excellent crop for the lowland tropics, especially if hybrids between the individual species were developed. Utilising the traits found in this complex, high yielding plants of small stature with large fruit clusters could be selected as an ideal tree crop for tropical agriculture. In the past Brazil exported 'patauá' oil in substantial quantities — from 1939 to 1949 a total of 924,392 kilos (Pereira-Pinto, 1951). Over-exploitation with little regard to future production has resulted in the decimation of once large stands in many areas and action must be taken if this important food source is to be utilised for wider human benefit.

19.2.7. *Lonchocarpus utilis* Killip & Smith; *L. urucu* Killip & Smith; *L. nicou* (Aubl.) DC.

Common name: 'Timbó' (Brazil).

Fish poisons derived from plants are common in Amazonia. Indigenous peoples utilise these materials by soaking the leaves and stems in a dammed up body of water, temporarily paralysing the fish which then float to the surface and are easily caught. Fish not collected soon recover and swim off as the dose used is usually just enough to stun rather than kill. In this way the river ecosystem is not destroyed, but rather it is preserved through selective harvesting. Rotenone is the principal active component of *Lonchocarpus utilis*, *L. urucu* and *L. nicou*, three species of fish poison from the Amazon Valley.

Rotenone is a colourless, odourless, crystalline solid poison, with a chemical formula of $C_{22}H_{22}O_6$. It is very toxic to cold-blooded animals. Because of its selective toxicity, rotenone is of great value as an insecticide, as it kills insects but is relatively harmless to mammals. The best source of rotenone is from the roots of *Derris* species from Indonesia, up to 12% by weight. However, *Lonchocarpus* is a

Fig. 19.11. Selection of wild rubber growing in a nursery in the Bolivian Amazon.

Fig. 19.12. Rubber tapper collecting from wild trees in the Bolivian Amazon. Harvest of rubber from wild trees still represents an important industry in the Amazon Valley, despite the advent of cultivated rubber elsewhere in the world.

commercially valuable source of rotenone, 2 – 4% by weight (Brady and Clauser, 1977). In 1946, the United States imported 11 million pounds of this product from Brazil and Peru (Purseglove, 1974). Brazil produced 30 tons of 'timbó' root in 1979, exclusively from the State of Pará (IBGE, 1979).

One interesting use of 'timbó' in Brazil was to eliminate or control populations of the 'piranha' fish in waters that could otherwise be filled with more valuable fish. It was discovered that 'timbo' in a proportion of three parts per million would totally eliminate the 'piranha' and its eggs within 15 minutes, causing minimal damage to other fish species. Between 1957 and 1961, 'piranha' was eliminated from some 48,000 km^2 of water systems, primarily in the State of Ceará. Apparently this technique was duplicated in the United States to restore balanced fish populations in waters affected by pollution (Rizzini and Mors, 1976). As the true lethal nature of more and more of the synthetically

Fig. 19.13. Rubber germ plasm collection and experimental plantation in the Venezuelan Orinoco.

produced chemical pesticides is discovered it is important to realise that the Amazon Valley offers a wide spectrum of toxic plants whose derivatives could help fill an important role in our food production systems.

19.2.8. *Orbignya martiana* Barbosa Rodrigues; *O. speciosa* (Mart.) Barb. Rodr.; *O. oleifera* Burret; *O. phalerata* Martius.

Common names: 'Babaçú'(Brazil); 'Cusi' (Bolivia) (Figs. 19.19 – 19.21).

While this palm is native to the Amazon Basin, its major concentration occurs in areas somewhat peripheral to this region — in the states of Maranhão, Goiás, Piauí, Brazil and Santa Cruz, Bolivia. Here it forms the dominant vegetal cover over millions of hectares of dry grassland or 'cerrado' forest vegetation. No single specific epithet can be assigned to this palm as its present taxonomy is very unclear. Brazilian species have been called *Orbignya martiana*, *O. speciosa* or *O. oleifera*, while Bolivian populations are referred to as *O. phalerata*. Recent fieldwork in both countries leads me to suspect that the large, heavily fruited species in these two countries represent a single species or a very closely related group of species.

'Babaçú' is truly a remarkable palm for many reasons. It yields an industrial raw material (fruits) that can be processed into a plethora of useful products. In addition, its aggressive nature and tolerance of stressed habitats makes it an ideal tree for use in degraded ecosystems. When established, 'babaçú' forms a cover not only providing useful products but offering a home for economically important animal species, including people. A myriad of products can be derived from its fruits (in per cent by weight): oil, 3.85%; feed cake, 3.15%; fertiliser cake, 2.9%; flour, 1.5%; animal ration, 3.5%; charcoal, 17.4%; methyl alcohol, 0.87%; tar, 4.64%, and acetic acid, 4.64% (Gonsalves, 1955). These numbers

Fig. 19.14. Experimental plantation of rubber in the Venezuelan Orinoco, underplanted with legumes to control weeds and provide a source of nitrogen for the trees.

can vary somewhat, depending on the end use desired, e.g. through fermentation of starch in the mesocarp, increased yields of methyl alcohol can be obtained (Carioca *et al.*, 1978).

'Babaçú' fruits look like small coconuts, borne in clusters of a few dozen to several hundred. These fruits are hard, brown, vary in size from that of a plum to an orange, and weigh approximately 150 – 400 g each. Some *Orbignya* trees are recorded to yield one-half ton of fruits per year, but an average yield of ca. 15.6 tons per hectare of wild palms is sometimes cited (Carioca *et al.*, 1978). However, a study recently carried out by the State Babaçú Institute, offered evidence of much lower yields in a survey of 800 random points of babaçú distribution throughout Maranhão. According to that study, average production of babaçú in native stands in that state was about 1800 kg per hectare, with some sample plots yielding three times that amount (SUDENE/Estado do Maranhão, 1981).

'Babaçú's' special role may be yet to come — the reforestation of degraded tropical ecosystems with an economically important plant. When scattered on the soil surface, the fruits sprout and develop into seedlings which quickly and effectively establish themselves in the ecosystem. In fact, attempts at clearing 'Babaçú' forests with fire and machete usually result in the springing back to life of the younger trees as they are so hard to kill. In this era when resources are known to be finite, 'Babaçú' has potential as an inexhaustable source of a coal-like fuel (its charcoal is higher in volatile material and lower in ash

Fig. 19.15. *Jessenia bataua* growing along the river's edge in the Amazon Valley of Colombia. These plants stand about 15 metres tall. Reprinted from *Economic Botany* 35(3) 1981.

Fig. 19.16. Large fruiting panicles of *Jessenia bataua* are borne just below the leafy crown. Reprinted from *Economic Botany* 35(3) 1981.

than some mineral coals), methyl alcohol (from the mesocarp and endocarp), other industrial products (including plastics), food (edible oil, animal feed) and may be yet another important contribution from the tropical forest to our industrial society.

19.2.9. *Paullinia cupana* H.B.& K. and *P. cupana* var. *sorbilis* (Mart.) Ducke.

Common names: 'Cupana' (Venezuela and Colombia); 'Guaraná' (Brazil) (Figs. 19.22 – 19.24).
'Guaraná' is a scandent shrub in the Sapindaceae growing to a maximum of 10 m in height. Its large, glossy green leaves form great contrast to the terminal panicles of fiery orange – red capsules containing

Fig. 19.17. Fruit of *Jessenia bataua* with the epicarp removed to reveal the oil-rich mesocarp. Reprinted from *Economic Botany* 35(3) 1981.

fleshy white arils and chocolate-brown seeds. When mature, these fruiting clusters seem like an aggregation of 'eyes'. The two varieties used to produce 'Guaraná' can be distinguished by their fruit size — those of *Paullinia cupana* var. *sorbilis* are about one-third the volume of the typical *P. cupana*. 'Guaraná' is considered native to areas around the Madeira, Maués and Ramos rivers, as well as the upper Orinoco and Negro rivers (Machado, 1946).

The seeds of this shrub are highly valued as a stimulant, due to their high caffeine content of 4.3% — some 3 – 5 times as much as coffee. Tannic acid content is also high with a range of 5 – 10% (Winton and Winton, 1939). Local people use this plant by harvesting the seeds and preparing them into thick sticks of dry, hardened paste which can be stored and transported. The ripe seeds are collected and sun-dried, their fleshy arils removed and the seeds baked. These are ground into a fine powder and with the addition of a small amount of water acquire a dough-like consistency. A few coarsely ground seeds are then mixed in and the mass kneaded into sticks approximately 5 – 8 inches long and 1 inch thick. Heat from the cooking fire ensures that the product will store well. Re-constitution involves simply rasping the stick against a rough object; in Brazil the tongue of the 'pirarucu' fish is used for this purpose. The resulting powder can be mixed with water and consumed either hot or cold.

'Guaraná' is a tremendously popular beverage in Brazil, sold as a carbonated, bottled beverage under a variety of names. Consumer demand is spreading into other countries in Latin America as well as the United States. In 1979, Brazilians consumed over 15 million bottles of 'Guaraná' soda per day. Coca Cola markets a 'Guaraná' product, known as 'Taí', and exports to Paraguay, Uruguay and the United States are envisioned. In the first 8 months of 1981, Coca Cola (Brazil) produced 51 million litres of 'Taí' and 3.8 million litres of 'Fanta – Guaraná' (B. Holder, pers. com.; Hoge, 1979). Folk-medicinal uses for 'Guaraná' in the Amazon include as a powerful tonic for general well-being, analgesic, aphrodisiac, against diarrhoea, for conditions of the heart, and a myriad of uses. It is not uncommon for an Amazonian to begin his or her day with a drink of hot 'Guaraná' — a few teaspoons of this powder mixed into a cup of steaming water.

Literature reports from 1889 mention 'Guaraná' included in medical pharmacopoeias (Simmonds, 1889). Recent advertisements in the North American media have offered 'Guaraná' pills as both diet aids and as an exotic natural stimulant, providing that 'little something extra — whether its dancing till dawn or making it through those incredibly slow days at the office, you should try Guaraná!' (Cosvetic Labs, 1980). Such interest has stimulated demand beyond local capacity and shortages in the market have resulted in a large jump in wholesale and retail prices. From 375 – 500 kg can be produced per acre each year, and in 1980/81 Brazil had plans to be producing 1215 tons, up some 275% over the 1976/77 level of 324 tons (Anon., 1977). Increased consumer use in the Amazon and elsewhere is expected to make 'Guaraná' an extremely important crop plant.

19.2.10. *Pourouma cecropiaefolia* Mart. ex Miq.

Common names: 'Imbauba do vinho', 'Mapati' (Brazil), 'Uvilla' (Colombia, Peru) (Fig. 19.25).

'Uvilla' is a medium-sized tree 10 – 15 m in height found in Amazonian Colombia, Peru, and Brazil. Its habit and leaf shape are similar to *Cecropia*, a common second growth tree of the Neotropics. The leaves of this member of the Moraceae are cordate-rotund and radiately parted, with obovate to oblong-lanceolate segments green above and white-scurfy beneath (MacBride, 1937).

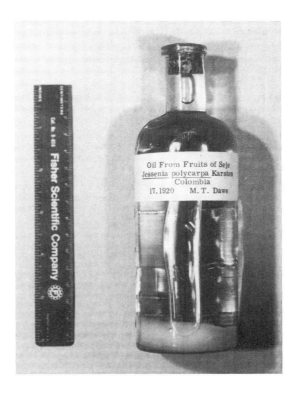

Fig. 19.18. A jar of *Jessenia bataua* oil collected in Colombia in 1920. From the Economic Museum, Royal Botanic Gardens, Kew.

TABLE 19.1. A comparison of the Fatty Acid composition of *Jessenia bataua* oil and olive (*Olea europaea*) oil.*

Fatty Acid	*Jessenia bataua*** samples, %	Olive oil samples, %
Palmitic	13.2 ± 2.1	11.2
Palmitoleic	0.6 ± 0.2	1.5
Stearic	3.6 ± 1.1	2.0
Oleic	77.7 ± 3.1	76.0
Linoleic	2.7 ± 1.0	8.5
Other	1.6 (range 0.2 – 4.6)	—

  * (Balick and Gershoff, 1981).
 ** Values given as the mean ± standard deviation of 12 separate samples.

The most important product of this tree is its purplish, round, sweet, juicy fruits which are the size of a small plum. The fruits are borne in clusters of a few dozen each and begin to appear 3 years after planting. While the outer covering is somewhat bitter, the fruits are readily consumed by sucking the pulp and spitting out the seed. 'Uvilla' is often found cultivated near indigenous villages in the Amazon Valley and also harvested from the wild. In addition to its fruits, the leaves are burned to ash which is then used as an admixture to powdered coca.

While not difficult to grow, Indians have told me that seeds will not germinate if sucked into the mouth with the pulp. This has not been tested scientifically, but there is some indication that germination may be affected by certain as yet unknown factors. To-date there are no published results of agronomic trials, but domestication programs have been observed in Manaus, Brazil and Iquitos, Peru.

Perez Arbelaez (1947) pointed out that a related species, *Pourouma sapida* (Aubl.) Karst. yielded grape-like fruits which could be dried like raisins and also used to produce a fine wine. It would seem that 'uvilla' would make a good jam or an excellent fruit drink. Very little is known of the nutritional value of this fruit, chemistry of its flavouring, or overall industrial potential. Investigations on such aspects of 'uvilla' would certainly yield a wealth of new and valuable data on a plant which deserves far greater utilisation.

19.2.11. *Theobroma cacao* L.

Common name: 'Cacao'

The genus *Theobroma* is considered by Purseglove (1974) to have probably originated in the Amazon Basin. There are 22 species according to Cuatrecasas (1965), all of which are in the Neotropics. Ducke (1940) listed 9 species as Amazonian. While the cultivated forms of *Theobroma cacao* are primarily native to Central America and Mexico, one taxon, *T. cacao* L. subsp. *sphaerocarpum* (Chev.) Cuatrecasas is found in the Amazon Valley, and referred to as 'Amazonian Forastero'. This is the most widely cultivated cacao throughout the world.

Because of the early recognition of its economic importance long before the Spanish conquistadores set foot on the continent, cacao had been widely dispersed and cultivated in Mexico and Central and South America. The Spaniards were introduced to cacao in the court of Montezuma (Dahlgren, 1923). It is a commonly cultivated crop throughout the Amazon Valley, and provides substantial revenue for the countries in this region. Along the more remote rivers, 'semi-wild' cacao or that from small holdings is collected and sold.

There are a number of important cacao research programs in the tropics, with the goal of increasing yield, developing new cultivation systems, lessening disease problems, and improving flavour. The genetic base of this crop plant is not very great. Cacao is particularly susceptible to Black Pod Disease (*Phytophthora palmivora*) which among other things causes the pods to rot (Purseglove, 1974).

Fig. 19.19. *Orbignya* sp. in Bolivia.

Much remains to be accomplished in the collection and utilisation of all the wild and cultivated forms of cacao for commercial use. Germ plasm collecting projects have shown good results, such as the 1937 collections by Pound in Amazonian Ecuador and Peru which obtained clones resistant to Witches' Broom Disease. Exploration programs currently in Brazil and a number of Amazonian countries are collecting, cataloguing, and cultivating some of the great diversity within this genus. In addition to *Theobroma cacao*, *T. bicolor* H. & B. is grown for its seeds and edible, sweet pulp, *T. angustifolium* Moc. & Sessé seeds are sometimes mixed in the cacao for commercial use, and pulp from *T. grandiflorum* (Willd. ex Spreng.) K. Schum. is the source of a sweet beverage in Brazil known as 'cupuaçu'.

19.3. IDENTIFYING USEFUL SPECIES AND THE ROLE OF THE ECONOMIC BOTANIST

Much of the knowledge concerning the useful plants of the Amazon Valley is not available in books, professional journals, newspapers, or on film. This information is in the possession of the many indigenous peoples inhabiting this region. They do not catalogue their data in the traditional way; rather it is passed down from generation to generation, guarded by selected individuals who utilise it to benefit the entire community. In an ideal situation, that is without the influence of outsiders and other 'civilising' forces, the information is refined over generations, and the end product is an excellent panorama of uses for local plants. Most of the indigenous knowledge, in the early stages at least, is obtained through a system of trial and error. From the first trials some plants proved fatal, while others had a positive effect upon the person. With time, people came to know which plants had strong activity, such as against a disease or what was perceived to be an evil spirit lurking inside the body causing the disease or other affiliation. Those species of culinary value were also identified.

The study of plants either useful or harmful to people is known as economic botany. A subdiscipline of this field, known as ethnobotany, is the investigation of plants employed by people indigenous to a particular area. Thus it is through ethnobotanical inquiry that many useful plants from the Amazon have been identified and put to wider use. Curarine, an important alkaloid used to relax muscle tissue prior to surgical incision was discovered through analysis of the Amazonian Indian arrow poison known as curare.

But yet our modern utilisation of plants from the Amazon represents only the tip of a huge beneficial 'iceberg' of possibilities present in the Amazonian flora. Only through an accelerated program of field

Fig. 19.20. Low density stand of *Orbignya* sp. scattered in the forest. In some areas, *Orbignya* stands comprise almost 100% of the canopy vegetation.

Fig. 19.21. Grinding the kernels of *Orbignya* sp. to produce oil, in Bolivia.

inquiry, coupled with laboratory testing and agronomic domestication programs, will people directly benefit from the plants of this great forest. The current pace of research in this field is not proceeding with the sense of urgency needed to build up a program with inertial movement to achieve results. Far greater numbers of multidisciplinary studies must be initiated with the aim of identifying, evaluating and bringing into wider use the plethora of useful plants found in the Amazon.

19.4. PROGRESS IN GERM PLASM CONSERVATION OF AMAZON FOREST RESOURCES

The popular and scientific press has been all too full in the last decade with coverage of the 'problem' of the Amazon Valley. In analysing any dynamic system, whether it be a corporation, country, government, city or ecosystem, it is always easiest to speak of the problems. Indeed, it almost seems that human nature dictates an emphasis in this area. Far more difficult, but much more important, is a creative analysis of the possible solutions or actions relating to the 'problem'. In the case of the Amazon

Valley, the continued, even pedantic insistence by some scientists that nothing short of halting all human activity in that vast ecosystem tends to reduce the opportunity for creative analysis of possible solutions in the search for rational and sustainable systems of exploiting this resource. The current epidemic of negativism, especially in the First World media, only serves to demoralise scientists and policymakers actively working on developing sustainable resource systems and new plant introductions from the Amazon rainforest and to fragment and diminish their resources with which to do so. Emphasis must be shifted to covering the 'positive' research on sustainable rainforest utilisation, along with the realisation of the irreversibility of continued human impact at some level in the Amazon Valley, short of regional catastrophe.

Brazil, which contains much of the Amazon Valley within its borders, has made a serious commitment to inventory and preserve as much of the genetic diversity contained within the Amazon rainforest as possible, especially of currently and potentially useful plant species. Policymakers and

Fig. 19.22. *Paullinia cupana*, planted in an open field in Belém, Brazil. In this environment, 'Guaraná' becomes shrub-like in habit.

scientists in that country are undertaking a coordinated program of germ plasm collection, the creation of living germ plasm banks, and exchange programs designed to get new material into Brazilian agriculture and distribute existing stock to other countries.

CENARGEN, the Brazilian National Center for Genetic Resources (Centro Nacional de Recursos Genéticos) was created in 1974 as a unit of EMBRAPA, the Brazilian Enterprise for Agricultural Research (Empresa Brasileira de Pesquisa Agropecuária). Realising the paucity of genetic resources for use in improving Brazilian agriculture, CENARGEN was given the mandate to implement a continuing system of organisation for introducing, conserving, and documenting germ plasm. As part of this mandate CENARGEN is to collect and study germ plasm from forest plant species, both related to commonly cultivated crops and potentially useful new crop species. As of 1980 there were some 47 'active germ plasm banks,' or areas where genetically diverse collections of economic plant species were

Fig. 19.23. Close-up view of the ripe fruit of 'Guaraná'. Note the fleshy white arils which surround the shiny dark seeds.

being developed and expanded. These included commonly cultivated plants such as soybeans and rice to regional specialities such as 'Guaraná' (EMBRAPA, 1982). Priorities were established relating specifically to the Amazon Valley in 1981, with the addition or acceleration of activities in germ plasm collection and banking for 'Babaçú', *Elaeis oleifera*, rubber, and cashew to name a few (CENARGEN/EMBRAPA, 1981). Many of these programs are international in scope and involve the collaboration of scientists from a number of countries. For example, scientists from the New York Botanical Garden Institute of Economic Botany assisted in the creation of a germ plasm bank for 'Babaçú' in 1981, which is located in Bacabal, Maranhão. This external collaboration was supported by the Charles A. Lindbergh Fund and U.S. Agency for International Development. Through an agreement with CENARGEN, the 'Babaçú' germ plasm banks are managed by agronomists from the State Institute for 'Babaçú' (INEB — -Instituto Estadual do Babaçú) in Maranhão and the State Unit for Field Research in Teresina, Piauí (UEPAE de Teresina) and comprises germ plasm of this palm from many areas of Brazil, including that now in threatened ecosystems such as dam sites, as well as from other countries where 'Babaçú' is native, such as Bolivia. There is a great interest in conserving genetic resources in other Amazonian countries, although Brazil probably has the largest network of germ plasm banks at present.

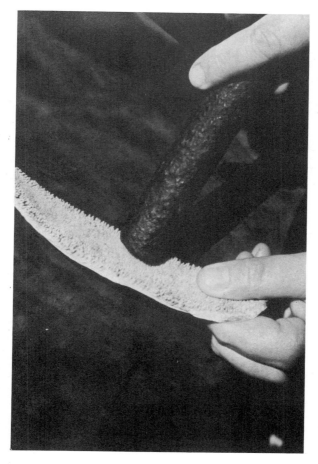

Fig. 19.24. A stick of 'Guaraná' being grated against the tongue of the 'Pirarucu' fish, to produce a fine, water-soluble powder.

Fig. 19.25. *Pourouma cecropiaefolia* planted next to an Indian dwelling in the Northwest Amazon Valley of Colombia.

19.5. CONCLUSION

Many people derive their sustenance from the products of the Amazon rainforest. Although low in actual population density, this forest does support large numbers of inhabitants, dispersed along the many rivers and small cities of the region. Table 19.2 offers an interesting perspective on just how extensively used the native Amazonian flora is, outlining some of the many products derived from the forests of Amazonian Brazil (although not exclusively Amazonian in origin or distribution) and used in commerce. Many of the commercial products presently derived from this region are from forest trees which could be utilised on a far greater sustained basis. Policymakers and scientists from Amazonian countries and elsewhere must begin to address the options for sustained usage of this fragile resource. At the same time research on many broad fronts relating to the further utilisation of Amazonian economic plants must be intensified: basic biology, agronomy, anthropology, chemistry, ethnobotany,

TABLE 19.2. Native plants, primarily Amazonian, utilized commercially in Brazil* (harvested from the wild during 1979)

Commodity	Tons	Value in 1000 Cruzeiros**
RUBBER		
Castilla ulei Warb. (''caucho'')	994	32,445
Hevea (coagulated)	20,269	836,987
Hevea (liquid latex)	1,288	30,208
Hancornia speciosa Gomez (''mangabeira'')	16	272
NON-ELASTIC GUMS		
Manilkara bidentata (DC.) Chev. (''balata'')	358	10,913
Achras zapota L. (''chicle'')	6	75
Manilkara elata (Fr. All.) Monac. (''maçaranduba'')	435	8,855
Couma hileianas (''sorva'')	5,197	72,543
Ecclinusa balata Ducke (''ucuquirana, coquirana'')	1	13
WAXES		
Copernicia cerifera (''carnaúba'')	19,920	695,717
FIBRES		
Mauritia flexuosa L.f. (''buriti'')	394	9,546
Urena lobata L. (''guaxima'')	27	191
Sida rhombifolia L. (''malva'')	66	536
Attalea funifera Mart. (''piaçava'')	55,186	551,770
Astrocaryum tucuma Mart. (''tucum'')	95	1,657
Stryphnodendron barbadetiman (Vell.) Mart. (''barbatimão'')	2,712	7,158
Rhizophora mangle L. (''mangue'')	405	1,177
OILS		
Carapa guianensis Aubl. (kernel) (''andiroba'')	277	469
Orbignya sp. (kernel) (''babaçu'')	250,913	2,591,082
Copaifera spp. (oil) (''copaíba'')	33	921
Dipteryx odorata (Aubl.) Willd. (''cumaru'')	41	2,855
Astrocaryum murumuru Mart. (seed) (''murumuru'')	24	24
Astrocaryum spp. (kernel) (''tucum'')	11,724	88,688
Virola surinamensis (Rol.) Warb.; *V. sebifera* Aubl. (kernel) (''ucuuba'')	84	374
FOODS		
Euterpe oleifera (seed) (''açaí'')	54,507	203,627
Bertholletia excelsa H. B. K. (''castanha-do-Pará'')	43,242	460,298
Hancornia speciosa Gomez (fruit) (''mangaba'')	1,101	3,645
Euterpe edulis Mart. and other palms (heart) (''palmito'')	31,358	116,158
Hymenaea spp. (resin) (''jatoba,'' ''jutaicica'')	23	354
Lonchocarpus urucu Killip & Smith (root) (''timbo'')	30	126
Bixa orellana L. (fruit) (''urucu'')	538	10,452

* Source: IBGE, 1979.
** The approximate dollar value for the Cruzeiro during 1979 was CR$ 42.33/US$ 1.00 (personal communication, Bank of Brazil).

entomology, forestry, nutrition, pathology, zoology and other fields. Regional agencies must form networks to benefit not only from interaction with each other, but actively seek to increase collaboration of scientific and technical counterpart agencies throughout the world. One such network was recently established in the Amazon region — REDINAA (Red de Investigación Agraria para la Amazonia) a group comprising six Amazonian countries committed to strengthening agricultural research capabilities in this region.

A report by Boyer (1982) pointed out that while the genetic potential exists for high yields in today's conventional crops, actual yields fall far short of their potential. This is primarily due to the inability of traditional crop plants to adapt to the less than optimum environments which comprise 88% of U.S. agricultural lands. Among the major environmental limitations in the U.S. are drought, shallowness of soil profile, cold, and wet soils. He concluded that much more work needs to be done on adapting plants to environments that are less than optimal for growth. While this study was done in the temperate zone, the data and conclusions are equally valid for the tropics. Tropical ecosystems are less than ideal environments for conventional agricultural crops and work must proceed in identifying and developing plants able to tolerate such conditions, while still offering economic and sustainable yields. Many of the native Amazonian economic species are such plants. What is needed now is an increased commitment towards developing these multipurpose species to help feed, clothe, shelter, and provide fuel for our ever-growing global family. Indeed, as we are now coming to realise, the future is in the forest.

ACKNOWLEDGEMENTS

This paper is fondly dedicated to my friends and colleagues in the Neotropics undertaking research involving the identification and utilisation of resources from the tropical forest. While they often work in relative obscurity, as this kind of research is not one of the most visible nor colourful of today's sciences, their contributions will be some of the most important to the future of both the developing and developed worlds. Dr. G. T. Prance kindly provided Figs. 6 – 8, Dr. J. L. Zarucchi kindly provided Fig. 15, and Mr. Rupert Hastings offered much-valued assistance in photographing Figs. 2 and 18. Figures 2 and 18 are reprinted with the permission of the Director, Royal Botanic Gardens, Kew.

The author would like to thank the following national organisations for facilitating recent studies in South America. Bolivia: Centro de Desarrollo Florestal — Departmento Vida Silvestre, Parques Nacionales, Caza y Pesca; Instituto Boliviano de Tecnología Agropecuario (IBTA); Instituto de Ecologia, Universidad Boliviana, Universidad Mayor de San Andrés; Ministerio de Asuntos Campesinos y Agropecuarios (MACA). Brazil: Centro Nacional de Recursos Genéticos (CENARGEN); Consejo Nacional de Desenvolvimento Científico e Tecnológico (CNPq); Empresa Brasileira de Pesquisa Agropecuária (EMBRAPA); Instituto Estadual do Babaçu (INEB); Instituto Nacional de Pesquisas da Amazônia (INPA); Museu Paraense Emílio Goeldi; UEPAE de Teresina. Venezuela: Ministerio del Ambiente y de los Recursos Naturales Renovables (MARNR) Zona 10. I would also like to acknowledge financial support from the following organisations: The Charles A. Lindbergh Fund; The National Science Foundation — Projeto Flora Amazônica; The Rockefeller Foundation; The U.S. Agency for International Development.

REFERENCES

Anonymous (1977) As saudáveis perspectivas do guaraná. *Amazônia*, Fevereiro.

Balick, M. J. (1976) The palm heart as a new commercial crop from Tropical America. *Principes* 20, 24 – 28.

Balick, M. J. (1980) The Biology and Economics of the *Oenocarpus-Jessenia* (Palmae) complex. Ph.D. Dissertation, Dept. of Biology, Harvard University.

Balick, M. J. and Gershoff, S. N. (1981) Nutritional evaluation of *Jessenia bataua*: source of high quality protein and oil from Tropical America. *Econ. Bot.* 35, 261 – 271.

Boyer, J. S. (1982) Plant productivity and environment. *Science* 218, 443 – 448.

Brady, G. S. and Clauser, H. R. (1977) *Materials Handbook*, Eleventh Ed. McGraw-Hill Book Co., New York.

Burchard, R. E. (1975) Coca chewing: a new perspective. In *Cannabis and Culture*. Ed. V. Rubin, pp. 463 – 484. Mouton Publishers, The Hague.

Carioca, J. O. B., Scares, J. B. and Thiemann, W. H. P. (1978) Production of ethyl alcohol from babassu. *Biotechnology and Bioengineering* 20, 443 – 445.

CENARGEN/EMBRAPA (1981) Coordenação de exploração botânica e coleta de germoplasma. (Typewritten report).

Chaves, J. M. and Pechnik, E. (1947) Tucumã. *Revista de Quimica Industrial* 16, 5 – 19.

Cosvetic Labs. (1980) Advertisement for Guaraná — 800.

Cuatrecasas, J. (1965) Cacao and its allies: a taxonomic revision of the genus *Theobroma*. *Contrib. U.S. Nat. Herb.* 35, 379 – 614.

Dahlgren, B. E. (1923) Cacao. *Field Mus. Nat. Hist., Dept. Bot., Leaflet no. 4.*

Ducke, A. (1940) As espécies Brasileiras de cacau (gênero *Theobroma* L.) na botânica, sistemática e geográfica. *Rodriguesia* 13, 265 – 276.

Duke, J. A., Aulik, D. and Plowman, T. (1975) Nutritional value of coca. *Bot. Mus. Leaflet* 24, 113 – 119.

EMBRAPA (1982) *Relatório Técnico Anual do Centro Nacional de Recursos Genéticos 1980.* EMBRAPA, Brasilia.

Gonsalves, A. D. (1955) *O Babaçú, consideracões científicas, técnicas e economicas.* Série Estudios e Ensaios No. 8. Ministerio da Agicultura, Rio de Janeiro.

Hoge, W. (1979) Coca-Cola's subsidiary in Brazil joins the guaraná generation. *The New York Times*, Saturday, Nov. 3.

IBGE (1979) *Produção Extrativa Vegetal – -1979. Vol.7.* Fundação Instituto Brasileiro de Geografica e Estatística, Rio de Janeiro.

Johannessen, C. L. (1967) Pejibaye palm: physical and chemical analysis of the fruit. *Econ. Bot.* 21, 371 – 378.

MacBride, J. F. (1937) Flora of Peru, Part II, No. 2. *Field Mus. Nat. Hist., Bot. Ser.* 13, 257 – 661.

MacBride, J. F. (1960) Flora of Peru, Part I, No. 2, Palmae. *Field Mus. Nat. Hist., Bot. Ser.* 16, 321 – 418.

Machado, O. (1946) Contribução ao estudo das plantas medicinais do Brasil — o guaraná. *Rodriguesia* 10, 89 – 110.

National Academy of Sciences (1975) *Underexploited Tropical Plants with Promising Economic Value.* National Academy of Sciences, Washington, D.C.

Pereira-Pinto, G. (1951) O oleo de pataua. *Bol. Tecn. do Inst. Agron. do Norte* 23, 67 – 77.

Perez-Arbelaez, E. (1947) *Plantas utiles de Colombia.* Contraloria General de La Republica, Bogota.

Plowman, T. (1979) The identity of Amazon and Trujillo coca. *Bot. Mus. Leaflet* 27, 45 – 68.

Plowman, T. (1980) Coca. *Field Mus. Nat. Hist. Bull.* 51, 17 – 21.

Prance, G. T. and Mori, S. A. (1979) Lecythidaceae — Part I. *Flora Neotropica Monograph* No. 21.

Purseglove, J. W. (1974) *Tropical Crops: Dicotyledons.* John Wiley and Sons, New York.

Rivier, L. (1981) Analysis of alkaloids in leaves of cultivated *Erythroxylum* and characterization of alkaline substances used during coca chewing. *J. Ethnopharm.* 3, 313 – 335.

Rizzini, C. T. and Mors, W. B. (1976) *Botânica Economica Brasileira.* Editoria Pedagogica e Universitaria Ltda., São Paulo.

Schultes, R. E. (1977) Wild *Hevea*: an untapped source of germplasm. *J. Rubb. Res. Inst. Sri Lanka* 54, 227 – 257.

Simmonds, P. L. (1889) *Tropical Agriculture.* E. and F. N. Spon, London.

SUDENE/Estado do Maranhão (1981) *Mapaeamento das Ocurrencias e Prospecção do Potencial Atual do Babaçu no Estado do Maranhão.* São Luis.

Ulman, N. (1982) Brazil pursues Amazon's riches with a project on a huge scale benefiting the region's vastness. *Wall Street Journal*, Thursday, October 28, page 56.

Winton, A. L. and Winton, K. B. (1939) *The Structure and Composition of Foods.* Vol. IV. John Wiley and Sons, New York.

CHAPTER 20

Forestry in the Brazilian Amazon

JUDY McKEAN RANKIN

Department of Ecology, Instituto Nacional de Pesquisas da Amazônia, C.P. 478, 69.000 Manaus, Brazil

CONTENTS

20.1. INTRODUCTION

Forestry, or the management of forests, involves far more than simple wood production. Broadly interpreted, forestry includes the state of health and productivity of the environment as a whole, including both the site of wood production and its surrounding forest, agricultural and urban lands (Lanly and Clement, 1979). This definition is particularly appropriate for forestry activities in tropical rainforest areas such as the Amazon Basin. Such a holistic view is essential when considering rainforests where interdependency among components of the biological community and physical environment is at its highest (*see* preceding contributions on hydrological and nutrient cycles, climate and biological interactions). Whether broadly or more narrowly defined, forestry is not yet practised in the Amazon on an industrial scale, with the exception of a single plantation enterprise in northern Brazil covering a fraction of 1% of the Basin. Whereas much timber exploitation takes place, not one commercial timber tract of lowland tropical rainforest is being intensively managed on sustained yield basis in any of the six nations with significant territory in the Basin (Bolivia, Brazil, Colombia, Equador, Peru, Venezuela) or the adjacent Guianas (Guyana, Surinam, French Guiana), an area encompassing approximately 5 million km² of tropical rainforest.

Several events in the last decade have combined to raise doubts about the direction of forestry in the Amazon and the future of the Amazon forests themselves. The demand for wood products of all types has grown at an increasing rate both in the countries of the Basin and the world in general; Brazil for example is a net importer of forest products despite its huge southern tree plantations and major share of the Amazon rainforest (Eckholm, 1979). Projections indicate that Brazil's consumption of wood could double during the last quarter of the century (Reis, 1978). Recent trends in the increased use of multispecies lots of tropical hardwoods in species tolerant (amenable to a diversity of species) industrial processes such as paper pulp, particle board and charcoal have significantly increased the volume of wood which can be harvested per hectare from native tropical rainforests. Road building and government sponsored and spontaneous colonisation booms begun in the 1960s and 1970s have opened the previously remote Amazonian uplands and have brought large numbers of small farmers and extensive cattle ranching operations, dramatically increasing the rates of forest depletion and deforestation (Myers, 1980a; Fearnside, 1982). At the same time, projects have been launched in the Amazon for the implantation of silvicultural monocultures of uncertain economic and ecological viability along, with the establishment of industrial complexes with high demands for wood raw materials which must be met either by the plantations or the native forests. Together these events have created the prospect that significant portions of the Amazonian rainforest may be degraded beyond the point of economic recovery. The establishment of rational forest land-use policy and adequate forest management techniques has thus become *the* priority for governments in the region if the Amazon is to be developed for greater human use without incurring severe ecological and economic consequences in the near future.

This review of forestry in the Amazon will concern itself with the history and prospects of the management of native lowland tropical rainforest (also described as tropical moist or tropical evergreen forest) and of tree plantations established within this vegetation type. It will focus on the forestry situation in the Brazilian Amazon, although many of Brazil's experiences apply to the other Amazonian countries as well. Brazil occupies by far the greatest portion of the Basin, over 60%, including all but the northern and western margins; the country has a history of forest exploitation, inventories, silvicultural research and private entrepreneurial incentive in industrial forestry more extensive than that in the other countries in the Basin; and finally, while great pressures are being brought to develop the Brazilian Amazon at all costs, there exists in certain segments of Brazilian society the concept that the Amazonian forests must be conserved and managed as a renewable resource if they are to be developed for the long-term benefit of the country. Whereas it is obvious that different forest management systems will have to be developed to suit the different biological and socioeconomic conditions to be found throughout the region, the fate of forestry in the Amazon and of the Amazon itself will depend in a large part on what happens in Brazil.

20.2. HISTORICAL OVERVIEW

Forestry and forest-based industry in the Brazilian Amazon have developed more or less independently along three relatively distinct trajectories: (1) highly selective, uncontrolled timber extraction from native forest without provisions for obtaining a future crop of the species exploited; (2) private entrepreneurial efforts in industrial scale plantation silviculture; and (3) experimental government programs in permanent sustained yield management of native tropical rainforest.

Selective logging of only the most valuable timber species has the longest and most continuous history of these three activities. This utilisation pattern reflects the high species diversity and low number of individuals of any given species per unit area characteristic of the tropical rainforest community and the large number of tree species with dense, silicious, resinous, crossgrained or otherwise difficult-to-work wood. This form of forest exploitation has been practised almost unchanged to the present day, first in the inundated várzea (whitewater river) and igapó (black or clearwater river) forests on the river

Fig. 20.1. Inundated igapó forest such as this on the Rio Negro has traditionally been the target for logging activities in the Amazon.

margins (Fig. 20.1) and since the early 1970s in the non-inundated terra firme upland forests. With the construction and colonisation of a massive network of highways penetrating the uplands and the subsequent purchase of sizeable forest tracts by large Brazilian and multinational companies, the scale on which logging is practised has expanded by the selective nature of this activity remains unchanged.

Attempts at industrial plantation silviculture, initiated with the Fordlândia rubber (*Hevea brasiliensis*) plantations established by Henry Ford in the 1920s, have been sporadic and for the most part unsuccessful with the exception of Jari Florestal e Agropecuária Ltda. (Jari Forestry, Agriculture and Cattle Ranching Ltd.), an integrated plantation forestry, cattle raising and rice operation established in 1968 by American billionaire shipping magnate Daniel K. Ludwig on a 1.6 million hectare estate on the Jari river in Pará and Amapá. Despite the progress made in the last 10 years in the development of plantation silviculture at Jari, this project has also experienced a number of serious biological and economic problems, and the permanent sustainability of its plantations has yet to be confirmed. Other experimental and industrial plantations of hardwoods, softwoods, nut trees and native rubber ranging from tens to thousands of hectares have been established by diverse government agencies and private companies over the last 30 years. However, the total area in silvicultural plantations is small compared to the extent of the Brazilian Amazon, and most plantations are either abandoned, under-utilised or too recently established to play an active role in commercial forestry in the region.

The management of native tropical rainforest on an economic and permanent sustained yield basis has been an illusive goal in the Amazon as elsewhere in the humid tropics. Work in this area has been conducted exclusively on an experimental scale under the auspices of diverse government agencies. The first experimental work done in Brazil on tropical rainforest management by means of natural (self-seeding) and artificial (enrichment planting) regeneration, as well as on other aspects of tropical silviculture, began in the 1950s but the initially promising results were not experimentally or commercially pursued. Although frequently cited by government agencies as the most desirable management option for developing the region's timber resources, active experimental work was only reinitiated in the mid-1970s. By 1980 three experimental programs on permanent sustained yield native forest management had been established, including the first integrated program of forest and watershed management for commercial forest utilisation. The preliminary inventories of all these studies suggest that the biological potential for managed natural regeneration exists in each of the forest areas surveyed. However, the economic viability of such management plans is still unknown and commercial application is still years away.

20.3. TRADITIONAL LOGGING ACTIVITIES

Uncontrolled extraction of forest products, such as valuable hardwoods, latex and essential oils from wood, has been taking place in the Amazon since the advent of European colonisation 350 years ago. Until the ambitious road building projects of the 1960s and early 1970s, the picture for logging activities was essentially the same throughout the Amazon. Logging was highly selective and was concentrated in the areas of easiest access, the seasonally inundated várzea and igapó forests on the margins of the Amazon and its tributaries. Even as late as 1973, these forests supplied 80% of the wood harvested in the Amazon (Volatron, 1976). Only a small number of species were harvested, amounting to approximately 10% of the comparatively low 90 m³ standing wood volume (Pandolfo, 1978; Schmithüsen, 1978). In 1951, 6 species accounted for 89% of the approximately 115,000 m³ harvested from seasonally inundated forests and the adjacent terra firme, with louro inhamhui (*Ocotea cymbarum*) accounting for 24% of the total volume, followed by cedro (*Cedrela odorata*) 19%, Assacu (*Hura crepitans*) 16%, jacareuba (*Calophyllum brasiliense*) 15%, aguano or mahogany (*Swietenia macrophylla*) 9%, and andiroba (*Carapa guianensis*) 6%, with the remaining 11% made up of ucuuba (*Virola* spp.) and others (Gachot *et al.*, 1953). All logging was done by hand within 10 to 200 m of the mean annual high water mark. Trunks were cut into 4 m lengths and rolled by hand over poles to dry creek beds to be rafted downstream to the distant mills when the waters rose. Most logging was conducted by small independent operators who supplied sawmills on a demand basis: a mill might receive logs from as many as 100 loggers during the year from sites 200 to 2,000 km distant (Schmithüsen, 1978), with 60% of all logs coming from more than 1,500 km (Gachot *et al.*, 1953). The seasonal nature of the operation led to losses of logs waiting in the forest exposed to damage by insects and fungi. Many logs were also lost if flood waters did not reach expected levels. Mill owners were forced to tie up capital in log stocks to assure adequate supplies for running the mills during the dry season. Aside from supply problems, sawmills were plagued by old equipment, inefficient layout, and lack of capital, skilled labour and replacement parts (Volatron, 1976; Palmer, 1977).

Representing only 2.2% of the lowland tropical rainforest in the Amazon (Palmer, 1977; Myers, 1980a), the várzea and igapó forests have suffered serious depletion of those tree species favoured by the wood industry, with seed bearing trees or whole adult populations of *Manilkara huberi* (the source of *balata* gum) and *Virola surinamensis* having been eliminated throughout much of these forest types (J. Palmer, cited in Fox, 1976). Even so, 60% of the wood harvested in the Brazilian Amazon continues to come from the várzea forests harvested in the traditional manner (Carvalho, 1981).

The forests of the non-inundated terra firme uplands account for 95% of the tropical rainforest in the Amazon (Myers, 1980a); they have both a greater number of tree species and a higher standing volume than the seasonally inundated forests, averaging 178 m³/ha (Pandolfo, 1978) for the Legal Amazon (approximately 5 million km, including the Brazilian Amazon and pre-Amazonian parts of the states of Maranhão and Goiás), yet up to the end of the 1960s they remained virtually unexploited due to their inaccessibility. The construction of highways such as the 1,900 km Belém − Brasília in 1963 and the 4,900 km Transamazônica in 1970 led to the occupation of sizeable tracts of terra firme forest by small agriculturalists and large cattle ranches, the latter ranging from 3,000 ha to several hundreds of thousands of hectares. A small number of private holdings in the terra firme were also obtained by local and multinational companies, such as Georgia − Pacific (approximately 400,000 ha), Toyomenka (approximately 300,000 ha) (Myers, 1980b), and Atlantic Veneer (300,000 ha) (J. Bruce, pers. comm., 1982) for the logging of native species for veneer, plywood and chipboard production (Fig. 20.2).

The availability of access, the depletion of native forests in southern Brazil and, to a small extent, the várzea, plus SUDAM (Superintendency for Development of the Amazon) incentives for sawmills and forestry operations in the Amazon, resulted in increased logging of terra firme forests and exponential growth in the number of sawmills in the Legal Amazon: numbering less than 300 in 1970, there were 1,639 sawmills operating in the region in 1982 (Pandolfo, 1974; Brazil, Ministério de Agricultura, IBDF, 1982). In the colonisation area of the western state of Rondônia alone, hundreds of sawmills sprang up almost overnight accompanying the colonisation boom as it pushed forestward from the margins of the main Porto Velho − Cuiabá road (P.M. Fearnside, pers. comm., 1982).

The growth in the timber industry and the availability of financing has not been accompanied by increases in sawmill efficiency and timber quality. Many mills continue to operate at about 40% efficiency and still suffer from lack of skilled labour and raw materials and poor production layout, with few having the saws and kilns to produce finished, dried lumber of standard quality (Palmer, 1977). This situation persists to the present day. More importantly, SUDAM fiscal incentives have been dedicated almost exclusively to promoting the extraction and processing of timber, technologies already relatively well known, rather than to the lesser known operations of management and regeneration of logged forests. Incentives for reforestation administered by IBDF (Brazilian Institute for Forestry

Fig. 20.2. Selective logging of the upland forests provokes little environmental impact but severely depletes stocks of desirable commercial species.

Development, the agency responsible for overseeing all forest utilisation and conservation in the country) in conjunction with the 1965 Forestry Code stipulating the planting, anywhere in the Legal Amazon, of four seedlings of any tree species for each tree harvested, have also proved totally inadequate to safeguard the future productivity of the exploited native forests. In practice, these requirements have often been fulfilled by contracting out the replanting task to 'forest condominiums', companies which establish monocultures of native or exotic species with no defined eventual industrial end. The second largest timber tree plantation in the tropical rainforest zone of the Brazilian Amazon, Santa Isabel near Belém, is the result of such a 'condominium'. No new research or industrial application of natural forest management was financed or conducted in the Brazilian Amazon and much previous work stagnated during the 20 year period between the inauguration of silvicultural research under a bilateral agreement between FAO (United Nations Food and Agriculture Organisation) and SPVEA (Superintendency for the Economic Valorisation Plan of the Amazon, founded in 1953 and later reorganised as SUDAM in 1966) at the Curuá-Una Experiment Station in the late 1950s and the initiation of the fieldwork in the Tapajós National Forest under a 1973 bilateral agreement between FAO and IBDF's Project for Development and Research in Forestry (PRODEPEF), later including EMBRAPA/CPATU (Brazilian Enterprise for Agriculture and Cattle Ranching/Center for Agricultural and Cattle Ranching Research in the Humid Tropics) despite insistence by SUDAM that the sustained yield utilisation and management of the Amazon forests were desirable and in fact feasible (e.g. Pandolfo, 1974).

The contribution of timber from terra firme forests climbed to approximately 40% by the mid-1970s, but logging continued to be highly selective as in the várzea and igapó, concentrating on one or two valuable species such as cedro (*Cedrela odorata*) and mahogany (*Swietenia macrophylla*) (Schmithüsen, 1978). Despite the large clearings for agricultural holdings, less than 0.5% of the standing wood volume (estimated at 178 m^3/ha total and 45 m^3/ha for commercial species by SUDAM) was used for timber or fuel as late as 1979 (Myers, 1980a). In such operations, the bulk of the forest biomass is burned on the site to provide nutrient-rich ash for fertilising the future crop (*see* Fearnside, this volume). An estimated 3.11 million hectares of the Brazilian Amazon had been partially or completely deforested by 1981 (Anon., 1981). The rate of non-lumbering deforestation of tropical moist forest by 1979 in Brazil has been estimated at 10,000 km^2/year (Myers, 1980a).

Some increase in the number of tree species utilised by the timber industry has come about due to economic pressures at the local level to keep sawmills from standing idle for lack of logs and, to a small extent, due to increased enforcement of the IBDF directive requiring utilisation of timber on land to be converted to non-forest uses (Anon., 1977). Cattle ranches and other land clearing enterprises with centralised operations near the state capitals of Belém and Manaus have been most affected. In other areas this directive is generally unenforceable due to the limited number of IBDF staff. In the state of Amazonas, for example, IBDF has a total of 80 staff members, only 8 − 10 of whom are forest officers responsible for all parks, reserves and forestry operations for an area of 1.6 million km^2. Twenty to forty species are currently accepted by local sawmills. The largest sawmill operating on terra firme in the state of Amazonas in forests being converted to cattle pasture accepts 22 species of the more than 400 found on the 15,000 ha property. This mill occasionally experiments with other non-commercial species that are sent in by the logging foreman and has found some to have adequate commercial properties. Since almost all of the lumber sold from the mill is by prior order, little success has been achieved in introducing new species into the local market.

Whereas even fewer species are sold on the international market, this situation may soon change with IBDFs vigorous campaign to improve timber quality and grading consistency [Brazil (Presidência da República), 1982] and to promote little-known Brazilian timbers through export incentives, improved infrastructure for transport and storage, and meetings with foreign buyers (*A Critica*, 16 de dezembro de 1982). Finally, greater utilisation of wood from native forests can be expected to expand in the region with the growth of industries based on species-tolerant industrial processes, such as charcoal, chipboard, and pulp. For example, cement factories, such as one currently under construction in Manaus, will be fueled with charcoal by federal decree. The Manaus plant, with an estimated consumption of 200 MT of charcoal per day (da Silva and Corrêa, 1983), will be supplied entirely from native forests exploited by independent contractors. This amounts to between 900 and 1,500 ha per year if all trees larger or equal to 25 cm DBH (diameter at breast height) are utilised. No provisions currently exist for the eventual establishment of plantations to supply wood for charcoal for this plant (A. Corrêa, pers. comm., 1983). Other industries, such as steel mills and mining concerns, will also contribute to this consumption (see Forest Resource Inventories).

20.4. FOREST RESOURCE INVENTORIES

In addition to the remoteness of forest resources and the lack of infrastructure and private incentive in the timber industry, early economic development of forestry in the Amazon was hampered by lack of forest inventories permitting a realistic assessment of the extent of and biological potential of resources present. In 1953 the Superintendency for the Economic Valorization Plan of the Amazon (SPVEA) was founded to promote the economic development of the region and most forestry-related activities came to be overseen by this organ. In the same year FAO and SPVEA began a joint program to inventory a large area of tropical rainforest in the state of Pará, to begin silvicultural experiments and to train foresters in tropical silvicultural techniques appropriate for the Amazon. From 1956 to 1961 some 210,000 km^2 just south of the lower Amazon River in the state of Pará were surveyed by the FAO teams (Heinsdijk, 1957; Rollet and Queiroz, 1978). These inventories were never put to industrial use due to the reduction of FAO presence in 1962 after the founding of the National School of Forests in Curitiba, and the later emphasis on the development of the more remote interior uplands through highway colonisation programs (Palmer, 1977).

The Projeto RADAM survey (Radar Survey of the Amazon of Brazil, later known as RADAMBRASIL covering the whole country) was conducted in Amazonia by the Ministry of Mines and Energy from 1968 to 1977. This massive program attempted to catalogue all aspects of the biological and mineral resources of Brazil's Legal Amazon. Synthetic aperture side looking radar imagery was utilised to produce descriptive texts, forestry inventories and maps of the geology, mineral deposits, soils, vegetation and potential land use of the region. Although supported by data from thousands of scattered site visits, ground truth information provided was sparse due to the region's vast area.

The RADAM surveys have led directly to the discovery and subsequent exploitation of many important concentrations of valuable minerals, including more than 100 'alkaline chimneys' frequently associated with deposits of valuable metals like niobium, copper, manganese etc., and the world's purest deposit of bauxite with reserves estimated at 4.5 billion MT located on the Trombetas River, a northern tributary of the Amazon (de Almeida, 1978), providing strong motivation for the establishment of a variety of industrial activities in the region. RADAM maps have been used extensively by SUDAM for planning and development of the agency's Large Project Poles emphasising mineral exploitation, such as Projeto Grande Carajás (Brasil, 1977) (see Plantations) and for defining potential areas for forest exploitation (e.g. Pandolfo, 1978) (see Government Administration of Forestry Activities on Public Lands).

Other forestry inventories were conducted during the late 1960s and 1970s by IBDF and other government institutions, concentrating mainly on the western state of Acre, on the region between the Juruá and Purús Rivers near milling centres at Tefé and Coari in the state of Amazonas, and on the Trombetas River north of the Amazon in western Pará. These inventories cover approximately 1.8

million km^2 and, with the exception of the 12,000 km^2 survey on the Ilha de Marajó at the mouth of the Amazon, do not include significant areas of várzea forest (Rollet and Queiroz, 1978).

The availability of these forest inventories has not greatly influenced the forestry-oriented utilisation of the Amazon rainforest in Brazil or led to a reasonable evaluation of its potential either in terms of the present standing crop or future regeneration possibilities. The reasons behind this are related to the surveys themselves as well as to other socioeconomic factors at work in the region. Most surveys have not permitted more than a static estimate of wood volume actually present. Since the work of the FAO mission at Curuá-Una in the 1950s, only two inventories have included the seedlings and saplings less than 25 cm DBH necessary for evaluating the forest's capacity for natural regeneration. One of these was conducted in 1975 on an experimental scale in the Tapajós National Forests (de Carvalho, 1980) and the other in 1981 by INPA (National Institute for Research in the Amazon) in the 'Ecological Management of Tropical Rain Forest' watershed study area north of Manaus (Higuchi et al., 1982). Problems also exist with the botanical accuracy of most of the large scale forest inventories. With the exception of a small survey conducted by the botanical staff at INPA in the region of Manaus, the identifications of most tree species in published surveys have been based on common names provided by local informants, with matching to scientific names being done later. This practice can lead to errors in species identifications as great as 90% (Pires, 1979).

At the industrial level, many independent operators ignore existing inventories in their areas and log selectively to meet market demands. Similarly, the great productivity and timber wealth of the terra firme forests often cited in the forestry-oriented publications of SUDAM (e.g. Pandolfo, 1969, 1978) seems to ignore repeated results showing high species diversity, low volumes per species per hectare and high wood densities except in certain areas containing high volumes of a few desirable species (e.g. the mahogany-rich area south of Curuá-Una). This exaggerated enthusiasm to promote forestry as the vocation of the Amazon appears to be an over-reaction to the ill-conceived promotion by the Brazilian government in the 1970s of vast cattle pastures in the midst of the world's largest remaining tropical rainforest. Combined with inaccuracies in the surveys themselves, overly optimistic claims have caused repercussions that have set back the cause of forestry in the region. This appears to have played a part in the problems associated with the first large government logging concession in the Brazilian Amazon, a 65,000 km^2 tract associated with the Tucuruí hydroelectric dam basin in southern Pará. Initially estimated at 11 million m^3, this figure was soon reduced to 9 million^3, then to 6 million^3, and finally to 1.7 − 2.7 m^3 of standing commercial timber. To compensate for the concessionaire's losses due to this much reduced volume, the Brazilian government ceded logging rights to a further 93,000 ha located in the Pucurii and Parakana Indian Reserves, bringing the final volume of the contract to around 3 million m^3 (Pereira, 1982). However, this move came too late to rescue the concessionaire from serious financial difficulties (see Government Administration of Forestry Activities on Public Lands).

20.5. GOVERNMENT ADMINISTRATION OF FORESTRY ACTIVITIES ON PUBLIC LANDS

The promotion of organised and sustainable commercial logging in the Brazilian Amazon has floundered despite increased accessibility and information on forest resources. The major impediments to organising ecologically and economically sustainable forestry activities in native Amazonian forests have been the number of government agencies involved in the various aspects of forest utilisation, none with complete authority to approve, integrate, implant and oversee projects, the lack of federal forest reserves and the lack of regulations adapted to the realities of the Amazon forest, including an explicit Forestry Code and plans for silviculture and management governing the use and management of forest lands in the public and private domain.

The first Brazilian Forestry Code, established in 1939, provided powers for the establishment of permanent forest reserves but contained few concrete directives concerning forest utilisation and protection. A Federal Forest Council existed but was not active in the Amazon. This Code was supplanted in 1965 by the version which continues in effect at present. While more specific than its predecessor, it is strongly oriented toward the forestry situation in southern Brazil and contains only two articles specifically related to land use and forest management in the Amazon. These prohibit the 'empirical' exploitation of native forests in the Amazon Basin until such time as a technical management plan is legally adopted (Art. 15 Código Florestal Lei No. 4.771, 15 de setembro de 1965) and requires that clear cutting in what is now the Legal Amazon be limited to 50% of each property, with the remaining 50% to be left in unspecified 'tree cover' (Art. 44). 'Tree cover' has been variously interpreted as timber plantations, logged forest, and perennial crops such as fruit trees and the 50% requirement has been circumvented by subsequent division and sale of properties. Under the aegis of this Code some 20 million hectares in the Legal Amazon have been designated by IBDF as multiple-use forest reserves. However, to date only two such reserves have actually been demarcated on the ground: Tapajós National Forest (600,000 ha) and Caxiuanã National Forest (200,000 ha), both in the state of Pará. Only the Tapajós reserve has a defined land use plan (Reis, 1978).

Since 1979 Brazil has been on the brink of revising its forest policy for the Amazon. In May 1979 an interministerial commission was appointed by presidential decree to draw up an Integrated Forest Policy to replace the 1965 Code. Working papers to aid the commission were solicited from virtually all research institutions, universities and other agencies in the Legal Amazon as well as other parts of the country. The final draft document gave great emphasis to forestry and severely limited cattle ranching in the tropical rainforest zone of the Legal Amazon. This draft was subject to further revision in 1980 by a second commission which reintroduced a strong emphasis on cattle ranching (P.I.S. Braga, pers. comm., 1980). Neither of these versions has yet received final approval. In September 1982, the president of IBDF, Mauro S. Reis, assured participants at a conference on native timber species that an unspecified proposal for the Integrated Forest Policy for the Amazon was under consideration at the level of the office of the President of the Republic (*Journal de Brasilia*, 14 de setembro de 1982). The current situation remains unchanged.[1]

Despite the lack of an explicit Amazonian forest policy, several proposals exist for the development of commercial forestry in native forests in the public domain. One of the more widely divulged proposals has been that of Income Forests (*Florestas de Rendimento*) promoted by SUDAM. Under this plan, twelve regional income forests or reserves for commercial logging concessions encompassing 39.5 million hectares would be operated under the supervision of a vaguely defined government company (Pandolfo, 1978). This organ would be responsible for all aspects of the operations, including some of the actual logging, supervision of the activities of private concessionaires and all post-logging management of the forests. An untested management scheme based on the 'recomposition' of the native forests calls for enrichment of the logged stands by replanting with seedlings of the same species removed by logging and by favouring natural regeneration through unspecified silvicultural treatments.

Whereas the stated goal of this proposal is the utilisation of native forest on a permanent sustained yield basis, the provisions set forth in the SUDAM document are inadequate to guarantee its achievement. Little consideration appears to have been given in the selection of the income forests in light of necessary preconditions for successful natural regeneration management, such as detailed knowledge of initial species composition, population structures, tree distributions, reproductive frequency and seed germination and seedling growth characteristics (*see* Liew and Wong, 1973; Fox, 1976). These factors will dictate to a large extent, not only the forest regeneration potential under commercial use but also the nature of that use. While intensive logging with little control over damages to the remaining stand has been recognised as one of the major impediments to successful natural regeneration management and forest resource protection (Meijer, 1970; Liew and Wong, 1973; Fox,

1976; Hopkins *et al.*, 1976; Ewel and Conde, 1980), the Income Forest plan does not provide an explicit mechanism for overseeing extraction and enforcing limitations to logging damage. Finally, little consideration is given to the capital investments necessary for both the establishment and maintenance of enrichment plantings in native forests or to the persistent silvicultural problems associated with those species most likely to be logged and replanted in this context [*see* Brazil (Ministério do Interior), 1979]. The clause in recent versions of the Income Forest proposal (*see* Superintendência do Desenvolvimento da Amazônia *et al.*, 1978) permitting concessionaires the option of doing the actual replanting or paying the costs of replanting to the government agency makes no provision for the long term maintenance needed to ensure the success of enrichment plantings. Concessionaires can be expected to be tempted to minimise their investments in replanting operations for whose ultimate success they will not be responsible. Pitt (1961), in his pioneering work on enrichment plantings at Curuá-Una, states that 'if [enrichment plantings] are not kept clean and fairly open the plants put out just do not develop and the whole effort is wasted.'

Parallel to the SUDAM promotion of Income Forests, another concession system for developing of commercial logging in the Brazilian Amazon has been proposed by IBDF. This plan for Forest Utilisation Contracts or 'risk contracts' is an outcome of studies conducted in the mid-1970s by the joint IBDF/FAO/UNDP program Project for Development and Research in Forestry (Schmithüsen, 1978). Specified in less detail than the SUDAM proposal, risk contracts would grant the right to private logging companies to exploit timber from certain public lands over a defined period of time, ranging from 1 to 20 years. The final project report does not specify whether such concessions would be managed on a permanent sustained yield basis but cautions that one of the major drawbacks to such contracts is the lack of control afforded over logging intensity and extraction practices which could jeopardise future forest productivity. A strong Forest Service and explicit forestry legislation are stated as prerequisites for risk contract utilisation (Schmithüsen, 1978). Whereas risk contracts were envisioned by the original report as only one of several types of logging concessions to be used in the Brazilian Amazon, they received a great deal of negative publicity at the time of announcement in late 1978 due to public fears that they would be used to hand over large tracts of the Amazon forest to multinational companies. It is largely due to this negative public opinion that this proposal has not been put into practice.

The first major public logging concession in the Brazilian Amazon was granted in 1980 by Eletronorte, the government power utility for the Legal Amazon, for the extraction of commercial timber from 65,000 ha of the more than 300,000 ha reservoir basin of the Tucuruí hydroelectric dam on the Tocantins River, a southern tributary of the Amazon in the state of Pará. Despite the purely salvage nature of the operation, requiring no care in logging practices or subsequent silvicultural treatment, this concession has been a complete failure with severe repercussions for the Brazilian timber industry at home and overseas. It also raises serious doubts about the management of future concessions, such as those envisioned by SUDAM, supposedly to be operated on a permanent sustained yield basis. Two major problems plagued the Tucuruí concession: the granting of the concession to a company lacking the necessary experience and financial reserves to successfully undertake the logging operation, and the lack of adequate inventory data to permit a realistic evaluation of the concession area's timber potential. Difficulties were allegedly experienced in finding a company willing to work the Tucuruí concession, with smaller interested Amazonian timber companies judged to have inadequate financial resources while larger companies were unwilling to accept the risks of the venture. The concession was eventually granted to Capemi Agropecuária S/A (Capemi Cattle Ranching, a subsidiary of CAPEMI — Caixa de Pecúlios, Pensões e Montepios-Beneficientes, a southern Brazilian firm specialising in private pension plans), having one tenth the financial resources considered necessary for successful development of the concession and with no previous experience in logging (*Veja*, 09 de fevereiro de 1983). Initiation of activities in the concession soon showed that commercial timber reserves were only 10% of those originally estimated by IBDF and SUDAM, severely reducing the possible rate of wood extraction from the concession area (*see* section on Forest Resource Inventories).

Capemi's growing indebtedness and inability to work the concession have had an impact beyond the limits of the individual company and concession. Initially, members of the timber industry associations in the states of Pará and Amazonas alleged that their export activities to European markets were damaged by buyers holding off purchases in expectation of a flood of logs and sawn lumber from the Tucuruí concession which is exempt from certain restrictions on the export of unprocessed logs (*Folha de São Paulo*, 11 de setembro de 1982). Later, cancellation of the contract to supply wood to the French firm Maison Lazard Frères due to Capemi's inability to fulfil contract obligations has raised doubts about the Brazilian timber industry in European import circles (*Veja*, 09 de fevereiro de 1983). Capemi's activities at Tucuruí are currently suspended and the Brazilian government is taking steps to transfer the concession to another logging consortium (*A Crítica*, 04 de fevereiro de 1983). These experiences with the managerial mistakes at the Tucuruí concession, combined with the lack of definition of a Forest Policy for the Legal Amazon and functional management plans for designated forest reserves, make the prospects for forestry activities on public lands dim unless major changes are instituted.

20.6. PLANTATIONS

Plantation silviculture has been repeatedly seized upon as a solution to the economic, silvicultural and logistic problems associated with utilising native tropical rainforests for wood production. Tree plantations in the tropics offer many obvious advantages but also have serious biological and economic drawbacks, making the evaluation of a large number of factors necessary before any conclusion that tree plantations are indeed the most efficient management solution for wood production in a given context.

The main advantage of tropical silvicultural plantations is their great productivity. Plantation species typically have much higher growth rates and shorter rotation times than most native forest species. Annual growth rates for tropical plantations are between $25-35$ m^3/ha, whereas logged tropical rainforest averages only about $1-3$ m^3/ha (Johnson, 1976). Short generation times permit rapid improvement of tree characteristics on a large scale (Dubois, 1979). Plantation species also are capable of developing greater final wood volume per unit area than native species due to their narrower crowns and thus their lower crown-to-bole ratios (Palmer, 1975; Wadsworth, 1981). Such concentrated productivity permits reductions in transportation costs and in the capital investments required for land purchase. Savings can also be realised to some extent by mechanisation (Dubois, 1979). Finally most of the techniques of plantation establishment are well known and relatively simple to employ, although subsequent monitoring of stand development and changes in environmental quality may require corrective measures which are less well understood.

At the regional planning level, silvicultural plantations offer an important alternative to uncontrolled forest exploitation and can be used to take logging pressure off native forests while appropriate management plans are still being developed.

The most serious disadvantages associated with plantations is the significant possibility of environmental deterioration, involving changes in the local hydrological regime, decline in soil fertility and changes in microclimate. These changes may not only affect plantation production but may have negative effects on the surrounding areas as well. Increased risks from pests and diseases, a feature common to all tropical monocultures, also pose significant threats to productivity. Removal of the original forest implies a loss in genetic resources and in future options to utilise other forest products. Finally, the known high cost of plantation establishment, estimated to be US$250/ha (Johnson, 1976), and the eventual unknown costs of maintaining plantation productivity indefinitely, are other important considerations in evaluating the plantation silvicultural option.

Fig. 20.3. South American leafblight disease (*Microcyclus ulei*) has been the major impediment to the successful development of native rubber plantations in the Brazilian Amazon.

The classic examples of the pitfalls in the management of monocultures in the tropics is also the single major entrepreneurial effort in Amazonian tree plantations made before 1968: the plantations of native rubber (*Hevea brasiliensis*) established in 1928 by Henry Ford at the Fordlândia estate on the lower Tapajós River in the state of Pará to guarantee rubber supplies for the North American market (*see* Fearnside, this volume). Throughout its existence, the operation was plagued by plant disease problems, compounding an already difficult administrative situation. The decreased distances between individual trees in the plantations of this normally disperse member of the Amazonian tropical rainforest led to a high incidence of the South American leaf blight disease caused by the native fungal pathogen *Microcyclus ulei* (Fig. 20.3). Latex productivity, in turn, was reduced to the point where the operation, with over US$15 million invested (Goodland and Irwin, 1975), was abandoned in the late 1940s. Large scale tree plantations were not undertaken again in the region during the next 20 years.

The largest and at the present time the only operational industrial scale tree plantation in the Amazon is that of Jari Florestal e Agropecuária Ltda., a private enterprise established in 1968 by American billionaire shipping magnate Daniel K. Ludwig of National Bulk Carriers. Activities including native timber extraction for lumber, fuel wood and paper pulp, tree plantations of exotic pulp species, silvicultural experiments, kraft pulp manufacture, cattle raising, mining, and rice are being developed on the project's 1.6 million hectare holdings located on the Jari River in the state of Pará and the Federal Territory of Amapá. At the present time Jari is the only operational industrial scale tree plantation in the Amazon. Virtually since its inception, Jari has been repeatedly suggested by Brazilian planners as a model for large scale development projects in the Amazon, despite its obviously monumental capital investment requirements, reportedly totalling US$ 1 billion at the end of 1981 (*Veja*, 13 de janeiro de 1982), and the initial uncertainty of the success of the various tropical monocultures on which most of the project rests (Fearnside and Rankin, 1980, 1982a). Emphasis on the 'Jari model' and the physical and economic dimensions of the project make the details of its development and its ultimate success or failure as a biological and economic entity of great importance for forestry in the region.

Jari's silvicultural plantations are dedicated to three introduced softwood tree species, *Gmelina arborea*, *Pinus caribaea* var. *hondurensis* and *Eucalyptus deglupta*, known for their rapid growth and desirable characteristics both for paper pulp and solid wood products. During the first decade of its existence and before the start-up of the estate's pulp mill (Fig. 20.4) in 1979, Jari's efforts were concentrated on plantation establishment. Initially the existing native tropical rainforest was felled and burned without salvaging the timber. Heavy machinery was used in felling and site preparation but this practice was later abandoned when resulting soil compaction was found to have a negative influence on the growth of the future tree crop (Fearnside and Rankin, 1980). Beginning in 1980, 60 – 90% of the native timber on sites cleared for plantations was harvested for use in the company sawmill, and as fuel to supplement the diesel-fired thermoelectric generators, and in pulp manufacture. Pressed by the necessity to compensate for low plantation yields, Jari has pioneered research on incorporating native species into their paper pulp mixture: in 1980 some 83 native species were being used to supplement 15% of the *Gmelina*-based pulp (F.J. de Almeido Neto, pers. comm., 1980).

Gmelina (Fig. 20.5) was originally intended as the base for the entire plantation program, however early experiences showed that this species did poorly on all but the project's most fertile clay soils. Many of the original *Gmelina* plantations were subsequently converted to *Pinus* on sandy soils, and to *Eucalyptus* on less fertile clays. Plans called for the establishment of 106,000 ha of plantations by 1981, including 53,000 ha of *Gmelina*, 37,000 ha of *Pinus* and 5,000 ha of *Eucalyptus* (J. Welker, pers. comm., 1980). The project's silviculturalists assume that the final plantation area will be between 100,000 and 200,000 ha, depending on plantation productivity, the demands of the pulp mill, generators and sawmill and plans for future industrial expansion, as well as the general direction of the project.

The Jari project has conducted research on a number of ways by which it might broaden its operations so as to increase biological and economic stability. The potentials of native and other exotic tree species are being tested for possible future incorporation of these species in plantations. Some 32 species have

Fig. 20.4. The Jari kraft pulp mill, with a 750 MT/day capacity currently depends on wood from native forests to supplement plantation output for pulp and fuel.

Fig. 20.5. Mature *Gmelina arborea* at Jari with two Brazil Nut trees (*Bertholetia excelsa*) spared at the time of plantation clearing demonstrates the great difference in biomass between plantation species and the original rainforest. (*Interciencia*)

been set out in trial plantings, and the behaviour of 76 native species appearing spontaneously in the plantations is under observation wherever these species occur (J. Welker, pers. comm., 1980). The first experimental result to be promoted on an industrial scale was the substitution of *Pinus caribaea* for *Gmelina arborea* on sandy soils. Progress has been made in genetic improvement of *Gmelina* trunk form and disease resistance (Woessner, n.d. and pers. comm., 1980). Research was also initiated on soil changes, nutrient cycling and plantation biomass production by independent investigators in collaboration with the project's forestry sector.

Jari has also experimented with agroforestry, combining the cultivation of food crops such as manioc, maize and beans with the tree crops in the first years of plantation development. Such mixed plantings have not jeopardised the growth of the tree plantations, at least in the same rotation, and have the advantage of multiple land use which decreases the project's dependency on food stuff imported from other parts of the country. Beef cattle have been raised in the *Pinus* plantations, beginning once the seedlings are large enough to resist trampling. This combination has been economically successful on a pilot scale, although the economics of *Pinus* plus cattle on an industrial scale are still unknown. Further development of the *Pinus*/pasture combination has been limited by the lack of water in the plantations and by project policy changes.

The long-term biological and economic viability of Jari's silvicultural plantations is still unknown. This will depend largely on changes in soil fertility under the plantation regimes and on losses due to pests, diseases and fires, all of which can have serious effects on future yields. The existing plantations are still not sufficient to support all pulp manufacture and energy generation, both operations continuing to depend to a significant degree on timber from the estate's native forests. In the future, plantations will not only have to maintain current yields but will have to supply wood currently being harvested at a rate of from 96 to 158 m^3/ha from native forests to meet these demands (based on figures from Woessner, 1980). The total area of plantations that will ultimately have to be established to support industrial activities and the future capital investments necessary to maintain plantation productivity depends on factors common to all tropical silvicultural plantations — not just the specific situation at Jari.

Most essential nutrients in tropical rainforest ecosystems are found in the biomass or located within the topmost layers of the soil. The intensive harvesting of native timber and the subsequent repeated harvesting of pulp trees planned for the Jari plantation sites will remove essential nutrients from the system to the point where future yields may be jeopardised. This is especially true for limited vital nutrients such as phosphorus (Johnson, 1976). *Gmelina*, like many other fast growing timber trees, makes heavy nutrient demands on the soil. Short rotations such as those practised at Jari have a greater impact on certain nutrients than longer rotations (Chijicke, 1980). Deterioration is greatest on sandy soils when *Gmelina* is grown on a coppice rotation (second and third crops obtained from stump sprouts), a fact discovered by trial and error at Jari (Fearnside and Rankin, 1980). Estimates for nutrient loss from *Gmelina* plantations and the cost of nutrient replacement through fertiliser inputs show that this will be a significant figure on Jari's future balance sheets, with complete replacement of four essential nutrients alone running over US$100/ha/year (Fearnside and Rankin, 1982a). Field studies monitoring changes in soil and biomass nutrient stocks under *Gmelina* during the first rotation at Jari have shown significant losses in calcium (Russell *et al.*, 1982). A slight decrease in *Gmelina* growth rates during the second rotation has already been noticed by Jari foresters (Fearnside and Rankin, 1982a). The eventual necessity of fertilising has now been recognised by the silvicultural staff: *Eucalyptus deglupta* now being planted on poor *Gmelina* sites will receive fertiliser inputs (D. Oren, pers. comm., 1982). Whereas biological productivity may be successfully maintained with fertilisers, the economics of this practice will be determined by the future prices of these materials, many of which are petroleum derived, and by the prices of the pulp so produced. Pulp prices have been observed to be more strongly controlled by the market factors of supply and demand than by the true costs of investment for past and future productivity (Fearnside and Rankin, 1982a).

Attacks by pests and diseases are among the other factors that may reduce productivity of silvicultural plantations in the tropics, where constant high temperatures and abundant moisture permit year-round biological activity. Unlike the native tropical rainforest where species densities are low per unit area and species diversity is high, tropical monocultures have high concentrations of individuals of a single species, facilitating the spread and establishment of pathogens (Janzen, 1973). Pests and diseases are present in most tropical plantations; plantations established on inappropriate sites, preventing vigorous development of the tree species of interest, are particularly vulnerable (Johnson, 1976). Although the pests and diseases observed in the plantations of *Gmelina* and *Pinus* at Jari have not yet caused serious economic losses, their continued presence is cause for concern and requires careful continuous monitoring. Limited outbreaks of the canker-producing fungal pathogen, *Ceratocystis fimbriata* (Fig. 20.6), have been noted in Jari's *Gmelina* plantations (Muchovej *et al.*, 1978). The wide distribution of *Ceratocystis* on other introduced and native tree species throughout the Amazon means that its complete eradication from *Gmelina* plantations at Jari or elsewhere in the Basin is unlikely (Fearnside and Rankin,

Fig. 20.6. The fungal pathogen *Ceratocystis fimbriata* has caused trunk cankers (black) in a number of *Gmelina* plantations at Jari. (*Interciencia*)

1980). Control has been partially achieved at Jari through changes in plantation management techniques such as eliminating the branch trimming that appeared to facilitate spread and establishment of this disease.[1] Silviculturalists at Jari are also working to develop *Ceratocystis*-resistant strains of *Gmelina* (R.A. Woessner, pers. comm., 1980). Several limited attacks by defoliating lepidopteran larvae have been observed over the years, the most severe of which defoliated approximately 300 ha of *Gmelina* in 1974 (Fearnside and Rankin, 1980). Leafcutter ants (*Atta* spp., Fig. 20.7) are frequent in the *Pinus* plantations and can cause serious harm to young trees. Significant expenditures on myrmicides are required to control damage (Ribeiro and Woessner, 1978).

The *Eucalyptus deglupta* plantations at Jari have not developed serious pest problems to date. However, this species has suffered attacks by defoliating insects [leaf cutter ants (*Atta* spp.) and bagworms (Lepidoptera)] and by a fungal pathogen in experimental plantings in Manaus (D. Arkcoll, pers. comm., 1983). Recent serious outbreaks of defoliating insect larvae in the vast *Eucalyptus* spp. plantations in the Brazilian state of Minas Gerais, south of the Amazon Basin, should also be of great concern. In Minas Gerais 60,000 ha of trees were defoliated during a single attack, and damage estimates on the order of US$ 15 million have caused speculations that any further defoliation losses will put an end to *Eucalyptus* reforestation in that region (*Folha de São Paulo*, 16 de setembro de 1982). It is significant to note that the defoliating larvae are known to have been present in the plantations at least one and a half years before the massive outbreak (*Folha de São Paulo*, 17 de setembro de 1982).

Environmental impacts, especially those contributing to changes in the hydrological cycle, are a final aspect of the biological viability of large plantations in the tropical rainforest. Along with the possibility

[1]A subsequent visit to the Jari silvicultural project revealed significant and widespread infestation of *Ceratocystis fimbriata* in the *Gmelina arborea* plantations, a fact concealed by the previous administration (*vide* Fearnside, P. M. and J. M. Rankin 1985. Interciencia 10(3): 121 – 129).

Fig. 20.7. Leaf cutter ants (*Atta* spp.) are the most serious pests of *Pinus caribaea* at Jari.

of regional changes in the hydrological cycle (*see* both Salati and Lovejoy this volume) resulting from the removal or substitution of native forest, changes may be expected in local run-off patterns and water table levels. Differences exist in the capacity of plantations and tropical rainforests to absorb, retain and recycle water. Low surface soil and litter humidity and unpredictable fluctuations in water tables may be two consequences of increased water discharge from the local system under extensive plantations. This is of special concern for *Pinus* plantations typically established on well-drained sandy soils. The major growth-limiting factor for *Pinus* is inadequate soil moisture (Chijicke, 1980); changes in local hydrological characteristics which would decrease soil moisture thus pose a possible threat to plantation productivity. Plantation fires caused by spontaneous combustion and accidental ignition of dry needle litter may also lead to severe losses at any stage of plantation development and may disturb production rhythm both by the absolute area of plantation lost and by the unbalancing of yields from plantations with different harvest schedules. Despite these possible problems, the *Pinus caribaea* var. *hondurensis* plantations at Jari (Fig. 20.8) are judged to be outstanding by many silvicultural experts (C.B. Briscoe, G.S. Hartshorn, R.G. Lowe, pers. comms., 1980–1982). Fire prevention and monitoring of changes in water tables are priorities if this performance is to be maintained on an industrial scale.

The biological success of the Jari plantations and the project's economic health are separate and distinct problems, with the fulfilment of one not necessarily guaranteeing the other (Fearnside and Rankin, 1980). At the present time the project is encountering difficulties with both. Jari Florestal e Agropecuária Ltda. was sold in 1982 to a consortium of 27 Brazilian companies (*Veja*, 13 de janeiro de 1982). Legal, regulatory, and financial problems were involved in Ludwig's decision to sell, as well as the fundamental problem of lower plantation yields than originally expected. Despite the Brazilian government's apparent willingness to extend a variety of favours to national businesses, most of the companies now involved in the project were reluctant to assume responsibility for the venture, with some entering the deal only after being 'convoked' by the Minister of Planning, rather than on the basis of the economic prospects of the project (*Veja*, 13 de janeiro de 1982). While no firm definition of the project's future direction has yet been declared, the effective head of the present consortium has suggested that greater future emphasis will be placed on cattle ranching (*Gazeta Mercantil* 17 de setembro de 1982). If retrenching takes place in the silvicultural operations, then the final results of the Amazon's largest silvicultural plantation experiment may never be obtained, and the tendency to abandon attempts at silvicultural management of plantations and native forests in favour of non-sustainable land use practices offering more immediate financial returns for lower capital investments will be significantly reinforced.

While the future of Jari and its appropriateness as a development model for the Amazon are being debated, the opportunity to apply this model has thrust itself upon Brazil in connection with the discovery of the world's largest iron ore deposit, estimated at 18 billion metric tons, in the Serra de Carajás located in the state of Pará south of the Amazon River. Development of this resource as foreseen by the Projeto Grande Carajás includes the initial harvest of 1.5 million hectares of native tropical rainforest and the eventual development of 2.4 million hectares of *Eucalyptus* plantations to provide charcoal to be used to smelt some of the ore into steel (Fearnside and Rankin, 1982b). With a total project area of 80 million hectares, Projeto Grande Carajás will involve the human use of 16% of

Fig. 20.8. *Pinus caribaea* such as this 8-year-old stand has shown good growth at Jari.

Brazil's Legal Amazon. Development of the Carajás silvicultural plantations will proceed without many of the intrinsic advantages of the Jari project, such as relatively high soil quality, nearby deep water port, project establishment before the 1973 increases in petroleum prices, extensive and easily expended reserves of liquid capital, multinational business and shipping network to ensure supplies and reasonable prices (Fearnside and Rankin, 1980). The planned Carajás plantations, 24 times as large as those of Jari, carry all the risks associated with large tropical silvicultural monocultures. Given the current situation of the Jari project and the pest problems appearing in the *Eucalyptus* plantations elsewhere in Brazil, there is reason to speculate that the silvicultural plantations of Carajás may either never be established or, if established, that they may fail biologically and/or economically. In either case, the wood to meet needs for fuel and other uses would continue to be harvested from native forest for which no sustained yield management system currently exists.

20.7. SILVICULTURAL MANAGEMENT OF NATIVE TROPICAL RAINFORESTS

Sustained yield management of native tropical rainforest has been declared by silviculturalists and government planners to be a desirable and necessary goal for its successful development and conservation (*see* Pandolfo, 1978; Reis, 1980; Wadsworth, 1981). It is the only form of management which can guarantee the renewability of the resource base without the negative side effects of marked environmental deterioration and the loss of genetic stocks accompanying other resource utilisation options (Dubois, 1979). It can also provide a source of desirable timber species which may not be amenable to plantation cultivation (*see* Fox, 1976). The fact that this form of management is not more widely practised throughout the tropical rainforest zone attests to the significant biological, economic and sociopolitical difficulties encountered in its implantation and maintenance. Persson (1974, cited in Wadsworth, 1981) estimated that less than 3% of the tropical forests in the world are being managed on a permanent sustained yield basis. It is currently practised in Brazil on a purely experimental scale amounting to no more than a few hundred hectares (Dubois, 1979; Carvalho, 1980).

The problems associated with permanent sustained yield management are to a certain extent just the opposite of those of silvicultural plantations: slow growth rates, long rotations, low densities of desirable species and commercial volume per unit area, variable log quality, need for detailed ecological and taxonomic knowledge in the development of an often complex management plan requiring skilled labour, and high transport and road maintenance costs (*see* Palmer, 1975; Dubois, 1979; Wadsworth, 1981). Without strict control over the individuals logged in each rotation, genetic stocks may degenerate due to the negative selection of seed producing trees (Palmer, 1975; Wadsworth, 1981). Harvesting itself involves high rates of damage due to wounding or crushing of unharvested trees and seedlings, jeopardising potential future stock (Meijer, 1970; Liew and Wong, 1973). Where human population densities create land scarcities, sustained yield forests may enter into direct conflict with other non-renewable uses of the tropical rainforest, such as shifting cultivation (Fearnside, 1983). Examples of this are unfortunately common. For example, the Tropical Shelterwood System of management practised in Nigeria was abandoned in part due to competition with oil and food crops (Lowe, 1977) while itinerant agriculturalists and hunters in Papua New Guinea destroyed two forest reserves after only 4 years of successful management on a sustained yield natural regeneration basis (Fox, 1976).

While the economics of permanent sustained yield management of native forest have been debated (Johnson, 1976; Leslie, 1978; Spears, 1979), it remains a fact that this is the only forestry practice which has the potential to guarantee the maintenance of environmental quality, forest genetic stock, and other biological resource utilisation options. Were the costs of the losses of these features to be taken into consideration, along with calculations for costs related to establishment and maintenance of permanent

Fig. 20.9. *Goupia glabra* has demonstrated excellent natural regeneration capacity in the 1963 experimental plots at Curuá-Una.

sustained yields from plantations, based on other than the unrealistic 'no problems' scenario currently used, the economic viability of this option would be more apparent.

The first silvicultural research program in the Brazilian Amazon, initiated in 1955 under the auspices of the FAO – SPVEA bilateral agreement, was based at the Curuá-Una Experiment Station, east of Santarém, Pará and just south of the Amazon River. There FAO silviculturalist John Pitt began work on native forest management by conducting surveys of the natural regeneration (the smaller saplings and seedlings), as a complement to the previous FAO – SPVEA inventory work (Heinsdijk, 1957) on trees greater than or equal to 25 cm DBH. Pitt (1961) concluded that sufficient stocking of young plants existed to permit the development of a forest management scheme based on the natural regenerative capacity of the native species. He also initiated planting trials for native tree species such as cedro (*Cedrela odorata*), mahogany (*Swietenia macrophylla*) and andiroba (*Carapa guianensis*) plus the exotics *Pinus caribaea* and *Eucalyptus citriodora* planted in the open and in lines cut in native forest (enrichment plantings) with the objective of developing management plans based on artificial as well as natural regeneration and for identifying appropriate species for silvicultural plantations. These are the oldest silvicultural experiments in the Amazon. Despite a promising start in experimental forestry, these lines of research were not vigorously pursued after the FAO – SPVEA project terminated in the early 1960s and no further research on natural regeneration and native forest management was conducted until the mid-1970s.

Active research on native forest management was reinitiated at Curuá-Una under another FAO – SUDAM agreement in 1973. Re-evaluation of the original plots established by Pitt (1961) show successful natural regeneration of species such as *Goupia glabra* (Fig. 20.9) and further natural regeneration inventories and experimental logging are currently underway. A similar experimental program was begun in 1975 at the Tapajós National Forest under the auspices of IBDF, EMBRAPA/CPATU and FAO. The lack of previous exploitation records in the Tapajós forest detailing dates and intensities of logging hamper translation of the natural regeneration inventories (de Carvalho, 1978, 1980) into a meaningful management program, but the presence of abundant regeneration of commercial species is promising. This project is also now in the experimental logging and subsequent inventory phase.

The first integrated program of forest and watershed management for commercial forest utilisation was begun in 1980 by INPA and FAO at the INPA Tropical Silviculture Experiment Station (EEST) 60 km north of Manaus in the state of Amazonas. Here data is being collected on hydrology, soils, nutrient cycling, microclimate, fauna and vegetation structure and composition in experimental and control watersheds prior to experimental logging scheduled to begin in 1983. Parallel ecological and silvicultural studies will continue to monitor the future developments in the two watersheds. Pre-exploitation inventories of the natural regeneration on the experimental watershed suggest that the potential for permanent sustained yield management exists (Higuchi et al., 1982) but little is yet known about the reproductive behaviour and seedling characteristics of desirable timber species. The unique combination of integrated ecosystem and silvicultural studies in this project are intended to speed the accumulation of this essential information.

Based on the promising results of the natural regeneration inventories at the Tapajós National Forest and at Curuá-Una, SUDAM and IBDF have declared that sustained yield natural regeneration management of native forest can now be considered a feasible management technique for the forests of the Amazon (Superintendência do Desenvolvimento da Amazônia et al., 1978; Reis, 1980). While admittedly encouraging, such results should not overshadow the fact that successful sustained yield natural regeneration management depends on much more than having adequate seedling stocks before or just after the first logging cycle. Details of subsequent management activities will have to be adapted to changes in tree population behaviour over time and administration agencies will have to have the resources and flexibility to respond effectively. There will not be a single 'canned' management plan which can be applied to all forest areas in the Amazon (see Lowe, 1981), a fact underscored by differences in the results of the Manaus and Tapajós regeneration inventories as well as the differences in structure and taxonomic composition of the Amazon forests recognised throughout the Basin. The true biological success of programs in sustained yield management for native forests based on natural regeneration will be known only after the successful appearance of forest regeneration in the second logging cycle. Finally, the successful implantation of sustained yield native forest management systems will depend to a large extent on the administrative agencies' ability to apply the management plans on a large scale, to control the activities of loggers and to resist pressures to convert managed forest areas to other uses.

Agroforestry, one of the most recent developments in forestry in the Brazilian Amazon, may indirectly contribute to the viability of managed forest reserves. A mixed management strategy combining timber and food crops, agroforestry is directed at the creation of a broader biological and economic base for production with greater guarantees of permanent sustained yields than with either logging, plantations or annual crops alone. It also offers reduced environmental deterioration from that occurring with the latter two land uses. This system is currently being tried on a pilot project basis under the direction of IBDF near the first National Forest on the Tapajós River in an attempt to stabilise spontaneous colonisation on the Forest's boundary and thus protect this managed timber tract from invasion by itinerant agriculturalists (Eden, 1982). As the population of the Amazon and the demands for food stuffs and wood products grow, this form of management will undoubtedly become an important means of maintaining the quality of life for the inhabitants of the region while at the same time affording significant protection to vulnerable managed forest reserves.

20.8. PERSPECTIVES

The future direction of forestry in the Brazilian Amazon is uncertain. While recent developments in both plantation forestry and sustained yield management of native forests are promising, the ultimate success of either option is subject to many conditions and qualifiers which go beyond the basic questions of their biological viability, an aspect itself subject to many preconditions. Research and industrial application are still in their initial stages and more time and effort must be invested in these, as well as in the legal and administrative details of operation, before the successful utilisation of these forestry options is assured. Similarly, the establishment of forest reserves necessary to guarantee the resource base for forest management must also be accelerated. In the meantime, the conversion of the Amazon tropical rainforest to non-forest uses and uncontrolled logging continue, while new industries with high demands for wood raw materials are being established in the region without adequate provisions for their future supply. It remains to be seen if what has been called the 'Faustian bargain' in forestry (Richardson, 1978) will be struck in the Brazilian Amazon, trading future potentially permanent returns from these forests for immediate but ephemeral gain.

ACKNOWLEDGEMENT

I thank Philip M. Fearnside for his many helpful comments on this manuscript.

REFERENCES

Anon. (1977) IBDF adota rigidas medidas para evitar o uso irracional das florestas Brasileiras. *Brasil Florestal* 8(29), 12 – 14.
Anon. (1981) Brazil: Brazilian Amazon — just how much deforestation? *Commonw. For. Rev.* 60(3), 169 – 170.
Brazil, Ministério da Agricultura, Instituto Brasileiro de Desenvolvimento Florestal (IBDF) (1982). *Programa de Entrepostos Madeireiros para Exportação - PROMAEX.* IBDF, Brasília.
Brazil, Ministério do Interior, Superintendência do Desenvolvimento da Amazônia (SUDAM) (1977) *Amazônia.* SUDAM, Belém.
Brazil, Presidência da República, Secretaria de Planejamento, Conselho Nacional de Desenvolvimento Cientifico e Tecnologico (CNPq), Instituto Nacional de Pesquisas da Amazônia (INPA) (1982) *Amazonian Woods — CPPF: Information Bulletin of the Forest Products Research Center of the National Institute for Amazonian Research (INPA).* 01. INPA, Manaus.
Brazil, Ministério do Interior, Superintendência do Desenvolvimento da Amazônia (SUDAM) (1978) Estudo ténico de recomposição florestal em florestas de terra firme na Estação Experimental de Curuá-Una. *Silvicultura 14* 'Anais do 3 Congresso Florestal Brasileiro, volume II.', 442 – 443.
Brazil, Ministério do Interior, Superintendência do Desenvolvimento da Amazônia (SUDAM) (1979) *Caracteríticas silviculturais de espécies nativas e exóticas dos plantios do Centro de Tecnologia Madereira — Estação Experimental de Curuá-Una.* SUDAM, Belém.
Carvalho, J. C. de M. (1981) The conservation of nature and natural resources in the Brazilian Amazon. *CVRD Revista (Companhia Vale do Rio Doce)* 2 (Special edition).
Chijicke, E. O. (1980) *Impact on Soils of Fast-Growing Species in the Lowland Humid Tropics.* FAO Forestry Paper 21. United Nations Food and Agriculture Organization (UN-FAO), Rome
A Crítica (Manaus) (16 de janeiro de 1982) 'Brasil ampliará em 30% sua participação em madeira.' Cad. 1, p.10.
A Crítica (Manaus) (04 de fevereiro de 1983) 'Capemi em situação dificil vai deixar área de Tucuruí.' Cad. 2, p.4.
da Silva, D. A. and Corrêa, C. M. (1983) *Pesquisas para a utilização de carvão vegetal na Amazônia.* (ms.).
de Almeida, H. (1978) *O Desenvolvimento da Amazônia e a Política de Incentivos Fiscais.* SUDAM, Belém.
de Carvalho, J. O. P. (1978) Inventário diagnóstico da regeneração de uma área na Floresta Nacional do Tapajós. *Silvicultura 14* 'Anais do 3 Congresso Florestal Brasileiro, volume II', 409 – 414.
de Carvalho, J. O. P. (1980) Inventárió diagnóstico da regeneração da vegetação em área da Floresta Nacional do Tapajós. *EMBRAPA/CPATU Boletim de Pesquisa 2*, Empresa Brasileira de Pesquisas Agropecuárias/Centro de Pesquisas Agropecuárias do Tropico Umido (EMBRAPA/CPATU), Belém.

Dubois, J. (1979) Los sistemas de producción mas apropriados para el uso racional de las tierras de la Amazónia. Paper presented at the Seminário sobre los Recursos Naturales Renovables e el Desarrollo Regional Amazonico, May, 1979, Bogotá.

Eckholm, E. (1979) Forestry for human needs. *Interciencia* 4(4), 207 – 213.

Eden, M. J. (1982) Silviculture and agroforestry developments in the Amazon Basin of Brazil. *Commonw. For. Rev* 61(3), 195 – 202.

Ewel, J. and Conde, L. F. (1980) Potential ecological impact of increased intensity of tropical forest utilization. *BIOTROP Special Publication* No. 11. Southeast Asian Ministers of Education Organization (SEAMED) Regional Center for Tropical Biology (BIOTROP), Bogor, Indonesia.

Fearnside, P. M. (1982) Deforestation in the Brazilian Amazon: How fast is it occurring? *Interciencia* 7(2), 82 – 88.

Fearnside, P. M. (1983) Development alternatives in the Brazilian Amazon: an ecological evaluation. *Interciencia* 8(2), 65 – 78.

Fearnside, P. M. and Rankin, J. M. (1980) Jari and development in the Brazilian Amazon. *Interciencia* 5(3), 146 – 156.

Fearnside, P. M. and Rankin, J. M. (1982a) The new Jari: risks and prospects of a major Amazonian development. *Interciencia* 7(6), 329 – 339.

Fearnside, P. M. and Rankin, J. M. (1982b) Jari and Carajás: the uncertain future of large silvicultural plantations in the Amazon. *Interciencia* 7(6), 326.

Folha de São Paulo (São Paulo) (11 de setembro de 1982). 'Madeireiros recusam substituir ou ajudar a Capemi em Tucuruí p.18.

Folha de São Paulo (São Paulo) (16 de setembro de 1982). 'Lagarta ameaça 60 mil hectares de eucaliptos.' p.21.

Folha de São Paulo (São Paulo) (17 de setembro de 1982). 'Comissão verá como combater as lagartas.' reprinted in *Sumário de Noticias CNPq (Brasília)* 172, 18.

Fox, J. E. D. (1976) Environmental constraints on the natural vegetation of tropical moist forest. *Forest Ecol. Manage.* 1, 37 – 65.

Gachot, R., Gallant, M. N. and MacGrath, K. P. (1953) *Report to the Government of Brazil on Forest Development in the Amazon Valley.* FAO Report 171. United Nations Food and Agriculture Organization (UN-FAO), Rome.

Gazeta Mercantil (Brasília) (17 de setembro de 1982) 'As diretrizes que Antunes sugere para a região do Jari.' p.10.

Goodland, R. J. A. and Irwin, H. S. (1975) *Amazon Jungle: Green Hell to Red Desert. An Ecological Discussion of the Environmental Impact of the Highway Construction Program in the Amazon Basin.* Elsevier Scientific Publishing Co., New York.

Heinsdijk, D. (1957) *Report to the Government of Brazil on a Forestry Inventory in the Amazon Valley (Region between Rio Tapajós and Rio Xingú).* FAO Report 601. UN-FAO, Rome.

Higuchi, N., Jardim, F. C. S., dos Santos, J. and Alencar, J. da C. (1982) *Bacia 3: Inventário Diagnóstico da Regeneração Natural.* Report on the INPA/BID/FINEP project. (ms.).

Hopkins, M. S., Kikkawa, J., Graham, A. W., Tracey, J. T. R. and Webb, L. J. (1976) An ecological basis for the management of rain forest. In *The Border Ranges: A Land Use Conflict in Regional Perspective.* Eds. R. Monroe and N. C. Stevens, pp. 57 – 66, Brisbane.

Janzen, D. H. (1973) Tropical agroecosystems: habitats misunderstood by the temperate zones, mismanaged by the tropics. *Science* 182, 1212 – 1219.

Johnson, N. E. (1976) Biological opportunities and risks associated with fast-growing plantations in the tropics. *J. Forestry* 74(4), 206 – 211.

Journal de Brasília (Brasília) (14 de setembro de 1982) 'IBDF anuncia politica florestal para Amazônia.' p.8.

Lanly, J. P. and Clement, J. (1979) Present and future natural forest and plantation areas in the tropics. *Unasylva* 31(123), 12 – 20.

Leslie, A. (1978) Where contradictory theory and practice co-exist. *Unasylva* 29(115), 2 – 17.

Liew, T. C. and Wong, F. O. (1973) Density, recruitment, mortality and growth of Dipterocarp seedlings in virgin and logged-over forests in Sabah. *Malayan Forester* 36, 3 – 15.

Lowe, R. G. (1977) Experience with the Tropical Shelterwood System of regeneration in natural forest in Nigeria. *Forest Ecol. and Manage.* 1(3), 193 – 212.

Lowe, R. G. (1981) Initiation of an investigation into the effects of exploitation and silvicultural treatment on growth, recruitment and mortality in natural lowland tropical forest of Amazonia. Paper presented at the UFRO Forestry Meetings, Manila.

Meijer, W. (1970) Regeneration of tropical lowland forest in Sabah, Malaysia forty years after logging. *Malayan Forester* 33, 204 – 229.

Muchovej, J. J., de Albuquerque, F. C. and Ribeiro, G. T. (1978) *Gmelina arborea* — a new host of *Ceratocystis fimbriata. Plant Disease Reporter* 62(8), 717 – 719.

Myers, N. (1980a) *Conversion of Tropical Moist Forests.* National Academy of Sciences Press, Washington, D.C.

Myers, N. (1980b) Preservation and production: Multinational timber corporations and tropical moist forests. *Council on Economic Priorities Newsletter* 5.

Palmer, J. R. (1975) Towards more reasonable objectives in tropical high forest management for timber production. *Commonw. For. Rev.* 54(3 + 4), 273 – 289.

Palmer, J. (1977) Forestry in Brazil — Amazonia. *Commonw. For. Rev* 56(2), 115 – 130.

Pandolfo, C. (1969) *Amazonia — the Great Potential of its Natural Resources and Opportunities for Industrialization.* Superintendência do Desenvolvimento da Amazônia (SUDAM), Belém.

Pandolfo, C. (1974) *Estudos básicos para o estabelecimento de uma política de desenvolvimento dos recursos florestais e do uso racional da terras da Amazonia.* Superintendência do Desenvolvimento da Amazônia (SUDAM), Belém.

Pandolfo, C. (1978) *A Floresta Amazônica Brasileira: Enfoque Econômico-Ecológico*. Superintendência do Desenvolvimento da Amazônia (SUDAM), Belém.

Pereira, F. (1982) 'Tucuruí: já retirados 15% da madeira.' *Gazeta Mercantil* (Brasília), 06 de outubro de 1982, p.11.

Pires, J. M. (1979) A política florestal para o desenvolvimento da Amazônia. *Acta Amazonica* 9(4) *Suplemento*, 131 – 140.

Pitt, J. (1961) *Report to the Government of Brazil on the Application of Silvicultural Methods to some of the Forests of the Amazon.* Expanded Technical Assistance Program, FAO Report 1337. United Nations Food and Agriculture Organization (UN-FAO), Rome.

Reis, M. S. (1978) Uma definição técnico-política para o aproveitamento racional dos recursos florestais da Amazonia Brasileira. Paper presented at the 3rd Congresso Florestal Brasileiro, 4 – 7 December, 1978, Manaus. (ms.).

Reis, M. S. (1980) Present situation. Presentation of the Brazilian Delegation. United Nations Environmental Program (UNEP) Meeting on Tropical Forests, 26 February, 1980. Nairobi.

Ribeiro, G. T. and Woessner, R. A. (1978) Teste da eficiência com seis (6) saúvacidas no controle de saúvas (*Atta* spp.) na Jari, Pará, Brasil. Paper presented at the V Congresso Brasileiro de Entomologia, Seção de Controle Químico, July, 1978. Ilheus and Itabuna, Bahia. (ms.).

Richardson, S. D. (1978) Foresters and the Faustian bargain. In *Papers for Conference on Improved Utilization of Tropical Forests, 21 – 26 May, 1978, Madison, Wisc.* U.S. Forest Service Forest Products Laboratory, Washington, D.C.

Rollet, B. and Queiroz, W. T. (1978) Observações e contribuições aos inventários florestais na Amazônia. *Silvicultura 14* 'Anais do 3 Congresso Florestal Brasileiro, Volume II', 405 – 408.

Russell, C. E., Jordan, C. F. and North, R. M. (1982) Nutrient cycling and stand stocking in native and plantation forests at the Jari Project, Pará, Brazil. Paper presented to the Ecological Society of America at the 33rd Annual AIBS Meetings, Pennsylvania State University, University Park, Penn., 8 – 12 August, 1982.

Schmithüsen, F. (1978) *Contratos de Utilização Florestal com Referência Especial a Amazônia Brasileira.* PNUD/FAO/IBDF/BRA/76/027 Serie Técnica 12, Brasília.

Spears, J. S. (1979) Can the wet tropical forest survive? *Commonw. For. Rev.* 58(3), 165 – 180.

Superintendência do Desenvolvimento da Amazônia (SUDAM), Empresa Brasileira de Pesquisas Agropecuária/Centro de Pesquisas Agropecuáias do Tropico Umido (EMBRAPA/CPATU), Associação das Industrias Madeireiros do Estado do Pará e Amapá (AIMP), Faculdade de Ciências Agrárias do Pará (FCAP), Associação Florestal do Pará e Amapá (AFPA), Federação das Industrias do Estado de Pará, and Centro das Industrias do Estado do Pará (1978) A racionalização das atividades de exploração madereira na Amazônia. *Silvicultura 14* 'Anais do 3 Congresso Florestal Brasileira, Volume II', 401 – 404.

Veja (São Paulo). (13 de janeiro de 1982). 'O pais afinal comprou o sonho do Jari.' No. 697, 68 – 73.

Veja (São Paulo). (9 de fevereiro de 1983). 'Um tombo na selva.' No. 753, 83 – 84.

Volatron, B. (1976) La mise en valeur de richesses forestieres en Amazonie Brésilienne et en Colombie. *Bois et Forets de Tropiques* 166, 55 – 70.

Wadsworth, F. H. (1981) Principles of management for sustained yield: evaluation and prospects. In *Simposio Internacional sobre las Ciencias Forestales y su Contribucion al Desarrollo de la America Tropical*. Ed. M. Chavarria, pp. 81 – 88. Editora EUNED.

Woessner, R. A. (1980) Forestry operation and wood utilization at Jari. Paper presented at the World Woods Conference, December, 1980, Santiago, Chile. (ms.).

Woessner, R. A. (n.d.) *Gmelina arborea* Roxb. genetic improvement program at Jari. (ms.).

CHAPTER 21

Agriculture in Amazonia

PHILIP M. FEARNSIDE

Department of Ecology, National Institute for Research in the Amazon-INPA, Caixa Postal 478, 69.000 Manaus-Amazonas, Brazil

CONTENTS

21.1. AGRICULTURAL TYPES: PATTERN AND TRENDS

21.1.1. *Terra Firme*: the vast uplands

21.1.1.1. *Shifting cultivation*

Shifting cultivation or swidden is the traditional method of farming Amazonia's vast unflooded uplands known in Brazil as *terra firme* (Span: *tierra firme*). Indigenous populations have used such 'slash-and-burn' agriculture for many centuries as a means of obtaining plant-based foodstuffs from Amazonia's infertile soils, with a minimum of human effort spent on fending off the relentless competition of weeds and crop pests (Carneiro, 1960; Harris, 1971; Gross *et al.*, 1979). Large land areas relative to the human populations have allowed employment of long fallow periods, usually several decades, between brief farming periods of 1 − 2 years. During the fallow period, woody second growth (Port.: *capoeira*, *juquira*, or *quisasa*; Span.: *purma*, *rastrojo*, or *barbecho*) takes over the temporarily 'abandoned' fields, accumulating nutrients in the tree biomass, restoring the soil's porosity and other physical structure characters degraded through farming, and increasing the organic matter content of the soil as reduced soil temperatures shift the balance between accumulation and decomposition of soil humus. Soil fauna, greatly depleted during the farming period, returns with consequent resumption of nutrient cycling and other roles in the forest ecosystem.

The *caboclos*, or poor Portuguese-speaking inhabitants of the Amazonian interior, also employ a similar system (Wagley, 1976; Moran, 1974). *Caboclos* generally do not move their residences together with their fields, as indigenous groups often do, but are still able to move their plantings over sufficiently wide areas to have long fallows. Most of the region's river and stream banks now occupied by the *caboclo* population have only been farmed by these racially and culturally mixed residents on the order of one century, in contrast to the much longer history of occupation, very often of the same choice riverside sites, by Amerindian groups. *Caboclos* lack the complex of cultural mechanisms which have been found in many parts of the world to result in long fallows among traditional practitioners of shifting cultivation.

When either primary forest or a second growth stand is cut for farming in Amazonia, it is essential that the downed vegetation be burned. Burning removes the physical obstruction of the dead vegetation, releases needed plant nutrients into the soil (especially phosphorus and cations such as calcium, magnesium and potassium), and, of particular importance, raises the soil pH. The extremely acid soils of the region yield only stunted crops if burning is poor. Low soil pH has a synergistic effect with the low phosphorus levels, reducing the availability to plants of what little phosphorus exists.

During the farmed period, crop yields usually decline as a combined result of exhausted soil fertility and the increased inroads of weeds and pests. The relative importance of the different factors depends on the initial fertility of the soil (Sánchez, 1976). Where soil is extremely infertile, as in the white sand areas of the upper Rio Negro, the end of nutrient supply, especially organic matter from decomposition of the thick mat of forest roots, is believed to be critical (Herrera *et al.*, 1978). In rich volcanic soils of Central America the invasion of weeds is credited with at least equal impact on yield declines (Popenoe, 1960). The question of what causes shifting cultivators to 'abandon' a given field can easily become sterile academic debate, as farmers themselves are not concerned with levels of phosphorus, organic matter, or any other soil nutrient, but rather with the net result in terms of yield obtained from their labour. Increased labour demands of weeding, combined with declining yields per area, make moving to a new location more and more attractive as farmed period lengthens. The per area yield declines are themselves the combined result of the many individual agricultural setbacks, a kilogram lost to pests being just as unavailable to feed the farmer as a kilogram lost to stunted crop growth.

Yields, and their declines, are exceedingly erratic depending on weather, biological problems, and many other factors. Sometimes yields will be better in the second year than the first, or *vice versa*, a large sample being needed to draw valid conclusions. Yields of some crops, such as maize, may increase in the second year of cultivation in comparison with the first (Jessup, 1981), although evidence is conflicting. Others report the more traditional view of yields declining steadily from the first year (Penteado, 1967; Watters, 1971, 101, 106; Cowgill, 1962; Sánchez, 1976, 375; UNESCO, 1978, 472 − 73). One contributing factor to an increase in the second year would be the disappearance, as the farmed period progresses, of downed vegetation occupying some of the land area. The soil itself may provide some explanation if allelopathic chemicals released into the soil by the original forest trees have a role in inhibiting crop growth in the first year after clearing. Information on such possible effects is scant and conflicting.

It is important to note that many indigenous groups are believed to move their residences, with consequent 'abandonment' of swidden fields, as an adaptation to exploiting game and fish populations over a wide range of territory (e.g. Gross, 1975; Roosevelt, 1980). For many indigenous groups the distinction is often blurred between an actively cultivated garden and an 'abandoned' or fallow field, as tree crops planted in the field (or spared the axe during the initial clearing) may be harvested for many years after active cultivation has ceased.

Shifting cultivation is condemned by many agronomists for its inability to provide sufficient surpluses to allow its practitioners entry into the cash economy (e.g. Alvim, 1978), as well as for its leading to deforestation and erosion (United Nations F.A.O., 1957; Watters, 1966, 1971). Advantages of the system include its successful record for supporting human populations over millenia (provided population densities remain low), as well as its self-sufficiency and high productivity per unit of human labour (Leach, 1959; Nye and Greenland, 1960; UNESCO, 1978: 467 – 476; Sánchez, 1973, 1976). It is well to point out that most clearing in Amazonia today is the result of large-scale cattle ranching rather than shifting cultivation, although clearings from both large and small operators can have negative effects. Small clearings with short farmed times regenerate far more quickly than large pastures (Uhl, 1982; Uhl *et al.*, 1982a), but true shifting cultivation with small isolated clearings and long fallows is becoming a rarity in the region. With the present rapid disappearance of indigenous groups (Davis, 1977; Hanbury-Tenison, 1973; Goodland and Irwin, 1975; de Oliveira *et al.*, 1979) shifting cultivation can be expected to disappear. Pioneer agriculture by small farmers, both squatters and government-sponsored colonists, resembles shifting cultivation superficially but has profound differences which render it unsustainable.

21.1.1.2. Pioneer smallholder annual crops

The thousands of pioneer farmers who have entered the Amazon in recent years from other regions employ agriculture with many essential differences from the traditional long-cycle shifting cultivation of Amerindian and *caboclo* populations. The new migrants come from areas such as drought-prone Northeast Brazil, and from the former coffee and food-crop lands of Paraná and other southern Brazilian states where mechanised soybean and wheat cultivation, along with vast sugar cane plantations for alcohol production, are driving out the former sharecroppers and small landowners. In the case of migration to the Amazonian portions of Bolivia, Peru, Ecuador, Colombia, and Venezuela newcomers come from Andean areas. The flow of migrants has swollen as a combination of worsening conditions in the source areas and the opportunity to obtain land in Amazonia by taking advantage of the many new highways constructed in the region. Pioneers are settled in government-sponsored colonisation areas, as well as both private and public lands where squatters have entered on their own initiative. The new arrivals fell and burn the forest, much as do traditional shifting cultivators in the first step of a swidden cycle, but thereafter the differences in the two classes of systems become more apparent. A few of the pioneers are from *caboclo* backgrounds in other parts of Amazonia; these carefully select the land to be cleared based on indicator tree species present, and plant a diversified array of crop plants (Moran, 1979a). They also are more skilful in timing the felling and burning operations to obtain the best burns, as well as in making the many agricultural decisions from deciding how much to plant of crops like rice (*Oryza sativa*) requiring intensive periods of seasonal labour as compared with more traditional staples like manioc (*Manihot esculenta*) which spread the labour requirements over much of the year (Fearnside, 1978).

Most of the new arrivals from other ecological regions find adaptation to the new environment difficult. Many of the responses lead them gradually to adopt some of the solutions long practised by the area's residents (Moran, 1981). The speed and path of the adaptation process varies greatly, however, depending in part on the colonist's background before arrival (Moran, 1979b, 1981; Fearnside, 1980a).

Pioneer farmers do not plant the wide variety of crops employed by traditional shifting cultivators (Smith, 1978, 1981a,b). The more homogeneous and larger fields planted are both more susceptible to pest and disease problems, and represent a more devastating blow when problems do arise. The TransAmazon Highway colonists, for example, suffered a severe setback when virtually the entire rice crop failed in 1973 as a result of an untested rice variety distributed by the government colonisation agency. Colonists in government-sponsored areas such as the TransAmazon Highway expand their planting far beyond what their family's labour supply would permit, through hired hands for felling and harvesting paid by bank financing. The bureaucratic delays and other institutional problems associated with financing can often result in colonists' agricultural efforts failing both agronomically and economically (Wood and Schmink, 1979; Moran, 1981; Bunker, 1980; Fearnside, 1980a). Good burn qualities, largely predictable from meteorological data, and felling and burning dates, are critical to obtaining a good yield (Fearnside, nd-b); delayed felling for bureaucratic reasons, or ignorance of the associated risks, can often result in poor burns and failed crops.

The most striking difference between pioneer agriculture and traditional shifting cultivation is lack of the cultural traditions which lead swidden farmers to leave their fields in second growth for long periods before returning for a subsequent crop. Pioneers clear young second growth only one or 2 years of age with high frequency, not a practice that could be expected to continue for long. Colonists have no intention of using a sustainable cycle of shifting cultivation as the basis for their agriculture. Rather, annual crops planted in the early years of settlement are seen as a temporary solution to their immediate needs for cash, while the settler waits for a change to other sources of income such as cattle pasture, perennial crops, or selling the land at a good price to someone else who will develop one of these longer-term uses. By far the greatest share of the land area, both in areas of small colonists and in large land holdings, is rapidly being converted to cattle pastures.

Pasture is the most common land use in terms of area even in settlement zones that have been the focus of the most intense promotion of perennial crops. In the Ouro Preto colonisation project in Rondônia, for example, 105 lots surveyed in 1980 by Furley and Leite (nd.) had 39% of deforested land under pasture, while 100 lots surveyed in the same year by Léna (1981) had 49% of cleared area under pasture. Much of the recently-cleared land eventually tends to be planted to pasture after an initial period of time in other land uses (Fearnside, 1983a). In the much larger areas of the Amazon Region where large cattle ranches rather than small colonists predominate, the fraction of cleared land going into cattle pasture is closer to 100%.

Annual cropping by small farmers cannot continue indefinitely in its present pattern, given the unsustainable features of the system. Traditional long-fallow shifting cultivation also becomes impossible when population density increases, as is rapidly occurring in Amazonia.

21.1.1.3. Cattle ranching

Cattle ranching, by far the most important agricultural activity in Amazonian rainforest, is growing at such a rate that it can be expected to dominate Amazonian landscapes in all parts of the Basin (Fearnside, 1982). Even in areas where intensive government programs promote perennial crops, such as colonisation projects in Rondônia, much greater areas are planted to pasture every year.

Ranching is widespread both on the 15 million hectares of 'natural' upland grasslands and in the rapidly increasing areas of planted pastures. Beef productivity is low, but, far more importantly, it is unlikely to prove sustainable in the planted pastures (Fearnside, 1979a). The dry weight of pasture grasses produced per hectare per year is small largely due to poor soil, available phosphorus having been found to limit grass yields in several locations on typical Oxisols and Ultisols (Serrão et al., 1971; Koster et al., 1977; Serrão et al., 1979). Pastures are quickly invaded by inedible weeds, better adapted than the grasses to the poor soil, in addition to being spared the grazing pressure of the cattle (Serrão et al., 1971, 19; Simão Neto et al., 1973; Fearnside, 1979a). Of 2.5 million hectares of planted pastures in the Brazilian Amazon by 1978, 20% were considered 'degraded', or invaded by second growth (Serrão et al., 1979, 202).

The question of how soils change under Amazonian pastures is one of more than academic importance in Brazil. Massive governmental programs subsidising pasture in the region have been encouraged by claims that pasture improves the soil, and, by implication, is sustainable indefinitely. In 1974 the head of the principal government agricultural research institute in the Brazilian Amazon announced that comparisons of soils under virgin forest with soils under pastures of various ages both on the Belém-Brasília Highway at Paragominas and in ranching areas of northern Mato Grosso had shown that:

> Immediately after burning (of forest) the acidity is neutralized, with a change in pH from 4 to over 6 and aluminum disappearing. This situation persists in the various ages of pastures, with the oldest pasture being 15 years old, located in Paragominas. Nutrients such as calcium, magnesium, and potassium rise in the chemical composition of the soil, and remain stable through the years. Nitrogen falls immediately after the burn but in a few years returns to a level similar to that existing under primitive forest. (Falesi, 1974, 2.14, my transl.)

The soil changes led to the conclusion that:

> The formation of pastures on latosols and podzolics of low fertility is a rational and economic manner in which to occupy and increase the value of these extensive areas. (Falesi, 1974, 2.15, my trans.)

The data on which these conclusions were based (Falesi, 1976), when examined more closely, reveal that the soil does not improve from the point of view of pasture growth. Available phosphorus, the element limiting pasture growth in these areas, decreases over the period (Fearnside, 1980b). A more detailed study of soil change in the Paragominas ranching area also confirms that the soil degrades, rather than improves, from the point of view of pasture growth (Hecht, 1981, 1982b). Brazilian government agencies concluded in 1977 that the soil improvements they had noted were not sufficient to maintain pasture productivity without the addition of phosphate fertilisers but that adding 50 kg/ha of phosphorus (about 300 kg/ha of superphosphate) would solve the problem of nutrient deficient growth limitation (Serrão et al., 1979; Serrão and Falesi, 1977; Toledo and Serrão, 1982).

Adding phosphorus is not in itself sufficient to render pasture sustainable, as other soil characters continue to deteriorate until they limit production. Soil compaction is a major problem. Exposure of the soil to sun and the trampling of cattle in pastures quickly results in the soil becoming hard and dense, with reduced pore volume and water infiltration capacity (Schubart, 1977; Schubart et al., 1976; Dantas, 1979). Success has often not been great in fertilised pastures in other tropical areas. In Peru researchers found that 'with time, these mixed pastures lose productivity because of soil compaction by animal hooves, disease in legumes and probably deficiencies of nutrients not provided by single superphosphate. The proposed management alternative considered is to revert back to crops, fertilise heavily and start the cycle over again' (Sánchez, 1977 citing results of Peru, IVITA, 1976). Pasture growth is reduced as the compacted soil restrains the plants' roots, and soil erosion increases as rain water runs off rather than sinking into the soil. Vital to the phosphorus fertilisation program has been heavy subsidisation of its cost by the government, through attractive loans with long grace periods and negative interest rates in real terms.

Brazilian government recommendations regarding cattle ranching have changed several times as additional problems have come to be known. After the 1974 theory of self-improving pastures was changed to one of pastures sustainable with limited phosphorus inputs, the drawbacks of Guinea grass

(*Panicum maximum*), the recommended species occupying 85% of the planted pasture area in the Legal Amazon by 1977 (Serrão and Falesi, 1977) became evident. The grass's disappointing performance on the poorest soils, inability to re-seed itself under many conditions, and bunchy habit facilitating invasion of second growth (as well as erosion), led to the official change to promoting creeping signal grass (*Brachiaria humidicola*) in about 1979. *Brachiaria humidicola* has the advantage of forming a low dense cover, but has low yields and is not, as was at first believed, immune to the attacks of the homopteran bug known as *cigarinha* (*Deois incompleta*, Cercopidae) that destroyed many pastures planted with the congeneric species signal grass (*Brachiaria decumbens*) along the Belém-Brasília Highway in the early 1970s (de Brito Silva and Magalhães, 1980; Hecht, 1982b).

Would phosphate fertilisation, as recommended by the Brazilian government (Serrão and Falesi, 1977), make cattle ranching a sustainable undertaking in Amazonian terra firme? The question is a vital one given the continued rush to convert forest to pasture. If fertilised pasture is unsustainable, or is sustainable only with the present government subsidies of fertiliser purchase and application, then the possibility of fertilising may prove to be little more than an illusion. Planners may be led to advocate continuation of the rush to pasture on the assumption that these areas can always be made productive at a later date. Phosphate applications produce immediate and dramatic improvement in degraded pasture but it is well to remember that the number and magnitude of nutrient deficiencies to be supplied, as well as the cost of steps needed to counter the deterioration of soil physical structure, will increase as pasture use is prolonged. Ultimately, the cost and availability of the inputs needed to maintain a significant portion of Amazonia as fertilised pasture may restrain reliance on fertilisers. Even with generous subsidies available for pasture fertilisation, most ranchers presently prefer to concentrate their resources on clearing larger areas rather than improving their pastures. A survey done in 1977 of 92 ranches in northeastern Pará found only one ranch (1.08% of the sample) using any kind of fertiliser on pasture (Homma *et al.*, 1978, 18).

Pasture is attractive to landowners for a number of social and institutional reasons, production of beef often being a minor consideration. A major factor is pasture's capacity to occupy a large land area quickly with a minimum labour and capital expenditure. Amazonia's land tenure system is based almost entirely on physical possession of the land. Formal documentation of land titles normally occurs only after the 'owner', or his representatives, have occupied the claimed area. Violence and fraud are commonplace in eliminating less powerful competitors for claims, especially small farmers or Amerindians (Mueller, 1980, 1982; Martins, 1980; Davis, 1977; and many others).

Clearing land is considered an 'improvement' (*benefitoria*), and pasture is the easiest means of keeping land from reverting to secondary forest once cleared. Land has a tremendous value as a speculation, which accrues both to large land holders drawn to the region by potential capital gains and to smaller farmers who come with the intention of making a living through agricultural production. Pastureland prices in northern Mato Grosso increased at a rate of 38% annually during the 1970 – 75 period, after discounting inflation (Mahar, 1979, 124). No agricultural production system can match these rates of return. Even small farmers who do not view themselves as speculators are tempted to sell their holdings to receive the financial reward obtainable for having occupied a site — a reward which is usually much more than they have ever made through their farming efforts. The lure of speculative profits hinders agricultural development by raising land prices to a point where more productive small farmers are excluded, and by channelling land use decisions toward unproductive pasture rather than intensive management of smaller areas. Ironically, it is the initial lower price of land (relative to other inputs) which leads to extensive use patterns and little concern for sustainability. Land prices rise to levels far higher than would be justified by the value of land as an input for production (*see* Found, 1971). The skyrocketing prices are partly due to the land's function as a store of value, providing protection from Brazil's triple digit inflation. Expectation of future price increases is an immediate motivation for many purchases; the anticipation of uninterrupted expansion and improvement of road access, as well as the continued influx of new arrivals in the region, underlie these hopes. In the case of pasture developed with governmental incentives, the value of land as a key giving access to this rich trove of tax exemptions and concessionary financing adds greatly to its value.

Incentives for pasture projects approved by Brazil's Superintendency for Development of the Amazon (SUDAM) are a major contributing factor to deforestation for ranching (Mahar, 1979; Fearnside, 1979b). Approved projects allow their owners to invest up to 50% of the income tax these individuals or firms would have otherwise had to pay to the government. The decision to invest is logical for tax reasons alone' for anyone with significant income, even if the pasture schemes are economic failures when viewed separately. In addition, an approved project allows borrowing from the government-supported Bank of Amazônia, Anonymous Society (BASA) with no interest, although principal is adjusted yearly to compensate for inflation (usually by a percentage below real inflation). No payments need be made during a grace period of 5 years; formerly the grace period extended for 7 years. Moreover, inspection of the remote ranching projects is lax, allowing many to invest substantial parts of the subsidised financing in more profitable ventures elsewhere.

The generous terms of incentive arrangements not only offer a pull to attract investors to Amazonian lands but are themselves a contributor to the inflation that pushes investors to seek shelter in real estate. Brazil's agricultural incentives are viewed by economists as one of the major factors in the country's notorious inflation, according to former Brazilian finance minister O.G. de Bulhões (Gall, 1980). Inflation occurs any time large amounts of money are spent on unproductive endeavours, thereby putting money in the pockets of consumers without contributing a corresponding flow of products to the economy to satisfy resulting demand.

A change of policy in 1979 has restricted new incentivated ranching projects to parts of Legal Amazonia outside the area defined as 'high forest'. Contrary to popular belief, the change in SUDAM policy has not halted the subsidised expansion of ranching. The hundreds of SUDAM projects already approved for the 'high forest' area continue to receive their full incentives, and most of these have hardly begun to clear their forested area. At the same time, new projects are approved for the large areas classified as 'transition forest' along the southern fringe of Amazonia, already the focus of the most intensive ranching activity.

Many forces leading towards the rapid spread of ranching suggest that this land use, of dubious sustainability, will continue to predominate in the expanding clearings in Amazonia.

21.1.1.4. Perennial crops

Perennial crops, such as cacao (*Theobroma cacao*), coffee (*Coffea arabica*), rubber (*Hevea brasiliensis*), and black pepper (*Piper nigrum*), are seen by many planners as holding great promise for producing sustainable yields in Amazonia (e.g. Alvim, 1978, 1981). Other perennial crops in earlier phases of expansion as commercial planting include African oil palm (*Elaeis guineensis*), various native and introduced fruit trees, and guaraná (*Paullinia cupana*), the Sapindaceous woody climber used in a Brazilian soft drink and as a sex stimulant. Sugar cane (*Saccharum* spp.) is also officially classed as a perennial crop due to its ability to sprout back for subsequent croppings after harvest, although its herbaceous nature and need to be replanted after every 2 − 3 crops in order to maintain full productivity make it more like an annual crop in ecological terms, while its highly seasonal labour requirements make it more like many annual crops in social terms.

Principal reasons for hopes that perennials will prove sustainable are that (1) the products' value, in contrast to annual crops such as rice and maize, justifies the cost of supplying nutrient requirements through fertilisers, rather than relying on the small and quickly exhausted stocks in the soil (Alvim,

1973), (2) plant nutrient losses are minimised, as compared with annual crops, due to better recycling within the agroecosystems, since leaves fall to the ground to contribute to soil fertility in plant root zones, and (3) the soil is protected from direct impact of sun and rain in the case of tree crops such as cacao and rubber. In the case of black pepper, a vine crop grown on posts in the open sun, erosion and other effects are much more akin to annual crops than is the case with arborescent crops like cacao (Fearnside, 1980c).

Perennial crops are affected by a variety of diseases, raising serious doubt about some of the plans for large plantations of these crops. 'Permanent crops', as perennials are euphemistically designated in Brazil, are often anything but permanent. Rubber is the best known example. This native Amazonian tree grows wild as scattered individuals. Wild trees dispersed throughout the rainforest are susceptible to the fungus *Microcyclus* (formerly *Dothidella*) *ulei*, causing South American leaf blight, or 'SALB', but the impediment of many trees of other species separating each individual rubber tree from others of its own species prevents the disease from ever reaching epidemic proportions. Susceptibility to pest and disease attacks of monospecific stands in comparison with scattered individuals in a diverse forest has been suggested as a selective pressure leading to the evolution of such sparsely distributed patterns of rainforest tree species (Janzen, 1970a). When rubber is planted in monocultural plantations, the fungus passes easily from tree to tree, resulting in death or low productivity of susceptible plantations in regions favourable to the fungus. Fordlândia, the Ford Motor Company's plantation begun on the Tapajós River in 1926, was attacked by *Microcyclus*: it became uneconomic in the mid-1930s, was carried on a few years due to Henry Ford's persistence plus the advent of World War II when rubber was produced at all costs to compensate for supplies unavailable from Southeast Asian plantations. After World War II the Fordlândia plantation was abandoned, and the second Ford plantation at Belterra 100 km downstream, begun in 1934 in an attempt to avoid the fungus, was turned over to the Brazilian government as a money-losing proposition (Sioli, 1973). Although attacked by *Microcyclus*, Belterra still functions today, with continual government subsidy and a constant battle of grafting and spraying to combat losses to the fungus. The best solution to the fungus problem has been found to be locating plantations in areas where a sufficiently harsh dry season causes the trees to lose their leaves once a year, combined with the expensive process of grafting resistant tops to high yielding root stock, and a battery of fungicides to control the disease. Brazil, once the world's principal source of rubber, is forced to import two-thirds of its natural rubber needs from Southeast Asia, despite a sustained program of research, extension, and government subsidies to encourage production in the Amazon region.

Black pepper, introduced to Amazonia by Japanese immigrants in 1933 (Loureiro, 1978, 282 − 84), produced large and valuable harvests in areas of Japanese settlement in the 1950s and 1960s. The fungus *Fusarium solani* f. *piperi* first appeared in 1960 at Tomé-Açú (de Albuquerque and Duarte, 1972), later spreading to other pepper-growing locations in the Brazilian Amazon. The result has been devastation of the crop at one location after another, now affecting the most recent plantations on the TransAmazon Highway (Fearnside, 1980d). As long as pepper prices remained high, replanting or moving to new locations was a practical means of dealing with the disease. No resistant varieties have yet been found, and spraying has proved unsatisfactory as a means of control. Falling world market prices for pepper have contributed to making pepper less attractive, although many government financed pepper plantings exist.

Cacao, a native Amazonian plant, is also susceptible to local fungal diseases. Witches' broom disease (*Crinipellis perniciosa*, formerly *Marasmius perniciosus*), attacks plantations, even those of relatively resistant seed varieties produced by government breeding programs in the State of Bahía, the traditional cacao producing region of Brazil located outside of Amazonia and away from the native range of the *Crinipellis* fungus. Breeding programs for resistance to fungal disease suffer from the disadvantage of such programs for any tree crop, in that the much shorter generation time of the fungus in relation to the tree allows the disease organisms to evolve ways of breaking the resistance faster than the trees can evolve new means of resisting attack, even with the help of plant breeders (Janzen, 1973). Witches' broom was a major factor in the demise of cacao production in the State of Pará at the end of the nineteenth century (Pará, SAGRI, 1971 cited by Morais, 1974). The recent government financing and extension programs for cacao on the TransAmazon Highway and in Rondônia have resulted in marked increases in planted areas. Witches' broom attacks have led to some farmers abandoning their plantations, to some following government advice to spray and remove affected branches and fruits, and to many others taking an attitude of waiting to see how the disease will progress.

Disease will undoubtedly be a major factor affecting the extent to which cacao and other perennial crops spread in Amazonia. Disease attack can be expected to have an additional effect to falling market prices in restricting the spread of cacao. Since controlling witches' broom is expensive, requiring both a large amount of labour to remove affected branches by hand and costly copper-containing fungicide sprays, growers can be expected to have less motivation to incur these expenses as cacao prices fall. Once disease foci become well established in neglected plantations, losses and control costs can be expected to increase in surrounding areas, further weakening motivation to control the disease. Disease and pest problems can also be expected to increase as the size of monocultures of perennial crops increases. The world price of cacao has been falling since the peak reached in 1977. World Bank estimates of the future course of the decline indicated FOB cacao prices dropping, in constant 1980 US dollars, from the observed $3,489/metric ton in 1979 to a projected $2,837 in 1984 and $2,073 in 1989 (International Bank for Reconstruction and Development, 1981: 100). Increased world cacao production, partly from expanding plantations in Amazonia, is one factor contributing to the expected decline (Skillings and Tcheyan, 1979), as is anticipated progress in producing substitutes for cacao in chocolate (International Bank for Reconstruction and Development, 1981, 79). The rise in price in 1983 caused by a severe drought in cacao-producing areas of West Africa cannot be expected to continue over the long term.

Irrespective of the biological problems of perennial crops, economic limits are sure to prevent these land uses from occupying a significant portion of the vast area of Amazonia, although the relatively small area that could be planted to these crops without saturating world markets could provide a significant income for the region.

21.1.1.5. Mechanised annuals

Mechanised cultivation of annual crops in terra firme has been increasing in recent years but still represents only a tiny fraction of the total planted to such crops as rice and beans. Wealthier newcomers to the region arriving from areas in Southern Brazil where tractors and other machinery are commonplace have increasingly brought with them the cultural orientation and knowledge, as well as the machinery and financial resources, needed to employ this form of technology. Mechanisation avoids the headache of obtaining hired hands to do manual labour at the seasons of peak labour demand. Since most people come to the new areas with the intention of staking out their own claim rather than working for others, the relatively few workers available for hire find a sellers' market for their labour.

Mechanisation has disadvantages as well. The isolated settlers find much higher costs for obtaining spare parts and skilled maintenance for the equipment than they had experienced in the highly developed South. At the same time, farm gate prices of cereal crops are lower, since the cost of transportation to distant markets is far greater. Use of tractors is also difficult in much of the Amazon where land is dissected into steep slopes, contrary to the popular illusion that the area is as flat as it appears from the air. Removing rainforest tree stumps and partially burned trunks is a costly prerequisite for using tractors in agricultural operations. De-stumping almost always requires bulldozing the land, thus removing the most fertile upper layer of soil, as well as contributing to soil compaction (Van der Weert,

1974; Seubert et al., 1977; Uhl et al., 1982). Ploughing the fields has the disadvantage of bringing less fertile lower layers to the soil surface, in contrast to many temperate zone farming systems where topsoil is deep and lower layers consist of relatively unweathered material rich in plant nutrients.

The influx of Southern Brazilians to the Amazon can be expected to increase the number of these new arrivals wanting to apply their capital to mechanisation. Improved transportation and urban infrastructure, such as asphalting of the Cuiabá — Porto Velho Highway in 1984, make today's frontier areas increasingly attractive to these wealthy farmers. Better transportation will make the products more marketable, as will the progressive disappearance of staple food crops from Brazil's South, where these land uses are now being quickly replaced by export crops such as soybeans. At the same time, rising land values will make investing capital in equipment more attractive than in land clearing as currently. Forces that can be expected to hold any explosion of mechanisation in check include continued migration of manual labourers to the region, presumably to lead to a drop in wages from present levels which are far above those in other rural areas of Brazil. Increasing fuel costs as fossil fuel supplies dwindle will also slow mechanisation, as will the disadvantages of soil and topography already mentioned. The tremendous amount of capital that would be required to convert any significant portion of Amazonia to mechanised agriculture ensures that cheap, quickly installed land uses like pasture will dominate for the foreseeable future.

21.1.1.6. Horticulture

Growing vegetables has become a profitable venture for enterprising farmers located near large cities in the Amazon. Market prices for such commodities as tomatoes are as much as seven times higher in Manaus than in São Paulo, and much of the produce sold is actually flown in from São Paulo, over 2600 km away. Around major cities such as Belém and Manaus, as well as many smaller towns such as Altamira on the TransAmazon Highway, farmers specialised in horticulture are often of Japanese origin. These farmers have a cultural tradition of intensively cultivating small areas, together with liberal use of fertilisers, pesticides, and other costly inputs, practices foreign to most of Amazonia's other inhabitants. The high price of inputs has been compensated by high value products, and the ventures have often proved economic successes.

Horticulture is much more difficult in the tropics than in other regions, due to greater losses to diseases and pests. Rural residents grow what few green vegetables they include in their diet in raised windowbox-like structures called *hortas*. The legs of the *hortas* are protected against rats (*Rattus rattus*), and sometimes against leaf-cutter ants (*Atta* spp.) as well. Soil in the box is fortified with ash, black 'Indian earth' (*terra preta do indio*), or other nutrient-rich supplements. Production of green onions (*Allium cepa*), collard greens (*Brassica oleracea* var. *acephala*), and other vegetables is meagre, but supplies an important addition to the usual meal of manioc flour, rice and, when available, beans.

Commercial horticulture must combat plagues of insects, slugs, rats, and other pests, as well as disease-causing fungi, bacteria, and viruses. One successful system for growing tomatoes is employed commercially by a Seventh Day Adventist agricultural school 92 km from Manaus. Open-sided greenhouses with polyethylene roofs shield the crop from rain, thus avoiding removal of heavy doses of pesticides and fungicides from the leaves and fruits. The greenhouses also buffer the crop from rapid changes in temperature and humidity, believed to be the cause of tomatoes grown in the open having a tendency to split before ripening. Soil in wooden troughs containing the plants is sterilised prior to planting, and irrigation is done by periodic flooding of small ditches in the soil in each trough, to prevent loss of protective chemicals and to avoid creating disease-favouring humid conditions for the aerial portion of the plant. Division of the plantation into separate greenhouses also helps prevent the spread of diseases, as do elaborate procedures for disinfecting and controlling use of garden tools. Large quantities of reasonably well-qualified but low-paid labour from students is required.

Another commercial scale horticultural enterprise near Manaus is run by the municipal government. Settlers have been assigned individual small plots in Iranduba, on land fertilised with processed garbage from the city of Manaus. The scheme provides for irrigation, transportation, supply of chemical inputs, agronomic advice, marketing arrangements, and housing in a planned village. Tomatoes (*Lycopersicon esculentum*), cabbage (*Brassica oleracea* var. *capitata*), green peppers (*Capsicum annum*), and other vegetables are grown for marketing at a cycle of weekly markets in different parts of the city of Manaus. Yields and product quality are somewhat lower than under the Seventh Day Adventist system, but the product forms an important addition to the city's food supply.

The many Japanese immigrants engaged in raising vegetables near Amazonian cities do so with intensive application of fertilisers and manure, especially chicken manure often obtained from poultry raising ventures on the same farms. Chickens are raised on a diet of pre-mixed food grains imported from southern Brazil. Land is often tilled with micro-tractors or hand-pushed motorised tillers. Pesticide use is extremely heavy. Japanese embassy staff offer technical support, conducting surveys and giving farmers Japanese language computer outputs with individualised reports and advice. More important to the success of these farmers is the close-knit network of information exchange and mutual assistance offered by the Japanese immigrant community itself. Strong cultural emphasis on thrift, sober planning, and hard work have also been essential to the accumulation of capital and information needed to pursue this form of agriculture.

21.1.2. *Várzea*: Amazonian floodplains

21.1.2.1. *Annual crops of smallholders*

In the past, Amazonian indigenous populations made extensive use of the Amazon's várzea, or floodplain, during the period of each year when river water level is low (Lathrap, 1970; Meggers, 1971; Denevan, 1966; Gross, 1975; Roosevelt, 1980). Várzeas have been used to a far lesser extent by the *caboclos* occupying these areas since most riverside Amerindian populations disappeared in the years immediately following European contact. While várzea soils are more fertile than almost all terra firme soils, the most important difference is not that várzea yields are higher when a crop is harvested. Far more significant is the possibility várzea offers for a sustainable yield without the lengthy fallows (or heavy fertilisation) required to make annual crops produce for more than 1 or 2 years on terra firme. Annual flooding in the várzea deposits a fresh layer of fertile silt and leaves the land virtually free of weeds and pests at least once per year, at the moment when the water recedes: 'the river is the plough'.

Várzea areas can be subdivided into horizontal zones such as mud bars, levees, backswamps, and beaches (Denevan, 1982). Only the levees are unflooded year round. Soils, crops, and timing of agricultural activities differ for each zone. Bergman (1980) describes a typical crop zonation from a Shipibo village on the Ucayali River in Peru: rice and beans on the beaches; maize, sugar cane, and jute on the levee foreslope; bananas, manioc, and fruit trees on the levee tops; jute and sugar cane on the levee back slopes; and beans and pasture in the backswamps farthest from the river. *Caboclo* exploitation of várzea on the Guamá River near Belém has a similar zonation of crops; the addition of an associated zone with supplementary plantings of perennial crops on nearby terra firme has been suggested as making the pattern a model for Amazonian settlements (de Carmargo, 1958).

The timing of the rise and fall of water levels dominates every aspect of várzea agriculture. Years when the water level begins to rise earlier than normal, or rises to higher than normal flood levels, can be disastrous to várzea cultivators. These uncertainties have been hypothesised to explain a wide array of cultural adaptations of indigenous várzea groups, as well as limits to várzea as a base for 'cultural development' (Meggers, 1971, 149), although not all anthropologists agree with this interpretation (Roosevelt, 1980, 23).

The continuing deforestation of Amazonia can be expected to result in higher and less regular flooding. Indeed, some evidence exists that such changes may have already begun in the Upper Amazon (Gentry and López-Parodi, 1980, but *see* Nordin and Meade, 1982; Gentry and López-Parodi, 1982). Among many negative effects, these changes will make cultivation of annual crops in the Amazonian várzea increasingly more difficult. Deforestation of the floodplains will affect the productivity of the Amazon fishery (Chapter 14, this volume).

21.1.2.2. *Mechanised rice*

Mechanised cultivation of irrigated rice is being pursued commercially in one location in várzea of the lower Amazon as a part of the Jari project (Fearnside and Rankin, 1980, 1982). The potential, or lack of potential, of this form of capital intensive high yield agriculture is a question with importance far greater than the relatively insignificant area of the present 3062 ha under cultivation, or the 14,165 ha to which the plantation is eventually expected to expand if probable ownership changes do not alter the previous planning. The rice project is not included in U.S. shipping magnate D.K. Ludwig's sale of silvicultural and mining operations at Jari to a group of Brazilian firms (*Veja*, 27 de janeiro de 1982, 92).

Rice is currently grown on a rolling schedule, with different fields being planted and harvested at different times. Any given field produces two crops per year, although experiments underway may eventually permit about 30% of a full crop's yield to be harvested from a ratoon or stubble crop during the interval between the two crops planted from seed. Yields in most years have been on the order of 8 tons of rice (with husks) per hectare per year. A drop to around 7 tons/ha/year in 1979 caused great concern among the technical staff and company officials. Several drops in yield have occurred and for the most part been countered by management changes. A sulphur deficiency was discovered (Wang *et al.*, 1976) and corrected by changing the nitrogen fertiliser used from urea to ammonium sulphate. Iron toxicity contributed to a sharp fall in yields in 1979 to about 7 tons/ha/year. Various insect pests, especially army worms (*Spodoptera frugiperda*) and stink bugs (*Oebalus poecilus*), are also believed to have contributed to the drop. When completed, an improved canal system and regrading of fields are expected to allow the fine-tuned water management needed to minimise these problems. Rice variety changes, increased pesticide use, and greater attention to a host of management details are hoped to reverse the decline. In the future, yields are expected to improve with the construction of a canal to allow changing the irrigation source from the Araiolôs River to the less acid and more nutrient-rich Amazon. A variety of insect pests, mites (Acari), nematodes, weeds, and fungal diseases exact some toll on rice production. Perhaps more important are the diseases, weeds, and pests that have not yet arrived at Jari's rice project in São Raimundo. The rice plantation has been enjoying the honeymoon from coevolved pest and disease organisms that has been a repeating pattern for newly introduced species throughout the world (*see* Janzen, 1973; Elton, 1958). Neighbouring countries have biological problems in irrigated rice which can eventually be expected to reach Jari, such as 'hoja blanca' virus in Venezuela and two major graminaceous weeds in Surinam (*Leptochloa scabea* and *Ischaemum rugosum*). Jari was able to use the IR-22 rice variety as its mainstay for 6 years, even though this high-yielding variety is highly susceptible to rice blast (*Piricularia oryzae*). When the fungus arrived, IR-22 was already being phased out in favour of more resistant varieties. The most effective response to disease problems is generally a switch to more resistant varieties, chemical treatments representing only a temporary measure. Managing large monocultures is a constant race, pitting human efforts to breed, identify and propagate appropriate varieties against the ever-changing array of biological problems. The outcome of this contest is never guaranteed.

Irrigated rice of the type planted at Jari fails to take advantage of the Amazon várzea's major advantage: the annual renewal of soil fertility by flooding and siltation. Instead, the fields are isolated from the river's water level fluctuations by a polder — a dike surrounding the fields, into which water must be pumped both in and out. The soil enclosed in the polder has essentially been mined for nutrients in these early years since many nutrients have been removed in the crop without being fully replaced through fertilisation, in the same way that the mining of ore deposits removes the resource without replacement. Compensating increases in fertiliser-supplied inputs can restore the balance, but at an increased cost.

The dependence of mechanised agriculture on nonrenewable resources may prove to be a long-term problem making it less attractive in the future.

21.1.2.3. Horticulture

Várzea areas near urban markets are increasingly being cultivated for vegetable production. The farmers are usually from *caboclo* backgrounds, with many changes in their agricultural methods in comparison with the traditional largely subsistence agriculture of the scattered *caboclo* residents of more remote areas. Many have come to these areas from other parts of the region. Government extension agencies provide advice to producers within ready boating distance of the agents' posts. The agencies also help in obtaining seeds, insecticides, sprayers, and other necessities. Impact of extension agencies appears to be much greater with introduction of this novel and demonstrably profitable technology than are similar efforts with subsistence crops more familiar to the farmers. Horticulture among these well-located várzea residents is generally profitable and is expanding, although many failed attempts at individual plantings can also be seen. Defending these crops against diseases and pests requires a large store of knowledge to be able to recognise and treat a given problem as soon as it arises, as well as stocks of chemical remedies readily at hand.

21.1.2.4. Fibre crops

Jute (*Corchorus* spp.) and malva (*Malva rotundifolia*) are common várzea crops among small farmers. Jute was first introduced to the region in 1934 by Japanese immigrants (Soares and Libonati, 1966), although most jute farmers today are not of Japanese origin. Jute is most prominent in the várzeas of the middle Amazon, while malva is most common in the tidally influenced várzeas in the Zona Bragantina of Pará, as well as in the floodplains in the lower portions of the Solimões (Upper Amazon) River. Malva is sometimes also planted on terra firme, but it exhausts the soil quickly and does better in the fertile floodplain. Jute and malva can be processed into bales of saleable fibres by hand labour, can be stored and transported without spoilage and can be sold for cash.

21.1.2.5. Cattle and water buffalo

Zebu cattle (*Bos indicus*) are grazed on natural várzea grasslands in many parts of the Brazilian Amazon, especially in the lower part of the Rio Solimões (Upper Amazon) and in the várzeas near the Amazon's mouth. Productivity is quite low in part due to poor quality fodder, but more importantly due to stress in months when water level is high and grazing land nonexistent. During this critical period the cattle are herded together either on isolated hilltops still above water, on raised wooden platforms (*marombas*), or on floating barges. The cattle tenders bring as much fodder as possible, carrying by boat or towing loads of macrophytes cut from the river's 'floating meadows', from semisubmerged grasses along the river margins, or from terra firme. Cattle become emaciated and frequently die during the flood period. Cattle tenders try to sell as many animals as is practical as the water level rises in order to keep their herds at a manageable size during the flooded period. When water levels fall again, there is a superabundance of pasture area.

Water buffalo (*Bubalus bubalis*) were first introduced to Brazil from Asia in 1895, and since the early 1960s the population of these animals has been exploding at an estimated 10%/year (do Nascimento, 1979). The várzeas of the enormous Ilha do Marajó at the mouth of the Amazon have been the focus of most water buffalo ranching. Water buffalos are better adapted than zebu cattle to the wet conditions of the várzea, being well equipped for swimming and wading during the flood season. Much of the Marajó herd is raised for meat, but Brazilian government agricultural research efforts both in Pará and Amazonas states are most enthusiastic about water buffalo as a source of dairy products such as milk, butter, and cheese. Water buffalo milk is richer and produced in larger quantities per animal than is cows' milk, and each litre yields 50% more cheese or 43% more butter (do Nascimento, 1979). It is well to note, however, that water buffalo in commercial operations, such as those in much of the Jari Project's várzea area, are noticeably less fat and healthy than are those in government experiments. Nevertheless, replacing the zebu cattle presently grazed on várzea grasslands with the clearly superior water buffalo could significantly increase the production of dairy products in the region.

21.2. ALTERNATIVE MANAGEMENT: IMPEDIMENTS AND PROSPECTS

21.2.1. Fertilisers and continuous cultivation

Agronomists working at Yurimaguas, near Pucalpa in Amazonian Peru, have directed their efforts towards devising a system that would permit continuous cultivation of annual crops by small farmers in terra firme (North Carolina State University Soil Science Department, 1975, 1976, 1978, 1980). The system developed has produced two crops per year from the same field over a 10 year period using a rotation of upland rice, maize, and soybeans (Nicholaides *et al.*, 1982).

Although the Yurimaguas experimenters are enthusiastic about the system's potential for implementation by small farmers over vast expanses of terra firme (Sánchez, 1977; Nicholaides *et al.*, 1982; Sánchez *et al.*, 1982; Valverde and Bandy, 1982), several drawbacks may make any such expansion more difficult and less rewarding than imagined. The system requires continuous inputs of fertilisers. Although present prices for these inputs in Peru are apparently low enough to be justified by the yields so far, the long-term costs and availabilities of these are a major cloud on the horizon for fertiliser-based agriculture worldwide. Projections of global trends from 1976 indicate potash being exhausted by the year 2027 and mineable phosphate rock by the year 2062 (United States, Council on Environmental Quality and Department of State, 1980; *see also* Institute of Ecology, 1972). Although the trends of the recent past cannot continue through all of this period due to other restraints on population and cultivated area (Wells, 1976), unprecedented price increases can be expected as supplies of these resources, nonrenewable on a human time scale, dwindle. Nitrogen, generally the major nutrient deficiency for tropical agriculture (Webster and Wilson, 1980, 220), is an element whose supply depends heavily on the world's vanishing reserves of fossil fuels if plant requirements are to be met through fertilisation.

A major practical problem in implementing the 'Yurimaguas technology' on a wide scale in Amazonia is the need for a continuous input of technical information. As soil nutrients are exhausted in any given field, the balance of nutrients added must be continuously changed. After 8 years, the experimental plantings require supply of all essential elements with the exception of iron and chloride (Nicholaides et al., 1982). Soil samples must be taken every year from every field, chemical analyses performed, and the results interpreted and explained to the farmer in terms of fertiliser requirements. Even the staff of qualified agronomists at Yurimaguas have experienced sharp yield declines in years when nutrient balances were not spotted and remedied in time. The prospect is slight of semiliterate farmers doing as well when dependent on a frail chain of poorly qualified extension agents as their link to information sources on constantly changing input requirements. The present infrastructure of soil analysis laboratories in the Amazon has difficulties in processing a few thousand samples for research purposes; the barriers to expanding this infrastructure sufficiently to cope with the millions of samples needed to apply the Yurimaguas system to a significant portion of Amazonia would be tremendous in the foreseeable future.

In the long term, agronomic problems other than the nutrient deficiencies countered in the present scheme are likely to become increasingly difficult to solve. Soil compaction is one such problem (Cunningham, 1963; Baena and Dutra, 1979), as is the decline in organic matter indicated in the Yurimaguas data (Nicholaides et al., 1982). Erosion, apparently not a significant problem on the 'flat Ultisol' of the Yurimaguas station, is likely to be a major problem if extended to much of Amazonia where many areas of intensive settlement are far from flat. The experimenters point out that the system has 'low erosion hazard except during periods of intense rainfall' (Nicholaides et al., 1982), but just such periods of intense rainfall are characteristic of Amazonia.

Profitability of the system, even in the short term, may well be less than the Yurimaguas results would indicate. The substantial costs of supplying the technical information required to maintain the system, including performing soil analyses and communicating their results and significance, are not included in calculations of the system's profitability. Also, both the experiment station staff and the 11 farmers described as 'respected farm leaders' who have tried the system can be expected to obtain better results than the masses of less well qualified farmers that would use the system if expanded on a large scale.

The problem of devising annual cropping systems for terra firme is an important one deserving intense research. It is essential to remember that a practical and sustainable system of this type has yet to be devised. One should be wary of placing faith in the future development of such technology to save tropical peoples from the consequences of unwise forest clearing and land use decisions being made today.

21.2.2. Diversity and sustainable management

Most of the history of human agricultural development has been one of finding ways to reverse or arrest the process of ecological succession (E.P. Odum, 1971). 'Climax' communities, usually diverse forests, are replaced with earlier successional stages such as low-diversity stands of herbaceous crop plants or pasture grasses. Earlier successional stages offer the advantages of quicker yields, of higher net primary productivity, and of a greater share of the plant's energy budget being allocated to producing the seeds and fruits that humans are interested in harvesting. An additional advantage of the simplified crop stands is the ease of applying energy supplements, such as fossil fuel inputs for mechanisation. This strategy can prove a cruel illusion. In Howard T. Odum's (1971, 115 – 16) classic statement: 'A whole generation of citizens thought that the carrying capacity of the earth was proportional to the amount of land under cultivation and that higher efficiencies in using the energy of the sun had arrived. This is a sad hoax, for industrial man no longer eats potatoes made from solar energy; now he eats potatoes made partly of oil.'

Such simplified farm ecosystems have many other disadvantages (see Dickenson, 1972; Janzen, 1970b, 1973; Fearnside, 1983b). The direct contribution of the farmer's production to his own diet is reduced, obligating him to rely on expensive, uncertain, and often lower quality products purchased through middlemen from other distant monocultures. The single stratum of the monoculture has less complete utilisation of the space and incoming sunlight, as bare earth is often unoccupied by photosynthetic material. Land is also left bare between crops. The unshaded soil leads to greater weed competition and labour (or fossil fuel) requirement to achieve control as well as to soil erosion. Open nutrient cycles allow greater losses of soil nutrients, in contrast to the relative effectiveness in minimising leaching afforded by the deep roots and well-developed detritus cycling of trees and their litter communities. Concentration on a single crop exposes farmers to international market fluctuations beyond their control, whereas having a variety of agricultural products gives them the insurance of income from the other crop species should the market plummet for any particular species. The same disadvantage applies to the farmer's hardship when faced with crop losses from bad weather, pests, or diseases. The chance of pest and disease outbreaks is itself increased by removal of both natural chemical defences and the protection afforded by spatial heterogeneity. Labour requirements for maintaining monocultures are usually far more seasonal than those for diversified plantings, thus making less use of family labour and fostering less socially attractive systems of migrant labour. The concentration of management and marketing decisions in distant elites can also prove a profound social disadvantage, as sugar cane growers on the TransAmazon Highway have discovered during a decade of worsening relations with a series of three successive mill management concerns. Frequent disagreements over acceptability, price, and payment schedules for cane, usually settled to the disadvantage of the producers, have led to a climate of mistrust and violence in the cane-producing area.

Although as yet only in its infancy as a field of research, attempts are being made to develop sustainable and diverse crop associations for tropical areas (e.g. Bishop, 1978, 1979, 1982 in Ecuador; Gleissman et al., 1978, 1981; Gleissman, 1979 and Alarcón, 1979 in Mexico; May and Momal, 1981 in Indonesia). In the Brazilian Amazon systems are under development by the Brazilian Enterprise for Research in Agriculture and Cattle Ranching: EMBRAPA (de Andrade, 1979), The Commission for Promotion of Cacau Growing: CEPLAC (Bazán et al., 1973), and the National Institute for Research in the Amazon: INPA (Arkcoll, 1979). Many are based on the modification of traditional systems which have had the benefit of centuries of trial and error by indigenous populations (see Clarke, 1976, 1978). Better designs of polycultural systems are needed (Kass, 1978), especially including effects which reduce insect attacks through increased diversity (Root and Tahvanainen, 1972; Risch, 1980). Theoretical approaches can help save time and resources needed for trial-and-error testing of possible intercropping combinations (Vandermeer, 1981). Increased agricultural intensity and decreased diversity (Pool, 1972) and decreased interfield spacing (Janzen, 1972) also increase vulnerability to insect attack. The presence (Popenoe, 1964; Janzen, 1972, 5) or absence (Price, 1976 cited by Gleissman, 1979; Janzen, 1974) of nearby woody vegetation can increase agricultural pest problems depending on their role as reservoirs for populations of insect pests or biological control agents.

Some attempts have been made at modifying shifting cultivation to produce higher returns. Suggestions include eliminating some of the fallow period (Guillemin, 1956; Andreae, 1974; Ahn, 1979). The 'corridor system', begun by Belgian administrators in Zaïre before independence (Martin, 1956; Ruthenberg, 1971) has not been tried elsewhere or continued after the end of Belgian rule in its original site. Unfortunate rigidity in the planning of the scheme brought on many problems avoided by the flexibility in locating and timing cropping that is the hallmark of traditional systems. Social pressures also led to overly shortened fallow periods, the Achilles' heel of shifting cultivation in many locations (e.g. Vermeer, 1970 in Nigeria; Freeman, 1955 in Sarawak, *see also* Nye and Greenland, 1960; Watters, 1971; UNESCO, 1978). Adding carefully chosen 'modern' inputs, such as herbicides, has also been suggested as a way of 'bringing the green revolution to the shifting cultivator' (Greenland, 1975).

Interest has been high in variation of the taungya system, or agri-silviculture (King, 1968; Mongi and Huxley, 1979; Hecht, 1982a; Dubois, 1979). Taungya, a system with a long history of application in Southeast Asia, involves planting annual crops together with silvicultural tree species such as teak (*Tectonia grandis*). The trees take the place of second growth in the shifting cultivation cycle, giving a valuable yield at the end of each cycle although they do not supply the ash of burned secondary vegetation as in unmodified shifting cultivation. The necessity of clearing forest for taungya has environmental costs which limit the extent to which this or other systems requiring clearcutting should be promoted, but advantages exist for employing agri-silvicultural systems on land already cleared for low productivity uses such as pasture (*see* Fearnside, 1983b). Taungya and systems like it are far from ideal: serious erosion can easily result over the long term (UNESCO: 1978, 464; see Bell, 1973 on erosion under teak plantations in Trinidad). One of the important features of taungya for supporting human populations is its appropriateness for use by small farmers. Farm size is itself one of the major determinants of land use choices, and the ability of agriculture to support human populations.

21.2.3. Farm size and agricultural populations

The question of land tenure distribution lies at the root of any discussion of agricultural land use and production in Amazonia. Land tenure in Brazil has traditionally been extremely skewed, with most of the land in a small number of large properties or *latifundios*. In 1975, 0.8% of Brazil's 'rural establishments' were over 1000 ha in area and represented 43% of the land, while 52% were under 10 ha representing only 3% of the land (Brazil, IBGE, 1980, 314 – 16). Regional differences in land quality make the concentration even greater in terms of its ability to support agriculture: the National Institute for Colonization and Agrarian Reform (INCRA) cadastre for 1972 revealed that 72% of all farms were *minifundios*, or establishments with less than one 'rural module' of land, a unit unique to each region officially defined as the size required to absorb the year-round labour of the farmer and his family, while large enough to permit 'social and economic progress of the domestic unit' (with supplementary hired labour) (da Silva, 1978, cited by Wood and Wilson, 1982). The degree of land concentration varies between the regions of Brazil, being highest in the Northeast and in Amazonia. Within Amazonia great variation exists: properties over 1000 ha in area account for 85% of the total farm area of Mato Grosso, but only 33% in Rondônia (Mahar, 1982). Within Rondônia, the state where the most government colonisation projects have been located, land concentration varies from areas of 100 ha colonist lots in the older settlement projects (50 ha in the ones now being implemented), to areas where 3000 ha ranches are auctioned from public lands, to areas of much larger holdings. The Gini coefficient, an index of land tenure concentration, has been increasing in Brazil, rising from 0.842 in the 1950 – 1960 period to 0.844 in 1970 and 0.855 in 1975 (Wood and Wilson, 1982) indicating an increase in larger holdings. High indices, of around 0.86, dominate in ranching areas in the Amazonian parts of Goiás and Maranhão, while low indices of around 0.28 are typical of old areas of small farmer settlement in the Zona Bragantina near Belém (Hébette and Acevedo, 1979, 117 – 21). Forms of agriculture employed vary with the size of the holdings. Large landowners are more likely to engage in ranching, while smallholders are more likely to plant annual crops.

As a general rule, small properties do not produce consistently more or less per cultivated hectare than large properties on land of the same quality planted with the same type of crop, but produce far more per unit of total area, according to a World Bank study of six tropical countries including Brazil (Berry and Cline, 1976, cited by Eckholm, 1979, 17 – 18). The smaller units produce more because of cultivating a greater fraction of the land area, as well as by more intensive techniques such as double cropping in some areas. In northeast Brazil, where land tenure concentration is notorious, the World Bank study argues that redistribution of the land into small holdings would give an 80% increase in agricultural production. A similar situation appears to be developing in Amazonia, where 'replication' of northeast Brazilian land tenure arrangements has been noted by many social scientists (e.g. Ianni, 1979a,b). The process is only one of several in changing land tenure patterns in Amazonia, others including the breakup of large claims of rubber 'barons' (see Cardoso and Müller, 1978, 74 – 76), a statistic largely an artifact of boundary readjustments and the subdivision of farmers' small plots into ever smaller *minifúndios* as the land is divided through inheritance (Hébette and Acevedo, 1979; Martine, 1980). Unevenness of land tenure can be expected to increase in much of the region once the first wave of pioneers has passed. Land tenure concentration occurs through the takeover of squatters' claims by large ranches, as occurred along the Belém-Brasília Highway (Valverde and Dias, 1967; Mahar, 1979, 78), or through a process that does not appear in government statistics: the purchase in the names of wives, children, or other relatives of a number of adjoining or nearby properties by wealthier newcomers as in colonisation areas like those on the Transamazon Highway. Concentrated land tenure results in both lower overall production and the favouring of crops not eaten locally, in addition to a greatly reduced contribution of what is produced to supporting the human population (Durham, 1979 for an excellent example from Central America).

21.3. LIMITS TO AGRICULTURE: HUMAN CARRYING CAPACITY

Human carrying capacity refers to the density of people that can be supported indefinitely in an area at an adequate standard of living without environmental degradation, given appropriate assumptions concerning productive technology, consumptive habits, and criteria for defining an adequate standard of living and acceptable environmental degradation. Criteria can include adequate security of a given family meeting the standards in any year. Since exceeding carrying capacity leads to failure to maintain adequate levels of consumption and environmental quality, achieving a balance at a density below carrying capacity is of supreme importance for the long-term future of the region's inhabitants. Intense flows of migrants are currently entering the Amazon region especially in Rondônia. The population of Rondônia rocketed by 331% from 116,620 in 1970 to 503,125 at the 1980 census (Brazil, IBGE, 1981, 5). The northern region (Rondônia, Acre, Amazonas, Roraima, Pará, and Amapá) grew by 65% while the country as a whole grew by 28% during the same period. The rapid increase in population in areas like Rondônia, combined with the exclusion of settlers from much of the land area by owners and other claimants already there, mean that population densities can be expected to quickly exceed carrying capacity in settled areas.

The individual agricultural systems discussed in previous sections of this chapter all have finite limits, as does agriculture everywhere. That the limits are often lower than recent arrivals to the region or overly enthusiastic government planners envision is far less important than the fact that limits exist. Amazonia is a land of many illusions, both of infinite area and of infinite agricultural 'potential'. These illusions lead governments to propose, and the public to accept, roadbuilding and agricultural colonisation as solutions to such national problems as poverty and social unrest due to overpopulation, highly unequal land tenure distribution, and rural unemployment precipitated by coffee-killing frosts and changes in agricultural patterns to mechanised agribusinesses.

The combination of overpopulation and skewed land tenure had been noted as a prime motive for the migrations to colonisation areas in the Amazonian portions of Bolivia (Nelson, 1973), Peru (Aramburú,

1982), Ecuador (Uquillas, 1982), and Colombia (Carrizosa U., 1982), in addition to alleviating social tensions in Northeast Brazil in prompting Brazil's National Integration Program for establishing the TransAmazon Highway colonisation schemes (Kleinpenning, 1975, 1979; Ianni, 1979a). Despite the fanfare often accompanying the launching of colonisation initiatives, their role in absorbing displaced populations has been minimal, being dwarfed by migration to urban slums. In Brazil, the National Integration Program absorbed only 7,839 families, or 0.3% of the rural exodus during the 1970s (assuming that the virtually paralysed program absorbed no more net immigration after 1977), while the 24,242 families settled in the entire Northern Region during the decade represent less than 1% of the rural exodus during the period (Wood and Wilson, 1982).

The notion that agricultural development in Amazonia is capable of providing long-term solutions, such as the 'Solution for 2001' as the TransAmazon Highway was enthusiastically christened (Tamer, 1970), has been doomed from the start. If one were to make the improbable assumption that all of Brazil's Legal Amazonia were distributed as 100 ha (1 km^2) lots in the manner done in colonisation areas along the TransAmazon Highway, only 5 million families, or about 25 million people, would fill the entire region. This represents less than 8 years of growth for Brazil's 119 million 1980 population increasing at the current 2.4%/year.

In discussing the merits of different forms of agricultural development, one must be very clear about what the objectives of development are. Conflicting objectives commonly cause divergent views on what forms of agriculture are most appropriate. Many proposals for Amazonia are directed at solving problems outside the Amazon Region, such as alleviating rural poverty in migrant source areas, urban squalor aggravated by the flow of new arrivals in cities like São Paulo, providing products for markets in other parts of the country, producing export earnings to lessen national debts, and providing investment opportunities for speculators and businessmen from more capital-rich regions. Farming the Amazon is a difficult and poorly understood challenge, and supplying the needs of the Amazon's residents alone is not an easy task if it is to be done on a sustainable basis. The suggestion has been made that Brazil's development effort be directed to other regions, such as the central Brazilian scrubland or *cerrado* (Goodland *et al.*, 1978; Goodland, 1980). At the least, I would suggest, the portion of the agricultural development effort in Amazonia motivated by problems outside of the region should be applied instead to addressing the problems directly in those regions.

Exponentially growing national problems cannot be solved for long by exploiting a finite resource such as Amazonia. Even problems which do not grow can only be solved if the agricultural systems employed are sustainable. Recognising the limits of agriculture is the first and most essential step in redirecting development policies as a whole, so that the human population can be maintained at an adequate standard of living on a sustainable basis. Estimating human carrying capacity is an essential element in any such redirection (Fearnside, 1979c, 1983d). Devising sustainable agroecosystems is also essential, and is a task which will require a sharp reorientation of the present emphasis in agronomic research priorities. Presently, agricultural research usually aims at obtaining higher and higher crop yields, or, more accurately, at producing higher monetary returns on money invested in agriculture. Producing the greatest profits is not necessarily consistent with sustaining production (Clark, 1973, 1976; Fearnside, 1979b). Researchers should strive to produce sustainable systems, even if yields and profits are lower. Agroecosystems also need to serve the needs of family consumption, producing the diverse array of products required for local consumption, and doing so with a premium on the security of obtaining an adequate harvest. Technologies that increase yields at the cost of security may make sense to government planners who see only aggregate statistics, or to wealthy investors who can afford to gamble on risky ventures to maximise 'expected monetary value' (*see* Raiffa, 1970), but such risky agricultural choices are far less wise for the small farmer who depends on the yield to feed his family from year to year. When a crop fails on an agricultural experiment station, the agronomists in charge receive their salaries at the end of the month as usual, but when a small farmer's crop fails his family goes hungry. The difference in perspective needs to be incorporated into decisions about research priorities and the promotion of new technologies.

The available development choices for Amazonia, both agricultural and non-agricultural, have widely differing prospects in terms of agronomic and social sustainability, competitiveness without subsidies, self-sufficiency, fulfilment of social goals, retention of development options, effects on other resources, and macro-ecological effects (Fearnside, 1983b). What is needed is a patchwork of areas in different land uses, fulfilling different needs and restricted by different standards for environmental quality (*see* Margalef, 1968; E.P. Odum, 1969; Eden, 1978; Fearnside, 1979b). Agricultural development must be pursued in the context of an interlocking system of components, no one of which can be changed without affecting the others, and no one of which can alone be expected to achieve goals such as sustaining an adequate standard of living for the region's population. Agroecosystems must be sustainable, concentration of land holdings must be limited, total consumption must be limited, and the population must be maintained below carrying capacity.

ACKNOWLEDGEMENT

I thank Judith G. Gunn for her careful reading and correction of the manuscript.

REFERENCES

Ahn, P. M. (1979) The optimum length of planned fallows. In *Soils Research in Agroforestry: Proceedings of an Expert Consultation held at the International Council for Research in Agroforestry (ICRAF) in Nairobi, March 26 – 30, 1979*. Eds. H.O. Mongi and P.A. Huxley, pp. 15 – 39. ICRAF, Nairobi, Kenya.

Alarcón, M. A. (1979) La base ecologica de la tecnología agricola tradicional y su aplicacion en el manejo de los agroecosistemas tropicales. In *La Tecnología Latinamericano. Seminário sobre nutrición y Vivienda III*. [Cuadernos del Centro Internacional en Ciencias Ambientales (CIFCA), No. 17], pp. 31 – 40. CIFCA, Madrid.

Alvim, P. de T. (1973) Desafio agricola da região Amazonica. *Ciência e Cultura* 24(5), 437 – 43.

Alvim, P. de T. (1978) Perspectivas de produção na região Amazônica. *Interciencia* 3, 253 – 51.

Alvim, P. de T. (1981) A perspective appraisal of perennial crops in the Amazon Basin. *Interciencia* 6(3), 139 – 45.

Andreae, B. (1974) Problems of improving the productivity in tropical farming. In *Applied Science and Development*, Vol.3, pp. 124 – 42. Institute for Scientific Cooperation, Tübingen, F.R. Germany.

Aramburú, C. E. (1982) La expansion de la frontera agraria y demografica en la Selva Peruana: paper presented at the conference on 'Frontier Expansion in Amazonia,' Center for Latin American Studies, University of Florida, Gainesville, Florida. February 8 – 11, 1982.

Arkcoll, D. B. (1979) Nutrient recycling as an alternative to shifting cultivation: paper presented at the 'Conference on Ecodevelopment and Ecofarming,' Science Foundation, Berlin, F.R. Germany.

Baena, A. R. C. and Dutra, S. (1979) Densidade aparente e porosidade do solo no desenvolvimento do milho. *Comunicado Técnico No. 24*, Empresa Brasileira de Pesquisa Agropecuária-Centro de Pesquisa Agropecuária do Trópico Úmido (EMBRAPA-CPATU), Belém.

Bazán, R., Páez, G., Soria V. J. and Alvim, P. de T. (1973) Estudo comparativo sobre a produtividade de ecosistemas tropicais sob diferentes sistemas de manejo. Instituto Interamericano de Ciencias Agrícolas da O.E.A., Programa Cooperativa para o Desenvolvimento do Trópico Americano (IICA-TROPICOS), Belém.

Bell, T. I. W. (1973) Erosion in the Trinidad teak plantations. *Commonwealth Forestry Review* 52(3), 223 – 33.

Bergman, R. W. (1980) *Amazon Economics: the Simplicity of Shipibo Indian Wealth*. Dellplain Latin American Studies No. 6. University Microfilms International, Ann Arbor, Michigan.

Berry, R. A. and Cline, W. R. (1976) Farm size, factor productivity and technical change in developing countries. In *Land Reform in Latin America: Bolivia, Chile, Mexico, Peru and Venezuela (Summary)*. Eds. S. Echstein *et al*. World Bank Staff Working Paper No. 275, International Bank for Reconstruction and Developing, Washington, D.C. (1978).

Bishop. J. P. (1978) The development of a sustained yield agro-ecosystem in the upper Amazon. *Agro-Ecosystems* 4, 459 – 61.

Bishop, J. P. (1979) Producción ganadera-forestal en el trópico húmedo hispanoamericano. In *XII Conferencia Anual sobre Ganaderia y Avicultura en América Latina*, sponsored by the University of Florida, Gainesville.

Bishop, J. P. (1982) Agroforestry systems for the humid tropics east of the Andes. In *Amazonia: Agriculture and Land Use Research*. Ed. S.B. Hecht, pp. 403-16. Centro Internacional de Agricultura Tropical (CIAT), Cali, Colombia.

Brazil, Presidência da República, Secretaria de Planejamento, Fundação Instituto Brasileiro de Geografia e Estatística (IBGE), (1980). *Anuário Estatístico do Brasil 1979.* Vol. 40. IBGE, Rio de Janeiro.

Brazil, Presidência da República, Secretaria de Planejamento, Fundação Instituto Brasileiro de Geografia e Estatística (IBGE), (1981) *Sinopse Preliminar do Censo Demográfico: IX Recenseamento Geral do Brasil — 1980.* Vol. 1., Tomo 1, No. 1. IBGE, Rio de Janeiro.

Bunker, S. G. (1980) Barreiras burocráticas e institucionais à modernização: o caso da Amazônia. *Pesquisa e Planejamento Econômico* 10(2), 555 – 600.

Cardoso, F. H. and Müller, G. (1978) *Amazônia: Expansão do Capitalismo.* 2a. Ed. Editora Brasiliense, São Paulo.

Carneiro, R. L. (1960) Slash-and-burn agriculture: a closer look at its implications for settlement patterns. In *Men and Cultures: Selected Papers of the Fifth International Congress of Anthropological and Ethnological Sciences, Sept., 1956.* Ed. A. F. C. Wallace, pp. 229 – 34. University of Pennsylvania Press, 1960.

Carrizosa U., J. (1982) Expansión de la frontera agropecuária en el área de Caquetá-Colômbia. In *Anais do Seminário 'Expansão da Fronteira Agropecuária e Meio Ambiente na América Latina'; Brasília, 10 a 13 de Novembro de 1981.* Vol. I. Fundação Universidade de Brasília, (UnB.) Departmento de Economia, Brasília.

Clark, C. B. (1973) The economics of overexploitation. *Science* 181, 630 – 34.

Clark, C. B. (1976) *Mathematical Bioeconomics: the Optimal Management of Renewable Resources.* Wiley-Interscience, New York.

Clarke, W. C. (1976) Maintenance of agriculture and human habitats within the tropical forest ecosystem. *Human Ecology* 4(3), 247 – 59.

Clarke, W. C. (1978) Progressing with the past: environmentally sustainable modifications to traditional agricultural systems. In *The Adaptation of Traditional Agriculture: Socioeconomic Problems of Urbanization.* (Development Studies Centre Monograph No. 11.) Ed. E. K. Fisk, pp. 142 – 57. Australian National University, Canberra, Australia.

Cowgill, U. (1962) An agricultural study of the Maya lowlands. *American Anthropologist* 64, 273 – 96.

Cunningham, R. H. (1963) The effect of clearing a tropical forest soil. *J. Soil Sci.* 14, 334 – 44.

Dantas, M. (1979) Pastagens da Amazônia Central: ecologia e fauna de solo. *Acta Amazonica* 9(2) supplemento, 1 – 54.

da Silva, J. F. G. (ed.) (1978) *Estrutura Agrária e Produção de Subsistencia na Agricultura Brasileira.* Hucitec, São Paulo.

Davis, S. H. (1977) *Victims of the Miracle: Development and the Indians of Brazil.* Cambridge University Press, Cambridge, U.K.

de Albuquerque, F. C. and Duarte, M. de L. R. (1972) Relação entre *Fusarium solani* f. *piperi* e o mal de mariquita da pimenta do reino. Instituto de Pesquisas Agropecuárias do Norte (IPEAN) Indicação Preliminar de Pesquisa. Comunicado No. 18. IPEAN, Belém.

de Andrade, E. B. (1979) Sistemas de produção com plantas perenes em consórcio: paper presented at the Simpósio Amazônia e seu Uso Agrícola, 16 – 17 de julho de 1979, XXXI Reunião da Sociedade Brasileira para o Progresso da Ciência (SBPC), Fortaleza, Ceará.

de Brito Silva, A. and Magalhães, B. P. (1980) Avaliação do grau de resistência de gramíneas forrageiras à cigarrinha. *Pesquisa em Andamento* No. 22 Empresa Brasileira de Pesquisa Agropecuária-Centro de Pesquisa Agropecuária do Trópico Umido (EMBRAPA-CPATU), Belém.

de Camargo, F. C. (1958) Report on the Amazon Region: in United Nations, Education and Scientific Organization (UNESCO). *Problems of Humid Tropical Regions,* pp. 11 – 24. UNESCO, Paris.

Denevan, W. M. (1966) A cultural ecological view of the former aboriginal settlement in the Amazon Basin. *Professional Geographer* 18, 346 – 51.

Denevan, W. M. (1982) Ecological heterogeneity and horizontal zonation of agriculture in the Amazon Floodplain. Paper presented at the conference on 'Frontier Expansion in Amazonia' Center for Latin American Studies, University of Florida, Gainesville, Florida. February 8 – 11, 1982.

de Oliveira, A. E., Cortez, R., van Velthem, L. H., Brabo, M. J., Alves, I., Furtado, L., de Silveira, I. M. and Rodrigues, I. (1979) Antropologia social e a política florestal para o desenvolvimento da Amazônia. *Acta Amazonica* 9(4) supplemento, 191 – 95.

Dickenson, J. C. III (1972) Alternatives to monoculture in the humid tropics of Latin America. *Professional Geographer* 24, 217 – 72.

do Nascimento, C. N. B. (1979) Criação de búfalos na Amazônia: paper presented at the Simpósio Amazônica e Seu Uso Agrícola, 16 – 17 de julho de 1979, 31a. Reunião da Sociedade Brasileira para o Progresso da Ciência, Fortaleza, Ceará.

Dubois, J. (1979) Los sistemas de produccion mas apropriados para el uso racional de las tierras de la Amazonia. In *Seminário sobre los Recursos Naturales Renovables y el Desarrollo Regional Amazonico, Bogotá, Colombia, 28 – 30 mayo 1979.* Instituto Interamericano de Ciencias Agricolas (IICA-TROPICOS) Belém.

Durham, W. H. (1979) *Scarcity and Survival in Central America: Ecological Origins of the Soccer War.* Stanford University Press, Stanford, California.

Eckholm, E. (1979) *The Dispossessed of the Earth: Land Reform and Sustainable Development.* Worldwatch Paper No. 30. Worldwatch Institute, Washington, D.C.

Eden, M. J. (1978) Ecology and land development: the case of Amazonian rainforest. *Transactions of the Institute of British Geographers, New Series.* 3(4), 444 – 63.

Elton, C. S. (1958) *The Ecology of Invasions by Animals and Plants.* Methuen, London.

Falesi, I. C. (1974) O solo na Amazônia e sua relação com a definição de sistemas de produção agrícola. In *Reunião do Grupo Interdisciplinar de Trabalho sobre Diretrizes de Pesquisa Agrícola para a Amazônia (Trópico Umido).* Vol. I, pp. 2.1 – 2.17. Brasília, May 6 – 10, 1974. EMBRAPA, Brasília.

Falesi, I. C. (1976) Ecossistema de pastagem cultivada na Amazônia Brasileira. Boletim Técnico do Centro de Pesquisa Agropecuária do Trópico Umido (CPATU) No. 1, CPATU, Belém.

Fearnside, P. M. (1978) *Estimation of Carrying Capacity for Human Populations in a Part of the Transamazon Highway Colonization Area of Brasil.* (Ph.D. dissertation in biological sciences, University of Michigan, Ann Arbor, Mich.), University Microfilms International, Ann Arbor, Michigan.

Fearnside, P. M. (1979a) Cattle yield prediction for the Transamazon Highway of Brazil. *Interciencia* 4(4), 220 − 25.

Fearnside, P. M. (1979b) The development of the Amazon rain forest: priority problems for the formulation of guidelines. *Interciencia* 4(6), 338 − 43.

Fearnside, P. M. (1979c) *The Simulation of Carrying Capacity for Human Populations in the Humid Tropics: Program and Documentation.* Instituto Nacional de Pesquisas da Amazônia — INPA, Manaus.

Fearnside, P. M. (1980a) Land use allocation of the Transamazon Highway colonists of Brazil and its relation to human carrying capacity. In *Land, People and Planning in Contemporary Amazonia.* Ed. F. Barbira-Scazzocchio, pp. 114 − 38. University of Cambridge Centre of Latin American Studies, Occasional Paper No. 3, Cambridge, U.K.

Fearnside, P. M. (1980b) The effects of cattle pastures on soil fertility in the Brazilian Amazon: consequences for beef production sustainability. *Tropical Ecology* 21(1), 125 − 37.

Fearnside, P. M. (1980c) The prediction of soil erosion losses under various land uses in the Transamazon Highway Colonization Area of Brazil. In *Tropical Ecology and Development: Proceedings of the 5th International Symposium of Ecology, 16 − 21 April 1979, Kuala Lumpur, Malaysia.* Ed. J. I. Furtado, pp. 1287 − 95. International Society for Tropical Ecology-ISTE, Kuala Lumpur, Malaysia.

Fearnside, P. M. (1980d) Black pepper yield prediction for the Transamazon Highway of Brazil. *Turrialba* 39(1), 35 − 42.

Fearnside, P. M. (1982) Deforestation in the Brazilian Amazon: How fast is it occurring? *Interciencia* 7(2), 82 − 88.

Fearnside, P. M. (1983a) Land use trends in the Brazilian Amazon as factors in accelerating deforestation. *Environmental Conservation* 10(2), 141 − 48.

Fearnside, P. M. (1983b) Development alternatives in the Brazilian Amazon: an ecological evaluation. *Interciencia* 8(2), 65 − 78.

Fearnside, P. M. (1983c) Stochastic modeling and human carrying capacity estimation: a tool for development planning in Amazonia. In *The Dilemma of Amazonian Development.* Ed. E. F. Moran. In press. Westview Press, Boulder, Colorado.

Fearnside, P. M. (nd-a.) *Human Carrying Capacity of the Brazilian Rainforest.* Columbia University Press, New York.

Fearnside, P. M. (nd-b) Burn quality prediction for simulation of the agricultural system of Brazil's Transamazon Highway Colonists for estimating human carrying capacity. (In press). In *Ecology and Resource Management in the Tropics.* Eds. K. C. Misra, H. V. Pandy and G. V. Govil. International Society for Tropical Ecology-ISTE, Varanasi, India.

Fearnside, P. M. and Rankin, J. M. (1980) Jari and development in the Brazilian Amazon. *Interciencia* 5(3), 146 − 56.

Fearnside, P. M. and Rankin, J. M. (1982) The new Jari: risks and prospects of a major Amazonian development. *Interciencia* 7(6), 329 − 39.

Found, W. C. (1971) *A Theoretical Approach to Rural Land-use Patterns.* Edward Arnold, London.

Freeman, J. D. (1955) *Iban Agriculture: A Report on the Shifting Cultivation of Hill Rice by the Iban of Sarawak.* (Colonial Research Studies No. 18). Her Majesty's Stationery Office, London.

Furley, P. A. and Leite, L. L. (nd.) Land development in the Brazilian Amazon with particular reference to Rondônia and the Ouro Preto Colonization Project. In *Change in the Amazon Basin: the Frontier after a Decade of Colonization.* Ed. J. Hemming. In press. Manchester University Press, Manchester, U.K.

Gall, N. (1980) Why is inflation so virulent? *Forbes*, October 13, 1980, pp. 67 − 71.

Gentry, A. H. and López-Parodi, J. (1980) Deforestation and increased flooding of the Upper Amazon. *Science* 210, 1354 − 56.

Gentry, A. H. and López-Parodi, J. (1982) Deforestation and increased flooding of the Upper Amazon. *Science* 215, 427.

Gleissman, S. R. (1979) Some ecological relationships of traditional agroecosystems in the lowland humid tropics of Southern Mexico: paper presented at the symposium on 'Mexican Agro-systems. Past and Present', International Congress of Americanists, Vancouver, Canada, August 4 − 11, 1979.

Gleissman, S. R., Espinosa, R. G. and Alarcon, M. A. (1978) *Modulo de Produccion Diversificada, um Agroecosistema de Produccion Sostenida para el Trópico Calido-Humédo de México.* Secretaria de Agricultura y Recursos Hidraulicos, Colegio Superior de Agricultura Tropical H. Cardenas, Tabasco, Mexico.

Gleissman, S. R., Garcia, E. R. and Amador, A. M. (1981) The ecological basis for the application of traditional agricultural technology in the management of tropical agro-ecosystems. *Agro-Ecosystems* 7, 173 − 85.

Goodland, R. J. A. (1980) Environmental ranking of Amazonian development projects in Brazil. *Environmental Conservation* 7(1), 9 − 26.

Goodland, R. J. A. and Irwin, H. S. (1975) *Amazon Jungle: Green Hell to Red Desert? An Ecological Discussion of the Environmental Impact of the Highway Construction Program in the Amazon Basin.* Elsevier, New York.

Goodland, R. J. A., Irwin, H. S. and Tillman, G. (1978) Ecological development for Amazonia. *Ciência e Cultura* 30(3), 275 − 89.

Greenland, D. J. (1975) Bringing the green revolution to the shifting cultivator. *Science* 190, 841 − 44.

Gross, D. F. (1975) Protein capture and cultural development in the Amazon Basin. *American Anthropologist* 77(3), 526 − 49.

Gross, D. R., Giten, G., Flowers, N. M., Leoi, F. M., Ritter, M. L. and Werner, D. W. (1979) Ecology and acculturation among native peoples of central Brazil. *Science* 206, 1043 − 50.

Guillemin, R. (1956) Evolution de l'agriculture autochthone dans les savannes de l'Oubangui. *L'Agronomie Tropicale* 11(1), 39 − 61; 11(2), 143 − 76; 11(3), 279 − 309.

Hanbury-Tenison, R. (1973) *A Question of Survival for the Indians of Brazil.* Angus and Robertson, London.

Harris, D. R. (1971) The ecology of swidden cultivation in the Orinoco Rainforest, Venezuela. *Geographical Review* 61(4), 475 – 95.

Hébette, J. and Acevedo, R. (1979) Colonização para Quém? *Série Pesquisa* 1(1), 1 – 173. Universidade Federal do Pará, Núcleo de Altos Estudos Amazônicos (NAEA), Belém.

Hecht, S. B. (1981) Deforestation in the Amazon Basin: magnitude, dynamics and soil resource effects. *Studies in Third World Societies* 13, 61 – 108.

Hecht, S. B. (1982a) Agroforestry in the Amazon Basin: Practice, theory and limits of a promising land use. In *Amazonia: Agriculture and Land Use Research*. Ed. S. B. Hecht, pp. 331 – 71. Centro Internacional de Agricultura Tropical (CIAT), Cali, Colombia.

Hecht, S. B. (1982b) The environmental effect of cattle development in the Amazon Basin: paper presented at the Conference on 'Frontier Expansion in Amazonia', Center for Latin American Studies, University of Florida, Gainesville, Florida, February 8 – 11, 1982.

Herrera, R., Jordan, C. F., Klinge, H. and Medina, E. (1978) Amazon ecosystems: their structure and functioning with particular emphasis on nutrients. *Interciencia* 3(4), 223 – 31.

Homma, A. O., Sá, F. T., do Nascimento, C. N. B., de Moura Carvalho, L. O. D., Mello Filho, B. M., Morreira, E. D. and Teixeira, R. N. G. (1978) Estudo das caracteristicas e análises de alguns indicadores técnicos e econômicos da pecuária no Nordeste Paraense. *Comunicado Técnico No. 13*. EMBRAPA-CPATU, Belém.

Ianni, O. (1979a). *Colonização e Contra-Reforma Agrária na Amazônia*. Editora Vozes Ltda., Petropolis.

Ianni, O. (1979b) *Ditadura e Agricultura: o Desenvolvimento do Capitalismo na Amazônia: 1964 – 1978*. Editora Civilização Brasileira, Rio de Janeiro.

International Bank for Reconstruction and Development (World Bank) (1981). *Brazil: Integrated Development of the Northwest Frontier*. World Bank, Washington, D.C.

Institute of Ecology (1972) Cycles of elements. In *Man and the Living Environment*, pp. 41 – 89. University of Wisconsin Press, Madison, Wisconsin.

Janzen, D. H. (1970a) Herbivores and the number of tree species in tropical forests. *American Naturalist* 104, 501 – 28.

Janzen, D. H. (1970b) The unexploited tropics. *Ecological Society of America Bulletin* 51(3), 4 – 7.

Janzen, D. H. (1972) Interfield and interplant spacing in tropical insect control. In *Proceedings Annual Tall Timbers Conference on Ecological Animal Control by Habitat Management, February 24 – 25, 1972*, pp. 1 – 6.

Janzen, D. H. (1973) Tropical agroecosystems: habitats misunderstood by the temperate zones, mismanaged by the tropics. *Science* 182, 1212 – 19.

Janzen, D. H. (1974) The role of the seed predator guild in a tropical deciduous forest, with some reflections on tropical biological control. In *Biology in Pest and Disease Control, the 13th Symposium of the British Ecological Society, Oxford, January 4 – 7, 1972*. Eds. D. P. Johnes and M. E. Solomon, pp. 3 – 14. Blackwell Scientific Publications, Oxford, U.K.

Jessup, T. C. (1981) Why do Apo Kayan shifting cultivators move? *Borneo Research Bulletin 1981*, 16 – 32.

Kass, D. C. L. (1978) Polyculture cropping systems: review and analysis. (Cornell International Agriculture Bulletin 32), Cornell University, Ithaca, New York.

King, K. F. S. (1968) *Agri-silviculture. The Taungya System*. Department of Forestry, University of Ibadan, Ibadan, Nigeria, Bull. No.1.

Kleinpenning, J. M. G. (1975) *The Integration and Colonisation of the Brazilian Portion of the Amazon Basin*. Institute of Geography and Planning, Nijmegen, Holland.

Kleinpenning, J. M. G. (1979) *An Evaluation of the Brazilian Policy for the Integration of the Amazon Basin (1964 – 1975)* Publikatie 9, Vakroep Sociale Geografie van de Ontwikkelingslanden, Geografisch en Planologisch Instituut, Nijmegen, Holland.

Koster, H. W., Khan, E. J. A. and Bosshart, R. P. (1977) Programa e resultados preliminares dos estudos de pastagens na região de Paragominas, Pará, e nordeste de Mato Grosso, junho 1975 – dezembro 1976. Ministério do Interior, Superintendência do Desenvolvimento da Amazônia (SUDAM), Departmento de Setores Produtivos, Convênio SUDAM/Instituto de Pesquisas IRI, Belém.

Lathrap, D. W. (1970) *The Upper Amazon*. Praeger, New York.

Leach, E.R. (1959) Some economic advantages of shifting cultivation. *Proceedings of the 9th Pacific Science Congress (Bangkok, 1957)* 7, 64 – 66.

Léna, P. (1981) Dinâmica da estrutura agrária e o aproveitamento dos lotes em um projeto de colonização de Rondônia. In *Expansão da Fronteira Agropecuária e Meio Ambiente na América Latina*. Ed. C. C. Mueller. (Irregular pagination). Departamento de Economia, Universidade de Brasília, Brasília, 2 vols.

Loureiro, A. J. S. (1978) Síntese da História do Amazonas. Imprensa Oficial, Manaus.

Mahar, D. J. (1979) *Frontier Development Policy in Brazil: a Study of Amazonia*. Praeger, New York.

Mahar, D. J. (1982) Public international lending institutions and the development of the Brazilian Amazon: the experience of the World Bank: paper presented at the conference on 'Frontier Expansion in Amazonia,' Center for Latin American Studies, University of Florida, Gainesville, Florida, February 8 – 11, 1982.

Margalef, R. (1968) *Perspectives in Ecological Theory*. University of Chicago Press, Chicago.

Martin, R. (1956) Les paysannats en Afrique Centrale. *L'Agronomie Tropicale* 11(3), 362 – 77.

Martine, G. (1980) Recent colonization experiences in Brazil: expectations versus reality. In *Land, People and Planning in Contemporary Amazonia*. Ed. F. Barbira-Scazzocchio, pp. 80 – 94. Centre of Latin American Studies Occasional Publication No.3, Cambridge University, Cambridge, U.K.

Martins, J. de S. (1980) Fighting for land: Indians and *posseiros* in Legal Amazonia. In *Land, People and Planning in Contemporary Amazonia*. Ed. F. Barbira-Scazzocchio, pp. 95–105. Centre of Latin American Studies Occasional Paper No.3, Cambridge University, Cambridge, U.K.

May, B. and Momal, P. (1981) Forest for Food. Phase I Report including TOR for Phase II. Transmigration Area Development Project (TAD), Samarinda, Indonesia.

Meggers, B. J. (1971) *Amazonia: Man and Culture in a Counterfeit Paradise*. Aldine, Chicago, Illinois.

Mongi, H. O. and Huxley, P. A. (eds.) (1979) *Soils Research in Agroforestry: Proceedings of an Expert Consultation held at the International Council for Research in Agroforestry (ICRAF) in Nairobi, March 26–30, 1979*. ICRAF, Nairobi, Kenya.

Morais, V. H. F. (1974) Fatores condicionantes e perspectivas atuais de desenvolvimento de cultivos perenes na Amazônia Brasileira. In *Reunião do Grupo Interdisciplinar de Trabalho sobre Diretrizes de Pesquisa Agrícola para a Amazônia (Trópico Umido), Brasília, Maio 6–10, 1974*. Vol.2, pp. 7.1–7.37. Empresa Brasileira de Pesquisa Agropecuária (EMBRAPA), Brasília.

Moran, E. F. (1974) The adaptive system of the Amazonian caboclo. In *Man in the Amazon*. Ed. C. Wagley, pp. 136–59. University Presses of Florida, Gainesville, Florida.

Moran, E. F. (1979a) Strategies for survival: resource-use along the Transamazon Highway. *Studies in Third World Societies* 7, 49–75.

Moran, E. F. (1979b) Criteria for choosing successful homesteaders in Brazil. *Research in Economic Anthropology* 2, 339–59.

Moran, E. F. (1981) *Developing the Amazon*. University of Indiana Press, Bloomington, Indiana.

Mueller, C. C. (1980) Recent frontier expansion in Brazil: the case of Rondônia. In *Land, People and Planning in Contemporary Amazonia*. Ed. F. Barbira-Scazzocchio, pp. 141–45. Centre of Latin American Studies Occasional Publication No.3, Cambridge University, Cambridge, U.K.

Mueller, C. C. (1982) O estado e a expansão da fronteira agrícola no Brasil. In *Anais do Seminário 'Expansão da Fronteira Agropecuária e Meio Ambiente na América Latina'; Brasília, 10 a 13 de novembro de 1981*. Vol. I. Fundação Universidade de Brasília (UnB.) Departamento de Economia, Brasília.

Nelson, M. (1973) *The Development of Tropical Lands Policy Issues in Latin America*. Johns Hopkins University Press, Baltimore, Maryland.

Nicholaides, J. M. III, Bandy, D. E., Sánchez, P. A. and Valverde, C. S. (1982) Continuous cropping potential in the Amazon: paper presented at the conference on 'Frontier Expansion in Amazonia', Center for Latin American Studies, University of Florida, Gainesville, Florida, February 8–11, 1982.

Nordin, C. F. and Meade, R. H. (1982) Deforestation and increased flooding of the Upper Amazon. *Science* 215, 427–27.

North Carolina State University (NCSU), Soil Science Department (1975) *Agronomic-Economic Research on Tropical Soils: Annual Report for 1974*. NCSU, Raleigh, N.C.

North Carolina State University (NCSU), Soil Science Department (1976) *Agronomic-Economic Research on Tropical Soils: Annual Report for 1975*. NCSU, Raleigh, N.C.

North Carolina State University (NCSU), Soil Science Department (1978) *Agronomic-Economic Research on Soils of the Tropics: Annual Report for 1976–1977*. NCSU, Raleigh, N.C.

North Carolina State University (NCSU), Soil Science Department (1980) *Agronomic-Economic Research on Soils of the Tropics: Annual Report for 1978–1979*. NCSU, Raleigh, N.C.

Nye, P. H. and Greenland, D. J. (1960) *The Soil Under Shifting Cultivation*. Commonwealth Bureau of Soils, Harpenden, U.K.

Odum, E. P. (1969) The strategy of ecosystem development. *Science* 164, 262–270.

Odum, E. P. (1971) *Fundamentals of Ecology*, 3rd Ed. W.B. Saunders Co., Philadelphia.

Odum, H. T. (1971) *Environment, Power, and Society*. Wiley and Sons, New York.

Pará, Secretaria da Agricultura (SAGRI) (1971) *Projeto Cacau*. SAGRI, Belém.

Penteado, A. R. (1967) *Problemas de Colonização e de Uso da Terra na Região Bragantina do Estado do Pará*. Universidade Federal do Pará, Belém.

Peru, Instituto Veterinario de Investigación del Trópico y Altura (IVITA) (1976) Instituto Veterinario de Investigación del Trópico y Altura: presentation to the Ministro de Alimentación. Universidad Nacional Mayor de San Marcos, Lima.

Pool, D. (1972) Insect Leaf Damage as Related to the Intensity of Management in Tropical Wet Forest Successions. MS thesis in Agriculture, University of Florida, Gainesville, Florida.

Popenoe, H. (1960) Effects of Shifting Cultivation on Natural Soil Constituents in Central America. Ph.D. dissertation in Agriculture, University of Florida, Gainesville, Florida.

Popenoe, H. (1964) The pre-industrial cultivator in the tropics. In *The Ecology of Man in the Tropical Environment*, pp. 66–73. IUCN, (IUCN New Series No.4), Morges, Switzerland.

Price, P. W. (1976) Colonization of crops by arthropods: non-equilibrium communities in soybean fields. *Environmental Entomology* 5, 605–11.

Raiffa, H. (1970) *Decision Analysis: Introductory Lectures on Choices under Uncertainty*. Addison-Wesley, Reading, Massachusetts.

Risch, S. (1980) The population dynamics of several herbivorous beetles in a tropical agroecosystem: the effect of intercropping corn, beans and squash in Costa Rica. *J. Appl. Ecol.* 17, 593–612.

Roosevelt, A. C. (1980) *Parmana: Prehistoric Maize and Manioc Subsistence Along the Amazon and Orinoco*. Academic Press, New York.

Root, R. B. and Tahvanainen, J. O. (1972) The influence of vegetational diversity on the population ecology of a specialized herbivore, *Phyllotreta cruciferae* (Coleoptera: Chrysomelidae). *Oecologia* 10, 321–46.

Ruthenberg, H. (1971) *Farming Systems in the Tropics*. Clarendon Press, Oxford, U.K.

Sánchez, P. A. (1973) Soil management under shifting cultivation. In *A Review of Soils Research in Tropical Latin America*. Bulletin No. 219. pp 46 – 67. North Carolina Agricultural Experiment Station, Raleigh, N.C.

Sánchez, P. A. (1976) *Properties and Management of Soils in the Tropics*. Wiley-Interscience, New York.

Sánchez, P. A. (1977) Advances in the management of OXISOLS and ULTISOLS in tropical South America: in *Proceedings of the International Seminar on Soil Environment and Fertility Management in Intensive Agriculture*, pp. 535 – 566. The Society of the Science of Soil and Manure, Tokyo, Japan.

Sánchez, P. A., Bandy, D. E., Villachica, J. H. and Nicholaides, J. J. III (1982) Amazon basin soils: management for continuous crop production. *Science* 216, 821 – 27.

Schubart, H. O. R. (1977) Critérios ecológicas para o desenvolvimento agrícola das terras-firmes da Amazônia. *Acta Amazonica* 7(5), 559 – 67.

Schubart, H. O. R., Junk, W. J. and Petrere, M. Jr. (1976) Sumário de ecologia Amazônica. *Ciência e Cultura* 28(5), 507 – 9.

Serrão, E. A. S., Cruz, E. de S., Simão Neto, M., de Sousa, G. F., Bastos, J. B. and Guimarães, C. de F. (1971) Resposta de três gramíneas forrageiras (*Brachiaria decumbens* Stapf., *Brachiaria ruziziensis* Germain et Everard e *Pennisetum purpureum* Schum.). *Instituto de Pesquisas Agropecuária do Norte (IPEAN) Série: Estudos sobre Forrageiros na Amazônia* 1(1).

Serrão, E. A. S. and Falesi, I. C. (1977) *Pastagens do Trópico Umido Brasileiro*. Empresa Brasileira de Pesquisa Agropecuária-Centro de Pesquisa Agropecuária do Trópico Umido (EMBRAPA-CPATU), Belém, 63 pages.

Serrão, E. A. S., Falesi, I. C., de Veiga, J. B. and Teixeira Neto, J.F. (1979) Productivity of cultivated pastures on low fertility soils in the Amazon of Brazil. In *Pasture Production in Acid Soils of the Tropics*. Eds. P. A. Sánchez and L. E. Tergas, pp. 195 – 225. Proceedings of a Seminar held at CIAT, Cali, Colombia April 17 – 21, 1978. Centro Internacional de Agricultura Tropical, Cali, Colombia. Series 03 EG-5.

Seubert, C. E., Sánchez, P. A. and Valverde, C. (1977) Effects of land clearing methods on soil properties of an ultisol and crop performance in the Amazon jungle of Peru. *Tropical Agriculture* (Trinidad) 54(4), 307 – 21.

Simão Neto, M., Serrão, E. A. S., Gonçalves, C. A. and Pimentel, D. M. (1973) Comportamento de gramíneas forrageiras na região de Belém. *Comunicado Técnico No. 44 do Instituto de Pesquisa Agropecuária do Norte (IPEAN)*. IPEAN, Belém.

Sioli, H. (1973) Recent human activities in the Brazilian Amazon Region and their ecological effects. In *Tropical Forest Ecosystems in Africa and South America: a Comparative Review*. Eds. B. J. Meggers, E. S. Ayensu and W. D. Duckworth, pp. 321 – 34. (ATB) Smithsonian Institution Press, Washington, D.C.

Skillings, R. F. and Tcheyan, N. O. (1979) *Economic Development Prospects of the Amazon Region of Brazil*. Center of Brazilian Studies, School of Advanced International Studies, Johns Hopkins University, Baltimore, Maryland.

Smith, N. J. H. (1978) Agricultural productivity along Brazil's Transamazon Highway. *Agro-Ecosystems* 4, 415 – 432.

Smith, N. J. H. (1981a) *Rainforest Corridors: the Transamazon Colonization Scheme*. University of California Press, Berkeley, California.

Smith, N. J. H. (1981b) Colonization: lessons from a rainforest. *Science* 214, 755 – 61.

Soares, L. P. and Libonati, V. F. (1966) Problemas atuais da juticultura Amazônica. *Pesquisa Agropecuária Brasileira* 1, 1 – 6.

Tamer, A. (1970) *Transamazônica, Solução para 2001*. APEC Editora, Rio de Janeiro.

Toledo, J. M. and Serrão, E. A. (1982) Pasture and animal production in Amazonia. In *Amazônia: Agriculture and Land Use Research*. Ed. S. B. Hecht, pp. 281 – 309. Centro Internacional de Agricultura Tropical (CIAT), Cali, Colombia.

Uhl, C. (1982) Recovery following disturbances of different intensities in the Amazon rain forest of Venezuela. *Interciencia* 7(1), 19 – 24.

Uhl, C., Clark, H., Clark, K. and Maquirino, P. (1982a) Successional patterns associated with slash and burn agriculture in the Upper Rio Negro region of the Amazon Basin. *Biotropica* 14(4), 249 – 54.

Uhl, C., Jordan, C., Clark, K., Clark, H. and Herreira, R. (1982b) Ecosystem recovery in Amazon caatinga forest after cutting, cutting and burning and bulldozer clearing treatments. *Oikos* 38, 313 – 20.

United Nations Educational Scientific and Cultural Organization (UNESCO)/United Nationals Environmental Programme (UNEP)/United Nations Food and Agriculture Organization (UN-FAO) (1978) *Tropical Forest Ecosystems: a State of Knowledge Report*. UNESCO/UNEP, Paris.

United Nations, Food and Agriculture Organization (FAO) (1957) Shifting cultivation. *Tropical Agriculture* (Trinidad) 34, 159 – 164.

United Nations, Food and Agriculture Organization (FAO) (1959) Shifting cultivation — FAO's position and course of action. *Proceedings of the 9th Pacific Science Congress (Bangkok, 1957)* 7, 71.

United States, Council on Environmental Quality and Department of State (1980) *The Global 2000 Report to the President*. Pergamon Press, New York.

Uquillas, J. E. (1982) Colonización y assentamientos esponaneos en la Amazonia Ecuatoriana: paper presented at the conference on 'Frontier Expansion in Amazônia', Centre for Latin American Studies, University of Florida, Gainesville, Florida, February 8 – 11, 1982.

Veja (27 de janeiro de 1982). 'Jari com a cortina aberta', pp. 90 – 92. São Paulo.

Valverde, O. and Dias, C. V. (1967) *A Rodovia Belém-Brasília*. Instituto Brasileiro de Geografia e Estatística (IBGE), Rio de Janeiro.

Valverde, S. C. and Bandy, D. E. (1982) Production of annual food crops in the Amazon. In *Amazonia: Agriculture and Land Use Research*. Ed. S.B. Hecht, pp. 243 – 80. Centro Internacional de Agricultura Tropical (CIAT), Cali, Colombia.

Van de Weert, R. (1974) Influence of mechanical forest clearing on soil conditions and the resulting effects on root growth. *Tropical Agriculture* (Trinidad) 51(2), 325 – 31.

Vandermeer, J. H. (1981) The interference production principle, an ecological theory for agriculture. *BioScience* 31, 361 – 64.

Vermeer, D. E. (1970) Population pressure and crop rotational changes among the Tiv of Nigeria. *Annals Association of American Geographers* 60(2), 299 – 314.

Wagley, C. (1976) *Amazon Town: a Study of Man in the Tropics*. Oxford University Press, London.

Wang, C. H., Liem, T. H. and Mikkelsen, D. S. (1976) *Sulfur deficiency — a limiting factor in rice production in the lower Amazon Basin. I. Development of sulfur deficiency as a limiting factor for rice production*. (IRI Research Institute, Inc., Bulletin No. 47). IRI Research Institute, New York.

Watters, R. F. (1966) The shifting cultivation problem in the American tropics. In *Reunion Internacional Sobre Problemas de la Agricultura en los Tropicos Humedos de America Latina, 22 de mayo, 1966 (Lima) 14 de junio, 1966 (Belém do Pará)*, pp. 1 – 16, Lima.

Watters, R. F. (1971) Shifting cultivation in Latin America. *FAO, Forest Development Paper No.17*, Rome.

Webster, C. C. and Wilson, P. N. (1980) *Agriculture in the Tropics* 2nd ed., Longman Group Ltd., London.

Wells, F. J. (1976) *The Long-run Availability of Phosphorus: a Case Study in Mineral Resource Analysis*. Johns Hopkins University Press, Baltimore, Maryland.

Wood, C. and Schmink, M. (1979) Blaming the victim: small farmer production in an Amazon colonization area. *Studies in Third World Societies* 7, 77 – 93.

Wood, C. H. and Wilson, J. (1982) The role of the Amazon frontier in the demography of rural Brazil: paper presented at the conference on 'Frontier Expansion in Amazonia', Center for Latin American Studies, University of Florida, Gainesville, Florida, February 8 – 11, 1982.

CHAPTER 22

Over-exploited and Under-used Animals in the Amazon Region

MARC J. DOUROJEANNI

Universidad Nacional Agraria, Lima, Peru

CONTENTS

22.1. INTRODUCTION

Of the almost three thousand species of land vertebrates living in the Amazon region, only a little more than a hundred have directly benefited man and, of the millions of species of terrestrial invertebrates, the proportion utilised is minimal. Nevertheless, the contribution made by the relatively small number of animals used has been very significant for the economy of the region and, in particular, for the well-being of the local people.

In the present chapter, the species of mammals, birds, reptiles and batrachians of the Amazon and Orinoco regions commonly used by man in these and other parts of the world will be reviewed, with special emphasis on the consequences of exploitation and the possibility of their populations being managed scientifically with a view to sustained production without risk of extinction.

TABLE 22.1. Average daily consumption per capita of fresh meat (soft meat) from wild animals in different sites of the Amazon region in Brazil and Peru.

Country Site	Average daily consumption per capita (Gr.)	Year in which observations took place	Author
BRAZIL			
Nova Fronteira	25.9	1973 – 1974	Smith (1976)
L. da Vinci	42.1	1973 – 1974	,, ,,
Coco Chato	6.6	1973 – 1974	,, ,,
F.N. Tapajóz	246.0	1978	Dourojeanni (1978)
PERU			
Pachitea River	460.0	1965	Pierret & Dourojeanni (1966)
Ucayali River	52.0	1966	Pierret & Dourojeanni (1967)
J. Herrera	75.8	1971 – 1972	Rios *et al.* (1973)
R. Pichis	64.9	1980	Gaviria (1981)

22.2. USE OF WILD FAUNA

22.2.1. Human food

The fauna of the Amazon, as anywhere else, was first used as food for man. This is, even today, the main contribution made by the fauna to the rural population, whether natives or old and new settlers. However, its importance has greatly diminished for the urban population of the Amazon region, where it has come to be a luxury or contraband article in most countries.

The contribution made by the fauna as human food has different characteristics from country to country and from place to place, according to the type and size of the human settlements, their age and density, their ethnic composition and, obviously, the impact made by hunting and other human activities on the fauna population. It also varies, as is logical, according to the wildlife's environment, such as the climatic, topographic, edaphic, hydric and ecological characteristics of the hunting areas or fields corresponding to each human settlement.

In general, the fauna provides less protein for the inhabitants of the high parts of the Amazon Basin than for those living in the middle or lower part. In fact, between the line of trees at approximately 3,700 m above sea level on the eastern slope of the Andes and those at 600 m, the fauna of interest for food value is less both in terms of diversity and density. Moreover, the Amazon forests on the eastern slope of the Andes in Venezuela, Colombia, Ecuador, Peru and Bolivia have been severely exploited, or completely destroyed over a few tens of millions of hectares. This is due to agriculture and cattle ranching developed during the last 50 years and which is growing in intensity.

The only country which possesses consolidated statistics about the meat production from wild animals is Peru, which, in 1976, estimated production at 13,100 MT (Peru, Direccion General Forestal y de Fauna, 1977). Table 22.1 summarises information pertaining to Brazil and Peru on the daily consumption *per capita* of fresh meat from wild animals in different places, years and conditions. As pointed out by Smith (1976) and Pierret and Dourojeanni (1967), the smallest contribution corresponds

TABLE 22.2. Meat consumption from wild animals and other sources of animal protein in the Amazon region of Peru (in grammes of fresh meat daily per capita).

Sources	From Pucallpa to Nauta (Ucayali River)	In Jenaro Herrera (Ucayali River)
Fish	135.6	158.3
Game	52.0	75.8
Farmyard birds	22.1	25.7
Pigs	12.0	10.2
Cows	insignificant	insignificant
TOTAL	221.7	270.0

Sources: Pierret and Dourojeanni (1967) and Rios *et al.* (1973).

to the sites occupied for greater lengths of time, where hunting and other human activities have driven the fauna away. The greatest contributions, as in the Pachitea river in Peru (Pierret and Dourojeanni, 1966) or in Tapajós National Forest in Brazil (Dourojeanni, 1978) correspond to areas of low population density and recent human occupation. The study by Pierret and Dourojeanni (1967), which is particularly significant because of the importance of the statistical sample, and that by Rios *et al.* (1973) which concentrates on part of the same area, must represent results that come closest to an average for a great part of the lowland Amazon region not serviced by roads.

For the Aguaruna natives of the northern Amazon region of Peru (Berlin and Berlin, 1978) and for the Campa of the central Amazon region of the same country (Denevan, 1971) wild birds and mammals represent 19.1 g and probably about 10 g respectively, daily food *per capita*. Denevan (1971) shows that, during the three days of his observations, an adult man consumed 90.6 g daily of protein deriving from a deer, but on the fourth day he only ate part of a pigeon and on the fifth he did not eat meat. Denevan's observations were shown by Pierret and Dourojeanni (1966, 1967) to also apply to settlers who, due to their ignorance of techniques to conserve meat, consume the latter in enormous quantities when available and then go for days without eating any. Natives now living under pressure from 'civilisation' undoubtedly eat less meat than the settlers.

Various studies on hunting and fishing in the Amazon area demonstrate that these sources of protein are the main ones, bringing more than 85% of the meat consumed despite the availability of cows, pigs and farmyard birds (Table 22.2), Pierret and Dourojeanni (1966, 1967), Rios *et al.* (1973) and Gaviria (1980). The reason for this is, essentially, the high price of meat from domestic animals, especially cows, which are produced exclusively for sale to urban centres.

Most studies undertaken demonstrate that small animals or small game constitute 50% or more of the meat of wild animals that is consumed (Table 22.3). However, Smith (1976) in Brazil, and Campos (1977) in Peru, have reached notably different results. The former shows that the tapir (*Tapirus terrestris*), the peccary (*Tayassu pecari*), the deer (*Mazama americana*), the collared peccary (*Tayassu tajacu*) and other large species can provide as much as 87.8% and 92.7% of meat consumed. However, these results can be a consequence of biased replies to survey questions. According to Campos (1977), one tribal group, Shipibo, obtained and consumed 74.6% of its meat from large animals. Yet small species are more abundant than large, and the favourite and more expensive meats are usually those from the species of primates, agoutis (*Dasyprocta* and *Cuniculus*) and birds. The species of *Tayassu* and *Mazama* do also fetch high prices. In contrast, the meat of *Tapirus terrestris* is considered second class, and that of *Hydrochoerus*, except in the case of Venezuela where it is eaten a great deal in cities during Holy Week (Ojasti, 1971), is often openly despised. Of course during shortages, inhabitants hunt for species that they would not normally eat, among them the smallest, as in the case of the Campa Indians in Peru (Denevan, 1971) and the oldest of the three villages studied by Smith (1976).

TABLE 22.3. Rate of contribution made by each game species on rural food in the Amazon region of Peru.

Species	Pachitea River[1]	Ucayali River[2]
Big Game		
Tapirus terrestris	6.8	10.1
Tayassu pecari	3.1	21.1
Tayassu tajacu	16.6	12.6
Mazama americana	17.4	8.1
Hydrochoerus hydrochaeris	5.4	—
Small Game		
Dasypus	2.1	5.1
Dasyprocta	5.7	5.8
Cuniculus paca	16.5	14.8
Geochelone	17.2	9.9
Monkeys	6.6	9.3
Birds	2.5	3.1

Sources: [1]Pierret & Dourojeanni (1966);   [2]Pierret & Dourojeanni (1967).

The favourite primates are those of the *Ateles* and *Lagothrix* genera,[*] but numerous specimens of *Alouatta* and *Pithecia* are also consumed. Castro *et al.* (1976) showed the inhabitants can eat any species of monkey in Iquitos, in the Amazon region of Peru[*]. They also found that, in 1973, for some primate species the number consumed was almost as high as that exported for biomedical research. However, primates constituted only 4.3% of the meat market from wild animals in Iquitos. The birds consumed most usually belong to the *Mitu*, *Penelope*, *Ortalis* (Guans and Curassows), *Crypturellus*, *Tinamus* (Tinamou), *Columbina* (Doves), *Psophia* (Trumpeters) and *Odontophorus* genera. The important role played by the land turtle *Geochelone denticulata* as human food in Peru and other Andean countries deserves special note.

The water turtles (*Podocnemis*), previously very important human food in the Amazon region (Brazil, Ministry of Agriculture, 1973) and in the Orinoco region (Ojasti and Rutkis, 1965, 1967), have declined in importance due to excessive game hunting and egg collecting. Various crocodilians, especially *Caiman crocodilus*, are hunted as food by the Indians of certain tribes and some settlers.

The land invertebrates may represent a significant percentage of animal protein consumed (from 3 to 7%) as much by the natives as by the settlers. Among the species most consumed, and considered as delicacies, are the larvae of certain palm-tree beetles (*Rynchophorus*, *Rhinostomus*) and the queen ants of the *Atta* and *Acromyrmex* genera. Various molluscs, such as those of the genus *Strophoceilus* (Dourojeanni, 1965) are also eaten.

22.2.2. Hides and skins

Comprehensive evaluations of the volume of wild animal hides and skins produced in the Amazon and Orinoco regions are not available, but a few national statistics give an idea of the enormous volume it has been and, doubtless, still is, despite recent protection measures adopted by nearly all the countries of the area, which, moreover, have been endorsed by the Convention on International Trade of Species Threatened by Extinction (CITES)

In Table 22.4, the main species whose hides and skins were exported from the Amazon region of Peru between 1962 and 1966 are displayed. These official figures, as shown by Dourojeanni (1972), must

[*] For the English names of the primate species *see* Table 16.1 of Chapter 16.

TABLE 22.4. Species of wild fauna producing skins and hides in the Amazon region of Peru between the years 1962 and 1966

Species	Number	%
Skins		
Felis pardalis	61,445	4.4
Lutra amazonica	41,410	3.0
Potos flavus	9,607	0.7
Felis wiedii	9,364	0.7
Panthera onca	4,406	0.3
Pteronura brasiliensis	2,390	0.2
Hides		
Tayassu tajacu	690,219	49.5
Tayassu pecari	239,472	17.2
Mazama americana	169,775	12.2
Caiman crocodilus	93,015	6.7
Melanosuchus niger	44,251	3.2
Hydrochoerus hydrochaeris	27,126	1.9
TOTAL	1,392,680	100.00

Sources: Dirección General Forestal, de Caza y Tierras del Perú.

correspond to no more than 60% of what really left the country. During the period 1965 − 76 475,000 skins and more than 5 million hides were exported legally (Peru, Direccion General Forestal y de Fauna, 1977). Twice as many are likely to have been slaughtered if damaged hides and skins, contraband and subvaluation at customs are taken into account.

Bolivian statistics demonstrate that, in 1966, from the provinces of Beni and Santa Cruz alone, more than 325,000 skins and hides were produced, of which 223,000 were crocodiles, 50,000 peccaries and 39,000 *Felis pardalis*. From 1960 to 1969 Bolivia exported, legally, 919 MT of dried and cured skins and hides (Bejarano, 1973).

In Paraguay, from 1960 to 1978, 2,937 MT of dry hides and skins of wild animals were exported (Dourojeanni et al., 1979). The volume of exports tended to decline, as in other countries, but their value rises a great deal. Much of that exported by Paraguay comes from Bolivia. In the Pantanal of Mato Grosso, Brazil alone, it is estimated that almost one half million specimens of *Caiman crocodilus* are slaughtered annually. Blohm (1973) reveals that, from 1929 to 1934, 2,025 MT of hides of *Crocodylus intermedius* were exported from Venezuela and that this traffic continued afterwards.

The figures cited above reveal the extraordinary importance of the traffic of hides and skins from animals in the Amazon region. However, it is necessary to recognise that its magnitude has diminished considerably, particularly in the last 5 years.

In Table 22.4, the species of the Amazon region in Peru with highest consumption on the world market are indicated.

22.2.3. Live animals

No less than 150 species of live animals have been regularly exported from the Amazon and the Orinoco regions. Of the total exported, however, about 90% corresponded to ornamental birds (especially Psittacidae) and primates for pets or biomedical research. The remaining species were exported essentially to zoos and also, to a lesser degree, for scientific research.

From Iquitos, Peru, 1,958,000 specimens were exported legally between 1965 and 1973 (Peru, Direccion General Forestal y de Fauna, 1977), the year in which this trade was definitively prohibited.

In 1964, of the 69,533 animals exported legally from Iquitos, 39% were Psittacidae, 38% exclusively *Saimiri sciureus*, 4.9% other ornamental birds and 12% other monkeys of the *Cebus*, *Lagothrix*, *Saguinus*, *Cebuella*, *Ateles*, *Aotus*, *Cacajao*, *Pithecia* and *Callicebus* genera. Speaking exclusively of primates, Soini (1972) informs that from 1962 to 1971, 321,784 monkeys were exported legally of which 79% were *Saimiri*, 6% *Cebus* and *Saguinus*, respectively, and 5% *Lagothrix*. This author and Castro (1975), among others, reveal the considerable mortality rate as much through the simple act of capture, as from captivity and transportation. Just as in the case of skins and hides, official statistics did not represent much more than half of what in fact left the country, avoiding the payment of taxes at Peruvian customs.

The data registered above, pertaining to one country alone, give a good idea of the enormous trade of live animals carried out in the Amazon region. Nowadays, because of restrictions adopted by governments, most of the traffic of live animals, especially primates, is undertaken through Bolivia and Paraguay and, more recently, also through Surinam and Guyana.

Primates are essential for the advance of biomedical science, although the latter, obviously, has never required such a great number as has been leaving the countries. Whitney (1976) points out that of the 47,345 specimens of South American primates which entered the U.S.A. in 1982, only 11,300 were so used, of which half were *Saimiri sciureus*, followed closely by *Aotus trivirgatus* and *Saguinus mystax*. Each species is useful for particular purposes. The *Saimiri* are used for general research, the testing of medicines and nutrition and cardiovascular experiments; the *Saguinus* are essential for research into hepatitis, viral oncology, immunology and reproduction physiology; *Aotus* for the chemotherapy of malaria, immunology and studies in vision (PAHO/WHO, 1976). According to PAHO, in the year 2000, some 29,000 neotropical primates will be needed worldwide for biomedical research, of which the greatest proportion will continue to be *Saimiri*, *Saguinus*, *Cebuella*, *Cebus*, *Callithrix* and *Aotus* (Muckenhirn and Cohen, 1978; U.S. Department of Health, Education and Welfare, 1978; Dourojeanni, 1980).

22.2.4. Other direct uses of fauna

Numerous species of birds, and lepidoptera and other insects, are used when mounted, as ornaments. Pictures, fans and all kinds of objects, even musical instruments, are made with the feathers, wings, teeth, bones, elytra, shells and other parts of the animal bodies. The amount of trade generated in this fashion is not negligible and can be very significant locally as in the case of the *Morpho* butterflies, in Brazil and Peru, or armadillos, especially in Bolivia.

Another form of use of the fauna of the Amazon region is, obviously, for medicine and magic, which covers a vast range of species like the dolphins (*Sotalia*, *Inia*), coati (*Nasua*), various snakes, etc.

Equally significant has been the production of guano and organic matter suitable as a fertiliser, brought about by the activity of the oil bird *Steatornis caripensis*, a bird which besides is in great demand for its meat and fat (Bordon, 1959; Dourojeanni and Tovar, 1972).

22.2.5. Indirect uses of fauna

Game hunting as a sport has not developed in the Amazon region and its present day importance is minimal. The reasons for this are as much the difficulty in finding the prey as the unsporting nature of the kill, as well as the lack of desirable trophies. The few game hunters that venture into this region look mainly for spectacled bears in the upper Amazon region; jaguars and pumas and, to a lesser extent, tapirs and peccaries, in the middle and lower region.

Much more important than hunting for sport is, without doubt, the attraction the fauna has for the national or international tourist who visits the now important network of national parks and protected areas in the Amazon and Orinoco regions in which there were, at the close of 1980, no less than 24 units which covered more than 15 million hectares (Dourojeanni, 1980). Since then, new protected areas have been created in Brazil and one more has been extended in Peru. Of these national parks, the most famous or important are Canaima (Venezuela), Manu and Pacaya-Samiria (Peru), Amazonia, Jau, and Pico de Neblina (Brazil) and Serrania de la Macarena and El Tuparro (Colombia), but many of the others, like those recently established, are able to provide notable sites of wild fauna and can be the base for the increasingly important influence of tourism.

Another aspect worth mentioning is that, regrettably, almost all the skins and hides have been exported from the Amazon region to other regions or countries without any industrial transformation *in situ*; wasting opportunities to create local employment and benefit from the added asset thereby created.

22.3. CONDITION OF WILD FAUNA

Paradoxically, the species in greatest danger of extinction by the year 2000 are not those of the greatest economic importance now, but rather many others, which are less conspicuous, whose habitats are destroyed essentially on the periphery of the tropical rainforests of South America, in particular between the eastern slopes of the Andes, and in the east and the southeast of Brazil, where the growth of the agricultural border is flattening forests that cover areas of extensive endemism. It has been estimated that by the end of the century, as many as a third of the species of the humid tropics of the continent could disappear, mainly insects and other invertebrates, but also birds, reptiles and batrachians.

The statistics for the production and export of the main species used for food and for their hides seem to demonstrate that the population of some species, on the basis of the countries in which such information is available, react well under the pressure of hunting to which they are exposed. Such would be the case with the *Mazama americana*, *Tayassu pecari* and *T. tajacu* species, among many others. However, this reflects in part, a rise in the pressure of hunting and the incursion into new or virgin territory. If the likelihood of species like those mentioned above disappearing in the next 20 years is small, it is certain that their populations will diminish to levels that will render difficult any attempt to manage them rationally.

In the case of fur species like the various felines such as *Panthera onca*, as well as *Lutra amazonica* and *Pteronura brasiliensis*, the available statistics demonstrate that the populations are already definitely over-exploited, although some more so than others. For example, *Felis pardalis* seems to resist better than all the other fur bearers. Exploitation of the crocodilians *Caiman crocodilus*, *Crocodylus intermedius*, *C. acutus* and *Melanosuchus niger* also seems, according to the statistics, to be exhausting stocks.

Despite the frequent violations of the important protection measures adopted essentially by Brazil, Colombia, Peru and Venezuela in the last decade, there is evidence that they have brought about a certain reduction of pressure in hunting exerted on species not used for food. The most recent edition of the IUCN Mammal Red Data Book lists 44 species of the tropical rainforests of South America with threatened, vulnerable, rare or indeterminate populations mentioned (Thornback and Jenkins, 1982). Fifty-seven per cent of this list is made up by primates of the genera *Callithrix*, *Saguinus*, *Leontopithecus*, *Callimico*, *Chiropotes*, *Alouatta*, *Lagothrix*, *Ateles*, *Callicebus*, *Cacajao* and *Brachyteles* affected more by alteration of habitat than by hunting. In addition to monkeys, the Amazon species of economic interest that are most threatened up to the year 2000 are, in the opinion of the author, *Trichechus manatus*, *Tremarctos ornatus*, *Tapirus pinchaque*, *Pteronura brasiliensis* and *Podocnemis expansa*. Among the threatened species, despite their having no economic interest whatsoever, two members of the Canidae should be included, *Atelocynus microtis* and *Speothos venaticus* whose populations are naturally reduced.

The recent discoveries of the the yellow-tailed woolly monkey (*Lagothrix flavicauda*) in the northeast of Peru, which was believed extinct (Macedo and Mittermeier, 1979) as well as the similarly considered *Catagonus wagneri* peccary (Wetzel *et al.*, 1975) in Chaco, clearly demonstrate how little, even now, is known of the real nature of the populations of many American tropical species. However, these cases as well as the rediscovery of the white winged guan (*Penelope albipennis*) (Macedo, 1978) on the north coast of Peru, cannot obscure a picture that is, overall, far from optimistic and worse still if one considers how little is known about birds, reptiles and batrachians and how practically nothing is known about invertebrates, especially insects.

22.4. OPTIONS FOR OPTIMISED USE

22.4.1. General aspects

The fauna of the Amazon region can be managed as much on an extensive as on an intensive and superintensive level. The technical difficulties are considerable but not necessarily insuperable; in the case of many species of great economic importance, there is clearly enough information to begin rational management. The main obstacles are the usual ones in underdeveloped countries, rooted in social and economic problems.

Management of the Amazon fauna should encompass virgin forests, forests under forestry control, large forests fragmented by agricultural areas, areas of pasture, on river banks and areas of open water and, also, in semiartificial or artificial conditions as in many propagation centres. Or again, management can be on the species level including groups of useful species or of the entire fauna of an area.

The control of fauna in virgin forests will, for a long time to come, remain on a general basis, that is, without precise census data on populations. Forests can be divided into zones, each with an administrative unit, on the basis of characteristics of physiographic and ecological homogeneity among other criteria, as well as water availability. The fauna of each zone is examined and a comparative appraisal of their populations is made, particularly to find possible reserves and areas for repopulation. Annual hunting quotas can be estimated on the basis of regular investigations of how much wild animal meat in the region is consumed by the local populations, and also from statistics of animals taken, if permits are granted. In addition, game controls must include permanent or regional closed seasons and the establishment of minimum sizes for prey, quotas by sex, strategically placed animal preserves, restrictions on the type of arms (calibre, munition) and use of traps and bait, as well as authorisation for hunting by night, among other options. Year by year, these measures are adjusted in line with the results (Dourojeanni, 1981).

In forests under forestry management the procedure is similar to that applying in virgin forests, although there are better opportunities for carrying out a more intense fauna management. In effect, such forests are patrolled, have a better layout, and besides, possess, infrastructure such as roads which make it easier to census some species. However, in both cases the financial resources for carrying out generalised censuses of fauna are very limited. Wildlife management could coincide with felling zones. Whatever the most appropriate forest rotations (which range between 20 and 70 years) there are appropriate conditions for simultaneous exploitation of forest and game. The operations of tree removal can, contrary to popular belief, be favourable for some fauna species of great economic importance since the clearings left behind allow the proliferation of grasses which nourish some herbivores (*Mazama*, *Tapirus*) (Dourojeanni, 1978a, 1981).

In these forests it is possible to manage the habitat up to a point by logging and silvicultural methods as long as not less than 10% of the area has no form of tree removal. This percentage must be reserved in the form of well-distributed lots, and also along rivers and brooks, as well as on uneven spots. In the reserved areas there must be a strict ban on hunting so that they may serve as places of refuge. Some forestry methods which raze the trees to the ground in strips interspersed with others left intact, ensure the conservation of the whole genetic stock of flora, and therefore of fauna, including even species not subject to management (Dourojeanni, 1978b).

Brazilian, as Peruvian, legislation obliges farmers to reserve a significant percentage (15 to 50%, as the case may be) of their plots as natural or artificial woodland, preferably along watercourses and on steep inclines. This requirement, if fulfilled, establishes a mosaic of agricultural and pasturing areas with forest areas, and ones intermediate between natural and seminatural and artificially managed ecosystems, or, in other words, a series of ecotones beneficial for some small fauna highly sought after for food and fur. Among them, those of the genera *Dasyprocta*, *Dinomys*, *Cuniculus*, *Dasypus*, *Geochelone*, primates, guans and currasows, partridges, pigeons, parrots, iguanas. They include also small predators like *Felis pardalis* the abundance of which depends on the size of the woodland plots and the number of available prey (Dourojeanni, 1981).

Under these conditions extensive management can be put into effect, but intensive management is also possible, orientated towards more valuable species such as primates, in planting in woodlands of adequate size, for example, fruit-bearing species in suitable places and adequate proportions.

In natural or cultivated pasturelands, it is possible to maintain, in at least ecotone areas and sometimes in the whole area, species like *Mazama* or *Hydrochoerus hydrochaeris*. Finally, on river banks or open waters, there are opportunities to manage populations of important species such as *Caiman crocodilus*, *Melanosuchus niger*, *Lutra amazonica*, *Pteronura brasiliensis*, *Podocnemis* spp. and *Trichechus inunguis*. In the case of the latter intensive management is possible, with population censuses and management to eliminate or reduce restrictive factors such as food, shelter, predation, parasitism and trace elements.

Finally, of course, it is possible to carry out a superintensive management by establishing breeding centres for species that are particularly valuable, such as primates, crocodiles or *Morpho* butterflies.

22.4.2. Experiments in wildlife management

South America has seen some of the most successful examples in the world of wildlife management such as the management of guano birds and vicuña, both in Peru. In the Amazon and Orinoco regions, the experience is more recent, and not so spectacular, although they are encouraging and point to auspicious prospects for the survival of some of the most valuable species.

However, hardly anything has been done as regards extensive or intensive management of useful fauna collectively in virgin forests or forestry areas. Game regulations have been issued which are normally ignored. Nevertheless there is limited experience in intensive management of particular species in natural forests and also with certain species which occur in savannahs and in natural and artificial pastures, and on river banks and open waters. Experience in captive propagation is also increasing.

The species for which there is the most work is, undoubtedly, the capybara (*Hydrochoerus hydrochaeris*) in Venezuela. Since 1953 there have been attempts to develop management, apparently successfully since 1968, after a 5-year ban (Ojasti and Medina, 1972). Ojasti (1968, 1970a, 1970b, 1971, 1973) had conducted basic research to demonstrate the technical and economic viability of production of meat and

TABLE 22.5. Hypothetical comparative data for the development of capybaras and cows in the conditions of the Pantanal in Mato Grosso, Brazil.

Species	Individuals for each 3 hectares	Age at withdrawal (years)	Weight at withdrawal (kg)	Median weight gained (g/day)	Median Wt. gained in each 3 hectares (g/day)
Cow	1	4.5	490	283	283
Capybara	18	1.5	35	63	1,134

Source: Negret (1979) based on the studies by Ojasti and collaborators carried out between 1968 and 1978.

hides on the plains of Venezuela. The average weight of the capybara is 44.2 kg of which 51.5% is meat. The estimate of its net annual productivity is as high as 34%, since it is possible to exploit 30% of the populations when moderately dense, and more in the case of higher density. Table 22.5 shows the undoubted superior productivity of capybara as compared with cattle. Numerous other studies by Ojasti (1978, 1980a,b), Cordero and Ojasti (1981), Escobar (1973), Escobar and Gonzalez (1976), Gonzalez (1972, 1974, 1977), Gonzalez and Parra (1973), among others have analysed various aspects of production and management of this species in Venezuela, confirming that in theory as in practice the capybara is a manageable resource. In other countries there is also an interest in the capybara. In Brazil, studies by Schaller (1980), Schaller and Crawshaw (1980), Schaller and Vasconcelos (1978) and Schaller et al. (1979) indicated the possibility of its management in the Pantanal of Mato Grosso, as discussed also by Negret (1979), Dourojeanni (1980) and more recently Ojasti (1981), although not all that is known from Venezuela is applicable to other sites.

The management of primates took on great importance in the middle of the 1970s because of the drastic export bans on live animals which various Amazon countries adopted, among them primates for biomedical research. Since then, major progress has been made in Peru, where, today, primates are managed in natural forests using semi-intensive methods, for example, in forested island and a propagation centre both at Iquitos. Specialists have developed census techniques appropriate for various species: Castro et al. (1980), Castro and Soini (1977), Encarnacion et al. (1977), Neville et al. (1976). The following have begun to use them: Castro et al. (1975, 1978), Flores et al. (1977), Freese et al. (1976, 1977), Heltne et al. (1980), Kinzey et al. (1977), Janson (1980) with excellent results. In propagation centres even more advances have been made (PAHO-WHO, 1976; Kleiman, 1977). In Brazil, equally, work has been carried out on breeding of the Leontophitecus, Saguinus and Callithrix species with appreciable success (Coimbra-Filho, 1965; Coimbra-Filho and Magnanini, 1972; Coimbra-Filho and Maia, 1976, 1977) and also on their management in natural areas (Coimbra-Filho and Mittermeier, 1973; Magnanini, 1977).

Another section of important current development is the management of Podocnemis expansa tortoises which has achieved notable success in Brazil's river Trombetas programme of the Brazilian Institute of Forestry Development (Instituto Brasileiro de Desenvolvimento Florestal = IBDF). The method used is simple since it consists basically of protecting the beaches, on which the turtles build their nests, as well as the eggs and the recently hatched turtles so as to reduce the enormous mortality rate typical during these periods (Padua, 1981). Moreover, efforts are made in the situation to disperse the population adequately and repopulate overexploited rivers (Brazil, Ministry of Agriculture, 1973; Alfinito et al., 1976; Mittermeier, 1978). In Venezuela (Ojasti and Rutkis, 1965, 1976) identical conclusions have been arrived at, although the programme initiated has not progressed as far as in Brazil. The experience gained would be valuable for other species such as Podocnemis unifilis, P. sextuberculata, P. erythrocephala and others (Mittermeier, 1978).

Other species which, although not yet managed anywhere, have aroused great interest and been the subject of a good deal of study, include the Caiman crocodilus and Melanosuchus niger and, to a lesser extent, *Crocodylus acutus* and *C. intermedius* crocodiles. In Venezuela concrete proposals for the management of *Caiman crocodilus* and *Crocodylus intermedius* have been put forward, and there has been valuable results with various experiments (Rivero, 1970, 1973; Blohm, 1973). In Peru, where various commercial proposals to establish breeding centres were rejected in the last decade for lack of technical guarantees, a good deal of progress in basic information has been made with the studies by Otte (1979) on *Melanosuchus niger*, by Vasquez (1981) and Verdi *et al.* (1980) on *Caiman crocodylus*, and by Hofmann (1968) on both. In Colombia the studies and proposals for rational use by Medem (1960, 1963, 1969) referring for these same two species are well known. Finally, in Brazil interest has developed in the control of *Caiman crocodilus yacare* in the Pantanal of Mato Grosso (Dourojeanni, 1979a), on the basis of studies by Schaller and Crawshaw (1979a), Crawshaw and Schaller (1979) and Crawshaw *et al.* (1980).

A species with a potential for great economic importance, despite its diminished population is the manatee (*Trichechus inunguis*). Research on its control and use carried out in Guyana (Guyana, National Research Council, 1974) and, recently, in Brazil (Brazil, INPA, 1979) throws light on a more promising future for this species.

There is undoubtedly sufficient information to manage a number of species including *Cuniculus paca* (Mondolfi, 1972) for which, pamphlets about conservation and rearing have even been published and distributed in Colombia (Otero, 1980), *Tapirus terrestris* (Mondolfi, 1971) and various others that Nogueira-Neto (1973) also describes, particularly *Dasyprocta*, *Mazama*, *Tayassu*.

Important recent studies on the biology and ecology of *Pteronura brasiliensis* (Duplaix, 1980), *Panthera onca* (Schaller and Crawshaw, 1979b), *Tremarctos ornatus* (Peyton, 1980, 1981) suggest definite possibilities for management of species for the valuable fur, as in the first two and for game, as the last two.

Nogueira-Neto (1973) underlines the possibility of rearing several economically valuable species that are not mammals. He refers to various reptiles and birds. One of the former which, through local experiments in Peru, seems promising, is the land tortoise *Geochelone denticulata*. In Colombia, Otero (1978) has prepared an important document on rearing the boa (*Boa constrictor*) to produce hide and human food. Studies like these by the mentioned authors and others by various primatologists are part of the trend of those who consider superintensive management or breeding as a more feasible option than extensive or intensive free management. The construction of state experimental breeding centres in Manaus, Brazil and in Jenaro Herrera and Iquitos, Peru is a response to this trend.

22.5. THE FUTURE

Prior to 1973 the exploitation of fauna in the Amazon region of Peru generated an internal gross product comparable to forestry exploitation (Dourojeanni, 1972). However, the rate of exploitation was exhaustive, and for that reason an absolute ban on commercial game was declared. Now, as we have seen in the preceding text, there is evidence that management could restore the wild fauna to the economic and social importance it once possessed, while eliminating the risks of extinction brought about by indiscriminate game-hunting.

The overall economic importance of the wild fauna of the Amazon and Orinoco regions has been illustrated also by numerous other writers (Moro, 1972; Ojasti, 1970c). Dourojeanni (1968, 1976, 1978b, 1979a, 1979b, 1980, 1981) has analysed the definite possibilities of integrating its management with regional development plans, and with whole and integrated versions of rural development, clearly showing the technical viability and the economic advantages of doing so.

It is important to understand that one of the best guarantees of survival of species of economic interest is their optimised use by local populations.

A great deal has been achieved in scarcely 20 years. The new focus given to research in the Amazon fauna is succeeding and is attracting the attention of those concerned with development of that region.

REFERENCES

Alfinito, J., Martius, C., Ferreira, M. M. and Rodrígues, H. (1976) Transferencia de tartarugas do rio Trombetas para o rio Tapajoz. *Brasil Florestal* 7(26), 49 − 53.

Bejarano, G. (1973) *La extincion de los félidos en las selvas bolivianas y el desequilibrio ecológico.* Manaus, Brasil. Symposium Internacional sobre Fauna Silvestre, Pesca fluvial y lacustre Amazónica 26 nov. − 1° dic. 1973. 4 p + anexos estadist.

Berlin, B. and Berlin, E. A. (1978) Etnobiología, subsistencia y nutrición en una sociedad de la selva tropical: Los Aguaruna (Jíbaro). In *Salud y Nutrición en Sociedades Nativas.* Compiled by A. Chirif, pages 13 − 47. CIPA, Lima.

Blohm, T. (1973) *Conveniencia de criar crocodílidos en Venezuela con fines económicos y para prevenir su extinción.* Caracas, Asoc. Nac. Df. Naturaleza, 30 pages.

Bordón, C. (1959) Breves notas sobre la fauna entomológica de la Cueva del Guacharo. Caracas. *Bol. Soc. Ven. Ciencias Naturales* 95, 62 − 76.

Brasil. INPA (1979) *Projeto Peixe-Boi. Brazilian Manatee Project.* Manaus. Instituto Nacional de Pesquisas da Amazônia, Departamento de Biología de Mamíferos Aquaticos, 42 pages.

Brasil. Ministerio da Agricultura (1973) *Preservação da tartaruga amazônica.* Belém, Ministerio da Agricultura. DEMA/PA, IBDF, 110 pages.

Campos, R. (1977) Producción de pesca y caza de una aldea Shipibo en el río Pisqui, Lima. *Amazonía Peruana-Ecología* 1(2), 53 − 74.

Castro, N. (1975) *Lineamientos para la conservación de los primates en el Perú.* Lima, Dirección General Forestal y de Fauna, 45 pages.

Castro, N. (1978) Diagnóstico de la situación actual de los primates no humanos en el Perú y un plan nacional para su utilización racional. Lima, Universidad Nacional Mayor de San Marcos, 204 pages (Tésis para optar al título de Biólogo).

Castro, N., Encarnación, F., Lescano, L., Valverde, L., Ugamoto, M. and Maruyama, E. (1980) Censo de primates no humanos en Iberia e Iñapari, departamento de Madre de Dios. In *Seminario sobre Proyectos de Investigación Ecológia para el Manejo de los Recursos Naturales Renovables del Bosque Tropical Húmedo.* Iquitos, 12 − 18 de octubre de 1980 Dirección General Forestal y de Fauna/ORDELORETO/COTESU/MAB Peru. Pages 157 − 169.

Castro, N., Revilla, J. and Neville, M. (1976) Carne de monte como una fuente de proteínas en Iquitos, con referencia especial a monos. Lima, *Rev. Forestal del Perú* 6(1 − 2), 19 − 32.

Castro, R. and Soini, P. (1977) Field studies on *Saguinus mystax* and other Callithrichids in Amazonian Peru. In *The Biology and Conservation of the Callitrichidae.* Ed. D. G. Kleiman, pages 73 − 78.

Coimbra-Filho, A. F. (1965) Breeding lion marmosets *Leontideus rosalia* at Rio de Janeiro Zoo. *Int. Zoo. Yearbook* 5, 109 − 110.

Coimbra-Filho, A. F. and Magnanini, A. (1972) On the present status of *Leontopithecus*, and some data about new behavioural aspect and management of *L. r. rosalia*. *Proc. WAPT, Golden Lion Marmoset Conference.* Ed. D. G. Bridgewater, pages 59 − 69.

Coimbra-Filho, A. F. and Maia, A. de A. (1976) Hibridismo entre o *Callithrix jacchus* o *C. geoffroy* e criação artificial de filhote hibrido. *Brasil Biol.* 36(3), 665 − 73.

Coimbra-Filho, A. F. and Maia, A. de A. (1977) A alimentação de sagüis em cativeirio. *Brasil Florestal* 29, 15 − 26.

Coimbra-Filho, A. F. and Mittermeier, R. A. (1973) Distribution and ecology of the genus *Leontopithecus* Lesson 1840 in Brazil Inuyama. *Primates* 14(1), 47 − 66.

Cordero, G. A. and Ojasti, J. (1981) Comparison of capybara population of open and forested habitats. *J. Wildl. Management* 45(1), 267 − 71.

Crawshaw, P. G., Dalponte, J. C. and Carbosa de Oliveira, L. F. (1980) *Dados adicionais sobre a nidifição de Caiman yacare en Pocone, M.T.* Brasília, IBDF 12 pages + graficos (mimeograph).

Crawshaw, P. G. and Schaller, G. B. (1979) Nesting of Paraguayan caiman (*Caiman yacare*) in Brazil. Brasília, *IBDF REPORT No. 11*, 17 pages (mimeograph).

Denevan, W. M. (1971) Campa subsistence in the Gran Pajonal eastern Perú. *Geographical Review* 61(4), 496 − 518.

Dourojeanni, M. J. (1965) Denominaciones vernaculares de insectos y algunos otros invertebrados en la selva del Perú. Lima. *Rev. Per. Ent.* 8(1), 131 − 7.

Dourojeanni, M. J. (1968) Consideraciones sobre las interinfluencias entre la fauna, su manejo y la zootecnia, con referencia especial al Perú. *Rev. For. Peru, Lima* 2(1), 34 − 45.

Dourojeanni, M. J. (1972) Impacto de la producción de la fauna silvestre en la economía de la amazonía Peruana. *Rev. For. Peru, Lima* 5(1 − 2), 15 − 27.

Dourojeanni, M. J. (1976) Una nueva estrategia para el desarrollo de la amazonía Peruana. *Rev. For. Peru, Lima* 6(1 − 2), 41 − 58.

Dourojeanni, M. J. (1978a) *Ecological aspects and wildlife conservation requirements for the management and development of Tapajoz National Forest, Brazil.* Brasília/Belém FAO-TCP Proyect OG/BRA/OS/1, 10 pages (mimeograph).

Dourojeanni, M. J. (1978b) L'amenagement integré de la faune forestiere comme source de proteines pour las populations rurales. Jakarta, Huitième Congres Forestier Mondial, 16 − 28 oct 1978. Doc. FFF/8-0 Memoire General, 15 pages.

Dourojeanni, M. J. (1979a) *Desarrollo y conservación en el pantanal Matogrossense (Brasil), con especial referencia al manejo de la fauna.* Brasília D. F., Proyecto PNUD/FAO BRA 78/003 Set. 1979, 58 pages + supplement.

Dourojeanni, M. J. (1979b) Desarrollo rural integral en la Amazonía Peruana con especial referencia a las actividades forestales. Roma. In *Seminario FAO/SIDA sobre el papel de la Silvicultura en el Desarrollo Rural de América Latina Anexo al Informe,* pages 109 – 28. Doc. FOR:GCP/RLA 50 (SWE).

Dourojeanni, M. J. (1980) *Situation and Trends of Renewable Natural Resources of Latin America and the Caribbean.* Lima, World Wildlife Fund/US AID, 419 pages + bibliography.

Dourojeanni, M. J. (1981) Fauna and wild area management in the Palcazu Valley, Peru. In *Central Selva Resources Management Lima, J.R.B. Assoc.* Vol. II Appendices App. E., pages 1 – 64.

Dourojeanni, M. J., Torres, H., Child, G. and Poore, D. (1979) *Manejo de Parques Nacionales y Vida Silvestre.* Asunción, Servicio Forestal Nacional Proyecto PNUD/FAO/PAR/79/004, 139 pages (Draft Report).

Dourojeanni, M. J. and Tovar, S. A. (1972) Notas sobre el ecosistema y la conservación de la Cueva de las Lechuzas (Parque Nacional de Tingo María, Perú). *Rev. For. Perú, Lima* 5(1 – 2), 28 – 45.

Duplaix, N. (1980) Observations on the ecology and behavior of the giant river otter *Pteronura brasiliensis* in Surinam. *Paris, Rev. Ecol. (Terre & Vie)* 34, 495 – 620.

Encarnación, F., Castro, N., Heltne, P. and Valverde, L. (1980) Censo de primates no humanos entre los ríos Tahuamanu y Manuripe. In *Seminario sobre Proyectos de Investigación Ecológica para el Manejo de los Recursos Naturales Renovables del Bosque Tropical Húmedo.* Iquitos, 12 – 18 octubre 1980 Dirección General Forestal y de Fauna/ ORDELORETO/COTESU/MAB Perú. Pages 170 – 2.

Escobar, A. (1973) Diagnóstico técnico económico de la explotación comercial del chigüire (*Hydrochoerus hydrochaeris*) Estudio de un caso. *Proyecto CONICIT DF 030 Informe Anual 1972 – 73.*

Escobar, A. and González Jiminez, E. (1976) Estudio de la competencia alimenticia de los herbívoros mayores del llano inundable con referencia especial al chigüire (*Hydrochoerus hydrochaeris*). *Agronomía Tropical* 26(3), 215 – 28.

Flores, M., Freese, C. H. and Revilla, J. (1977) Feeding ecology of the pygmy marmoset, *Cebuella pygmaea*, in Northeastern Peru. In *The Biology and Conservation of the Callitrichidae.* Ed. D. G. Kleiman, pages 91 – 104.

Freese, C. H., Freese, M. A. and Castro, N. (1977) The status of Callitrichids in Peru. In *The Biology and Conservation of the Callitrichidae.* Ed. D. G. Kleiman, pages 121 – 30.

Freese, C. H., Neville, M., Castro, R. and Castro, N. (1976) The conservation status of Peruvian primates. *Laboratory Primate Newsletter* 15(3), 1 – 9.

Gaviria, A. (1981) La fauna silvestre y su aprovechamiento por las comunidades. *Rev. For. del Perú* 10(1), 192 – 201.

González, E. (1972) Exploracion industrial del chigüire (*Hydrochoerus hydrochaeris*). *Venezuela, Dinámica Empresaria* 1(4), 28 – 30.

González, E. (1974) *El potencial ecológico del chigüire o capibara (Hydrochoerus hydrochaeris) para la producción de carne en el llano inundable.* Maracay, Univ. Central de Venezuela Facultad de Agronomía Monografía, 9 pages (mimeographed).

González, E. (1977) The capybara. An indigenous source of meat in tropical America. *World Animal Review* 21, 24 – 30.

González, E. and Parra, R. (1973) The capybara a meat producing animal for the flooded areas of the tropics. *III World Conference on Animal Production, Melbourne, Australia* 1(b), 1 – 8.

Guyana. The National Science Research Council (1974) *An International Centre for Manatee Research.* Georgetown, Report of a Workshop held 7 – 13 February 1974, 34 pages.

Heltne, P., Moya, L., Ruiz, R., Moro, J. and Malaga, C. (1980) *Plan de manejo de fauna silvestre en semicautiverio en la Isla de Iquitos y Padre Isla.* Iquitos, ORDELORETO/UNMSM/OMS, Proyecto Primates, 23 pages + 6 supplements + maps.

Hofmann, R. K. (1968) Posibilidades para una mejor protección de los lagartos en el Perú. *Rev. For. Perú, Lima* 2(2), 69 – 78.

Janson, Ch. (1975) *Ecology and population densities of primates in a Peruvian rainforest (Parque Nacional del Manu).* Princeton University, Department of Biology, 96 pages.

Kinzey, W. G., Rosenberger, A. L., Heisler, P. S., Prowse, D. L. and Trilling, J. S. (1977) A preliminary field investigation of the yellow handed titi monkey, *Callicebus torquatus torquatus*, in northern Peru. *Primates* 18(1), 159 – 81.

Kleiman, D. G. (editor) (1977) *The Biology and Conservation of the Callitrichidae.* Washington, D.C., Smithsonian Institution Press. (A symposium held at the Conservation and Research Center, National Zoological Park, Smithsonian Institution, August 18 – 20, 1975), 354 pages.

Macedo, H. de (1978) Redécouverte du Cracidé *Penelope albipennis* dans les forets seches du nordouest de Pérou. *Paris, C.R. Acad. Sci.* 287, 265 – 67 (Série D).

Macedo, H. de and Mittermeier, R. A. (1979) Redescubrimiento del primate Peruano *Lagothrix flavicauda* (Humboldt 1812) y primeras observaciones sobre su biología. *Lima, Rev. de Ciencias.* Univ. Nac. Mayor de San Marcos 71(1), 78 – 92.

Magnanini, A. (1977) Progress in the development of Poço Das Antas Biological Reserve for *Leontopithecus rosalia rosalia* in Brazil. In *The Biology and Conservation of the Callitrichidae.* Ed. D. G. Kleiman, pages 131 – 136. Smithsonian Institution Press, Washington, D.C.

Medem, F. (1960) Datos zoo-geográficos y ecológicos sobre los Crocodylia y Testudinata de los ríos Amazonas, Putumayo y Caquetá. Bogotá. *Caldasia* 8(38), 341 – 51.

Medem, F. (1963) Osteología craneal, distribución geográfica y ecología de *Melanosuchus niger* (Spix) (Crocodylia, Alligatoridae) Bogotá, *Rev. Acad. Colomb. Cienc. Exactas, Físicas y Naturales* 12(45), 5 – 20.

Medem, F. (1969) Estudios adicionales sobre los Crocodylia y Testudinata del Alto Caquetá Río Caguian. Bogotá. *Caldasia* 10(48), 329 – 53.

Mittermeier, R. A. (1978) South America's river turtles: Saving them by use. London, *Oryx* 14(3), 222 – 30.

Mondolfi, E. (1971) La danta o tapir. Caracas. *Defensa de la Naturaleza* 1(4), 13 – 20.

Mondolfi, E. (1972) La lapa o paca. Caracas. *Defensa de la Naturaleza* 2(5), 4 — 16.

Moro, M. (1972) La fauna amazónica como un recurso natural. Lima, IVITA, Univ. Nac. Mayor de San Marcos. *Boletín Divulgativo* No. 12, 32 pages.

Muckenhirn, N. A. and Cohen, A. L. (1978) Trends in primate imports into the United States. *ILAR News, Institute of Laboratory Animal Resources* 21(2), 17 — 19.

Negret, R. (1979) *Possibilidades do Aproveitamento Zootécnico da Capivara (Hydrochoerus hydrochaeris) na Bacia do Alto Paraguai, Mato Grosso.* Brasília, EDIBAP, 33 pages + map (mimeographed).

Neville, M., Castro, N., Mármol, A. and Revilla, J. (1976) Censusing primate populations in the reserved area of the Pacaya and Samiria rivers, Department Loreto, Perú. *Primates* 17(2), 151 — 81.

Nogueira-Neto, P. (1973) *A criação de Animais Indigenas Vertebrados.* São Paulo. Ed. Tecnapis, 327 pages.

Ojasti, J. (1968) Notes on the mating behavior of the capybara. *J. Mamm.* 49(3), 534 — 5.

Ojasti, J. (1970a) Sobre el crecimiento individual del chigüire (*Hydrochoerus hydrochaeris*). *Acta Científica Venezolana* 21(1), 28 — 9.

Ojasti, J. (1970b) Datos sobre la reproducción del chigüire (*Hydrochoerus hydrochaeris*). *Acta Científica Venezolana* 21(1), 27.

Ojasti, J. (1970c) La fauna silvestre produce. In *La Ciencia en Venezuela.* Caracas, Edited at Univ. de Carabobo, pages 277 — 94.

Ojasti, J. (1971) El chigüire apureño. Caracas, *Informe al MAC y al FNIA* 315 pages (mimeographed).

Ojasti, J. (1973) *Estudio Biológico del Chigüire o Capibara.* Caracas, Edit. Sucre FONAIAP, 271 pages.

Ojasti, J. (1978) The relation between population and production of the capybara. Univ. of Georgia, Ph.D. Dissertation, 217 pages.

Ojasti, J. (1980a) Ecology of capybara raising on inundated savannas of Venezuela. *Tropical Ecology and Development 1980*, 287 — 93.

Ojasti, J. (1980b) Papel ecológico de mamíferos en sabanas inundables. Caracas, *Boletín Soc. Venez. Cienc. Naturales* 35(139), 59 — 66.

Ojasti, J. (1981) *Informe sobre las posibilidades de manejo de la capivara (Hydrochoerus hydrochaeris) en el Pantanal del Matogrosso, Brasil.* Informe FAO al IBDF.

Ojasti, J. and Medina, G. (1972) The management of capybara in Venezuela. In *Transaction of the 37th North American Wild life and Natural Resources Conference* March 12 — 15, 1972, pages 268 — 77.

Ojasti, J. and Rutkis, E. (1965) Operación tortuguillo, un planteamiento para la conservación de la tortuga del Orinoco. Caracas, *El Agricultor Venezolana* 26(228), 33 — 7.

Ojasti, J. and Rutkis, E. (1967) Consideraciones sobre la ecología y conservación de la tortuga *Podocnemis expansa* (Chelonia, Palomedusidae). In *Simposio sobre Biota Amazônica, Belém* Brasil 1966. Atas Rio de Janeiro, Conselho Nacional de Pesquisas 1967 V7, pages 201 — 6.

Otero, R. (1978) *La boa. Su cría y aprovechamiento económico.* Manizales, Ed. La Patria, 153 pages.

Otero, R. (1980) *Proteja y cría la boruga.* Bogotá, Corporación de Araracuara, 46 pages.

Otte, K. D. (1979) *Unterseechungen zur Biologie des Mohrenkaiman (Melanosuchus niger Spix 1825) aus dem National Park Manu (Peru): Beiträge zur Morphologie, Physiologie, Ethologie und Okologie.* Otte, München und Lima, 311 pages.

Padua, L. F. (1981) Biologia da reprodução, conservação e manejo da tartaruga-da-Amazonia-*Podocnemis expansa* (Testudinata Pelomedusidae) na Reserva Biológica do rio Trombetas, Pará. Instituto de Ciências Biológicas, Univ. de Brasília, 133 pages.

Pan American Health Organisation (1976) *First Inter-American Conference on Conservation and Utilization of American Non-human Primates in Biomedical Research (Lima, Peru 2 — 4 June 1975).* Washington, D.C. Pan American Sanitary Bureau, Regional Office of the World Health Organisation, 252 pages (Scientific Publication No. 317).

Perú. Direccion General Forestal y de Fauna (1977) *Vademecum Forestal.* Lima. Ministerio de Agricultura, 133 pages.

Peyton, B. (1980) Ecology, distribution, and food habits of spectacled bears, *Tremarctos ornatus*, in Peru. *J. Mamm.* 61(4), 639 — 52.

Peyton, B. (1981) Spectacled bears in Peru. London, *Oryx* 16(1), 48 — 56.

Pierret, P. V. and Dourojeanni, M. J. (1966) La caza y la alimentación humana en las riberas del río Pachitea, Perú. *Turrialba* 16(3), 271 — 7.

Pierret, P. V. and Dourojeanni, M. J. (1967) Importancia de la caza para alimentación humana en el curso inferior del río Ucayali, Perú. *Rev. For. Peru, Lima* 1(2), 10 — 21.

Ríos, M., Dourojeanni, M. J. and Tovar, A. (1973) La fauna y su aprovechamiento en Jenaro Herrera (Requena, Perú). *Rev. For. Peru, Lima* 5(1 — 2), 73 — 92.

Rivero, C. V. (1970) Situación de la baba y los caimanes. Efectos de la explotación comercial. Recomendaciones en el Manejo de las especies. Caracas, *Pononcia al Foro sobre Protección y Fomento de la Fauna Silvestre* 16 — 17 julio 1970.

Rivero, C. V. (1973) Ensayo monográfico sobre los hábitos reproductivos de la baba o jacare-tinga, *Caiman crocodilus*, en los llanos de Venezuela y las posibilidades de manejo en semicautividad, con sugerencias sobre las posibles aplicaciones de la metodología de manejo al caimán negro o jacare-açu, *Melanosuchus niger* de las cuencas del Amazonas y Río Negro. Manaus. *Simposio Internacional sobre Fauna Silvestre y Pesca Fluvial y Lacustre Amazonica* 26 nov. — 1° dic. 1973, 16 pages + supplements.

Schaller, G. B. (1980) *Mammals and their biomass on a Brazilian ranch.* Brasília, Instituto Brasileiro de Desenvolvimento Florestal, Report No. 16, 57 pages + graphs and plates (mimeographed).

Schaller, G. B. and Crawshaw, P. G. (1979a) *Fishing Behavior of Paraguayan caiman (Caiman crocodilus).* Brasília, Instituto Brasileiro de Desenvolvimento Florestal, 11 pages + graphs (mimeographed).

Schaller, G. B. and Crawshaw, P. G. (1979b) *Movement Patterns of Jaguar*. Brasília, Instituto Brasileiro de Desenvolvimento Florestal (A report), 18 pages + tables + figures (mimeographed).

Schaller, G. B. and Crawshaw, P. G. (1980) *Social Organization in a Capybara Population*. Brasília, Instituto Brasileiro de Desenvolvimento Florestal, Report No. 15, 30 pages + graphs and plates (mimeographed).

Schaller, G. B., Crawshaw, P. G. and Eberhard, A. (1979) *Dynamics of a Capybara Population in the Pantanal*. Brasília, Instituto Brasileiro de Desenvolvimento Florestal, Report No. 13, 5 pages + plates (mimeographed).

Schaller, G. B. and Vasconcelos, J. M. C. (1978) Jaguar predation on capybara. Hamburg y Berlin, *Z. Säugetierkunde* 43, 296 – 301.

Smith, J. H. (1976) Utilization of game along Brasil's transamazon highway. Manaus, *Acta Amazônica* 6(4), 455 – 66.

Soini, P. (1972) The capture and commerce of live monkeys in the Amazonian region of Peru. In *International Zoo Yearbook 12*. Eds. J. Lucas and N. Duplaix-Hall, pages 26 – 36, Zool. Soc., London.

Thornback, J. and Jenkins, M. (compilers) (1982) *The IUCN Mammal Red Data Book Part 1*. Gland, IUCN, 516 pages.

U.S. Department of Health, Education and Welfare (1978) National Primate Plan. Washington, D.C., Public Health Service, National Institutes of Health *DHEW Publication No. (NIH) 80-1520*, 81 pages.

Vásquez, P. (1981) *Bases bio-ecológicas para el manejo de los Alligatoridae en Jenaro Herrera (Requena-Perú)*. Lima, Universidad Nacional Agraria 205 pages + supplement (Thesis).

Verdi, L., Moya, L. and Pezo, R. (1980) Observaciones preliminares sobre la bioecología del lagarto blanco *Caiman crocodilus* (Linnaeus, 1758) (Alligatoridae) en la cuenca del río Samiría, Loreto, Perú. Iquitos, *Seminario sobre los Proyectos de Investigación Ecológica para el Manejo de los Recursos Naturales Renovables del Bosque Tropical Húmedo. del 12 al 18 de oct. 1980*, 37 pages.

Wetzel, R. M., Dubos, R. E., Martin, R. L. and Myers, P. (1975) *Catagonus*, an 'extinct' peccary, alive in Paraguay. *Science* 189, 379 – 81.

Whitney, R. A. (1976) International requirements for non human primates in medical research. In *First Inter-American Conference on Conservation and Utilization of American Non-human Primates in Biomedical Research. Lima, 2 – 4 june 1975*, pages 242 – 6. PAHO/WHO Sc. Pub. No. 317.

Index

KEY ENVIRONMENTS

Other Titles in the Series